Why Food Matters

ALSO AVAILABLE FROM BLOOMSBURY

Food, Warren Belasco

The Food History Reader, Ken Albala

Food Studies, Willa Zhen

Why Food Matters

Critical Debates in Food Studies

EDITED BY
MELISSA L. CALDWELL

BLOOMSBURY ACADEMIC
LONDON • NEW YORK • OXFORD • NEW DELHI • SYDNEY

BLOOMSBURY ACADEMIC
Bloomsbury Publishing Plc
50 Bedford Square, London, WC1B 3DP, UK
1385 Broadway, New York, NY 10018, USA
29 Earlsfort Terrace, Dublin 2, Ireland

BLOOMSBURY, BLOOMSBURY ACADEMIC and the Diana logo are trademarks of
Bloomsbury Publishing Plc

First published in Great Britain 2021

Cover design by Adriana Brioso
Cover image: Genetically engineered wheat growing in the greenhouse.
(© inga spence / Alamy Stock Photo)

A catalogue record for this book is available from the British Library.

Library of Congress Control Number: 2020950619

ISBN: HB: 978-1-3500-1143-4
PB: 978-1-3500-1142-7
ePDF: 978-1-3500-1144-1
eBook: 978-1-3500-1145-8

Typeset by Newgen KnowledgeWorks Pvt. Ltd., Chennai, India
Printed and bound in Great Britain

To find out more about our authors and books visit www.bloomsbury.com
and sign up for our newsletters

For Woody and Rubie Watson

Contents

Acknowledgments xi

Permissions xiii

Introduction: Why Does Food Matter? 1
  Melissa L. Caldwell

PART ONE Revaluing Food in a Global Economy

Introduction 15

1 Willing (White) Workers on Organic Farms? Reflections on Volunteer Farm Labor and the Politics of Precarity 19
  Julie Guthman

2 Grocery Auction Games: Distribution and Value in the Industrialized Food System 27
  Micah Marie Trapp

3 The Labor of *Terroir* and the *Terroir* of Labor: Geographical Indication and Darjeeling Tea Plantations 45
  Sarah Besky

4 Famine Talk: Communication Styles and Socio-Political Awareness in 1990s North Korea 65
  Sandra Fahy

5 Blaming the Consumer—Once Again: The Social and Material Contexts of Everyday Food Waste Practices in Some English Households 83
  David Evans

6 Alimentary Dignity: Defining a Decent Meal in Post-Soviet Cuban Household Cooking 95
  Hanna Garth

Suggested Additional Readings 111

PART TWO The Power of Food: From Politics to Microbiopolitics

Introduction 113

7 Power at the Table: Food Fights and Happy Meals 115
Richard Wilk

8 Postsocialist Spores: Disease, Bodies, and the State in the Republic of Georgia 129
Elizabeth Cullen Dunn

9 Everyday Approaches to Food Safety in Kunming 153
Jakob A. Klein

10 Digestive Politics in Russia: Feeling the Sensorium beyond the Palate 169
Melissa L. Caldwell

11 Resistance is Fertile! 189
Anne Meneley

Suggested Additional Readings 203

PART THREE New Bodily Realities in a Techno-Science World

Introduction 205

12 "Lose Like a Man": Gender and the Constraints of Self-Making in Weight Watchers Online 209
Emily Contois

13 Everyday Translation: Health Practitioners' Perspectives on Obesity and Metabolic Disorders in Samoa 223
Jessica Hardin

14 Sensorial Pedagogies, Hungry Fat Cells and the Limits of Nutritional Health Education 237
Emilia Sanabria

15 The Environmental Account of Obesity: A Case for Feminist Skepticism 255
Anna Kirkland

16 Who Defines Babies' "Needs"?: The Scientization of Baby Food in Indonesia 271
Aya Hirata Kimura

Suggested Additional Readings 287

PART FOUR More than Human, More than Food

Introduction 289

17 Waste, Incorporated 293
Chika Watanabe

18 Arts of Inclusion, or How to Love a Mushroom 303
Anna Tsing

19 How to Taste Like a Cow: Cultivating Shared Sense in Wisconsin Dairy Worlds 313
Katy Overstreet

20 FCJ-142 Spectacles and Tropes: Speculative Design and Contemporary Food Cultures 325
Carl DiSalvo

Suggested Additional Readings 337

Index 339

Acknowledgments

This project originated from a conversation with Mark Graney and James L. (Woody) Watson. Together we envisioned a follow-up to *The Cultural Politics of Food and Eating*, which Woody and I had published in 2005 (Blackwell). Mark got the ball rolling with this project, before handing it off to Jennifer Schmidt at Bloomsbury. Since that hand-off, I have been fortunate to work not just with Jennifer but also with Miriam Cantwell, Lucy Carroll, and Lily McMahon. I am grateful to all of them for their help and support along the way. I also want to thank the many colleagues who have suggested potential readings and talked through ideas that helped me develop and frame this book. I especially appreciate the conversations I have had with Julie Guthman, Jakob Klein, Rebecca Feinberg, Katy Overstreet, and the students in my Anthropology of Food courses. As editor of *Gastronomica: The Journal of Critical Food Studies*, I was very fortunate to have a broad view of the entire field of food studies and to be introduced to authors, ideas, and debates that I might not have encountered otherwise. Those influences are also represented here. Finally, as always, I am deeply endebted to Andy and Kaeley Baker for their assistance, great and small, and their patience as they have endured yet another project in our house.

Permissions

The author and publisher gratefully acknowledge the permission granted to reproduce the copyright material in this book.

1. Julie Guthman. 2017. "Willing (White) Workers on Organic Farms? Reflections on Volunteer Farm Labor and the Politics of Precarity." *Gastronomica: The Journal of Critical Food Studies* 17(1): 15–19.

2. Micah Marie Trapp. 2018. "Grocery Auction Games: Distribution and Value in the Industrialized Food System." *Gastronomica: The Journal of Critical Food Studies* 18(1): 1–14.

3. Sarah Besky. 2014. "The Labor of *Terroir* and the *Terroir* of Labor: Geographical Indication and Darjeeling Tea Plantations." *Agriculture and Human Values* 31: 83–96.

4. Sandra Fahy. 2012. "Famine Talk: Communication Styles and Socio-Political Awareness in 1990s North Korea." *Food, Culture & Society* 15(4): 535–55. Reprinted by permission of the publisher Taylor & Francis Ltd, http://www.tandfonline.com.

5. David Evans. 2011. "Blaming the Consumer—Once Again: The Social and Material Contexts of Everyday Food Waste Practices in Some English Households." *Critical Public Health* 21(4): 429–40. © 2011 Taylor & Francis Ltd. http://www.tandfonline.com | http://dx.doi.org/10.1080/09581596.2011.608797.

6. Hanna Garth. 2019. "Alimentary Dignity: Defining a Decent Meal in Post-Soviet Cuban Household Cooking." *The Journal of Latin American and Caribbean Anthropology* 24(2): 424–42. © 2019 by the American Anthropological Association. All rights reserved. DOI: 10.1111/jlca.12369

7. Richard Wilk. 2010. "Power at the Table: Food Fights and Happy Meals." *Cultural Studies ↔ Critical Methodologies* 10(6): 428–36. © 2010 SAGE Publications. http://csc.sagepub.com. Reprints and permission: http://www. sagepub.com/journalsPermissions.nav DOI: 10.1177/1532708610372764

8. Elizabeth Cullen Dunn. 2008. "Postsocialist Spores: Disease, Bodies, and the State in the Republic of Georgia." *American Ethnologist* 35(2): 243–58. Reproduced by permission of the American Anthropological Association. Not for sale or further reproduction.

9. Jakob A. Klein. 2013. "Everyday Approaches to Food Safety in Kunming." *The China Quarterly* 214: 376–93. Reproduced with permission from Cambridge University Press. DOI: 10.1017/S0305741013000325.

10. Melissa L. Caldwell. 2014. "Digestive Politics in Russia: Feeling the Sensorium beyond the Palate." *Food and Foodways: Explorations in the History and Culture of Human Nourishment* 22(1–2): 112–35. Reproduced with permission from Taylor & Francis Ltd.

11. Anne Meneley. 2014. "Resistance Is Fertile!" *Gastronomica: The Journal of Critical Food Studies* 14(4): 69–78. © 2014 the Regents of the University of California. All rights reserved. DOI: 10.1525/GFC.2014. 14.4.69.

12. Emily Contois. 2017. "'Lose Like a Man': Gender and the Constraints of Self-Making in Weight Watchers Online." *Gastronomica: The Journal of Critical Food Studies* 17(1): 33–43. © 2017 the Regents of the University of California. All rights reserved. DOI: HTTPS://DOI. ORG/10.1525/GFC.2017.17.1.33.

13. Jessica Hardin. 2015. "Everyday Translation: Health Practitioners' Perspectives on Obesity and Metabolic Disorders in Samoa." *Critical Public Health* 25(2): 125–38. © 2014 Taylor & Francis. Received 21 Sep 2013, Accepted 14 Mar 2014, Published online: 16 Apr 2014.

14. Emilia Sanabria. 2015. "Sensorial Pedagogies, Hungry Fat Cells and the Limits of Nutritional Health Education." *BioSocieties* 10: 125–42. © 201 S Macmillan Publishers Ltd. 1745–8552. www.palgrave-1ournals.com/biosoc/

15. Anna Kirkland. 2011. "The Environmental Account of Obesity: A Case for Feminist Skepticism." *Signs* 36(2): 463–85. Republished with permission of University of Chicago Press. Permission conveyed through Copyright Clearance Center, Inc.

16. Aya Hirata Kimura. 2008. "Who Defines Babies' 'Needs'?: The Scientization of Baby Food in Indonesia." *Social Politics: International Studies in Gender, State and Society* 15(2): 232–60. Published by Oxford University Press. All rights reserved. DOI: 10.1093/sp/jxn008.

17. Chika Watanabe. 2015. "Waste, Incorporated." *Gastronomica: The Journal of Critical Food Studies* 15(4): 6–13. © 2015 by the Regents of the University of California. All rights reserved. DOI: 10.1525/GFC.2015.15.4.6.

18. Anna Tsing. 2010. "Arts of Inclusion, or How to Love a Mushroom." *Manoa* 22(2): 191–203.

19. Katy Overstreet. 2020. "How to Taste Like a Cow: Cultivating Shared Sense in Wisconsin Dairy Worlds." In *Making Taste Public: Ethnographies of Food and the Senses*, edited by Carole Counihan and Susan Højlund, pp. 53–67. London: Bloomsbury.

20. Carl DiSalvo. 2012. "FCJ-142 Spectacles and Tropes: Speculative Design and Contemporary Food Cultures." *The Fibreculture Journal* 20: 109–22.

Introduction: Why Does Food Matter?

Melissa L. Caldwell

Why does food matter? This may seem like a self-evident question. Food is one of the few universal human necessities: everyone needs to eat to survive. Beyond that immediate biological requirement, however, there are few, if any, things that are universal about food, its use, or its meaning within people's daily lives. How people assign worth to food, how they use food, how they acknowledge and appreciate the sensory experiences of food, and even what they count as food has varied significantly around the world and through time. Perhaps most intriguingly, despite food's reputation as something comforting, pleasurable, and desirable, the reality is that many foods—and by extension, many people's experiences with food—can often be messy, unpredictable, and, frankly, unpleasant.

Despite food's singularity as a human necessity, food is, in fact, an elusive, even contradictory thing. It may be both comforting and discomforting, and both familiar and strange, all at the same time. It is this capacity of food to settle and unsettle simultaneously that makes it such a powerful, meaningful, and essential part of daily life for people everywhere. It is also what makes food such a fruitful topic for research into the human condition. Not only does careful examination of food shed light on people's experiences and how they make sense of their daily lives and the social worlds in which they live and through which they move, but the study of food also invites possibilities for critically interrogating our own scholarly belief systems and for inviting new theoretical insights and methodological approaches.

Why Food Matters takes up these intriguing ambiguities and paradoxes in order to consider what makes food so meaningful and powerful, and to shed light on how questioning the very nature of food itself offers possibilities for reconsidering what we think we know about ourselves, other people, and the world around us. The framing questions of this collection are the otherwise ordinary questions "what is food?" and "why does food matter?" Through these provocations, the chapters presented here individually and collectively converge around longstanding debates about the nature of human existence while also reexamining and moving beyond established theories in the social sciences and humanities. Consequently, these chapters and the volume as a whole encourage new conversations that rethink the boundaries, possibilities, and eventual futures of food, food practices, and food beliefs. In different ways, the authors of these chapters illuminate the possibilities and potentialities not merely of what food is, but of what food could be.

Why Food Matters Now

This is an excellent moment to rethink the nature of food. Over the past two decades, food studies has established itself as a robust, multidisciplinary, and even interdisciplinary field. This is a relatively recent development, however. In the early 2000s, when James L. Watson and I published *The Cultural Politics of Food and Eating* (2005), we were inspired by the scholarship on food that had appeared in the late 1990s and early 2000s. Studies of food were certainly not new at that time, as scholars in the social sciences and humanities had long found food to be a particularly fascinating and productive research topic for understanding fundamental questions about identity, community formation, ritual, tradition, and social dynamics more generally (e.g., Douglas 1966; Goody 1982; Harris 1987; Lévi-Strauss 1969). What was novel at that time, however, was that this emerging and expanding scholarship on food was coalescing around shared critical interventions that used empirically rich research and sophisticated social theory to examine larger social and cultural phenomena. Through nuanced case studies, these scholars looked to food topics as opportunities to understand some of the most pressing and timely cultural, political, and intellectual issues of the period: for instance, the spread of transnational food cultures (Miller 1998; Mintz 1986; Watson 1997), the implications of spreading American-style fast-food cultures and the responding emergence of the Slow Food Movement (Ritzer 1996; Wilk 2006), the underlying cultural and structural issues behind global food anxieties (Freidberg 2004; Ritvo 1998), the invention of so-called traditional and even heritage cuisines (Pilcher 1998; Wilk 1999), the promises and limits of organics and other alternative food movements (Belasco 1990; Guthman 2004), and the ongoing manipulation of food as a political instrument and expression of power (Mintz 1997; Poppendieck 1988), among many other topics. Perhaps most importantly, scholars working on these and related topics were also at the forefront of scholarship that crossed disciplinary boundaries while also focusing attention on parts of the world that had either largely been overlooked or had only recently emerged, such as the formerly state socialist world (e.g., Caldwell 2004; Dunn 2004; Watson 1997; Yan 2000). These new approaches to scholarship on food were transformative because they both represented the cutting edge of intellectual conversations within their respective disciplines and offered insights that enabled comparative debates and research across disciplines and regions.

Since then, studies of food, both within individual disciplines and within the broader field of food studies, have come to be commonplace.[1] Courses on food and food-related topics are frequent—and often oversubscribed—at all levels of the curriculum, from elementary school to PhD-level seminars. Publication and outreach venues have expanded from the more traditional journals, magazines, and books to include blogs, museum exhibits, plays and ballets, and technology-infused hackathons.

Yet even as food has become recognized as a valuable, perhaps even necessary, object of scholarly and popular investigation, it has to a great extent become taken for granted. As food has become *the* thing to study, its very obviousness has increasingly belied its complexity and opacity. In other words, once food becomes mundane, it becomes easy to presume that we already know the important questions to ask, and so the most important, and most fundamental question of all—*what is food, really?*—recedes to the background. Consequently, it is an important moment both to pause and revisit some of the most enduring questions in studies of food and society and to consider the possibilities of emerging and future topics and trends in studies of food. Above all, rethinking the obviousness of food challenges us to consider the potentialities evinced through the unmaking of food as a thing, a necessity, and an ontological concept.

Making, Unmaking, and Remaking Food

Scholars of food who have taken seriously the challenge of unmaking food and questioning what we think we know about food have inspired exciting conversations on pressing intellectual and social issues in economics, politics, ritual, social organization, identity, critical race studies, gender studies, health, world-making, science and technology, and knowledge politics, to mention a few key areas. Despite the diversity of topics across these fields, a persistent and unifying refrain has been the question of how and why food is made meaningful at different moments. In other words, what makes food valuable and what gives it value? In most societies, food exists as something with value and meaning, yet how values and meanings come to be defined depends on the particular social, economic, political, and religious contexts in which they exist. In some cases, foods acquire economic value depending on qualities such as scarcity, abundance, seasonality, desirability, or even the labor needed for production or preparation (Dickinson 2019; Garth 2020; Holmes 2013; Wilson 2013). In other cases, foods acquire moral or ethical value depending on the particular ideologies that make up the beliefs and practices of a society (Jung, Klein, and Caldwell 2014; Leung and Caldwell 2020; Veit 2015). Rules about who can prepare, use, or consume which foods, when, and with whom are all informed by moral regimes that reflect ideals about propriety, need, and deservingness. In still other cases, food is itself a thing that circulates through, holds together, or even rips apart economic systems ranging from barter economies and state socialist economies to neoliberal capitalist systems and democratic social welfare systems (Jung 2019; Reese 2019; Wilson 2013).

What counts as food is also highly variable. In Asian health traditions, the boundaries between food and medicine are blurred (Chen 2008), whereas in other societies ideas about "real food" may set up distinctions between fast food and manufactured foods, on the one hand, and organic, natural, or "whole" foods on the other (Sexton 2016; Wurgaft 2019). The line between food science and food art is perhaps even more indistinct, as artists find inspiration in food as a physical medium for painting, sculpture, textiles, and music, while chefs and artisans bring artistic techniques and aesthetic sensibilities to their dishes, kitchens, and serving plates (Paxson 2011; Roosth 2013). Even food's presumed materiality is up for grabs. From miniaturization practices that have made possible food in pill form (Belasco 2010) to modernist cuisine and molecular gastronomy techniques that transform foods from their solid states into vapors or deliberately transfer the flavors, colors, or other properties of one food into another (Myrhvold, Young, and Bilet 2011; This 2005, 2006), the physical, material properties of food are rarely fixed or even predictable.

Whether food will even continue to exist is another issue that both vexes and motivates people around the world. On the one hand, concerns with climate change and population pressures are connected to real and perceived declines in food safety, the degradation of agricultural productivity, and challenges to environmental sustainability (Wheeler and von Braun 2013). On the other hand, innovations in science and technology are recovering ancient or extinct seeds, crops, and foods, thereby generating appreciation for heritage foods and cuisines (McDonell 2015; Montenegro 2016). These same innovations are also enabling the industrial production of alternative food sources, such as insects or seaweed, or synthetic foods that are edible, nutritious, and even tasty (Looy, Dunkel, and Wood 2014; Wurgaft 2019). It is not merely the future of food that is at stake, however, but also food's past and present. When lab-grown meats and synthetic nutrients land on grocery shelves and kitchen plates, consumers may start to question such cherished qualities as authenticity, heritage, and tradition. And once beef, pork, and shrimp can be made from plant material and no longer require actual animals (Samuel 2020), what happens to important morally infused choices such as vegetarianism or veganism or even to religious traditions such as kashrut and halal?[2]

The intersection of new technologies and politics further invites deliberation about the moral regimes in which foods are entangled. In the last two decades, the global geopolitics between Russia and other formerly state socialist countries, on the one hand, and the countries that have joined the European Union, on the other, have frequently played out through competing policies over food safety, agricultural innovation, and labelling (Gille 2016; Klumbytė 2010; Mincyte 2014). Similar geopolitical differences have existed between China and the United States as both countries have oscillated between their roles as producer and consumer. At more regional levels, new technologies in viticulture and dairying have enabled the recuperation of "traditional" recipes for culturally privileged commodities such as cheese, wine, and cured meats, as well as their global circulation (Black and Ulin 2013; Grasseni 2014), even as regional, national, and supranational political movements have motivated protracted legal battles over which communities are morally and culturally entitled to claim and name foods (e.g., champagne, Parma ham, feta cheese, and hummus, to name just a few) as their own (Avieli 2016; Brulotte and Di Giovine 2014; Guy 2007).

Meanwhile, these moral-technological-political entanglements extend to new, more nuanced discussions about personhood, especially moral personhood. Moving beyond earlier discussions that questioned the agency of consumers in a context of globalization and cultural imperialism (e.g., Ritzer 1996), recent research has examined the responsibilization of citizen-consumers. When consumers are presented as ethical citizens with both rights and responsibilities, their food choices can be understood in very different ways that trouble perceptions about desire, demand, and deservingness (Carney 2013; Dickinson 2017; Jung, Klein, and Caldwell 2014). By extension, when researchers have turned their attentions to the individual bodies that produce, consume, and dispose of food, they have asked profound questions about what constitutes appropriate bodies and how those bodies should exist in and move through the world (Biltekoff 2013; Guthman 2011; Guthman and DuPuis 2006). More critical awareness of bodies has invited both scholarly and activist attention to the moralities informing bodily shape and size. Nutritionism, healthism, and sizeism have emerged as critical issues in how we understand different cultural ideals about what appropriate bodies should look like and their place in the world (Guthman 2014; Scrinis 2013).

Critical interrogation of the autonomy and boundedness of bodies, both individual and social, has also informed very different debates about the innermost workings of the body as well as how bodily experiences might extend beyond a single person or even beyond people altogether. Increasingly, researchers have considered the microbiome as a fascinating site for understanding how the mechanics of biological processes are themselves culturally produced, as well as for how cultural practices are influenced by biological activities. Microbes, bacteria, and other gut flora represent the inner frontiers of food microbiopolitics (Landecker 2013; Paxson 2008), while moral, cultural, and even political sensibilities can be expressed through bodily responses such as taste preferences and digestive processes (Caldwell 2002, 2014; Klumbytė 2010). More holistic treatment of the body has also dethroned the palate's position as the dominant arbiter of taste and pleasure and instead has drawn attention to other sensory experiences such as touch and sound as channels through which people interact with food and experience pleasure and displeasure (Harris 2015; Mann, Mol, Satalkar, et al. 2011).

Finally, this unsettling of food and the human body encourages us to revisit enduring questions about the labors through which food is produced and consumed. Scholars of food labor have increasingly complicated discussions about fairness, equity, and justice by unpacking dichotomies between work, service, and voluntarism. From volunteer brigades that grow, prepare, and serve food to others, sometimes as a prerequisite for their own eligibility to receive supplemental food, to the global growth of flexible and casual labor in the sharing economy, the work of producing and delivering food has upset prevailing hierarchies of value (Dickinson 2017; Guthman 2017). At the same time, discussions of food labor have expanded beyond the person so that the question of "who makes our food" looks very different when viewed through the vantage points of animals, insects, and bacteria, who are no longer sources of food but credited as producer-workers (Grasseni 2005; Overstreet 2018). The conversations change again when considered through the perspectives of nonliving entities such as robots, drones, or algorithms and other forms of digital technology and artificial intelligence (Caldwell 2018; Kera, Denfeld, and Kramer 2015; Schneider, Eli, Dolan, et al. 2018).

As these and many other developments in contemporary studies of food show, food matters because it challenges our very assumptions about the nature of food and its place and meaning in our lives. The constancy of food is, in many ways, its lack of constancy.

Organization of the Volume

Why Food Matters takes up these intriguing new directions and possibilities through twenty chapters that cover an impressive diversity of topics and regions: for instance, food waste in England, food safety and daily shopping in China, food and health in Samoa, the scientization of baby food and motherhood in Indonesia, botulism and state control in the former Soviet Republic of Georgia, the political economy of brewing *terroir* in the Indian tea industry, the ethics and practices of culinary dignity under conditions of food scarcity in Cuba, the micropolitics at play around the American family dinner table, the macropolitics of resistance in Palestine, consumer negotiations at American grocery auctions, the digital worlds of dieting and gendered bodies, the recirculation of food and food waste in Myanmar, and the appropriation of tasting on behalf of nonhuman others among American dairy farmers.

Although not all of the chapters are written by card-carrying anthropologists, they all prioritize ethnographically grounded case studies. This empirical depth, coupled with topical and regional diversity, highlights how similar issues and topics might look quite different when viewed from multiple vantage points. As such, collectively, the chapters featured in this volume invite critical comparisons across topics, regions, methods, and theories, which in turn situate the authors in shared conversations about enduring topics and questions in anthropology and social theory while also illuminating emerging and future directions in scholarly inquiry.

The book is organized into four sections. Each section coalesces around a shared thematic focus, with each chapter presenting a different analytical approach to these themes in order to illuminate both ethnographic, methodological, and theoretical points of intersection as well as important disagreements and divergences. These groupings are intended to provoke conversations and debates around questions and insights. There are certainly other thematic overlappings and groupings that transect these sections, and readers are encouraged to move across all of the chapters and find other points of intersection and disagreement. In many respects, this book invites a kaleidoscopic approach that reveals new possibilities depending on how pieces are put together.

Part One, "Revaluing Food in a Global Economy," addresses some of the most enduring issues and debates in economic anthropology and the political economy of food more generally. Building on foundational scholarship and theories about exchange, systems of circulation, commodity chains, value production, globalization, consumer demand, scarcity, and labor, the authors pose challenging questions about how economic practices and values come to be and the ways in which they are embedded in local communities and with what effects. How do moral regimes shape economic beliefs and practices? How do positionality and intersectionality inform the choices and actions of producers and consumers? How do food systems and commodity chains change shape and meaning as they move from production to disposal, especially within circuits of reappropriation and redistribution? When does food work transform into aesthetic performances or even leisure? How do nation-state policies affect consumers' abilities to access food? What is the interplay between access to food and consumer-citizens' material and affective experiences? And how do economic aspects inform ideologies of personal choice, responsibility, and pleasure?

The value of food, its meaning, and its role within local communities vary significantly, depending on its use. By looking at the many relationalities that cohere between moments of production, consumption, and disposal, and between producers, sellers, and consumers, the chapters in this section question the very nature of food and how it comes to be made as something with value. In some cases, the meanings associated with food emerge from particular forms of labor, such as when unpaid volunteers appropriate the spaces and work occupied by poorly paid, migrant laborers, provocatively blurring distinctions between leisure and labor, and between desire and need (Chapter 1, Guthman). Labor also shifts registers when it is tied to particular forms of knowledge and connection to place, such as when tea growers, pickers, blenders, and marketers collectively, but not necessarily cooperatively, produce the aesthetic and financial qualities assigned to tea (Chapter 3, Besky). Food labor is a performative act that transforms both producers and consumers, as well as the nature of food itself.

The transformation of food is especially apparent as it moves through presumed economic networks, beginning with production and continuing through consumption and on to its eventual disposal. Yet what happens to food after its consumption is ambiguous, as food often gets diverted into alternative pathways and remade into new things with new social lives. For instance, grocery auctions reveal the ways in which food surpluses are redistributed—and revalued—through alternative disposal networks in which prices are set by performative bidding among small business owners and ordinary consumers in search of a bargain (Chapter 2, Trapp). In other cases, individual consumers struggle with the financial and ethical burden of food surplus, as they try to prevent food waste, including by diverting food to other purposes (Chapter 5, Evans). Food surplus does not always automatically turn into food waste but can become redirected back to earlier stages in the food chain.

Whereas attention to food surplus opens up important questions about the materiality of food and food production, in other cases it may be the absence of food that sheds light on the on-the-ground implications and effects of different economic systems, most notably differences between capitalist and state socialist systems. Access to food is not guaranteed, and how people access food that is both nutritionally and culturally appropriate as well as desirable sheds light on the ways in which economic activities of exchange are enmeshed within other ideologies and policies about personal and societal rights and responsibilities, as well as the ways in which states intervene in economic activities to support or repress their citizens, as in the case of North Korea (Chapter 4, Fahy). Above all, as Hanna Garth shows for the case of Cuba (Chapter 6), it is access to the "right" foods—foods that are familiar, comforting, and desired—that is often most important because they enable experiences of pleasure and dignity.

Part Two, "The Power of Food: From Politics to Microbiopolitics," moves beyond political economies to examine the power dynamics and relationships that inform food practices and experiences. Collectively, the authors examine how power, control, authority, risk, regulation, and resistance shape people's food experiences with food and how these experiences contribute to particular forms of social order from the level of the community to the level of the nation-state. As each of the authors shows, power is a multisited and multiscalar phenomenon that connects and disconnects people and communities in overlapping and often conflicting ways. Building from Mary Douglas's insights about the relationships and dynamics that cohere between the physical body and the social body (Douglas 1970), the authors move our attention back and forth from states to citizens and into the most interior spaces of citizens' bodies. How do people articulate political beliefs through their food practices? How do states and individuals negotiate important issues around risk and safety? How do states and individuals monitor, regulate, and police one another? And how does food move from being something that enhances commensality and solidarity to something that disrupts social order?

Food is often presented as a medium for community building: sharing food brings people together and strengthens social bonds. Yet the commensal qualities associated with food are never neutral but are instead forged through interactions between individuals who occupy different positions of power and authority. As such, the outwardly congenial appearance of meals and other acts of food sharing may obscure contentious debates and conflicts. The family meal is perhaps the most obvious space of contestation in many parts of the world, especially in the United States. Despite its revered status in American mythology as the facilitator of family harmony, personal health, and community solidarity, mealtimes are just as often highly contested, disruptive, and even unpleasant events when parents and children wrestle for control and personal autonomy (Chapter 7, Wilk). Meals and other food events are thus transformed from spaces of presumed safety to spaces in which risk, danger, and unrest are made apparent. At larger scales, food events can acquire significance as sites where individuals and states make competing claims on political legitimacy and demonstrate either adherence or resistance to each other's beliefs and status. Yet if control over food, especially the withholding of food, can be presented as acts of violence by states against its citizens, as in North Korea (Chapter 4, Fahy), conflicts over food can also provide the channel for nonviolent, but no less symbolically potent, acts of resistance, such as in the West

Bank of Palestine, when consumers use food choices to articulate their views and allegiances within the politics of Israeli occupation (Chapter 11, Meneley).

When politics moves into the realm of control, regulation, and governance, interactions between states and individuals do not necessarily remain in public, even civic, spheres but can move to more private and personal spaces like private homes, kitchens, and individual bodies. Individualizing qualities such as autonomy, self-control, and agency take on new forms and meanings when the state appropriates the personal health and well-being of individual persons for its own purposes, or when individuals experience and interpret their interactions with the state through the most personal activities of their home life and in the most intimate spaces of their bodies. Even though states may present themselves as guarantors of public safety, they can also cause harm by ceding their responsibility for safety, leaving ordinary people to take on those responsibilities as well as to suffer the consequences. For instance, China's political and economic transformations of the past three decades have produced a series of food-related environmental health scares. Chinese consumers have responded by relying less on official information and products and more on local cultural beliefs and networks in their food shopping strategies (Chapter 9, Klein).

Meanwhile, in the formerly Soviet Republic of Georgia, the collapse of the state's economic system, and especially its food manufacturing, resulted in an outbreak of botulism as ordinary people attempted to revive home canning practices, thereby bringing the state—or its absence—directly into the bodies of its citizens (Chapter 8, Dunn). If extreme cases of food poisoning bring the state into people's bodies, far more routine bouts of indigestion, constipation, biometrics such as elevated blood pressure, and other biological processes keep the state and its citizens connected in more prolonged political interactions, such as with Russian consumers who narrate their political beliefs, and especially their commitment to nationalist, patriotic ideals, through their daily bodily responses to food (Chapter 10, Caldwell). When states and their citizens encounter each other both through external markets and through the most interior parts of the body, then deliberate consumer choices and innate biological processes are equally opportunities for civic activity and even protest. As food moves through the body, politics likewise moves from biopolitics to microbiopolitics.

Part Three, "New Bodily Realities in a Techno-Science World," extends this theme of microbiopolitics through chapters that address the new types of persons and bodies that are constituted through food, with specific attention to the new technologies, knowledge regimes, and forms of expertise that are at play in today's global world. Individually and collectively, the chapters in this section consider how food practices and food experiences have been transformed by contemporary techno-bureaucratic innovations. Health and wellness form one cluster of themes in these studies, while another cluster converges around discussions of gender and age. Yet another cluster encompasses questions about the role of experts—scientists, environmentalists, health professionals, and policy makers, among others—in determining what appropriate bodies should look like and how they should exist in and move through the world.

One of the curious consequences that occurs when new technologies inform food experiences is that those experiences may be distanced from the immediacy of people's lives and bodies and instead are mediated by anonymous digital technologies, such as happens with online weight loss programs like Weight Watchers, which has introduced radically different online programs and idealized bodies and lifestyles for its male and female members (Chapter 12, Contois). More intriguingly, scientific knowledge and biomedical technologies have pathologized bodies in ways that require intervention and regulation by outside observers. Whether it is through health education programs geared at reducing body size, such as with medical programs that target not only Samoan bodies but also Samoan beliefs about wealth, status, and well-being (Chapter 13, Hardin), or through international development programs promoting fortification of baby food that displace mothers as the experts about their own children (Chapter 16, Kimura), outside experts and knowledge producers are using food choices as a means to create idealized notions of healthy, productive bodies that, in turn, further distance and disenfranchise local communities from their own knowledge and ways of living. In so doing, structures of domination are reproduced through techno-bureaucratic projects of "assistance" and "improvement."

Yet this privileging of scientific, technological interventions is limited, as consumers themselves have very different experiences and knowledge systems that inform their realities. In some ways, both deep within the body and at larger social levels, there are alternative feedback loops within and across the body and local communities that often exert greater influence over the choices that consumers make. Aesthetic values, sensory pleasures, and even personal preferences all inform not just what foods people eat but also how they interpret and assign meaning to their bodily forms and sensations. For instance, French eaters who emphasize the pleasures and displeasures of the sensory experiences of eating over scientific information force public health agents to reconsider how to accommodate what Csordas (1993) has called "somatic modes of attention" in public health policies (Chapter 14, Sanabria). Perhaps even more importantly, processes that acknowledge, classify, and regulate bodily experiences and bodily health by subjecting bodies to quantitative measures and by making them into objects requiring intervention reveal the extent to which science, medicine, and technology are themselves never absolutely objective but are instead subjective moral regimes with preferences and biases. Embedded within many of the ostensibly noble efforts to prevent and compensate for the global "obesity epidemic" are actually moral concerns about the values and lifestyles of the non-elite (Chapter 15, Kirkland).

Lastly, Part Four, "More than Human, More than Food," brings the volume full circle by providing four different meditations on the very essence of food. Contributing to diverse debates in multispecies theories, animal-human and more-than-human approaches, and critical design studies, the chapters in this section disrupt expectations about the boundaries of food, human communities, and humanness itself. Person-centric encounters with food give way to larger musings on the social lives and social worlds that foods and people inhabit, sometimes alongside one another and sometimes separated from one another.

Moving beyond analyses that either put humans at the center of food experiences or privilege the thingness of food challenges us to think about how food activities bring us into multiply tangled and complicated relations with many other beings. Humans are not the only beings that eat and use food; animals and other plants are also eaters of sorts with their own preferences and lifeworlds. Many of us think carefully about our animal companions and how best to respond to their own individual food needs and preferences. How might including them, both as fellow members of a community of eaters and as social actors with their own ability to demonstrate food preferences, expand our understanding of food, its meaning in social encounters, and its value? How we access those other eaters and their preferences and experiences requires us to find new points of connection with them, such as by observing animals' taste preferences and trying to recreate them with our own, human palates, as happens among Wisconsin dairy farmers who try to accommodate their cows' taste preferences (Chapter 19, Overstreet). In other cases, decentering the human requires shifting our gaze and carefully observing and noticing the independent social lives of the beings that share our worlds and may eventually end up on our tables. Fungi are an excellent example of living beings that form their own social worlds and relationships with others and thus require our respect and attention (Chapter 18, Tsing). We could just as easily think about bees, yeasts, or bacteria as entities that create their own social communities that both feed on and feed others.

Shifting our gaze to new modes of subjectivity also encourages us to rethink the materiality or thingness of food, with particular attention to the speculative nature of food experiences and the potentialities that are inherent in foods and food encounters. Food is not merely a known thing but it is also, and perhaps more significantly, a source or inspiration for things not-yet-known or not-yet-realized. Food waste is not simply an endpoint for a set of relationships but rather it inspires and makes possible new relationships to come in the future, as it moves from bodies back into the soil in order to generate and grow new foods for future generations of eaters, such as when human and animal waste is redeposited as fertilizer into the soil in an agricultural program in Myanmar (Chapter 17, Watanabe). In these circulations and recirculations, both foods and eaters reconstitute one another while making possible new beings and new possibilities. It is these possibilities that show that unbounding food actually makes possible new forms, new modes, and new imaginaries. The potentialities inherent in food disrupt and reconfigure boundaries between art and science, desire and need, reality and fiction in ways that challenge us not just to imagine but also to make alternative presents and futures and ponder what food could be (Chapter 20, DiSalvo).

Ultimately, this final section also encourages us to revisit the previous chapters and think about how the issues they covered might be reexamined through a more-than-human and more-than-food lens. How do power dynamics change when nonhuman entities are included as social actors capable of expressing some kind of agency? How might questions of danger, risk, safety, and stability look differently when viewed from the vantage point of bacteria, microbes, and naturally occurring foodstuffs rather than from the perspective of eaters or health and safety officials? When food is recirculated through the body and into the soil and back into the food that goes into the body, how might we reimagine food and commodity chains, as well as the values attached to food surplus and food waste when disposal is the starting point and not the ending point? Who qualifies as an expert when animals and plants are making their own preferences known? And lastly, how might we reimagine how and why food will continue to matter in the future? Will foods' inconstancy remain its most constant quality?

Notes

1 More recently, "critical food studies" has emerged as a new and vibrant direction within food studies. "Critical food studies," which emerged from intellectual debates that were primarily located among American west-coast food scholars, notably a cluster of scholars from within the University of California community, emphasizes the need to look critically—carefully and analytically—at food in order to see beyond its aesthetics and pleasurable aspects and instead think about its many facets, including its unpleasant ones (Caldwell 2019: vi).

2 For more information from Impossible Foods about their new pork product, see https:// impossiblefoods.com/pork/. Accessed February 9, 2020.

References

Avieli, Nir. 2016. "The Hummus Wars Revisited: Israeli-Arab Food Politics and Gastromediation." *Gastronomica* 16(3): 19–30.

Belasco, Warren. 1990. *Appetite for Change: How the Counterculture Took the Food Industry—and What Happened When It Did, 1966–1988*. New York: Pantheon Books.

Belasco, Warren. 2010. "Future Note: The Meal-in-a-Pill." *Food and Foodways* 8(4): 253–71.

Biltekoff, Charlotte. 2013. *Eating Right in America: The Cultural Politics of Food and Health*. Durham, NC: Duke University Press.

Black, Rachel E., and Robert C. Ulin. 2013. *Wine and Culture: Vineyard to Glass*. London: Bloomsbury.

Brulotte, Ronda L., and Michael A. Di Giovine. 2014. *Edible Identities: Food as Cultural Heritage*. London: Ashgate.

Caldwell, Melissa L. 2002. "The Taste of Nationalism: Food Politics in Postsocialist Moscow." *Ethnos* 67(3): 295–319.

Caldwell, Melissa L. 2004. *Not by Bread Alone: Social Support in the New Russia*. Berkeley: University of California Press.

Caldwell, Melissa L. 2018. "Hacking the Food System: Re-Making Technologies of Food Justice." In *Digital Food Activism*, edited by Tanja Schneider, Karin Eli, Catherine Dolan, and Stanley Ulijaszek, pp. 25–42. London: Routledge.

Caldwell, Melissa L. 2019. "Editor's Letter." *Gastronomica* 19(1): iv–x.

Carney, Megan A. 2013. "Border Meals: Detention Center Feeding Practices, Migrant Subjectivity, and Questions on Trauma." *Gastronomica* 13(4): 32–46.

Chen, Nancy N. 2008. *Food, Medicine, and the Quest for Good Health*. New York: Columbia University Press.

Csordas, Thomas J. 1993. "Somatic Modes of Attention." *Cultural Anthropology* 8(2): 135–56.

Dickinson, Maggie. 2017. "Free to Serve? Emergency Food and Volunteer Labor in the Urban U.S." *Gastronomica* 17(2): 16–25.

Dickinson, Maggie. 2019. *Feeding the Crisis: Care and Abandonment in America's Food Safety Net*. Oakland: University of California Press.

Douglas, Mary. 1966. *Purity and Danger: An Analysis of the Concepts of Pollution and Taboo*. London: Routledge & Kegan Paul.

Douglas, Mary. 1970. *Natural Symbols: Explorations in Cosmology*. New York: Pantheon Books.

Dunn, Elizabeth Cullen. 2004. *Privatizing Poland: Baby Food, Big Business, and the Remaking of Labor*. Ithaca, NY: Cornell University Press.

Freidberg, Susanne. 2004. *French Beans and Food Scares: Culture and Commerce in an Anxious Age*. New York: Oxford University Press.

Garth, Hanna. 2020. *Food in Cuba: The Pursuit of a Decent Meal*. Stanford, CA: Stanford University Press.

Gille, Zsuzsa. 2016. *Paprika, Foie Gras, and Red Mud: The Politics of Materiality in the European Union*. Bloomington: Indiana University Press.

Goody, Jack. 1982. *Cooking, Cuisine, and Class: A Study in Comparative Sociology*. Cambridge: Cambridge University Press.

Grasseni, Cristina. 2005. "Designer Cows: The Practice of Cattle Breeding Between Skill and Standardization." *Society & Animals* 13(1): 33–49.

Grasseni, Cristina. 2014. "Re-Localizing Milk and Cheese." *Gastronomica* 14(4): 34–43.

Guthman, Julie. 2004. *Agrarian Dreams: The Paradox of Organic Farming in California*. Berkeley: University of California Press.

Guthman, Julie. 2011. *Weighing In: Obesity, Food Justice, and the Limits of Capitalism*. Berkeley: University of California Press.

Guthman, Julie. 2014. "Introducing Critical Nutrition: A Special Issue on Dietary Advice and Its Discontents." *Gastronomica* 14(3): 1–4.

Guthman, Julie. 2017. "Willing (White) Workers on Organic Farms? Reflections on Volunteer Farm Labor and the Politics of Precarity." *Gastronomica* 17(1): 15–19.

Guthman, Julie, and Melanie DuPuis. 2006. "Embodying Neoliberalism: Economy, Culture, and the Politics of Fat." *Environment and Planning D: Society and Space* 24: 427–48.

Guy, Kolleen M. 2007. *When Champagne Became French: Wine and the Making of a National Identity.* Baltimore, MD: Johns Hopkins University Press.

Harris, Anna. 2015. "The Hollow Knock and Other Sounds in Recipes." *Gastronomica* 15(4): 14–17.

Harris, Marvin. 1987. *The Sacred Cow and the Abominable Pig: Riddles of Food and Culture.* New York: Simon and Schuster.

Holmes, Seth. 2013. *Fresh Fruit, Broken Bodies: Migrant Farmworkers in the United States.* Berkeley: University of California Press.

Jung, Yuson. 2019. *Balkan Blues: Consumer Politics after State Socialism.* Bloomington: Indiana University Press.

Jung, Yuson, Jakob A. Klein, and Melissa L. Caldwell, eds. 2014. *Ethical Eating in the Socialist and Postsocialist World.* Berkeley: University of California Press.

Kera, Denisa, Zach Denfeld, and Cathrine Kramer. 2015. "Food Hackers: Political and Metaphysical Gastronomes in the Hackerspaces." *Gastronomica* 15(2): 49–56.

Klumbytė, Neringa. 2010. "The Soviet Sausage Renaissance." *American Anthropologist* 112(1): 22–37.

Landecker, Hannah. 2013. "Postindustrial Metabolism: Fat Knowledge." *Public Culture* 25(3): 495–522.

Leung, Angela Ki Che, and Melissa L. Caldwell, eds. 2020. *Moral Foods: The Construction of Nutrition and Health in Modern Asia.* Honolulu: University of Hawai'i Press.

Lévi-Strauss, Claude. 1969. *The Raw and the Cooked.* New York: Harper & Row.

Looy, Heather, Florence V. Dunkel, and John R. Wood. 2014. "How Then Shall We Eat? Insect-Eating Attitudes and Sustainable Foodways." *Agriculture and Human Values* 31: 131–41.

Mann, Anna, Annemarie Mol, Priya Satalkar, et al. 2011. "Mixing Methods, Tasting Fingers: Notes on an Ethnographic Experiment." *HAU: Journal of Ethnographic Theory* 1(1): 221–43.

McDonell, Emma. 2015. "Miracle Foods: Quinoa, Curative Metaphors, and the Depoliticization of Global Hunger Politics." *Gastronomica* 15(4): 70–85.

Miller, Daniel. 1998. "Coca-Cola: A Black Sweet Drink from Trinidad." In *Material Cultures: Why Some Things Matter*, edited by Daniel Miller, pp. 169–87. Chicago, IL: University of Chicago Press.

Mincyte, Diana. 2014. "Raw Milk, Raw Power: States of (Mis)Trust." *Gastronomica* 14(4): 44–51.

Mintz, Sidney J. 1986. *Sweetness and Power: The Place of Sugar in Modern History.* New York: Penguin Books.

Mintz, Sidney J. 1997. *Tasting Food, Tasting Freedom: Excursions into Eating, Power, and the Past.* Boston, MA: Beacon Press.

Montenegro, Maywa. 2016. "Banking on Wild Relatives to Feed the World." *Gastronomica* 16(1): 1–8.

Myrhvold, Nathan, Chris Young, and Maxime Bilet. 2011. *Modernist Cuisine: The Art and Science of Cooking.* Bellevue, WA: Cooking Lab.

Overstreet, Katy. 2018. " 'A Well-Cared-For Cow Produces More Milk': The Biotechnics of (Dis)Assembling Cow Bodies in Wisconsin Dairy Worlds." PhD dissertation, University of California, Santa Cruz.

Paxson, Heather. 2008. "Post-Pasteurian Cultures: The Microbiopolitics of Raw-Milk Cheese in the United States." *Cultural Anthropology* 23(1): 15–47.

Paxson, Heather. 2011. "The 'Art' and 'Science' of Handcrafting Cheese in the United States." *Endeavour* 35(2–3): 116–24.

Pilcher, Jeffery M. 1998. *Que vivan los tamales!: Food and the Making of Mexican Identity.* Albuquerque: University of New Mexico Press.

Poppendieck, Janet. 1998. *Sweet Charity? Emergency Food and the End of Entitlement.* New York: Penguin Books.

Reese, Ashanté M. 2019. *Black Food Geographies: Race, Self-Reliance, and Food Access in Washington, DC.* Chapel Hill: University of North Carolina Press.

Ritvo, Harriet. 1998. "Mad Cow Mysteries." *American Scholar* 67(2): 113–22.

Ritzer, George. 1996. *The McDonaldization of Society: An Investigation into the Changing Character of Contemporary Social Life*. Thousand Oaks, CA: Pine Forge Press.

Roosth, Sophia. 2013. "Of Foams and Formalisms: Scientific Expertise and Craft Practice in Molecular Gastronomy." *American Anthropologist* 115(1): 4–16.

Samuel, Sigal. 2020. "Impossible Foods' New Pork is 0% Pig. That's a Big Deal." Vox. January 7, 2020. https://www.vox.com/future-perfect/2020/1/7/21054910/impossible-pork-sausage-plant-based-meat. Accessed February 9, 2020.

Schneider, Tanja, Karin Eli, Catherine Dolan, and Stanley Ulijaszek, eds. 2018. *Digital Food Activism*. London: Routledge.

Scrinis, Gyorgy. 2013. *Nutritionism: The Science and Politics of Dietary Advice*. New York: Columbia University Press.

Sexton, Alexandra. 2016. "Alternative Proteins and the (Non)Stuff of 'Meat.'" *Gastronomica* 16(3): 64–76.

This, Hervé. 2005. "Modelling Dishes and Exploring Culinary 'Precisions': The Two Issues of Molecular Gastronomy." *British Journal of Nutrition* 93(1): S139–46.

This, Hervé. 2006. "Food for Tomorrow? How the Scientific Discipline of Molecular Gastronomy Could Change the Way We Eat." *EMBO Reports* 7(11): 1062–6.

Veit, Helen Zoe. 2015. *Modern Food, Moral Food: Self-Control, Science, and the Rise of Modern American Eating in the Early Twentieth Century*. Chapel Hill: University of North Carolina Press.

Watson, James L., ed. 1997. *Golden Arches East: McDonald's in East Asia*. Stanford, CA: Stanford University Press.

Wheeler, Tim, and Joachim von Braun. 2013. "Climate Change Impacts on Global Food Security." *Science* 341(6145): 508–13.

Wilk, Richard R. 1999. "'Real Belizean Food': Building Local Identity in the Transnational Caribbean." *American Anthropologist* 101(2): 244–55.

Wilk, Richard R., ed. 2006. *Fast Food/Slow Food: The Cultural Economy of the Global Food System*. Lanham, MD: Altamira Press.

Wilson, Marisa. 2013. *Everyday Moral Economies: Food, Politics, and Scale in Cuba*. Malden, MA: Wiley-Blackwell.

Wurgaft, Benjamin Aldes. 2019. *Meat Planet: Artificial Flesh and the Future of Food*. Oakland: University of California Press.

Yan, Yunxiang. 2000. "On Hamburger and Social Space: Consuming McDonald's in Beijing." In *The Consumer Revolution in Urban China*, edited by Deborah S. Davis, pp. 201–25. Berkeley: University of California Press.

PART ONE

Revaluing Food in a Global Economy

Introduction

What makes food meaningful? This is a question that encourages us to recognize the tremendous variation that exists around the world in terms of how people and communities decide which foods are useful, edible, desirable, and pleasurable for whom and under what circumstances. Both the elevation of some foods to a special, perhaps privileged status, and the denigration of other foods—or even the same foods—reflect different sets of beliefs, principles, practices, and priorities. Paying attention to the diversity of meanings that foods acquire at different times and places opens up important questions about how and why people and their communities come to hold particular beliefs and attitudes about specific foods and food practices.

Entangled in these questions about what makes food meaningful and significant is a related but slightly different question: What makes food valuable? In some cases, the significance of a food or food practice may be represented by the monetary or cultural value placed on it, such as with scarce or luxury foods that attract both high prices and high prestige because of their rarity or singularity. In other cases, the personal or cultural significance of a food eludes easy social or economic valuation, such as a family recipe that can be fully appreciated only by members of that family who remember not just the taste of the dish but also the conversations, jokes, and dinners that were part of their experiences with the dish. The cost of ingredients, the experience of a skilled cook, and the care and personal histories invested in and made possible by a family dinner cannot be neatly calculated as elements with equal or convertible value. Examining the ways in which foods are valued or devalued sheds light on the types of value that are at play—financial, social, emotional, cultural, or even political—and the hierarchies in which these values are arranged. Does financial value supersede cultural value, or vice versa? When does a food have more value as a political symbol than it does as a commercial product?

Economic activities have long occupied a privileged position within studies of the value of food, as researchers have examined the systems of production, distribution, consumption, and disposal that move foods from farms or factories to markets and on to tables, as well as the forms of labor and types of laborers required to move those foods along those networks. As foods move through those relationships, they also change from one state to another, as well as acquire (or change or lose) value: from crop to commodity to dinner, or from object of necessity to object of desire, or from raw material to commodity to gift, or from fresh to expired to rotten. Tracking food as it moves through these different relationships has long been an important topic for researchers interested in studying a broad range of economic topics: access, demand, production, distribution, manufacturing, labor, pricing, scarcity, entitlement, welfare, and charity, among many others.

Recognizing that value can be understood from multiple directions helps us think about food beyond cost, price, or access. Attention to the values attached to food, as well as the moments when value is added or lost, helps us rethink the nature of economic systems, as well as how these economic systems have been studied. In many ways, the ordinariness of food in everyday life and its necessity for biological sustenance can obscure the reality that people's access to food and the choices they make about which foods to consume are deeply embedded in extensive and convoluted economic systems that bring together many different people, communities, and traditions into relationships of dependency and obligation across multiple scales.

Studies of food invite exciting possibilities for rethinking not only what we know about the economic systems that make up food practices but also what alternative economic systems might look like. The chapters in this section present new vantage points from which to reconsider some of the most enduring issues and debates in economic anthropology and the political economy of food more generally. Drawing on scholarship and theories about exchange, systems of circulation, commodity chains, value production, globalization, consumer demand, scarcity, and labor, these chapters develop those ideas and methods and connect them fruitfully to critical discussions about ethics, morality, positionality and intersectionality, performance, agency, choice, and pleasure. Collectively, the conversations and disagreements forged through these chapters are multiscalar, as they shift registers between the very local to the national and the transnational, and simultaneously reveal new synergies and divergences among economic systems in different parts of the world.

Potential Questions to Guide Reading and Discussion

What is "value" and how does "value" change depending on the context?

What are the circumstances under which "value" comes to be an important quality?

Who determines what counts as "valuable" and for what reasons?

How does comparison of food practices across different societies reveal different types of value and hierarchies of value?

How does attention to value shape our understanding of the many different people and activities involved in making, distributing, consuming, and disposing food?

What other qualities are associated with, or embedded within, the quality of "value"?

How does attention to "value" help us understand the structures and ideologies that constitute different economic systems such as state socialism, market capitalism, or gift exchange and barter?

How do the values attached to foods and food practices change at different moments in their movement through economic processes or their life cycles?

How can we understand differences between use value and exchange value?

How does waste become revalued?.

How are ethical or moral qualities attached to economic activities?

What is a moral economy?

1

Willing (White) Workers on Organic Farms? Reflections on Volunteer Farm Labor and the Politics of Precarity

Julie Guthman

A not uncommon ambition of young adults these days is to work on organic farms as volunteers and interns. Many do so through programs such as Worldwide Opportunities on Organic Farms/ Willing Workers on Organic Farms (WWOOF); opportunities abound where I am located, as well. In the United States, most of these volunteers come from middle-class backgrounds, they are generally white, and they have grown up around or have been educated in progressive university towns. The San Francisco Bay Area and central coast of California, where I do much of my research and teaching, is a fountain of such interest, replete with deep foodie culture and histories of social experimentation. In the course of my teaching at UCSC, I have worked with many students who want "to put their hands in the soil" or otherwise hang out with farming and gardening. I have learned from countless conversations and papers that they seek unalienated labor, a chance to connect with others, and the opportunity to grow their own food.

I have an inkling about what makes *food* work so attractive. American foodie icons such as Alice Waters, Mark Bittman, and Michael Pollan have extolled going back to the kitchen as a way to reconnect with both the pleasures and health-giving properties of food. Waters, for example, rejects convenience discourses because they omit what Waters sees as meaningful work. Trying to save time by not cooking or shopping, she claims, misses out on "one of the few worthwhile pleasures in life—not in getting away from work but in doing good work that means something" (cited in Biltekoff 2013: 101). Enacting her vision no doubt enhances one's status. Emma Maris (2014) has noted that the labor devoted to food preparation has replaced scarce ingredients as the way to indicate gourmet food. At the same time, it is an ideal that many find difficult to attain (Bowen et al. 2014).

As we also see in Waters's statement, food work conflates with good work and even hints of philanthropy. As I have written (2008, 2011), the missionary practice of teaching others how to garden, cook, and eat has become a common mode of activism for those who want to effect social justice in food systems, albeit a mode that often reflects the desires of the givers much more than those of the recipients. Waters's own biography in trying to align the city of Berkeley's public schools, and now the University of California, with her own vision of teaching food further indicates a conflation of food work and philanthropy. (Here I allude to Waters's imprint on the university's Global Food Initiative.)

Yet, I have still wondered what exactly about *farmwork* is so attractive to these young people—especially when it is unwaged. After all, this work is extremely demanding, painful, and has been historically demeaning. How has it apparently become a source of pleasure, reward, and even status? And always cognizant of political economy, I have also wondered about whether those who volunteer have considered the potential impacts of their unwaged labor on those who are relegated to doing farm labor for a living. What is the relationship between privilege and precarity in this realm of action? To begin to answer these questions, I interviewed several UCSC students about the meanings of volunteer farm labor for them. I did this as my contribution to a UC working group, funded by the Mellon Foundation, on Rethinking the Purpose of Work through the Pleasures and Displeasures of Food. What I learned confirms some of my suspicions about their privileged positionality, yet upon further reflection suggests some lines of flight, including their pursuit of creative ways to piece together a life. In that way I think these students' desires and trajectories open up much broader questions about the blurring of productive and reproductive labor, the meaning of precarity, and how living the precarious life works as politics in a very uncertain world.

* * *

All of those I interviewed were pursuing voluntary farmwork "for the experience," and to some extent to learn new skills, including those that could not be attained in formal university training. These are motives that other researchers have identified for nonwaged farmwork (McIntosh and Bonnemann 2006; Mostafanezhad 2016; Schugurensky and Mündel 2005). These were skills they would not necessarily include on their resumes, although with today's emphasis on "service learning" would make for feathers in their caps nonetheless (Cody 2016).

Several mentioned that they hoped WWOOFing, in particular, would give them the ability to travel very cheaply, a finding noted by MacIntosh and Campbell (2001), as well. None expected to be very good at farm labor, and none expected to do it for a living. They were fully cognizant of the privilege of dabbling in farmwork as a way to enrich their own lives and, for that matter, that it required considerable social and economic capital (Ekers et al. 2015).

In terms of the pleasures and pains they would experience, some (the men especially) were excited about the idea of engaging in physically demanding labor. In that way, their desires were reminiscent of masculine hobby work, which is often productive and physical, but performed at a self-determined pace. Others viewed the labor they would provide as a necessary trade-off for the other benefits they would receive.

Surprisingly, I found that few had seriously thought about the implications for paid labor on the farms they had worked or would work (see Gray 2013 on this point). None had worked side by side with migrant farmworkers or were even aware of their presence on the farms they had or would work—even if they were in regions where migrant farmworkers are a mainstay, such as California. When I pressed, a few mentioned that they could see how voluntary farm labor could possibly negatively affect wages or morale for waged workers.

I was also curious about how they saw this work in comparison to other work in the food sector. Although a couple of interviewees had worked in restaurants, they did not see farmwork as comparable, and none would consider volunteering in a restaurant. Neither would they consider volunteering on a conventional farm. They had not really reflected on the subsidy they were effectively providing to the organic farming sector, despite that having nonwaged labor is one of the primary motivations for farm hosts of WWOOF farms (Cody 2016; Ekers et al. 2015; McIntosh and Campbell 2001).

This subsidy, by the way, has not gone unnoticed by conventional farmers, who, in California and Oregon, have reported "informal" labor arrangements in the form of internships or apprenticeships as violations of state and federal labor laws. Small farmers have paid some steep fines for this practice and so it is diminishing in California (Alcorta et al. 2013). One of the criteria for determining if such work is illegal is whether it has the potential to displace waged workers. For their part, the interns do not expect be covered by labor laws, as they see themselves as learning from the experience more than contributing to the viability of the farm. Their physical separation from waged workers reinforces a sense that their role on the farm is distinct and perhaps not deserving of remuneration. Nevertheless, their inattention to the subsidy they provide and how that might reverberate in the so-called formal economy sheds some light on similar blind spots regarding the so-called sharing economy of Uber and Air B&B: many users do not think twice about how they may be contributing to the deregulation of waged work and health and safety standards through purchasing services that are cheaper precisely because they are casualized.

Despite these real issues of unwitting exploitation of self and others (Perlin 2012), arguably this phenomenon reflects that young adults these days are developing much different relationships to work than their middle-class parents enjoyed. Perhaps they are responding to a postwar Fordist, suburban way of life that may no longer appear desirable. Writing on the centrality of oil for making that other way of life possible—oil was important not just for the roads and cars but also the energy-saving household machines, and even the food and modes of provisioning food—Huber (2013) argues that the essential Fordist postwar bargain (for the white middle class) was a rote and unpleasant job for a good home life. The sphere of social reproduction became where freedom was experienced and where meaning was made, making for a clear separation of "life" and "work." So, in wanting meaningful, even if unpaid work, these young people are effectively rejecting that separation—and that bargain. In wanting to embrace muscle power, and perform what was once considered drudgery (not only through hard work but also through, for example, bicycle transportation), they also are rejecting (or at least suspicious of) reliance on cheap energy and automobility.

Or perhaps they are recognizing that the old middle class life would be attainable if they did want it. Opportunities for volunteering and interning are proliferating at a time when professional jobs are becoming scarcer—at least outside of the tech sectors—creating a sort of white-color precarity. Unfortunately, many employers take advantage of labor market conditions by offering unpaid internships as stepping-stones to real jobs, opportunities in which, of course, only those who can afford to forego income can participate (Perlin 2012). Many of my students wonder whether they will ever have a steady income, much less professional employment.

Whether by desire or necessity, many of my former students are piecing together their livelihoods: working in less than professional jobs (often related to food!), pursuing artistic endeavors, and doing a good deal of DIY as both pleasure and to develop quasi-survival skills. Their interest in survival skills is not incidental: In a class several years ago, I noticed many of my students were knitting or had brought their homemade kombucha. I asked them at the time about their attraction to DIY practices, and they admitted that their interest was both proto-anarchist and in preparation for the apocalypse. (All of a sudden I felt that I was the most optimistic person in the room!) In the context of these sorts of uncertainties, if not fears, self-food provisioning provides a number of solaces: sociability, sharing, and a better chance of having something on the table come what may.

*　*　*

What, then, are the politics of piecing together a life with DIY and other pursuits that erase boundaries of production and social reproduction? In writing about the growth of casual and informal work, Michael Denning (2010: 80) refutes the idea that waged labor is the norm from which capitalist life has veered. As he puts it, "the fetishism of the wage may well be the source of capitalist ideologies of freedom and equality, but the employment contract is not the founding moment. For capitalism begins not with the offer of work, but with the imperative to earn a living." For him, [...] "the informal economy precedes the formal, both historically and conceptually." In that way the realm of social reproduction, including household food provisioning, is not the relic other of real capitalist production but its basis, suggesting that defining human worthiness through participation in wage labor concedes too much to capitalism. Anna Tsing (2015: 20) similarly sees precarious living as the norm, as the "center of the systematicity we seek."

In offering a capacious idea of what does *not* count as work, Denning also suggests that "the wageless life" exists not only for so much of the world's extreme poor (Agamben's [1998] "bare life") but for many others. In a similar vein, Guy Standing (2011) has coined the term "the precariat" to refer to "the multitude of insecure people, living bits-and-pieces lives, in and out of short-term jobs, without a narrative of occupational development." Among the precariat, he includes the "millions of frustrated educated youth who do not like what they see before them." If we follow Tsing's (2015:2) definition of precarity as a "life without promise of stability," which depends on "noticing what is available," then, indeed, these students are part of the precariat.

So, I want to suggest that for these students there is also a kind of politics, albeit perhaps only an imminent one, in seeking unalienated, material labor or in refusing (or not prioritizing) waged work. In *The Problem with Work*, Kathi Weeks (2011) challenges the presupposition that work, or waged labor, is inherently a social and political good. Writing in a similar vein as Dunning, Weeks notes that we have accepted waged work as the primary mechanism for income distribution, as an ethical obligation, and as a means of defining ourselves and others as social and political subjects. Weeks argues for work refusal and proposes a post-work society that would allow people to be productive and creative rather than relentlessly bound to the employment relation. Growing and preparing food would no doubt be a central activity in such a society, since a nonwage economy would no longer make workers a commodity and therefore no longer make food a commodity. Many of these young people are experimenting in this kind of living.

*　*　*

And yet ... I can't help but juxtapose their situations and desires with those of the strawberry pickers who are the objects of my primary research these days. Their work is arduous. Paid primarily on piece rates, these farmworkers pick while bent over and when their boxes are full they literally run through the fields to get their boxes weighed and tabulated, only to start again. They are routinely subjected to a cocktail of chemicals, as well.

As mainly undocumented workers they have little ability to contest or improve conditions in their workplaces. Neither bare life nor classic waged workers, they work in these conditions out of economic necessity, indeed take the risk of crossing the border out of economic necessity. As Seth Holmes (2013) puts it, not earning a livelihood poses the much larger risk. For these workers, and many others in farm and food work today, the labor conditions are no basis for romanticization, notwithstanding the pride they may take in their work, given the substantial skill involved in truly arduous farmwork (Bardacke 2012; Holmes 2013).

So what strikes me is that these farmworkers are also part of the precariat. Yet, they obviously have a very different relationship to waged work and precarity than my former students and WWOOFers—so much so that Standing's capacious definition of the precariat seems to fall apart. In that light, it may be useful to engage recent work on surplus populations and disposability. Collard and Dempsey (2016), for example, differentiate those who are "officially valued" for their labor, even waged, but are otherwise of little consequence biopolitically—in Foucaultian thinking they do not count as part of the population deserving of protection. These "necropolitical subjects" are generally racially marked subjects who are useful as laboring bodies but whose futures are not protected precisely because of the existence of surplus populations (McIntyre and Nast 2011). Many food and farmworkers, not only those working in California strawberry production, are such necropolitical subjects.

In contrast, the privileged precariat, as we might call the students and WWOOFers, are inversely valued. That they are biopolitically recognized is evident in the security and protection they receive from, for example, remaining state safety nets, legal and regulatory protections, and relatively friendly policing. (They are not let to die, in Foucaultian terms.) And it is arguable that their biopolitical privileges make it possible for them to refuse capitalism. At the same time, they are of little use as waged workers—particularly in farming! This suggests an important distinction between biopolitical precarity and livelihood precarity. Biopolitical precarity, that experienced by farmworkers, is much more useful to capitalism, as it makes for more compliant and efficient workers.

These distinctions are by no means static, though. As it happens, strawberry growers are now faced with a labor shortage, thanks to the tightened border that once served them so well. Consequently, they are paying much more attention to field conditions to attract workers (Guthman 2016). If the current political climate against undocumented immigration continues, existing workers' and their children's lives could come to matter even more. Growers would then need to do more to protect workers, for instance with better pay, working conditions, access to health services, and perhaps less toxic exposures. In other words, workers may come to receive biopolitical recognition.

As for the privileged precariat of educated, middle-class (white) young adults, only time will tell if their precarity and their purposeful blending of work and leisure will continue to be a choice or if their various state and familial safety nets will fall away. One thing seems clear, though: their voluntary presence on farms does little to bring about biopolitical recognition for traditional farmworkers, other than remind employers that paid employees are more reliable and better trained. So the young adults who today volunteer on farms and engage in other acts of self-provisioning may indeed be engaged in a politics of work reconfiguration, but theirs is not a politics of solidarity.

Acknowledgments

Research for this project was made possible by the Mellon Foundation under the Changing Conceptions of Work initiative. This paper was strengthened from comments by members of the Changing Conceptions of Work through the Pleasures and Displeasures of Food working group, Lissa Caldwell, Seth Holmes, and Lisa Jacobson, as well as participants in the Sydney Environment Institute's symposium on Bodies | Caring | Eating: Gender in food provisioning.

References

Agamben, Giorgio. 1998. *Homer Sacer: Sovereign Power and Bare Life.* Stanford, CA: Stanford University Press.

Alcorta, Marisa, Jessy Beckett, and Reggie Knox. 2013. *California Guide to Labor Laws for Small Farms.* National Center for Appropriate Technology and California FarmLink.

Bardacke, Frank. 2012. *Trampling Out the Vintage: Cesar Chavez and the Two Souls of the United Farm Workers.* New York: Verso Books.

Biltekoff, Charlotte. 2013. *Eating Right in America: The Cultural Politics of Food and Health.* Durham, NC: Duke University Press.

Bowen, Sarah, Sinikka Elliott, and Joslyn Brenton. 2014. "The Joy of Cooking?" *Contexts* 13(3): 20–25.

Cody, Kevin. 2016. "Organic Farming and International Exchange: Participant Perceptions of North-South Transferability." *International Journal of Agricultural Sustainability* 14: 1–13.

Collard, Rosemary-Claire, and Jessica Dempsey. 2016. "Capitalist Natures in Five Orientations." *Capitalism Nature Socialism*, published online July 5.

Denning, Michael. 2010. "Wageless Life." *New Left Review* 66: 79–97.

Ekers, Michael, et al. 2015. "Will Work for Food: Agricultural Interns, Apprentices, Volunteers, and the Agrarian Question." *Agriculture and Human Values*, 1–16.

Gray, Margaret. 2013. *Labor and the Locavore: The Making of a Comprehensive Food Ethic.* Berkeley: University of California Press.

Guthman, Julie. 2016. "Paradoxes of the Border: Labor Shortages and Farmworker Minor Agency in Reworking California's Strawberry Fields." *Economic Geography*, published online July 13.

Guthman, Julie. 2011. *Weighing In: Obesity, Food Justice, and the Limits of Capitalism.* Berkeley: University of California.

Guthman, Julie. 2008. "Bringing Good Food to Others: Investigating the Subjects of Alternative Food Practice." *Cultural Geographies*, 15 (4), 431–447.

Holmes, Seth. 2013. *Fresh Fruit, Broken Bodies: Migrant Farmworkers in the United States.* Berkeley: University of California Press.

Huber, Matthew T. 2013. *Lifeblood: Oil, Freedom, and the Forces of Capital.* Minneapolis: University of Minnesota.

Maris, Emma. 2014. "Beyond Food and Evil: Nature and Haute Cuisine after the Chez Panisse Revolution." *Breakthrough Journal*, http://thebreakthrough.org/index.php/journal/past-issues/issue-4/beyond-food-and-evil.

McIntosh, Alison, and Tamara Campbell. 2001. "Willing Workers on Organic Farms (WWOOF): A Neglected Aspect of Farm Tourism in New Zealand." *Journal of Sustainable Tourism* 9(2): 111–27.

McIntosh, Alison J., and Susanne M. Bonnemann. 2006. "Willing Workers on Organic Farms (WWOOF): The Alternative Farm Stay Experience?" *Journal of Sustainable Tourism* 14(1): 82–99.

McIntyre, Michael, and Heidi J. Nast. 2011. "Bio(necro)polis: Marx, Surplus Populations, and the Spatial Dialectics of Reproduction and 'Race'." *Antipode* 43(5): 1465–88.

Mostafanezhad, Mary. 2016. "Organic Farm Volunteer Tourism as Social Movement Participation: A Polanyian Political Economy Analysis of World Wide Opportunities on Organic Farms (WWOOF) in Hawai'i." *Journal of Sustainable Tourism* 24(1): 114–31.

Perlin, Ross. 2012. *Intern Nation: How to Earn Nothing and Learn Little in the Brave New Economy*. New York: Verso Books.

Schugurensky, Daniel, and Karsten Mündel. 2005. "Volunteer Work and Learning: Hidden Dimensions of Labour Force Training." *International Handbook of Educational Policy*. Springer International Handbooks of Education series, vol. 13, 997–1022.

Standing, Guy. 2011. "The Precariat - the New Dangerous Class". *Policy Network*, http://www.policy-network.net/pno_detail.aspx?ID=4004

Tsing, Anna L. 2015. *The Mushroom at the End of the World: On the Possibility of Life in Capitalist Ruins*. Princeton, NJ: Princeton University Press.

Weeks, Kathy. 2011. *The Problem with Work: Feminism, Marxism, Antiwork Politics, and Postwork Imaginaries*. Durham, NC: Duke University Press.

2

Grocery Auction Games: Distribution and Value in the Industrialized Food System

Micah Marie Trapp

"Willing to Play the Dating Game with Your Food? Try a Grocery Auction"
— SERRI GRASLIE, *THE SALT* BLOG POST TITLE, NPR, AUGUST 23, 2012
"THE UNIVERSE BEGINS HERE!"
— COLONEL KIRK'S GROCERY AUCTION, MYGROCERYAUCTION.COM

The auction house was packed and steamy as a thunderous, steady rain pounded on the aluminum roof. Nestled within a maze of rural highways, farmland, industrial production facilities, and big-box stores along the Eastern Seaboard of the United States, the auction house provided welcome shelter from the brewing storm outside. More than a hundred bidders were scattered throughout the large room, sitting on folding chairs, surrounded by boxes and coolers full of food. Bidders chatted, laughed, and made trips to the concession stand, but managed to remain attentive to the flow and distribution of groceries. Bidding cards rose and fell in rhythmic succession as the price for a case of twelve strawberry and blueberry Stonyfield organic yogurt cups quickly reached six dollars. The winning bidder, a woman firmly planted in her metal folding chair, opted for two cases and tucked them into the already full cooler at her side. The remaining yogurt cases entered the pass-out phase, where other bidders could claim a share for the same price. As a few bidders waved cards in the air for yogurt, the grocery dealer and a couple of auction runners—those who helped the auctioneer spot bids from the audience, brought items up to the auction block, and carried items to winning bidders—wheeled an entire pallet of several hundred cases of the yogurt into the room.

The auctioneer boomed into his microphone: "Who wants yogurt? A dollar fifty per case." Bidding cards *shot* up into the air. Runners would typically carry the yogurt to the winning bidder, but the sheer volume brought the crowd to its feet as they formed a line to get the yogurt. An air of festivity exploded in the room; plastic spoons were plucked from the concession stand at the far end of the auction hall as people tasted and confirmed that the yogurt, despite its looming expiration date, was quite good. The yogurt had been a good deal at $6, but at $1.50 this was a savings of 93 percent based on retail price at the time of the auction. In the wake of this spectacular deal the crowd calmed down and bidding continued as usual: meat, soda, processed and frozen foods sped down the wheeled ramp from the refrigerated truck to the auction table and into the coolers of bidders. As the barely discernible chant of the auctioneer washed over me, my mind raced with questions: Why were there so many cases of yogurt? How did they get here? How could they be sold so cheaply?

Grocery auctions, as an outgrowth of the inefficiencies of the industrialized food system, repurpose unwanted, damaged, and overstock food that has been removed from the primary market (i.e., grocery stores, restaurants). Distributors, or grocery dealers, source these unwanted goods and bring them to the auction house, where the public is able to engage in the collaborative and competitive process of bidding to determine the value and distribution of the groceries. Jeffrey Cohen and Susan Klemetti (2014) described a grocery auction in Ohio as a site where bidders, dealers, and auctioneers collaborated to set prices well below the established retail value of food in the grocery store, but "the auction is not a place where bidders critique power and authority. Rather, the auction is a place where shared cultural norms … are performed, embraced, and given voice and where an alternative framework for action is constructed around shared tastes and values" (85). In the capitalist industrialized food system, retail price and food labels such as expiration dates and brand operate as key mediators of value as food travels across lengthy supply chains. But at the grocery auction many foods are approaching or have reached their expiration date or remain unfamiliar to bidders; new or intermediary markers of value are needed. How, then, do grocery auctions turn the spoils and waste of the capitalist industrialized food system into valued food? How is the value of a deal generated?

In *The Mushroom at the End of the World: On the Possibility of Life in Capitalist Ruins*, Anna Tsing (2015) examines the emergence, disappearance, and convergence of value forms as she contemplates what it is that can survive in the ruins of capitalism. Capitalism, for Tsing, is a "translation machine" (133), suturing or "patching" (62) meaning and value across space and time. For example, mushrooms—organisms that feed off of dead organic matter—and the people who pick them intersect in "contaminated diversity" (30), an encounter that enables transformation and collaborative survival. Mushrooms thrive in ruined forests, such as those devastated by logging; Hmong refugees who pick these mushrooms find freedom and build livelihoods in these same forests. In a fitting parallel, yogurt—whose bacteria feed on sugar, an icon of excess and ruin in the industrialized food system—is one of the few *living* foods we purchase, and it made regular appearances at the grocery auctions I attended. Yet, its life on the auction block was a precarious one: rapidly approaching expiration dates raised fears of spoilage, and cartons of yogurt rescued from a tractor-trailer spill—indeed, a compelling icon of the ruined landscape of the industrialized food system—were more or less given away. Yogurt deals at the grocery auction thus become an apt vehicle for thinking about the dynamic nature of value in the industrialized food system.

The grocery auction, as a site where consumers (bidders) and distributors (dealers, auctioneers) collaborate to give meaning and value to the discards of the industrialized food system, also presents a rare opportunity to study how processes of *distribution* in the capitalist industrialized food system influence the value of the food. During the competitive play of bidding, the divergent needs and motivations of distributers and consumers intersect and collectively determine the value of food. Thus, distribution, rather than production, emerges as a central force in the creation of value. Here, I argue that the social dimensions of distribution enacted through bidding expose the products of the industrialized food system as contested sites of engagement rather than hegemonic markers of value. The contaminated diversity of making deals at the grocery auction reveals cracks and slippage in the otherwise seamless narrative of value in the capitalist industrialized food system.

I begin by situating the grocery auction within a politics of distribution. Next, I describe my research methodology and discuss the "business" of getting food to the auction house. Following this, I draw on ethnographic and survey data to introduce the demographics, behaviors, and motivations of bidders. I then analyze bidding and the creation of deals as a strategy for resolving uncertainties in value; in doing so, I show how value is defined through capitalist notions of profit and savings, but also derives from the social relations of distribution. I also demonstrate how the social processes of distribution engage, expose, and may even transform existing markers of value, such as a brand, in the industrialized food system. Finally, I examine two deals, pork and probiotics, to consider how the complex social interplay of bidding may generate visibility of the value-making process and inspire reflection upon the value of food. The article concludes by resituating the grocery auction universe within the ruins of the industrialized food landscape.

From Invisible to Visible: Value and the Politics of Distribution

Extensive research has focused on the role of producers and consumers in shaping the value of food, particularly in alternative food movements. Distribution processes and channels have generally remained invisible and marginalized despite ongoing declarations (Arce and Marsden 1993; Dixon 1999; Ilbery and Maye 2005) and attempts (Cook and Crang 1996) to consider their significance in adding value to food. Conceptual frames such as "the social life of things" (Appadurai 1986), "commodity biographies" (Kopytoff 1986), following the thing (Bestor 2004), "commodityscapes" (Cook 2004; Foster 2008; Lundy 2012), and "supply chain capitalism" (Tsing 2009) have rendered distribution processes visible to some extent, and in the latter case, have revealed the exploitative and marginalized dynamics of distribution. Tsing's (2015) more recent account of the mushroom industry is one of few anthropological studies to consider distribution in the capitalist industrialized food system as engaged, social processes of exchange.

Distribution has featured much more prominently in discussions of "alternative food," such as the local food and slow food movements, where the focus on shorter supply chains and linking consumers directly to producers emerges as a restorative function. However, this focus on shorter supply chains may contribute to the invisibility of distribution. In Heather Paxson's (2013) study of value in the American artisanal cheese industry, for example, distribution is treated nominally, and then only as a negative factor—i.e., unreliable UPS trucking services—in constructing the value of food (100). Nonetheless, the shorter and social supply chains of alternative food remain situated as a mechanism for repairing the ills of the industrialized food system. Critics have questioned the extent to which alternative food movements based on environmental sustainability, fair labor practices, and shorter supply chains have actually changed the structure of the capitalist, industrialized food system (Fonte 2013; Guthman 2004; Harris 2009), embedded economic and racial inequalities (Allen 1999; Guthman 2008), and fetishized relationships to food production processes (Gunderson 2014: 111). Efforts to repair the industrialized food system (Grey 2000: 147; Gregory and Gregory 2010: 104) remain thwarted by a central, unresolved paradox surrounding distribution: despite extensive surplus production, massive amounts of food are wasted while people remain hungry (Bloom 2010; Patel 2007).

When distribution does appear as a point of value making in the capitalist industrialized food system, it is primarily through the lens of redistribution. For example, soup kitchens, food banks and pantries, and food recovery programs redistribute unused food as charity, but these efforts do not change the underlying inequalities and inefficiencies wrought by the capitalist industrialized food system (Poppendieck 1998). In his study of the circulation of "devalued value" in food banking, George Henderson (2004: 508) explains how hunger, as a lowest common denominator, "articulates" and creates connections across a broad range of political interests, but ultimately works against the interests of those who are hungry. The diverse political interests represented on the food bank's board—all of whom work to help the hungry—prevented the executive director from advocating for living wage legislation, a policy that would help to alleviate hunger. Henderson thus characterizes food banking as a "dilemmatic space" (Honig 1996 in Henderson 2004: 509): while premised on the value of relieving hunger, the food bank ultimately reproduces the exploitative dimensions of capitalist labor relations that generate hunger. More recent framings of redistribution, such as Ferguson's (2015) distributive political economy, draw on webs of reciprocity to frame distribution as a vital form of survival in the postindustrial economy marked by high unemployment rates and grave inequalities. Here, my aim is not to propose the grocery auction as a mechanism of repair for solving the inequalities of the capitalist industrialized food system. Rather, my analysis of the grocery auction situates distribution as a central factor in the creation of value; in doing so, this research charts new terrain for understanding the generative potential of value.

Researching Distribution

In her work on coffee in Papua New Guinea, Paige West (2012: 195) argues that anthropologists have not studied distribution to any notable extent, given the difficulties of safety and health regulations on transport vehicles and high-stress labor conditions. More significantly, she argues, a study of distribution would expand the ethnographic field of vision so much so that anthropologists would behave like journalists, catching only glimpses of distribution. Considering the limitations raised by West, I have focused on one site of distribution—the grocery auction—and a small number of distributors as well as consumers (bidders) to cultivate an understanding of how the distribution of food impacts its value. Numerous sites (distribution centers, storage facilities), processes (procurement, road travel), and actors (grocery and distribution center staff) inevitably and regrettably remain left out of my ethnographic field of vision.

My ethnographic research was conducted at ten grocery auctions in Maryland and Mississippi. Auctions were selected based on convenience and do not represent a generalizable account. The bidding component of auctions lasted from three to eight hours, but the time before and after formal auction activities proved to be vital components of my participant observation as I used this time to talk with dealers, auctioneers, other auction staff (runners, clerks), and bidders about their bidding and cooking plans. The majority of my participant observation during the auction consisted of bid-alongs, which I adapted from Beall's (2010) shop-along technique, a method where the researcher accompanies a shopper to ask questions as consumption decisions are made. I selected twenty-three bid-along participants based on convenience and approachability; bid-alongs ranged from several minutes to several hours and were invaluable for understanding the social dynamics among bidders, auctioneers, and dealers. In many instances, bid-alongs also resulted in my own bidding, which kept my refrigerator and freezer stocked throughout the duration of my research, but also helped me to understand the complex social dynamics that emerge during bidding exchanges. In one auction, I also spent a sustained period of time working on the distribution truck, sending goods to the auction block. In another, I filled in as an auction runner, holding up items as the bidding took place, calling bids to the record-keeper (which required shouting to be heard in the large auction hall), and carrying items to the winning bidder. I also conducted interviews with six dealers and seven auctioneers and auction staff.

After attending several auctions, I drew on insights from my participant observation to develop a survey, which I field-tested with thirty-two bidders. Following the field test, I constructed a series of Likert scales to assess auction behavior and bidding motivation, including questions that asked about food preferences and familiarity, brand, packaging, saving money, "getting a deal," entertainment, food waste, health, winning, group influence, and buying for others. The survey also collected demographic data and included questions about auction attendance, grocery and auction budgets, as well as use of auction food. At each auction, I set up a survey table, but most participants were individually approached in the seating area for bidders. Prior to the start of an auction, auctioneers also introduced my research and encouraged bidders to participate. The results of this survey (n=171) represent bidders from five of the auctions I attended in Maryland; research conducted in Mississippi primarily provides additional ethnographic context and detail. Here, I draw on this body of qualitative and quantitative data to reveal how the complex dynamics of distribution created and transformed the value of food.

Hidden Circuits of Value: Getting Groceries to the Auction House

In 2009, journalists started reporting on the "new" phenomenon of grocery auctions as a fun way to stretch food dollars during tough economic times (Associated Press 2009; Graslie 2012), but one dealer in my research reported supplying a grocery auction since 1995. Data posted on the nationwide website Auctionzip.com reveals a sizable grocery auction landscape. In June 2015, 143 grocery auctions were held in 21 different states, concentrated in the Midwest, Northeast, and Southeast, and with few exceptions, grocery auctions occur in rural areas and smaller towns.[1] … In this section, I provide an overview of the "business" of distributing food through the grocery auction.

My first interview took place in a truck where I found Fred, a boisterous auctioneer in his sixties, napping before the start of an auction. Within moments of waking, Fred animatedly described his lifelong love of auctions, but cautioned that the grocery dealer would need to grant research permission. When I later approached the dealer's refrigerated truck "office," the telltale pair of feet sticking out the window indicated that he was also taking a nap. Tim, a veteran grocery dealer who had worked as a food distributor on the primary market for three decades, agreed to my research as long as I did not ask where the food came from. However, after attending several auctions where Tim distributed groceries, we developed a comfortable rapport. One night after a five-hour auction, we chatted as he waited for the auctioneer to pay him his cut of the sales. When I caught myself mid-sentence asking Tim where he had managed to get so much yogurt, he offered a pointed smile and proceeded to explain that he had recently been called to pick up a thousand cases of Fage yogurt from a truck that had overturned; while the manufacturer and trucking company remained in dispute over who was at fault for the accident, Tim was called in to clean up the perishable mess. In addition to cleaning up messes along the road or in stores, salvage dealers often sourced food directly from retail stores and vending machines by removing products nearing their sell-by date from the shelves. Tim's business thus hinged upon the successful transformation of this discarded food waste into a valued food commodity.

In a rather literal version of "salvage capitalism" (Tsing 2015: 63)—where capitalists generate value from what they do not control—dealers realize surplus value from the embedded expectations of waste within the industrialized food system. When Tim worked as a distributor for Eckrich—a meat brand owned by Smithfield Foods—his company assumed and allowed a three percent margin for product loss on the goods he distributed. Tim now operates within and extracts value from this three percent margin. Salvage may offer deep savings in food — "I basically name my own price," explained Tim — but salvage dealers have "no choice [in product] whatsoever. They call me and I take the whole lot." Tim put it simply, "You [the dealer] make money when you buy it [food]," and he used his expansive and encyclopedic knowledge of food prices and preferences to determine how he would distribute a thousand cases of yogurt, an entire pallet of baked beans, or three hundred pounds of whole bean coffee.

Dealers worked and took care to acquire a stock of goods with the potential for high exchange value; providing bidders with foods consistent with their tastes resulted in higher profit margins. Tim achieved this through diverse sourcing tactics: direct from manufacturers, overstock distribution centers, wholesale auctions, liquidation sales run by distributors, and salvage; his extensive contacts in the food industry; and his deep knowledge of consumer preferences. Less experienced dealers intentionally avoided salvage goods as a testimony to the high quality of their products. As Mark, a new dealer, explained: "When I see the trucks, [a] tractor-trailer overturned on the highway, I don't chase it. That's called salvage. The stuff that's ready for the dumpster. It's like six months or a year out of date Some people do buy it, and some people do sell it. But I would never sell something that's a year out of date or two years out of date." During the auction, as I will discuss, dealers and auctioneers worked together to help bidders negotiate the sometimes ambiguous value of the foods.

Inside the Auction House: Playing the Bidding Game

Inside the auction house endless amounts of food appear, seemingly out of nowhere, in the raised arms of auction runners and eventually disappear into the loaded coolers of bidders. Groceries travel along a "food line," which at one auction consisted of a long hallway stacked with boxes of food, largely outside the view of bidders. In other auctions, the food slid down a wheeled conveyor belt to make its way from a refrigerated truck to the bidding table or perishables hid inside coolers and freezers at the front of the auction house.[2] An excerpt from my field log reflects a wide array of industrialized food products sold in fifteen minutes: a twenty-pound box of spicy chicken nuggets; five-pound boxes of breaded chicken breast patties; cans of V8; five-pound boxes of precooked ground beef; fifteen pounds of frozen egg omelet; cases of meatless meatballs; eight-pound containers of potato salad; cases of Odwalla orange juice; and five-pound bags of frozen, headless cleaned whiting fish. Auctioneers worked closely with dealers to peddle such food and bidders paid a "buyer's premium," usually ten percent in the auctions I attended, on top of the winning bid to compensate the auctioneer. In this section, I draw on survey data to describe the demographics, motivations, and behaviors of bidders who were ready (or not) to bid on these groceries.

Harry and Sue, a couple in their fifties dressed in jeans, T-shirts, and sneakers, ran their own carpet cleaning business and were keenly aware of retail food prices and like the majority of bidders I surveyed (85%), they approached the auction as an opportunity to save money on food because the distribution of food at the grocery auction frequently resulted in prices that were drastically below retail norms. Though united by the motivation to save money, bidders represented a wide array of occupations—farmers, service industry jobs, teachers, and federal contractors— and income levels, with the lowest concentration (4%) earning less than $20,000 and the highest concentration (24%) more than $100,000 annually.[3] Findings from my survey reveal that bidders skewed toward middle-aged and older: 48% were aged 35-54 and 39% were aged 55 and older. Just 13% reported that they were aged 18-34.

While bidders exhibited some economic diversity, bidders generally constituted a fairly homogenous and privileged group, particularly in Maryland. Bidders were primarily white, though a small number of African Americans attended some of the auctions that I studied. In Maryland, quite a few Mennonites attended and purchased large amounts of food at grocery auctions that they loaded onto horse-drawn carts. Grocery auctions were time consuming and required leisure time to participate; thus, the grocery auction may reproduce inequalities, allowing only those with time to spare to benefit from such great deals. In some instances, as I will discuss below, unemployed individuals approached the grocery auction as a form of important work that helped them stick to a small food budget. However, more frequently, bidders came to the auction to be social *and* to save money while doing so.

The auction was marked by a general, shared sentiment of thrift and getting the best deal possible, regardless of income or wealth. Harold and Madge had been going to auctions at the Cat's Cradle Auction House for the past twenty years, but now only attended grocery auctions to buy food for their large, extended family, including their dog, four children, five grandchildren, and one great-grandchild who lived nearby. Years earlier, Harold had received a multimillion-dollar worker's compensation settlement for a debilitating accident, but they remained concerned with paying as little as possible for their groceries. Harold and Madge had installed three freezers in their house so that their kids can come over and "shop." On the day that we talked, they had specifically purchased croissant sandwiches for their daughter, hot dogs for their son-in-law (and dog—"the dog eats better than I do," claimed Harold), paper cups for their son, and forty pounds of ribs for the cookout they were having with their neighbors the next day.

The grocery auction primarily supplemented rather than supplanted regular grocery shopping; fresh fruits and vegetables in particular rarely appeared at the auction. Almost half of the bidders

(46%) spent from $50–149 at a grocery auction, while the median reported monthly grocery budget ranged from $300-399. Most bidders (60%) had attended a grocery auction one to three times in the past year; 20% attended one every few months; and 17% attended a grocery auction every other month or more. Bidders varied quite significantly in the amount and variety of food they purchased, with some—especially newcomers—purchasing just a few items.[4] It was common for bidders to fill coolers, and one family remarked that they only shopped at the grocery store to purchase staples such as eggs, milk, and bread that were generally not available at the auction.

Relying substantially on the grocery auction required strategies for storing large quantities of food; twenty-six bidders (15%) reported they had purchased an extra refrigerator or freezer after attending an auction. Anecdotally, bidders mentioned having multiple refrigerators and freezers (or borrowing space in a neighbor's freezer) and had sophisticated techniques of packaging, logging, rotating, and storing food. However, storing large amounts of food did not solely result from the auction; living primarily in rural areas, the majority of bidders (78%) traveled less than thirty miles to attend a grocery auction and tended to store food at home because the nearest grocery store was often far from home.

For many bidders, the grocery auction was a social event and form of entertainment. After a couple filled a *massive* cooler with meats and frozen foods, they explained that they usually spent $300 per grocery auction. While they approached their monthly trip to the auction house as a pragmatic endeavor—they had two teenage daughters who ate a lot and buying in bulk helped them stay within their $500 monthly grocery budget—they described their evening as "date night at the grocery auction." Unlike shopping at a store, purchasing food through the auction gave them the opportunity to simultaneously socialize and save. Harry and Sue explained: "We'd spend sixty dollars if we went out anyway, so it doesn't really matter if we spend sixty dollars at the grocery auction." By attributing bidding to multiple budget categories—food and entertainment—bidders approached the grocery auction as an opportunity to spend money on food in ways that went beyond stocking their freezer. Since they were having fun, Harry and Sue felt free to deviate from their regular grocery budget and bought food for others: caramel sauce for Sue's mom, snacks for her sister and nieces, and probiotic water for their church. In the next section, I draw on the social dimensions of bidding to demonstrate how distribution occupies a central role in the construction of value.

The Deal: The Social Dimensions of Distribution

"There's [sic] two reasons people go to auctions," proclaimed Fred, "One, to get a commodity product or whatever they can't get anywhere else. … That's not the reason they come [to a grocery auction]. Second reason is they come to get a good deal. And that's why they come here. They come to get a good deal." Indeed, nearly all bidders (98%) agreed that they would bid on an item because it was a "deal."[5] Fred and other auctioneers I interviewed disagreed with Smith's (1989: 164) theory that auctions serve the ritual purpose of transforming an object of unknown value into a known value: people know what food costs. Bidding is a collective and competitive process for determining the price and allocation of goods; at the grocery auction, bidding resolves the uncertainty surrounding the quality and distribution of the discarded products of the capitalist industrialized food system. In this section, I analyze bidding and the creation of deals as a strategy for resolving uncertainties in value; in doing so, I show how value is defined through capitalist notions of profit and savings, but also derives from the social relations of distribution.

Dealers, auctioneers, and bidders occupy conflicting roles and motivations in the grocery auction business: dealers and auctioneers want to realize profits while bidders seek savings. The auctioneer, as an interlocutor between seller and buyer, must create a sense of community among an otherwise disjointed group of bidders in order for winning bids to be accepted by all (Smith 1989: 55) and frequently uses humor to create a collective spirit and to entice bidding (see Cohen and Klemetti 2014). As I held up a gallon jar of spicy horseradish sauce for bidding, the auctioneer exclaimed: "It's great on ice cream!" When a pork butt came up for bid, a runner shouted: "BUTT!! steak," causing the crowd to roar with laughter. Auctioneers also made explicit efforts to unite bidders: "At this auction house, we share. If the person next to you looks hungry, open 'em up and give 'em a spoon," urged Robert as he launched into selling a pallet of yogurt. Indeed, grocery auctions are social events: bidders and auction staff frequently referred to their "auction friends" and "auction family." As I interviewed an auction clerk before the start on an auction, we frequently had to pause our interview because so many people greeted her: she had worked at the auction house for decades and described the bidders as her "auction family." Later, during the auction, I sat in the front row with Sandra, who had called ahead to reserve her seat. She had been coming to the auction house for years and explained that the auctioneer was such a good man, she kept coming back because he was "like family."

During the bidding process, grocery dealers also stirred excitement by creating combined deals that generated savings and profit. Tim frequently combined boxes of steaks with cases of soda because when auctioned on its own, soda would only sell for a few dollars, but when combined with meats the deals usually exceeded $20. While I chatted with Sandra she won a deal that included a bag of a dozen three-ounce crab cakes and a case of Diet Coke for $17. As she packed the crab cakes inside her cooler, Sandra commented to me: "Maybe it's not the best deal." If a dealer noticed this kind of frustration among bidders, he might call back the price to produce an undeniable and irresistible deal: when the bidding on Farmland honey-cured quarter spiral hams had ended at $15, Tim cut the price back to $7.50. Such drastic reductions in price were seen almost as a gift, or at the very least an act of goodwill that compelled bidders to pack their coolers full. During bid-alongs, I regularly heard bidders talk of "helping" the auctioneer or dealer to get rid of the food. Nonetheless, in the midst of excitement surrounding such prices, bidders attempted to mediate and assess the quality and value of an item. When a fifty-pound double pork loin appeared on the auction block, the auctioneer yelled, "Folks, this is what's called eating high on the hog!" As it sold for $45, the man sitting next to me called out, "Is it bull hog?" I quickly asked him to explain. "It's an old breeder hog that smells nasty and tastes nasty too." In his assessment, this could be the only explanation for why such a large cut of meat would be available for that price.

Bidders' familiarity with the groceries generally neutralized questions about the sourcing of the food, but expired or unfamiliar foods—such as frozen cassava — or prices that were very low—such as the bull hog—could generate uncertainty among bidders. Dealers thus became key figures in vouching for food quality. At the start of an auction, the grocery dealer or auctioneer typically commented on the source and quality of the food, including a promise to announce if and when a food item was expired. First-time grocery auction-goers were often unsure of how to assess the quality of the food; as one runner explained, "Some people have the misconception that the 'best if used by' dates is [*sic*] actually an expiration date, but it's not. It's just a taste standpoint.... It's not something that's regulated by the FDA or anything like that from my understanding."[6] In my survey, only twelve (34.3%) first-time bidders stated they would bid on expired food, while nearly half (44.3%, 35) of bidders who had attended more than one auction were willing to bid on expired food, suggesting that bidders either became comfortable with expired food or did not return to the auction. However, when cracks and questions surrounding the quality of food did emerge, dealers employed active remediation strategies. For example, Tim set up a "free sample" table of vending-machine chips after someone had complained that they were out of date and stale. In another auction, a runner opened a gallon container of peeled, hardboiled eggs and bit into one to prove to the audience that they were okay; but after spending the evening in the refrigerator truck, the egg was partially frozen and he immediately spit it out, causing the crowd to scream with glee. Some items—a box of one hundred airline meals—simply never became a deal.

As tensions surrounding the quality of food suggest, the generosity and goodness of "auction family" feeling was not seamless; the tactics of the auctioneer and dealer could become coercive and getting a good deal required an attentive bidder. Bidders were generally knowledgeable about the retail price of food and exhibited "smart" bidding behavior, reflecting the principles of an "efficient housewife": organized, disciplined to withstand impulse buys, staying within budget, and making rational decisions (Koch 2011: 69). Embracing their roles as consumers in a capitalist system, one mother and daughter attended auctions together so that the daughter, who worked in a grocery, could advise on retail prices. When bidding on beef jerky ended at $10 and was further cut back to $5, the daughter advised it was still cheaper at Walmart. Some bidders brought store ads for reference, while others used their phones to check retail prices. As Sandra explained, "I try not to go overboard. I look at sales ads to see what things are going for. You can get food anywhere."

Before the start of one auction, I chatted with Chelsea, an especially "smart" bidder, while she clipped coupons. A year earlier, she had lost her job and now invested a substantial amount of time and labor into using coupons to manage on a tight budget. Chelsea was interested in meat products because there are rarely coupons for meat, and in bulk deals such as big boxes of vending-size chips. When bidding on chips ended at $12.50, Chelsea had been careful to come in as the backup bidder—the last person to be bidding against the winner—thereby ensuring that she would be the second person to select chips if the winning bidder did not take all of the chips, which was unlikely in this case given that the dealer had at least half a dozen cases on the auction block. Chelsea's focus on being a backup bidder transformed the chips into a deal: she had been able to get her preferred assortment of chips, but did not drive up the price of the chips by engaging in a bidding war. "Smart" bidders like Chelsea often became frustrated with "stupid" bidders, those who continued to drive up the price of a product when it was clear that the dealer had plenty of an item. One evening two people were suddenly caught in an unexpected, brief, and furious bidding war over four one-gallon containers of Heinz white vinegar. The victorious woman paid $15 (plus a 10% buyers' premium and sales tax), or just over $4 per gallon of vinegar. After a quick calculation, it appeared that this was higher than most retail stores. As one of the auction runners stacked the vinegar next to the victorious woman, her expression was riddled with ambiguity. Was this really a deal? Auctioneers described such moments as getting caught up in "auction fever."

While bidders could "overpay"—a concept frequently discussed—most transformations were celebrated as amazing deals, and the auction was viewed as a place to save money. Some distributors even viewed the transformation from salvage to food as a service; as Fred the auctioneer explained:

> He [the dealer] has a sign that the coffee's out of date.... But there's nothing wrong with that coffee ... but, they can't retail it, you know? So what are they going to do with it? Throw it in the dumpster? Take it down to [the] Bay and open it up and [laughs] have some crab feed or what? [The auction is] a service ... [a way of] liquidating the product without having to discard it in a landfill or ... flushing it down in a water system somewhere.

Cohen and Klemetti (2014: 85) maintain that "the auction does not create a 'moral economy' where justice replaces competition." However, approached through a framework of contaminated diversity, the grocery auction contains elements of capitalist profiteering *and* justice. For example, Mark, a grocery dealer who also acted as his own auctioneer, narrated the service of the grocery as a form of opposition to corporations and subsequently as a mechanism for obtaining consumer justice. The grocery auction is "a *public* service to help people save money from the big guys" (emphasis mine). "It is tough out there," explained Mark, "a lot of people are still out of work, [and] ... you can't make it on a Walmart salary because they don't pay forty hours. 'Cause they cut their corners by [paying] no benefits." Mark continued, "If we get juice for $1.25, Walmart is buying that same juice, but buying an entire truckload. They are going to get it even cheaper, but charge that much more. Their profits are huge." While Mark adamantly described his efforts to distribution food as a form of justice, he was still careful to generate profits while simultaneously redistributing industrial food waste and surplus to pass the "savings" on to consumers.

Risky Business: From Trash Value to Refurbished Commodities

In the capitalist industrialized food system, brand operates as the primary symbol of quality and distinction. On the surface, the grocery auction is no different: auctioneers, dealers, and bidders all relied on brand as a symbol of value. As one auctioneer boasted during an interview: "There have been times that we have had not only steaks, but high-end roast beef, lunch meats, lots of pizza." An auction runner piped in: "DiGiorno. All brand name stuff." When Frito-Lay chips were on the auction block, Harry shook his head and turned to me: "I'm an UTZ man." He later opted out of bidding on tuna: "We only buy Sunkist." Other brands smell "too fishy," and Sunkist, Harry added, "is dolphin free." Indeed, Cohen and Klemetti (2014: 85) have argued that bidders preferred certain brands and shopped "according to their tastes." At grocery stores, consumers become unconsciously subject to corporate constructions of value through weekly sales promotions, and the intentional placement of products (Koch 2011), but at the grocery auction, the dynamic process of distribution presents an opportunity to expose the unstable and malleable process of brand loyalty (Foster 2007). While nearly half (49%, 84) of the respondents in my survey agreed they would bid on an item because it was brand name, almost a third (32%, 54) *disagreed* that brand influenced their bidding. In this section, I demonstrate how the social processes of distribution engage, expose, and may even transform existing markers of value, such as a brand, in the industrialized food system.

While dealers were the first to acknowledge that the grocery auction had little impact on the overall food system, they were, nonetheless, players in a threatening game. Corporations protect their products from the cannibalization of demand—the ability of the secondary market to destroy consumer desire for branded goods on the primary market—by developing legal codes that restrict the circulation and distribution of branded products. While it was difficult for corporations to enforce these codes, grocery dealers strategically negotiated the limitations of selling branded goods on the secondary market. For example, Tim did not allow news crews to record his auctions because he imagined how an executive might react if he saw a DiGiorno pizza being auctioned for $2.50. Such fears were not unfounded: a corporate lawyer had contacted Mark: "Some products I sell are not meant to be mentioned what they are. ... I've already had a confrontation with a lawyer once." In fact, after selling squeeze bottles of Miracle Whip for a dollar, Mark joked, "They'd probably sue me if they knew I was sellin' it that cheap. They'd put me in jail." In another instance, he held up a box of Italian Ice and announced: "Freezer pops is what the hell they are. Three dollars?" When no one raised a card to bid, he proclaimed: "I can't steal this stuff, I gotta buy it." Mark's jokes demand visibility and compensation for his risky labor, but he also used them to simultaneously capitalize upon and challenge the brand as a mechanism for determining value.

Mark held up unlabeled bags of ground coffee: "Real Dunkin Donuts coffee, premium house blend," he called, and the bidding started as Mark explained that the coffee was for restaurants and thus not labeled with a commercial logo. Moments later, he once held up another set of unmarked coffee: "I can't say the name. My friends bought three trucks of this. There's a place in [Boone] County that relabels it. It had to be repackaged. I'm not allowed to say the name. I'm gonna give you a hint: sitting on the porch at night, looking up at the sky." When a bidder purchased both types of coffee, Mark suggested the bidder could alternate his morning coffee routine: "Dunkin. Stars. Dunkin. Stars." In this instance Mark exploited brand value to increase bidding and sales, but also corporate tactics of brand protection, such as the removal of the Starbucks logo. At a later point in the auction, Mark further exposed the construction of brand value. When a case of Valley Gem baked beans came up for bidding, Mark launched into a fictional narrative about the non-English-speaking factory worker who was operating the labeling machine. As he dramatically turned over the can of Valley Gem beans, Mark exposed an ink stamp that boasted the Busch's Baked Beans slogan on the bottom of the can. Mark explained that this error had allowed him to acquire the beans, which not only tasted like, but *were*, Busch's Baked Beans. In constructing this narrative, Mark reified and resisted brand value.

In her study of American artisanal cheese, Heather Paxson (2013) characterizes artisanal cheese as an *unfinished commodity*. Unlike finished commodities—those with established and collectively recognized value, i.e., established retail prices—consumers do not know how much artisanal cheese should cost. Instead, the unfinished nature of the commodity presents an opportunity for the values of producers and consumers to inform and shape the value of the cheese. Similarly, the value of food at the auction must be—and is—made by consumers, but bidders know the retail price of the food; it is not an unfinished commodity. The value of grocery auction deals derives through other means. In contrast to the emergent value-making of unfinished commodities, in "Following Things of Rubbish Value: End-of-Life Ships, 'Chock-Chocky' Furniture and the Bangladeshi Middle Class Consumer," Gregson et al. (2010) look "down" the value chain to consider how value emerges in the disassembling of things and subsequent transformation into new object and value forms.

The grocery auction similarly operates "down" the supply chain and manages to generate value from rubbish; however, unlike the movement from ship breaking to furniture making (Gregson et al. 2010), the grocery auction is not the work of destruction. At the grocery auction, foods appear as salvage and waste; the process of making value is rooted in ruin, survival, and repair generated through processes of *distribution*. In this way, the emergence of value at the grocery auctions takes shape in the action of refurbishment. Mark's narration of the afterlives of industrialized food commodities, whether true or not, exposed the simultaneous importance and fallacy of corporate branding as a marker of value. Mark's work at the end of the industrialized food supply chain reveals the interdependence and overlap of participants along the supply chain and also shows how distribution remains simultaneously embedded in capitalism (Mark profits from the auction), social relations (Mark implores bidders to help him deal with the glut of industrialized food waste), and justice (Mark helps bidders to avoid the exploitation of corporate branding). Dealers such as Mark do not merely reproduce, but engage, curate, and may even transform existing markers of value in the industrialized food system.

Pork and Probiotics: Making Value Visible

"What most people come here for!" shouts the auctioneer as his runners hold up fifteen-pound boxes of bacon. Bacon appeared at many auctions I attended and the fifteen-pound boxes of bacon typically sold for $30—40. One evening, Kevin—a single man in his twenties who had learned about the auction from his co-worker at the mechanic shop — won sixty pounds of bacon. When I asked what his plans were, Kevin laughed and said he did not realize how much bacon he had won. He initially bought a single box of bacon, but then won several combined deals that included more bacon. Kevin speculated he would take a lot of bacon-related dishes—a "bacon explosion" and bacon prepared with an apple butter and cinnamon rub — to share with his co-workers and help him reduce his bacon stockpile. Fred's insistence that the purpose of the grocery auction centers on "how much food can you get for as little as possible" resonates. Cohen and Klemetti (2014: 83-85) argued that the social dimensions of the auction limited excess and greed at the auction, but in this section, I extend analysis of the social dimensions of distribution to consider how bidding impacts the value and meaning of food.

In "It Is Value That Brings Universes into Being," David Graeber (2013) outlines an "ontological gambit": people move between multiple, contradictory worlds and systems of value because they do not care about the nature of reality; rather, people participate in "as-if play." They invest in the players of a game and thus adopt the attendant values and reality of that social world. Graeber's analogy of the game is a particularly apt metaphor for unpacking value at the grocery auction: bidding *is* a game. Indeed: 86 percent of bidders surveyed agreed that they attended grocery auctions because they are fun; 27 percent agreed that they bid to win; and one auction house was invited to tape a pilot reality TV show, but declined out of fear that the show would not reflect the "family values" of the auction. At first glance, the grocery auction is a game that promotes getting a good deal and boundless consumption; however, upon closer inspection, the game is quite a bit more complex.

In Graeber's ontological gambit, the nature of social reality only becomes significant when worlds collide and ontological claims are made to cement the status of one universe over another. The domination of one system of value over another occurs through the creation of "metavalues," which emerge by "taking the tacit *interior* values that inform *how* one goes about pursuing value within certain fields … and reassembling them as an explicit value in themselves" (233; emphasis in original). For example, in a capitalist industrialized food system marked by weekly sales and double coupons, getting a deal operates as a metavalue, an end in and of itself. While the grocery auction is firmly rooted in the capitalist industrialized food system, at the grocery auction—where buyers and sellers collaborate, despite competing needs—the process of value formation is altered: the capitalist metavalue of the deal also exists as an interior value enacted through the practice of bidding. Bidding—the *making* of deals — is the method of determining value. As a communal and visible process, the interior value of making a deal can expose and test the limits of its status as a metavalue and consuming just to get a good deal. I return to the ubiquity of bacon to explain.

As a dealer pulled box after box of bacon from the truck, a few bidders raised their cards for bacon, but I heard a mutter: "I still have some from last time." "It comes out in strips!" yells the dealer, hoping his humor might inspire more bids. "We know what bacon is," shouts the auctioneer, "get back in the truck!" The crowd bursts into laughter as the bacon stays in the truck and the bidding moves on to one-pound containers of guacamole. The excess of bacon and the visibility of the labor required to distribute it, to make it into a deal, presents opportunities for disruption, inquiry, and reflection: Do I want bacon? Why is there so much bacon? Where should all this bacon go? Swept up in the action and game of the auction, Kevin did not ask these questions when bidding; but as the winner and owner of sixty pounds of bacon, Kevin most certainly faced that question of what he would do with all the bacon. However, other bidders refrained from buying bacon they did not need, despite its appearance as a record low deal for the fifteen-pound boxes that night. In an attempt to explain the sudden devaluation of bacon, the auctioneer exclaims, "People are trying to get healthy!"

Making deals became more laborious for dealers, auctioneers, and bidders when unfamiliar foods arrived on the auction block, but these instances also generated opportunity for further reflection on the meaning and value of food, in some cases generating critical insight on industrial food supply chains. When giant boxes of frozen, bulk dim sum items appeared on the auction block, the dealer described the delicious, shrimp-stuffed cabbage rolls as a delicacy served in a restaurant in Washington, DC, to entice bidders. At the time I was sitting next to Sue, who turned to me and said: "It's the waste from the city. We get the food that they throw away."

In other instances, the interior value of the deal could transform such waste into value. At several points throughout one auction, cases of Kevita probiotic coconut water appeared on the auction block. "I don't know what it is, but for two dollars a case, you can find somebody to take it," the auctioneer pronounced. And some bidders did, but later in the auction, the remaining Kevita appeared again in a combined deal: five cases of Kevita and five bags of frozen Alexia French fries for $10. Running a quick calculation, I estimated a retail cost close to $400 ($3.99 per bag of fries, $2.99 per bottle of Kevita). I commented to Harry and Sue that *this* really *was* a good deal. "Only if you need that much," they quickly responded. The deal did not resonate with the bidding crowd, who remained largely unfamiliar with the Kevita brand. At the end of the auction, the Kevita water appeared again for a dollar a case and Harry and Sue decided to buy three cases. In response to my surprised inquiry about their purchase, they explained that somebody needed to buy it and they would donate it to their church, or, as Sue pointed out, a good recycling program would value the glass bottles for more than a dollar. At four cents each, the unknown bulging bottles of probiotic water had became food — if only for charity—or worst-case scenario would be transformed into an entirely new commodity form that could extract surplus value through recycling.

Value emerges from the collision of multiple sets of food values—affordability and thriftiness, preventing food waste, social obligations to the dealer, charitable food aid—that come into contact in the moment of bidding. In this instance, the metavalue of consuming in order to get a good deal became less important than the social negotiations of *making* a deal. Harry and Sue certainly considered the cost and thriftiness of the probiotic water, but the deal emerged through the social value of the water, which allowed Harry and Sue to fulfill their obligations as bidders, congregants, and citizens of a planet full of waste. Similarly, the supply chain of the frozen dim sum from the city to the countryside—and the attendant perception of inequalities — prevented it from becoming a worthy food. The social role of bidders—and distribution processes more generally—resulted in a form of contaminated diversity that could inspire reflection and even transform the meaning and value of food.

The Universe of Distribution

Colonel Kirk, a grocery auctioneer, once boasted online: "THE UNIVERSE BEGINS HERE!" Indeed, the grocery auction charts new territory in understanding the role of distribution in shaping value within the capitalist industrialized food system. Distribution, rather than production, emerges as a visible and central player in the creation of value at the grocery auction. In an odd moment of convergence, Colonel Kirk's ploy to entice new bidders to attend his grocery auction also resonates with Graeber (2013). In Graeber's ontological gambit, "as-if play" facilitates the uptake of new, conflicting values and brings universes into being as long as the conflicting worlds *do not* collide. But the grocery auction is a site of collision: the risks of live foods fight against the extended shelf-lives of frozen and processed foods; the low prices and thrift of the secondary market clash with the retail prices and brand values of the primary market; dealers and auctioneers chase profits while bidders seek savings; and alternative food values of ecological and human sustainability confront the inefficiencies and waste of the industrialized food system. Following Graeber, these collisions prevent the sustained uptakes of new values, and for the most part this was true at the grocery auction: bidders bought the foods they liked, often bought more food than they "needed," and sometimes even paid *more* than retail price if they got caught up in the game-time heat of bidding. But the contaminated diversity of Tsing's mushroom offers another model for understanding the creation of value at the grocery auction: contamination is an encounter that enables transformation and collaborative survival.

At the grocery auction, the social dimensions of distribution were at play in each collision, enabling survival. Dealers mediated and generated value through expiring date labels and brand, while the auction became a social venue, befitting of date night. As contaminated diversity, both forms of dating realize the value of food: as labor, distribution generates economic value; as a social project, distribution is fun and may even reallocate savings to consumers, not corporations. Perhaps more significantly, these forms of survival generated visibility of the value-making process itself. Bidders did not always, but *could*, remain critical of whether or not they really got a good deal, or reflect on whether they even needed the food. Dealers' attention to the limits of labeling could spark inquiry and reflection on the capitalist industrialized food system among consumers (who knew there were de-branding facilities that allowed a second life for Starbucks coffee?). Such ethnographic details demand attentiveness to the relationship between "meta" and "interior" values, suggesting that they may coexist, eliding into one another, and that neither maintains hegemony over the value and consumption of food. Consider, then, the possibilities for collaboration: 25 percent of bidders surveyed reported that they had thrown out auction food at least once, but a remarkable 75 percent of bidders agreed that they attend grocery auctions to prevent waste. Although preventing food waste was, at best, a secondary motivation for participating in the auction, could the distribution of food at the grocery auction instill, or perhaps, distill new—albeit imperfect—forms of practice centered on reducing waste from within the capitalist industrialized food system?

Acknowledgments

I am deeply grateful to all the distributors, auctioneers, auction staff, and bidders that welcomed me at the grocery auction and were patient with my endless questions. Roman Sehling and Kristen Douglas were tireless friends, joining me on many long auction adventures and providing keen insight on the experience of bidding. Numerous colleagues supported the development of this manuscript; thank you Kay Zagrodny, Katherine Lambert-Pennington, and Jennifer Simpson for your input. I would also like to thank Dr. Melissa Caldwell, the editing team at *Gastronomica*, and the anonymous reviewers for their valuable feedback on this work

Notes

1 Seventy-nine of the listed auctions exclusively sold groceries, while sixty-four sold groceries within the wider context of a general auction.

2 Some dealers without a refrigerated truck installed chest freezers into a truck to transport frozen food.

3 The concentration of households earning more than $100,000 annually reflects the availability of middle-income earning opportunities in Maryland. Survey research in other regions would provide a much-needed comparison.

4 Cohen and Klemetti (2014: 83) reported that bidders could save, on average, 43 percent on food costs at a chain supermarket. Moreover, women saved an average of 17.6 percent more than men on meat purchases.

5 In a mundane sense, a deal could refer to what was up for bid, such as one bottle of ketchup or an entire case of frozen breakfast sandwiches, while the more meaning-laden deal referred to an item purchased below its primary market retail value.

6 The runner accurately articulates the lack of regulation of dating food products; see Nestle (2002) and Bloom (2010) on food labeling.

References

Allen, Patricia. 1999. "Reweaving the Food Security Safety Net: Mediating Entitlement and Entrepreneurship." *Agriculture and Human Values* 16(2): 117—29.

———, Margaret FitzSimmons, Michael Goodman, and Keith Warner. 2003. "Shifting Plates in the Agrifood Landscape: The Tectonics of Alternative Agrifood Initiatives in California." *Journal of Rural Studies* 19: 61-75.

Appadurai, Arjun, ed. 1986. *The Social Life of Things: Commodities in Cultural Perspective.* Cambridge: Cambridge University Press.

Arce, Alberto, and Terry K. Marsden. 1993. "The Social Construction of International Food: A New Research Agenda." *Economic Geography* 69(3): 293-311.

Associated Press. 2009. "Thrifty Shoppers 'Sold!' on Grocery Auctions." *NBC News*, March 25. Accessed March 23, 2014. www.nbcnews.com/id/29865090/?gt1=43001#.U_ukB_ldU-A

Barndt, Deborah. 2007. *Tangled Routes: Women, Work, and Globalization on the Tomato Trail.* Lanham, MD: Rowman and Littlefield.

Beall, Anne E. 2010. *Strategic Market Research: A Guide to Conducting Research That Drives Businesses.* Bloomington, IN: iUniverse.

Bestor, Theodore. 2004. *Tsukiji: The Fish Market at the Center of the World.* Berkeley: University of California Press.

Bloom, Jonathan. 2010. *American Wasteland: How America Throws Away Nearly Half of Its Food (and What We Can Do About It).* Cambridge, MA: Lifelong Books.

Cohen, Jeffrey, and Susan Klemetti. 2014. "The Social and Economic Production of Greed, Cooperation, and Taste in an Ohio Food Auction." *Economic Anthropology* 1: 80–87.

Cook, Ian. 2004. "Follow the Thing: Papaya." *Antipode* 36(4): 642–64.

——— and Philip Crang. 1996. "The World on a Plate: Culinary Culture, Displacement and Geographical Knowledges." *Journal of Material Culture* 1(2): 131–54.

Dixon, Jane. 1999. "A Cultural Economy Model for Studying Food Systems." *Agriculture and Human Values* 16(2): 151–60.

Ferguson, James. 2015. *Give a Man a Fish: Reflections on the New Politics of Distribution.* Durham, NC: Duke University Press.

Fischer, Edward, and Peter Benson. 2006. *Broccoli and Desire: Global Connections and Maya Struggles in Postwar Guatemala.* Palo Alto, CA: Stanford University Press.

Fonte, Maria. 2013. "Food Consumption as Social Practice: Solidarity Purchasing Groups in Rome, Italy." *Journal of Rural Studies* 32: 230–39.

Foster, Robert J. 2007. "The Work of the New Economy: Consumers, Brand, and Value Creation." *Cultural Anthropology* 22(4): 707–31.

———. 2008. *Coca-Globalization: Following Soft Drinks from New York to New Guinea.* New York: Palgrave Macmillan.

Graeber, David. 2013. "It Is Value That Brings Universes into Being." *HAU: Journal of Ethnographic Theory* 3(2): 219–43.

Graslie, Serri. 2012. "Willing to Play the Dating Game with Your Food? Try a Grocery Auction." *The Salt* blog, National Public Radio, August 23, 2012. Accessed September 3, 2013. www.npr.org/blogs/thesalt/2012/08/23/159601015/willing-to-play-the-datinggame-with-your-food-try-a-grocery-auction

Gregory, Nicole, and Robin Gregory. 2010. "A Values-Based Framework for Community Food Choices." *Environmental Values* 19(1): 99–119.

Gregson, N., Crang, M., Ahamed, F., Akhtar, N., and Ferdous, R. 2010. "Following Things of Rubbish Value: End-of-Life Ships, 'Chock-Chocky' Furniture and the Bangladeshi Middle-Class Consumer." *Geoforum* 41(6): 846—54.

Grey, Mark A. 2000. "The Industrial Food Stream and Its Alternatives in the United States: An Introduction." *Human Organization* 59(2): 143–50.

Gunderson, Ryan. 2014. "Problems with the Defetishization Thesis: Ethical Consumerism, Alternative Food Systems, and Commodity Fetishism." *Agriculture and Human Values* 31(1): 109–17.

Guthman, Julie. 2002. "Commodified Meanings, Meaningful Commodities: Re-thinking Production-Consumption Links through the Organic System of Provision." *Sociologia Ruralis* 42(4): 295–311.

———. 2004. *Agrarian Dreams: The Paradox of Organic Farming in California*. Berkeley: University of California Press.

———. 2008. "Bringing Good Food to Others: Investigating the Subjects of Alternative Food Practice." *Cultural Geographies* 15(4): 431–47.

Harris, Edmund. 2009. "Neoliberal Subjectivities or a Politics of the Possible? Reading for Difference in Alternative Food Networks." *Royal Geographic Society* 41(1): 55–63.

Henderson, George. 2004. " 'Free' Food, the Local Production of Worth, and the Circuit of Decommodification." *Environment and Planning D: Society and Space* 22: 485–512.

Ilbery, Brian, and Damian Maye. 2005. "Alternative (Shorter) Food Supply Chains and Specialist Livestock Products in the Scottish-English Borders." *Environment and Planning* 37: 823–44.

Koch, Shelley L. 2011. *A Theory of Grocery Shopping: Food, Choice and Conflict*. New York: Berg.

Kopytoff, Igor. 1986. "The Cultural Biography of Things: Commoditization as Process," In *The Social Life of Things: Commodities in Cultural Perspective*, ed. Arjun Appadurai, 64–91. Cambridge: Cambridge University Press.

Lundy, Brandon. 2012. "Playing the Market: How the Cashew "Commodityscape" Is Redefining Guinea-Bissau's Countryside." *Culture, Agriculture, Food, and Environment* 34(1): 33–52.

Nestle, Marion. 2002. *Food Politics: How the Healthy Food Industry Influences Nutrition and Health*. Berkeley: University of California Press.

Patel, Raj. 2007. *Stuffed and Starved: The Hidden Battle for the World Food System*. London: Portobello Books.

Paxson, Heather. 2013. *The Life of Cheese: Crafting Food and Value in America*. Berkeley: University of California Press.

Poppendieck, Janet. 1998. *Sweet Charity?: Emergency Food and the End of Entitlement*. New York, New York: Penguin Books.

Smith, Charles W. 1989. *Auctions: The Social Construction of Value*. Berkeley: University of California Press.

Tsing, Anna. 2009. "Supply Chains and the Human Condition," *Rethinking Marxism* 21(2):148–76.

———. 2015. *The Mushroom at the End of the World: On the Possibility of Life in Capitalist Ruins*. Princeton, NJ: Princeton University Press.

West, Paige. 2012. *From Modern Production to Imagined Primitive: The Social World of Coffee from Papua New Guinea*. Durham, NC: Duke University Press.

3

The Labor of *Terroir* and the *Terroir* of Labor: Geographical Indication and Darjeeling Tea Plantations

Sarah Besky

Abbreviations

AOC   *Appellation d'origine côntrolée*
DTA   Darjeeling Tea Association
GI   Geographical Indication
TRIPS Trade Related Aspects of Intellectual Property Rights

Introduction

In the spring of 2009, as florescent green buds were sprouting up on the tea bushes after a winter of dormancy, in what is known as the "first flush," I was sitting outside the manager's office of a large tea plantation in Darjeeling, India, high in the Himalayan foothills. While I was waiting to interview the manager, I chatted with the office *didī* (literally, "older sister") over a cup of tea. In Darjeeling plantations, the office *didī* was a hybrid position of secretary and servant, and depending on the plantation, her role leaned to one or the other of these poles. Here, she held a more secretarial position. We joked about the state of the desk in the foyer, where she often had to work, examining random pieces of scratch paper with cryptic notes or lists of numbers without qualifiers. Managers would dump these papers and unmarked files on the desk as they passed through. A glossy piece of paper poking out from under a stack of file folders caught my eye, and I slowly pulled it towards me, trying not to disrupt the desk's stratigraphy. It was a poster, with trails of more cryptic numbers scratched on it. I asked what it was for. She said that the *sahib* (manager) gave posters like this one out to visitors to the factory. These kinds of marketing materials frequently arrived from Kolkata with instructions about display or distribution. She told me to take this one home with me.

An antique-looking scroll unfurled on the poster asked:

What is it that makes the world's tea aficionados rush to Darjeeling during springtime to "book" the first flush teas?

The answer?

… Darjeeling Tea just happens.
The reports blame it on the mixed soil, the pristine air, the well orchestrated rainfall, the lofty altitude, the optimum humidity levels—and how they have all come together uniquely to make Darjeeling Tea *Darjeeling Tea*.

To science, Darjeeling Tea is a strange phenomenon. To the faithful, it is a rare blessing.

… Darjeeling Tea, hand-plucked by local women with magician's fingers … is manually sorted, packaged and begins its world tour. The only problem with Darjeeling Tea is that there is never enough of it to satisfy the connoisseurs around the world.

But then, the finest things on earth are like that—very very rare—or they would not be considered the finest.

This was one of the first of many encounters I had with such Darjeeling tea advertisements, which the Tea Board of India, the government regulator of the tea industry, distributed. The advertisements were part of the Tea Board's efforts to market Darjeeling's "Geographical Indication," or GI, an international legal distinction that protects Darjeeling tea as the "intellectual property" of the Indian government. In a global market that is calling for locally sourced, socially responsible, and environmentally friendly commodities, Darjeeling tea planters and the Tea Board looked to GI to distinguish their product from other Indian, African, and blended teas on the market. GI is a nationally and internationally regulated property rights regime that legally protects a wide range of products, from artisan cheese to fruits to handicrafts. Notable GI beverages include Champagne, Cognac, Tequila, Scotch, Bordeaux, and Kona coffee. The producers of these products (and the governments of the states or countries in which they are produced) advocate for GI status on the grounds that their products can only be made in certain locales by certain groups of people. The assignment of GI status to foods rests on the assumption that they possess a unique *terroir*, or "taste of place." *Terroir* derives not only from biophysical conditions but also from distinct production practices. Marketing for *terroir* products tends to emphasize the roles that both unique ecological landscapes and skilled artisans play in creating them.

Over the course of ethnographic fieldwork I carried out in Darjeeling and Kolkata between 2006 and 2012, the Tea Board petitioned the European Union (an important market for fine teas) to recognize Darjeeling's GI. Darjeeling's tea plantations date back to the British colonial era, and as I show in this article, the organization of landscape and labor in the region has been remarkably consistent from the British era to the present. Since the designation of Darjeeling tea as a GI product in 1999, the region's tea industry has witnessed a resurgence: closed plantations have reopened, and tea is fetching higher prices. GI enables place to stand in for a product. Many of us know that Champagne is sparkling wine, that Roquefort is cheese, that Scotch is whiskey, and that Vidalias are onions, without being told so. The Tea Board and the Darjeeling Tea Association (DTA) wanted consumers to associate "Darjeeling" with these GIs—*luxury* products with territorial distinction. This association was often quite overt. Another remarkably stark poster, which the office *didi* dug out from under a stack of papers after I expressed interest in the first one, featured a picture of three glasses labeled: "Cognac. Champagne. Darjeeling!"

The poster continues:

Our very own Darjeeling Tea joins the global elites.

The whole world now recognizes the fact that this magical brew owes its unique eloquence to its place of origin, the misty hills of Darjeeling.

Darjeeling Tea has now been registered as a GI (Geographical Indication) in India. Which officially places Darjeeling Tea in the esteemed company of a Cognac or Champagne—other famous GIs.

The unique geographic conditions of Darjeeling help make its teas such a rarity. Just the way Cognac and Champagne are rare because they can only come from specific regions in France.

To celebrate this new rise in status for India, just raise your cup!

How did an industrial plantation crop with a less than savory colonial past become a product with an authentic *terroir*, placed uncritically next to Champagne and Cognac? One answer to this question lies in the way the Tea Board framed tea plantation labor. An arduous and exploitative productive process had to be replaced with something else: something craft-like. To make this replacement discursively and materially possible—and thereby to make plantation production palatable in the world of *terroir* products—required contemporary plantation owners and Tea Board officials to resolve what their colonial forbears called the "Labor Question." Colonial planters' Labor Question concerned how to maintain a settled and reasonably healthy labor force in burgeoning Indian tea districts (Chatterjee 2001). The contemporary Labor Question does not focus on the *acquisition* of labor, but instead on how planters, hoping to export to international markets for boutique tea, worked to *recast* the unpleasant colonial legacy of plantation production as a palatable national heritage of craft production. In asserting a luxury distinction for Darjeeling tea, as well as a natural connection between laborers and tea plants, the language of *terroir* embedded in GI marketing and promotional materials produced a sanitized image of Indian plantation life and labor.

GI marketing materials and legal structures certainly do produce ideas about place and labor that diverge to a great extent from the realities of plantation life, but as GI has taken hold in Darjeeling, laborers themselves have become willing participants in the materialization of *terroir*. Laborers worked not only to produce tea but also to make manifest the images of "naturally" intertwined place, product, and labor that GI discourses and marketing materials evoked when they referred to Darjeeling plantations as "gardens." Establishing *terroir* would seem to be a challenge on tea plantations, where buildings, machinery, and even plants date back to the mid-1800s, the height of British colonialism, and where the management of Nepali laborers by non-Nepalis largely mirrors colonial forms. Nevertheless, in Darjeeling, plantation labor and its colonial past were far from ignored or hidden from view: instead, they were, rather successfully, packaged and performed as "heritage."

GI is part of a complex set of practices that enrolls tea planters, marketers, and even low-wage plantation laborers in producing *terroir*. Drawing on anthropological analyses that link luxury consumption practices, discourses about qualities of food production, and the "invention" of national or regional food "traditions," I argue that the distinction of Darjeeling as a unique *taste* was legally and performatively tied to the governance of Darjeeling and the activities of tea laborers, as part of a bounded *place*. I draw primarily on interviews with tea planters; officials from the Indian Tea Association, the Darjeeling Tea Association, the Tea Board of India; and Kolkata-based tea brokers, tasters, and distributors. I contextualize these interviews in insights from fieldwork on Darjeeling tea plantations and an analysis of GI-related marketing materials. In the next section, I situate my argument in social scientific critiques of GI and *terroir*. The third section provides background on Darjeeling's GI. The two sections that follow explore a conceptual dyad that frames how British colonial officials, the Indian state, and international consumers have understood Darjeeling and its signature commodity. Since the colonial era, these actors have conceived Darjeeling as both an idyllic "garden" space and an industrial "plantation" space. As I show through an analysis of GI marketing materials and interviews with planters, pluckers, and tourists who visit Darjeeling plantations, this dyad maps in surprising ways onto labor relations. While planters and marketers' discourses tend to emphasize the "garden," laborers' investment in GI lay primarily in an active—if also ambivalent—embrace of the plantation, encapsulated in the Nepali word "*kamān*."

Placing Taste: The Cultural Production of *Terroir*

The analysis of GI in this article highlights the work of *protection* and *perception* that this legal and market distinction performs. GI's supporters in India claimed that it protected Darjeeling tea from imitation; that it protected a unique agricultural landscape and the people who worked in it from being engulfed by competition in an undifferentiated marketplace; and that it protected Indian national economic interests by differentiating Indian tea from other varieties. At the level of perception, GI sought to reshape how consumers understood the taste of Darjeeling tea. GI asserted that Darjeeling had a *terroir*. Descriptions of the environment of Darjeeling—the rainfall, the altitude, the humidity, and the "magical" fingers of local women tea workers— defined that *terroir*. In a classic understanding of *terroir*, taste is endowed by the geology and climate of the region in which food is grown (see Wilson 1998), but in my analysis of Darjeeling tea GI promotional materials, I want to underscore that *terroir*—the "taste of place" that GI protects—is a cultural, rather than a natural phenomenon. GI depended on a perception of tea-producing labor as making a unique and inimitable contribution to *terroir*.

Terroir and Luxury Consumption

In a growing market for goods marked "organic," "fair trade," or "local," consumers appear to be searching for value from three interrelated sources: bureaucratic or legal certification, the sensory "taste" of food quality (and by extension, environmental quality), and the cultural "taste" of class "distinction" and refinement (Bourdieu 1984). *Terroir* products protected by

GI legislation and embossed with a GI label meet this tripartite standard of value. Appeals to geographical distinction play into the desires of Northern consumers who are demanding more of a global food system in which food " … comes from a global everywhere, yet from nowhere that [consumers] know in particular. The distance from which their food comes represents their separation from the knowledge of how and by whom what they consume is produced, processed, and transported" (Kloppenburg et al. 1996, p. 34). In consuming Champagne over sparkling wine, Roquefort over blue cheese, and Darjeeling over generic English Breakfast, buyers can see themselves as supporting "traditional" forms of craft food production as well as imbibing luxury distinctions associated with place. Distinction and rarity have a price. GI products are more expensive precisely because they come from somewhere in particular and because they must travel across the globe in sophisticated networks to make it into consumers' cups (Heath and Meneley 2007).

Critical analyses of the link between the construction of *terroir* and practices of luxury consumption have pointed to what Guy (2011, p. 460–461) calls the "immaterial labor" of building images of "authenticity" and "naturalness" into *terroir* products. Consumer beliefs about authenticity occlude the work of marketing and branding that go into the making of *terroir,* as well as the "material" labor of food production. Discourses about *terroir* "[minimize] the place of labor and … workers, whether these are artisanal cheese and wine makers or seasonal migrant laborers" (Guy 2011, p. 462; see also Laudan 2004). Guy's critique of the immaterial labor of *terroir* in the making of Champagne resonates with anthropological analyses of coffee by West (2012) and Roseberry (1996), and of olive oil by Meneley (2004, 2007, 2008). These scholars all argue that the pursuit of distinction through place-based products actually depends upon a radical change in the perception of the qualities of those products. In the case of olive oil, as Meneley has shown, the religious and ritual significance of the substance in Mediterranean contexts differs significantly from the scientifically based claims about its healthful qualities in Western fad dieting (Meneley 2008). Nevertheless, consumers of olive oils, like consumers of "relationship coffees" from small specialty roasters (Doane 2010), see themselves as buying qualities directly associated with specific people in specific places (see also Trubek 2008).

As Weiss (2011) showed in an anthropological study of "local" "heritage" pork, consumers must *learn* the taste of place. In the Piedmont region of North Carolina, this learning took place in farmers markets, restaurants, and exclusive tasting events and was transmitted by specialists trained in the dietary habits of pigs and in the growing genre of "meat science" (Weiss 2011, p. 446). As Weiss explains, "[heritage pork] (and its taste) is an amalgam of animal husbandry, marketing strategies, and social networking" (Weiss 2011, p. 452). Similarly, as I show below, consumers and connoisseurs have learned to regard Darjeeling tea, with its light smoky flavor, as the "Champagne of teas." The Tea Board of India's marketing materials were educational and instructional, not only in the how-to details of brewing, steeping, and storage, but more importantly in messages about how to enjoy Darjeeling tea as a distinguished good. The advertisements taught consumers of this high-end GI to reconcile their desire to purchase a luxury good with the knowledge that tea was grown on colonial plantations. As in Guy's descriptions of Champagne, a product whose *terroir*-related discourses hid the material conditions of labor in plain sight, Darjeeling's *terroir* created "a retreat into a nostalgia for the past that works to create a bundle of silences around agricultural labor" (Guy 2011, p. 462).

Terroir and the Quality of Production

Without the work of marketing, it would be difficult to see Darjeeling tea as simultaneously good to drink and "good to make" (Paxson 2012). Consumers learn to see the foods most commonly associated with *terroir*, including fine wine, farmstead cheese, heritage pork, olive oil, and *foie gras*, as artisanal products, not as colonial or industrial goods. Anthropological studies of foodways and taste have long called attention to the interface between imaginative and symbolic practices surrounding the consumption of plants and animals and the material organization of their production (e.g., Mintz 1985). GI-based marketing promotes a perception of an agricultural landscape that highlights relationships between craftspeople and the things they make, but not every producer counts as a craftsperson. The elaborate discourse about the *terroir* of French wine and Wisconsin cheese, for example, certainly does not include the seasonal or migrant labor that goes into their production (Guy 2011, 1997). On Darjeeling plantations, however, wage laborers were too prominent to be cut out of the marketing picture. The Tea Board of India and planters, in advocating for Darjeeling's GI protection, recast tea's *industrial* production as *craft* production—a process done in small batches by "magical fingered women," not disenfranchised interchangeable labor. In Darjeeling, GI recast the plantation as a landscape in which tea workers and tea bushes lived in symbiotic unity. According [to] the GI narrative, laborers acted as stewards for the "natural" potential of Darjeeling tea. Everything else, as the poster describes, "just happened."

As Paxson (2006, 2012) notes, what makes farmstead cheeses and other *terroir* products taste *good* is related to the values embedded in explanations for why these cheeses are "*good to make*." Such explanations of goodness and appeals to social values, as Weiss (2011) shows, appear in the repeated and highly structured way in which consumers and sellers learn about the foods they exchange. Paxson describes the attempts by cheesemakers in Vermont and Wisconsin to "reverse engineer" *terroir:* to devise strategies for making cheese that seemed compatible with particular environmental conditions. This required developing particular cheesemaking "skills" or "place-making practices" (Paxson 2010, p. 453). Most *terroir* products, however, are not reverse engineered. In the case of Darjeeling, the values of *terroir* were assigned to ongoing productive practices, rendering field labor into traditional knowledge. As Heath and Meneley (2007) have argued, when place-based products enter a global marketplace, claims to distinction based on the qualities of productive practice tend to be imbricated in global productive and consumptive processes (such as the monitoring of chemical "quality"), which are underwritten by decidedly placeless technical and scientific authorities.

Terroir and the Invention of Tradition

Crafting products, as Terrio (2000) has suggested, means crafting history. *Terroir* emerges not only from luxury consumption practices and ideas about the qualities of production but also from "invented" national or regional traditions of food production (Hobsbawm and Ranger 1983; Trubek et al. 2010; Ulin 1995). Eric Hobsbawm defines "invented tradition" as "a set of practices ... which seek to inculcate certain values and norms of behavior ... which attempt to establish continuity with a *suitable historic past*" (Hobsbawm 1983, p. 1, emphasis added). Contemporary Darjeeling tea production under GI was selectively linked to colonial plantation production. Darjeeling's colonial past did not disappear, but it was revalued and made "suitable" for contemporary consumers. An association with quality of taste and quality of production is essential to *terroir*, but that association tends to be based upon assumptions about historical continuity.

Boisard, in his examination of Camembert, what he calls "the odorous emblem of France" (2003 [1992], p. xi) and a recognizable *terroir*-based product, argues that this product, *naturally* associated with Frenchness, is actually embedded in "national myths" about the French nation-state. Similarly, Guy (2003) in her study of Champagne, another comestible symbol of the French nation-state, describes how the production of uniquely French wines was tied up in rural populations' integration into the nation. Though France can be most readily identified with discussions of taste and its relationship to place, *terroir* has become a global commentary on the values, histories, and characteristics of certain foods, as consumers become more aware of the origins of their food (Trubek and Bowen 2008).

Political Economic Critiques of *Terroir*, GI, and Food Labeling

In this article, I analyze how tea, an industrial plantation crop whose production owes as much to colonial labor organization as to skilled artistry, has become a legally protected GI, complete with a *terroir* that consumers recognize and seek to experience for themselves. This question is especially pressing, since *terroir,* food localism, and GI have been associated with movements *against* the globalization of the food system and the exploitation of farm labor, and *for* the conservation of sustainable environments and traditional practices (Trubek 2008; Bowen 2010). Even if *terroir* is as much a process of class distinction as it is a "natural" feature (Bourdieu 1984), wage laborers (and issues of political economy more generally) rarely make it into social scientific depictions of *terroir* food production, even though many GI products are industrial food crops (e.g., Washington apples, Vidalia onions). As West (2012) notes, the producers of commodity food crops (in West's case, Papua New Guinean coffee) actually become re-fetishized through place-oriented marketing. In a similar critique of the tendency among scholars and activists to see GI, fair trade, organic, and other labels as successful instances of consumer-based resistance to commodification, Guthman (2007) argues that such labels create markets (for craft labor, place, and ecological conditions) where none previously existed. By creating new markets, such labels necessarily change the nature of labor itself.

For conscientious consumers, the locally bounded craft of artisans contrasts with the regimented (and arguably place-less) labor of industrial agricultural workers (Meneley 2007). As Bowen and Gaytán (2012) suggest with reference to the assignation of GI status to tequila in Mexico, the confluence of nationalism, globalized marketing, and state support has allowed large tequila distillers to hijack the *terroir* discourse at the expense of the small "artisan" agave producers GI is at least partly meant to benefit. Thus, GI has serious limitations as a strategy for rural "development" (Bowen 2010). Bowen argues elsewhere that the "embeddedness" of products in places can be destabilized by the very processes of certification and labeling that attempt to maintain it (Bowen 2011).

GI and its attendant *terroir* discourse thus often fail to protect the small farmers they claim to be helping, and in the case of industrial crops, perceptions of *terroir* underwritten by labels may occlude labor conditions altogether (Guy 2011). Elsewhere, Guthman (2004) has argued that "local food" and organic movements create an "agrarian imaginary" of farm labor that does not hold up to empirical scrutiny and elides rather than addresses the inequalities that persist at all levels of the food system. This critique is important for understanding how GI becomes a legitimate label for former colonial crops, such as Darjeeling tea, that are grown and processed under conditions that have changed little since the colonial era. As I argue below, the GI scheme in Darjeeling attempted to recast tea plantations as "gardens," as sites of luxury consumption and craft production. The implications for laborers were considerable. They began to recast themselves in line with these discourses, working not only to produce tea but to perform *terroir*, paradoxically working to mask the conditions of tea's production even as they produced tea. First, however, I provide further background on how Darjeeling tea became a GI.

Making Darjeeling a Geographical Indication

A promotional film distributed by the Tea Board of India to tea retailers opens with a British tea shop owner sitting in her London café, reflecting: "I grew up thinking that Darjeeling was just a tea …" (DTA 2001). Then, with the exaggerated movement of a cursor on a map, we follow her from London to foothills of the Indian Himalayas, where she climbs aboard the "Toy Train," the narrow gauge railroad that has transported tea and tourists since the 1860s, and begins a slow journey up the mountainside to Darjeeling.

The next day, while shopping for tea in the market, she meets a tea plantation manager, Mr. Kumar. Over a pot of Darjeeling tea, the scratchy and stilted, dubbed-in voice of Mr. Kumar describes Darjeeling's Geographical Indication status:

> The reputation, the characteristics, of the renowned tea that has been produced over here are essentially attributable to the geographic location, climate, and even the soil … That's the magic of Darjeeling.

Mr. Kumar whisks her down to a tea plantation. They stop on the side of a plantation access road. Grabbing a handful of wet dirt, Mr. Kumar explains, "This is the soil that produces the sweet brew of Darjeeling … see?" The teashop owner gingerly pinches the soil. As they walk behind a large group of female laborers, Mr. Kumar continues: "Tea leaves are handpicked by tea garden workers, 70 % of whom are women. Perhaps it is the warmth of their touch that gives the brew such sweetness."

Mr. Kumar and the tea buyer watch the women, clad in bright red *chaubandis*. (Red is the color of fertility, and *chaubandis* are the "traditional" female dress of a united Hindu Nepal. For the record, I usually saw them wearing men's button down shirts to work, never *chaubandis*.) As the rains start, the laborers break out into trilled folksongs, mimicking a Bollywood musical aside. The women smile from ear to ear while they toss handfuls of green leaf into the baskets strapped to the top of their heads. Rhythmic claps punctuate the song as well as their tea plucking movements.

Later in the film, the tea buyer muses: "I started … exploring the mountains that are home to rhododendrons, wild orchids, and a thousand other flowers. Oh! And the birds … some six *hundred* kinds. When you drink a cup of *pure* Darjeeling, you drink all of this in."

We see the tea buyer later that afternoon, writing in her journal on the verandah of a Raj-era palace-turned-hotel. Excerpts from her journal refer not to the tea, but to the people and the environment that produce it: the "breathing mountains," "musical brooks," "hardened exteriors," "smiles of genuine people with genuine pride." After a long sip of amber tea, she remarks: "Mr. Kumar made me realize the significance of the laws protecting Darjeeling tea. It is thanks to these laws that the flavor of *pure* Darjeeling has worked its magic for me."

In the film's descriptions, the environment of Darjeeling—the rains, the mists, the loamy soils, *and* the beautiful Nepali tea laborers—are integral to the taste, quality, and *terroir* of Darjeeling tea. The viewer-consumer of this advertisement is reassured that the environment is not only natural and pristine (despite their application, agrochemicals never figure into discussions of the *terroir* of any product) but also populated by female workers who have such an idyllic work environment that they are compelled to dance and sing throughout the day. The film implies that "the laws protecting Darjeeling tea" protect the purity of female tea laborers as well.

Wines, liquors, and cheeses have long been the objects of place-based distinctions and governance. In broad terms, a "Geographical Indication" is any material or linguistic symbol used to establish that a product comes from a particular location. Contemporary national and international GI laws descended from national laws aimed at curtailing the imitation or falsification of products whose values were linked to place of origin and traditional forms of production. Though it has undergone several transformations throughout the twentieth-century, one of the first systems for the protection of the Geographical Indication of food products is the French *appellation d'origine côntrolée* (AOC), first codified in 1905. Food items that meet AOC regulations that verify that they are made in a particular geographical location (one that confers a distinct *terroir*) can have a French government issued stamped on them (Colman 2008). By the middle of the twentieth-century such national laws had spread outside of France, and in 1958, the Lisbon Agreement created a common "appellation of origin" protection for products originating in signatory countries, mostly from Europe.

The 1994 World Trade Organization Trade Related Aspects of Intellectual Property Rights (TRIPS) agreement reaffirmed and extended the right of national governments of member states to grant GIs. Under the Indian Geographical Indications Act of 1999, Darjeeling Tea became the first of India's now almost 200 registered GIs (GOI 2013). Other agricultural products now governed by Indian GI legislation include Basmati rice and Alphanso mangoes. The 1999 legislation also protects a large number of handicrafts, such as Kullu shawls and Kancheepuram silk (GOI 1999). This national legislation endowed the Tea Board, and by extension the Government of India, with "ownership" over the words "Darjeeling" and "Darjeeling tea" as well as the Darjeeling tea logo. ....[1]

The 1999 Indian GI Act recast the name "Darjeeling" and the logo as certified trademarks owned by the Government of India, and regulated by the Tea Board of India. The Tea Board describes Darjeeling's status as a GI:

> Darjeeling tea is India's treasured Geographical Indication and forms a very important part of India's cultural and collective intellectual heritage. It is of considerable importance to the economy of India because of the international reputation and consumer recognition enjoyed by it (Tea Board n.d.).

According to the Tea Board of India, "Darjeeling tea" is only produced on 87 plantations in the Darjeeling district of West Bengal.

Mr. Kumar's narration in the film I described above echoes the definition of Geographical Indication in Article 22, Paragraph 1 of the TRIPS Agreement, which defines GIs as "indications which identify a good as originating in the territory of a Member, or a region or locality in that territory, where a given quality, reputation or other characteristic of the good is *essentially attributable* to its geographical origin" (emphasis added). India's 1999 legislation regarding Darjeeling's GI echoes that definition. A report of the World Intellectual Property Organization, an agency of the United Nations that manages global patents, defines Darjeeling's GI with reference not only to the plantations, with their "perfect soils and environmental conditions for tea cultivation," including wind speed, clouds, fog, and amount of sunshine, but also with reference to the "traditional knowledge" of female tea plantation laborers (WIPO 2011). The report states:

> Because the tea bushes in the Darjeeling region are the rare *camellia sinensis* … two leaves and a bud must be picked. The traditional knowledge the women possess ensures that they can … pick Darjeeling tea while being careful to protect … the bushes from any undue stress … the traditional knowledge and production practices … [differentiate] Darjeeling tea from other teas …[2]

With the labor of plucking tea on plantations couched as "traditional knowledge," GI lent support to ideas about a natural connection between plants and people.

Indian Tea Board officials touted the conversion of Darjeeling tea into intellectual property as, above all, a means of "protecting" the product from imitators. Nepal, which lies only a few miles west of many Darjeeling tea plantations, has a similar climate, sloping mountain tea fields, and, of course, a large population of Nepali laborers. Darjeeling's GI, as the Darjeeling Tea Association Secretary and numerous Darjeeling planters told me, exists in large part to protect Darjeeling tea from Nepal tea. These officials, along with tea retailers, argued that Nepal tea could not have the same taste as Darjeeling because the conditions of its production were fundamentally different. Still, planters claimed, tea retailers continued to pass off Nepal tea, often mixed with other teas, as "Darjeeling." The DTA Secretary often claimed that there were over twenty tons of "so-called Darjeeling" produced each year, but less than ten tons actually grown and manufactured in Darjeeling. Figures like this, drawn from planters' estimates, provided a key justification for the 1999 law granting Darjeeling a Geographical Indication. One Canadian tea buyer I interviewed, who buys both Nepal and Darjeeling tea and markets them separately, maintained that this "myth of overproduction" was a deliberate strategy to stimulate demand. He and other tea buyers argued that Nepal tea was just as good—grown in the same environmental conditions with younger bushes, with an added bonus. Nepal tea was cheaper because it did not carry the "Darjeeling" label (Rao 2005).

Gardening the *kaaman*: GI, Traditional Knowledge, and Craft Production

In her office in the towering Tea Board of India building in the heart of old Kolkata, a Tea Board executive responsible for the administration of Darjeeling's GI speculated in an interview with me that the region's history may have made the Darjeeling "brand" easier to "position":

It just so happens that Darjeeling has developed a market of its own … So, when we started off on the GI exercise, the brand had actually already been positioned. Maybe because of certain activities that have taken place historically or because of the fact that it is a product with certain benefits and attributes which have … been liked by people.

The job of GI marketers, she explained, was to link people's tastes—what they already liked about Darjeeling—to a specific place. She continued:

If somebody thinks that Champagne is just a sparkling wine, then France will find it very difficult to protect Champagne as a GI because America would say that Champagne has got nothing to do with origin and is just a sparkling wine and would taste a certain way and that's it. You need to communicate. You need to promote. You need to tell people what it's all about. You need to convey the fact that a GI has something to do with the origin, reputation, quality, characteristics … So, you have the legal side, you have the administrative side, [and] you have the side that's linked with promotion.

Legal, administrative, and promotional activity certainly figured heavily in Darjeeling's GI, but the Tea Board official's cryptic reference to "certain activities that have taken place historically" signals that *terroir* depends upon the mixing of timeless environmental qualities (soils, air, climate) with a sense of return to a mode of production that belongs somewhere in the historical past.

Unlike coffee, tea is a rather geographically undifferentiated market. Consumers frequently drink teas from Malawi, Java, Bangladesh, or Cambodia, but these teas are rarely distinguished as such. Tea from across the globe is instead commonly blended into varietals, such as "Earl Grey," "English Breakfast," and "Russian Caravan" which can be sourced from any tea-growing region or grade. These teas, blended from broken leaf and dust grades, make up the bulk of the international tea market. There is little demand within India for Darjeeling tea, as the price is exponentially higher than the price of tea produced in Assam, the Dooars, or other Indian tea-producing regions. Darjeeling tea workers and town residents I met actually preferred these cheaper, extra-local teas. Tea workers frequently reminded me that Darjeeling tea was grown for foreign consumption. Foreigners, they explained, liked *halkhā chiyā* ("light tea"). Workers also explained that foreigners preferred tea grown in the mountains. Workers knew the place of production was significant.

Darjeeling's distinction as a good tea thus comes from its associations with a pleasant *taste* and a restful *place*. The town of Darjeeling, surrounded by some 87 plantations, was established by the British initially as a sanitarium for convalescing soldiers to recover in the cool mountain airs. The refuge quickly grew and developed into a "hill station" and the summer capital of British India. Regarded for its recuperative airs and misty mornings, Darjeeling has long existed in Indian and Western imaginaries as a place of purity, an accessible Shangri-la. Since 1835, when Darjeeling was established, the region has been simultaneously conceived of as both a site of industrial agriculture and as a site of rest and leisure. The opening of E.C. Dozey's popular history-cum-guidebook to Darjeeling describes the recuperative powers of the Darjeeling hills:

In the strenuous days when the struggle for existence shackles men to their desks, or keeps them tied to counters in the sweltering heat of the plains, the very mention of Darjeeling recalls memories of the last but too short week-end during which as much of the pleasure as was possible was pressed into it (1922, p. 1).

Darjeeling guidebooks and gazetteers, at the same time, describe the regimentation and productivity of Darjeeling's plantations:

> The plantations were models of neatness and order, and the planters are always willing to explain each process and the reason for it to visitors. The Nepalese coolies, too, are very interesting. In spite of a pretty liberal coating of dirt, some of the women are good-looking, and men and women alike are a happy-go-lucky lot, cheerful and in good condition ... They are well paid and well housed, and each family has its little patch of cultivation rent free (Newman & Company 1900, p. 50–51).

Darjeeling's dual identity as a site of both industry and refuge is encapsulated in a linguistic dynamic, between the Nepali word for "plantation," *kamān*, used by workers to describe their work place, and the English word "garden," used both historically and by the Tea Board's GI marketing materials to describe tea plantations. *Kamān* is of disputable linguistic origin, derived from the English words "command" or "common," or perhaps even colonial British planters' use of the imperative "Come on! Come on!" to communicate with workers. *Kamān* evoked the oppressive aspects of plantation life: the repetitive plucking, pruning, and maintenance of a commodity crop. *Kamān* also signals the materiality of the plantation and an industrial mode of production: the factories, machines, and division of labor as well as the rugged physical topography, heat, and rains that make tea plucking so difficult. The use of *kamān* reminded my interlocutors of the plantation land tenure system, managed by affluent men and staffed by thousands of low-paid wage laborers of Nepali origin, who live in cramped villages amidst the sweeping fields of tea (*kamān busti*). The word *kamān* evoked regimented work schedules, repetitive labor, and routine submission to the weights and measures of management. On the *kamān*, nothing is "natural." Even the tea bushes, *camellia sinensis*, were imported from China to Darjeeling in the mid-nineteenth-century to satisfy British consumers' demand in the wake of the Opium Wars. For Darjeeling tea to become a GI, this colonial agricultural legacy had to be repackaged, not removed.

The DTA and Tea Board believed that by thwarting the blending of Darjeeling tea with other teas—particularly Nepal tea—GI has given struggling plantations a better market. Nepal and Darjeeling tea are remarkably similar in every way—the taste, climate, topography, and bushes. But there is one clear difference: the *kamān*. Nepal tea is not grown on a *kamān*. The word for a tea cultivation landscape in Nepal is *bāri* (literally, "non-irrigated or dry field"). Producing communities in Nepal are relatively new; they are not the product of British colonialism. Nepal tea-growing operations hire laborers from the villages that surround the *bāris*. Darjeeling tea plantations, on the other hand, are staffed by the descendents of pluckers recruited by British planters beginning in the mid-1800s. Darjeeling plantations are relatively larger and vertically integrated. Each plantation is staffed by 600 to 1,000 permanent workers, who labor under the supervision of field managers who answer to more powerful plantation managers (or "planters") and ultimately to plantation owners.

As shown in the quotations above, the word "Darjeeling" has long been associated with restful, garden-like qualities. Contemporary GI-based promotions harness these garden images to discursively supplant those of the *kamān*. One promotional brochure, in text set next to a picture of a demure Nepali woman, head dropped towards the tea bush, describes "Life on the Gardens":

> It's an idyllic existence close to nature's heartbeat. That's what makes this tea so unique. The tea pluckers sing of the tiny saplings which bend in the wind as they work. A melody of greenness surrounded by blue skies and the sparkle of the mountain dews. And tied to the circle of life, the tea bushes sustain themselves, day in and out, season after season, through the years. Life on a plantation is a completely natural, refreshing state of being (DTA n.d.).

Another GI marketing poster hails the connection between "gardeners" and tea:

> Thankfully, the Darjeeling Tea Estates have always lived by their faith—by humbly accepting this unique gift of nature and doing everything to retain its natural eloquence.
>
> So, Darjeeling Tea, hand-plucked by local women with magician's fingers, withered, rolled and fermented in orthodox fashion, with the sole intention of bringing out the best in them [sic] (DTA n.d.).

Marketing, of both female tea workers and the plantation environment they inhabited, thus supplemented legal boundary-making to render a complex production system and relationships between tea bushes, labor, and management into a single, fetishized, feminized element of mystical "nature."

In her ethnography of female tea laborers on a Dooars plantation, to the south of Darjeeling, Chatterjee (2001) describes a similar process, whereby popular tea brands like Brooke Bond and Celestial Seasonings sexualize female tea workers and fetishize their delicate hands. Chatterjee notes the way in which the feminization of tea merges ideas of labor and leisure, as the soft hands of tea pluckers (juxtaposed against their hard bent backs) echoes the soft touch of the genteel colonial female tea drinker. The marketing strategy for Darjeeling's GI goes one step further, transforming female laborers into "ecologically noble," hyper-fertile features of a timeless landscape (Doane 2007). This combination of legal definition and market imagery was largely directed at bulk buyers in the EU and USA who might otherwise have "unscrupulously" adulterated Darjeeling tea with Nepal tea. Ironically, however, the marketing materials abounded with pictures of women dressed in traditional Nepali *chaubandis* and depicted with the features that made Nepali women desirable not only to British colonial appetites but also to contemporary Indian ones: light skin, bright eyes, and glossy black hair.

Talk of a limited number of "gardens" bounded by discrete borders not only produced the impression that "true Darjeeling" was rare, it also gave a physical location to the "traditional knowledge" on which the Tea Board's claims to intellectual property were based. It was not only the landscape but also the natural connection between land, labor, and product that planters and bureaucrats referred to when they discussed Darjeeling's *terroir*. GI marketing materials were replete with descriptions of the environment of Darjeeling—an environment of which the rainfall, the altitude, the humidity, *and* the warm fingers of local women tea workers were all parts.

Tasting Tea, Tasting Labor: "Heritage" Tourism and the Performance of *Terroir*

Despite the meticulous reference to plantations as "gardens" (GI promoters I interviewed used the terms *kamān* or "plantation" as rarely as Nepali workers used the term "garden"), the persistence of the *kamān* in the postcolonial era was central to Darjeeling's distinction. Unlike GI promoters, tea workers were surprisingly vocal about the importance of maintaining the *kamān* system. As I noted above, for Nepali tea pluckers, *kamān* referenced not only a site of highly regimented work but also the location of their homes and villages. In the decades after Indian Independence and prior to the establishment of the GI, many tea plantations closed or scaled back production. In the 1970s and 1980s, starvation deaths, landslides, and outmigration took a toll on life in the *kamān busti*. Many former tea laborers and their children began migrating to Darjeeling town, Delhi, and Kolkata (and even back to Nepal) in search of work.

Beginning in 2008, I made regular visits to laborers at Kopibari Tea Estate,[3] a plantation that had been closed for three years. A new owner had pushed its tea through fair trade and organic certification. He intended to capitalize on those labels, as well as GI, to turn Kopibari into a "tea resort." Tourists who visited Kopibari were given tours of the tea-processing factory, a coal-fired plant whose machines, the tourists were told, dated to the British era. (Coal, too, is an important element of Darjeeling's *terroir* and heritage. Tasting experts in Kolkata claim that coal-operated machinery imparts Darjeeling's special "muscatel" flavor). Tourists were also given the opportunity to meet a retired tea plucker, Bishnu, who would invite them into an old one-room village shack she had converted into a small café. There, she would demonstrate the "proper" way to brew and drink Darjeeling tea.

Bishnu called herself "the Five Second Lady" because she could prepare a cup, she said, in just "five seconds." She brewed broken Darjeeling leaf from her monthly ration for tourists. If you swish that grade of tea in hot water for five seconds, the brew will attain the light amber color seen in the promotional pictures. As she drank a cup of the five second tea with visitors, Bishnu would extol its health benefits and remind them that they could find this very tea in Harrods department store in London. She would also remind visitors that the proper way to consume Darjeeling was lightly brewed, with no sugar or milk. It was, she said, an "acquired taste."

Even in the absence of tourists, workers like Bishnu were regular consumers of Darjeeling tea. In fact, drinking Darjeeling tea (with milk and sugar, or with salt) was part of how labor was reproduced. Pluckers received 350 g of low-grade broken leaf Darjeeling tea (produced at Kopibari's factory, but not deemed fit for international circulation) as part of their monthly food ration. Throughout a day in the field, workers sipped sugar or salt tea from reused liter-sized "XXX Rum" bottles. On afternoons and weekends, I would sit with female workers as they would steep this ration tea (or, after the 350 g ran out, cheap tea produced in the plains of India and purchased in the local bazaar) into a strong, dark brew. They knew that a cup of Darjeeling tea in the United States cost more than they made in a day (just over $1.00 in 2010). Tourists and tea buyers who visited the plantation told them this. On days off, plantation workers would go to town to the bazaar and see the faces of Darjeeling tea workers—of women just like them—plastered onto billboards. . . .

The model Darjeeling tea workers on the billboards were smiling, dressed in *pukka Nepali* ("totally Nepali") clothes: in red *chaubandis*, handing the implicit consumer a cup of light amber tea. Workers ridiculed the *chaubandi* as the dress of old Nepali women or villagers who migrated to town in search of piecework, and they found such lightly brewed tea (presumably without sugar) unappetizing. But even as they mocked such images, pluckers on plantations like Kopibari, where tourism was as important as tea production, worked to reproduce them.

Both domestic and international tourists traveled to Darjeeling to consume Darjeeling tea on Darjeeling tea *gardens*. But they also wanted to see the material elements of *kamān*—the factory, the antique machinery, the hand-plucked tea, and the bungalows. In Darjeeling, these colonial legacies of the *kamān* were discursively recast as "heritage." "Heritage" tea plantation tourism emphasized the experience of the plantation, where the colonial means of tea production—the coal-fired processing factories, the 8-h plucking days, and female laborers with bent backs portering tea leaves—were stops on the tour. These material symbols of British colonial development and domination over the tea industry are essential to both the high market value of Darjeeling tea and the tourist experience. Tourism provided a confirmation that Darjeeling plantations were not imaginary: that there were aspects of both the "garden" and the *kamān* that could be experienced materially. Whereas on a winery or brewery tour, tourists come to view the technologies of production in action, "heritage" tourists come to witness "living history," "the simulation of life in another time" [Anderson (1983) quoted in Handler and Saxton 1988, p. 242]. Active, visible laborers were required to provide both of these experiences. Tea pluckers could not simply work; they had to *pose as workers*. They had to present themselves both as *contemporary* tea producers and as plausible simulators of *past* tea producers. The set pieces for this performance were already in place; again, the mode of tea production in contemporary Darjeeling is largely the same as in the colonial era. On Darjeeling plantations with tourism projects, workers posed for pictures, let tourists borrow their *tāukoris* (head baskets used for collecting tea), described how "peaceful" the plantation was, and even sang a song or two. GI couched tea pluckers as possessors of traditional knowledge that was tuned to a delicate ecosystem. In tourism, workers willingly played the role of "gardener" for tourists, against the background of the *kamān*. While GI media made the plantation hyper-real, tourism sutured the experience of consuming tea to that of consuming place.

In recent years, tea plantation tourism has boomed. Plantations are converting bungalows into tourist lodging and encouraging visitors to see tea production and experience the Darjeeling distinction for themselves. They can, as a *New York Times* travel reporter writes, "compare styles and improve their palates" and immerse themselves in "a teetotaler's version of a Napa Valley wine tour" (Gross 2007). In order for the plantation to be itself consumable, it had to be remade further, from relic of an oppressive colonial past to proud regional "heritage." A heritage tourist experience depended on reminders of the spatial and class divisions of the *kamān*. One planter explained to me that tourists wanted a "colonial experience," and that in order to compete with other plantations, he needed to provide this for them. At Lindendale Tea Estates, for example, a double occupancy room complete with bed tea, picnics, bird watching, and day trips to Kalimpong and Darjeeling runs between $400 and $500 a night. A review of Lindendale in *Condé Nast Traveller* reports:

[The bungalow] stands as an unselfconscious reminder of an era when graciousness effortlessly prevailed … The guests who stay now are given the opportunity to see the day-to-day workings of the estate … and its labor-intensive routines (*which don't appear to have changed in centuries*) … Visiting [Lindendale] is like arriving in a little corner of heaven—and almost as remote (Blackburn 2006, p. 70, emphasis added)

Tourists, too, worked to perform *terroir*. As a visitor to Windsor Tea Estate put it when I asked her why she came to that particular garden, "We drink their tea, and we wanted to know more about it." Many of Darjeeling's GI marketing materials echo the strategies and mimic the rhetoric pioneered by Keshav Roy, Windsor's owner. Beginning in the early 1990s on an otherwise marginal plantation, Roy helped make Darjeeling India's first GI through both advocacy with the Tea Board and tourist projects. In a multifaceted fetishization project, he turned the workers and the environment of Windsor into consumables. In the process, he remade himself, as a Raj-era planter incarnate, as well as the workers and the soils, elements critical to Darjeeling's *terroir*, all consumable in a cup of Darjeeling and knowable by experiencing that cup on his plantation.

Every day at Windsor, tour groups filtered in and out. If they were lucky, they would have an audience with Roy himself, a captivating storyteller. I followed some of these tours around the factory and tasting room to hear Roy wax to visitors about the "rhythms of nature," the "terrestrial infirma," and how they had become "harmonious" at Windsor. He peppered narratives about tea manufacturing with memorable and provocative one-liners, such as "they are looking for favor in the balance sheet, not flavor in life" (a biting criticism of other tea plantation owners). If guests asked for sugar or milk, Roy would chastise them: "Would you put milk in your glass of Champagne?"

At Windsor, visitors could not only learn to drink tea from Roy, a fourth generation plantation owner who preferred meeting guests in his khaki safari suit, but also help laborers in "volunteer projects" such as repairing houses and building latrines. The tourist experience made GI's "garden" imaginary material, but by literally re-building plantation villages and residing in Raj bungalows above them, tourists, planters, and laborers together materially reproduced the *kamān*.

Conclusion: *Terroir* and the Obliteration of Labor

While legal administration and promotion have helped establish Darjeeling's garden image at an imaginative level, then, the *terroir* to which the GI label attests depends upon materiality and visibility, manifested ironically in the *kamān*. A colonially derived production process, along with geographical ideas, had to become tangible and digestible. An ugly colonial past had to be repackaged into a garden "heritage," something that was itself consumable through tea tourism. Ethnographies of artisanal food production highlight the affective relationships farmers *and consumers* have towards products as well as to the agricultural environments that produce them. In her study of American farmstead cheese, Paxson (2010, p. 445) shows how cheese makers "reverse engineer" *terroir*, using the idea of an intimate connection between environment, producer, and product—the same ideas invoked in Darjeeling's GI—to create new agricultural practices that are suited to particular places (or ideas about those places). In post-GI Darjeeling, tourism required Darjeeling tea laborers to physically manifest the imaginaries presented in marketing materials and stipulated in GI law. In the context of tea tourism, laborers viewed their work not as the transformation of the plantation into an idyllic garden but as a revitalization of the *kamān*. Tea workers did not participate in tourist projects because they were coerced, or because they had any particular investment in ideas of ecological purity or "traditional knowledge." Nor were tea laborers "reverse engineers," working to make their practices suitable to the landscape. Instead, they were rebuilders. Their acquiescence to the imaginaries surrounding GI amounted to a knowing performance: a plantation version of the industrial worker's strategic "consent" to self-exploitation (Burawoy 1979). This consent was a response not only to the will of management but also to the material realities wrought by a volatile tea market. It was evidence of workers' longstanding participation in the ideological construction of Darjeeling as both refuge and industrial space that predates GI by some 150 years. More than anything else, it was laborers who embodied the dualism of *kamān* and garden, and it was labor—colonial plantation labor— that was essential to the *terroir* of Darjeeling tea.

Workers saw the revitalization of the plantation—the revitalization of the *kamān*—through new marketing schemes and tourism projects as allowing them to stay in their villages on the plantations. Before the market upturn brought on by GI, fair trade, organic and other international certification schemes, plantations closed and women were forced to find work in town, breaking rocks and portering luggage. By most accounts I collected, these jobs netted them more money than plantation work. Workers, however, returned to work on reopened plantations. I asked why. Time and again, I was told that manual labor in town was not desirable, because it took workers away from the *kamān busti*, from homes and family. Workers knew that international consumer demand was critical to the stability of the plantation. The revitalization of the tea industry through GI allowed the *kamān* to once again become a stable site of both home and work.

With the increased popularity of alternative agriculture movements that are framed as resistance to the inequities in the global food system, scholars have begun to interrogate how the ideals of alternative agriculture intersect with the material conditions of food production (Guthman 2004; Lyon 2011; West 2012). In this article, I have shown how, through GI, wage laborers become meaningfully engaged in value as a legal, sensory, and "distinctive" practice as well as an economic one. The post-colonial Indian tea plantation offers a chance to investigate the place of old (and often disquietingly inequitable) regimes of labor in new regimes of value, including GI as well as organic, fair trade, and biodynamic. Previous scholarship has linked food localism and *terroir* to either the fetishization of labor or its wholesale erasure in favor of "agrarian imaginaries" (Guthman 2004). While it is true that GI marketing and legal codes offer a misleading view of the plantation labor process, I have shown in this article that the power of taste comes not just from "invented" consumer imaginaries but also from material conditions that workers themselves knowingly reproduce.

Darjeeling's GI and its attendant marketing reconcile and repackage several dualities: *kamān* and garden; industry and ecological refuge; production and consumption. The language of GI yokes these dualities into a coherent image of a palatable place and product. In Darjeeling, both the culturally constructed "nature" of the tea "garden" and the labor relations of the *kamān* became the intellectual property of the Tea Board of India. Through GI, Nepali laborers, who were often ostracized within their own country as "outsiders," were all of a sudden included within the Indian nation state as the holders of the "traditional knowledge" behind Darjeeling tea—a piece of national patrimony and intellectual property.

Acknowledgments

In addition to the helpful comments from the editor and the two anonymous reviewers, I would like to thank Kirin Narayan, Jane Collins, Jill Harrison, Paul Nadasdy, Claire Wendland, Katherine Ewing, Laura-Anne Minkoff-Zern, and Alex Nading for their comments on drafts of this article. A version of this paper was presented at the 2011 American Anthropological Association annual meetings. I would like to thank Virginia Nazarea, Jonathan Padwe, and the other panel participants for their helpful feedback. Research for this article was supported by the Fulbright Hays Doctoral Dissertation Research Abroad Program, the American Institute of Indian Studies, and the Land Tenure Center at the University of Wisconsin-Madison. An Andrew W. Mellon/American Council of Learned Societies Dissertation Completion Fellowship and the Michigan Society of Fellows supported the writing of this article. All errors are my own.

Notes

1 The Darjeeling tea logo is available in the Darjeeling Tea Association's Media Kit: http://darjeelingtea.com/files/media.asp.htm (Accessed February 4, 2013).

2 The Tea Board claims the *camellia sinensis* bush—the finer, lighter, and exotic *jat* (variety) of tea—is part of Darjeeling's *terroir*. The monocropped landscape of Darjeeling tea was not so homogenous, however. Tea laborers knew how to differentiate between the smaller, coarser leaves of the "*chiniya jat*" (*camellia sinensis*) from the glossier, greener, and more prolific leaves of the "*assame jat*" (*camellia assamensis*).

3 All personal names and plantation names are pseudonyms.

References

Anderson, B. 1983. *Imagined communities: Reflections on the origin and spread of nationalism.* New York, NY: Verso.

Blackburn, J. 2006. The perfect tea break. *Condé Nast Traveler* August: 69–70.

Boisard, P. 2003 [1992]. *Camembert: A national myth.* Trans. Richard Miller. Berkeley, CA: University of California Press.

Bourdieu, P. 1984. *Distinction: A social critique of the judgment of taste.* Trans. R. Nice. London: Routledge.

Bowen, S. 2010. Development from within? The potential for geographic indications in the global South. *The Journal of World Intellectual Property* 13(2): 231–252.

Bowen, S. 2011. The importance of place: Re-territorialising embeddeness. *Sociologica Ruralis* 51(4): 325–348.

Bowen, S., and M.S. Gaytán. 2012. The paradox of protection: National identity, global commodity chains, and the tequila industry. *Social Problems* 59(1): 70–93.

Burawoy, M. 1979. *Manufacturing consent: Changes in the labor process under monopoly capitalism.* Chicago, IL: University of Chicago Press.

Chatterjee, P. 2001. *A time for tea: Women, labor, and post/colonial politics on an Indian plantation.* Durham, NC: Duke University Press.

Colman, T. 2008. *Wine politics: How governments, environmentalists, mobsters, and critics influence the wines we drink.* Berkeley, CA: University of California Press.

Doane, M. 2007. The political economy of the ecological native. *American Anthropologist* 109(3): 452–462.

Doane, M. 2010. Relationship coffees: Structure and agency in the fair trade system. In *Fair trade and social justice: Global ethnographies*, ed. S. Lyon, and M. Moberg, 229–257. New York: NYU Press.

Dozey, E.C. 1922. *A concise history of the Darjeeling district since 1835*. Calcutta: R.N. Mukherjee.

Darjeeling Tea Association (DTA). 2001. *Darjeeling tea: A Geographical Indication* [Film].

Darjeeling Tea Association (DTA). n.d. *Overwhelm your senses*. Kolkata.

Government of India (GOI). 2013. State wise registration details of G.I. applications 15th September, 2003–31st March, 2013. New Delhi: Geographical Indications Registry. Intellectual Property India. http://ipindia.nic.in/girindia/. Accessed 28 May 2013.

Government of India (GOI). 1999. The Geographical Indications of Goods (Registration and Protection) Act, 1999. No. 48 of 1999. New Delhi: Ministry of Law, Justice, and Company Affairs (Legislative Department).

Gross, M. 2007. High tea, India style. *New York Times* October 14: 51.

Guthman, J. 2004. *Agrarian dreams: The paradox of organic farming in California*. Berkeley, CA: University of California Press.

Guthman, J. 2007. The Polanyian way? Voluntary food labels as neoliberal governance. *Antipode* 39(3): 456–478.

Guy, K.M. 2003. *When champagne became French*. Baltimore, MD: The Johns Hopkins University Press.

Guy, K.M. 1997. Wine, work, and wealth: Class relations and modernization in the champagne wine industry, 1870–1914. *Business and Economic History* 26(2): 298–303.

Guy, K.M. 2011. Silence and *savoir-faire* in the marketing of products of the *terroir*. *Modern & Contemporary France* 19(4): 459–475.

Handler, R., and W. Saxton. 1988. Dyssimulation: Reflexivity, narrative, and the quest for authenticity in "living history". *Cultural Anthropology* 3(3): 242–260.

Heath, D., and A. Meneley. 2007. Techne, technoscience, and the circulation of comestible commodities: An introduction. *American Anthropologist* 109(4): 593–602.

Hobsbawm, E. 1983. Inventing traditions. In *The invention of tradition*, ed. E. Hobsbawm, and T. Ranger, 1–14. Cambridge: Cambridge University Press.

Hobsbawm, E., and T. Ranger (eds.). 1983. *The invention of tradition*. Cambridge: Cambridge University Press.

Kloppenburg, J., J. Hendrickson, and G.W. Stevenson. 1996. Coming into the foodshed. *Agriculture and Human Values* 13(3): 33–42.

Laudan, R. 2004. Slow food: The French *terroir* strategy and culinary modernism. *Food, Culture & Society* 7(2): 133–144.

Lyon, S. 2011. *Coffee and community: Maya farmers and fair trade markets*. Boulder: University of Colorado Press.

Meneley, A. 2004. Extra virgin olive oil and slow food. *Anthropologica* 46: 165–176.

Meneley, A. 2007. Like an extra virgin. *American Anthropologist* 109(4): 678–687.

Meneley, A. 2008. Oleo-signs and quali-signs: The qualities of olive oil. *Ethnos* 73(3): 303–326.

Mintz, S. 1985. *Sweetness and power: The place of sugar in modern history*. New York: Penguin Books.

Newman & Company. 1900. *Newman's guide to Darjeeling and its surroundings, historical & descriptive, with some account of the manners and customs of the neighbouring hill tribes*. London: W.H. Allen and Company.

Paxson, H. 2006. Artisanal cheese and economies of sentiment in New England. In *Fast food/slow food: The cultural economy of the global food system*, ed. R. Wilk, 201–218. Lanham, MD: AltaMira Press.

Paxson, H. 2010. Locating value in artisan cheese: Reverse engineering *terroir* for new-world landscapes. *American Anthropologist* 112(3): 444–457.

Paxson, H. 2012. *The life of cheese: Crafting food and value in America*. Berkeley, CA: University of California Press.

Rao, C. N. 2005. Geographical Indications in Indian context: A case study of Darjeeling tea. *Economic and Political Weekly* October 15: 4545–4550.

Roseberry, W. 1996. The rise of yuppie coffees and the reimagination of class in the United States. *American Anthropologist* 94(4): 762–775.

Tea Board of India. n.d. *Darjeeling—The best: A quest for intellectual property rights*. Kolkata.

Terrio, S.J. 2000. *Crafting the culture and history of French chocolate*. Berkeley, CA: University of California Press.

Trubek, A.B. 2008. *The taste of place: A cultural journey into terroir*. Berkeley, CA: University of California Press.

Trubek, A.B., and S. Bowen. 2008. Creating the taste of place in the United States: Can we learn from the French? *GeoJournal* 73: 23–30.

Trubek, A.B., K.M. Guy, and S. Bowen. 2010. *Terroir*: A French conversation with a transnational future. *Contemporary French and Francophone Studies* 14(2): 139–148.

Ulin, R.C. 1995. Invention and representation as cultural capital: Southwest French winegrowing history. *American Anthropologist* 97(3): 519–527.

Weiss, B. 2011. Making pigs local: Discerning the sensory character of place. *Cultural Anthropology* 26(3): 438–461.

West, P. 2012. *From modern production to imagined primitive: The social world of coffee from Papua New Guinea*. Durham, NC: Duke University Press.

Wilson, J. 1998. *Terroir: The role of geology, climate, and culture in the making of French wines*. Berkeley, CA: University of California Press.

World Intellectual Property Rights Organization (WIPO). 2011. Managing the challenges of the protection and enforcement of intellectual property rights: Darjeeling tea. http://www.wipo.int/ipadvantage/en/details.jsp?id=2540. Accessed 23 Feb 2012.

4

Famine Talk: Communication Styles and Socio-Political Awareness in 1990s North Korea

Sandra Fahy

During the 1990s, several factors led to a famine emerging in North Korea.[1] Estimates place the number of deaths anywhere between 200,000 and 3 million.[2] Although hundreds of thousands of North Koreans died, the government system survived despite expectations and anticipations that it would collapse (Kaplan 2006; Martin 2004; Noland 2004; Oh and Hassig 1999). The famine represented the first substantial internal threat to national security in North Korea's history. Like any sovereign nation, North Korea took actions to minimize the impact. Rarely affecting more than 5 percent of a population (Sen 1981), famines tend not to result in whole or even partial changes in political leadership. As such, managing population responses does not require nationwide levels of control, but rather control of those areas most harshly affected by the famine. Thus, where they do occur, punishments for coping strategies such as migration, defection or other crimes are harsh. Alongside such punishments in North Korea, however, a "famine discourse" operated at a public and individual level, supporting the innocence of the government as an agent in the crisis. As a result, a de facto language filter ensured that any information on the famine or any discussion of famine, hunger or starvation did not implicate the government. Indeed, any discourse that approximated the truth was largely avoided as the use of such language would be met with death threats. North Koreans were well aware of these language restrictions. Informants interviewed for the present research discussed at length the limits within which they could articulate themselves. This paper examines these discourse limits and discusses their impact on the articulation of experience post-famine. The speech of survivors demonstrates the lasting impact of North Korea's socio-political cosmology in both the articulation of famine experience at the time of its happening, and after the fact when living safely in a different country.

The collection, archiving and study of oral accounts from survivors of famine is a relatively new and unchartered field.[3] Indeed, the notion of a famine survivor is to a certain extent oxymoronic. This paper contributes to the literature on collective social suffering and famine theory by demonstrating that socio-political cosmologies in place at the time of atrocity shape discourses of suffering and thus personal accounts both during and after survival.

Famine and Silence

Censorship and the control of language have a long and involved history with famine, as they do with other rights violations (Article 19 1999; Devereux 1993; Leshuk 2000; Sen and Drèze 1999). Famine has historically been accompanied or exacerbated by lack of free speech, limited access to information and the manipulation of language, resulting in a dearth of information flowing from the famine location. This may explain why the word "silent" appears so frequently in descriptions of the North Korean famine (e.g. Natsios 1998, 2002; Skelton 1997; see also Lautze 1997: 5, 6, who describes state-level silence as well). Other descriptions include the words "slow" (Natsios 2002; Norgaard and Valfells 2003) and "invisible" (Natsios 2002). These phrases have lasting power, reappearing in more recent social history books of North Korea and Korea more generally (Flake and Synder 2003; Yun and Shin 2006). More recently, Cuff and Goudie (2009: 260) employ the example of North Korea to illustrate how the term "silent famine" is used to describe famines that are little known to the rest of the world. In short then, when it comes to descriptions of the North Korean famine, the word "silent" is apt. This begs the question: if the famine is so little known beyond the borders, what knowledge exists within? Just how deafening is the silence on the inside?

Within North Korea, official terms for the famine were used to actively shape perception of the situation. Outside of the country, we commonly refer to it as the North Korean famine whereas inside it was known as *Konan-ŭi haenggun* [The March of Suffering]. Historically, the "March of Suffering" refers to Kim Il Sung's march with guerrilla fighters against Japanese imperialism in Manchuria in 1938–39, yet it is the most common term of reference for the famine of the 1990s. Among the thirty interviewees, everyone, without exception, used the term. In fact, when I used the Korean word for famine, I was asked to clarify, "You mean the March of Suffering?" by three-quarters of my informants. The other quarter merely began, "Ah, you want to know about the March of Suffering." Some North Korean official literature, including the leading newspaper, also used the term *pulgŭn ki chaengch'wi undong* (the Red Banner Spirit); and for a time in 1998, the Forced March to Final Victory, *ch'oehu-ŭi sŭngni rŭl wihan konan-ŭi haenggun*. Significantly, each of these historical references is characterized by national usurpation of foreign powers.[4] At the very least, these terms operate euphemistically, hiding or erasing truth (Todorov 2003: 115). Terms loaded with cultural and historical significance are not used arbitrarily, but are part of the cosmology or social atmosphere. In fact, such expressions can be so culturally bound as to be almost incomprehensible without contextual or historical knowledge. Despite how incongruous they may in fact be, they are operational in reinforcing existing socio-political ideals while simultaneously disarming the emergence of threats to those ideals.

Famine theorists have made connections between names given to famine periods, noting the political motivation behind labels (de Waal 1989; Kelleher 1997; Sen 1981; Yang 1997). Such metaphoric descriptions can affect overall perception of the ongoing process of the famine, how people understand causal factors as well as public reaction at the time and how it is spoken about afterwards, if at all. In China, what is now known as the Great Leap Forward Famine of 1959–62 was at the time officially called the "Three-year Natural Calamity" (Yang 1997: 59). Such terminology can further exacerbate confusion both within the country and abroad, leading to botched humanitarian aid activities and untimely response. Thus, the terms can effectively silence accurate discussion or knowledge of famine where those inside the country are just as confused as those beyond its borders. In North Korea, ordinary people had less information about real famine causes, consequences and conditions than those of us on the outside for several reasons: the government obscured accurate reporting, the transmission of information between individuals was highly controlled and the verification of information was highly unreliable. However, as we will see shortly, although people lacked accurate information about the famine, survivor accounts collected during my field research demonstrate a self-conscious awareness of the power of speech in shaping individual survival.

Given the intersections of censorship, language control and famine, what happens to language and memory under such conditions? Scholars working in the field of collective social suffering have demonstrated that trauma plays a role in the accounts of survivors; sometimes trauma can silence permanently. Traumatic experience and its explicability have been the topic of research within the social sciences for some time (Caruth 1995, 1996; Friedlander 1992; Kelleher 1997; LaCapra 2001; Ortega 2003; Spence 1982). Emotionally arousing events activate the amygdala, a portion of the brain responsible for emotional learning and memory; this may be the reason they are stored in memory longer than less emotionally arousing events, thus forming long-term memories (McGaugh 2005).[5] It is possible that this is why the "flashbulb memories" of truly shocking events are stored in memory and reappear (Brown and Kulik 1977).[6] Not to be overlooked is the fact that survivors themselves remark on the changes that took place for them on the level of language as well as their difficulties with explicability after their survival of particularly traumatic events. To explore this I turn briefly to two examples, from the Soviet Union and China respectively, before turning back to survivors from North Korea.

Explicability: Soviet and Chinese Examples

Writing about his experience in the Soviet forced-labor camps of Kolyma, in the north-eastern area of Siberia, Shalamov explained that the words he used during imprisonment were stripped of all unessential communication:

> My language was the crude language of the mines and it was as impoverished as the emotions that lived near the bones. Get up, go to work, dinner, end of work, rest, citizen chief, may I speak, shovel, trench, yes sir, drill, pick, it's cold outside … These few words were all I needed for years. (Shalamov 1994: 74)

In many ways, emotional trauma alone may be so harsh as to produce these language fractures. The impoverished emotions that live near the bones are far from those that live in the heart, and the language he used was likewise far from the heart. At the same time, a socio-political impetus from authorities had a vested interest in controlling Shalamov's speech. Zhang (1994: 61–2, 82) has observed this same authorial concern over language. This social environment promotes a type of language that obfuscates accurate descriptions of the atrocity, making it palatable, endurable and normal.[7]

Xianlang Zhang, a writer imprisoned during China's Great Leap Forward famine, kept a highly coded and ambiguous diary during those years—it had to be highly coded and ambiguous so as not to alert the attention of authorities who would kill him. He later used these diaries to jog his memory and write two autobiographies. In the first of these, *Grass Soup*, he explained that a new set of circumstances produced new semantic structures:

> At times of the year when there was less farm work to do, the leaders would pick a time when they thought it would be alright for us not to go to work and they would allow us not to go to work. This sentence sounds awkward, but there isn't a better way of putting it. You will find similar sentences in what follows. A new set of social circumstances has to produce a new semantic structure. (Zhang 1994: 61)

Scholars in the fields of anthropology, science and medicine have considered the impact of trauma on memory and speech (Caruth 1995, 1996; Friedlander 1992; Kelleher 1997; LaCapra 2001; Ortega 2003; Spence 1982). However, for the initial trauma site to come into being (whether it be a gulag, prison camp, or famine) there must also be a socio-political discourse that generates, reproduces and reinforces preselected "truths" that simultaneously make accurate information unverifiable. In fact, one might say that violence sends out from itself a type of discourse that has the ability to affect others—we can see this in the domestic and international realms where ways of speaking about violence rationalize, obfuscate and sometimes even popularize the abuse of power.

In the prison camp where he lived, [Shalamov] explained that he needed very few words for many years, but what happened to his communication after release? Of course, we have the literature he wrote, but how did the former gulag-language facilitate or hinder the expression of his suffering? In many ways, the paucity of emotion in his language provides a picture of stoicism necessary to survive such conditions. However, as Zhang indicates, sometimes this awkward language requires explanation. My concern is twofold: firstly, whether or to what extent the language used to articulate suffering, during and after survival, is indirectly controlled by the political apparatus that produced the suffering in the first place. Secondly, survivors demonstrate a degree of agency despite the repressive and vigilant regime that controlled them; by what means do they achieve this?

For some survivors, the fact that their expressions are rooted and informed linguistically by the traumatic past exacerbates suffering. They write about survival in a language touched through by the authority that facilitated their oppression. This positions the survivor in a kind of double bind because to articulate suffering they must use the language born in the context of their suffering. The work of Zhang and Shalamov demonstrates that survivors are aware of the impact of atrocity on language. Traces of the former ways of speaking do re-emerge in later accounts of survival. Their work also demonstrates how language born in the context of suffering reveals aspects of their individual agency in self-expression, despite authoritarian forces.

North Korean Famine Talk

Turning to North Korean famine survivors, what traces remain of their former communication styles? What do these reveal about the linguistic enclosures placed on the experiences of individuals? Although certain types of communication were enforced, did alternative, coded and ambiguous expressions or grammars emerge to ease accurate communication into life? As evidenced by the oral accounts of survivors I recorded, despite the linguistic enclosures existing in North Korea, a vibrant lexicon was in use that rendered the famine experience and enabled, contradictorily, "escape within the enclosure." This lexicon was in use by ordinary people and it was distinct in meaning from that used by the state. However, due to severe restrictions placed on accurate famine talk, coded communication had to be extremely subtle. Often the very terms provided by the government were used, but their meanings were remade. Context and contrast were often the two variables necessary to identify the hidden meaning.

First I will explore the linguistic enclosure placed on North Koreans from the state level. Survivor accounts demonstrate that this form of communication was indeed received; how it was enforced is also revealed. However, according to survivors, these state initiated terms were used in ordinary, private discourse, yet people managed to manipulate their meanings just enough to secure a degree of linguistic freedom. Because these manipulated terms re-emerge in the oral accounts of survivors, there are implications for how the famine is remembered and the accuracy of articulation post-famine.

Government linguistic practices informed the type of language used to discuss the famine, and consequently any suffering that resulted from the famine was expressed in ways consistent within those linguistic practices. Using printed text as an example, it is evident that both popular media as well as literature represented the famine according to the desires of the state. There are, for instance, many cases of short and long fiction in North Korea representing the famine according to government interpretations; such texts favored representations of the famine as a food shortage, as a time when potatoes were nutritious and healthier than meat (Gabroussenko 2009). However, the extent of influence of these texts is questionable. Few ordinary North Koreans own books privately (Ryang 1996: 289) so their social influence may be negligible. For many people in the North, their greatest contact with the written word is through the newspaper of the day, exhibited in window cases on the streets. The North's leading newspaper, the *Rodong Shinmun* carried expressions that many of my interviewees might have encountered during those years.

Newspapers provided the population with information about how to interpret and cope with the famine. In the spring and summer of 1999, when the famine was still well underway, the *Rodong Shinmun* published several articles outlining practical ways of coping. Heading the list of coping mechanisms was loyal adherence to Juche farming methods, a seed revolution, taking better care of young plants, double cropping, substitution of corn for rice, and the "right crop in the right soil in the right season."[8] Many informants mentioned that doubt and denial were their first responses to the famine. It is possible that messages from the newspapers engendered trust in the population. Many North Koreans said they doubted things could get worse, or that the government would allow things to get worse. Strengthening this sense, the government helped the population to understand and rationalize the famine. The interface of language and socio-political control is most glaring in how the famine itself was termed. Never referred to as a famine, the words *kikŭn* (famine) and *kia* (hunger in famine) were almost totally unknown to the survivors I interviewed. Among the thirty interviewees, only those who lived abroad in Seoul or Tokyo for more than a handful of years (approximately ten persons) used the term "famine," but their application of the term to North Korea was an affectation. All interviewees readily used the phrase "food shortage" instead. Several informants told me that use of the word "famine" did not apply to what happened in North Korea because that term, they explained, more readily described Africa (indicating no specific country) or South Korea. Like many other negative terms, these refer to the failings of non-socialist countries (Ryang 1996). However, what was taking place in the country did need some term of reference. Through the term, the *Konan-ŭi haenggun* (March of Suffering),[9] the North Korean government drew instant correlation between the plight of ordinary North Koreans and Kim Il Sung's fight against Japanese imperialism in Manchuria. The term appeared as many as four or five times a day in Korean Central News Agency articles.[10] Yet it is not enough to demonstrate the state's use of such terms. It is necessary that we see the extent to which these terms appeared in the daily communication of ordinary people.

The fact that informants repeatedly referred to the famine as the *Konan-ŭi haenggun* indicates the widespread use of the term. As I will demonstrate shortly, several other expressions used by both the government and among individuals, hid the reality of the situation just as the term *konan ŭi haenggun* did. Milroy and Milroy (1991) have established that written language is much more easily codified than the spoken word. The government provided a written linguistic framework to guide the population that operated as a kind of "protective shield" (Argenti-Pillen 2000: 88, 89) to individuals, but more importantly to the nation itself. Within this linguistic framework the collective experience of famine or starvation could be "made sense of" within cultural frames familiar to the reader or listener. Through these messages, the previously established cultural context of such histories provided the population with ways to intellectualize and familiarize themselves with how to cope, how to survive. Thus, the former struggles (the original March of Suffering, as it were) strengthened reliance on culturally conditioned ways of engaging with tried and tested means of surviving struggles. These codified and culturally conditioned ways of speaking appeared in the ordinary speech of informants, but they also underwent a liberating metamorphosis as well. I will turn my attention to this last point shortly. At this stage it is important to consider first how official state terms were enforced.

Enforcement of this discourse had two main outcomes. First, the official terminology became more widespread; second—and simultaneously—the government drew attention to unacceptable phraseology in its process of weeding out such expressions. Of the thirty North Koreans, five identified disappearances during the famine, and explained that they knew this could happen to them too if they were not careful. When discussing disappearances in oral accounts, survivors attributed the cause of disappearance to what the victims had said or what they were rumored to have said. Mr. Ŏm explained that his neighbor disappeared. When he told me this, he did not begin with the disappearance story directly, but rather with what the old woman had been saying the day before. Structured in this way, it is evident that for the speaker, the old woman's speech and her disappearance were situationally linked in relevant ways. With the events juxtaposed it is conveyed that the "antecedent event somehow gives rise to or affords the possible occurrence of the subsequent event" (Ochs 2004:271). This establishes the disappearance as an event naturally correlated to speech. However, the truth of the correlation cannot be verified. Mr. Ŏm explained:

So a senior citizen was going about—an 80-year-old hungry senior was going about saying, "My gosh, I'm so hungry how am I supposed to live? This, at my age? I wish I were young." That night, for saying that [lit: for doing that] she was taken somewhere. There in *Hamgyŏngbuk-to* they were not giving out food. One kilogram of food was usually given, but they didn't give any so the senior woman was very hungry, "How are we supposed to live?" Having said this [lit: this way of speaking], she was captured and taken away. Who took her in the night? It was likely the police, in *Onsŏng, Hamgyŏngbuk-to*. You just couldn't say those things. Even if I were so hungry I was dying, "I'm so hungry, I'm dying" you couldn't make that sound. I'm in so much pain I'm dying' that's how you talk. (Mr. Ŏm)

Other survivors observed a correlation between speech and disappearance. For example: "I could not say that my grandfather died of hunger, because if we say that they'll take us away. The party will have my family and close acquaintances banished" (Mr. Kim, November 2006). Being aware of political prison camps meant that North Koreans made the connection between the camps and the disappearances. Just as it had in other regimes, this worked to regulate behavior (Todorov 1999; 2003), most obviously in citizens' choice of language and type of expression.[11] The earlier extract from the interview with Mr. Ŏm shows not only that he had identified a correlation between speech and consequence, but he had also identified alternative ways of communicating, removing the possibility of being disappeared: *I'm in so much pain I'm dying, that's how you talk.* Rather than subvert the ideological apparatus, as some might presume, knowledge of these double realities kept North Koreans behaving and speaking in ways that ensured their survival along with, perhaps sometimes inadvertently, the system that constituted their suffering. Among my informants, all had complex emotional responses to the difficulties of life in the North, both during the famine and in post-famine life. Despite the horrendous difficulties suffered, the norm was to demonstrate loyalty to the nation (real or fabricated loyalty) and eke out an existence via the highly limited coping strategies available.

It was difficult for people to verify information in this environment of inaccurate and indirect communication, which led to delays in coping strategies. These forms of speech may also indicate that denial emerged as the earliest coping strategy, which would not be unusual. Like other cultural systems, terror has an underlying structure where shared denial gives way to defensive rationalizations.[12] These may also be natural responses to the outpouring of unreality generated by traumatic experiences (Scarry 1985); such responses can serve to bolster a wavering sense of insecurity. At the beginning, denial of the famine came hand in hand with complete faith in the government. All thirty interviewees reported this: it was a temporary lull in supply; it would right itself. People trusted the repeated assurances from the government that faith in it would pull them through—the government would do as it had always done and take care of its people. In fact, this had been the case. The famine was the first instance where the government failed to uphold its promises on a sustained basis. The famine began with misperceptions on behalf of the government and people on the ground. Denial was the first response of many North Koreans, both in the government and on the ground. During the latter stages of the famine, when its effects were finally visible in Pyongyang, informants who lived in those areas were shocked to find famine dead on their doorsteps. Prior to this high visibility, it was easier to deny the famine.

These types of response are typical. It has been shown that a common reaction to major and painful life changes is to draw on cultural beliefs and create new mental worlds, perhaps in an effort to justify events and maintain a sense of security (Argenti-Pillen 2000). Although doubt and denial were the earliest reactions to the famine, when the food shortages continued and there was no fulfillment of government promises, people began to see a difference between the government discourse and their daily lives.

Perceiving the double reality in which they lived, passing through the earliest phase of the famine when doubt and denial were the strongest reactions, people began to remark upon the incongruities with uncertainty and delicacy. The social environment in North Korea lends itself to a sustained lack of accurate information regarding factors that led to the famine and subsequent rights violations such as public execution and disappearance, for instance. Lacking a means by which to access sustained clarity on events engendered uncertainty and doubt within the population, such that explanations and justifications for such horrendous actions emerged. Zhang's observation that hunger was counter-revolutionary (Zhang 1994), is echoed in the writings of Mr. Jang. A member of the elite when he lived in Pyongyang, and an official poet of the government, Mr. Jang is not representative of my interview sample, but he nonetheless accurately identified a common observation throughout the informants' testimonies when he wrote, "our very lives are illegal."[13] Genuine lived experience was illegal if articulated as such.

People omitted words like "hunger," "famine" and "starvation" from spoken and written vocabulary and replaced them with neutral or more acceptable words such as "pain," "illness" and "food poisoning." These replacements had such currency as to appear in the testimony of informants from as far south as Pyongyang and as far north as Onsŏng—the length of the nation. Accurate terms were life-threatening. To say you were "dying of starvation" was often more immediately life-threatening than starvation itself. The skill of knowing what not to know (Suarez-Orozco 1990: 367) or in the North Korean case, knowing what not to talk about, was a life-saving coping mechanism.

Free Speech within Limits

If trauma systematically silences (Desjarlais *et al.* 1995: 175; Jenkins 1998: 187) and if the context of suffering provides the victim with a limited linguistic framework to express themselves, how does the survivor negotiate survival against these extreme limitations? Language is about relationships, likewise survival. The two must meet to negotiate a chance at living through an atrocity. How did this happen in North Korea? Coded and indirect communication patterns emerged and articulation of experience was confined to these boundaries because to do otherwise would mean death. As such, these coded terms demonstrate two things simultaneously: the awareness of potential dangers and the need to maintain harmony (Argenti-Pillen 2003a, 2003b). We will return to this point in the conclusion as it continues to influence the survivor testimonies given in Seoul and Tokyo. In North Korea, people knew what they could discuss openly and what they could not. Though it was difficult to verify information because of very practical limitations of geography, infrastructure and so on, the survivor accounts reveal an awareness of and participation in a double-discourse.

Awareness of a double-discourse, which we can identify as one thing speaking in place of another, surfaces across the testimonies just as it does in the independent writing of defectors. Mr. Jang, the poet who lived well in Pyongyang, wrote about public executions in this fashion:

>Bullets hurl words in these times..
>the most brutal, the most long-lasting decree
>is said in three syllables
>from the gun barrel
>the military first policy proclaims it: Kim Jong Il.

The limits placed on free articulation suggest that the methods by which genuine thought and experience are transmitted must out of necessity be highly specialized and refined much more so than the relatively blunt instrument of *samizdat*. Evidence of highly specialized communication appeared in the oral accounts. Other scholars have observed similar tendencies in similar contexts (Argenti-Pillen 2003a; Burke 1989; Humphery 1994; Scott 1998).

Indeed, the testimony of Mr. Lee demonstrates that even discussions about the suffering of others had to be highly ambiguous, minimized and made light of so as not to hint at guilt or implication of victim/perpetrator. Typically, the word "hunger" was substituted for other, less damning terms of reference. Notice how the cause of death in this account switches from hunger to cold when Mr. Lee speaks with the official over the phone and his co-workers:

>In 1997, when I was living in Pyongyang, I was leaving the house for work one morning and there in the front entrance of the building was a woman and a child, dead from hunger. It was morning. It was December. Seven o'clock in the morning. When I went out it was bitterly cold. Everything was fully frozen. I went back into the house and phoned what we call the district administration office, "Ah! here." I gave them my address and said that on the first floor at the entrance there were two people who had frozen to death, and would they come and take care of them. I said that and then, "Alright," they said, and put the phone down as if it were of little importance. But I was thinking that two people are dead, and how could they just be careless like that? So I phoned them back. "Yeah, a comrade has died. How can you just respond like that?" Then he said, "Sir, who are you?" "I'm the one responsible for the area," I said, to which he replied, "We've got lots of dead people. So far this morning we have dozens of people who have died. You've called us, but we have many places to go to collect the bodies. We will come and collect them." So then—ah!—so a lot of people are dying. Then I knew. Our area was an upper-class neighborhood, so I hadn't any idea there were that many dying. So, then I went to work at the Northwest office, "Ah, this morning I came out of the house and found some mother and her child frozen to death outside!" And they replied, "You're just starting to notice that now? Outside of the Unification office we have been seeing dozens dead every day." Ah! And then I knew. I had been abroad and had friends who helped me with money, so I could live without worry over eating. So, because of that, I hadn't any idea. So, through the policy of the government these numbers of people were dying of starvation. (Mr. Lee, September 2006)

One can see from the above account that death could be openly discussed, so long as the cause of death was not identified. This pattern is emblematic of the thirty interviewees. Mr. Lee begins this portion of his testimony by telling me unambiguously that the mother and child had died from hunger. Then he describes the scene, focusing on the extreme cold. He uses reported speech to describe the phone call with the local authorities, in which he explains that the two had died of cold. The phrasing ensures no one is implicated in their death, whether state or individual.

Hunger or starvation death was not possible in the socio-political context of North Korea so it was articulated as death by freezing or cold. At the local government office, Mr. Lee's interlocutors are similarly engaged in an act of obliteration, not over the fact of multiple deaths in the city that morning, (*We've got lots of dead people. So far this morning we have dozens of people who have died* and *You're just starting to notice that now? Outside of the Unification office we have been seeing dozens dead every day*) but rather in the meaning ascribed to the deaths: *two people who had frozen to death* and *we have many places to go to collect the bodies. We will come and collect them.* The meaning of their deaths (government negligence) is altered (cold) and divorced from the fact of their deaths (starvation).[14]

These expressions indicate that some North Koreans were not only aware of their circumstances, or that articulation of that awareness required clandestine and careful means of communication, but also that they sat uncomfortably at the interface of these truths. The expressions point to a human need, regardless of conditions, to articulate observed incongruities and received confirmation of what is observed. Safety is negotiated within these articulations; they simultaneously maintain pre-existing relationships of inequality with real or potential perpetrators (because they must, at risk of death) and the necessary articulation of experience between those beyond the realm of privilege as it is structured within North Korean society. It has been observed that limits placed on political discourse also limit political thought (Bourdieu 1991: 172); however, the accounts of famine survivors indicate the presence of value systems and perceptions alternative to those dictated by official ideology. Limits placed on political discourse resulted in alternative speech that carried traces of socio-political dissatisfaction.

Recollecting Survival with Limited Speech

When famine survivors do speak in post-famine times, in places like Seoul or Tokyo, what traces remain of the former context of censorship and limited speech? When survivors shared their experiences with me, the very act of speaking openly and at length about the famine inverted the original social norms that were in place when the famine took place. This being the case, it follows that ways of speaking during famine are embedded in the oral testimonies. What are the implications of this for the telling of survival experiences? How is it possible to communicate things that were off-limits to articulation at the time they were experienced? Furthermore, in the narrowly circumscribed linguistic spaces of safety that were carved out, is the memory of famine mixed or muddled in some way? How is it possible to remember that which was not officially sanctioned to remember (after Burke1989:100)?

These questions are particularly relevant to research on North Korea because the vast majority of information gathering relies on survey and interview work with former North Koreans. When using such methodology, how informants remember and render their memory of events in language is an important consideration. If the articulation of experience was restricted, surely this will influence the recollection of things after the fact. As shown through the above examples from informants, coded communication could be exchanged with greater safety than free speech. In the following lengthy example and analysis I will show that some coded ways of speaking while in North Korea continued to appear in post-famine accounts, making complex and almost indecipherable the meaning attributed to survival in North Korea. As observed, accurate expressions could spark disapproval or violence and thus required ambiguous expressions to maintain a safe distance from reality. I use the following account from Mr. Kim to demonstrate how the safety-net created by indirect and ambiguous speech can continue to obfuscate, confuse and baffle the listener in post-famine contexts.

In the following example, Mr. Kim shares his metaphorical reference to a body destroyed by frostbite to explain to me how the famine happened in North Korea. Although this is an unusual route to describe famine, he switches into this metaphoric description easily and sustains it until the end of the story. Echoing an observation of Ochs (2004), the events are narrated to convey that the antecedent event (chilblains) gave rise to the occurrence of the subsequent event (death). The prevalence of this metaphoric conversion from hunger to cold, from starvation death to freezing death, is repeated throughout several unrelated accounts across the spectrum of survivors I interviewed. Connections between cold weather, dropping body temperature and hunger are invariably intertwined at latitudes such as North Korea's. Famines kill principally through making a population sufficiently nutritionally deficient to become vulnerable to disease, illness and inclement weather. People perish more quickly through these than strictly through starvation alone.

> When a person is cold, the freezing starts at the end of their fingers and then their feet freeze, later it comes to about here [points to mid-chest]. Why? They are far from the heart, the heart is far away so the blood that comes out at first is hot, but it cools as it goes out. It gets colder. So the fingers freeze. In North Korea, likewise, we call Pyongyang the heart. Near to Pyongyang they are giving out the food relief [the government's Public Distribution System—PDS]. Then, further away at the tips of the fingers far away in Hamgyŏngbuk-to, Yangkangto and so on from 1991, 1992 they weren't giving PDS. Then by February of 1996 little by little they weren't even able to give out any PDS in Pyongyang, the blood was starting to freeze, by about February 1996 the relief had stopped even as far as Pyongyang. So if you think of it as a person, if they are frozen up to here, to the heart, then they are going to die. Then at that time the warehouses were nearly run empty and Kim Jong Il took a countermeasure against it. From that time on, Kim Jong Il was telling the population, "Yeah, because of our natural enemy, the bastard Americans, we are unable to farm and so there is no food, so it is difficult to give the PDS." (Mr. Kim, November 2006)

Mr. Kim's account mirrors nationalist discourse about how the famine is best understood and interpreted: as one national body suffering in concert. The progression of the famine in North Korea is depicted through the metaphor of a body (the nation) gradually overtaken by chilblains (the famine), where only the heart (Pyongyang) is scarcely saved (to save the whole, as a consequence, unnecessary extremities must be sacrificed). On one level, we have the associated articulation of the national experience of suffering. On the other we have the articulation of an individual experience of suffering. Both of these pain expressions are separate from starvation experience; instead, chilblains is selected as a metaphorical carrier perhaps because it provides the handy convenience of drawing a relatively clear image of gradual, fatal and inevitable exposure to "the elements."[15] The experience of the individual in starvation is extracted from this metaphor; reference to the famine appears in the form of cessation of food ration delivery and then is draped in the metaphor of blood flowing from the heart. It might not be possible, from this metaphor, to say that the famine was a shared experience as the notion of the inevitable and wholesale loss of non-vital parts is explained as a biological (scientific and therefore logical) process.[16] The countermeasures taken against the food shortage were merely to explain the perceived source of the problem, reinforcing perceptions of the suffering as inevitable. If we take Mr. Kim's metaphor to its ultimate end, the treatment for the most severe chilblains would indeed be to cut off the affected areas so that infection does not set in and destroy the person entirely. A partial death is unfortunate—it is complicated, there are inconveniences, one ought to have taken precautions in the first place and so on— but it is favorable to total death. The causes of famine (nature and external enemy forces) and the inevitable survival methods (sacrifice of non-essential parts for the good of the whole) were rationalized and understood through roughly this type of narrative structure. This type of narrative always ends in the same way; under threat of total death, parts have to be sacrificed.[17]

This analogy of chilblains appeared only in my interview with Mr. Kim. Although Mr. Kim takes the story to a pitch unprecedented among my interviewees, it is entirely consistent with the general theme I found in the accounts, namely the abstraction of cause and effect. My attention to this pattern, a method influenced by the work of Thomson (1977: 9), recognizes the frequency which established a consistent general view of things. The only difference in Mr. Kim's account is that he does not offer the self-awareness seen in other interviews, where speakers reveal their awareness of "putting on" a particular reality. This may be due to his being a resident of Pyongyang where there was, indeed, a more palatable reality well into the 1990s while the rest of the country suffered severely.

The ideological apparatus of North Korea, like that of many socialist and capitalist states, maintains a rather liberal relationship between language, meaning and truth (Todorov 2003: 44; Watson 1994: 1). It should naturally follow then that similar types of communication will appear in the language of those who lived within such ideology. Intentionally or otherwise, Mr. Kim's metaphor communicates the government mentality that pervaded the socio-political space: it justifies government inaction and the countless lives lost. Given how far the metaphor moves from the subjective experience of starvation, it is interesting that the body is mentioned at all. But the body was essential. The means by which North Korea attempted to manage the famine manifested itself most clearly in how it managed the bodies of its population: how they farmed, where they farmed; where they lived, moved, escaped; how they spoke and what words they used. Furthermore, the use of human anatomy to explain political structures, in particular the Juche idea, is standard in North Korea (Lee 2003: 111). The people, the bones and muscles of this metaphoric national body, execute the orders given down by the nervous system (the party) and the brain (the Great Leader) (Oberdorfer 1997: 20).

Therefore, when the body (the hungry body, the national body) appears in the metaphoric articulations of the famine, particularly in ways of managing, it is not unusual for it to appear the way it does. The control of bodies passing in and out of the country, the control of verbal communication between bodies, the control of criminal bodies in prisons and re-education facilities, the displayed execution of bodies as a means to teach criminal wrongs, even down to where bullets were placed in those bodies and gags or stones in the mouths of prisoners to stop them speaking before death—all of this was regulated, the details were intentional and socio-politically significant. As observed elsewhere, violence is rooted in a "pattern and ideology of behavior" and the articulated memories reveal the enduring structures of violence that created them (Triulzi 2006: 123). The fact that Mr. Kim chose to speak about the nation undergoing famine as a body experiencing inevitable suffering is not incidental.

Writing on culture and narrative, Bruner (1987: 15) explains that "one important way of characterizing a culture is by the narrative models it makes available for describing the course of a life." In North Korea, the narrative models available are singular in that they are about the defeat of the Imperialists by the North Koreans—also expressed as Kim Il Sung and by extension Kim Jong Il's defeat of the enemy. More significant for this research are the narrative models available to informants for articulating their experience of the famine and what these say about how the famine was understood, experienced and remembered.

Though the survivor emerges from the famine with the language of that context, language operates as a linguistic package providing insights into the structures that sustained and generated the famine. Another type of history is produced through the oral history of subordinate groups and their written testimonies, because the "narrative home" is different (Connerton 1989: 19). Within the field of psychology, the articulation of traumatic pain through narrative therapy is said to be an effective means of overcoming and resolving trauma (Herman 1997; Merscham 2000; Walsh and Keenan 1997; White and Epston 1990). However, accounts from North Korea demonstrate the complex nature of survivor accounts, the variety of positions from which a speaker speaks.

Conclusion

Discussions of survival techniques while in North Korea were of necessity highly coded and clandestine. Talk of suffering and death emerged in manipulated and ambiguous expressions. This famine talk was so widespread among those affected that it emerged almost endemically. The years of the famine, arguably a decade, ensured a period of time wherein these expressions could take shape, gaining in popularity and in use. In addition, they remain in the oral accounts of survivors many years post-famine. However, North Korean famine survivors remain in an ambiguous space when recollecting their lives in the North. The suffering they experienced did not equal their wholesale rejection of the country. In this way their memory of events and its articulation is highly complex. Caruth (1996: 9) wrote that trauma is at once the survival of a catastrophic event and the incomprehensibility of survival, arguing that a new mode of reading and listening is necessary to understand these experiences. For North Koreans, the trauma may also result from experiencing a kind of political betrayal. The confluence of loyalty to the nation and to the family were two features which shaped how suffering unfolded, and these two features were later associated with the greatest instances of post-traumatic stress (Woo et al. 2005). Witnessing the failure of socialism, they explained, was a traumatic experience.

The limited linguistic frameworks available to North Koreans, as evidenced in the oral accounts of survivors, reveal the popular mentality during the famine years, both of the government and what ordinary people were expected to uphold. The government used pre-existing narratives of national persecution and victimhood to provide a ready-made interpretation of events and prescribe appropriate coping strategies and ways of speaking. To further support this type of communication, any direct reference to famine, hunger or starvation were off limits precisely because those experiences were incongruous with national self-image and incongruous with nationalist narratives. Kim Il Sung's march with guerrilla fighters against Japanese imperialism involved pain and death, but famine, hunger and starvation are inconsistent with this narrative.

The coded and ambiguous famine talk of survivors reveals to some extent the existence of alternative thought systems. The expressions demonstrate a lack of confidence in the ideological structure, an accurate perception of things as they were as opposed to what they were said to be. They show an active participation in ambiguous rather than direct forms of articulation and an awareness of the danger involved with free forms of communication. The accounts show the active choice to speak within these life-preserving codes and metaphors.

There are other issues specific to their case that complicate the communication of North Korean famine survivors. North Korean defectors speak about their experiences of rights violations while these same violations continue against their family, friends and comrades still in the North; indeed there is also survivor guilt. Any talk has the potential to threaten the lives of those back home. Consider too, North Koreans have lived with anti-South Korean and anti-Japanese indoctrination. North Koreans may experience condemnatory speech about the homeland as shameful, even if they are grateful to have survived; they may cling to the coded speech as a way of cushioning reality. Oftentimes, adding insult to injury, North Koreans experience prejudices from South Koreans which invariably shape their recollections of home and how they talk about it.

In a co-authored autobiography by two young North Korean defectors titled *Kulmchulim poda Musŏun Kŏsŭn Huimangŭlll hŏpŏlinŭnll imnida (More Frightening than Starvation is the Loss of Hope)* the authors write:

> We didn't escape from North Korea because we hated it. That is the country in which we were born and raised. I have so many memories that upon reflection bring tears flowing from my eyes. If I had been able, I would have lived in North Korea. It is regretful, but right now North Korea has no means by which to give us life. (Bak and Bak 2000: 141)

Indeed, some of the greatest difficulties North Koreans face in articulating their experiences occur in their conflicted relationship to their homeland, for which they have *aechŭong*, meaning both love and hate.

Acknowledgment

I would like to thank my two anonymous reviewers for their helpful remarks on this paper.

Notes

1   North Korea's famine is evidence of this era of "new famines" described by Devereux (2007). These famines are characterized by the political failure of local, national and international response and accountability. For a detailed discussion of the multiple causal factors leading to the 1990s famine in North Korea see Natsios (2002).

2   Between 200,000 and 3.5 million people are said to have died in the famine. These figures are clearly very rough estimates. The low end represents North Korean government figures, and the high end the estimates of aid agencies; the former is not transparent in its information gathering,

while the latter is restricted by the North Korean government in information gathering. For the most informative text on the 1990s deaths, see Natsios (2002). The number of people who perished from famine-related disease or punishments related to famine coping strategies is unknown.

3   I conducted my doctoral field research in 2005–06 in Japan and Korea. In Korean, I interviewed thirty famine survivors living in Seoul and Tokyo. The brevity of this article limits the number and amount of testimonies used; I have selected examples from four informants to use throughout this analysis, all of whom lived in Seoul. The Japan-based defectors are an interesting point of comparison, which I will address in a future publication. I changed the names of my interviewees to ensure their safety. There are two other records of famine from the point of view of survivors. Zhang (1994, 1996) wrote about his experience of surviving the Great Leap Forward famine several years postfamine. The Ukrainian Canadian Research & Documentation Centre collected the oral testimonies of Ukrainian famine survivors of the 1921–23, 1932–33, 1946–47 famines, respectively. For more information, see: http://www.ucrdc.org/index.html (accessed September 9, 2011).

4   For information about the Red Banner Spirit or the Red Flag Movement used in 1995, see Korean Central News Agency (2005) and Lee (2005). See also Oh and Hassig (2000: 32).

5   For a review of memory studies within anthropology, see Berliner (2005).

6   The flashbulb memory results from witnessing (directly or through other means) a shocking and consequential public event—the authors provide the example of the assassination of JFK. This may also explain why the research of Woo et al. (2005) showed the highest incidence of trauma to be related to visual experiences of shocking events such as public executions and witnessing someone starve to death.

7   This tendency is not unique to China, Russia or North Korea. Consider the predominant term in American English, referring to the atomic explosion of Hiroshima and Nagasaki as a "mushroom cloud" (see Maclear 1999). In this case, words for ordinary, benign things— mushrooms, clouds—identify something unprecedented on the scale of instant death and widespread mass suffering.

8   For further details on this, see Gabroussenko (2009).

9   *Pukhan Tae Sajŏn* (1999). On the "march of hardships," see Kim (2005).

10   For an excellent discussion of how the North Korean state media and literature frame rural experiences, see Gabroussenko (2009).

11   Such control over the expression of experience happens inside of the prison camps, as well as outside of them. In his memoir of life inside Kaech'ŏn No.14 Political Prisoner Complete Control Camp, Shin wrote that there were whole groups of words he did not know, many of them expressions of happiness and joy (Shin 2007: 327–60).

12   Denial was one of the first coping strategies to emerge during the Dirty War in Argentina, which subsequently led to the internalization of terror. For further details, see Suarez-Orozco (1990)

13   This manuscript is in the author's possession as an unpublished monograph. However, information about the recent publication under the title "I sold my Daughter for 100 Won" can be found at: http://www.rfa.org/korean/c9c0b09c-d504b85cadf8b7a8/poem_jang-09292008161208.html?searchterm=None (last accessed February 14,2012).

14   After Todorov (2003: 1): "Facts don't come with their meanings attached."

15   Rubie Watson demonstrates the propensity for this idea of (scientific/biological) inevitability to find itself a place in the history, policies and leaders of communism, and the supposed inevitability of communism itself (1994).

16   For further discussion on socialism's relationship to science, see Todorov (2003: 33).

17   In times of war, or war-readiness, governments evoke the economics of survival as rational.

References

Argenti-Pillen, A. 2000. The Discourse on Trauma in Non-Western Cultural Contexts: Contributions of an Ethnographic Method. In A. Shalev, R. Yehuda and M.D. McFarlane (eds) *International Handbook of Human Response to Trauma*. New York: Kluwer Academic/Plenum, pp. 87–102.

Argenti-Pillen, A. 2003a. The Global Flow of Knowledge on War Trauma: The Role of the "Cinnamon Garden Culture" in Sri Lanka. In Johan Pottier, Alan Bicker and Paul Stillitoe (eds) *Negotiating Local Knowledge, Power and Identity in Development*. London: Pluto Press, pp. 189–214.

Argenti-Pillen, A. 2003b. *Masking Terror: How Women Contain Violence in Southern Sri Lanka*. Philadelphia, PA: University of Pennsylvania Press.

Article 19. 1990. Starving in Silence: A Report on Famine and Censorship. Available from: http://www.reliefweb.int/rw/lib.nsf/db900SID/OCHA-6NMTSW?OpenDocument (accessed September 12th 2011).

Bak, S. H. and C. S Bak. 2000. *Kulmchulimpoda MusŏunKŏsŭn Hŭimangŭl Ilhŏpŏlinŭnll imnida* [More Frightening than Starvation is the Loss of Hope]. Seoul: Sidae chŏngsin.

Berliner, D. C. 2005. The Abuses of Memory: Reflections on the Memory Boom in Anthropology. *Anthropological Quarterly* 78(1): 197–211.

Brown, R. and Kulik, J. 1977. Flashbulb Memories. *Cognition* 5: 73–99.

Bruner, J. 1987. Life as a Narrative. *Social Research* 54(1): 11–32.

Bourdieu, P. 1991. *Language and Symbolic Power*. Cambridge: Polity Press.

Burke, P. 1989. History as Social Memory. In T. Butler (ed.) *Memory, History, Culture and the Mind*. Oxford: Basil Blackwell, pp. 97–113.

Caruth, C. 1996. *Unclaimed Experience, Trauma, Narrative, and History*. Baltimore, MD: Johns Hopkins University Press.

Caruth, C. (ed.) 1995. *Trauma: Explorations in Memory*. Baltimore, MD: Johns Hopkins University Press.

Connerton, P. 1989. *How Societies Remember*. Cambridge: Cambridge University Press.

Cuff, D. J. and A. Goudie (eds). 2009. *The Oxford Companion to Global Change*. Oxford: Oxford University Press.

De Waal, A. 1989. *Famine that Kills, Darfur, Sudan, 1984–1985*. Oxford: Clarendon Press.

Desjarlais, R., Eisenberg, L., Good, B. and Kleinman, A 1995. *World Mental Health: Problems and Priorities in Low-income Countries*. New York: Oxford University Press.

Devereux, Stephen. 1993. *Theories of Famine, From Malthus to Sen*. Hemel Hempstead: Harvester Wheatsheaf Publishers.

Devereux, S. (ed.) 2007. *The New Famines, Why Famines Persist in an Era of Globalization*. New York: Routledge.

Flake, G. L. and Snyder, S. (eds). 2003. *Paved with Good Intentions: The NGO Experience in North Korea*. Mansfield Centre for Pacific Affairs, Praeger Publishers: Westport, CT.

Friedlander, S. (ed.) 1992. *Probing the Limits of Representation: Nazism and the "Final Solution."* Cambridge, MA: Harvard University Press.

Gabroussenko, T. 2009. North Korean "Rural Fiction" from the Late 1990s to the Mid-2000s: Permanence and Change. *Korean Studies* 33: 69–100.

Herman, J. 1997. *Trauma and Recovery, The Aftermath of Violence from Domestic Violence to Political Terror*. New York: Basic Books.

Humphery, C. 1994. Remembering an "Enemy": The Boyd Khan in Twentieth-Century Mongolia. In Ruby S. Watson (ed.) *Memory, History and Opposition under State Socialism*. Santa Fe, NM: School of American Research, University of Washington Press, pp. 21–44.

Jenkins, J. H. 1998. The Medical Anthropology of Political Violence: A Cultural and Feminist Agenda. *Medical Anthropology Quarterly* 12(1): 122–31.

Kaplan, R. D. 2006. When North Korea Falls. *The Atlantic Monthly*, October. Available from: www.theatlantic.com/doc/200610/kaplan-korea (accessed September 12, 2011).

Kim, Kapsik. 2005. 1990-nyŏndae "konan ŭi haenggun" kwa "sŏn'gun chŏngch'i," Pukhan ŭi insik kwa taeŭn [March of Hardships and Military First Policy: North Korean Attitude and Responses]. *Hyŏndae Pukhan yŏn'gu* 8(1): 9–38.

Kelleher, M. 1997. *The Feminization of Famine*: *Expressions of the Inexpressible?* Durham, NC: Duke University Press.

Korean Central News Agency. 2005. *3tae hyŏongmyoŏng pulgoŭn ki chaengch'wi undong paldan 30 to is*. KCNA, November 18. Available from: http://www.kcna.co.jp/calen dar/2005/11/11–18/2005-1118-004.html (accessed March 8 2012).

LaCapra, D. 2001. *Writing History, Writing Trauma*. Baltimore, MD: Johns Hopkins University Press.

Lautze, S. 1997. The Famine in North Korea: Humanitarian Responses in Communist Nations. Feinstein International Famine Centre Working Paper, School of Nutrition Science and Policy, Tufts University. Available from: http://repository.forcedmigration.org/show_ metadata.jsp?pid=fmo:1 744 (accessed February 20, 2012).

Lee, G. 2003. The Political Philosophy of Juche. *Stanford Journal of East Asian Affairs* 3(1): 105–11.

Lee, J. 2005. '3tae hyŏngmyŏng pulgŭn ki chaengch'wi undongun'Noemul undong. Daily NK, June 29. Available from: https://www.dailynk.com/korean/read.php?catald=nk00700&num=7828 (accessed March 8, 2012).

Leshuk, L. 2000. *Days of Famine, Nights of Terror, Firsthand Accounts of Soviet Collectivization 1928–1934*, 2nd edn. Translated by Raimund Rueger. Washington, DC: Europa University Press.

Maclear, K. 1999. *Beclouded Visions*: *Hiroshima-Nagasaki and the Art of Witness*. New York: State University of New York Press.

Martin, B. K. 2004. *Under the Loving Care of the Fatherly Leader, North Korea and the Kim Dynasty*, New York, Thomas Dunne, pp. 553–5.

McGaugh, J. L. 2005. Neuroscientists Identify How Trauma Triggers Long-lasting Memories. 26 July. Available from: http://www.universityofcalifornia.edu/news/article/7355#content (accessed September 12, 2011).

Milroy, J. and Milroy, L. 1991. *Authority in Language, Investigating Language Prescription and Standardisation*. New York: Routledge.

Natsios, A. S. 2002. *The Great North Korean Famine, Famine, Politics, and Foreign Policy*. Washington, DC: United States Institute of Peace Press.

Natsios, A. S. 1998. The Silent Famine in North Korea. Why Should We Care? Available from: http://www.worldvision.org/worldvision/pr.nsf/217a1c6d85845c0085256475000cc4b9/b2b09b779f4cf4a3 882564f4006ea7e2!OpenDocument (accessed September 9, 2011).

Noland, M. 2004. *Korea after Kim Jong-II*. Washington, DC: Institute for International Economics.

Norgaard, L. and Valfells, J. 2003. A Slow Silent Famine. *Magazine of the International Red Cross and Red Crescent Movement*. Available from: http://www.redcross.int/EN/mag/ magazine1997_3/10–11 html (accessed September 12, 2011)

Oberdorfer, D. 1997. *The Two Koreas*. Reading, MA: Addison-Wesley.

Ochs, E. 2004. Narrative Lessons. In A. Duranti (ed) *A Companion to Linguistic Anthropology*. Oxford: Blackwell, pp. 269–89.

Oh, K and Hassig, R. 1999. North Korea between Collapse and Reform. *Asian Survey* 39(2): 287–309.

Ortega, F. A. 2003. Trauma and Narrative in Early Modernity: Garcilaso's Comentarios reales (1609–1616) *Modern Language Notes* 118(2): 393–426.

Pukhan Tae Sajŏn. 1999. *Pukhan Tae Sajŏn* [Dictionary of North Korea]. Soul T'ukpyolsi: Pukhan Yon'guso.

Ryang, S. 1996. Do Words Stand for Faith? Linguistic Life of North Korean Children in Japan. *Critique of Anthropology* 16(3): 281–301.

Scarry, E. 1985. *The Body in Pain*: *the Making and Unmaking of the World*. New York & Oxford: Oxford University Press.

Scott, J. C. 1998. *Seeing Like a State, How Certain Schemes to Improve the Human Condition Have Failed*. New Haven, CT: Yale University Press.

Sen, A. 1981. *Poverty and Famines: An Essay on Entitlements and Deprivation.* Oxford: Clarendon Press.

Sen, A. and Drèze, J. 1999. *The Amartya Sen & Jean Drèze Omnibus, Poverty and Famines, Hunger and Public Action, India, Economic Development and Social Opportunity.* Oxford: Oxford University Press.

Shalamov, V. 1994. *The Kolyma Tales.* Translated by John Glad. Harmondsworth: Penguin.

Shin, T. H. 2007. *Chŏngchi'pŏp suyongso wanchŏn t'ongche kuyŏk sesange pakŭlo naoda pukhan inkwŏn chŏngpu sen t'ŏ* [Out into the world: North Korean Complete Control Zone]. Seoul: Chonshin Sidae chulpansa.

Skelton, R. 1997. The Young Victims of N Korea's "Silent" Famine. *Sydney Morning Herald.* 26 July. Available from: http://reliefwebint/node/31741 (accessed February 14, 2012).

Spence, D. P. 1982. *Narrative Truth and Historical Truth: meaning and interpretation in Psychoanalysis.* New York and London: W. W. Norton and Co.

Suarez-Orozco, M. M. 1990. Speaking of the Unspeakable, Toward a Psychosocial Understanding of Responses to Terror. *Ethos* 18(3): 353–83.

Thomson, O. 1977. *Mass Persuasion in History: An Historical Analysis of the Development of Propaganda Techniques.* New York: Crane, Russak & Company.

Todorov, T. 1999. *Voices from the Gulag.* Translated by Zaretsky. Pennsylvania, PA: Penn State Press.

Todorov, T. 2003. *Hope and Memory, Reflections on the Twentieth Century.* Translated by David Bellos London: Atlantic Books.

Triulzi, A. 2006. The Past as Contested Terrain: Commemorating New Sites of Memory in War-torn Ethiopia. In Preben Kaarsholm (ed.) *Violence, Political Culture and Development in Africa.* London: James Currey, pp. 122–38.

Walsh, W. M. and Keenan, R. 1997. Narrative Family Therapy. *The Family Journal, Counseling and Therapy for Couples and Families.* 5(4): 332–6.

Watson, R. S. (ed.). 1994. *Memory, History and Opposition under State Socialism.* Santa Fe, NM: School of American Research.

White, M. and Epston, D. 1990. *Narrative Means to Therapeutic Ends.* New York: W. W. Norton & Co.

Woo, T. J., C. H. Hong, C. H. Lee, D. K. Kim, M. Y. Han, S. K. Min. 2005. Correlation between Traumatic Events and Posttraumatic Stress Disorder among North Korean Defectors in South Korea. *Journal of Traumatic Stress* 18(2): 147–54.

Yang, R. 1997. *Spider Eaters: A Memoir.* Berkeley, CA: University of California Press.

Yun. P. W. and G. W. Shin (eds). 2006. *North Korea: 2005 and Beyond.* Stanford, CA: Brookings Institute Press.

Zhang, X. 1994. *Grass Soup.* Translated by Martha Avery. London: Secker & Warburg.

Zhang, X. 1996. *My Bodhi Tress, Prison Diaries from a Chinese Gulag.* Translated by Martha Avery. London: Secker & Warburg.

5

Blaming the Consumer—Once Again: The Social and Material Contexts of Everyday Food Waste Practices in Some English Households

David Evans

The Debate about Food Waste in the UK

It is estimated (WRAP 2009) that UK households throw away 8.7 million tonnes of uneaten food each year and that at least 5.3 million tonnes are avoidable. The annual financial cost of this avoidable waste is estimated at £12 billion (£480 per household) and the environmental impact is equivalent to 20 million tonnes of carbon dioxide emissions.[1] Whilst prominent commentators (e.g. Stuart 2009) do not lay the blame solely at the door of consumers; public and policy imaginations are focused disproportionately on domestic waste. Within these debates, recommendations appear to be limited to interventions that target knowledge, attitudes and the behaviours that individuals choose to undertake. For example, Stuart (2009, p. 77) stresses the need to raise awareness of the 'non-financial costs of wasting food' (environmental impacts, world hunger). Similarly, WRAP's lovefoodhatewaste campaign[2] aims to raise awareness about the consequences of food waste and provide information that will help individuals to change their behaviour. These suggestions are refreshingly well-intentioned and non-judgemental; however, they continue to individualise responsibilities for affecting change and so miss the ways in which so-called 'waste behaviours' relate to the dynamics of everyday life. It is this tendency that initiated the study discussed below.

Before turning to the study, a brief note on terminology is required. I view waste as a consequence of how something is disposed as opposed to an innate characteristic of certain objects. In this view, surplus matter is not necessarily the same as waste insofar as it could conceivably be placed in conduits of disposal (Gregson *et al.* 2007) that save it from wastage. It follows that something is wasted when it is disposed of through a trajectory that connects it to the waste stream. The empirical work that informs this analysis found that surplus food was routinely disposed of through the waste stream via the bin (Evans 2012) as opposed to being handed down, handed around or otherwise saved from wastage (e.g. through composting).[3] For the purposes of the discussions that follow, then, surplus food is treated as synonymous with food waste. When referring to food, I refer only to that which could have been eaten – I am not referring to things that UK households tend not to eat (such as tea bags or apple cores) nor am I referring to things that are discarded in the preparation of food (such as fruit and vegetable peelings). Finally, for reasons of brevity and consistency – when referring to specific meals, I refer only to evening meals.

The Study

The analysis that follows is based on a broadly ethnographic study in which I adopted a material culture approach to the research design (Evans 2011). The fieldwork involved 8 months (November 2009 to July 2010) of sustained and intimate contact with the residents and households encountered on two 'ordinary' streets – pseudonymously called Rosewall Crescent and Leopold Lane – in and around South Manchester. I use the term 'ordinary' to signal that the streets were chosen because, following Miller (2008), I had no particular reason to chose them other than attempting to encounter everyday lives as they are found without recourse to the categories of social/sociological analysis. As a study of material culture, the emphasis was on the logic of stuff itself (the passage of 'food' into 'waste') and not the reasons why particular 'types' of household waste food. Participants were recruited by dropping information leaflets through doors and following this up with successive rounds of door knocking. In total, 19 households participated in the study and whilst this sample is by no means representative, the heterogeneous nature of the areas in which I was working ensured a reasonable spread of income band, age, housing structure, housing tenure and household composition.

The study was undertaken to explore household food waste; however, I anticipated that a narrow focus on disposal would be problematic in terms of recruiting and retaining respondents. Moreover, in order to explore the passage of 'food' into 'waste', I decided to focus on the broader processes, dynamics and relations that accompany this movement. Accordingly, the study explored the ways in which households plan for and shop for food; how they prepare, consume and eat it; how they store it; and ultimately the ways in which they dispose of the food that they do not eat. In terms of carrying out the fieldwork, I utilised a range of qualitative of approaches. I conducted repeat in-depth interviews (Mason 2002) with respondents in which we discussed the various ways in which they shop for, prepare, eat, store and dispose of food. I also spent a lot of time 'hanging out' in respondents' homes, their streets and the areas in which the study took place. Additionally, I adopted a range of less familiar techniques. These included diary records; 'going along' (Kusenbach 2003) with participants as they shop for and prepare food; cupboard rummages and fridge inventories; and kitchen and home tours (Pink 2004).

Feeding the Family

Throughout the study, respondents were found to routinely overprovision food such that they were often left with a certain amount of food that they struggled to then find a use for. Typically, this situation arose when a particular item of food was purchased for a specified purpose but the volume in which it could be purchased exceeded the volume required. For example, Julia is in her early 30s and lives with her husband and two young children on Rosewall Crescent. Talking though the items in her fridge, she explained:

J: I got that to do a, a cauliflower cheese last week but I didn't need the whole thing um floret […] and if I am honest, I don't really know what I'll do with it or can

I: I see

J: and [laughing] cauli just isn't the same without cheese, none of us really like it on its own without erm, yeah so there isn't anything we do that uses it […] and I worry a lot, not being able to use the food that we have bought.

Such items are at risk of not being eaten and interventions targeted at reducing household food waste are sensitive to this predicament. For example, the lovefoodhatewaste campaign website has a 'recipes' section that gives suggestions on how to find a use for leftover ingredients.[4] For the respondents encountered in this study, however, the problem was not one of lacking knowledge about what to do with the food that needs using up. To the contrary, they had very clear ideas about how leftover ingredients might be saved from wastage, but were unable to put these ideas into practice given the domestic context in which they provision food. For example, Suzanne is a single mother in her 30s who lives on Rosewall Crescent with her two children. Going through her fridge, she discussed a bag of spinach with about ¼ of the contents remaining:

S: If it was just me, it would be easy enough I would I dunno do something with it like omelette. Something quick that uses it up.

I: If it was just you?

S: Yeah, I mean it would be it doesn't need to be great and I don't have to bother but my lot probably aren't going to be all that impressed if I put I spinach omelette down for their tea [laughs]

I: Why's that then?

S: for a start [laughing] they are fussy buggers […] well I suppose that they do eat different things but it takes a while to get there as there is a definite, definitely prefer tried and tested recipes that they've had before and know they like.

In common with many respondents, Suzanne's food practices are located in a household context where the culinary repertoire is relatively fixed and provisioning highly routinised (DeVault 1991). It is well-understood that in feeding the family, the work of caring requires those responsible (usually women) to subsume their preferences to those of others within the household (DeVault 1991, Burridge and Barker 2009). Given that Suzanne's family are unlikely to be receptive to new introductions, especially 'improvised' foods that do not constitute a 'proper meal' (on which more below), it is perhaps not surprising that she would go for a 'tried and tested recipe' over something that would use the spinach up. However, as a consequence, this spinach was rendered obsolete and in turn, wasted.

Eating 'Properly'

Just as the process of feeding the family is well-understood in terms of practising care and devotion towards significant others, it can also be noted that the provisioning of 'proper meals' has been identified as the appropriate means of doing so (Murcott 1983, Charles and Kerr 1988, Jackson 2009). The empirical material gathered here supports this idea. For example, Sarah lives on Rosewall Crescent and is a married mother of two in her early 30s. Having returned to work as a result of her youngest child starting school, she explained:

S: [b]efore I went back they always had good, proper food and ate well but it becomes a little bit harder to do when I am not at home so much and so what I do is spend Sunday cooking meals for the week ahead [...] and that doesn't stretch the whole week and but a night of junk food is alright and for the rest I try to mix proper things in with easy things.

The imperative to eat 'properly' also emerged in the accounts and experiences of those not living as part of a family (however defined), but in these cases, the emphasis was on healthy living (Peterson *et al.* 2010) and practising an ethic of caring for the self. For example, Pete is in his early 20s and living with 'a bunch of randoms' in a houseshare on Leopold Lane. Talking about how his work takes him 'on the road' a lot, he explained:

P: [i]t would be all to easy when you all over the shop to just pick up a takeaway or, god, there have been times that I've just survived on microwaved stuff from the garage but it's no good. You have to look after yourself, don't you and I don't want to turn into a fat bas- so yeah I now try and eat a bit better.

This of course raises the question of what constitutes 'proper' food and existing researches suggest that it is understood to encompass fresh, healthy ingredients that are used to prepare cooked meals from scratch whilst incorporating a variety of flavours and ethnic cuisines (Douglas 1972, Murcott 1983, Charles and Kerr 1988, Mitchell 1999, Bugge and Almas 2006, Short 2006, Halkier 2009). Again, the empirical material gathered here suggests that respondents recognised these as appropriate procedures and engagements with practices of food provisioning. The following excerpt from my field diary is drawn from a Sunday that I spent with Sarah as she prepared meals for the upcoming week:

Sarah opens up the fridge and announces that it looks right and good to have all of these fresh ingredients in and she sets about moving some ingredients [peppers, lean steak mince, garlic] over to the chopping board. These are joined by onions and a carrot from the cupboard. She tells me how she is going to cook a lasagne as that can easily be put in the fridge and reheated 'on the night' and served with a salad to create a proper meal in minutes [...] she chops up all three peppers in the packet and I ask if she is planning to use them all in the lasagne to which she replies that she is chopping them ready to be used in a Moroccan dish that she is going to cook later and here she explains that it is important that they have something 'lighter' and 'healthier' in the week and that her children should have exposure to flavours from other cultures. (Field diary March 2010)

These understandings and definitions of 'proper food' were also recognised by respondents who did not themselves adhere to the attendant procedures and engagements. For example, Ceri is a single mother of three and is in her early 20s. She lives on Rosewall Crescent in a housing trust home. The following extract from my field diary is drawn from an occasion when I accompanied her to the supermarket:

> *As we walk down the frozen food aisle, she tells me that this is where she fills her trolley up. She jokes about how she doesn't really pick up much in the fruit and veg aisle. Various freezer doors are opened and frozen chips, fish fingers, pizzas and pies go into her trolley. She looks at me and tells me that she knows that I think it is all ok but also states that she feels like a 'first rate failure'. I ask her why and she says that she feels like one of those people 'doing it all wrong on the Jamie Oliver show'. With this she tells me that she knows that she should be cooking like he suggests but points out that it isn't 'how her life is' and she can't 'live up to it' [...] Moving down the aisle a little, she picks up lots of frozen vegetables and jokes that even when she cooks right, she cheats. (Field diary June 2010)*

Not only does Ceri define her own food practices in relation to dominant understandings of competence, but she also appears very troubled by not 'living up' to them.

It is instructive to note that biomedical interventions in health promotion – such as healthy living guidelines (Lindsay 2010) – play a role in shaping these definitions of proper food. For example, fresh fruits and vegetables were positioned as good, whilst processed foods that are high in salt or sugar were seen as bad. Without wishing to comment on the legitimacy or nutritional significance of these expectations, they can be viewed as helping to shape the routines in which households end up wasting food. Notably, a lot of 'proper' food is perishable and so at risk of being wasted if it is not eaten within a particular timeframe. Viewed as such, the materiality of foodstuffs themselves assume importance in terms of organising the practices through which they must be used or otherwise wasted.

Materiality and Temporality

This section considers waste as a consequence of the ways in which the materiality of food intersects with the broader socio-temporal context of food practices. Where public debates intimate that food waste arises when individuals do not have enough time to cook 'properly', the respondents encountered here reveal a more subtle mismatch between the materiality of food and the rhythms of everyday life. For example, Tamsin is in her mid-20s and lives alone on Leopold Lane. She explained that she tries to eat properly but that this often involves buying '5 different ingredients' for a particular recipe and that these are not available in quantities that are suitable for a single person living on her own. Additionally, she explained how her employment requires her to travel away from Manchester frequently such that she 'does not know where she is going to be from one moment to the next':

T: So when I go away, right, I simply have no memory um recollection of what's going on in my fridge [...] so when I get back into Manchester, the train gets in and all I really know is that I am tired and hungry and in desperate need of food

I: so what do you do?

T: Well, generally one of two things. Either I go for something quick and easy from the local supermarket – perhaps a ready meal and a bagged up salad or if it's the weekend, I can justify a cheeky takeaway […]

I: […] and what about the ingredients that you already had in

T: um, well very often I end up not getting to make anything from them before they are too far gone […] it's actually very hard to stay on top of it all.

The problem of keeping on top of ingredients in various states of decay was not exclusive to persons living alone and managing an erratic work schedule. Respondents who provisioned food within a family context were found to do so at relatively fixed intervals, typically every 7–10 days. Even allowing for the proliferation of 'mini' supermarkets where 'bits and bobs' could be picked up 'as and when', the vast majority of grocery shopping tended to be acquired via a 'big shop' at a large out of town supermarket. Through going along with participants on these shopping trips, I discovered that they tended to buy roughly the same things at each visit. Whilst very few households planned what would be eaten meal by meal, there was certainly a tacit expectation that certain dishes would be eaten (recalling the preference for a relative fixed culinary repertoire) at some point within the period between visits (see also DeVault 1991). However, these habituated routines of food provisioning were easily thrown out of balance by the rather more fluid nature of the ways in which lives are lived. As Julia explained:

J: There is always something gets in the way of what I was going to d-

I: you plan out what you are going to eat each night?

J: um- I suppose no, not but I think I have a sense of what I might do throughout the week

I: sorry, I just threw you right off [laughing] – you were saying that something always gets in the way

J: oh, um, yeah like if I know I've some greens that need using – I'll think I can do them with some chops or wh- you know one night in the week […] but other things always come up

I: like?

J: oh god, anything like if there is something on at school or one of us has something else on we might not have what I was thinking.

She went on to explain what would happen to the 'greens' that ended up not being eaten:

J: If they don't get used before a new bag comes in they will go

I: thrown out?

J: bad but they go when the new ones come in

I: why is that?

J: well they didn't get used and I am definitely not going to use them if there is a newer pack that I could, um, need to use before that starts getting old.

In this example, food gets displaced and wasted as a result of a mismatch between the food that is provisioned and the food that is eaten within a given period of 7–10 days. Again, the lovefoodhatewaste campaign is attuned to this situation and gives advice on planning meals such that they mirror more closely the food that is provisioned when going shopping.[5] However, this advice is not sensitive to the temporal dynamics of everyday life nor does it appear to recognise that the materiality of food (and the temporalities of its decay) render it unable to accommodate disruptions to household provisioning routines.

Of course, it might reasonably be assumed that the domestic freezer might operate as a 'time machine' (Shove and Southerton 2000) to help households circumvent some of the tensions created at the intersection of food's materiality and the rhythms of everyday life. However, food that is well-suited to the freezer tended to be viewed as undesirable on the grounds that it does not constitute 'proper' food. For example, in discussing the amount of work she does on Sundays to ensure that her family eat 'properly', Sarah pointed out that:

S: It would definitely be easier if I was one of those Mums that go to Iceland[6] [laughing] you
     know, getting all that stuff for a fiver … god, would save loads of money and I bet I wouldn't
     ever chuck anything out as that stuff is pumped so full of crap that it never goes off
I: you are never tempted to start doing that?
S: um maybe but I never would, couldn't um I wouldn't give that to my family as it isn't food
I: how would you feel about frozen vegetables then?
S: they are better but really they can't compare to fresh.

In this example – and throughout the study – the refusal of certain foodstuffs extends beyond concerns about eating healthily to incorporate class-based processes of classification and distinction on the grounds of taste in food (Warde 1997). More generally, it is instructive to highlight that the imperative to eat 'properly' (discussed above) leads to the provisioning of foodstuffs that are at risk – against the backdrop of the routines and rhythms discussed in this section – of wastage. Viewed as such, a picture of household food waste as the fall out of everyday life begins to emerge.

Food Risk and Anxiety

This section picks up on the idea that food waste arises as a consequence of households juggling the complex and contradictory demands of day-to-day living. In addition to the aforementioned concerns about healthy and 'proper' eating; the respondents encountered were found to be negotiating concerns about food safety and storage. Throughout the study, respondents were quite explicit that once food has 'past its best', it is no longer fit for human consumption and as such, should be cast as 'waste'.[7] There is not the space here to discuss the ways in which respondents evaluated food as 'past its best' but suffice to say, the processes and practices varied across households and according to foodstuff. For example, some households observed dates and labels stringently, whilst others rejected them in favour of 'trusting their nose'. Some evaluated food according to its aesthetic qualities ('it's gone all wrinkly') whilst others used *ad hoc* knowledge about how long it had been 'kicking about'. Some foodstuffs were positioned as highly risky (meat, poultry, fish and dairy) whilst others were thought to be more 'forgiving' with their riskiness limited to the potential for a decline in quality (onions, herbs and spices). Others still were thought to be salvageable in the sense that signs of being past their best could be removed to prevent the rest of the item being contaminated (e.g. cutting mould out off a corner to rescue a block of cheese). The unifying feature across households and in respect of all foodstuffs was an acute awareness that food harbours the potential to make people ill and that this risk accelerated evaluations of food as past its best. For example, Faye is in her late 20s and living with her boyfriend on Leopold Lane. Narrated retrospectively, she discussed some chicken breasts that they had thrown out the previous week:

F: It costs doesn't it and well something died for that and we didn't eat it […] such a waste. Not good.

I: how come it didn't get eaten?

F: just kind of forgot about it and to be honest yeah, when I came to it I thought it had been there are while so I thought to check the date

I: was it in date?

F: No it was probably a few something like a few days gone so I ummed and ahhed about it but it's chicken so you've got to be careful

I: uh huh

F: and I wasn't going to risk it as you're going to know about it if you eat bad chicken.

Similarly, Natalie is a divorcee in her mid-40s who lives on Rosewall Crescent with her two teenage children. Whilst talking about the items in her kitchen, I asked her about a saucepan that was on the stove:

N: That's from stew that I made a few nights ago […] I meant to put it in the fridge after it cooled, you know, and then have it another night […] but it's probably not safe to eat as its been out for a few days now […] crap, I really hate wasting food.

Both Faye and Natalie – in contrast to claims that modern consumers are anomalously profligate – are troubled by their acts of wasting food. More generally, virtually, every respondent informed me that 'it is wrong to waste food' and that they 'felt awful' about the instances in which they end up doing so. However, this section has shown that, again, biomedical interventions in health promotion are also being played out in the everyday lives of the households encountered here. It is instructive to note that throughout this study, discourses of food safety tended to 'win out' over anxieties about wasting food such that the imperative to ensure that unsafe food is not eaten appeared to provide adequate justification for acts of binning and wasting. It is certainly not my intention to question the legitimacy of concerns about food safety and storage, I am simply illustrating how they help create the context in which food is evaluated as past its best and consequently, constituted as waste.

Discussion

The preceding analysis does not dispute that current volumes of household food waste are problematic in a number of registers (developmental, environmental, financial). It does, however, suggest that it is overly simplistic to blame consumers for these problems or individualise responsibilities for solving them. [It] would be wrong, on the evidence here, to suggest that there is a need for attitudinal change insofar as the respondents encountered did not appear to have a careless or callous disregard for the food that they end up wasting. More generally, the analysis has demonstrated some of the ways in which waste is a consequence of the ways in which domestic food practices are socially organised. I have focused specifically on the role of biomedical interventions in health promotion (food safety and storage, healthy eating) but more generally, I have paid attention to the broader social (family relations, socio-temporal context, tastes) and material (domestic technologies, the organic vitality of food, infrastructures of provision) conditions through which food is provisioned. Taken together, it seems somewhat perverse to position food waste as a matter of individuals making negative choices to engage in behaviours that lead to the wastage of food. Indeed, the analysis here suggests that food waste arises as a consequence of households negotiating the contingencies of everyday life and as such, it recalls those who critique biomedical models of health promotion (Ioannou 2005, Lindsay 2010).

It has not been my intention to systematically evaluate existing policies or interventions and the prescription of alternatives based on the small-scale exploratory analysis offered here is necessarily beyond the scope of this article. However, if pushed, I would be inclined to suggest that interventions in the material context of food practices are key. For example, if food was to be made readily available in different quantities (material infrastructures of provision), then the respondents encountered here may well end wasting less. Similarly, there may be some mileage in targeting the material properties of food itself by, for example, finding ways to normalise the provisioning of foodstuffs that are not susceptible to rapid decay. These recommendations are of course mere speculation and the take home message here is that any effort to reduce household food waste could usefully reach beyond the default position of blaming the consumer in order to target the social and material contexts through which food practices might be changed.

Acknowledgements

This research was made possible through funding from the Sustainable Consumption Institute at the University of Manchester. Additional writing was undertaken while I was a visiting researcher on the Economic and Social Research Council funded 'Waste of the World' programme (RES000232007). I thank Ulla Gustafsson, Liza Draper and Wendy Wills for their helpful guidance and editorial steer. I also thank two anonymous referees whose useful and insightful comments have no doubt strengthened this article. The usual disclaimers apply. Above all, I am indebted to those who accommodated my sustained presence in their homes during the course of the fieldwork.

Notes

1 The same impact as the emissions generated by ¼ of the cars on UK roads.
2 http://www.lovefoodhatewaste.com [Accessed 8 June 2011].
3 I am not claiming that households never do these things; I am simply highlighting the normativity of binning surplus food.
4 http://www.lovefoodhatewaste.com/recipes [Accessed 3 February 2011].
5 http://www.lovefoodhatewaste.com/save_time_and_money/two_week_menu [Accessed 7 February 2011].
6 Iceland is a food retailer in the UK that specialises in low-cost frozen foods.
7 Or more accurately, it is cast as excess at which point it is deemed appropriate to dispose of it through the waste stream (Evans 2012).

References

Bettinghaus, E., 1986. Health promotion and the knowledge-attitude-behaviour continuum. *Preventive Medicine*, 15, 475–491.

Bugge, A. and Almas, R., 2006. Domestic dinner: representations and practices of a proper meal among young suburban mothers. *Journal of Consumer Culture*, 6 (2), 203–228.

Bunton, R., Nettleton, S., and Burrows, R., eds., 1995. *The sociology of health promotion: critical analyses of consumption, lifestyle and risk*. London: Routledge.

Burridge, J. and Barker, M., 2009. Food as a medium for emotional management of the family: avoiding complaint and producing love. *In*: P. Jackson, ed. *Changing families, changing food*. Basingstoke: Palgrave Macmillan, 146–164.

Charles, N. and Kerr, M., 1988. *Women, food and families*. Manchester: Manchester University Press.

Delormier, T., Frohlich, K., and Potvin, L., 2009. Food and eating as social practice – understanding eating patterns as social phenomena and implications for public health. *Sociology of Health and Illness*, 31 (2), 215–228.

DeVault, M., 1991. *Feeding the family: the social organization of caring as gendered work*. Chicago, IL: Chicago University Press.

Douglas, M., 1972. *Implicit meanings*. London: Routledge.

Evans, D., 2011. Beyond the throwaway society: ordinary domestic practice and a sociological approach to household food waste. *Sociology* (awaiting issue). DOI: 10.1177/ 0038038511416150.

Evans, D. 2012. Binning, gifting and recovery: the conduits of disposal in household food consumption. *Environment and Planning D: Society and Space*, 30 (6), 1123–1137.

Giddens, A., 1984. *The constitution of society*. Cambridge: Polity Press.

Gregson, N., Metcalfe, A., and Crewe, L., 2007. Moving things along: the conduits and practices of divestment in consumption. *Transactions of the Institute of British Geographers*, 32 (2), 187–200.

Halkier, B., 2009. Suitable cooking? Performance and positionings in cooking practices among Danish women. *Food, Culture and Society*, 12 (3), 357–377.

Holm, L., 2003. Blaming the consumer: on the free choice of consumers and the decline in food quality in Denmark. *Critical Public Health*, 13 (2), 139–154.

Ioannou, S., 2005. Health logic and health-related behaviours. *Critical Public Health*, 15 (3), 263–273.

Jackson, P., ed., 2009. *Changing families, changing food*. Basingstoke: Palgrave Macmillan.

Kusenbach, M., 2003. Street phenomenology: the go-along as ethnographic research tool. *Ethnography*, 4 (3), 455–485.

Lindsay, J., 2010. Healthy living guidelines and the disconnect with everyday life. *Critical Public Health*, 20 (4), 475–487.

Mason, J., 2002. Qualitative interviewing: asking, listening and interpreting. *In*: T. May, ed. *Qualitative research in action*. London: Sage, 225–241.

Miller, D., 2008. *The comfort of things*. Cambridge: Polity Press.

Mitchell, J., 1999. The British main meal in the 1990s: has it changed its identity?. *British Food Journal*, 101 (11), 871–883.

Murcott, A., 1983. It's a pleasure to cook for him: food, mealtimes and gender in some South Wales households. *In*: E. Garmarnikow, ed. *The public and the private*. London: Heinemann.

Peterson, A., *et al.*, 2010. Healthy living and citizenship: an overview. *Critical Public Health*, 20 (4), 391–400.

Pink, S., 2004. *Home truths: gender, domestic objects and everyday life*. Oxford: Berg.

Røpke, I., 2009. Theories of practice – new inspiration for ecological economic studies on consumption. *Ecological Economics*, 68, 2490–2497.

Short, F., 2006. *Kitchen secrets: the meaning of cooking in everyday life*. Oxford: Berg.

Shove, E., 2003. *Comfort, cleanliness and convenience – the social organisation of normality*. Oxford: Berg.

Shove, E., 2010. Beyond the ABC: climate change policy and theories of social change. *Environment and Planning A*, 42 (6), 1273–1285.

Shove, E. and Southerton, D., 2000. Defrosting the freezer: from novelty to convenience. *A narrative of normalization. Journal of Material Culture*, 5 (3), 301–319.

Southerton, D., Chappells, H., and Van Vliet, B., eds., 2004. *Sustainable consumption: the implications of changing infrastructures of provision*. London: Edward Elgar.

Southerton, D., McMeekin, A., and Evans, D., 2009. *International review of behaviour change initiatives*. Available from: http://www.scotland.gov.uk/Publications/2011/02/01104638/0 [Accessed 7 February 2011].

Stuart, T., 2009. *Waste*: *uncovering the global food scandal*. London: Penguin.

Warde, A., 1997. *Consumption, food and taste*. Cambridge: Polity.

Warde, A., 2005. Consumption and theories of practice. *Journal of Consumer Culture*, 5 (2), 131–153.

Watson, M., 2008. The materials of consumption. *Journal of Consumer Culture*, 8 (1), 5–10.

WRAP, 2009. *Household food and drink waste in the UK*. Available from: http://www.wrap.org.uk/retail/case_studies_research/report_household.html [Accessed 7 February 2011].

6

Alimentary Dignity: Defining a Decent Meal in Post-Soviet Cuban Household Cooking

Hanna Garth

Quimara, a self-identified white middle-class woman in her mid-fifties from Santiago de Cuba, was one of the first people I approached when I began formally recruiting families into my study in January 2010.[1] Quimara often sat outside in the evenings awaiting friendly chats with neighbors and friends. I stopped to talk to her that night, trying to muster the courage to ask her to be part of my research. After some small talk I finally said, "You know that I am here studying the Cuban food system, right?" She nodded, for I had already explained this to her with varying degrees of detail. I then asked if she would let me spend a few weeks studying food practices in her home. She inhaled deeply and paused for a minute. Finally, she responded, "I would really like to help you out, but here in this house *there is no food*." I was puzzled by this answer and asked, "What do you eat then?" Quimara shrugged and said: "Crap. Whatever appears." I said, "Well then, that's exactly what I would like to study—how you turn 'crap' into food." I was intrigued by her assertion that they did not eat "real" food in her household; I felt it would make an instructive addition to my study, but no matter how much I explained this, Quimara declined to participate:

> It sounds like an interesting study, but what we eat here in this household is pure trash, it's not dignified. I would be ashamed to show you how we eat. No, I can't let you observe here. You'll have to find someone else who really eats Cuban food, but it will be difficult, so I wish you the best of luck.

Quimara's feeling that her household did not consume real food, that they ate "crap," or "whatever appeared," was centered on the notion of dignity, and shared by other Santiago families.[2] In my initial trips to Santiago in 2008 and 2009, I was confused by the paradoxical responses Santiagueros had to the Cuban food system. Cuba has virtually no reported malnutrition or hunger. Indeed, it was recently honored by the United Nation's Food and Agriculture Organization—the FAO—for maintaining extremely low levels of hunger and malnutrition (Delgado 2015). The FAO praised Cuba's national food ration, which still provides about half of an individual's monthly nutritional requirements at very little cost. The Cuban government also provides supplements and additional rationed items for children, the elderly, and those with certain chronic illnesses. At the same time, people seemed to regularly enjoy heaping plates of rice and beans served with pork, and fresh fruit juices. However, when speaking more generally about Cuban food and their consumption practices, people described what they ate as "crap" or "trash." People often set up a distinction between a decent meal and eating "crap" or "trash." Given this context, it puzzled me that people so often said, "There is no food."

After several trips to Cuba, I started to realize that when people claimed there was "no food," although in some instances they meant it literally, in most cases what they meant was that the food they had did not meet their expectations. I realized that their local notion of a dignified, decent cuisine was what they were often striving for with every meal.[3] The unraveling of this during the course of my research slowly revealed the complexity of this problem. Indeed, to be fully understood, the problem must be analyzed in practical terms (shifting food access) and in ideological terms (what counts as "real" food). These issues are key to considering what matters in the making of a "decent meal"—a category unpacked in this article—and the ways in which cuisine is connected to community life and the experience of sociopolitical change.

Santiagueros use the term "decent" to capture the desire to maintain what they conceptualize as a dignified cuisine, or what I call "alimentary dignity." Crucial for understanding food sovereignty, the concept of a decent meal involves a cuisine that not only provides adequate nourishment, but also implies the ability to assemble a meal that is perceived as categorically complete with starch, beans, meat, and vegetable components and the opportunity to serve an aesthetically plated meal. The decent meal contrasts with food that is somehow lacking in these elements, and would not be deemed appropriate to serve to others. Additionally, such a meal may potentially be a source of shame for the individual who must eat it. Drawing on Quimara's reflections, I use the notion of alimentary dignity as a broad framework that encompasses the myriad ways that Santiagueros reflect on their food, from the desire for a "decent" meal, for "authentic food," for "our food," to calling the food that they have "trash" or "not real."

The ethnographic material used in this article is based on long-term fieldwork in Cuba, beginning in 2008 and continuing through 2017. The majority of the data were collected during a period of sixteen months of ethnographic fieldwork in Santiago de Cuba, between 2010 and 2011. I studied twenty-two households across the city, selected to balance by geographic area, socioeconomic status, and skin color. These households varied in size and included a total of 107 individual participants. I spent twelve to eighteen hours a day for three weeks to one month in each household. The point of this intense observation was to be there for as much of the food acquisition, preparation, and consumption as I could, and also to observe the ways in which food acquisition affected social relationships.

In this article, to illuminate my construct of alimentary dignity, I argue that longing for a "decent" meal becomes a way of clinging to a social ideal of well-rounded, culturally appropriate, and nutritionally adequate meals. In analyzing the relationships between types of meals that do not meet local ideals for Cuban cuisine and those that are considered adequate, we can see that Cubans insist on categorizing food as "real" and meals as decent to give meaning to their experience of the changing Cuban food system. This practice is a way of upholding a categorically distinct and ideal cuisine that is rarely experienced in contemporary Cuba, in part due to the state's changing geopolitical position and shifting priorities at the level of the national economy. Achieving the decent meal may be even more rare in Santiago de Cuba, as the city and region suffer from increasing inequalities and resource scarcity. Santiagueros face a form of chronic (nonextreme) food scarcity, where certain ingredients are nearly impossible to acquire, and others are difficult to find, but something is almost always available to prevent hunger (Garth 2017). Alimentary dignity is negotiated through this discursive practice of only categorizing particular foods as "real." The categories of "real food" and the decent meal often index larger historical, social, political, and economic processes. Alimentary dignity is enacted in the practice of food acquisition. To further illuminate alimentary dignity, I specifically address two questions: "what is at stake in creating and maintaining the category of 'real' food and a decent meal"; and "what are the social meanings and cultural importance of establishing the boundaries of what counts as dignified cuisine?"

Alimentary Dignity

I use the concept of alimentary dignity to understand what is at stake when Cubans express culinary discontent even though they no longer experience drastic food shortages, and there is virtually no malnutrition or hunger in Cuba. Although there are sufficient calories available, for many Cubans there is no "real food." The notion of alimentary dignity addresses the aesthetic and moral imperative to meet cultural standards for food consumption and the ability to create meals that are desirable, enjoyable, and that one is proud to serve to others. Cross-cultural notions of food consumption and what constitutes a meal have long been concerns of anthropologists (de Certeau et al. 1994; Douglas 1966; Goody 1977, 1982; Mead 1943; Mintz 1985; Wilk 1999, 2013). Beyond its economic and nutritional roles, food consumption has important symbolic and socially meaningful aspects (Sahlins 1976; Sutton 2001). For instance, foods such as bread, wine, and honey have strong symbolic significance in our everyday lives, on special occasions, and during religious rituals. The concept of taste—which for Bourdieu (1979:190) is "an incorporated principle of classification which governs all forms of incorporation, choosing, and modifying everything that the body ingests and digests, and assimilates, physiologically and psychologically"—matters deeply in terms of our understanding of the social meaning of the meal. Eating in particular ways is often an index of civility. Elias (2000[1939]) documented the ways in which "civilized" society has been linked to certain tastes and standards for preparing and consuming food. According to Elias, the development and maintenance of certain ways of eating can be a marker for larger social identities and cohesions. Douglas (1972) crafted a meticulous analysis of the relationships between the components of a meal and the social meaning of sharing a meal. In *Deciphering a Meal*, she found that even in everyday settings, to serve a meal "worthy of the name supper" it must contain certain components, which vary cross-culturally. Douglas proposed that the formula of a proper meal must contain "A," which is a main course, plus some number of "unstressed" side courses, "B." These seemingly mundane categories of day-to-day cuisine are important for framing the ways in which food relates to larger social and cultural meanings.

Beyond food in the context of family dynamics, the meal also bears an important relationship to the ways in which communities deal with socioeconomic and political change. Although Cuba is still socialist, the body of work on food in postsocialist settings is useful here (Palmié 2004;

Verdery 1996). In the context of Russia, Ries documents the centrality of potato consumption for physical survival during periods of economic hardship, as well as this being what she calls a "cognitive resource," or "an object in the world 'coupled' to the social mind and thus an irreducible vehicle of thought about and action in the world" (2009:182). Therefore, in the context of Russia's transition from socialism to capitalism the potato serves as a symbol for Russians to reinterpret their changing world, while it simultaneously gives structure and meaning to their daily lives—it may seem that everything but the potato is changing. Caldwell (2002) shows that in post-Soviet Moscow the distinction between "our food" and "not ours" aligns with the notion that locally grown foods are superior to "new" imports. This is one of the ways that Muscovites make meaning of their shifting nation state's participation in the global food market. Similarly, Vann (2005) documents Vietnamese consumers' desires to consume local products and the forms of anxiety they feel as once-empty shops now fill with new products. In post-Soviet, socialist Cuba, the notion of alimentary dignity and insistence on consuming a decent meal is part of how Santiagueros make meaning out of Cuba's changing political and economic situation and the reductions in the socialist entitlement system. For some Santiagueros, the desire for alimentary dignity is also an implicit critique of unmet promises and the shifting relationship between the state and the people in Cuba.

Building on this previous work on food and social meaning, alimentary dignity frames the ways in which individuals or groups of people define their cuisine as meeting locally determined standards for a civilized, well rounded, calorically sufficient cuisine that also meets local standards of symbolic value. Alimentary dignity encompasses both a dignified cuisine that meets local standards, and the relationship of this cuisine to human dignity for those who are able to eat a dignified cuisine. Building on previous work on the ways in which the comingling of food and identity is mobilized as socially significant during times of change, my notion of alimentary dignity enables us to see the connections among local practices of food acquisition, discursive practices of categorizing food as "real," and notions of human dignity and civility as they all are wrapped up in the making of a meal.

This article argues that Cubans have internalized the notion that particular ways of eating are part of their understanding of civility, and that alimentary dignity and the decent meal indicate a certain level of modernity for Cubans. I argue that defining food as "real" or "not real" is part of the socially meaningful work of negotiating categories as a way of articulating the social value of such categories (Yates-Doerr 2015). Insistence on alimentary dignity is a moral stance that places a significant social value on local determinations of standards for cuisine (Zigon and Throop 2014); violations of this form of dignity lead to feelings of shame, humiliation, and the degradation of cuisine, as well as to related aspects of symbolic value in individual, familial, and social life. Put simply, to eat well is to live well.

To illuminate this argument, I document the ways in which Cubans draw on nostalgic longings for past periods of abundance, imagined or real, during the first decades of Cuban independence before the socialist revolution, and during the height of Soviet material aid in the 1970s and 1980s. Thus, rather than conforming to types of foods that are available and maintaining a certain "taste of necessity" (Bourdieu 1979), my research subjects continue to strive for particular forms of alimentary dignity even as they are increasingly difficult to achieve. Connecting to broader debates on food security and food sovereignty, I link desires for particular foods with notions of what it means to live a good life, and to be part of civil society.

Food in the Context of Cuban History

Contemporary desires and forms of longing are deeply entangled with Cuba's political relationships and economic policies over time. Food and agriculture have long been central to Cuban national and local identity (Benjamin et al. 1984; Dawdy 2002; Núñez González and González Noriega 1999; Núñez González 1999; Ortiz 1947[1995]; Pérez Firmat 1987; Pertierra 2012; Weinreb 2009). Despite fifty years of socialism, and limited trade with the United States, Cuba's food system is not completely detached from international market forces; it is entrenched within the global industrial food complex and has been since colonization (Hearn 2016; Mintz 1985). Cuba's colonial chattel slave society was established to produce sugar for the global market. Under Spanish colonial rule most foods were imported from Spain, and the local economy was based on agricultural production for export. Slaves with their own culinary traditions were brought to the region to work sugar and coffee plantations. In the nineteenth century, indentured Chinese, Trinidadian, and Guyanese laborers also left faint culinary influences. Over time, trade relationships shifted and, by the 1870s, products from the U.S. accounted for the majority of Cuban imports. The U.S. military occupation of Cuba that began immediately upon independence from Spain in 1899 was the beginning of over fifty years of neocolonial ties between Cuba and the United States.[4] During the postcolonial period, Cuban identity, *Cubanidad*, was developed alongside Cuba's mixed culinary heritage—a particularly modern cuisine comprised foods originating from all over the globe. Nevertheless, this food was seen as "Cuban food" (Garth 2013a). Food consumption was linked to cultural and national identity throughout the postcolonial period in Cuba (Gonçalves 2014).

After the 1959 revolution, Cuba eliminated the capitalist market-based economy and made efforts to establish egalitarian distribution systems. Cuba's food rationing system, still in place today, was officially established in 1962, which was the same year that the United States embargoed trade with Cuba (Benjamin et al. 1984). The transition to the socialist food system was not always smooth. In the early years, due to some resistance to agricultural reforms and some mismanagement of collective farms there were shortages of highly prized foods such as beef and pork (Enríquez 1994). These foods that were once consumed daily became luxury items. In the 1970s Cuba deepened ties with the Soviet Union, and joined in cooperation with several planned socialist economies. Although access to some foods improved with Soviet material aid in the 1970s, other items remained scarce. In the early Soviet era, while collectivist agricultural production and distribution still gained traction, Cubans longed for then scarce items such as onions, green peppers, and tomatoes, which were all viewed as central to "traditional" cuisine. Again, foods that were part of a seemingly mundane daily fare became a rarely achieved luxury for a brief period during this transition. However, from the late 1960s, 1970s, and 1980s many food imports from the Soviet Union were cheaply and conveniently available. Nutritional support during this era was crucial to developing Cubans' contemporary sense of alimentary dignity (Benjamin et al. 1984). Indeed, my research participants reflected nostalgically on this period as the height of socialist abundance.

After the collapse of the Soviet Union, during the 1990s, Cuba entered a period of extreme economic crisis known as "the Special Period in Time of Peace." Because Soviet imports had formed the basis of Cuba's food system and supplied inputs for agriculture since the 1960s, the food system radically changed. In the 1990s many food products became scarce and those that were available off the ration had prohibitively high prices (Garth 2009). The number of rationed products increased in the Special Period, from only nineteen items in the 1980s, to most food in the 1990s (Wright 2009). Food acquisition became a daily struggle (Eckstein 2003).

In order to deal with the food shortages, the state attempted to shift consumption practices by introducing new foods into the Cuban diet. For instance, soy and other vegetable proteins were substituted for meat, soy products were also substituted for dairy, and people were exhorted to eat more vegetables, tubers, and legumes. Along with rice, plantains, root crops, and beans have long been central to an ideal Cuban meal (Enríquez 1994), but more easily sourced plantains and root crops were encouraged in the Special Period. This history demonstrates some of the ways in which notions of Cuba's "traditional" food may simultaneously hold multiple meanings depending on which periods of history we look back to.

Today, every Cuban citizen is still eligible for a ration card, with which they can purchase basic food items. Prices are heavily subsidized, but households must pay the approximate equivalent of one U.S. dollar per month. As always, the items included in the ration fluctuate with national scarcities and surpluses.[5] The rationed foods are drawn from a mixture of imports, items locally processed from imported raw materials, and entirely locally produced foods (Wright 2009). Over the past decade, the quantity and quality of rationed foods has significantly decreased. While the ration still provides about half of monthly caloric needs, Cubans must turn to other outlets to supplement the rations (Garth 2009). With heavy reliance on food imports, Cuba's socialist food system continues to be deeply entrenched in the global industrial food system. Shifts in costs on the global market, or local issues with agricultural production can result in food scarcities or price increases, leaving some Cubans with little freedom to choose their ingredients.

The historical conditions laid out above have been factors in producing the ideal and traditional Cuban cuisine that many of my research participants refer to as their standard for "real food," and as well as providing the historical framework for understanding their sense of alimentary dignity. Periods of abundance and scarcity have shaped how Cubans understand their cuisine and continue to be factors in how Cubans assess the quality of their food (Garth 2009). As the following example with Alonzo's macaroni salad shows, based on these historical and remembered conditions people often have in mind that a dish must contain certain ingredients to be "real" or "truly Cuban."

Lo Que Aparaece: Eating "Whatever Appears" or "Crap"

On a June morning in 2008, Alonzo invited me to observe the process of preparing *ensalada fría* (macaroni salad)—a dish commonly served at birthday parties and on other special occasions in Cuba. He told me that he felt this was a "truly Cuban dish" that would be essential for my understanding of Cuban cuisine. Although it is a special dish, it is ubiquitous at Cuban birthday parties. The birthday that evening was for his best friend's wife; Alonzo projected that we should start the process of acquiring the ingredients and making the dish by 9:00 a.m. In typical Cuban fashion we started later than we had hoped, setting out at 10:00 a.m. Alonzo explained that we would need the following: a one-pound bag of macaroni, half a dozen eggs, a pint of oil, five cloves of garlic, salt, about two cups of cheese, a pineapple, and a pig's head.

First, we set out to find the pig's head from which Alonzo would extract the pieces of pork that would go in the salad. A person down the street ran a black market butcher's shop and the night before he had promised Alonzo that he would save the pig's head for him; alas, by 10:00 a.m. he had given up on Alonzo and sold the pig's head to someone else.

Few pig's heads remained at this hour because most people buy their meat very early in the day. Nonetheless, Alonzo's friend set out to scour one end of the barrio and we scoured the other. I asked if other pig parts would do, and Alonzo explained that the price per pound of the pig's head offered the most value. A head would allow use of various remaining parts for soup and beans later. Buying packaged ham was not worth the money to him; it was expensive and did not have as diverse utility as the pig's head. He argued that meat from a pig's head was the "real" way to make *ensalada fria*; anything else would not be "authentic." We spent two hours walking. Alonzo diligently stopped by each neighborhood butcher, state-run *carnicería*, and the homes of trusted friends who raised pigs or might know someone who did. He had butchers calling friends and searching the city high and low. We never found a pig's head that day and he never bought any other form of ham. The salad just went without ham, because Alonzo stuck by his belief that other forms of ham "*no valen la pena*" (are not worth the trouble) and are too expensive.

After giving up the search for a pig's head, Alonzo was ready to search for the other ingredients. Cheese was his next highest priority. He wanted to avoid having to buy cheese in the hard currency store, as that was the most costly point of sale. He went back to his local state-run *carnicería* and asked the person working there if they had any cheese. Cheese was not officially available in the ration, but the butcher's wife was selling some state-issued cheese that they had "found" (pilfered). We were directed to their house, where we quickly and cheaply acquired a block of cheese large enough for the salad and then some.

Alonzo told me that he preferred to add green olives to the salad, but he knew that without making a store purchase we would have to spend hours searching. Given the time we had lost in our search for a pig's head, he decided not to use green olives. Instead, we headed to the state-subsidized market to buy a pineapple. Pineapples were in season, so it was easy to find one at a good price.

From there we headed back toward Alonzo's house, stopping at two places along the way. The first was a house with a small piece of cardboard on its door with the faintly written words: *hay huevos* (there are eggs). We knocked and bought six fresh eggs sourced from the countryside nearby—technically, these were black market goods. We then stopped at another house, where Alonzo presented an old water bottle to the man who opened the door. He promptly filled it with oil and charged us ten pesos.

After three hours our food acquisition was done, and it was time to start on the preparations. Luckily for me, Alonzo had set the rice cooker and pressure cooker before we left, so we returned to his house for a quick lunch of rice and black bean soup. While we ate, Alonzo boiled water and cooked the macaroni. After we ate, we then turned to the making of the mayonnaise. I had originally thought it was all going to be made from scratch, but Alonzo started with about half of a jar of premade mayonnaise, "to add to the flavor," as he said. He put a bit of oil in the blender, added one egg, and blended. He then added more than five cups of oil, and four more eggs, one at a time, blending after each one. He poured this mixture over the pasta after it had cooled under the fan in the living room, and stirred. After cubing the cheese and chopping the pineapple he mixed them into the salad with his hands.

When it was all done, Alonzo looked down at his oily hands and sighed. He looked at me sternly, and said:

I do not want you to have the impression that this is *real ensalada fría*. It is important that you know that this is a bad version—a substitute for the real thing. But we had to work with whatever appears, and you saw that there was nothing. This is what we have to eat for the party, but it is not real.

He washed his hands and put the salad in the refrigerator to cool. He then threw his body onto a chair in the living room, slumped, and looked out of the window. He sighed deeply again, probably from a combination of exhaustion and shame.

The story of my search for ingredients with Alonzo illustrates several important aspects of food and everyday life in Cuba. First, this scenario of having to spend hours, or an entire day, searching the city for food is quite typical, even in cases that do not include special occasion foods. The scarcity of particular items that are out of season is common, and there are often shortages of certain food items for reasons of inefficiency in the socialist food system (Garth 2009). This is the daily experience of chronic (nonextreme) scarcity. The notion that a recipe requires particular ingredients is also a commonly held assumption in Cuba and in many places across the globe. This scene with Alonzo demonstrates the ways in which concessions may be made in trying to assemble the ingredients for a recipe under conditions of scarcity. It is central to this story that Alonzo, like many other Cubans, did not consider the dish to be complete or "real" unless all of the appropriate ingredients were available. It is also important to note that Alonzo still went through with making and serving the dish at a very high cost of his time and effort. However, he made sure to underscore that this was not a real version of the dish. This scene illuminates Alonzo's insistence on maintaining the boundaries of what constitutes a real *ensalada fria*: although he was willing to make do with whatever appeared, he refused to dignify the dish by calling it real. Alonzo upheld alimentary dignity both in his discursive practice of not calling it "real" ensalada fria, and in insisting on attempting to create a decent meal by way of his practice of food acquisition. His affective responses to the failure to achieve alimentary dignity are embodied in the way that he sighed and slumped in the chair, gazing out of the window after he had made the dish.

Making a Meal: The Essence of "Real" Cuban Food

In addition to standards for making particular dishes, I also found that many Cubans share ideas about the components that should be present to make a meal complete. Across the twenty-two households of various socioeconomic status, skin color, and location in the city that participated in this study, nearly every participant made attempts to describe and define Cuban meals to me. This act of defining and categorizing was often conducted in contrast to what was actually being eaten in the household. For instance, on my first day working with one of the Santiago families, Carla, the oldest household member and the one who cooked most often, made white rice with an okra sauce on it for lunch. As we were waiting for the rice to cook we sat in the living room and Carla turned to me and said, "I just want you to know that this meal is not real Cuban food." I asked her why it was not, and she explained:

It is just something I came up with (*inventé*) with what was available. There's no meat with the meal or in the sauce, and that is not how it should be. There are no *viandas* with the meal.[6] I guess since it is an okra sauce we do not need a salad, but normally there should be one.

In line with Douglas' (1972) observations that proper meals must contain certain necessary parts, comments like Carla's regarding the necessity of meat for a "real" meal were common across all of the households in my study. There appeared to be a shared notion of what a "real" or decent meal should constitute, which in practice was rarely achieved due to the scarcity of necessary ingredients or the money with which to purchase them (Garth 2013b).

One day, Omaro, who was fifty-eight years old, described the ideal Cuban meal:

> Well, if you are studying food in Cuba—Cuban food that is … all you need to know about is rice and beans—what we call here *Congris*—and then pork and *viandas*, that's all we eat because that is *our* food. What the Cuban people live, our way of living, is *congris*, pork, and *viandas*.[7]

The notion of a specifically Cuban diet, which consisted of a particular balance of different types of foods—meats, starches, and vegetables—was continually reified by many of my research participants in comments similar to those made by Omaro. The foods he mentioned are commonly viewed as "authentic" Cuban foods, which, when consumed together, comprised a decent meal and a dignified cuisine. … As his comments highlight, the role of the side dishes, or what Douglas (1972) termed "unstressed" dishes, may be just as important as the main meat dish. Omaro's inclusion of three starches—rice, beans, and tubers—was an ideal shared across Santiago families. These views establish a romanticized ideal of "real" Cuban food, which is enveloped in remembered traditions, local understandings, and histories of place (Garth 2009). Omaro also observed that this notion of a Cuban way of eating is also a way of living, a way of life—rendering it a broader category of social meaning that moves beyond the realm of just eating, or merely satisfying hunger, to an important part of what it means to be Cuban. However, as new products become available, some longstanding items become scarce, and old ways of production fall out of use, this ideal cuisine has become more difficult to regularly maintain in household cooking.

What We Eat Here Is Pig Slop

On a hot July morning I followed Marta, a sixty-seven-year-old, white, middle- to upper-class Santiaguera, to the neighborhood butcher to buy a pork leg. She explained that she would always be loyal to him because he set aside the best cuts for her. I helped her carry the large pork leg back to the house, and she instructed me on the proper way to trim the meat. She observed that the "scraps" from this meat would be important for adding flavor to beans, soups, and other dishes throughout the week. As she started preparing the pork leg for *carne mechada*, she described the proper process, step by step, and told me that cooking the "right way" and serving proper meals was a question of pride and self-respect. She felt that those who did not cook and serve meals in the proper way had suffered a certain form of poor upbringing (*mal crianza*)—a "deformation" that they would pass on to their children. She used the example of eating "crap" to illustrate her point:

> As many Cubans view it, the problem it just to fill up [*llenarse*], so Cuban women take the easy way out; they feed their families street food—grab a pizza or spaghetti, or even make it at home. Homemade pizzas can be very nice, and children love the taste. But what message does it send? Today in Cuba there is a huge lack of household education—manners, etiquette—children are spoiled. Before, it wasn't like this, people were proper and wanted to advance particular tastes

in their children, a household education, and not only among the rich. But these days people give their kids whatever they want; feeding them pizza fills them up and it's easier for the woman, but it does not teach them to do the right thing—both in terms of budgeting and what is right.

Marta's narrative reveals some of the ways in which the social practice of consuming a decent meal and the common understanding of alimentary dignity may be learned, habituated, and socialized over time. She also explained how these notions may *not* be being taught to or taken up by future generations as the practices of younger Cubans, the newest generation of heads of households, shift. Marta's reflections demonstrate the ways in which the social role of alimentary dignity is wrapped up with notions of respectability and values. It is part of how Cubans recognize and define one aspect of their self-worth, and it is an increasingly important way to recognize self-worth as the Cuban food system changes along with many other aspects of contemporary Cuban sociopolitical life. The data in this section illuminate the ways in which alimentary dignity is negotiated through the discursive practice of naming "real food" and "crap." … Certain foods may be consumed out of necessity to "fill up," but these foods are not placed in the same categories as dignified cuisine (Bourdieu 1979).[8]

Throughout my research on the realities of food acquisition and consumption in Santiago, I often heard consumers deprecate their food. For instance Yaicel, a young Black-identified Santiaguera, told me: "What we eat here is pig slop [*sancocho*], chicken fat, we waste nothing. People always look for money for their food, because how else are they going to live?"[9] By calling her food pig slop, like Quimara called her food trash, Yaicel set aside what she eats as undignified, as not good enough.

Gema, a low income Black-identified Santiaguera, talking about times of the month when rations ran low, told me:

Our preferred food is congrí with meat and *tostones*. If we do not have [the ingredients] we eat other stuff, like spaghetti with ham. If there is no food we go to the pizzeria and buy a pizza. This fills you up. Or it is enough to eat a roll of day old bread, or whatever (*lo que sea*). But we have to eat.

Like Quimara and Yaicel, Gema discusses what she is eating—pizza, spaghetti, day old bread—in contrast to "real food," which would be something more like the preferred meal of "congrl with meat and *tostones*." These three women across varied socioeconomic status frame what they are eating as merely something to fill them up, consumed only because they "have to eat" or because there are no other options.[10]

Alimentary Dignity and the Boundaries of "Real" Food

The ethnographic material presented above illuminates some of the ways in which Cubans today experience and make meaning of their current food distribution system vis-à-vis their previous food system. The accounts detailed here concern the social practices and meanings of food consumption beyond simply eating to survive: indeed, calories for filling up are obtainable; it is variety and consumer preference that are out of reach. Particular ways of eating are highly prized and there is a keen awareness of the necessary ingredients and processes for creating the ideal meal. Santiagueros are often quick to point out that their ideal has not been fully met.

The notion of alimentary dignity is brought to light when contrasted with the ways in which the Santiagueros featured here deprecate certain types of foods, or certain meals as not real.[11] As access to food items shifts, the key ingredients of a decent meal are harder to access and new, less desirable items appear, many Cubans do not accept the new ingredients or foods as "real." For instance, increased access to foods such as soy-based meat and dairy, juxtaposed with restricted access to beef, and constrained access to other "real" meats, become frustrating struggles for Cubans attempting to satisfy their desires to eat in particular ways—that is, to eat in dignified and socially significant ways. These forms of food consumption, while filling and potentially nutritious, mark a certain form of culinary discontent that is contrasted with the decent meal and the notion of alimentary dignity. Although in most cases there is enough to eat, meals with particular cultural relevance, which Cubans pride themselves on serving to friends and family in the proper way, are lacking.

The ways in which Cubans cling to the notion of a decent and dignified cuisine is clearly about more than just food. The category of "real" food and the decent meal have come to represent more than a mere meal but also "a cluster of promises" (Berlant 2011:16) around what it means to be civilized, living a certain "way of life," *Cubanidad*, family values, and countless other potential meanings. Here, the decent meal is symbolic of a sense of alimentary dignity and the cluster of promises that come with a dignified cuisine. Daily household consumption practices reflect a way of life—that is, a civilized cuisine that is also a symbol to indicate to oneself and others that one is living a decent quality of life. To serve decent meals is a matter of pride, or dignity, and a marker of respectability and self-worth that is communicated to other household members and friends, and passed on to children.

Across individuals, neighborhoods, and households there are many ways of maintaining or longing for alimentary dignity and all the promises it represents. Notions of what counts as real Cuban food range from romanticized views merging history and ecology, to imagined traditions, and childhood memories. Many desire imagined pasts they did not live through, gleaned from idealized notions of the ways their ancestors ate, or family lore about periods of abundance (Wirtz 2014). Others long for the types of foods consumed under Cuba's socialist food system during the height of Soviet material aid, with abundant imports from the Soviet Bloc during the 1970s and 1980s. As they remember and long for the abundance of low-cost food once available in the parallel market system of this era, these longings also include a desire for a functioning food system and an implicit critique of the current state of the Cuban socialist entitlement system.

Conclusion

My initial questions concerned the social meanings and cultural importance of establishing the boundaries of what counts as a dignified cuisine. It is not that Quimara's food did not exist, but that it did not exist outside the practices and categories in which the ideal meal had come to be defined. The story of a decent meal is not merely about categories and the varying ways in which groups of people classify things. Beyond the symbolic work of maintaining categories of "real food," alimentary dignity bears real meaning in people's lives in terms of their own sense of human dignity, self-esteem, and feeling satisfied with life. The insistence on defining certain food as "real" in efforts to maintain the notion of a decent meal is not a social commentary on nutritional deficiency, but a way of articulating deep-seated culinary discontent based on the incompleteness of the established category of the meal. Drawing on earlier work by Mary Douglas and Norbert Elias, I have suggested that Cubans have internalized the notion that particular forms of eating are part of civility, and that the maintenance of proper categories for a "decent meal" indicates a certain quality of life.

What else is at stake in establishing the boundaries of a decent meal in the ways described here? The concepts of alimentary dignity and the decent meal contribute to broader understandings of the ways in which people make meaning out of shifting life circumstances, including national and geopolitical change, and economic change. The accounts detailed here demonstrate some of the ways in which people maintain boundaries of cuisine and define social aspects of consumption. This is not to say that all those who consume food must do so in this way; indeed, many of the narratives here have alluded to others who are open to different ways of eating, whether it be an *ensalada fria* without olives or cheese or ham, homemade pizza, or a meatless meal. Rather, this article has demonstrated some of the social and emotional reasons for holding on to—indeed, insisting upon — particular standards for ways of living that people view as socially appropriate and respectable. Having said this, despite an insistence on maintaining particular ways of eating and living, the conditions of ongoing political and economic change may preclude households from attaining their own standards for living a good life. Nevertheless, the act of defining the decent meal and striving to maintain alimentary dignity represents an insistence on maintaining particular standards for living a dignified, decent life. This insistence on particular standards for food consumption sheds light on why people may cling to objects and ideals that they cannot actually achieve. The insistence on maintaining certain categories and ways of living is intended to indicate that there is still some level of decency and dignity in their daily lives. That they are aware of and want to maintain these aspects of their lives is in and of itself a form of maintaining their own sense of dignity.

More broadly, alimentary dignity is central to debates on food security and food sovereignty. As part of food sovereignty logics—of people's right to healthy, culturally appropriate foods, and the right to define their own food and agriculture systems—alimentary dignity provides a framework for capturing the centrality of the connections among a decent meal and identity, community, and local standards for a good life.

Alimentary dignity is part of a social process for living with ongoing forms of chronic food scarcity; it is a way of dealing with the uncertainties and difficulties of food access as the food system changes. Enacted through practices of food acquisition and negotiated through discursive practices, insisting upon alimentary dignity can be a way of critiquing political and economic change, and a demonstration of the living standards that people insist upon in the face of that change. Alimentary dignity is made visible and enacted in the daily household practices of food acquisition, preparation, presentation, and consumption, when people are not merely consuming calories but upholding important aspects of the sociality of eating and the signs of civility.

Acknowledgments

I would like to acknowledge my friends in Santiago who have made this project possible by sharing their stories with me. In particular, I thank the Casa del Caribe for supporting my work and sponsoring my visa. Earlier versions of this article were presented at UCLA and Spelman

College; I appreciated the audience engagement and comments that helped to improve the piece. I am grateful to Carole Browner, Mara Buchbinder, Lee Cabatingan, Leo Chavez, Hadi Deeb, Robin Derby, Raul Fernandez, Linda Garro, Akhil Gupta, Ellen Sharp, Mrinalini Tankha, and Jason Throop for comments on drafts. I thank JLACA Editor in Chief, Linda Seligmann and the anonymous reviewers for their insightful comments. This project was funded in part by the following organizations: UCDiversity Initiative for Graduate Study in the Social Sciences, UC Cuba Initiative Travel Grant, National Science Foundation, Social Science Research Council, UCLA Latin American Institute, UCLA Center for Study of Women, and UCLA's Department of Anthropology.

Notes

1   All names are pseudonyms to protect research participants' identities.

2   There might have been many other undisclosed reasons why Quimara did not want me to study the intimate contexts of her household food practices. However, my sense was that even if there were other factors, the feeling of shame that she felt about what she was able to feed her family was the primary factor in declining to participate.

3   Depending on specific contexts this may have been local in terms of the city, regional within the eastern provinces, or at the national level.

4   In early postcolonial Cuba, the influence of the U.S. was significant in shaping the local concept of *Cubanidad* (Pérez 1999; Pérez Firmat 1997). The U.S. occupied the island twice: 1899–1902 and 1906–1909. The Platt Amendment also restricted Cuban sovereignty (see Zeuske 2011).

5   In 2011, the monthly ration per person included five pounds of white rice, ten ounces of beans, three pounds of refined sugar, one pound of raw sugar, one kilogram of salt, four ounces of coffee, 250 milliliters of oil, and a roll of bread per day. Meat products consisted of six ounces of chicken, eleven ounces offish, ten eggs, and eight ounces of ground meat mixed with soy.

6   Viandas is a category of food that includes tubers such as sweet potatoes, yams, taro, cassava, and plantains.

7   Congrí is technically the correct spelling and pronunciation of the word, which refers to black beans and rice. It is common among lower income Santiago households to refer to the dish as "congris."

8   Marta's characterization of certain foods as real or proper and others as food for "filling up" is resonant of Bourdieu's distinction between the taste of necessity and the taste of freedom.

9   In Cuba, the word *sancocho* used to refer to a stew with beef or pork, plantains, taro, corn, and other vegetables, as it is in Colombia, Dominican Republic, Puerto Rico, and other places today. However, in Cuba the word has evolved to refer to household food scraps used as animal feed.

10   Although families often framed foods such as pizza and spaghetti as "crap" or "not real," I found that pizza and spaghetti were overwhelmingly common dishes. Most families in my study ate one or both these at least once a week.

11   Elsewhere I detail a similar phenomenon as a form of "discursive resistance" (Garth 2013c, 2017).

References Cited

Benjamin, Medea, Joseph Collins, and Michael Scott. 1984. *No Free Lunch*: *Food and Revolution in Cuba Today*. Princeton: Princeton University Press.

Berlant, Lauren. 2011. *Cruel Optimism*. Durham: Duke University Press.

Bourdieu, Pierre. 1979. *Distinction: A Social Critique of the Judgment of Taste*. New York: Routledge.

Caldwell, Melissa. 2002. "The Taste of Nationalism: Food Politics in Postsocialist Moscow." *Ethnos: Journal of Anthropology* 67: 295–319.

Dawdy, Shannon Lee. 2002. "*La Comida Mambisa*: Food, Farming, and Cuban Identity, 1839–1999." *New West Indian Guide* 76:47–80.

de Certeau, Michel, Luce Giard, and Pierre Mayol. 1994. *The Practice of Everyday Life, vol. 2: Living and Cooking*. Minneapolis: University of Minnesota Press.

Delgado, Sheyla. 2015. "The FAO Recognizes the Cuban Government for Efforts Toward Food Security." Accessed March 7, 2016. http://en.granma.cu/cuba/2015-10-08/the-fao-recognizes-the-cuban-government-for-efforts-toward-food-security.

Douglas, Mary. 1966. *Purity and Danger: Ananalysis of Concepts of Pollution and Taboo*. New York: Routledge.

———. 1972. "Deciphering a Meal." *Daedalus* 101: 61–81.

Eckstein, Susan. 2003. *Back From the Future: Cuba Under Castro*. New York: Routledge.

Elias, Norbert. 2000[1939]. *The Civilizing Process: Sociogenetic and Psychogenetic Investigation*. Revised edition. Oxford: Blackwell.

Enríquez, Laura J. 1994. *The Question of Food Security in Cuban Socialism*. Berkeley: Institute of International and Area Studies, University of California, Berkeley.

Garth, Hanna. 2009. "Things Became Scarce: Food Availability and Accessibility in Santiagode Cuba Then and Now." *NAPA Bulletin* 32: 178–92.

———. 2013a. "Cooking Cubanidad: Food Importation and Cuban Identity in Santiago de Cuba." In *Food and Identity in the Caribbean*, edited by Hanna Garth, 95–106. London: Bloomsbury Academic.

———. 2013b. "Disconnecting the Mind and Essentialized Fare: Identity, Consumption, and Mental Distress in Santiago de Cuba." In *Health Travels: Cuban Health(care) on and Off the Island*, edited by Nancy J. Burke, 54–84. San Francisco: University of California Medical Humanities Press.

———. 2013c. "Resistance and Household Food Consumption in Santiago de Cuba." In *Food Activism: Agency, Democracy and Economy*, edited by Carole Counihan and Valeria Siniscalchi, 47–60. London: Bloomsbury Academic.

———. 2017. " 'There is no food': Coping With Food Scarcity in Cuba Today." Hot Spots, Cultural Anthropology Website, Accessed March 23, 2017. https://culanth.org/fieldsights/1084-there-is-no-food-coping-with-food-scarcity-in-cuba-today.

Gonçalves, João Felipe. 2014. "The Ajiaco in Cuba and Beyond: Preface to 'The Human Factors of Cubanidad' by Fernando Ortiz." *HAU: Journal of Ethnographic Theory* 4: 445–80.

Goody, Jack. 1977. *The Domestication of the Savage Mind*. Cambridge: Cambridge University Press.

———. 1982. *Cooking, Cuisine, and Class: A Study in Comparative Sociology*. Cambridge: Cambridge University Press.

Hearn, Adrian H. 2016. *Diaspora and Trust: Cuba, Mexico and the Rise of China*. Durham: Duke University Press.

Mead, Margaret. 1943. "Dietary Patterns and Changing Food Habits." *Journal of the American Dietetic Association* 19: 1–5.

Mintz, Sidney. 1985. *Sweetness and Power: The Place of Sugar in Modern History*. New York: Penguin Books.

Núñez González, Niurka. 1999. "Algunas Concepciones Alimentarias de Los Cubanos." *Revista Cubana de Alimentación y Nutrición* 13(1): 46–50.

Núñez González, Niurka and Estrella Gonzalez Noriega. 1999. "Antecedentes etnohistóricos de la alimentación tradicional en Cuba." *Revista Cubana de Alimentación y Nutrición*, 13(2): 145–50.

Ortiz, Fernando. 1947[1995].*Cuban Counterpoint: Tobacco and Sugar*. Translated by H. De Onis. Durham: Duke University Press.

Palmié, Stephan. 2004. "Fascinans or Tremendum? Permutations of the State, the Body, and the Divine in Late-Twentieth-Century Havana." *New West Indian Guide* 78:229–68.

Pérez, Louis A. 1999. *On Becoming Cuban*: *Identity*, *Nationality*, *and Culture*. Chapel Hill: University of North Carolina Press.

Pérez Firmat, Gustavo. 1987. "From Ajiaco to Tropical Soup: Fernando Ortiz and the Definition of Cuban Culture Dialogue #93). *LACC Occasional Papers Series*" (. *Dialogues* (1980–1994). Paper 16. Accessed September 1, 2018. http://digitalcommons.fiu.edu/laccopsd/16.

———, 1997. "A Willingness of the Heart: Cubanidad, Cubaneo, Cubanía." *Cuban Studies Association Occasional Papers*. Paper 8. Accessed September 1, 2018. https://scholarlyrepository.miami.edu/csa/8.

Pertierra, Anna Cristina. 2012. "Sustenance in Special Times: Rice and Beans in Post-Soviet Cuba." In *Rice and Beans*: *A Unique Dish in a Hundred Places*, edited by Richard Wilk and Livia Barbosa, 35–60. London: Berg.

Ries, Nancy. 2009. "Potato Ontology: Surviving Postsocialism in Russia." *Cultural Anthropology* 24(2): 181–212.

Sahlins, Marshall. 1976. *Culture and Practical Reason*. Chicago: University of Chicago Press.

Sutton, David. 2001.*Remembrance of Repasts*: *The Anthropology of Food and Memory*. New York: Berg.

Vann, Elizabeth. 2005. "Domesticating Consumer Goods in the Global Economy: Examples From Vietnam and Russia." *Ethnos* 70: 465–88.

Verdery, Katherine. 1996. *What was socialism and what comes next*? Princeton: Princeton University Press.

Weinreb, Amalia.2009. *Cuba in the Shadow of Change*: *Daily Life in the Twilight of the Revolution*. Gainsville: University of Florida Press.

Wilk, Richard. 1999. "Real Belizean Food": Building Local Identity in the Transnational Caribbean." *American Anthropologist* 101: 244–55.

———. 2013. *Preface to Food and Identity in the Caribbean*, edited by Hanna Garth. London: Bloomsbury. 1–14.

Wirtz, Kristina. 2014. *Performing Afro-Cuba*: *Image*, *Voice*, *Spectacle in the Making of Race and History*. Chicago: University of Chicago Press.

Wright, Julia. 2009. *Sustainable Agriculture and Food Security in the Era of Oil Scarcity*: *Lessons From Cuba*. London: Earthscan.

Yates-Doerr, Emily. 2015. "Does Meat Come From Animals? A Multispecies Approach to Classification and Belonging in Highland Guatemala." *American Ethnologist* 42: 309–23.

Zeuske, Michael. 2011. "The Long Cuban Revolution," In *The Caribbean*: *A History of the Region and Its People*, edited by Stephan Palmie and Francicso A. Scarano, 507–22. Chicago: University of Chicago Press

Zigon, Jarrett and C. Jason Throop. 2014. "Moral Experience: Introduction." *Ethos* 42 (1): 1–15.

Suggested Additional Readings

Alex V. Barnard. 2011. " 'Waving the Banana' at Capitalism: Political Theater and Social Movement Strategy among New York's 'Freegan' Dumpster Divers." *Ethnography* 12(4): 419–44.

Lyna Fujiwara. 2005. "Mothers without Citizenship: Asian Immigrant and Refugees Negotiating Poverty and Hunger in Post-Welfare Reform." *Race, Gender & Class* 12(2): 121–41.

Julie Guthman and Melanie DuPuis. 2006. "Embodying Neoliberalism: Economy, Culture, and the Politics of Fat." *Environment and Planning D: Society and Space* 24: 427–48.

Yuson Jung and Andrew Newman. 2014. "An Edible Moral Economy in the Motor City: Food Politics and Urban Governance in Detroit." *Gastronomica* 14(1): 23–32.

Sarah Lyon. 2014. "The GoodGuide to 'Good' Coffee." *Gastronomica* 14(4): 60–8.

Brad Weiss. 2012. "Configuring the Authentic Value of Real Food: Farm-to-Fork, Snout-to-Tail, and Local Food Movements." *American Anthropologist* 39(3): 614–26.

Marisa Wilson. 2012. "Moral Economies of Food in Cuba." *Food, Culture & Society* 15(2): 277–91.

PART TWO

The Power of Food: From Politics to Microbiopolitics

Introduction

In many parts of the world, access to food is determined not simply by one's financial resources but rather by one's position within society. Whether a person has the ability to procure food—and more precisely, the ability to procure the right kind of food (safe, healthy, culturally appropriate)—reveals not only their status but also the degree to which they are empowered to act on their own behalf and in their own interests. Do they have the financial means to purchase food? Do they live in a neighborhood that has affordable food shops and restaurants, or does the neighborhood have food shops and restaurants at all? Do people have the ability to travel to get food, and if so, can they travel independently or are they reliant on public transportation? At an even more basic level, how people access food demonstrates the extent to which they have the knowledge necessary to navigate the world in which they live and, if necessary, to advocate for themselves.

Access to food does not, however, depend solely on the skills, resources, or agency of individual consumers and communities. It also depends on the nature of the social and economic systems that structure those communities. Which foods are available, to whom, and under what conditions, or whether food is available at all, reflects the ability of individuals, communities, and institutions to create, manage, and regulate production, distribution, and consumption. The provision of food, as well as the deliberate or accidental withholding of food, reflects the interplay of many forms and relationships of power.

Because food is deeply embedded in power relations, it is a political object that both enables power struggles and reveals them. Food and food practices are media through which political ideologies become tangible and realized, whether it is through people using food choices and taste preferences to articulate political ideologies (Eat local! Buy American! Support sustainable agriculture!) or through the efforts of governments to create categories of worthy and unworthy people by making food aid contingent upon certain behaviors or identities. Ordinary people can demonstrate their displeasure with political ideologies of political systems and engage in direct civic action through their food choices: boycotts, embargoes, and communal or solidarity kitchens have all emerged as important tools for social activism.

One of the reasons that food is such an effective conduit for expressing and articulating forms of power is that it mediates the personal and the political. Through food, people can engage with larger issues in the social intimacy of their own kitchens and the physical intimacy of their own bodies. Governments, corporations, and other regulatory institutions can also use food to promote their own interests. Governing forces have, at different times, both deliberately starved and fed their populations as forms of control, while ordinary people have deliberately starved themselves or consumed forbidden foods as forms of political resistance.

Focusing on food as an object that individuals, communities, and institutions try to control and regulate opens up critical questions about the nature of power and how it is wielded and experienced by different actors. This section examines food as both an object of power and a form of power in itself, with attention to the power dynamics and relationships that shape food practices and experiences. In different ways, the chapters in this section probe themes such as power and control, authority, regulation, and resistance to understand the dynamic, cooperative, and sometimes agonistic processes through which communities are constituted, controlled, and resisted. Individually within each chapter, and collectively across the chapters, the authors attend to the ways in which power dynamics shape forms of social organization at different scales and for different communities. This question of scale is particularly significant, as the authors illuminate how power dynamics can exist at the macro level of global politics and nation-states, in more small-scale domestic spaces like private homes, and even in the most intimate and personal spaces within individual bodies. By moving across these various scales and locations, the authors consider how individuals, citizens, institutions, and governments come to know one another and interact with one another through food and its regulation, as they navigate themes such as authority, choice, surveillance, privacy, risk, and security.

Potential Questions to Guide Reading and Discussion

What is power and how is it experienced through food and food practices?

How are power relations experienced by differently positioned actors?

What are the possibilities and limits of power when it is enacted through food?

How do food practices illuminate power differentials, especially in terms of control and agency?

What are the performative dimensions of political negotiations?

How does food help us understand questions about choice, force, coercion, and resistance?

What forms of governance and regulation emerge through food practices?

What kinds of interactions between individuals and institutions, including governmental bodies, emerge through food practices?

How and why does the body become a site for engaging with forms of power?

How does knowledge become a source of power and a site for political struggle?

7

Power at the Table: Food Fights and Happy Meals

Richard Wilk

The image of the happy family meal is culturally and politically exceptionally powerful. To a remarkable extent in the United States and other western countries, people share the notion that once upon a time, all families sat down together, mother put food on the table, and everyone said grace. The warm, encompassing circle of commensality drew everyone together around real food cooked with unique family recipes, teaching children religious values and respect for their elders, and brought order and comfort to a nation founded on family values. In the United States, government agencies, multinational firms, and religious organizations spend millions of dollars a year on publicity campaigns that exhort families to sit down together to share a happy meal.[1] Advice manuals and parenting magazines exhort parents to regularly bring the family together around the dinner table (e.g., Kalish, 2001). Academics have done their share, producing reams of papers and research which purports to show that family meals are healthy, universal, socially integrative, and an antidote to social evils of all kinds. Family meals are part of the official creed of the American Dietetic Association, which claims they promote better nutrition, reduce obesity, and help prevent drug use and antisocial behavior.[2] What political and social agendas lie behind these normalizing discourses? What is the power that drives such conformity and devotion, creating an ideological substrate so deep and solid that most North Americans, and even recent immigrants, can reproduce it without hesitation? This article seeks to understand how a powerful coalition of forces and agents has come together to make the family meal a part of the cultural politics of the contemporary United States.

In ethnographic interviews in the United States, when I ask people to describe "real" family meals, most can immediately recite some variation of the normative ideal of family commensality. Only later in the interview, when we are sharing personal family stories, are they willing to talk about the daily reality of their personal experiences, which rarely live up to the ideal. Like the nuclear family itself, the archetypal ideal is widely shared and has tremendous continuity despite the fact that the reality is rarely attained (Coontz, 1992). Like many deeply embedded normative cultural icons, it seems to be immune to experience or scientific observation. The famous 1956 study of people who believed the world was going to end *When Prophecy Fails* concluded that when expectations and strongly held beliefs are not verified by real events and experience, "the individual will frequently emerge, not only unshaken, but even more convinced of the truth of his beliefs than ever before. Indeed, he may even show a new fervor about convincing and converting other people to his view" (Festinger, Riecken, & Schachter, 1956, p. 3). The same thing might be said of family meals; the less the reality accords with the expectation, the more firmly emplaced and normative that expectation becomes.[3]

The uniformity of support and sentiment might be taken as no more than an instance of cultural conservatism and the willful continuity, which is often glossed as "tradition," but there are more active reasons why the family meal continues to be such an unassailable ideal. An enormous amount of political power has been brought to bear, at many levels and by many players, to reinforce the normative power of family meals. This political work has been so effective that the goodness of family meals is truly hegemonic, in the sense that alternatives are unthinkable. There is no oppositional position, no shading of opinion, and no praise of solitary eating. The industries that undercut family dining, and profit from hurried solitary eating, which must include most employers of hourly workers in the United States, not to mention the fast food and television industries, do so under an ideological cover of vociferous support for the togetherness of the normative family. Research begins with the presumption that family meals are socially, morally, and physically positive, and sets out to prove it. At an even more fundamental level, the research presumes that the majority of North American food consumption actually takes place during formal "meals" at a table, at a time when statistics show an ever-increasing amount of eating could better be described as auto-mobile snacking, liquid nourishment, or "grazing" (Frazao, 1999).

A less ideologically loaded approach suggests that the family dinner table is a place where public and private politics intersect, where the connections between gender and authority can be seen in all their pervasive and encompassing complexity (see Lakoff, 1996). Family meals are often the setting where imbalances of power based on age and gender are forced to the surface, events where authority is demonstrated and roles are enforced, where some people serve and obey while others make choices and arbitrary decisions, in other words, where individuals confront the power embedded in daily discourse, bodily habits, and the routines of everyday life (Neumann, 1996). Hierarchies are enacted and enforced by acts as subtle as passing the serving dish in a particular direction, or a disapproving glance at one's choice of a piece of meat. Rules for serving and sharing can be complex and contradictory, in ways that can be oppressive, lending structural power to some family members in ways that are difficult for an outsider to decode or understand (Shuman, 1981; Wilk, 2006).

Given the power of the family meal as a cultural ideal, and its complexity as a social phenomenon, it is quite remarkable how little serious scholarship has been devoted to the topic, particularly to the conflict and tension that so often surrounds the event, which do not fit the ideal. Such a lacuna is itself interesting, for it hints at the kinds of self-censorship and subtle shading of assumptions, which enforce political blindness to particular kinds of phenomena in the social sciences (Daly, 2003). The selection of "legitimate" research topics is one of the most effective ways that academic disciplines, through the mechanisms of funding and mentorship, police their boundaries and maintain intellectual continuity through generations in ways that are often strikingly conservative.

This article is based on preliminary fieldwork on table conflicts, which began with a project on children who are defined as "picky eaters," conducted in Berkeley, California in 2000–2001. I conducted 12 extended interviews with parents who self-identified as having children whose refusal to eat a "normal" diet was problematic. During these interviews, I was struck by the anguish of parents for whom every meal had become a struggle, full of tension and conflict. Part of their pain was caused by what they perceived as their failure to "live up" to the kinds of happy family meals they might remember from childhood, or which they expect other people are having. I found that during the interviews, once people understand I am not after the ideal, that I don't expect their family to be perfect, and reveal that many families share their problems, they are often eager to talk. In fact they seem relieved that someone is willing to listen, and interviews take on a kind of confessional tone. This is the only research I have ever done where people called me and asked to be interviewed and then expressed appreciation and relief afterwards. My initial sample was drawn from parents in the school my daughter attended, but it quickly snowballed to include a much broader and more diverse group. Since these initial interviews, I have opportunistically interviewed people I have met professionally and socially in six countries about their own lifelong experiences of family meals.

If people are so interested in the topic, why has there been so little research? First, there is the ideological power of the ideal image of the goodness of the family meal, usually held up by interpretations of the teachings of organized religions (Lakoff, 1996), and popular notions about American family history (Coontz, 1992). In surveying what has been written about family meals, I constantly found words like intimacy, integration, interaction, sociability, connection, foundation of society, togetherness, harmony, loving, and nurturing. Research on the idea of "home cooking" finds a similar degree of ideological loading and finds that family meals during holidays have become a central ritual in constructing family ideology and continuity in America (Moisio, Arnould, & Price, 2004). These feelings are compounded by ideals of universality, that one thing that binds all people of the world together is the power of shared meals as a kind of universal family glue. This perception is graphically bolstered by works like Peter Menzel's (2007) evocative and very popular photographs of meals around the world. In each one a family is posed together behind a display of all the food they eat during a typical week, creating a sense of universality that elides the actual diversity in families and their eating practices.

My colleagues in anthropology have not used their cross- cultural experience of the diversity of eating practices to question or relativise the prevailing ideology of meals as integrative events. This may be due to a functionalist bias, which interprets any kind of group event as a positive form of Durkheimian social solidarity, creating group identity through the magic of shared emotion. Nevertheless, while eating does seem to be a universal form of social life in every society anthropologists have studied, the nuclear family is not the unit of commensality in a majority of cases. Instead, the majority of the world's people eat together in age grades, in gender-segregated nonfamily groups, and in family groups both smaller and larger than nuclear families. In many cultures married couples eat separately—because they live in separate households. Even when they live together, men and women may regularly eat with other groups. Children do not always eat with two or even one parent. And in many cultures the numerical majority of meals are eaten in nonfamily groups, casually on the street, in crowds, while working, or in multifamily groups.

More people eat on the ground than at a table, and meals are often casual and utilitarian rather than formal, elaborate, or ceremonial.[4] The idea that in past cultures people were more likely to eat together in families than they are today does not find much concrete support in the historical or cross-cultural ethnographic literature, and group meals in many times were rare special events (Jones, 2008). As Coontz points out, the North American nuclear family beloved of the 1950s TV serial shows, was always more the exception than the rule (1992). In reality, "fast food" and individual or institutional eating are quite ancient, widespread, and "traditional" in many parts of the world. There are also many classic anthropological accounts of cultures where feasts are the scene of conflict and even violence, where eating in a group is a dangerous event that must be carefully controlled (e.g., the Yanomamo discussed by Chagnon, 1977). There are also good histories of the welfare state, which show how middle-class domestic mores were "scientifically" validated and imposed onto rural people, the poor, and ethnic minorities (e.g., Frykman & Lofgren, 1987).

This is not to say that the *ideal* of the congenial, socially integrative commensal family meal is not widespread, and anthropologists often hear it and find it convincing. Nevertheless, I can give an example from my own fieldwork with Q'eqchi' Maya farming villages in southern Belize in 1979–1980. Writing later about their household organization, I argued that shared cooking and meals were important practices that held extended families together, that eating from a common hearth was a metaphor for the social glue which turned a group of relatives living close together into a household as well as an example of daily sharing of labor and resources (1997, chap. 6). I never mentioned that families rarely ate together in a group. Related men and older boys would sit on benches or squat at one end of the house where they were usually served their food by women, while women and younger children squatted on the floor around the hearth at the other end of the house. The gender division was stricter at public events, feasts, and ceremonies. Only in the poorest and smallest families would a married couple ever eat together. I did talk about young men quarreling with their parents about marriage, money, religion, and work, and how some of them left home as soon as they could, and if I had been paying attention, I probably would have seen that some of these quarrels take place at meals. The truth in this case seems to be that households are held together by sharing a food supply, ownership of property, and by the labor exchanges necessary in subsistence farming, but not by the acts of consuming food together. One could speculate that meals may only acquire symbolic importance when the other things that hold families together have "withered away," but why should meals take on this role, when there are other forms of shared activities like driving, playing games, cleaning house, or listening to music, which might symbolically tie household members together.

These examples show how, when we assume that happy family meals are normal, anything else tends to become invisible, or if seen, interpreted as deviance or evidence of social decay. More seriously, when we do observe orderly formal group meals, we always interpret them as integrative, positive signs of a society which works. In an early work, Pierre Bourdieu (1970/1990) described the symbolic order of the Kabyle house, the formal rules that determined where each person ate, how food was to be passed from hand to hand, and who had precedence. Only much later did he start to question the authority and power that built this order, to portray the subordination, coercion, persuasion, and active discipline that maintained everyday life. In a similar way, the peaceful tableau of the modern American family table rests on invisible skeins of power that are rarely discussed except when they burst into visibility during quarrels or disputes when they are readily interpreted as "deviant." But there is strong evidence that the participants in family meals are quite aware that all is not peace and light.

Family Meals as a U.S. National Political Agenda

Before discussing the micropolitics of the family dinner table, it is important to recognize the interdependence of local and national cultural politics revealed by the case of the family dinner. The daily interaction at the family table always takes place under the shadow of normative expectations, so that anything beyond the norm is compared to a dominant hegemonic happy meal of harmony and social integration. The norm might change to closer reflect reality if it was not constantly reinforced by official organs of the state, cultural intermediaries in mass media, and religious authorities, abetted by paid academics who produce "research" that supports the norm. An example of the way this normative political apparatus generates expertise in the interest of the conservative "family values" agenda can be seen in the work of The National Center on Addiction and Substance Abuse at Columbia University.

The Center's roster of present and past directors is a collection of political royalty, including two First Ladies (Betty Ford and Nancy Reagan), influential members of Congress (Barbara Jordan) and a Secretary of Health, Education, and Welfare (Joseph Califano). The board of directors includes actress Jamie Lee Curtis, Columba Bush, wife of ex-Florida Governor Jeb Bush, university presidents, distinguished MDs, and the CEOs of many major corporations. They are funded by an alphabet soup of U.S. Government agencies, foundations, major corporations, media conglomerates, and rich individuals from William Bradley through Donald Rumsfeld to John Tishman.

The Center conducts regular surveys of teen drug abuse and underage drinking, and in 1996 they first "detected" a close association between the frequency of family meals with children and their likelihood of drug abuse.

Frequent family dining is associated with lower rates of teen smoking, drinking, illegal drug use and prescription drug abuse. Compared to teens who eat dinner frequently with their families (five or more family dinners per week), those who have infrequent family dinners (fewer than three per week) are

- three and a half times likelier to have abused prescription drugs,

- three and a half times likelier to have used an illegal drug other than marijuana or prescription drugs,

- three times likelier to have used marijuana,

- more than two and a half times likelier to have used tobacco, and

- one and a half times likelier to have used alcohol. (National Center on Addiction and Substance Abuse [NCASA], 2007, p. ii)

In his accompanying letter with the report, Joseph Califano states as follows:

The CASA survey and 15 years of my life devoted to understanding this problem lead me to this bottom line: Preventing America's drug problems is not going to be accomplished in court rooms, legislative hearing rooms, or classrooms by judges, politicians, or teachers. It will happen in living rooms and dining rooms and across kitchen tables—by the efforts of parents and families. (NCASA, 2007, p. iii)

This kind of personalization and individuation of social problems, devolving social responsibility onto individual citizens who can then make moral choices, is a consistent bedrock of conservative (neoliberal) policymaking, extended to everything from pollution to international development (see Lakoff, 1996; Maniates, 2002). Like the "antipolitics machine" identified by Ferguson (1990) in the context of impoverished Africa, this rhetoric renders the failure of policy and law invisible and denies the importance of inequality and social discrimination. It turns legitimate social problems into personal moral issues, which are addressed through exhortation and preaching, often glossed as "education."

The surveys sponsored by NCASA are released in short briefing papers, rather than being published in the scientific press. This allows the authors to imply that the statistical relationship between frequency of family meals and drug use is *causative*, a basic statistical error which would make publication impossible in a peer-reviewed journal. But it allows the authors to imply that if people would just have more family meals, their children would be less likely to use drugs. Any trained social scientist would know that the correlation may have no causal implications at all. It is probably an artifact of unmeasured covariables, like income, household size, marital status, or location.

The methodology used in the survey—telephone calls with lead-in questions—would also fail to meet any basic test of scientific rigor. But this does not stop them from being cited widely as scientific proof that family meals are an "antidrug." Each report on family meals issued by NCASA is picked up uncritically and approvingly by national newspapers and magazines, translated into headlines like "Family Dinners Give Kids a Message to Chew On, Too", and "Recipe for Drug-free Kids: Family Dinner". These popular messages, besides having very weak empirical support, stigmatize single parents, two-earner couples, and people from cultural or subcultural groups who do not share the dominant Anglo-American dinner custom, not to mention single people or those who live in institutional settings like schools, the military, prisons or nursing homes. Alternative forms of family and parenting become deviant and dangerous, conflict at meals a crime against society. Blended families, same-sex couples, multigenerational households, homeless families - all are pushed aside into other categories, so the quality of their dinner tables is marked as a product of their difference, in contrast with the normative center.

A Taste of Daily Life: "Real" Family Meals

The daily experience of mealtimes in families cannot be accurately elicited on survey forms because of the high normative power of family meals. When people are asked "How many times in the last week did your family eat a meal together around the dining table?" they are likely to respond with how they feel they should behave, not to mention the difficulty of accurate recall given hectic individual schedules and conflicting routines. The categories usually given on surveys about family meals are so broad and ambiguous that they can be interpreted many ways by respondents.

On a survey form, a meal where everyone shares jokes and tells stories is the same as one where everyone stares at their plate bolting food silently under the glare of an angry father. Even group interviews, participant observation, or short-term observational studies using videotape are subject to similar forms of error when concerned with an event so deeply loaded with meaning and expectations. Formal and survey techniques are notoriously unable to deal with the deeper emotional content and cultural significance of common events (Borneman & Hammoudi, 2009).

Marjorie DeVault tried to get around this by interviewing spouses separately, and then together - people told her about conflicts in the separate interviews, but when the couples got back together they denied what they had said, and returned to the normative story (1991). The result is easy to see in the literature. Discord at the dinner table is rarely seen, discussed, or analyzed.

Nevertheless, even the literature produced by advocates of family meals show that many events are experienced as unpleasant by the participants. When the National Center on Addiction and Substance Abuse report that 24% of surveyed teens wanted more frequent family meals, this suggests that 76% of teens said they did not want more of them (NCASA, 2005). In the same survey, 37% say the TV is usually on during family dinners and 14% admit that there is not much talking.

An article called "You will eat all of that!" reports on a survey of a college class, which found that 69% reported being forced to eat a food they did not like at a family meal and 57% reported threats and/or punishment about food at those meals (Batsell, Brown, Ansfield, & Paschall, 2002). In another paper, Story (2005) claims that family meals need to be promoted to improve nutrition because they are "essential for the unity of the family" and "transmit cultural and ethnic heritage." While 98% of parents "agreed that it was important for their family to eat at least one meal a day together," 25% of adolescents said family meals were "not enjoyable" and 33% reported "0–2" family meals in the previous week.

Why do some people dislike family meals and try to avoid them? What kinds of conflict are most common? Several surveys suggest that people go out to restaurants to avoid conflict over who should cook and clean up. Ethnographic studies like my work on children's food preferences give richer examples of the kinds of things that produce conflict in family meals, the daily politics of power that makes eating together into a theater fraught with tension. What appears to be an epidemic of picky eating among American children has spread to newly affluent groups in other countries including China (Jing, 2000) though it still appears to be rare in Europe. A plethora of self-help manuals advise North American parents on complex incentives and regulations they can use to persuade their children to eat (e.g., Piette, 2006). This hardly evokes a relaxed, sharing atmosphere at the table.

Disruptive behavior among children at the table is something American parents often talk about, a topic that appears frequently on message boards and blogs and in advice columns. But academics seem to have assiduously avoided studying this aspect of the dining experience. If mentioned, it is always seen as a symptom of some other problem, usually related to modernity, changes in gender roles, or the "time poverty" and overscheduling that afflicts suburban parents. Social science therefore performs a kind of sleight of hand, for when people perceive children's bad behavior at meals as a problem, academics tell them the children are responding to larger social forces, symptoms of the larger disruptions of family life caused by modern living. But when urban poor people try to deal with the bullying, gangs, and street violence their children face every day at school and in public places, they are told that the problem is *their* fault, because they are not providing enough family meals! The blame lands squarely on the shoulders of women, who already bear the double burdens of underpaid wage labor and responsibility for children.

The few ethnographic studies hint at the richness and depth of emotion involved in children's conduct at the table. One of Marjorie Devault's informants says she has to tell her children " 'Either sit up and eat, or leave the table.' And then the whole meal is ruined" (DeVault, 1991, p. 50). Carol Counihan collected the following quotes from some of her students:

The dinner table becomes a battleground every night about 5 p.m. I'm not home very often for dinner but when I am it's brutal. My mother is the worst. Every night at dinner we hear about how hard she works and how rotten we kids are (Counihan, 1992, p. 7)

Ever since third grade my father and I would always argue bitterly about how much I weigh ... I tended to eat less in front of my father, then I would eat more in secrecy" (Counihan, 1992, p. 8)

The dinner table is often a place where parents exercise authority over children, making it a common site for struggles over the impressions made by family members in public, standards of etiquette, and moral rules. Some of these issues have been taken up in the literature on eating disorders, dieting, and food anxieties (e.g., Nichter & Nichter, 1991). But this framing of the topic only furthers the marginalization of conflict at the table, with all its implications of deviance and medical pathology.

Even remembering happy family meals can evoke the sadness and guilt of failure or loss, a sense of inability to meet society's standards or the expectations of others. In a paper on home-made meals, Arnould and Price (2001) recorded the following reflections:

Oh, I always associated good food with my mother because she was a good cook and that's where you try to learn her cooking. But it seems like every time you want to be like that other person you never can be ... I don't know what they ever did but they always had some little thing they used to put in the food that was better than yours. But, I suppose my food is better maybe than my daughter's would be, you know. (p. 13) I might have hurt my mom's feelings a couple of times when I would ask her why she couldn't cook like grandma. (p. 14)

This regret can be related to the guilt, frustration, and defeat single parents, or those working two jobs feel when they cannot provide the idealized family dinner, or skip them because they become too complex or contentious (DeVault, 1991, pp. 51–53).

Parents often disagree about how to raise children, and these differences can erupt at family meals (Bove & Sobal, 2003 & Ellis, 1982). I have seen parents argue about everything from bottle feeding to the importance of eating vegetables. Feelings about food, particularly about apportioning, sharing, and wasting it, are strongly linked to moral philosophies. As George Lakoff (1996) says in *Moral Politics*, liberal and conservative political philosophies are fundamentally based on ideals of family politics. Lakoff argues persuasively that American conservatives follow strict father morality, whereas progressives frame their morals on a nurturing parent metaphor. The strict father gives orders, whereas the nurturant parent persuades and uses reason. In practice, most couples come into a marriage with different ideas, which must be negotiated and compromised in various practical ways, which are not always calm and reasoned.

Gender ideologies and gendered behavior set the stage for differences of many kinds around family meals. Besides the apportionment of chores in preparing, serving, and cleaning up after meals, conversation itself can be contentious. Marjorie DeVault discusses households where "talk at the dinner table was an item of contention between taciturn husbands and their wives, who were striving to construct the meal as a certain type of social occasion. As one woman said, "If I sit and start talking, he'll say 'what the heck, can't you ever shut up?'" (DeVault, 1991, p. 49; see also Neuhaus, 2003 and Pahl, 1989).

My work with the families of children identified as picky eaters revealed several cases where women found the food dislikes of their children were pushing them toward what they considered "traditional" gender roles, against their will. One woman told me that it had become so complicated preparing meals that catered to the complex dislikes and aversions of her children and husband that she gave up her job and went back to being a full time housewife. In another case where I was invited to share a family meal, the mother spent the entire mealtime cooking and serving different dinners for each child and adult, and never sat down to eat, explaining that she would have leftovers in the kitchen while cleaning up. Women are triply forced into complete liability for the eating behavior of their children, as the person still responsible for cooking most family meals in North American families, as the person who is still responsible for the majority of food shopping (which means remembering each family members' individual preferences), and as the person still responsible for daily family health and household hygiene: "nurse mom" (Bianchi, Milkie, Sayer, & Robinson, 2000; Coltrane, 2000).

The conflicts between adults around the dinner table are so rich and varied that they form the basis of many novels and dramatic works, especially when you include extended kin, multigenerational households, and festive meals that bring together family members who may be estranged from one another. It is hard to imagine a negative emotion or experience in family life which is not reflected, or instantiated at the dinner table. It is an anthropological truism that families are held together by exchange of gifts and labor, and that festive meals are stages where these exchanges are often remembered, enacted, and performed, where important family business takes place (Jones, 2008). But what happens when the exchanges are refused, when reciprocity breaks down, when the communal feast fails to heal disagreements and rifts?

In other cultures, anthropologists have documented how tensions over food and meals can lead to the division of complex stem families, joint families, nomadic bands, and urban extended families. In some patrilocal cultures, poor cooking skills can get a woman quickly divorced and sent home. Gracia Clark gives a wonderful description of how Ashanti men judge the state of their relationship with their wives by the quality of the food they get for dinner (Clark, 1999). Complaining is likely to make things worse.

This example points out especially well how conflict at the family meal can be both cause and symptom at the same time. It stands to reason that if meals are culturally and socially important events, the tensions, divisions, and conflicts in society will appear there too. The meal is both a powerful symbol of the family and an event that *makes* the family, so a great deal is at stake in all these conflicts.

There are other reasons why the family meal in North America has become such a highly charged arena for conflict over gender and authority. It is a setting where cultural stereotypes are dramatically juxtaposed with the increasingly diverse realities where few families ever approach the ideal. In addition, in the United States food is deeply laden with meanings of abundance, success, the bounty of nature, and progress (Belasco, 2006). The yawning gap between stereotype and performance creates a zone of maximum dissonance, a table where a hundred mass-mediated stereotypes are seated alongside real people, coping with a country where stable jobs that can support a family have become a vanishing memory. This implies that when gender roles and power structures within the family change, we should expect part of the renegotiation to take place in the one setting where the family regularly meets as a group. But rather than openly debating family roles and power relations, real families find visible issues and deal with the most immediate symptoms. Why should we expect them to do more?

Conclusion

To summarize, this article argues that out of the vast diversity of different ways that North Americans eat together, the idealized "family meal" has become a kind of cultural icon, a hegemonic collective representation of an ideal form of social behavior. The fact that few people actually achieve this ideal, or enjoy it in daily practice, does not seem to undercut its power or tarnish its image; it has the enduring power of mythology. I draw on personal experience, my own research, and narratives collected by others to expose the gap between the real and the ideal, to highlight the everyday unpleasantness of many family meals, and to raise the issues of power and gender, which often make the dining table a scene of social drama and conflict. To understand why the ideal meal has such resistance to practice, I follow Gramsci in looking at its role in political discourse and at the way it normalizes the practices of the white middle class.

From a scholarly point of view, one of the major problems with understanding family meals is that the event really does not belong in the traditional topical territory of any single discipline. In a form of "topical butchering" we cut up a phenomenon into pieces that belong to different academic fields, which ensures we can never put the whole animal back together again. Food studies, food science, and home economics usually stay in the kitchen, up to when the food goes through the dining room door. The way food is served and apportioned and the implements used may belong to some abstruse areas of food technology and family sociology, but they have not been anyone's central interest. Dieticians take over when people actually start eating, but cleaning up and doing the dishes goes to those who study housework and the gendered division of labor. The composition of the family that is eating is a toss-up between sociology, anthropology, and psychology. Children kicking each other under the table is a problem for family therapists. Kids who won't eat what they are served belong to child psychologists. This is a symptom of the general fate of food studies in academia. Although other emerging areas of trans- and interdisciplinary study like gender studies, human ecology, and sustainability research have found coherent institutional forms and programs, food studies floats somewhere in a space between food science, agriculture, gastronomy, history, and social science. It is something of a paradox that a subject so central to human existence has never become the focus of a single academic field.

The complex division of labor in food studies contributes in turn to a kind of normative invisibility, what Miller and Woodward (2007) call the "blindingly obvious." The everyday and mundane are often among the least noticed by scholars; this leads in turn to facile and premature assumptions about what is "normal," which tends to marginalize and stigmatize a great deal of daily practice. As I have found in previous work on household budgeting and money management, the normative invisibility of daily practice extends to popular perception; most people I interviewed wondered if their own practices, habits and systems were unique or typical. As a social scientist I could not really tell them, given the limited data available.

There are a number of important reasons why we need to pay more systematic attention to mundane events like daily meals, though clearly I do not agree that there is good evidence that doing so is likely to lead to great successes in pursuing public policies like drug prevention. Vernon (2007) provides abundant and detailed evidence of how well-intentioned political policies towards food, founded on partial and biased evidence and grounded in class prejudice, often backfire and increase the problems they attempt to solve. Yet careful and nuanced research could possibly lead to more informed and less simplistic public policy which takes account of cultural variability, and does not depend so thoroughly on moral assumptions defined as such mostly by white, heterosexual, middle-class, middle-age, and able-bodied European Americans.

Family meals represent an unusual nexus of local and national politics, of family and individual power, and the forces of ideologies and practices of gender, age, and cultural identity. They are worth studying in themselves, but that means being able to account for the moral rhetoric which has obscured real meals behind a rosy set of ideals, and paying close attention to negative emotions and behaviors at the dinner table without stigmatizing them or labeling them as deviant. The positive and negative sides of family meals are not just moral opposites; they are part of the same phenomenon and should not be divided up. This stance is in itself a political one, in that it counters the use of a normative "happy family meal" as a rhetorical tool for punishing those who lack the means or desire to conform to the cultural mores of a dominant class.

Declaration of Conflicting Interests

The author(s) declared no potential conflicts of interest with respect to the authorship and/or publication of this article.

Funding

The author(s) received no financial support for the research and/or authorship of this article.

Notes

1 For example, see Libby foods "Get Back to the Table" campaign (http://www.getbacktothetable.com/), the USDA "Food and Fun for Family" programs (http://www.nal.usda.gov/wicworks/Sharing_Center/gallery/fam_meals1.htm#fm15), and the Dobson's Focus on the Family ministry is just one of innumerable Christian groups which encourage family meals as the focus of religious practice (http://www2.focusonthe-family.com/focusmagazine/christianliving/A000000075.cfm). The Nutrition Education Network of Washington, funded in part by the Food Stamp Program, Food and Nutrition Service, United States Department of Agriculture, and administered by Washington

State University is just one example of the many organizations which promote family meals in the USA (http:// nutrition.wsu.edu/take5/07/200711.pdf) while UNICEF has taken up the task on an international basis.

2 The Association produces numerous publications in support of family meals, including many articles in the Journal of the American Dietetic Association which support family dining (e.g., Neumark-Sztainer, Hannan, Story, Croll, & Perry, 2003).

3 Some food marketing companies are now marketing small meals for "single diners," but again the very fact that they have to be singled out as a special category ends up normalizing the family meal as the unquestionable standard. A number of food bloggers have recently asserted that eating alone should no longer be stigmatized, but there is something plaintive about their tone (http://www.yelp.com/topic/austin-best-eat-alone-restaurant).

4 This is based on a quick review of the data collected in the Human Relations Area Files online (eHRAF, http://www.yale .edu/hraf/) as well as many years of reading ethnographies from all over the world.

References

Arnould, E., & Price, L. (2001, July 25–28). *Bread of our mothers. Ruptures and continuities in families and homemade food traditions.* Paper presented at the 8th Interdisciplinary Conference on Consumption, Université de Paris, La Sorbonne, France.

Batsell, W., Brown, A., Ansfield, M., & Paschall, G. (2002). "You will eat all of that!" A retrospective analysis of forced consumption episodes. *Appetite, 38,* 211–219.

Belasco, W. (2006). *Meals to come: A history of the future of food.* Berkeley: University of California Press.

Bianchi, M., Milkie, M., Sayer, L., & Robinson, J. (2000). Is anyone doing the housework? Trends in the gender division of household labor. *Social Forces, 79,* 191–228.

Borneman, J., & Hammoudi, A. (2009). *Being there: The fieldwork encounter and the making of truth.* Berkeley: University of California Press.

Bourdieu, P. (1990). The Kabyle house or the world reversed. In R. Nice (Trans.), *The logic of practice* (pp. 271–283). Stanford, CA: Stanford University Press. (Original work published 1970)

Bove, C., & Sobal, J. (2003). Food choices among newly married couples: Convergence, conflict, individualism, and projects. *Appetite, 40,* 25–41.

Chagnon, N. (1977). *Yanomamo, the fierce people.* New York: Holt, Rinehart and Winston.

Clark, G. (1999). Mothering, work and gender in urban Asante ideology and practice. *American Anthropologist, 101,* 717–729.

Coltrane, S. (2000). Research on household labor: Modeling and measuring the social embeddedness of routine family work. *Journal of Marriage and the Family, 62,* 1208–1233

Coontz, S. (1992). *The way we never were: American families and the nostalgia trap.* New York: Basic Books.

Counihan, C. (1992). Food rules in the United States: Individualism, control, and hierarchy. *Anthropological Quarterly, 65,* 55–66.

Daly, K. (2003). Family theory versus the theories families live by. *Journal of Marriage and the Family, 65,* 771–784.

deVault, M. (1991). *Feeding the family: The social organization of caring as gendered work.* Chicago: Chicago University Press.

Ellis, R. (1982). The way to a man's heart: Food in the violent home. In A. Murcott (Ed.), *The sociology of food and eating* (pp. 164–171). Aldershot, UK: Gower.

Ferguson, J. (1990). *The anti-politics machine: "Development," depoliticization, and bureaucratic power in Lesotho.* Cambridge, UK: Cambridge University Press.

Festinger, L., Riecken, H., & Schachter, S. (1956). *When prophecy fails—A social and psychological study of a modern group that predicted the destruction of the world.* Minneapolis: University of Minnesota Press.

Frazao, E. (Ed.). (1999). *America's eating habits: Changes and consequences* (Agriculture Information Bulletin No. AIB750). Washington, DC: United States Department of Agriculture.

Frykman, J., & Lofgren, O. (1987). *Culture builders: A historical anthropology of middle-class life.* New Brunswick, NJ: Rutgers University Press

Jing, J. (Ed.). (2000). *Feeding China's little emperors: Food, children, and social change.* Stanford, CA: Stanford University Press.

Jones, M. (2008). *Feast: Why humans share food.* New York: Oxford University Press.

Kalish, N. (2001). *Why family dinner is worth it. Parenting Magazine, 12,* 133–135.

Lakoff, G. (1996). *Moral politics.* Chicago: University of Chicago Press.

Maniates, M. (2002). Individualization: Plant a tree, buy a bike, save the world? In T. Princen, M. Maniates, & K. Konca. (Eds.), *Confronting consumption* (pp. 43–66). London: MIT Press.

Menzel, P. (2007). *Hungry planet: What the world eats.* Berkeley, CA: Ten Speed Press.

Miller, D., & Woodward, S. (2007). Manifesto for a study of denim. *Social Anthropology, 15,* 335–351.

Moisio, R., Arnould, E., & Price, L. (2004). Between mothers and markets: Constructing family identity through homemade food. *Journal of Consumer Culture, 4,* 361–384.

National Center on Addiction and Substance Abuse. (2005, September). *The importance of family dinners II.* Retrieved, April 30, 2010, from http://www.casacolumbia.org/ViewProduct.aspx?PRODUCTID={F547FA42-D19F-4a6d-9E06-3DF08477ADE1}

National Center on Addiction and Substance Abuse. (2007, September). *The importance of family dinners IV.* (2007). Retrieved, April 30, 2010, from http://www.casacolumbia.org/ViewProduct.aspx?PRODUCTID={296A5E1E-B68F-44fa-A64D-95ABC1FB6CA0}

Neuhaus, J. (2003). *Manly meals and mom's home cooking: Cook-books and gender in modern America.* Baltimore: Johns Hopkins University Press.

Neumann, M. (1996). *Collecting ourselves at the end of the century.* In C. Ellis & A. Bochner (Eds.), *Composing ethnography: Alternative forms of qualitative writing* (pp. 172–198). Walnut Creek, CA: Altamira.

Neumark-Sztainer, D., Hannan, R., Story, M., Croll, J., & Perry, C. (2003). Family meal patterns: Associations with sociodemographic characteristics and improved dietary intake among adolescents. *Journal of the American Dietetic Association, 103,* 317–322.

Nichter, M., & Nichter, M. (1991). Hype and weight. *Medical Anthropology, 13,* 249–284.

Pahl, J. (1989). *Money and marriage.* New York: St. Martin's Press.

Piette, L. (2006). *Just two more bites! Helping picky eaters say "yes" to food.* New York: Three Rivers Press.

Shuman, A. (1981). The rhetoric of portions. *Western Folklore, 40*(1), 72–80.

Story, M. (2005). A perspective on family meals. *Nutrition Today, 40,* 261–266.

Vernon, J. (2007). *Hunger: A modern history.* Cambridge, MA: Belknap Press.

Wilk, R. (1997). *Household ecology.* DeKalb, IL: Northern Illinois University Press.

Wilk, R. (2006). Serving or helping yourself at the table. *Food, Culture and Society, 9,* 7–12.

8

Postsocialist Spores: Disease, Bodies, and the State in the Republic of Georgia

Elizabeth Cullen Dunn

Teimuraz had gotten sick the night before. A strange sensation had come over him suddenly, and then his vision began to blur. Soon, his eyelids were drooping and his cheeks were slumping like a stroke victim's. His speech began to slur as he asked his wife for help. Together, they rushed to the local polyclinic, where the doctors took one look at him, realized the antidote to his disease was not to be had at any hospital nearby, and rushed him into an ambulance bound for Tbilisi, the capital of the former Soviet Republic of Georgia. Tbilisi was almost a hundred miles away over icy and potholed mountain passes, but the speed of the rickety ambulance was a matter of life or death: Teimuraz's breathing was becoming more and more labored, and the risk that he would suffocate to death before the ambulance could deliver him to antitoxin and a ventilation machine was high.[1]

At the Tbilisi Institute for Infectious Disease, Teimuraz lay on a hospital bed surrounded by physicians in heavy blue surgical gowns, epidemiologists from the Georgian National Center for Disease Control, and the team from the U.S. Centers for Disease Control (CDC) that I was working with as a consultant. He thrashed weakly as the doctors pried open his swollen eyes, and he tried feebly to move away from the bright light coming from the bulb that dangled from the exposed electrical wires above him. He wanted to speak, to tell them that the light hurt, but his tongue was thick in his mouth, and when he tried to talk, only strange noises came out. He felt nauseous and had difficulty breathing. Nearby, his wife sat in a chair, twisting the straps of her handbag and answering questions about what she had served Teimuraz for dinner the night before. Had Teimuraz eaten anything the rest of the family had not? Maybe the Bulgarian stuffed peppers, his wife said, or maybe he ate some tomatoes over at the neighbor's house, it was hard to remember. Where did the peppers come from? Who made the tomatoes? Teimuraz's wife had canned them herself, just like all the other women in all the other families in her apartment block. The doctors standing around the bed finished their examination of Teimuraz and went out into the cold, dim hall.

"Definitely botulism," said Jay Varma, one of the epidemiologists from the CDC who had come to the Republic of Georgia to investigate an outbreak of the disease. He turned to his colleagues from the Georgian National Center for Disease Control and asked, "How many cases is that this winter? Thirty-three since the first of December? And it's only March." Winter is the high season for botulism, and, clearly, many more cases were anticipated. To complicate matters, the botulism antitoxin, which Teimuraz received, was in short supply in the Republic of Georgia and not widely available outside Tbilisi.

Botulism is a potentially fatal disease. It is produced by *Clostridium botulinum* spores, which are ubiquitous in the air and in the soil in many places around the world. In an aerobic environment, the spores are harmless. But when they are placed in an anaerobic environment, they release a poisonous neurotoxin. The toxin causes a descending paralysis that can affect the muscles used in breathing; in severe cases, victims suffocate and die. In the United States, botulism is a rare disease, affecting fewer than one in three million people (an incidence rate of less than 0.01 per 100,000). In the Republic of Georgia, however, the rate is 90 times higher than in the United States. Adjusted for population size, the rate of botulism in the Republic of Georgia is the highest in the entire world (Varma et al. 2004). At the request of the Georgian government, the CDC had sent a team to investigate the reasons for the high incidence of disease, to ensure that cases were being properly diagnosed, and to recommend public health interventions to decrease the number of people contracting and dying from botulism. Because the CDC suspected that the origins of the disease were economic and social as much as biomedical, they had sought the help of an anthropologist who knew something about both food preparation and the former Soviet world, a search that led them to me. As an anthropologist, I had investigated charity and gift exchange in canneries owned by the Mormon Church (Dunn 1996), and I had spent 16 months exploring personhood, work, and labor activism on the shop floor of a formerly state-owned canning factory in Poland (Dunn 2004a). As is usual with CDC outbreak investigations, the team I joined had to work fast: We had scheduled just two short stays in Georgia of three weeks each. We traveled the country and interviewed women in their homes about their strategies for acquiring and preserving food, asking them to show us how they canned vegetables and photographing the equipment and materials they used. With the help of Georgian epidemiologists, I also held a series of 14 focus groups, in which over 100 women explored the feasibility of six different public health strategies we had devised.

The immediate question I address in my research is, of course, why Teimuraz and his countrymen and women are disproportionately affected by botulism and why, in postsocialist Georgia, it is so resistant to the technological solutions that have virtually eliminated the disease in advanced industrial nations. But I also focus here on a deeper question: What does Teimuraz's paralyzed body reveal about the Georgian postsocialist state, specifically, and the project of statehood, more generally? I argue that botulism is a window into modernist state projects and the new ways that states produce materially and socially variegated spaces. Attention to botulism reveals how the Soviet state project formalized particular forms of knowledge and spatially isolated them, highlights how material infrastructures were used to govern, and points out how Soviet power shaped people's tastes. But because botulism is not just a disease of the positive, shaping effects of governmentality but also one of collapse and disorder, it demands a more complex look at the operation of the ensembles of agents, practices, and representations that make up the postsocialist state project. As a disease that is peculiarly virulent in a postsocialist society, it points to what happens when the carefully ordered elements that make up a regulatory regime are thrown into disarray and how that affects the ways new forms of governmentality penetrate or isolate social spaces. Most importantly, the Georgian case points to distinctions between forms of state expansion and withdrawal. In this article, I argue that the Georgian case manifests three forms of statehood: first, the assemblage of practices that allowed the Soviet modernist state to inhabit and dominate new spaces; second, the neoliberal principles that claim to mandate state withdrawal while, in fact, inserting forms of domination into particular microspaces; and third, a collapsing state that is withdrawing from parts of social space not because it is adhering to neoliberal principles of self-regulation but because it is losing the capacity to order and regulate people and things.

Interest in collapsed states and disorder stems from recent arguments about the nature of "the state" inspired by James C. Scott's *Seeing Like a State* (1998). Scott argues that "high modernist" states govern by using techniques of representation to make both the social and natural worlds legible. He focuses on big state projects like collectivization and argues that "the state," which he sees as a reified actor, rules by abstracting data and turning them into highly stylized models that it then tries to make into reality.

Recently, anthropologists have criticized this vision of "the state" (see Ferguson 2005; Herzfeld 2005; Li 2005; Sharma and Gupta 2006). They argue that the high-modernist states Scott describes are on the wane and that they are being replaced by a distinctively neoliberal ethos of governance (Ferguson 2005). Advocates of neoliberalism, of course, say this trend marks a withdrawal of the nation-state, which leaves local institutions like "civil society" and "the market" to govern along with suprastate organizations such as corporations and international financial institutions (e.g., Ohmae 2005). But anthropologists do not necessarily buy the neoliberal claim that the state is being rolled back or even that "the state" exists as some sort of unitary entity that can be withdrawn from social life. Veena Das and Deborah Poole (2004), Aradhana Sharma and Akhil Gupta (2006), James Ferguson and Gupta (2002), and Janet Roitman (2004b), for example, take the Foucauldian view that even in the midst of the ostensible neoliberal rollback of the state, nonstate actors such as scientists, doctors, and NGOs are as responsible for creating webs of regulation as states are and that they act both directly and indirectly as state agents. Because, in this view, the state is an assemblage of actors and practices that far exceeds its own institutional boundary (see also Ong and Collier 2004), the resulting pluralization of figures of regulatory authority means that the neoliberal state is not actually withdrawing from social space but that social space is becoming even more "étatized" than it was in the era of modernist state projects (Roitman 2004a:213; cf. Verdery 1996).

The idea of seeing the state as an assemblage or ensemble of agents, objects, and practices—a move inspired perhaps by science-studies' actor-network theory—means that for Das, Roitman, and others, the boundary between "state" and "society" is analytically nonexistent. Even ostensibly antistate practices such as counterfeiting and smuggling are enmeshed with the state in this view, because they are a mimesis of state practice (see, e.g., Roitman 2004a). The problem, however, is that although this move creates a strong theoretical tool for understanding how the rapid proliferation of NGOs, international organizations, "voluntary" standards, and other mechanisms operate in statelike ways to regulate social behavior, it also leads to a remarkably un-geographical view of how state projects operate that glosses over the important spatializing effects of state activities by simply asserting that the state is everywhere.

Even places that appear to be free of state activity—because they are in the hinterlands of the nation-state or because they are arenas that state officials claim to have withdrawn from as a part of neoliberal policy making—show up in assemblage-based accounts as deeply infused by statist agents and practices. For example, Das and Poole say that areas that appear to be beyond the state are "not just spaces the state has yet to penetrate" but are "sites on which the state is continually formed in the recesses of everyday life" (2004:23). Likewise, Tania Murray Li argues that even ostensibly state-free social spaces are implicated in state practice. As she says, "There is … no spatial beyond of the state, and there are no subjects beyond power" (Li 2005:384). Although this dereification of the state is a welcome follow-up to Ferguson and Gupta's (2002) argument that the state is neither vertical nor encompassing, and although the concept of the state-as-assemblage shows that the state is not just "up there" but, indeed, deeply involved in the practices of daily life, such perspectives leave very little room to think about differences in the degree to which state projects regulate everyday life and the ways in which state projects enter, configure, bound, or leave different domains of social life.

Looking at the state as a set of explicitly spatial practices also means making it material. Here, the study of the postcommunist state is illuminating, and looking at botulism as a material phenomenon shows a great deal about the form that state takes. Looking at botulism as a material phenomenon borne by spores, vegetables, cans, and machines, however, challenges another currently popular idea about the state: that it is an illusion that comes purely from the representations of citizens or the semiotic practices of bureaucrats. This idea stems from Phillip Abrams's (1988) declaration that the state is one of the greatest ideological myths of modern power (see also Navaro-Yashin 2002:155). For Abrams and his followers, the state is not an objectively existing institution (singular) or even a loose grouping of practices, objects, and agents (plural) but a discursive construct that is reified in public speech and that prevents the dominated from understanding the true nature of their subjection (see also Mitchell 2006). This constructivist view of the state, however, does not do much to explain the constraints on the kinds of transformations states can undergo, particularly in situations of change as radical as the post-communist transformation has been. A view of the state as myth does little to help explain how and why the kinds of transformations that postcommunist states—and probably states of all kinds—can undergo are path dependent (Stark 1992). For this reason, I argue the importance of attending not only to discourses of state, to ideas of the state used as ideology, but also to the ways that state projects come together to create durable infrastructures and to impediments that may prevent them from doing so. This approach makes it possible to explore the interrelation of the semiotic and the material and the ways that this allows states to form not just space but the definite qualities of place that make transformations path dependent.

In short, then, the postsocialist Georgian state offers a unique opportunity to interrogate the twin claims that states are both mythic and omnipresent and to begin to see the state as an ensemble of concrete practices that are both material and spatial. To do so, I take up Michel Foucault's opening gambit in *Discipline and Punish* (1977) and examine the body of a suffering person to trace the relations between the body, regulatory practices, and state institutions to discover the relative effects of state power. By starting with the botulism sufferer's body and discovering how patients enter into a history of material production, codified regulation, spatial organization, and cuisine, I argue that botulism indexes places where the high-modernist state has failed and where the disciplinary practices of neoliberalism seem unable to take hold. In contrast to those who argue that the state is everywhere, I argue that, in some cases, states are highly spatially constrained and that practices of regulation are absent. I do so by discussing spaces in which a modernist state once existed but is now absent and by asking how political and material collapse constrains the ways that neoliberal state practices can enter social space. Finally, and most importantly, I ask how spaces that the state does not enter might matter in times of social transformation. In contrast to anthropologists who focus on the paradoxical effects of "development" and the ways that statist institutions deliver services and enforce regulation (e.g., Ferguson 1990; Friedberg 2004), I argue that the nondelivery of state services and the limits of global standards are equally ethnographically telling and that falling outside the state regulation of social spaces can be as harmful as falling under it.

A Culinary Disease

Understanding botulism begins with understanding how people eat. In Georgia, the food is absolutely superb, and the complex rules around food and dining are among the most culturally elaborated features in the construction of national identity. Georgians are famed for long, multicourse banquets, or *supra,* which often feature broiled eggplants with amazingly delicious sauces of walnuts and pomegranate seeds, deeply tangy plum sauce *(tkemali),* chewy flatbread stuffed with sharp melted cheese *(khachapuri),* rich dumplings stuffed with tantalizing broth *(khinkali),* delectable meatballs, and delicate wines, both red and white (Goldstein 1993).[2] Georgian cuisine also features salty pickled vegetables: not just cucumbers but also green tomatoes, peppers, and other foods marinated in brine. Prior to WWII, almost every household preserved these vegetables in wooden or clay casks, which were then buried in the ground for months before being exhumed and their contents eaten. This method, which is botulism safe because of the pH of the brine, was the only way of preserving vegetables for winter use: Although canned food was introduced in western Europe in 1809, industrially canned food was virtually unknown in the Caucasus until after WWII, 130 years later (Goody 1982:157–159; Shephard 2000:231).

At the end of the war, the Soviet Union launched into a second enormous wave of industrialization. As part of the drive to create an urban proletariat (while avoiding the famines of the 1920s and 1930s), Soviet planners attempted to rationalize the food supply. Under the Fourth and Fifth Five Year Plans, they designated Georgia the Soviet Union's primary source of fruits and vegetables and invested heavily in food processing in the southern Caucasus. This was an enormous project. Although Georgia had no canneries at all in 1945, by 1990 it had 58 huge canneries churning out 760 million cans of food per year—about two and a half cans of food for every Soviet citizen (cf. Smith n.d.).[3]

Not surprisingly, Soviet planners were intensely interested in canned food: Canning is one of the ultimate technologies of empire, as both the French and the British colonial empires knew (Goody 1982:157).[4] Canning allows armies to go on the march and bring their own food, thus at least partially freeing them from the threat of being cut off from their supply lines; permits sailors to go on long ocean voyages without fear of starving at sea; and makes it possible for colonists to feed themselves on the taste of home while reassuring themselves of their culinary superiority over the natives (Friedberg 2004; Shephard 2000:230–350). The Soviet empire found canning to be a particularly useful technology in another way, as well: By collecting food from many different regions, canning it, and redistributing it, the Soviet bureaucracy could begin to standardize diets that were dependent on local produce and regional cuisines. Even in Georgia, where the cuisine is highly valued, the substitution of Soviet canned goods changed the way people ate. For example, Georgian salted green tomatoes were increasingly replaced with plump red tomatoes packed in water, Bulgarian style. Likewise, the salted and pickled peppers that people once made at home were largely replaced by stuffed red peppers packed in oil. Although the techniques of pickling vegetables were not lost and people continued to consume some pickled foods, in general, Georgians followed changing patterns of consumption common to the entire Soviet Union and began incorporating new industrial foods into the way they cooked and ate.

Canned food also gave central planners increasing control over the Soviet Union's food supply by partially supplanting food sold by peasants with industrially processed foods only available from the state (Central Intelligence Agency, Office of Documents and Reports 1953:3). This was no mean addition to the source of Soviet power because, by controlling the distribution of industrially produced food, Moscow ensured that citizens depended increasingly on the state itself for daily sustenance. In Georgia, a site of industrial food production, both rural and urban populations had fairly steady access to this "state food." Urban people rarely experienced shortages of canned vegetables, and rural people often took raw produce into the factory and brought back canned food rather than preserving produce at home. Tomatoes in December and berries in February were the edible products of an industrial system that allowed Soviet citizens to disregard the weather and the seasons. The tin of vegetables was the product of a state that claimed to control nature, no different than the hydroelectric dam at Bratsk Station or the atomic bomb at Cheliabinsk-70.

The agroindustrial complex built by the Soviets was thus a classic "high modernist project" (Scott 1998), a streamlined system abstracted from the vagaries of actual production. The Ministry of Agriculture drew up plans for food production, the Ministry of Procurements gave state and collective farms orders to deliver a certain amount of raw produce to nearby factories, and the Ministry of Food Processing sent the factories planned inputs such as cans and jars.[5] The Ministry of Food Processing also sent down a detailed set of standards for food processing, known as *Sovstandardy*.

Like most standards, Sovstandardy were made with inputs from a wide variety of sources, including engineers, factory managers, and foreign experts. Once implemented throughout the Soviet Union, Sovstandardy created what Andrew Barry (2001) calls a "technological zone," a space in which the circulation of harmonized technologies enabled a greater flow of products. By ensuring that Georgian agricultural processing was conducted according to centrally mandated standards, Soviet planners enabled a much higher rate of trade between Russia and the other republics. Glass jars could be produced in standard sizes in Russia; filled and pasteurized according to standards in Georgia; capped with standardized lids made in, say, Armenia; and then shipped to Moscow in standardized pallets for transshipment to the rest of the Soviet empire. This was a relatively successful state project, if one thinks of states as assemblages of actors, ideas, and practices. Sovstandardy made use of expertise, linked a diverse set of institutions, and regulated practice well enough that metal lids made in one place fit well on jars made in another. They also, not coincidentally, dramatically increased the amount of food that got made.

Standards are always parts of power claims, and Soviet standards were no exception. Sovstandardy not only enabled the circulation of goods but also created the appearance of "the state" as a reified actor. They did so not only by enacting a sphere of legibility but also by representing an image of the state back to those who participated in the forms and practices of life that circulation made possible, that is to say, those who participated in production and consumption. The object itself—here, a jar of industrially canned food—promoted what Alfred Gell (1998:101) calls the "abduction of agency," or the assumption that behind every socially produced object is an agent who intended for the object to exist. Robert Layton illustrates Gell's complex theory of the abduction of agency in terms of a handy food-related example, describing how someone contemplating a boiled egg might abduct, or infer, the agent whose intentions produced the object: "If there were no breakfast-desiring agents, hens would not have been domesticated, saucepans invented, and eggs cooked. The real causal explanation for why there are any boiled eggs is that I, and other breakfasters, intend that eggs should exist" (2003:456).

In the case of the Soviet system, which did not assume the force of consumer desires to compel production, the existence of an industrially produced consumer good in the late socialist period could only imply one agent: the Soviet state. As Paul Manning puts it

Late socialism remained a unified semiotic regime in which orderly public manifestations were attributed to the one authorial source located in a state whose paternalistic relationship to society was manifested (however problematically) homologously across multiple dimensions of social life. ... The late-socialist order, then, was orderly in that it could be attributed to a single source. [2007:177]

Manning's use of the term *paternalistic* is not insignificant. Not only was the Soviet state seen as the agent whose centralized planning and command of technology could call objects into being, but it was also seen as the caring parent that thoughtfully provided for its citizen–children (Verdery 1996). If the object, canned food, was the proof that the agent, the reified state, existed, then Sovstandardy were the material proof of that state's intentions not only to produce food but also to care for its citizens by providing safe, healthy food.

Sovstandardy also fostered claims about who could control knowledge: In creating a uniform code of practice, the Ministry of Food Processing claimed explicitly to be the only body that could legitimately dictate production practice and to be the sole legitimate issuer, classifier, and disseminator of technical information. But this claim was more than representation or mythography; it was spatial and material: Planners used the industrial division of labor to confine production knowledge to the infrastructures controlled by the ministry. It collectivized the knowledge of how to make safe canned food by turning (nonpickled) canned food into a "black box," in Bruno Latour's (1987) sense, that is, into the nexus of a complexly interrelated network of actors, objects, standards, and documents whose workings were confined to the factory and hidden away from the end users of the product. Soviet consumers could assume their food was safe, knowing vaguely that the state had standards for production, without needing to know too much about how, precisely, the food was made.

One might object to the idea that the state collectivized production knowledge, pointing to the well-known fact that things in state socialist factories seldom worked according to plan. No one has any way of knowing how closely codes were followed in factories. Production processes have always diverged from their paper specifications, particularly in the socialist world, where workers and managers had to constantly deploy craft knowledge to cope with irregular inputs and broken machines. But my own research conducted on the line in a formerly state-run food processing plant in Poland suggested that workers took the issue of food safety seriously and very often deployed craft knowledge to meet standards, not to evade them (Dunn 2004a). Standards may not have been honored all the time, but the dramatically lower rates of botulism before 1990 suggest that lids usually fit well on jars and that appropriate pasteurization techniques were usually—although not always—followed.[6]

Soviet planners' high-modernist vision was of an entirely state-controlled food supply, and the central ministries attempted to gain control of agriculture even after the disastrous famines caused by Stalinist collectivization. Between 1964 and 1974, Leonid Brezhnev doubled the percentage of the state's budget devoted to agriculture. At 28 percent, it was one of the highest allocations in the developed world. But the official Soviet agricultural system was still unable to supply its citizens' demand and so tolerated semilicit markets of privately produced and traded food. By 1988, 26 percent of Soviet farm output came from private production (Gray 1989). The official response to the burgeoning private market in Russia was quite interesting: Central planners tried in some ways to étatize the gray market by enfolding it into the state's own technopolitical apparatus. State-owned factories started producing thin metal lids and a device known as a *mousakhoupi* that could be used to crimp lids onto recycled glass jars—thereby further endorsing and entwining state-sponsored production and unofficial production. But the technologies produced in statist spaces can be used apart from state-controlled space without necessarily undermining the state project. This was particularly true across the border in Georgia, where mousakhoupis had even fewer ties than in Russia to either the state or the black market: Although the tools filtered from Russia into Georgia in the late 1950s, they were mostly used by people canning fruit as a hobby, much as is commonly done in the United States, rather than as tools for survival.

Georgians' reliance on industrially canned food showed they had clearly developed a taste for the state. Industrially processed food was the product of a state that was an assemblage of the sort that Li and other anthropologists describe: It was pasted together of foreign machines and domestic experts, public health reports and culinary norms, factories and black markets. As it was materialized in mousakhoupis and cans, it was also a remarkably spatially dispersed state, too, that permeated private as well as public life. Like the Soviet infrastructures that Stephen Collier (2004) studied, which made people dependent on bureaucratically controlled thermostats and the municipal power grid, canned food also made people dependent on the infrastructure of the state food sector and let the logic of the state production permeate the cloistered space of the family. During the Soviet period, canned food helped to produce the coherence that is central to the claims and experience of state power because the very materiality of the product condensed the meanings of circulation and consumption and indexed the infrastructure that made it possible. The assemblage looked like a state because it functioned reasonably smoothly to organize the production and distribution of food and prevent foodborne disease. This relative success points to the ways that what people think of as "states" are, in important respects, spatializing projects. They involve the planned distribution of knowledge and resources in particular patterns and often make those patterns material in the form of infrastructures. They create new certainties, lifeways, and expectations about what "the state" will deliver. Like the physical manifestations of the state project in the former Soviet Union—the concrete apartment buildings, paved roads, and canned goods—these lifeways and expectations endured, at least in partial and decayed forms, even after the stable assemblage that was "the state" fell apart.

Dangerous Meals

The end of the Soviet period and the Georgian civil war dramatically altered the apparent solidity of the state. After the end of the "stagnant period" of late socialism and the dissolution of the Soviet Union in 1991, Georgia was wracked by a series of revolutions that left the country subject to what Manning (2007:176) calls "chaotic domination." The first revolution was led by Zviad Gamsakhurdia, who turned the technocratic socialist elites out of their posts in state institutions and replaced them with nationalist intellectuals (Manning 2007:176; cf. Derluguian 2005). The Zviadists launched a destructive series of civil wars in the breakaway republics of Abkhazia and South Ossetia, leaving those provinces decimated and causing 200,000 ethnic Georgians to become refugees in the wake of the defeat of Georgian forces. The refugees, seeking peace and stability, flocked to Tbilisi and took up residence in the old Intourist hotels, which quickly became (even more) dilapidated and crime ridden. But Tbilisi offered no sanctuary from violence. In the winter of 1992, a breakaway faction led by Jaba Ioseliani, the leader of a well-known paramilitary group, and Tengiz Kitovani, a failed sculptor turned strongman, launched a brutal coup d'état against Gamsakhurdia. The battle in the streets of Tbilisi was horrific and ravaged much of the physical infrastructure of the capital city, leaving a half-ruined landscape that municipal residents referred to ironically as "Kitovani's Exhibition." Throughout the next decade, during the entire time that Eduard Shevardnadze ruled Georgia at the invitation of Ioseliani and Kitovani, the ruination of the country continued to worsen because of lack of funds.

By 2002, the year the CDC team came for its first botulism-related visit, the physical infrastructure built in the Soviet project was collapsing. Concrete was falling off the huge apartment blocks in chunks, the roads were so potholed that in many places the concept of traffic lanes had been abandoned, and the power grid was so decayed that some Georgians had not had electricity in over a decade. The state-run medical system was in chaos, and many people avoided treatment because they were unable to pay for it privately. In the food sector, the situation was dire. The circulation that once gave the appearance of solidity to the state had ruptured as Soviet food production and distribution networks fell apart in the early 1990s, and it had not been restored. The Soviet ministries that once ordered food from Georgia for the other republics were gone, and no organized wholesaling structure appeared in their place. The civil wars in South Ossetia, Abkhazia, and Chechnya continued to impede Georgians from accessing major markets in Russia.

Not surprisingly, with few customers around, most of the factories had closed. By 2003, only 3 of Georgia's 58 canneries were operating, and they exported nothing. From producing 760 million cans a year, the industry now made only a little over one million cans, most of them without any government standards or inspection.[7] Derelict factories, once physical manifestations of the Soviet regulatory project, sat deserted on the landscape, their expensive machinery stolen and sold for scrap. "The state," in the sense of an institution that could organize physical infrastructure, use data to monitor production, or enforce norms of sanitation, had withdrawn from the food sector almost entirely. That dissolution had both material and symbolic effects: With the disintegration of the once tightly knit network of institutions, rules, growers, production experts, and standards writers, the apparent solidity of the state vanished, and the fragments of the state, now isolated from one another, presented only semiotic chaos. Because the collapse of the material industrial economy was also a collapse of the representational political economy, the fragmentation of the socialist state infrastructure led to both inscrutability and suspicions of conspiracy in the political domain and the fear of product adulteration among potential consumers of industrially produced food.

For most Georgians, the primary survival strategy in the face of economic collapse was involution, or a turn away from the market and toward nonmonetized production (see Burawoy 2001).[8] With a per capita income of only $591 in 2002 (Varma et al. 2004), most Georgians were forced to rely on products that were made at home, not in the factory. This dramatically changed what Michel-Rolph Trouillot (2001:126) has called the "spatialization effect" of states, or the boundaries and jurisdictions produced by state assemblages. Clearly, in Georgia, the boundaries the Soviet industrialization project had drawn between the city and the country were dissolving, as urbanites moved back to the country part time or began to undo the Soviet industrialization project on-site, by remaking the village in the city. By keeping chickens in pens outside apartment buildings, allowing pigs to forage on urban roadsides, or planting tomatoes in the land surrounding their old factory workplaces, people outside the capital began transforming urban industrial space into agrarian space. Preserving food at home was a key part of this strategy for most Georgian families, largely because they could not afford to buy out-of-season vegetables or commercially canned foods. Zhuzhuna, an unemployed 23-year-old from a village in Samogrelo, put it succinctly: "The doctors say that food made in factories is safer, but a small can is over a lari! We can make more at home for less money." That single lari (about 50 U.S. cents) was a substantial amount of money, especially for rural people who earned less than the national average income of $591.

Cost was not the only factor motivating people to can their own food, however. Although some women felt that industrially canned food was safer than home canned, others saw it as a serious risk, largely because they no longer felt they knew who was making it. For them, the can of food, once a material representation that allowed them to abduct the existence of a unitary authority, now was a symbol of potential fraud and deceit. This was not a phenomenon limited to the food sector but one that pervaded both social relations and material objects:

> With the disappearance of this general unified agency from material and cultural production alike, the world of appearances in all spheres of life increasingly was haunted by multifarious agencies, mediated by now separable economic and political media, money, and power, whose identities and motives were difficult to assign. Postsocialist Georgia, like Russia, was characterized by a failed state and a collapsed economy that corresponded to a more general collapse of semiotic orders: political corruption and manipulation were matched by the falsification of products and inscrutability of advertisements and the general disappearance of orderly, sincere, and "cultured" relationships between private persons. [Manning 2007:177]

As Magda, a sophisticated urbanite working for an NGO, put it, "For some people, commercially canned food is too cheap to be safe. For most people, others, it's too expensive to be affordable." Her statement was echoed by Omar Khacharava, the head of the Department of Food and Food Processing Industries at the Georgian Ministry of Agriculture, who said, "Georgians trust their own products more than the ones they find in the shops. If the quality of the products [in the shops] is good, then the price is high, and people can't afford it." Vardiko, a middle-aged woman from Borjomi, a mountain town famous for its industrially bottled spring water, was both ironic and succinct when she said, "We trust ourselves more than we trust a factory."[9]

Involution did not mean that Georgians returned to pre-Soviet cuisine, however. Although the average Georgian could not fix the roads or the power grid, one product of Soviet infrastructure could be replicated at home: canned vegetables. Many families continued pickling some of their foods—especially those that were not meant to be eaten directly but incorporated into dishes marked as specifically "Georgian." But the overwhelming majority of the more than 100 women I spoke to in focus groups refused to pickle exclusively. Canned food had clearly gained a place in both Georgians' daily cuisine and their ideological responses to the collapse of the state.[10] So, throughout the country, Georgians pulled out their mousakhoupis and began, jar by jar, to remake the red tomatoes of the socialist lifeworld. People's desire for the state, complete with the cohesion of elements that gave it the appearance of unitary authority, was thus made manifest as they tried to replicate the taste of socialism.

However, the disintegration of the state was evident in the decentralization of canning to home kitchens, and what actually happened in the preparation of those jars of tomatoes and peppers was a reproduction of state decay and the "chaotic domination" that characterized both politics and the economy (cf. Manning 2007). This was decidedly true during my first field visit in 2002, while Shevardnadze still reigned over a chaotic and dysfunctional state apparatus. But people's desire for order, their perceptions of chaos, and the material effects of state collapse remained startlingly apparent even after the "Rose Revolution" of 2003, when the pro-U.S. reformer Mikhail Saakashvili ousted Shevardnadze and assumed power. Although Saakashvili attempted to gather the fragments of state institutions together to recreate order, collapse and disorder continued to characterize political, industrial, and agricultural life. As late as 2006, most of the agroprocessing industry remained definitively moribund, and most of the citizenry still had to can its own food. The result was that just as the spores of socialism scattered through private kitchens in the form of jars, disembedded from industrial infrastructure, so too did deadly *C. botulinum* spores scatter through the food.

The central problem was that even after Saakashvili came to power and tried to reconstitute the state, the basic techniques of safe canning, once readily available as formalized standards in an industrial setting, were virtually unknown in the domestic sphere. Because the Saakashvili government did not have the financial resources to create some sort of state project to reinsert these technical standards in the domestic sphere—as agricultural extension does in the United States through agents who provide information about home canning—the family cupboard remained a space largely free of the state. Standards, like the cans, machines, and other pieces of infrastructure that had been disassembled and pulled out of the state project, did not function in the same way they had inside the state assemblage.

This became evident when the CDC team began to talk to home cooks about how they canned vegetables. Despite Georgian National Center for Disease Control efforts to transmit knowledge about botulism, many of the women I spoke with—even women who had personal experience with botulism and who had been contacted by public health officials and, thus, might have reason to know about it—had not received much in the way of information. Guliko, whose home I visited with a team of Georgian epidemiologists in the seaside town of Batumi, had recently gotten a severe case of botulism herself from eating smuggled fish at a banquet commemorating the anniversary of her husband's death. She obviously knew about botulism, told us that she had discussed botulism with both doctors and epidemiologists, and willingly invited us into her small, chilly, concrete-floored home to show us how she canned tomatoes. Despite her repeated contacts with epidemiologists and numerous discussions about botulism, she took a dusty jar off the shelf and put tomatoes directly in it, showing clearly that she had never been informed that botulism spores were found in dirt. The inability of the state project to extend itself in space (which is the basic principle behind "extension") and to inform her about the basic causes of botulism thus left her vulnerable to contracting the disease again.

In Koralistami, the next town over, we interviewed Dariko, a woman living in a once-grand but now decrepit white house in the center of a former tea plantation. Dariko was a less-experienced canner, having been a tea planter. In the Soviet period, she told us, she only served her family canned foods that had been industrially packed, having been too busy making money as a tea planter to waste time canning. However, we thought she might know about botulism because all three of her neighbor's children had contracted the disease from their mother's home-canned food and had died. Any knowledge about home canning and botulism that might have been given to the family of the stricken children clearly had not also been circulated more widely in the village of Koralistami. When we asked Dariko how the children had contracted the disease, she could only hypothesize that "they didn't cook carefully." When we asked her what she did if the lids of her home-canned jars bulged (which indicates that *C. botulinum* is producing neurotoxin and gas), she told us she pricked the lids with a needle, let the gas out, and then sealed the hole with candle wax and put the jar back on the shelf for future use. Obviously, knowledge about safe canning had not traveled along with the canned food itself or with the taste for the food the state once made. The once tightly bound elements of the state project had not dispersed together across social space in a way that mitigated disease.

Many women did know about botulism, and many had home remedies or culinary techniques they believed would prevent foodborne illness. They tipped the glass jars over steaming kettles to "sterilize" them and boiled filled jars for hours. Some of them added aspirin to the jars, again, in an attempt to sterilize them. But even our most knowledgeable informant—an elderly woman in Samogrelo who had been a food technologist in a canning plant before it closed but who now had to can as best she could over an old woodstove—knew no techniques that could make food ripped out of the state project completely safe. Killing *C. botulinum* requires superheating jars to 250 degrees Fahrenheit, which is something that can only be done reliably in a pressure cooker. Unfortunately, pressure cookers are products of a highly industrialized system, whether used in a canning factory or made for home use in a metal fabrication plant, and there were no commercially available pressure cookers in Georgia. This was not a case in which a rich store of folk knowledge could substitute for the abstract formal designs of the state project. Making industrialized food required industrialized knowledge, and this was not available to home cooks.

In a way that might have been predicted by Mary Douglas's (1966) analysis of purity and danger, then, the home cooks who knew about foodborne illness, not surprisingly, often portrayed food as a site of danger. Some women suggested reindustrialization as a solution. But other women, even those who believed that the food made in Soviet factories was safe, expressed real doubts about post-Soviet factories operating in markets devoid of regulation by a unitary and powerful state. Over and over again, they expressed their fears of nebulous shady dealings in an unregulated market and talked about how such lack of regulation might affect their health and well-being. "I'm afraid of industrially canned food," a woman named Sophiko told us in a focus group in Telavi, a region once noted for its wineries and fruit processing plants. "I'm afraid because … it won't be canned properly and we'll be poisoned." Her friend, Nato, expanded on Sophiko's words in a way that made it clear that the dissolution of the state-industrial system had left them unable to identify an agent responsible for food safety and had left the material object, the can, shrouded in a veil of mystery behind which corruption and contamination might lurk. She said, "We don't trust anyone. It's not a matter of money: It's that we don't know who is working there. Everyone lies to us. We can't trust a factory." This is another iteration of the widespread distrust and fear of the powers and unnamed agents who might lurk behind the appearances of objects: Whereas, once, material things, like cans of food, spoke in apparently straightforward ways about the state that produced them, they now seemed to index a shadowy and unknowable "they" who might cause great harm without being detected until it was too late.

State standards had functioned as a proxy for personal knowledge of the factory and allowed eaters to believe in the purity of their food. When they disappeared from food production, they took away certainty and left behind a strong flavor of danger. The sense of danger and disorder was made even worse by the randomness of botulism, a feature the disease shared with other risks from collapsing infrastructure, like the rising number of automobile crashes on decaying roads and asphyxiations caused by the gas heaters that many people used to replace central heating. Because people could do little to prevent botulism, it appeared to be like a random force of nature, beyond rational attempts to calculate risk and avoid it. As Sophiko, always quick to make a telling point, put it, "We have to be certain our food is safe. We have to be certain, but we don't know how to be certain." Here are people who once lived their lives in places strongly ordered by the infrastructure created by state projects, who are nostalgic for the certainty that order provided and who seek to replicate it, but who now find themselves outside the domain of state control and state order.

Paralyzed Infrastructures, Paralyzed Bodies

If Foucault (1977), who so brilliantly read the logics of French sovereign power from the body of the tortured criminal and the logics of governmentality from the body of the incarcerated prisoner, were to come to Georgia, he might immediately recognize the body of the botulism sufferer as a material mirror of the collapsing Soviet Leviathan, the patient's paralyzed nerves a replica of the paralyzed spaces of circulation that once gave the state the appearance of solidity. This body–state configuration is a different spatial configuration than either the one that characterized the high-modernist Soviet state or the flexible, fluid neoliberal one that characterizes contemporary state–industrial complexes like those in the United States or western Europe. The spores of *C. botulinum* are a very different technobiosocial complex than organisms like *Escherichia coli* 0157:H7 or *Listeria monocytogenes*, which flourish in the ecological niches created by consolidated agriculture in the United States. Rather, botulism is a disease of disintegration. The collapsing central nervous system of the patient and the progressive isolation of his or her face, lungs, and limbs mirror the ways that the formerly linked subsystems of the regulatory regime are falling away from each other and losing contact. Interestingly enough, however, each of the proposals to eradicate botulism has shown a different plan for a new kind of neurology, a new spatial configuration of infrastructure and regulation, and a new way to deal with uncertainty.

One proposal was first advanced by the Ministry of Agriculture, a mostly isolated fragment of the old Soviet state housed in a decaying building in Tbilisi. The ministry's proposal was to reinstate the high-modernist command and control mechanism. It wanted to reactivate the old Sovstandardy and restart the domestic canning industry so that the standards could be applied. This reactionary plan had little appeal for the Saakashvili crowd, however, which was intently focused on building relationships with the U.S. government, NGOs, and powerful supranational agencies, including the World Bank, the World Health Organization (WHO), and the Food and Agriculture Organization (FAO). Rather than reinstall Sovstandardy, the post–Rose Revolution government sought to eliminate the semiotic chaos that had led to suspicions of corruption by installing global codes of production and the neoliberal forms of standardization, documentation, and audit that characterize the forms of governmentality currently fashionable in the United States and western Europe. This approach was no surprise, given that Georgian state projects are largely driven by the interests of foreign donors, both private foundations and other nation-states (Koch 2006). Foreign donors showed little enthusiasm for the idea of reestablishing a state project in which the ministry dictated how food was processed and, instead, launched a set of reforms based on neoliberal spatializing projects that claimed to create new technological zones that would allow Georgian products to circulate in international markets (cf. Barry 2001 on similar projects in western Europe).

In a manner typical of many other development projects led by the World Bank, the new technological zones were based on the idea that harmonizing regulatory environments and production practices can overcome the boundaries of the nation-state. As part of a $25-million project, the World Bank financed the Georgian government's adoption of Codex Alimentarius, the global standards for food safety and hygiene that were developed jointly by the FAO and the WHO and that are required as a condition of membership in the WTO. Codex is a good example of the neoliberal "governance at a distance" that Peter Miller and Nikolas Rose (1990) have investigated: Rather than dictating how factories will produce, as Sovstandardy did, Codex uses an approach pioneered by the U.S. government's Hazards Analysis of Critical Control Points program to give managers the flexibility to create their own standards and methods within certain guidelines. After using "science" (in the form of published journal articles) to determine their own production codes, producers also create their own plans to monitor each of the "critical control points" in their production process, to record pertinent data, to rework production if it falls outside the self-determined limits, and to report all the monitoring data to in-house auditors and state regulators.

Because the system is based on the principles of audit and accountability (rather than prescriptive rules about production and subsequent inspection, as both Fordist–capitalist and state socialist production systems were), the new plan for reestablishing the Georgian canning industry did not envision having government inspectors oversee production or check the actual cans coming off the line. Rather, the system driven by international institutions envisioned modern factories in which producers could create their own recipes and canning procedures; record specifics of production like jar type, lid type, ingredients, and pasteurizing temperature; and then forward those records to state inspectors, who could audit the documents without ever touching product to see if a firm was living up to its self-set standards.[11] This is a method based on core neoliberal principles: self-regulation rather than mandates from a dictatorial state, disciplinary authority pushed up to the level of coordinating supranational bodies and given over to the local level instead of being vested in the nation-state, and change driven by the market response to consumer desires rather than by a parentified state eager to protect its citizens. In this sense, Codex Alimentarius is an almost textbook case of the pluralization of regulatory authority that Roitman (2004a, 2004b) and Li (2005) see as the hallmark of the postmodern state: a form of regulatory practice that worms its way into the microspaces of daily life, is advanced by an ostensibly nonstate agency, yet nonetheless links parts of state institutions in a complex network.

As a neoliberal project, Codex Alimentarius is used by the WTO to harmonize national food safety standards and to ensure that they do not create barriers to trade. Because common standards, common forms of audit and enforcement, and common forms of documentation seem to make it possible for a material object (e.g., a can of food) produced under the purview of one nation-state to be perceived by another as indexing a similar kind of state, the organizations that promote the use of Codex claim to be able to create a technological zone that overcomes geographic boundaries and links producers to distant markets. Whereas the Codex Alimentarius Commission claims that Codex standards are aimed at improving public health (FAO–WHO 2004:7), clearly, overcoming what the WTO calls "technical barriers to trade" posed by divergent national standards is also a key goal of Codex:

> The Codex Alimentarius has relevance to the international food trade. With respect to the ever-increasing global market, in particular, the advantages of having universally uniform food standards for the protection of consumers are self-evident. It is not surprising, therefore, that the Agreement on the Application of Sanitary and Phytosanitary Measures (SPS Agreement) and the Agreement on Technical Barriers to Trade (TBT Agreement) both encourage the international harmonization of food standards. Products of the Uruguay Round of multinational trade negotiations, these Agreements cite international standards, guidelines and recommendations as the preferred measures for facilitating international trade in food. As such, Codex standards have become the benchmarks against which national food measures and regulations are evaluated within the legal parameters of the World Trade Organization (WTO) Agreements. [FAO–WHO 2004:7]

Codex is thus an "immutable mobile," to use Latour's (1987) phrase, that claims to link far-distant places not only by being utterly devoid of the specificities of place itself but also by literally making different places, with all their peculiar facilities and habits and infrastructures, equivalent to one another. Codex claims to create new topographies of trade by flattening the particularities of place. For this reason, the Georgian government now holds Codex out as the path to reinvigorating rural economies: With Codex institutionalized in both the law of the nation-state and the physical infrastructure of the factory, Georgian farmers' produce could be processed and shipped to lucrative markets like the European Union. In this vision, Georgian produce standardized by Codex could flow freely once again among disparate places and people, just as standardized Bulgarian-style tomatoes used to circulate throughout the Soviet Union.

In theory, then, a neoliberal project could penetrate local space in the way that Li, Das, and Roitman suggest. This project would create new assemblages of local people, "scientific" techniques, supranational standards, and circulating objects that would, in the way Li suggests, create a new "contingent lashup" (2005:386) that would masquerade as a unitary and coherent state. The problem with this kind of regulatory terraforming, however, is that the collapse of both the economy and the state project has given postsocialist Georgia a peculiar and resistant terrain, one whose morphology does not mesh well with the First World state assemblage that produced

Codex. In the first place, Codex simply requires an entirely different physical infrastructure than the one Georgia has. It requires a high degree of sophistication in both food technology and information management that fits well with the computers, glistening steel tanks, and high-volume lines of Western agroprocessing, which allow large players to absorb costs that often drive smaller players out of the market. However, because Georgia's large canneries have mostly closed, and most of the few remaining agrofood processing firms are tiny startups, Georgians have neither the expertise nor the capital to create an infrastructure that would support Codex.

This was made absolutely clear when I visited a jam factory, one of the largest fruit and vegetable processing facilities in the country, outside of Gori: The factory was set up in the crumbling pig barn of an old collective farm. For equipment, it had only two hand pasteurizers without temperature gauges and a single rusting vat whose heating element cooked erratically. The information technology in the firm, whose owners were participating in a USAID-funded project designed to help them export to the European Union, consisted of a notebook, a pencil, and a colored marker.[12] Clearly, even with help from the Georgian government and foreign donors, it was nearly impossible for Georgian firms to create the kind of material infrastructure in which Codex could take root. Georgia's adoption of Codex, therefore, promises not to create new possibilities for international export of Georgian produce but, rather, very high barriers to Georgians' entry into world markets. Georgian entrepreneurs, who must rely on exports to gain a reasonable economy of scale, may find it difficult to found and grow new enterprises. This makes Codex unlikely to contribute to the development of a factory-owning middle class, reinvigorate the agricultural sector, or overcome Georgia's isolation from world markets.

If the goal of Codex is also, as the Codex Alimentarius Commission says, to uphold the "now universally accepted maxim that people have the right to expect their food to be safe, of good quality, and suitable for consumption" (FAO–WHO 2004:9), it faces yet another set of barriers. Codex is designed for industrial food production. It is so technically and bureaucratically complex that it cannot penetrate the most common space of food production in Georgia: the home kitchen. Georgia's adoption of Codex thus holds out no hope for improving the quality of the most commonly consumed canned foods, because it does not penetrate the nonindustrial, noncommodified spaces in which they are produced.

Worse yet, Georgians have discovered over the last year and a half that the neoliberal project that Codex is a part of can be used not only to incorporate new trading partners but also to exclude, to prevent certain kinds of goods and people from entering into regulated technozones. And this, of course, is exactly what has happened, even in the agricultural industries that have been able to attempt export. In the spring of 2006, Russia—which was in the process of adopting Codex as a part of its bid to join the WTO—declared that none of Georgia's wines met new Russian food safety standards and barred their import. Russian officials' claim that Georgian wines contained either heavy metals or pesticides was probably untrue, given that the United States tested samples of wine and found no threat to human health. At the time, Russia was trying to force Georgia to back off politically and militarily in Abkhazia and South Ossetia, so, although its deployment of food safety standards as a tool of international statecraft in this case was entirely within the rules, it was likely motivated more by geopolitics than by a concern for public health. Now, not only has Georgia lost the fantasy of exporting to the European Union, but it has also lost the $60-million market that was the destination for 90 percent of its wine production. With Codex in place, the export of low-margin goods like canned vegetables to either Russia or the European

Union seems unlikely, to say the least. Standards, the linchpins of the state assemblage once used to link Georgia to faraway consumers, are now being used to create a tight boundary around it, to ensure its isolation from emerging multinational state assemblages, to make the production of botulism-safe food even less likely, and to paralyze the networks of trade that might alleviate poverty in the crumbling country.

What this suggests is that, even though Georgia has a Western-leaning government and international organizations promote the growth of neoliberal projects in other parts of the world, a form of neoliberal governmentality is not penetrating all of Georgia's social space. Rather, although neoliberal projects colonize some of the spaces of Georgian social life very intensively—as Erin Koch (2006) demonstrated in her exploration of a WHO-funded tuberculosis treatment program in a Georgian prison—many other social spaces remain uncolonized, unpenetrated, and largely abandoned. Although the Saakashvili government clearly has the intention of reorganizing Georgia by enrolling international institutions to create new forms of regulation that can knit together people and objects in an assemblage that will allow people to assume the existence of "the state," it clearly has few financial resources, a very weak physical infrastructure, and less political clout than it had right after the Rose Revolution. As Manning points out, aside from a project to paint the buildings in Tbilisi, a few projects to pave the most potholed roads, and a campaign to reform the police, it is "difficult to pinpoint visible achievements of the Saakashvili regime" (2007:202). Despite a series of multimillion-dollar development projects, the Georgian government seems to have abandoned the problems of the countryside, of agroprocessors other than wineries, and of women canning fruits and vegetables. If Georgians fail to abduct authority when they look at their jars of canned food, it is perhaps because there is no coherent authority to abduct.

Haunted Tomatoes: The State in the Nonstate Space

So, in the end, what sickened Teimuraz? What forced his face to slump and his chest to struggle simply to rise with each breath? Why are Teimuraz and his fellow eaters, locked in a tiny postsocialist country, still so vulnerable to a disease that has technologically simple remedies? And why has the rate of infection tripled since the collapse of the Soviet Union in 1990? The explanation, narrowly defined, is given by the CDC epidemiologists making their report in *Emerging Infectious Diseases*: "Poverty likely drives more persons to conserve food; lack of reliable energy sources, clean water, and cooking supplies makes food preservation practices riskier; and food shortage compels persons to rely on preserved food for a larger proportion of their diet" (Varma et al. 2004).

This explanation, however, does not account for hyperendemic botulism in full: The problem is not just poverty and a lack of reliable infrastructure. If it were, botulism would be rampant in other poor countries, like Sierra Leone or Nepal. Rather, the root cause is a form of poverty particular to a postindustrial post-Soviet sphere. Teimuraz's botulism is, first of all, the product of a locally specific nostalgia, dietary desires evoked by a state that no longer exists. People who want canned red tomatoes are harkening back to the taste of the Soviet empire, to a world in which an industrial state provided food to its citizen–consumers as a way of linking them to the body politic. The yearning for red tomatoes thus is not just a longing for vegetables, no matter how tasty, but a culturally and historically specific longing for a lifeworld that was predictable (even if it was predictably awful), a state whose existence one could perceive in the material objects of daily life, and a regulatory environment that provided a measure of physical safety and existential security that no longer obtains. Canned tomatoes are haunted tomatoes, floating silently in jars in which specters of the past are as pervasive as spores of *C. botulinum.*

The ghosts that haunt the cans of vegetables on the dim basement shelves of the Georgian populace, though, are not the edited memories just of a past way of life but also of the policies, standards, factories, and distribution system that once made up the Soviet agrofood infrastructure. The spirits that swirl through the jars and cupboards include Josef Stalin, with his plans to industrialize the cities and turn peasants into a rural proletariat; Brezhnev, with his bloated budgets, pouring more and more money into the agricultural sector to meet ever-increasing demands from the Soviet population; and Gamsakhurdia, the post-Soviet president who led his country into a destructive civil war. Post-Soviet poverty is different than Third World poverty—and produces different diseases—precisely because the space built by Soviet leaders was founded on an enormous infrastructure that shaped the possibilities of production as well as the structures of desire. That assembled infrastructure—the cans, the pasteurizers, the factories, the cuisine, and even the workers who governed and produced—no longer coheres. That this infrastructure does not cohere, however, does not mean it has disappeared: The diverse elements that were once lashed together by the Soviet project now float in social space, unmoored by their previous sociopolitical matrix. The root cause of botulism is thus not poverty per se but the poverty caused by the black hole left behind by the collapsing Soviet red star, symbol of a state whose disintegrating material infrastructure pulled the force of its regulatory endeavors into nonexistence along with it.

Although the food, the land, and the cupboards are now nonstate spaces, they are nonstate spaces of a distinct kind. The state is gone, but the memory of the state is omnipresent in the growers' and canners' memories of state-produced goods and in their expectation that the Georgian state should be doing something to make the food safer. This means both the food and the infrastructure of agricultural production that surrounds it are not only characterized by the absence of the state but also by the postpresence of the state. Understanding that postpresence and its relationship to the variously integrative and disintegrating assemblages of the state is a means to complexify anthropological understandings of the state. The Georgian case suggests that, rather than assuming the ubiquity of the neoliberal state and proceeding to index it by pointing out the bits and pieces of state assemblages as they intrude into everyday life, it is important to see different kinds of state assemblages and their movements in and out of particular social spaces. This requires understanding their lingering historical effects and exploring the ways in which the debris left behind by old regimes sharply constrains the possibilities of the states that succeed them.

As powerful as the lingering ghosts of the past are, however, it would be a mistake to see the ongoing presence of the state in canned foods and the longings they evoke. The jars of vegetables that once were infused by the state are not elements reincorporated into neoliberal projects but have definitely become nonstate spaces free from regulation or standardization. This is what has turned the family cupboards once regulated by Soviet bureaucracy into zones of unpredictability and danger. The rate of botulism, which has tripled since 1990, indicates that the Georgian food sector has not become bound up in a transnational neoliberal project but, instead, has become a zone uncontrolled by the state. The existence of hyperendemic botulism thus challenges the assumption that neoliberal state projects are ubiquitous and all-encompassing. That argument is only about one kind of space: macroscale topographic space, the kind of space that can be delineated on a map. Li (2005) argues that every human being has some interaction with some form of state, if only in his or her imaginings and expectations of states, and, therefore, that there are no virgin territories of statelessness. She may well be right in this regard, but this vision of both space and statelessness is a very limited one. By looking at social spaces rather than topographic ones and examining space at different scales, it is clear that the state does not infuse all aspects of lived geographies. Although there may be no mountaintops that are sanctuaries from state projects, a look at sectoral spaces formed by production and circulation (or the lack thereof) and the microspaces of lived experience shows the existence of many nonstate spaces.

These stateless spaces in Georgia were first created by the implosion of the Soviet system, and they are now constantly replicated not by the collapse of the old state but by the disregard of the new one assembled from the weak Georgian national government, the World Bank, NGOs, standards including Codex Alimentarius, and the technologies and practices of global agricultural processing. This new state does little to penetrate the spaces of Georgian agriculture or to draw its dispersed elements back into a coherent arrangement; the food sector (with certain limited exceptions for winemaking and mineral-water bottling)[13] is abandoned territory, a space free from mobile neoliberal calculations because neither state agents nor capitalist firms choose to calculate there.

Georgian agriculture is thus one of the "exceptions to neoliberalism" discussed by Ong (2006b): neither integrated into the regime of global governance nor reduced to what Giorgio Agamben might call "bare life" (because even the institutions of bare life require a great deal of attention and activity by facets of the state assemblage) but, rather, left as disarticulated, unused, useless space. This is not to say that Georgia is entirely stateless or entirely outside the domain of neoliberal governance: As in many other places, Georgia has islands of tight regulation and frenetic statist activity interspersed in the sea of state withdrawal. Where transnational projects enroll the Georgian nation-state, in places like the area between the chain-link fences that surround the Baku–Tbilisi–Ceyhan oil pipeline or the prison hospitals for tuberculosis treatment sponsored by the WHO (Koch 2006), regulation is high, rules are enforced, and order is created. Outside those zones, though, large swathes of social space are deemed useless to the statist regulatory project and largely abandoned by both the nation-state and the concatenation of supranational agencies and NGOs that partially supplant it. Like the parts of Africa judged by 19th-century colonial administrators to be "inutile" or "unusable" (Ferguson 2005; Friedberg 2004), Georgia is spatially divided into zones "utile" and "inutile" for neoliberal governance. What this division creates, in the end, is not a homogeneous territory of national sovereignty—as Sarah Radcliffe (2001) suggests—but patchy and variegated spaces of differential regulation. As Ong puts it, "The logic of the exception fragments human territoriality in the interests of forging specific, variable, and contingent connections to global circuits" (2006b:19). Or of not forging such connections: Codex Alimentarius, despite claims that it facilitates inclusion, is used here as the knife that separates the economically useful wheat from the useless chaff. By imposing a set of rules so incompatible with the current infrastructure of Georgian food production, the regulatory framework that promises to create circulation in a common technozone, instead, sets up a boundary that excludes the majority of the people in Georgia who might seek to enter globalized spaces of agricultural trade. This counterintuitive outcome of global regulation requires one to ask how globalizing state projects, ones aimed at integrating places into a single system by making them alike or equivalent, often end up, instead, creating such wildly different kinds of social space. As Ong points out, neoliberalism is not "an ensemble of coordinates that will everywhere produce the same political results and social transformations" but "a migratory technology of governing that interacts with situated sets of elements and circumstances" (2006a:5). In entering into a specific historical and material milieu, here the debris left behind by the Soviet state in Georgia, neoliberal projects create not only arenas of tight inclusion into neoliberally governed circuits of exchange but also spaces and populations that are seen as not interesting enough, or not useful enough, to merit governance. In these spaces in which citizenship and sovereignty have been pried apart (Ong 2006b:19), people become subjects who must look beyond the state to safeguard not only their rights or their livelihoods but also their very lives.

Acknowledgments

I would like to thank Holly High, Michele Rivkin-Fish, Ziggy Rivkin-Fish, Jay Varma, Katrina Kretsinger, Jeremy Sobel, Tamar Zardiashvili, Neli Chakvetadze, Paata Imnadze, Jenny Smith, Kay Mansfield, the Georgian National Center for Disease Control, and the members of the colloquium series at Yale University's Center for Agrarian Studies for their help on this article.

Notes

1 To protect patient privacy, I use pseudonyms for all the individuals mentioned in this article. I have also amalgamated the very similar stories of two patients—both of whom I met in the same hospital on the same day—into a single story to eliminate any personally identifiable information.

2 For anyone interested in trying Georgian food—and I highly recommend it—Darra Goldstein's cookbook *The Georgian Feast* (1993) has not only fascinating discussions of regional cuisines but also tasty recipes that are easy to prepare. I own two copies: a clean one for my office and a well-spattered copy for the kitchen.

3 I owe thanks for these data to Omar Khacharava of the Georgian Ministry of Agriculture. Jenny Leigh Smith (n.d.) also suggests that the postwar period saw an enormous upswing in the introduction of food technology and the production of durable foods for distribution.

4 The canning process was invented by Nicholas Appert in 1795, in response to a call from the Napoleonic government to solve the problems of providing for soldiers on the march who could be cut off from supply lines. As Jack Goody (1982:157–158) explains, the industrial canning process was not introduced until 1809 but soon became important in supplying long sea voyages as well as the land armies that helped create empire.

5 I owe thanks to Stephen Wegren for this schema.

6 The rate of botulism in Georgia between 1980 and 1990 was 0.03 per 100,000. Incidence tripled after the collapse of the Soviet Union, however, to an annual average of 0.09 per 100,000 from 1991 to 2002 (Varma et al. 2004).

7 These data come from Omar Khacharava, Georgian Ministry of Agriculture.

8 After the "Rose Revolution" of 2003, there were some indications that both the United States and the European Union were attempting to assure Georgia's geopolitical loyalties by helping to reestablish agroprocessing. But this appeared to be mostly taking place in the wine sector, with no successful ventures in the processing of other fruits and vegetables.

9 Ironically, in 2006 Russian authorities banned the import of Borjomi brand water bottled in Vardiko's town. The Russians claimed not only that the product made in Borjomi was adulterated but also that counterfeiters were bottling water in unregulated factories, thus potentially contaminating it, and then slapping a Borjomi label on it and trying to sell it as the real thing. Vardiko may have been speaking from concrete knowledge when she said she trusted herself more than she trusted a factory. See also N. 13.

10 One of the reasons that Georgian cuisine is so robust, so varied, and so elaborated is that it plays a striking role in the creation of national identity. People very often consume foods that are explicitly marked as "Georgian" and thought to be traditional, and they do so at the supra that are held up as a unique feature of Georgian culture. Nonetheless, it is striking to see how many imported, industrially manufactured foods—some of them very explicitly marked as Soviet in origin—have been incorporated into Georgian eating habits and even into dishes that are said to be part of Georgia's national cuisine. One good example is canned peas, which are an essential component of very popular mayonnaise-based salads. Several of the women I interviewed and cooked with were adamant that the peas be industrially canned because home-canned peas failed to attain the degree of mushiness required for their incorporation in these salads. Thanks to Erin Koch for pressing me on this point.

11 See Dunn 2003, 2004b, and 2007 for more in-depth discussion of audit-based food safety systems in European and U.S. agriculture.

12 The jam factory was participating in a project run by ACDI–VOCA, a private development agency staffed by volunteers, which was funded by USAID.

13 And even in these cases, the degree to which any state assemblage, neoliberal or not, is governing is questionable. In 2006, the chief sanitary inspector of Russia declared that Georgian wine and water was tainted with pesticides and heavy metals. Additionally, he claimed that Georgian wines were "falsified," meaning that they were mixtures of alcohol, flavorings, and colorings rather than true wine fermented from grapes. Although most observers believed this was a political move designed to punish Georgia for creating close ties with Washington, D.C., and seeking to join NATO (e.g., Mainville 2006), even the Georgian government admitted that many products sold in Russia as Georgian wines are neither wines nor produced in Georgia

References Cited

Abrams, Philip
    1988 Notes on the Difficulty of Studying the State. Journal of Historical Sociology 11(1):58–89.
Barry, Andrew
    2001 Political Machines: Governing in an Anxious Age. London: Athlone.
Burawoy, Michael
    2001 Transition without Transformation: Russia's Involuntary Road to Capitalism. Eastern European Politics and Societies 15(2):269–291.
Central Intelligence Agency, Office of Documents and Reports
    1953 The Food Canning Industry in the USSR. Case Number EO-1999-00314. Electronic document, http://www.foia.cia.gov/princeton.asp, accessed January 12, 2006.
Collier, Stephen
    2004 Pipes. In Patterned Ground: Entanglements of Nature and Culture. Stephan Harrison, Steve Pile, and Nigel Thrift, eds. Pp. 50–52. Chicago: University of Chicago Press.
Das, Veena, and Deborah Poole
    2004 The State and Its Margins: Comparative Ethnographies. In Anthropology in the Margins of the State. Veena Das and Deborah Poole, eds. Pp. 3–34. Santa Fe: School of American Research Press.

Derluguian, Georgi M.
    2005 Bourdieu's Secret Admirer in the Caucasus: A World System Biography. Chicago: University
        of Chicago Press.
Douglas, Mary
    1966 Purity and Danger: An Analysis of the Concepts of Pollution and Taboo. London: Routledge.
Dunn, Elizabeth
    1996 Money, Morality, and Modes of Civil Society among Mormons. *In* Civil Society: Challenging
        Western Models. Elizabeth Dunn and Chris Hann, eds. Pp. 27–49. London: Routledge.
    2003 Trojan Pig: Paradoxes of Food Safety Regulation. Environment and Planning A 35:1493–1511.
    2004a Privatizing Poland: Baby Food, Big Business, and the Remaking of Labor. Ithaca, NY: Cornell
        University Press.
    2004b Standards and Person Making in East Central Europe. *In* Global
        Anthropologies: Governmentality, Technology, Ethics. Aihwa Ong and Stephen Collier, eds. Pp.
        173–193. London: Blackwell.
    2007 *Escherichia coli*, Corporate Discipline, and the Failure of Audit. Space and Polity 11:35–53.
Ferguson, James
    1990 The Anti-Politics Machine: "Development," Depoliticization, and Bureaucratic Power in
        Lesotho. Cambridge: Cambridge University Press.
    2005 Seeing Like an Oil Company: Space, Security and Global Capital in Neoliberal Africa. American
        Anthropologist 107(3):377–382.
Ferguson, James, and Akhil Gupta
    2002 Spatializing States: Towards an Ethnography of Neoliberal Governmentality. American
        Ethnologist 29(4): 981–1002.
Food and Agriculture Organization and World Health Organization (FAO–WHO)
    2004 Understanding Codex Alimentarius. Electronic document, http://www.codexalimentarius.net/
        web/index_en.jsp#, accessed April 14, 2006.
Foucault, Michel
    1977 Discipline and Punish: The Birth of the Prison. New York: Pantheon.
Friedberg, Suzanne
    2004 French Beans and Food Scares. Oxford: Oxford University Press.
Gell, Alfred
    1998 Art and Agency: An Anthropological Theory. Oxford: Oxford University Press.
Goldstein, Darra
    1993 The Georgian Feast. Berkeley: University of California Press.
Goody, Jack
    1982 Cooking, Cuisine, and Class: A Study in Comparative Sociology. Cambridge: Cambridge
        University Press.
Gray, Kenneth
    1989 The Soviet Food Complex in a Time of Change. National Food Review, Oct.–Dec. Electronic
        document, http://www.findarticles.com/p/articles/mi_m3284/is_n4_v12/ai_8274317, accessed
        April 24, 2006.
Herzfeld, Michael
    2005 Political Optics and the Occlusion of Intimate Knowledge. American Anthropologist
        107(3):369–376.
Koch, Erin
    2006 Beyond Suspicion: Evidence, (Un)Certainty, and Tuberculosis in Georgian Prisons. American
        Ethnologist 33(1):50–62.
Latour, Bruno
    1987 Science in Action. Cambridge, MA: Harvard University Press.
Layton, Robert
    2003 *Art and Agency*: A Reassessment. Journal of the Royal Anthropological Society 9(3):447–464.

Li, Tania Murray
 2005 Beyond "the State" and Failed Schemes. American Anthropologist 107(3):383–394.
Mainville, Michael
 2006 Sour Grapes: Georgian Wines Banned. Canadian Business, November 20. Electronic
  document, http://www.canadianbusiness.com/managing/strategy/article.jsp?cont
  ent=20061120_82714_82714, accessed May 14.
Manning, Paul
 2007 Rose-Colored Glasses? Color Revolutions and Cartoon Chaos in Postsocialist Georgia.
  Cultural Anthropology 22(2):171–213.
Miller, Peter, and Nikolas Rose
 1990 Governing Economic Life. Economy and Society 19(1):1–31.
Mitchell, Timothy
 2006 Society, Economy, and the State Effect. In The Anthropology of the State: A Reader. Aradhana
  Sharma and Akhil Gupta, eds. Pp. 169–186. London: Blackwell.
Navaro-Yashin, Yael
 2002 Faces of the State: Secularism and Public Life in Turkey. Princeton: Princeton University Press.
Ohmae, Kenichiro
 2005 The Next Global Stage. Philadelphia: Wharton/Pearson.
Ong, Aihwa
 2006a Neoliberalism as a Mobile Technology. Transactions 31:1–6.
 2006b Neoliberalism as Exception: Mutations in Citizenship and Sovereignty. Durham, NC: Duke
  University Press.
Ong, Aihwa, and Stephen J. Collier
 2004 Global Assemblages: Technology, Politics and Ethics as Anthropological Problems.
  London: Blackwell.
Radcliffe, Sarah
 2001 Imagining the State as a Space: Territoriality and the Formation of the State in Ecuador.
  In States of Imagination: Ethnographic Explorations of the Postcolonial State. Thomas Blom
  Hansen and Finn Stepputat, eds. Pp. 123–148. Durham, NC: Duke University Press.
Roitman, Janet
 2004a Fiscal Disobedience: An Anthropology of Economic Regulation in Central Africa.
  Princeton: Princeton University Press.
 2004b Productivity in the Margins: The Reconstitution of State Power in the Chad Basin. In
  Anthropology in the Margins of the State. Veena Das and Deborah Poole, eds. Pp. 3–34. Santa
  Fe: School of American Research Press.
Scott, James C.
 1998 Seeing Like a State: How Certain Schemes to Improve the Human Condition Have Failed.
  New Haven, CT: Yale University Press.
Sharma, Aradhana, and Akhil Gupta
 2006 Introduction: Rethinking Theories of the State in an Age of Globalization. In The Anthropology
  of the State: A Reader. Aradhana Sharma and Akhil Gupta, eds. Pp. 1–42. London: Blackwell.
Shephard, Sue
 2000 Pickled, Potted and Canned: How the Art of Food Preserving Changed the World.
  New York: Simon and Schuster.
Smith, Jenny Leigh
 N.d. Empire of Ice Cream: How Life Got Sweeter in the Postwar Soviet Union. Unpublished MS,
  History of Medicine and Science Program, Yale University.
Stark, David
 1992 Path Dependence and Privatization Strategies in Eastern and Central Europe. European
  Politics and Societies 6(1):17–54.
Trouillot, Michel-Rolph
 2001 The Anthropology of the State in an Age of Globalization. Current Anthropology 42(1):125–138.

Varma, J. K., G. Katsitadze, M. Moiscrafishvili, T. Zardiashvili, M. Chokheli, and N. Tarkhashvili
    2004 Foodborne Botulism in the Republic of Georgia. Emerging Infectious Diseases. Electronic
    document, http://www.cdc.gov/ncidod/EID/vol10no9/03-0806.htm, accessed June 10, 2006.
Verdery, Katherine
    1996 The Etatization of Time in Ceausescu's Romania. *In* What Was Socialism and What Comes
    Next? Pp. 37–53. Princeton: Princeton University Press.

9

Everyday Approaches to Food Safety in Kunming

Jakob A. Klein

In an August 2008 interview in her Kunming home, Ms Wang explained that after rinsing vegetables she had bought at the market, she would soak them for a while in water before cooking.

Klein: Why do you soak them?

Wang: Because of the pesticides nowadays.

Klein: Oh.

Wang: There could be some residues and that.

Klein: Oh.

Wang: Once I bought some cabbage (*baicai* 白菜). When I got home I put it in water and immediately it emitted a thick smell of pesticides. At first I didn't think much of it. I just felt the odour was weird. But still I boiled it. When we ate it, it just stuck in our throats, so we stopped eating it. I was so angry that time. This was cabbage I had bought at Zuanxin 纂新 [one of the largest covered markets in the city]. That time I even called "315" to complain [to the Yunnan Consumers' Association].

Klein: Really?

Wang: I don't think it made a difference. But since that event I have become especially careful when choosing vegetables.

Ms Wang's experience is part of what has been described as a growing concern with food safety among Chinese urban consumers.[1] This article investigates how urban Chinese have interpreted and acted upon food-related environmental health threats, particularly in the context of food shopping, and considers the ways in which concerns with food safety have shaped people's everyday life practices and impacted on their experiences of recent social change.

Ulrich Beck's depiction of a "risk society" may help us to understand experiences of food safety risks in China.[2] According to Beck, modern risk society is marked by a pervasive sense of uncertainty arising from hazards produced by technological industrialization itself. In China, the nature of food safety hazards has changed since the 1980s. In addition to long-standing problems with microbial contamination, prevalent problems now also include pesticide poisoning of farmers and consumers, heavy metal pollution from industries, the misuse of dangerous veterinary drugs, fungicides and other additives in animal feed, the use of harmful food additives, and animal-borne illnesses.[3] While some have attributed these problems to China's large number of small-scale food producers[4] or to the "fragmentation of regulatory authority among different government agencies,"[5] the country's food safety issues are also typical of a globalizing food system in which food supplies have become ever more divorced from their regional moorings and dependent on long distance trade and intensified production methods.[6] As with other hazards typical of a "risk society," many new food-related public health threats, from SARS to melamine-tainted milk powder, have been geographically dispersed, crossing regional and sometimes national boundaries. These threats have been hard for experts to identify and for authorities to contain, and they have been difficult – if not, following Ms Wang's account, always impossible – to detect with the senses. Thus, food-related risks in China are in many respects similar to those in the industrialized countries that are the focus of Beck's analysis, but are in other respects rather different. In his recent survey of food safety problems in China, Yunxiang Yan draws on and modifies Beck's theory to argue that "risk society" in China is, as elsewhere, characterized by a growing concern with "unsafe food" – for example the chemically contaminated foods typical of industrialized agriculture – but, unlike in industrialized countries, also by persistent worries about far-reaching food hygiene problems (not least in the catering industry), and an increasing focus on what Yan calls "poisonous foods" – the deliberate contamination of food by unscrupulous producers and traders.[7]

According to Beck and others, the uncertainty produced by technological industrialization is exacerbated by "individualization," a process by which people have become divorced from the institutions, cultural frameworks and authorities that had once provided some assurances in the face of risk.[8] According to Ms Wang's description, she must choose, soak and taste each vegetable for signs of pesticide residues. Although she has some recourse to a consumer watchdog, it is up to her to make the complaint. Bryan Tilt … argues that Chinese people in the reform era are indeed facing environmental health risks in a context of "individualization."[9] Tilt draws on the work of Yunxiang Yan, who maintains that this process has been led by the Party-state, and has involved the "untying" of the individual from collective institutions such as kinship groups and socialist work units.[10] Thus, under radical state socialism, the state organized the production and distribution of food, and was responsible for the adequacy and the quality of the food supply. In the cities, households were usually the main site of food consumption, but state and collective work units were important nodes in the rationing system and also provided many cooked meals, while uncooked food was purchased from state-run shops.[11] However, since the end of the 1970s, market forces have come to play an ever more crucial part in the food system, and since the 1990s, the importance of the work unit has greatly diminished. The responsibility for food safety and other aspects of the food supply have become distributed between the state, the food industries and consumers. New institutions, laws and management systems have been introduced to address food safety within the food industries.[12] At the same time, growing consumer choice has been accompanied by greater personal responsibility over what to eat, as emphasized through information campaigns in supermarkets, food markets, workplaces and residential neighbourhoods. The emphasis on personal responsibility for food safety parallels education campaigns in the areas of nutritional health and child rearing.[13]

Beck's emphasis on universalized uncertainties and individualized responses is a useful starting point which helps to frame some of my informants' experiences and also situates them within broader, global processes. The limitations of the "risk society" framework are suggested by accounts which highlight diversities in approaches to food-related risks. Caplan argues that degrees of distance to food producers informed consumer responses to BSE in the UK,[14] while Kjærnes, Harvey and Warde highlight the importance of national institutional contexts for shaping different degrees of trust in food across Europe.[15] Writing on China, some have argued that awareness of food safety risks and willingness to pay a premium for certified "safe" foods are shaped by levels of income and education.[16] An important recent study by Veeck, Yu and Burns on consumer approaches to food-related risk in four eastern cities emphasizes the significance of Chinese historical memories of food insecurity, and contends that amongst urban Chinese the "goods" of increased dietary abundance outweighed the "bads" of food safety risks.[17] Yan, by contrast, argues that the coexistence in China of different types of food safety problems, and especially the prevalence of "poisonous food," was contributing not only to a "deeply felt sense of insecurity,"[18] but significantly also to a "rapid decline of social trust."[19]

As these studies highlight, the way people make sense of and act upon risks related to food cannot be assumed, but needs to be investigated empirically. Here, I will compliment these approaches with a more localized attention to regional food culture and experiences of urban change. As a "risk society" approach would anticipate, people in Kunming did describe increasing uncertainties about food, and many viewed this as a result of a delocalization and intensification of the food supply. Further, in their daily food shopping practices, Kunmingers displayed limited trust in existing regulatory systems, relying instead on their own skills and experiences. Nevertheless, this article takes issue with the "individualization" argument. Shoppers did not interpret and act upon food safety threats as "untied" individuals. Instead, their approaches were informed by ties with family members and by cultural understandings of food. I complicate Yan's description of growing social distrust and argue that in the process of dealing with food safety risks, forms of trust reliant on new connections with people and to place have emerged. However, in contrast to the optimism of Veeck, Yu and Burns, I suggest that in Kunming concerns about the food supply were feeding into wider ambivalences about modernization and that this was especially acute among the economically disadvantaged, whose access to desired foods was being limited by stricter regulation of urban space.

Households

I carried out four months of ethnographic research in Kunming between 2006 and 2009.[20] Research included conversations and observations in food markets, shops, restaurants, and at "ecological" farms. My discussion relies especially on material collected through household food studies, mostly in the summer of 2008. These consisted of interviews with members of 25 households about food shopping, cooking and eating. The main shopper of the household was interviewed, and in many cases more than one person from the household took part. Most, but not all, principal shoppers were women, and in some households shopping was regularly undertaken by two or more members. Interviews took place in people's homes, at workplaces, cafes or restaurants, and lasted between 50 minutes and two hours. All but two of the interviews were recorded and transcribed. Follow-up meetings were arranged wherever possible. In 18 of the households the main interviewee completed a one-week food diary in which she or he recorded what they ate, where and with whom, what foods they bought and how much they spent on these.

… The majority of the households studied were nuclear and joint family households. In these households, shoppers articulated food choices and worries largely in terms of other family members, especially children. This sentiment was addressed in a billboard in a Kunming suburb which advertised "ecological" garden plots for rent. The billboard showed two children smiling at delicious-looking vegetables. The caption read: "Don't let your children eat any more vegetables fed on pesticides and chemical fertilizers" (*Bie rang nin de haizi zai chi nongyao huafei weida de shucai* 别让您的孩子再吃农药化肥喂大的蔬菜). The billboard voiced parents' concerns for their children's health, but the smiling children also highlighted the significance of good food as a source of family happiness. Among the families I met, enjoying good food together was considered to be an important part of family life, and on weekends and public holidays, family members, often from several households, would gather around food. Indeed, the garden plots advertised on the billboard were tended to by labourers during the week, and visited at weekends by middle-class families who would pick vegetables from their plot and often cook and eat them on the spot. Commensality has long been crucial to Chinese notions of family,[21] and as Yan has argued, in China "individualization" has not led to the demise of the family. On the contrary, with the dismantling of larger collective institutions, the family has become a key site for personal fulfilment and emotional attachment.[22]

Arguably, the centrality of food for the health, happiness and identity of the family has added to the seriousness of growing uncertainties surrounding the food supply, as suggested in the billboard described above. Certainly, the importance of food in family life contributed to the anxieties of food shopping for women such as Ms Ao, who described the difficulties of catering to the tastes and dietary needs of her husband and son on a limited budget. In other households, as mentioned, responsibilities were shared by two or more people, and in many households even everyday food shopping was a topic of shared discussion. While shared responsibility and debate could lead to conflicts,[23] it also meant that knowledge about food and shopping was not entirely "individualized." Ms Wang, for example, explained that while food shopping was a constant source of tension between the generations in her household, it was her live-in grandmother who taught her the many skills she used to choose, clean and cook food.

Cuisine and Urban Change

Shopping was done mostly in open-air or covered food markets, and at supermarkets. Most of the households I interviewed, including the low-income households, frequented both. They reported shopping daily or several times a week at food markets to purchase fresh food, and making occasional (monthly or weekly) visits to supermarkets to stock up on non-food items and on staple foods such as rice and cooking oil. On their trips to the market, shoppers used a number of methods for choosing "safe" vegetables. Ms Yang, a recently retired university librarian married to a professor, would look for leafy vegetables with insect holes, reasoning that if insects ate them they could not contain pesticides. Ms Liang, an office worker in a city government bureau, argued that cauliflowers should not be too white: "It feels like they have chemical fertilizers in them, that they exceed [prescribed limits]. You must choose the ones that are from the mountains, they are slightly yellow. They don't look pretty." Similarly, she told me, tomatoes should not be evenly red, as it suggests that they have been grown in a plastic greenhouse. Once home, both Liang and Yang would soak their vegetables in water before cooking them.

These strategies might be described as "individualized" in the sense that they had been developed by food shoppers aware that they were themselves responsible for ensuring the safety of their foods. However, such strategies also reflect knowledge, values and discussions about food shared both within and between households. They were informed by a "cuisine," in Mintz's sense of "the ongoing foodways of a region, within which active discourse about food sustains both common understandings and reliable production of the foods in question."[24] Cuisine in this sense is not static – indeed reliable production is not always sustained. Nevertheless, in Kunming changes to the food supply were mediated by everyday culinary practices, values and discourses on food.

The extent to which "food safety" strategies and discussions were embedded in regional cuisine was evident in the kinds of food people spoke about when discussing food safety concerns. Thus, while interviewees did mention concerns with a range of foodstuffs, including milk, oil, rice and dried goods, nothing was talked about as much as fresh vegetables and fresh meat, especially pork but also chicken and eggs.[25] A majority of the households ate pork two or more times each day, and it was a crucial food at most festive occasions. Chicken was the main ingredient in regional "signature foods"[26] like "steam pot chicken soup" (qiguoji 汽锅鸡). Kunmingers often highlighted with satisfaction that their mild climate allowed them to eat fresh leafy greens all year round, and many households reported regularly eating two or more vegetable dishes with midday and evening meals. Often, leafy greens were boiled in stock or simply in water, and served in the soup with a side dip of spices. This method was meant to bring out the "sweetness" of the vegetable itself and to achieve a mouth-melting texture, known in the local dialect as pa.

Not all foods important to the cuisine were regarded as equally risky. Rice is Kunming's main grain staple, and people hold strong opinions about its proper taste and texture, but the rice available in the city was rarely mentioned as a health risk. While recent migrants complained about the taste of the rice in the city, most native Kunmingers I spoke with agreed that the rice had become softer and more fragrant in the last 30 years. Kunming has, in fact, depended on imported rice since the 18th century.[27] By contrast, green vegetables, pork, eggs and chicken have until recently been supplied entirely locally, often from within the greater municipality. Thus, discourse on "food safety" reflected concerns with the disconnection of people from place.

The significance of cuisine was apparent also in the kinds of risks that people highlighted in conversations. Thus, although the majority of food safety incidents in China have involved microbial contamination resulting from poor hygiene practices,[28] and although hygiene was the main focus of public information campaigns, my interviewees rarely talked about these risks in relation to food shopping. Instead, they talked about risks associated with the industrialization of food production. All of the Kunmingers I spoke with expressed concern about the use of chemical fertilizers and pesticides in vegetable production. Other frequently mentioned concerns had to do with the use of growth hormones and chemical additives in animal feed.[29]

When it came to the health risks posed, few specified the dangers of particular chemicals or pollutants or distinguished between different kinds of agrichemicals. People talked in general terms about an increase in "cancers" or "illnesses" since the 1990s, and linked this to changes to the food supply. Informants claimed that foods had all become "polluted" (*wuran* 污染) and "unnatural" (*bu ziran* 不自然). By this, they referred not only to contamination by industrial pollution, agrichemicals or additives, but also to the increasing presence of non-seasonal vegetables, either imports from other regions or vegetables grown closer to the city but in plastic greenhouses, often called "greenhouse vegetables" (*dapeng cai* 大棚菜). For older informants in particular, eating seasonal foods underpinned the connection between people and the places where they lived, and was considered crucial to maintaining bodily balance between "heating" and "cooling." Mr Jia, a retired mechanic, argued that it used to be that every season had its proper vegetables, but now everything was "muddled" (*luantaole* 舌匚套了). Furthermore, "greenhouse vegetables," "feed pork" and other industrialized foods were described as having a bad taste and "mouth feel," and this was perceived to be connected to their healthiness. Ms Wu, a retired accountant who had recently become an enthusiastic customer and volunteer at a certified "organic" (*youji* 有机) farm near the city, explained that since they had started buying organic food, her husband had not only begun to enjoy eating vegetables, but had also been cured of his back pains and sleeping problems.[30]

Kunmingers' approaches to "food safety" were shaped in a social context of shared discourses on food, in which taste, health and place were interlinked. These discourses focused on foods that were important to everyday and festive diets and that were markers of regional identity. These were also foods which until recently had been supplied exclusively from the immediate surrounding countryside. Fears of ingesting residues of pesticides or growth hormones were conflated with generalized concerns about intensified production methods, described as "unnatural" or "polluted" because they defied what was perceived to be the proper order between food, people and place. Thus, concerns about the safety of foods were embedded in discussions about quality, taste and health.

Nevertheless, while "cuisine" provided a framework for approaching food safety hazards, the importance of cuisine could itself contribute to uncertainties over food. For example, while shoppers wanted to buy "natural" foods, they also valued "freshness" (*xinxian* 新舍羊). Freshness was regarded as a determinant of taste and healthiness, and it was the reason informants gave for taking daily or near-daily shopping trips to the market. Marketplace vendors insisted on the freshness of their produce and did their best to keep their vegetables looking bright, clean and pretty. However, there was a tension between these practices and the notion that vegetables that were too pretty contained too many agrichemicals. Furthermore, the attachment to region as a source of tasty, healthy foods itself contributed to feelings of disconnection. Thus, while people I met rarely spoke about concerns about fish, this was because fish had ceased to be an important part of their diet as a result of recent environmental degradation. Kunming is situated on the northern shores of Lake Dian (*Dianchi* 滇池). When people did talk about fish in relation to food safety, they mentioned that they used to eat more of it, but that now nobody dared to eat the fish from the polluted Lake Dian. Many recalled with nostalgia stories of catching and eating fish from the lake and from local streams.

The connection between food and place suggest that Kunmingers' experiences of changes to the food supply cannot be isolated from their experiences of wider social and spatial urban change.[31] A late developer, Kunming has been rebuilt since the mid-1990s in an effort to "catch up" with the eastern seaboard. It now boasts shopping malls with international chains and garden-style residential neighbourhoods for the new middle class. State-led modernization has included attempts to sanitize urban spaces, as in the 2009 campaign to transform Kunming into a "city of hygiene" (*weisheng chengshi* 卫生城市). Such campaigns, involving government bodies such as Kunming's city management bureau (*chengguanju* 城管局) and its hygiene bureau (*weishengju* 卫生局), have included food safety education and inspections of the city's food markets, as well as efforts to "cleanse" the city of street vendors, including farmers from nearby villages selling their own goods. With an official urban population of over three million, the city has doubled in size since the mid-1990s, encroaching on the surrounding countryside and exacerbating pollution and land conflicts. Increasingly, Kunming is marked by social divisions between the new rich and the urban poor, and between urban residents and rural migrants.

The ongoing significance of a regional cuisine provides Kunmingers with a cultural framework in which to interpret recent changes to the food supply. At the same time, the cultural importance given to food in connecting people with place contributes to the sense of rupture caused by rapid urban modernization.

Trust and Place

In response to the uncertainties surrounding the food supply, food providers, the state and consumers themselves have developed numerous strategies to increase trust in food. Government agencies have carried out visible and publicized controls in markets, and have backed a number of food certification schemes. Supermarkets use food safety messages in their strategies to attract customers, participate in government campaigns, construct conspicuously hygienic retail environments, and carry foods certified by government-backed schemes. The latter includes vegetables labelled as "organic," "green foods" (*lüse shipin* 绿色食品) or "no public harm" (*wu gonghai* 无公害).[32]

Interviewees often expressed some trust in supermarkets' claims to be selling safe foods. However, although some claimed to buy "no public harm" pork or "green foods," when they described concrete shopping decisions, it was often not the certificate they looked for. Instead, some interviewees put their trust in particular brands whose products were sold in the supermarkets. Ms Gong, a reporter who lived with her husband, two children, mother and a live-in maid in a gated villa community in the north of Kunming, told me that she used to buy pork from privately run stalls in the market but now regularly bought Shen Nong 神农 brand pork. For her, the fact that it was certified as "no public harm" was not irrelevant. More important, however, was the brand itself and the taste of the pork. She claimed that it was very popular and that if you wanted to buy tail bones for making soup you had to go very early. She explained:

> Compared to those market stalls that don't have any names, [the Shen Nong brand] feels like a bit of a guarantee. When it comes to eating, it's like that meat from the market stalls, sometimes it seems like it has water in it, that it is pork that has been injected with water.

Others put their trust in the supermarkets themselves. The supermarket sector in Kunming at the time of the interviews was dominated by multinational retailers, including Carrefour and Wal-Mart. One man in his 30s claimed to trust the supermarkets because they were not Chinese.[33] Another interviewee, Ms Li, who hailed from a village in nearby Shilin 石林 county, lived in the north of Kunming with her husband and their four-year old boy. She ran a small clothing shop near the city centre and often shopped at Wal-Mart. She bought pork there rather than in the food markets: "I feel like I don't have to worry … because foods that get into the supermarket need to be inspected first." She was aware that some of the pork in the supermarkets was certified as "no public harm," but she felt that this pork was too expensive and she did not believe that it was any better than the pork that was not certified. For her, all of the pork available in the city was about the same in taste, and was inferior to that from her home village.

Despite their stated trust, few of my interviewees claimed to purchase vegetables in the supermarkets more than occasionally, as these vegetables were not seen to be sufficiently fresh. Instead, they went to food markets. The "standardized" (zhenggui 正规) markets have fixed stalls and are often covered. Vendors at these markets are mostly specialized retailers who supply their stalls from wholesale markets. By contrast, the "informal" or "spontaneous" (zifa chengxing 自发成形) markets are open-air markets situated in low-income areas. Vendors at these markets are either middlemen who source their goods from wholesale markets or directly from farmers, or farmers selling their own produce. Informal vendors also operate on the peripheries of the standardized markets and in alleys near or inside residential neighbourhoods.

Generally, informal vendors' prices are lower than inside the standardized markets. The low-income households in my study regularly shopped in the spontaneous markets or from other informal vendors, and cited the lower prices as a key reason for doing so. However, price was not the only factor that determined where people shopped. While some informants were distrustful of the spontaneous markets owing to their lack of government inspection, others preferred to buy directly from farmers rather than from middlemen. Mr Xu and his wife, Ms Jiang, had recently retired from the city's environmental protection bureau and were now running an environmental consultancy firm. Although they often drove their car to farmers' markets in the countryside, when in town they preferred to buy from informal vendors who were more likely to be farmers selling their own produce. Less well-off shoppers similarly described shopping from farmers rather than from middlemen. Auntie Liu, a retired textile worker, shopped at the spontaneous market outside her former work unit, arriving early to shop from farmers selling their own goods since, she explained, the middlemen also operating at the market "are a bit cheaper, but they sell greenhouse vegetables and those are not good to eat."

In her study of food markets in Nanjing in the 1990s, Ann Veeck argues that Nanjing shoppers displayed an open lack of trust in food vendors, who were regarded as transient outsiders, and rarely entered into long-term ties with them.[34] In Kunming in the 2000s, I found a similar ambivalence towards vendors. However, there were signs that relationships of trust were being forged and that concerns over both being cheated on price and on food safety had something to do with this. Ms Yang, the retired librarian, lived within walking distance of an informal market in the north of the city where many of the vendors were farmers. When shopping at this market she would buy from vendors with whom she had become familiar. She felt she could trust them to sell her good quality, fresh vegetables, and that she did not need to haggle. Ms Liang had for several years been doing most of her shopping at one of the largest standardized markets in the city. She explained: "After all these years, [I am] clear about what the [food] is like in each stall. That is why, after shopping, we don't have to worry about eating it."

Among the Kunmingers I met, recreating trust in food hinged less on anonymous, government-backed certification schemes or systems of inspection, and more on faith in familiar brands, shops or individual vendors. Trust in food was inseparable from knowledge or perceptions of the agent providing the food.[35] Moreover, place was often crucial to constructing this trust. Foods that were seen as unsafe, tasteless, unhealthy or not fresh because of being disconnected from the regional food economy and its seasonal cycles were being reconnected by shoppers and retailers. The significance of place was apparent in shopping practices. Ms Yang would always go to vendors from Shalang to buy cabbage. Similarly, Auntie Liu bought vegetables from farmers from Tuanjie 团结 county and Baisha He 白沙河 village, and some vendors at the spontaneous market where she shopped would shout to passers-by: "Vegetables from Tuanjie, no chemical pesticides or fertilizers!" Several shoppers preferred to buy foods from poor, mountainous areas in Kunming's hinterland, reasoning that these had little industrial pollution and that farmers in these areas often could not afford agrichemicals.

For a number of Kunmingers, the kinds of food they desired were no longer available in the city itself. They sought out periodic markets in the countryside or peri-urban areas. While those with private cars could travel some distance from the city and combine these trips with farmhouse tourism, on weekends throngs of ordinary Kunmingers visited rural markets by bus, train or bicycle. Some supermarkets were becoming aware of Kunmingers' attachments to local places. In 2009, Metro introduced a line of vegetables advertised as "Yunnanese," and Carrefour began to sell vegetables they called "directly supplied by farmers" (*nongmin zhigong* 农民直供) and "local vegetables" (*bendi shucai* 本地蔬菜). I asked a section manager at Carrefour why customers would be interested in these foods. She replied: "Because they are vegetables from farmers' own homes. They use less chemical fertilizer and use farmyard manure instead. This is more natural (*tianran* 天然)." "What is good about that?" I asked. "If it is more natural, then it is healthier!" she replied, echoing a sentiment I had heard from many shoppers.

Social Stratification

Understandings of food were similar among informants of different economic means. However, in contrast to Beck's depiction of modern risks as universal,[36] in Kunming emerging social hierarchies have shaped the ways in which food safety issues are encountered, and the kinds of strategies people develop to deal with them. Observers have noted that rural food shops and markets have been particularly poorly regulated,[37] and some native Kunmingers reported being concerned about the safety of packaged foods when they visited the countryside. Differences were apparent within the city, too. Income was a real constraint on where and what people could buy. The retired textile worker, Auntie Liu, and a migrant worker from Sichuan, Ms Tao, did the bulk of their shopping in the spontaneous markets, and described this in part as an economic necessity. This was particularly the case for Ms Tao, who highlighted the recent rises in food prices. By contrast, Ms Gong, who lived in an up-market residential neighbourhood, did not think twice about paying a 30 per cent premium for Shen Nong-brand pork. Ms Wu, a retired accountant married to a successful entrepreneur, was able to buy all her vegetables from an "organic" farm.

In addition to pecuniary ability, practices of social distinction-making also shaped shopping patterns. I interviewed Ms Liang, the government office worker mentioned above, and her husband in her sister's flat, where they were staying temporarily. This flat was located in a working-class residential neighbourhood that was home to a large informal market. However, Ms Liang claimed to never shop at that market, even though it was just downstairs. Instead, she would walk through the market to get to a standardized market 15 minutes away on foot. Earlier in the conversation, her husband, Mr Gao, had explained that the government had begun to carry out random inspections in the standardized markets to measure pesticide residues in vegetables. Ms Liang now explained that she did not shop at the spontaneous market downstairs because the vendors there were farmers selling their own goods: "They grow them at their own homes, and after that they are not inspected – there are no procedures at all!" she exclaimed. She then added that the people who shopped there were all laid-off workers and poor pensioners. Liang and Gao claimed to avoid spontaneous markets because they were not inspected, although their trust in government inspections was in fact limited, as suggested by Liang's claims, mentioned earlier, that when shopping in the standardized market she only went to familiar stalls. Their preference for the standardized markets appeared to have as much to do with a mistrust of farmers and a wish to differentiate themselves from the urban poor as it did with a belief in government inspection.

While other interviewees appeared less worried about the spontaneous markets, where and what one shopped for had become a sign of one's social position. In particular, a conspicuous investment in one's own and one's family's dietary health was emerging as a mark of cultivation. Middle-class status, while rooted in income and residence, was increasingly contingent upon the ability to demonstrate refinement and education through consumption.[38] Working-class acquaintances told me that a concern for personal health was a sign that a person had "quality" (*suzhi* 素质). Master Chen, a roadside tailor from Sichuan province married to a Yunnanese, argued that while his family cooked simple foods, wealthy people cared about taste, nutrition (*yingyang* 营养) and hygiene (*weisheng* 卫生).

Nevertheless, although food safety has been described as an "increasingly salient issue for China's rising middle class,"[39] all of the households in my study, regardless of stated income, expressed concerns with "polluted" foods, and all developed practices, according to their means, to access food that they perceived to be safe, healthy and tasty. It could be argued that the link drawn by informants between an investment in dietary health and wealth and social status might be understood as critical commentary, not only on the differences between rich and poor, but also on the growing difficulties for the urban poor to access good-quality foods. Chen's comments were made in the context of a discussion about the impending closure of a major peri-urban market on which he and his family relied for vegetables and pork which, he explained, were both cheaper and fresher than those available in the city centre. Chen and his family had not yet figured out what they would do once the market had closed – they lived and worked in centre of the city but could not afford to buy food there.

The growing restrictions on public food vending were widely associated with Qiu He, who became Kunming's Party secretary in 2007. In the summer of 2008, informal vendors were regularly chased away from the city centre. In 2009, during the campaign to construct a "city of hygiene," a number of spontaneous markets in the city and periodic markets on the peri-urban fringe were closed down for reasons stated on public information boards which included the claim that these markets were threats to public order, hygiene and "food safety." While Qiu He's "cleansing" of the food markets and the peri-urban areas was popular with some Kunmingers, it was not so for the many urban poor, both recent migrants and Kunming natives, who depended upon these markets, or among other Kunmingers I met who similarly sought out foods that were thought to be fresher and more "natural" because they were sold by the farmers themselves.

Conclusion

In this article, I have explored how Kunmingers have interpreted and acted upon food-related environmental health threats. The discussion has been set against the backdrop of an increasingly market-led, intensified and delocalized food supply system on the one hand, and a state-led dismantling of collective institutions and emphasis on individual responsibility on the other. I have argued that while Kunming shoppers have indeed had to rely on their own devices, the practices they have developed to handle food-related risks and their understanding of what constitutes "safe" food has been developed within the frameworks of family ties and regional cuisine. Moreover, while food safety fears may indeed, as Yan argues, "have resulted in widespread social distrust of both food sellers and of the food industry as a whole"[40] and thereby have contributed to a wider decline of social trust, at the same time shoppers and purveyors of food have established relations which have rebuilt at least some trust in food and helped to remake some connections between people, food and place.

According to Veeck, Yu and Burns, in urban China individual strategies to create trust in food, together with the opportunities to enjoy new and abundant food choices in a country shaped by historical experiences of hunger, effectively offset "the fear of potential hazards in the food system."[41] Instead, consumers they studied in four eastern Chinese cities interpreted food safety risks as aberrations resulting from the "profit motives" of farmers and food retailers. In Kunming, too, people often contrasted the abundance of foods available today with the monotonous, often inadequate diets they themselves or their parents and grandparents had experienced. Moreover, distrust of specific foods was certainly often linked to mistrust of the people who sold them, just as trust in food often hinged on knowledge of specific vendors, supermarkets, brands and places. However, in contrast to Veeck, Yu and Burns, here I argue that, in Kunming, recent changes in the food supply were in fact a source of widespread discontent. First, as illustrated by Ms Wang's account at the beginning of the article, the shopping strategies people developed were often not adequate to dispel uncertainty about the food they ate. Not only did they not always prevent potentially harmful foods from being served at home, there was also an unresolved contradiction between a demand for pretty vegetables, which conveyed a culturally valued sense of freshness, and a suspicion of vegetables that were "too pretty," which suggested an overuse of chemical pesticides. Further, despite developing ties of trust with vendors or shops, people would nevertheless carefully check vegetables and meat for signs of chemicals and attempt to remove residues by soaking vegetables or par-boiling pork. The fact that people still regularly shopped at the markets cannot be read as a sign of confidence in the food supply or in the state's ability to regulate it. As one taxi driver, after lamenting the poor taste of pork and green vegetables in the city, put it to me: "There's nothing to be done. You've still got to eat!"

The cultural understanding of food as central to forging ties between people and place exacerbated the sense of disconnection produced by a rapidly delocalizing food system and a perceived deterioration in the quality of many foods. These sentiments fed into a wider ambivalence in Kunming towards a modernization project which had demolished the old city centre and its bustling street life, caused environmental degradation, and was giving rise to social distrust and polarization. Such ambivalence was particularly acute among the urban poor. While the new middle class had access to emerging types of "ecological" foods and were even using such foods in practices of social distinction, migrant labourers, laid-off workers and pensioners were often dependent on peri-urban periodic markets or informal markets in the city to access sought-after foods. However, as a result of Kunming's modernization project, which as in cities across the world has come to involve policies of "spatial cleansing,"[42] hawkers were being criminalized and informal markets eradicated, but without adequate alternatives being provided.

Nevertheless, few addressed their concerns about the quality of the food supply outside the domain of everyday food provisioning. Occasionally, people like Ms Wang did file complaints about individual traders with the Consumers' Association. However, there were to my knowledge no examples in Kunming of organized attempts to make demands on the state for improved regulation of the food supply. Writing … on netizen responses to tainted milk powder, Guobin Yang emphasizes that food safety is a politically sensitive issue and that public debate is actively contained by the state.[43] The NGOs and activist-entrepreneurs I have researched in Kunming were well aware of this sensitivity, and have focused on increasing consumer awareness of food-related health threats and encouraging people to buy "alternative" foods, often working in cooperation with government bodies and supermarkets.[44] In doing so, these groups have reinforced notions of individual consumer responsibility for their "food choices," and have helped mostly middle-class people navigate the food system. As mentioned, many middle-class consumers were also able to take their cars to farmers' markets further afield. Among the less well-off people I spoke to in 2009, some had access to peri-urban and informal markets that had not yet been closed, while others, like Master Chen and his family, were unsure of what to do. If citizen activism in the area of "food safety" was monitored by the state and further contained by the existence of "alternatives" to "unnatural" foods, it remains to be seen what will happen if access to such "alternatives" becomes further limited by the state's own public hygiene policies.

Notes

1 Tam and Yang 2005; Wang, Mao and Gale 2008; Yan 2012; Gong and Jackson 2012.

2 Beck 1992.

3 Ellis and Turner 2007; Ellis and Turner 2008; Hamburger 2002.

4 Xiu and Klein 2010.

5 Tam and Yang 2005, 10.

6 Mintz 2006; Broughton and Walker 2010.

7 Yan 2012.

8 Beck 1992; Giddens 1991; Beck and Beck-Gernscheim 2002.

9 Tilt 2013.

10 Yan 2009. In a recent discussion of food safety in China, Yan examines the impact of food safety problems on social trust, but he does not elaborate on the relationship between "risk society" and "individualization." See Yan 2012.

11 Croll 1983.

12 Wang, Mao and Gale 2008; Tam and Yang 2005.

13 Jing 2000; Gong and Jackson 2012.

14 Caplan 2000.

15 Kjærnes, Harvey and Warde 2007.

16 Wang, Mao and Gale 2008; Gale and Huang 2007.

17 Veeck, Yu and Burns 2010.

18 Yan 2012, 717.

19 Yan 2012, 707.

20 Fieldwork was funded by small research grants from the British Academy (SG-43053 and SG-50545), with additional support from the Universities' China Committee in London (UCCL) and from the SOAS Internal Research Grants scheme.

21 Stafford 2000, 99–109.

22 Yan 2003.

23 In their study of parenting practices in Chengdu in the wake of the 2008 melamine-contaminated powdered milk scare, Gong and Jackson argue that the feeding of infants was a frequent source of conflict between generations, contributing to the anxieties experienced by new mothers in particular. See Gong and Jackson 2012.

24 Mintz 1996, 107.

25 Most of my household interviews were conducted prior to the nationwide melamine milk scandal in September 2008. See Gong and Jackson 2012 for an account, based on focus group discussions, of how Chengdu families with infants responded to the scandal.

26 Mintz uses the term "signature foods" to refer to foods which come to stand for a region. See Mintz 1996, 95.

27 Lee 1982, 741.

28 Ellis and Turner 2008, 17.

29 The industrialization of the food supply in China has been a partial and uneven process. For example, according to one report, while concentrated animal feeding operations (CAFOs), promoted since the 1980s, accounted for over 75% of the country's chicken production and 68% of its eggs in 2005, the same report placed CAFO-produced beef and pork that year at around 30% and 37%, respectively, of domestic production. See Ellis and Turner 2007, 20. Yunnan is widely regarded as having less intensified food production than the eastern seaboard. However, pesticide use in the province more than doubled from 10,000 tons in 1990 to 25,000 tons in 2001. See Zhongguo nongyao fazhan baogao bianweihui 2005, 75–76.

30 On the connection between taste and efficacy in Chinese medicines and dietary therapies, see Lo 2005.

31 My discussion of these changes draws on Zhang 2006.

32 There were quite different requirements surrounding these "ecological" certifications, as discussed by Sanders 2006. In supermarket displays – and in popular discourse – the categories tended to get confused. No one I met commented on what the label "no public harm" might have implied about the rest of the food supply.

33 In their study of Chengdu families' responses to the powdered milk scandal of 2008, Gong and Jackson report high levels of loyalty to foreign supermarkets and department stores, as well as to foreign infant formula brands. See Gong and Jackson 2012, 562–64.

34 Veeck 2000.

35 Caplan 2000; Kjærnes, Harvey and Warde 2007.

36 Beck 1992, 36–39.

37 Tam and Yang 2005.

38 Zhang 2008; Klein 2015.

39 Tam and Yang 2005, 7.

40 Yan 2012, 717.

41 Veeck, Yu and Burns 2010, 233.

42 Herzfeld 2006.

43 Yang 2013.

44 Klein 2009. Some activists and activist-entrepreneurs I spoke with were privately critical not only of inadequate state regulation, but also of state economic interests in various domains of the food system, but this is not something I discussed with consumers.

References

Beck, Ulrich. 1992. *Risk Society: Towards a New Modernity*. London: SAGE.

Beck, Ulrich, and Elisabeth Beck-Gernscheim. 2002. *Individualization: Individualized Individualism and Its Social and Political Consequences*. London: SAGE.

Broughton, Edward I., and Damian G. Walker. 2010. "Policies and practices for aquaculture food safety in China." *Food Policy* 35, 471–78.

Caplan, Pat. 2000. "Eating British beef with confidence: a consideration of consumers' responses to BSE in Britain." In Pat Caplan (ed.), *Risk Revisited*. London: Pluto Press, 184–203.

Croll, Elisabeth. 1983. *The Family Rice Bowl: Food and the Domestic Economy in China*. London: Zed Press.

Ellis, Linden J., and Jennifer Turner. 2007. "Surf and turf: environmental and food safety concerns of China's aquaculture and animal husbandry." *China Environment Series* 9, 19–40.

Ellis, Linden J., and Jennifer Turner. 2008. "Sowing the seeds: opportunities for U.S.-China cooperation on food safety." China Environment Forum, Woodrow Wilson International Center for Scholars, *http://www.wilsoncenter.org/publication-series/sowing-the-seeds-opportunities-for-us-china-cooperation-food-safety*. Accessed 1 December 2010.

Gale, Fred, and Kuo Huang. 2007. "Demand for food quantity and quality in China." Economic Research Service, United States Department of Agriculture, *Economic Research Report* 32, *http://www.ers.usda.gov/publications/err-economic-research-report/err32.aspx*. Accessed 1 December 2010.

Giddens, Anthony. 1991. *Modernity and Self-Identity: Self and Society in the Late Modern Age*. Cambridge: Polity Press.

Gong, Qian, and Peter Jackson. 2012. "Consuming anxiety? Parenting practices in China after the infant formula scandal." *Food, Culture and Society* 15 (4), 557–578.

Hamburger, Jessica. 2002. "Pesticides in China: a growing threat to food safety, public health, and the environment." *China Environment Series* 5, 29–44.

Herzfeld, Michael. 2006. "Spatial cleansing: monumental vacuity and the idea of the West." *Journal of Material Culture* 11 (1–2), 127–149.

Jing, Jun (ed.). 2000. *Feeding China's Little Emperors: Food, Children, and Social Change*. Stanford: Stanford University Press.

Kjærnes, Unni, Mark Harvey and Alan Warde. 2007. *Trust in Food: A Comparative and Institutional Analysis*. New York and Basingstoke: Palgrave Macmillan.

Klein, Jakob A. 2009. "Creating ethical food consumers? Promoting organic foods in urban southwest China." *Social Anthropology/Anthropologie Sociale* 17 (1), 74–89.

Klein, Jakob A. 2015. "Eating green: ecological food consumption in urban China." In Kwang-ok Kim (ed.), *Tasteful Trends: Identity, Power and the Mobility of East Asian Food*. New York and Oxford: Berghahn Books, 238–262.

Lee, James. 1982. "Food supply and population growth in southwest China, 1250–1850." *The Journal of Asian Studies* 41 (4), 711–746.

Lo, Vivienne. 2005. "Pleasure, prohibition, and pain: food and medicine in traditional China." In Roel Sterckx (ed.), *Of Tripod and Palate: Food, Politics, and Religion in Traditional China*. New York and Basingstoke: Palgrave Macmillan, 163–185.

Mintz, Sidney W. 1996. *Tasting Food, Tasting Freedom: Excursions into Eating, Culture, and the Past*. Boston: Beacon Press.

Mintz, Sidney. 2006. "Food at moderate speeds." In Richard Wilk (ed.), *Fast Food/Slow Food: The Cultural Economy of the Global Food System*. Lanham, MD: Altamira Press, 3–11.

Sanders, Richard. 2006. "A market road to sustainable agriculture? Ecological agriculture, green food and organic agriculture in China." *Development and Change* 37 (1), 201–226.

Stafford, Charles. 2000. *Separation and Reunion in Modern China*. Cambridge: Cambridge University Press.

Tam, Waikeung, and Dali Yang. 2005. "Food safety and the development of regulatory institutions in China." *Asian Perspective* 29 (4), 5–36.

Tilt, Byan. 2013. "Industrial pollution and environmental health in rural China: risk, uncertainty and individualization." *The China Quarterly* 214.

Veeck, Ann. 2000. "The revitalization of the marketplace: food markets of Nanjing." In Deborah S. Davis (ed.), *The Consumer Revolution in Urban China*. Berkeley: University of California Press, 107–123.

Veeck, Ann, Hongyan Yu and Alvin C. Burns. 2010. "Consumer risks and new food systems in urban China." *Journal of Macromarketing* 30 (3), 222–237.

Wang, Zhigang, Yanna Mao and Fred Gale. 2008. "Chinese consumer demand for food safety attributes in milk products." *Food Policy* 33, 27–36.

Xiu, Changbai, and K.K. Klein. 2010. "Melamine in milk products in China: examining the factors that led to deliberate use of the contaminant." *Food Policy* 35, 463–470.

Yan, Yunxiang. 2003. *Private Life under Socialism: Love, Intimacy, and Family Change in a Chinese Village, 1949–1999*. Stanford: Stanford University Press.

Yan, Yunxiang. 2009. *The Individualization of Chinese Society*. Oxford and New York: Berg.

Yan, Yunxiang. 2012. "Food safety and social risk in China." *The Journal of Asian Studies* 71 (3), 705–729.

Yang, Guobin. 2013. "Contesting illness on the internet: the case of tainted milk powder." *The China Quarterly* 214.

Zhang, Li. 2006. "Contesting spatial modernity in late-socialist China." *Current Anthropology* 47 (3), 461–484.

Zhang, Li. 2008. "Private homes, distinct lifestyles: performing a new middle class." In Li Zhang and Aihwa Ong (eds.), *Privatizing China: Socialism from Afar*. Ithaca and London: Cornell University Press, 23–40.

Zhongguo nongyao fazhan baogao bianweihui (eds.). 2005. *Zhongguo nongyao fazhan baogao* (*Pesticide Development in China: A Comprehensive Report*). Beijing: Zhongguo huanjing kexue chubanshe.

10

Digestive Politics in Russia: Feeling the Sensorium beyond the Palate

Melissa L. Caldwell

Several summers ago, my husband and I enjoyed a late-summer trip to Russia. The visit was both professional and personal, as I planned to combine follow-up research on my summer gardens project with an opportunity to introduce my husband to friends I had made during that research. Because of the simultaneously social and professional nature of our trip, many of our visits with friends and colleagues focused on the pleasures of the palate. Visits to friends' homes or dachas (i.e. summer cottages) were often spent enjoying lengthy conversations and delicious meals prepared from garden-fresh produce. In several instances, friends who were excited about the emerging restaurant scene in their small cities treated us to dinner so that we could experience and share the latest trends in Russian culinary culture. In practically every case, the pleasures of our visits revolved around good food and good company.

Amid those enjoyable visits, one encounter stood out. An otherwise enjoyable afternoon party at a friend's dacha, filled with garden-fresh tomato and cucumber salads, a seemingly bottomless bowl of fresh berries, bottles of good wine, and plates of cakes and ice creams, ended with most of the guests suffering from severe gastric troubles. Because my husband and I were Americans who had been efficiently indoctrinated into a healthy suspicion of mayonnaise left out in hot weather, we were certain that the symptoms had resulted from the salads that had been served and left out in the 100°+ Fahrenheit heat. Our Russian friends, however, had a different perspective on the matter. Each individual was convinced that the cause of the problems was the ice cream that had been served for dessert. Our hostess had purchased an assortment of small cartons of sorbets and ice creams of various fruit flavors that had been divided for sharing. There was no one flavor that every person had tried, but each person who had become ill had sampled some of the same flavors. After many back-and-forth phone calls over the next several days, our friends compared notes to determine who had sampled which flavors and who was experiencing which symptoms, often in graphic detail.

Eventually, our friends came to the shared conclusion that the culprits were several cartons of cheaper and foreign-made ice creams and sorbets. As our friends explained, both individually and collectively, it had been risky for our hostess to purchase the foreign items, but the high-quality domestic ice creams that Russians were accustomed to buying were no longer as available as they had been in the past. Instead, consumers like our hostess were forced to buy cheaper and undoubtedly lower-quality ice creams that had replaced Russian brands. Curiously, despite the fact that while we had been eating the ice creams, our friends had commented enthusiastically on how flavorful and good they were, once they decided that the ice creams were to blame, their comments focused solely on their poor quality and dangerousness.

Even more noteworthy was that our friends' observations about taste, quality, and safety were framed as critical commentaries on changes in Russia's political economy. Our friends refused to assign personal responsibility to either the hostess who had purchased the ice creams or the guests who had eaten then. As they explained, it was not the fault of our hostess for purchasing substandard ice creams, nor was it the fault of the guests for not recognizing the poor quality of the ice creams and eating them anyway. In fact, our friends suggested that it was understandable, even acceptable, that we had all enjoyed the ice creams. The important point was that we were all victims of Russia's new capitalist economy, which had limited our options and forced us to consume poor-quality products.

Equally intriguing was that after articulating this critique of capitalism, our friends suggested that the proper response to this problem was not to focus on the palate but rather on the gut. They refused to treat their upset stomachs by restricting the foods they ate to bland foods, as my husband and I did by following the American trend of the so-called BRAT diet (e.g., bananas, rice, applesauce, and toast), coupled with weak broth and weak tea. Nor did they suggest that it was necessary to swear off ever consuming those ice creams again in the future. Instead, our Russian friends eagerly dug into huge quantities of grilled meats, oil- and mayonnaise-laden salads, spicy tomato and pepper dishes, and high-fat, dairy-based dishes. We watched in amazement as our friends suffered through the physiological consequences of their food choices but yet continued to state that they refused to sacrifice their taste buds. Instead, they claimed that the food choices they made were helping their bodies recover by forcing their stomachs to respond strongly and to familiar foods. Curiously, it seemed to be true: our friends seemed to recover about the same time that we did.

These gastric events raise intriguing questions about how eaters associate bodily sensations with cultural issues. In this case, these individuals interpreted the physiologically sensory effects of an apparent bout of food poisoning as the direct result of Russia's new political economy of market capitalism, which has been popularly blamed for replacing familiar domestic products that were believed to be safe and of high quality with low-quality foreign products (Patico). With their strategic use of fighting nausea and diarrhea with spicy foods, these eaters then further evoked particular sensory experiences as forms of engagement with, and even resistance to, these changes. As expressions of "somatic modes of attention," bodily experiences became the means by which these individuals engaged the particular social world that they inhabited—in this case, a new capitalist Russia (Csordas 138).[1]

This insight that sensory experiences are forms of engagement with the world is fundamental to understanding why eaters like these Russians interpret their own bodily responses as expressions of political engagement and critique. Food can merge the political and the personal, and even bring the political directly into the most personal spaces of the body, because of its capacity to evoke multiple sensory realities (De Silva; Ferrero; Seremetakis; Sutton, *Remembrance of Repasts*, "Food and the Senses"). Physiological sensations like taste, smell, hearing, and touch are all means of knowing, recognizing, remembering, and interpreting the world that one inhabits (Bourdieu; Herzfeld; Seremetakis; Stoller; Sutton, *Remembrance of Repasts*). As Constance Classen has noted, "we not only think about our senses, we think through them," a point echoed by David Sutton's statement that the sensory aspects of eating are means to access "whole worlds of experience and interpretation" (Classen 9; *Remembrance of Repasts* 15). Because "the body is a major repository of cultural memories," whereby past events and experiences are inscribed in bodily registers, flavors, aromas, sounds, textures, and appearances thus become powerful mnemonic triggers that document, reinforce, and convey experiences (Stoller 638).

Yet accounts of the relationships among food, body, and the worlds that eaters inhabit have typically prioritized moments of production and consumption as key sites of analysis. As Sidney Mintz has suggested in describing the unique relationship between humans and food choices, "nothing defines our nature as living creatures more dramatically than our ingestion" (Mintz 4). It is either ingestion—or the lack of ingestion as with non-eating, under-eating, or purging—that is presented as the moment that best captures how and when cultural values are consumed or repelled and that draws the attention of food reformers seeking to change or even "improve" eating habits (Mintz; Terrio; e.g., Lappé; Petrini; Pollan).[2]

Yet as the attitudes of my Russian friends suggest, this privileging of ingestion, and hence of the palate, might not be the only site to understand the relationships that exist between food and body, and between the health of individual bodies and the nation and state. Although less prominent than ingestion in food discourses, indigestion and other bodily processes further along the digestive tract have been prominent themes in my acquaintances' conversations about the significance of their dietary habits over the past two decades. From physicians and politicians who claim that Russia's declining work force is the direct result of broken bones caused by poor nutrition to social workers who have to consider matters such as hypertension and constipation when providing welfare services to their clients, digestion and excretion are themes within commentaries on politically salient matters in Russia. Thus, in many respects, the importance of food in Russia is very much tied not just to the palate but also to the gut.

Attending to processes of digestion and excretion demonstrates that bodily sensations are not confined only to the experiences of taste, smell, touch, and sound that occur at the point of entry to the body but in fact continue throughout the entire process as food moves through and is processed by the digestive track and is expressed through stomach pains, intestinal cramps, and other lower-body sensations. Moving beyond ingestion and the palate offers a productive new vantage point for rethinking what and where the sensory experiences associated with food occur (Hennion; Mann et al.). As the provocative "eating with fingers" experiment conducted by Anna Man, Annemarie Mol, and their colleagues revealed, how foods "taste" to eaters may change when those foods are touched by fingers and other body parts (Mann et al.). By expanding the range of types of contact with food beyond those that occur at the palate, the possibilities for types of sensory experiences also expand, reflecting Hennion's provocation to "feel the feeling of" as a form of subjective and active knowing that enables the feeler to understand and experience the thing that is felt—or tasted, in this case—in a wholly different but yet still wholly personal and individualized way (98).

In this article, I take up this concern with the sensory experiences evoked by food beyond the palate by examining how Russian eaters experience and interpret post-ingestion processes as means of engaging and responding to larger cultural phenomena, most notably events in Russia's political history. By recognizing and giving meaning to sensory experiences that occur further along the digestive track, Russian eaters engage at a deeply visceral level the larger cultural systems in which their bodies—and their foods—are embedded. This resonates with David Howes' observation that "any period of great cultural change will be a time of sensory confusion, for social revolutions are always sensory revolutions, [and which] may be experienced as an illness in the body of society or of the individual" (11). At the same time, Russian eaters prioritize different points of intervention into the body, thereby challenging prevailing notions that eating experiences begin or occur only at the mouth. Consequently, shifting this attention from the palate to the gut and to other peripheral body parts changes how Russian eaters conceive of the dynamics between the personal and the political. When the political becomes the gastric-political, entities like the state and the nation become invested in the most intimate spaces of their citizens' lives— that is, in the most intimate spaces of their bodies.

To address these themes, I begin by describing ways in which foods and their sensory dimensions have become channels through which Russians have experienced, understood, and explained the world they inhabit and the experiences through which they have lived. I then examine how Russians' own physical bodies have been shaped by acts of ingestion and other sensory experiences located further along the digestive track. Finally, I conclude by considering how this reorientation of where the sensory is most productively located might shed light on rethinking current food theories about taste preferences and consumer choice.[3]

Voting with One's Teeth and Stomach: Taste as Politics

Like eaters throughout the world, Russians have found food to be a particularly evocative symbol of political processes as well as a powerful medium through which those political processes take shape and become materialized. Both food production and consumption are highly politicized activities, as consumers can "vote" not simply with their feet but also with their teeth and stomach. In Russia, consumers have "voted with their teeth and stomach" in many ways, beginning in the 1990s with a backlash against the proliferation of foreign foods and the perceived Westernization of Russia—what Russians have derisively described as the "Snickerization" of their culture. Through forms of commercialized nationalism, Russians alternately rejected foreign products, including imported frozen chickens from America that Russian consumer-citizens pejoratively labeled "Bush Legs," and instead embraced food and other products that made claims on Russia's national heritage and culture (Caldwell, "The Taste of Nationalism").

In response, Russian food producers promoted a return to "traditional" food products and dishes that were familiar from different moments in the nation's political history. Russian manufacturers resurrected food brands and packaging from Soviet-era factories and used recipes promoted by Soviet dieticians and health reformers. Important historical moments and personages from Russia's past and present, ranging from ancient Rus' and Imperial Russia to the Soviet and post-Soviet eras, were used in branding and labeling to connote various aspects of Russian cultural life.[4] Peasants, bucolic villages, churches, revolutionary slogans, wartime battles, pre-Soviet novelists and artists, and Soviet and post-Soviet leaders have all emerged as markers that convey the more appropriately Russian, and hence presumably higher quality, taste, and reliability, of domestic food products.[5]

Vodka and chocolates have been especially noteworthy examples of how "national," and hence "traditional," themes and values have been used to promote products and the qualities of those products. The most prominent Russian candy companies—Red October, Red Front, and Bolshevik, among others—have routinely used pictures from traditional Russian fairy tales and paintings by Russian artists as decorations on the labels and boxes of their products. For the case of vodka, both historically important political figures and "traditional" modes of distilling have been promoted by marketers and vendors alike as distinguishing their products as superior to foreign products. One series of vodka advertisements featured famous Soviet aeronautic heroes with the slogan "When I return," while another enterprising vodka brand has capitalized on the hero worship of President Vladimir Putin with a brand of Putinka vodka. On different occasions in restaurants and liquor stores, when I have been considering which type of vodka to purchase, I have been advised by waiters or store clerks (and in one case by the drunken liquor store security guard) that I should buy only Putinka vodka because it was obviously the best quality and the most traditional "Russian" vodka. In the case of the drunken security guard, he also informed me that Putin himself monitored the vodka that came out under his name, so I could be assured that it was of the highest quality and cleanest flavor (e.g., with "clean" in this sense meaning that the vodka did not have any noticeable aromatics or flavors).

As public displays of religious practice have become more common over the past two decades, cakes, pastries, and other food items associated with Russian Orthodox religious holidays and rituals, or even pre-Christian rituals, became more visible in grocery stores and restaurant menus. After 70 years of severe restrictions against religious practice, today restaurants in Moscow frequently offer a special "Lenten menu" that follows Orthodox restrictions against dairy and meat. Both individual churches and monasteries and the denominational body of the Russian Orthodox Church have their own lines of food and beverages—some of which have been officially "blessed"—that they sell in commercial food retailers. Within this context of a "return to the nation," foods and beverages represent opportunities for Russians to express and ingest their cultural and even political values, especially their views about Russia's shift between its socialist past and its capitalist present.

The value of food for ingesting and expressing Russians' political sensibilities lies not simply in its communicative capacity as a cultural symbol. Rather, the more profound significance of food is in the extent to which consumers directly associate food with the physical effects of food in the bodies of both those who produce it and those who consume it. In multiple ways, political sensibilities are explicitly manifested in consumers' claims about preferring or disdaining certain sensory qualities of food. A university colleague recalled an occasion in the 1970s when she first tasted a banana and fell in love with the flavor. At that time, bananas were scarce and available only to elites who were allowed to shop in closed stores or eat in private cafeterias. My colleague was not a member of the elite class but had been invited to the private cafeteria after a special meeting. When she described the flavor to a friend, the friend chastised her for being "unpatriotic." By calling her "unpatriotic," the friend criticized her for enjoying an elite taste that was denied to ordinary citizens. For the friend, the very flavor of banana was a marker of a particular political identity or sympathy, and consequently a "good," "patriotic," and "ordinary" Soviet citizen was one who did not like the taste of banana and so did not eat it.

The cultivation of citizens' taste preferences was part of a Soviet project to regulate and improve both the country's food system and the diet of its citizens. As part of a civic project of disciplining citizens' bodies in order to cultivate a strong, healthy workforce and to encourage socialist values, socialist-era social reformers and officials targeted bodily dispositions. Through instructional guides, architectural styles, home furnishings, and other activities meant to train citizens' bodies in proper bodily behavior, citizens' bodies were conditioned in proper ways of walking and sitting, responding to weather conditions such as heat or cold, wet or dry, and recognizing and appreciating particular flavors and aromas (e.g., Buchli; Reid; Tura).[6] Personal health and hygiene manuals instructed parents on the proper foods to prepare and serve to their children, thereby ensuring that children learned to appreciate a particular flavor palate (Tura). The following section from a Soviet-era parenting manual is illustrative for the ways in which parents were instructed in how to teach their children to eat properly:

> Food should be tasty, appropriately hot, pleasantly composed. For example, a child might refuse soup with macaroni, but eagerly eat soup with macaroni in the shape of stars or little roosters. Beautifully presented food increases appetite. Therefore it is necessary to pay attention to the tastes of the child and his preferences. (Tura 87)

Additionally, the standardization of recipes in restaurants, food factories, and private kitchens, and the formal professionalization of food services, ensured a homogenized and rather narrow set of taste preferences and food styles (see also Shectman; cf. Jung, "From Canned Food..."). Even "exotic," "foreign" foods were heavily regulated and normed toward a standard by virtue of both the regulations on recipes and the limited supply of unusual spices. Today, Russian chefs and home cooks alike complain that Russian cuisine's emphasis on salt and vinegar has limited consumers' palates only to salty and sour, thereby making it difficult for both professional and amateur cooks to introduce alternative flavor profiles into their menus or homemade meals. During the course of my research, I regularly encountered complaints from women who wanted to try new recipes at home, including more "healthful" recipes that were lower in sodium or used olive oil instead of butter, but were stymied by husbands and sons who refused to eat those new foods because they did not have the "correct," that is familiar, flavor or texture.

Linking cultural values with physical sensations is one of the objectives of flavor chemists, R&D professionals with food corporations, restaurateurs, and food reformers alike, who are keen to identify the "flavor profiles" associated with distinct cultural groups (see also Rozin and Rozin). For the case of Russia, flavor chemists working in the Russian site of a major transnational food corporation claimed success when they achieved a mushroom flavoring that appealed to Russian preferences for earthiness and slight bitterness. As one of the chemists explained, his goal was to produce the right combination so that Russian consumers would recognize the product as "authentic" through the deeper, more unconscious awareness of their taste buds and not by appealing to a more superficial level of awareness through the visual cues of branding. Ultimately, the chemist and his superiors hoped that when Russians ate foods that contained this particular flavor profile they would feel comfortable that they were bringing "authentic" Russian experiences and values into their bodies.

Infused in these efforts to identify and cultivate "correct" sensory cues and responses is a concern with the morality of taste. Not only do taste preferences represent ethical or moral values, such as with concerns about labor, environment, and health that are promoted in ethical food movements, but taste preferences themselves might be understood as moral, as in the case of the

Soviet citizen who identified a taste preference for bananas as unpatriotic. In this instance, a dislike for bananas would have been the preferred, moral state (e.g., Guthman; Jung, Klein, and Caldwell).

In the post-Soviet period, taste preferences have become powerful conduits for moral codes about the Russian economy, most notably the values associated with Russia's new capitalist market. In Russia, much like in other parts of the state socialist world as officials, citizens, and corporations have negotiated the structures and values of socialism and capitalism, as well as the relationships between socialism and capitalism, food and taste preferences have emerged as prime sites for both debate and intervention (e.g., Caldwell, "The Taste of Nationalism"; Klumbytė; Mincyte; Patico; Shectman). In very tangible ways, the production and consumption of food have long been the frameworks for evaluative commentaries about Russian life—from the stories of bread lines that prompted the revolutions that led to the formation of the Soviet Union, through the accounts of starvation, cannibalism, and the ethics of responsible consumption during the Second World War, to the tales of "heroic shopping" for scarce food goods that Nancy Ries documented during the late Soviet period.

Continuing into the post-Soviet period, Russians' ambiguous relationships with market capitalism have been rendered alternately through the novelty and prestige afforded to Western foods and the denigration of foreign products and preoccupation with "nationalist foods" (Caldwell, "The Taste of Nationalism"; cf. Klumbytė). As an explicit project of food nationalism, Russian culinary nostalgia allays public anxieties about the potential loss of cultural heritage in the postsocialist period by directly linking consumers to their national past through familiar flavors, aromas, textures, and visual cues of "traditional" foods (Caldwell, "Tasting the Worlds…"). The reassurances offered by the familiar sensory cues of traditional foods are especially evident in Russian preferences for foods grown and processed in natural settings such as gardens, forests, and rural agricultural settings. These foods are presumed to be healthier, tastier, and more "nationally appropriate" than their industrially produced counterparts. In a series of interviews and surveys I conducted with Russian university students in the late 1990s, I asked why "traditional" foods were so important. One respondent succinctly summed up a perspective I had heard repeatedly from other respondents with her simple answer: "Russian taste buds prefer [Russian tastes]."

As expressions of political values and affiliations, sensory experiences such as taste preferences are powerful precisely because they transform the personal body into a civic body that is both a repository for and agent of national values and state processes. In Russia, the body that prepares, tastes, and consumes food is intrinsically a politically invested body, a detail that is apparent in one of Russia's most unusual political museums. The Museum of Public Catering (*Muzei Obshchestvennogo Pitaniia*) is a monument to Soviet history as told through the history of Russian cuisine and the professionals who have dedicated their lives to Russia's food industry. The museum is staffed by former chefs and restaurant managers who volunteer their time and expertise to preserve Russia's culinary history and pass that knowledge on to future generations through public lectures and cooking demonstrations.[7]

During my visits to the museum in the late 1990s before its reconstruction, my guides showed me extensive exhibits devoted to Russian food cultures from the 19th century to the present. Glass cases featured displays of cookware, dishes, and serving utensils taken from restaurants, public cafeterias, and private homes, as well as an exhaustive collection of personal and industrial appliances. Other displays contained carefully preserved documents such as ration cards, advertisements, and product labels. Ornate menus from restaurants and private gatherings document special events such as the inauguration of Soviet leaders. Photographs, plastic replicas, and other forms of artwork documented Russian foods ranging from simple fare served in peasant homes or taverns to lavish banquets served in the country's most elite restaurants and private dining rooms.

The halls of the museum were lined with formal portraits of chefs and foodservices officials dressed in their official uniforms and wearing Soviet medals denoting their culinary and political contributions, with special recognition given to foodservices workers who served their country during the war. Poems, stories, and drawings by both "hero chefs" from the war and by artists in their honor detailed their experiences and sacrifices. The careful arrangement of each item according to its appropriate time period and historical significance, combined with the guides' efforts to keep visitors on a strictly chronological tour of the museum, ensured an accounting of Russia's political history in which every event between the Imperial Period and the contemporary period was narrated through food. Although on most days the sensory emphasis is on the visual and textural evocation of Russia's past, on special days the museum hosts cooking demonstrations and tastings that allow visitors to connect the visual and textural representations of the past with the flavors and aromas of those pasts.

During my visits to the museum, I was escorted by Pavel Ivanovich, the retired manager of *Yar'*, an elite Moscow restaurant that has been in continuous operation since before the 1917 Revolution. As Pavel Ivanovich walked me around the museum, he described the various exhibits and the larger social contexts behind them: menus and plastic replicas of foods reminded him of meals that he had prepared for special occasions, such as the banquet he had hosted for visiting dignitaries from *Life* magazine in the 1960s or the dinner he had quickly put together when Soviet leader Nikita Khrushchev unexpectedly visited his restaurant. Pavel Ivanovich framed his recollections not simply on descriptions of past meals but more precisely on the particular sensory experiences of those meals. Interrupting his narratives to smack his lips and whisper reverently "*kak khorosho*! (how good!)" and "*Kak vkusno*! (how tasty!)," he recalled the precise tastes of specific meals and the wines and champagnes with which they had been paired.

What Pavel Ivanovich conveyed so elegantly with his shrugs, pursed lips, and facial expressions of ecstasy was that these stories could only be captured and conveyed through the flavors, aromas, and textures of each dish. For him, Russia's political past resided in and was expressed in the sensory nature of these foods. By appealing to the visceral, experiential quality of these events, Pavel Ivanovich opened up possibilities for his audience to grasp those events—and become intimate with the participants in those events—through their own bodies.

This appreciation for the sensorium as the place where political events, knowledge, and values reside and are expressed appeared frequently in interviews with ordinary Russians as well. Larisa Antonovna, a retired historian, similarly used the sensory experiences of food to document and communicate the two political moments that have the most significance for her: her childhood during World War II and the period of *glasnost* in the late 1980s. For Larisa Antonovna, these two series of events are necessarily correlated with the tastes of particular foods. For the case of World War II, the flavor of stinging nettles (*krapiva*) in homemade soups and teas instantly evokes the wartime deprivations she and her family endured. During the war, she and her sister were sent to live with their grandmother and, like many Russians, the three of them fed themselves by picking nettles and other wild plants. Later, during the food shortages of the glasnost period in the late 1980s, Larisa Antonovna began foraging for nettles to supplement her meager food supplies.

Larisa Antonovna was not unusual among Russians of her generation, as many people ate so much krapiva and other wild grasses during the war that they acquired a preference for the flavor, especially the flavor of young nettles that are at their freshest and most tender. In recent years, nettles have been resurrected as part of Russia's increasingly popular culinary nostalgia trends (Caldwell). Russian restaurants, cooking shows, and cooking magazines alike have featured nettles and other "deprivation" foods like wild grasses as a way to remind elderly Russians of their wartime experiences and connect younger generations with their country's history through its flavors and aromas.

For other Russians, the combination of taste and texture is equally significant as a sensory reminder of past events and experiences. Svetlana Andreevna, also an elderly survivor of World War II, has difficulty using basic kitchen utensils like spoons and forks because her fingers have permanently stiffened into a straight position. She explained that she suffered this disability during World War II, when she lived with her family in Leningrad. Owing to the personal sacrifices she made to help support her family during the Leningrad Blockade, most notably during the winter months, she suffered frostbite and her fingers froze. Today, she struggles to hold utensils, frequently spilling food on herself. As Svetlana Andreevna explained, this disability is a constant reminder and testimony to her experiences and those of her family during the Great Patriotic War. In a very visceral way, the legacy of the past comes through every day in her body as she attempts to feed herself.

As examples such as these show, the sensory aspects evoked by the ingestion of food inscribe political values and sensibilities into eaters' bodies, thereby transforming the political into the personal and transferring public politics into the most intimate personal spaces of individual citizens. Yet paying attention to the sensory qualities of foods only at moments of anticipation or consumption privileges qualities such as flavor, aroma, texture, and appearance as the catalyst for subsequent value-making activities and overlooks other ways in which bodily sensations might be responses to political issues. An intriguing question, then, becomes how might narratives of politics and value change as food makes its way through the body? In other words, how might refocusing attention further along the digestive track change our understandings of the sensory dimensions of cultural and political phenomena? Ultimately, how might processes of digestion and excretion provide a new way of thinking about what taste is and where it is located? These questions are the focus of the following section.

From the Palate to the Gut: Colon-izing Taste

Studies of taste have privileged the mouth and the nose—the palate—as the site where tastes are cultivated and recognized, where choice and agency are expressed, pleasure occurs, and responsibility is assigned (e.g., Brillat-Savarin; Korsmeyer; Petrini; Pollan).[8] Ultimately, because it is the palate where values enter the body and shape all that follows, taste and choice precede and produce particular types of bodies, a paradigm that contains an explicitly moral message: If individuals or institutions (governments, food producers, regulating bodies, etc.) do not exercise sufficient care with what goes into the mouth, then bodies suffer. This is the recurring perspective promoted in much contemporary food scholarship, especially in "health" studies, but also in other food studies focused on Slow Food, organics, Fair Trade, and sustainability. In these approaches, scholars, activists, and food enthusiasts present moralizing ideologies about the appropriate conditions that need to be met in order to ensure that consumers put into their bodies proper food that will produce bodies that are strong, healthy, thin, and cultured (Biltekoff; Guthman). Hence if bodily spaces like the mouth and palate are privileged as the spaces to be protected and rewarded with the ingestion of "good" and "tasty" foods, then other bodily spaces such as stomachs, colons, and body fat are to be feared, regulated, and even punished (De La Peña; Guthman; Nestle & Nesheim; Stearns).

An important alternative to this approach has emerged from anthropologists and other social scientists who are writing from science and technology approaches that are more attuned to the nuances of bodily politics as they play out in other bodily spaces and registers. Critiques of the so-called obesity epidemic have been especially significant for illuminating how the privileging of the palate has mischaracterized the social and political value of other body parts. As Guthman and DuPuis have argued, studies that identify body fat as social, economic, and political "problems" not only demonize that part of the human body but deliberately misrecognize the political work that body fat can contain and perform (Guthman and DuPuis). Guthman has convincingly demonstrated that when body fat, blood glucose, and other bio-markers are pathologized, the obvious solutions are directed at the act of ingestion, with strong preference for "alternative" or "real" foods (i.e. fresh, organic, artisanal, and sustainable, among other qualities) that prioritize the palate. By shifting the question to address why body fat, blood glucose, and other bio-markers are both culturally salient and politically productive, Guthman persuasively illustrates how bodily processes such as digestion and metabolism are thoroughly imbricated within political processes (Guthman; see also Biltekoff; Landecker; Nestle & Nesheim). In her research on the political history of milk in American society, Melanie DuPuis's observation that "the privileged discourse about the perfection of milk has left out those people—mostly people of color—who are genetically lactose-intolerant" (11) directly links presumed taste preferences with the sensory experiences of racial politics at the most basic, gut level. Thus attention to digestion and metabolism offers an important vantage point for understanding more clearly how politics are not simply ingested but embodied and evoked within the most intimate spaces and sensory experiences of the body.

In their own work on different dimensions of the politics of food and taste preferences, Elizabeth Dunn and Heather Paxson focus on the organisms that inhabit foods, be it the botulism spores that Dunn describes for canners in the formerly Soviet Republic of Georgia or the bacteria in cheese described by Paxson, thereby reorienting understandings of how and where acts of agency, choice, and responsibility occur, as well as of the precise relationship between the individual and the larger society in which that individual lives. As Paxson notes in her discussion of what she calls "microbiopolitics," "dissent over how to live with microorganisms reflects disagreement about how humans ought to live with one another. Microbiopolitics is one way to frame questions of food ethics and governance" (16). Elizabeth Dunn makes a related point in her argument that states may become apparent and active in both formal institutional structures as well as in micro-materialities like spores that move between foods and the bodies of those that consume those foods (244).

For the Russian case, it is through digestion and metabolism that political processes come to be inscribed physically in and on the bodies of citizens. This correlation became apparent in accounts related by informants who worked as physicians and who called my attention to how bodily experiences beyond the palate were crucial sites of national politics. Anatolii was a professor of orthopedic surgery at a university several hours south of Moscow. When Anatolii learned that I was researching food and political history, he argued, "There is no connection between food and history." Instead, he informed me, "you should study the connection between food and the skeleton."

By way of explanation, Anatolii commented that since the early 1990s, he had observed a sharp decline in the food-related health of his patients. During the Soviet period, his patients were primarily elderly persons who had suffered broken bones due to falls. In the post-Soviet period, however, his patients were more and more often young men in their twenties and thirties with broken bones. This apparent increase in bone injuries among young men was clearly visible in places like Moscow and St. Petersburg, where casts on arms and legs were so ubiquitous as to appear a fashion trend. Although popular wisdom typically blamed these injuries on violence (frequently alcohol-fueled), Anatolii suggested that these young men were also injured from falls. Anatolii argued that the increasingly frail bodies of Russia's young men were the direct result of the proliferation of foreign food products in Russian stores, thereby invoking the refrain of food nationalism that was prevalent in Russia at that time. Anatolii placed special blame on American foods, which he claimed were high in *konservanty*, or preservatives. It was this connection between food and the declining body that I should investigate, he said.

Several weeks later, I was visiting friends in another small city outside Moscow. Lena is also a physician at a state-run hospital, with a secondary, lucrative private practice in alternative medicine. Over dinner, Lena reflected on the escalating cost of groceries, and she noted how difficult it was for ordinary Russians to feed their families. Lena finished by commenting, "Today many people, children in particular, are just not getting the nutrition they need because prices are so high. It is really affecting their health." What Lena witnessed in her medical clinic were children with thin and frail bodies.

As both Lena and Anatolii suggested from their perspectives as physicians whose attentions are focused directly on the physical bodies of their patients, political processes can be borne out directly within consumers' bodies, such as in their bones and the strength of their muscles. By framing their medical assessments about the health conditions of Russian patients as commentaries on Russian political processes, Lena and Anatolii articulated a potent critique of Russia's transition to market capitalism by arguing that the new, foreign food products that were available to Russian consumers were of lower nutritional quality than their Russian equivalents. Consequently, foreign foods were bringing about the decline and frailty—both physical and symbolic—of Russians and, by extension, the Russian nation. These concerns have been mirrored at the national level in Russia, with growing public and governmental concern about the physical weakening of the country's military. Media exposés and soldiers' letters home to parents have documented inadequate food, which is resulting in illnesses and injuries. Mothers of conscription-age young men expressed their worries about how the food provided during their military service would weaken, and even break (literally), their sons' bodies.

Bodily frailties are experienced sensorily, as with the pains associated with broken and healing bones. But even healed injuries can still evoke sensory responses as food moves throughout the body. One memorable afternoon, I was visiting my elderly friend Aleksandra Petrovna for lunch. During an otherwise normal conversation about her adolescence during the Great Patriotic War (i.e. World War II), she asked me if I would like to see her scar. Curious, I assented. Without warning, Aleksandra Petrovna quickly unbuttoned her blouse and removed her undergarments.

Tracing a thick scar from just under her chin all the way down her chest and down to her groin, Aleksandra Petrovna narrated the story of how it came to be. During the war, she was sixteen and lived on the outskirts of Moscow with her mother and sister, while her father was at the front. The German army had advanced to a nearby position, and she and her neighbors had grown accustomed to the constant shelling. One day, as Aleksandra Petrovna was on her way to pick up her family's food ration, bombing caused a tree to topple over, pinning her beneath it. After she was eventually rescued, her stomach hurt terribly. Without medicine or access to a physician, her mother strapped tight bandages around her chest to relieve the pressure.

Years later, she continued to suffer pain in her chest and stomach, which worsened during and after meals. Only after her second son was born and Aleksandra Petrovna was being treated for post-delivery complications did a physician determine that her pains were due to her long-ago untreated injuries. Her stomach had been severed into two parts from the force of the tree on her, thereby preventing her from being able to fill her stomach with more than a few tiny bites at a time and further hindering digestion. A surgeon successfully tied off the smaller section of stomach and created an alternative esophagus to the more effectively functioning section. Now, although she still cannot eat more than a few bites at a time, she no longer endures extended bouts of indigestion.

In narrating this story, Aleksandra Petrovna reflected that because of the physiological symptoms of this past trauma, every bite of food that she ingests is a painful reminder of the past. She thus has to be careful about the food that she puts into her body because of the physiological sensations it might evoke. Foods with small pieces, such as breads, fruits, and chocolates with nuts and seeds, or fruits with high acidity levels, or even excessively hot foods will all cause her to feel pain. Yet despite the unpleasant effects of eating irritating foods, this does not stop her from consuming them altogether. Because these are foods that she enjoys for their flavors, she refuses to give them up entirely. Rather, she simply moderates the quantity and timing of her meals. She has thus found ways to manage her digestive processes so that she can continue to acknowledge and even pleasure different parts of her body.

Although Aleksandra Petrovna's story is extreme, it was not the only one like it that I encountered, as acquaintances gradually revealed long-ago injuries such as hers. More generally, though, Aleksandra Petrovna's careful attention to digestive ailments was commonplace. Other friends and acquaintances have repeatedly complained about stomachaches, nausea, and intestinal troubles related to the foods they have eaten. Bottled waters are particularly suspect for causing stomach distress, and friends have lamented the poor bottling processes that produce tainted water. Yet because tap water is not always safe to drink, consumers still buy bottled water, even when they know it will distress their stomachs and colons. Meanwhile, consumers' complaints about fast foods like McDonald's focus not on the flavors of the foods but on the subsequent physiological sensations caused by these foods. Acquaintances have described in great detail how their stomachs feel bloated and their skin feels flushed from excess sodium in these foods. While such comments are perhaps not unique to Russian consumers, as American acquaintances have also expressed such sentiments, it was noteworthy that Russian respondents did not usually also comment that the foods tasted poorly and thus should be avoided.

Other acquaintances have described the unpleasant bodily sensations of constipation and diarrhea that have resulted from eating unfamiliar foods served at "new" (i.e. not Russian) restaurants. Recipients in several Moscow food relief programs have not infrequently grumbled that the starchy foods and lack of fresh fruits and vegetables served in their hot meals and contained in their supplemental food bags frequently result in extended bouts of constipation, a complaint seemingly borne out by the grunts and howls of pain that relief workers and I have heard coming from the toilets used by recipients. A physician with a medical relief program serving low-income Moscow residents related that most of his clients suffered heart palpitations and other physical conditions from high blood pressure that was likely caused by the high-sodium foods they were given as part of their food relief packages.

Russians' concerns with their digestive processes are not unique but part of a longer historical trend both in Russia and elsewhere in which social reformers have focused on the gut, and on processes of digestion and indigestion, as the site for cultivating and transmitting moral values. American food moralists like Kellogg and Post—both Seventh-Day Adventists who contributed to the founding of America's cereal industry, and Graham, who invented the digestive biscuit the graham cracker—found their counterparts in Soviet and post-Soviet moral reformers who have taught citizens how to manage their colons as a way to become productive and compliant workers. By the mid-19th century, dietary advice focused on digestion, and excretion was a frequent topic in Russian medical and domestic hygiene texts. With recipes and tips that displayed a nationalist orientation, these texts encouraged readers to pay attention both to particular foods and the origins of those foods in order to protect and improve their digestive tracks (Smith 64–91). Cabbage was valued especially highly as part of the Russian diet, as evident in the Russian annotated translation of a French hygiene manual. In response to the French author's assertion that cabbage should be avoided because it is "difficult to digest, it agitates, and continued use of it may upset the stomach and even bring about the actual inflammation of it," the Russian translator inserted the comment that " 'in all likelihood, the author gives his opinion about cabbage simply from hearsay. In all of Russia those who eat shchi [cabbage soup], never complain about it, and even more would very unwillingly replace it with watery French soups" (quoted in Smith 64–65). Similarly, cured cheeses (also associated with French cuisine) were described as foreign, dangerous, and could only be eaten by those who had already ruined their digestion (Smith 66).[9]

This interest in how foods were processed by the digesting and excreting body continued into the Soviet period. Child-rearing manuals included tips about how children should chew and swallow their foods so as not to upset their stomachs:

> [Parents] need to teach children how to chew and not to swallow food directly with a beverage. This is dangerous because thick food gives off warmth and *kisel* [a fruit drink] or water is room temperature. As a result, it creates a rapid change in the temperature of the stomach, which impedes the process of digestion. (Tura 87)

From a young age, children were also taught to eliminate properly through individual and collective practice (e.g., Tura). Institutions such as schools and orphanages trained children to eliminate at certain times through group training. Images from the socialist era show groups of children sitting together in a neat line of training potties. In more recent periods, Russian hygiene reformers and advocates have begun promoting bariatric surgeries, colonics, and other digestion-focused interventions to create healthy Russian bodies.

Despite their complaints about the unpleasant digestive experiences associated with particular types of foods, today's Russian consumers do not necessarily choose to forego those foods.

Within the food relief programs described above, recipients who complain about constipation and heart palpitations nevertheless specifically request that their supplemental food bags continue to include bowls of instant ramen noodle soups, which contain high quantities of sodium. Hypertension is an increasingly problematic ailment among these recipients, and the physicians affiliated with the program are increasingly insistent that recipients need to reduce their sodium intake drastically. Nevertheless, recipients continue to demand the soups and explain that they will find other ways of managing their ailments, either with other medications or, more commonly, through homeopathic means.

In contrast to prevailing North American models of healthy eating that advocate vigilance to the types of food that one eats—notably, low-fat, low-sodium, limited red meat, preponderance of fruits and vegetables—Russian ideals of healthy eating have typically featured meat, starch (bread and potatoes), and dairy. American-trained physicians in Russia have complained that the high-sodium and high-fat content of much Russian food, coupled with high rates of alcohol consumption among certain populations, is directly leading to food-related health diseases like hypertension, high cholesterol, and malnutrition, as well as the brittle bones noted by Anatolii, the orthopedic surgeon.

Yet as the practices of my informants reveal, consumers tend to focus their interventions elsewhere, primarily on the stomach and the colon, which means that their dietary concerns are different. Russians' heavy reliance on dairy, especially dairy products with active bacteria cultures like yogurt and oatmeal, helps them cleanse and protect their digestive systems from harm. Respondents note that fruits, especially berries, can lower blood pressure and help with weight loss, thereby counteracting the effects of high-sodium and carbohydrate-heavy diets. In still other cases, if all else fails, herbal teas, dietary supplements, and medicines such as purgatives and charcoal can be consumed to control the stomach and the bowels. This refocusing came up clearly during a series of interviews I observed in spring 2011, when a health food company tried to understand how a group of Moscow consumers made choices about healthy eating. What the researchers in that project discovered was that many of their informants commented that while they knew that certain foods were not healthy for them, they chose to eat them anyway because they enjoyed them. They resolved the tension between enjoyment and unhealthiness by instead medicating their digestive processes through natural medicines, ingesting charcoal, and other foods.

Ultimately, Russians are using foods homeopathically for their healing qualities, and specifically for their ability to soothe the ailments of indigestion and constipation, as well as relying on medical interventions to compensate for the foods they put in their bodies. In so doing, they are creatively balancing the beneficial and potentially harmful qualities of different foods so that they can indulge the palate and compensate at the gut. Such practices reveal that consumers are not necessarily concerned with eliminating indigestion but rather are focusing their attentions on engaging indigestion itself. They privilege the gut as the site of sensory experience, and consequently also the site of intervention and management. As my informants have repeatedly emphasized, they do not intend to give up the foods they love. Rather, they look for ways to manage their body's responses to those foods. In so doing, they are not denying the sensory experiences that occur beyond the palate but rather acknowledging and including them in a more holistic awareness of how "taste" encompasses the entire body.

Gastri(c)Politics: The Microbiopolitics of Taste

What might a reorientation away from the palate and to the gut tell us about the political work of taste, both in Russia and more broadly? If prevailing moralities of taste in current foodist accounts have emphasized the palate as the point of entry to the body, then moral issues pertaining to appropriate behavior and appropriate values are associated with ideas about agency and control over what enters the body. As Guthman and DuPuis, among many others, have observed, consumers are exhorted to be mindful about what they eat, lest it have negative repercussions on their bodies. The pleasures of eating then become secondary to the pleasures of restraint. In many ways, restraint becomes a form of pleasure itself, especially in cases of extreme dieting (e.g., Griffith). Yet if the focus moves to the gut as the site of expression and management, and especially compensatory intervention, then this changes how notions of choice, agency, and even pleasure are configured and where they are located. Consumers do not have to exercise restraint at the moment of ingestion but can perhaps pleasure their palates, even at the expense of their stomachs, intestines, or hearts. Because ingestion is connected to, and not separated from, digestion and excretion, this longer process of moving food through the body allows for additional points of engagement and intervention.

Relocating agency and control further along the digestive process in turn changes concerns and practices of responsibility and blame. For nutritionism proponents, responsibility must occur before ingestion, whether it is that of the eater or that of the producer (see discussions by Biltekoff, Nestle & Nesheim). But can post-consumption, digestive management also be a form of responsible healthfulness? If one of the concerns about the health of the nation is tied up in the bodily health of its citizens, can a healthy nation be one in which the state is interested in managing its citizens' digestive processes, whether it is by advocating particular foods and healing treatments or by training their bodily processes? Given Russia's past history, in which Soviet health reformers did direct their attentions to the digestive processes of citizens, this is a question that could be productive for understanding health transitions elsewhere in the world, not least the United States, where digestive interventions are increasingly the norm for managing the country's health problems.

Finally, to return to the themes of microbiopolitics raised by Dunn and Paxson, what is the nature of the sensorium when taste is expressed and experienced so deeply inside the human body? At one level, sensory qualities such as flavor, aroma, texture, and appearance are inadequate for capturing the physical experiences associated with digestion and metabolism, which occur in body parts and bodily registers removed in space and time from the mouth. At another level, theories of how taste preferences are the external manifestations of deeply ingrained cultural values and practices overlook how taste preferences might in fact be the deeply ingrained physical manifestation of external cultural values (Bourdieu).

Here Hennion's inspiration to "feel the feeling of," coupled with the idea of "tasting with fingers" proposed by Mann et al., provides an important way into rethinking the sensorium beyond the palate because both concepts emphasize the encounter with food itself as the point of departure for understanding how bodies respond to and interpret what they encounter (Hennion 98). Eaters encounter and engage with food both outside and inside their bodies, through both willfully controlled acts such as touching, smelling, seeing, and tasting, and through involuntary, reflexive responses such as absorption, metabolization, and excretion. Stomachs, muscles, blood vessels, and colons are not empty spaces but rather spaces occupied by a plethora of other organisms, which are in turn inhabited by a plethora of cultures and politics. As such, there are multiple points and moments at which the sensorium is realized and expressed, a fact that Hennion notes in his comment that "taste" is perhaps best understood as "a situated activity … [that] points toward the contact, a situation of 'between-the-two'" (101). And if physical, sensory contact can occur in bodily registers beyond the palate, then so too can cultural contact. Consequently, just as the cultural politics of the sensorium can be evoked at the palate with the moment of ingestion, the sensorium evoked at the gut can illuminate much about the experience and consequence of a politically engaged body.

Acknowledgments

This essay has emerged from a series of conversations and presentations over the years, and I owe thanks to many people whose feedback has shaped this final product. I am grateful to Melanie DuPuis, Julie Guthman, Michael Herzfeld, Dan Linger, and Carolyn Martin-Shaw for helping me work through very rough ideas and even rougher early drafts. A more developed version was presented to the anthropology department at Texas A&M, and I deeply appreciate the comments and suggestions I received from my colleagues and their students there. I especially thank Cynthia Werner for the invitation to share my work. Yuson Jung and Nico Sesnier have been terrific colleagues who have thoughtfully (and firmly) pushed me to develop this into a more polished and developed analysis, and I greatly appreciate their guidance. And finally, I want to thank the two anonymous *Food and Foodways* reviewers for their suggestions, and especially Rachel Black for her editorial wisdom and assistance.

Notes

1 Csordas defines (138) "somatic modes of attention" as the "culturally elaborated ways of attending to and with one's body in surroundings that include the embodied presence of others."

2 See Mann et al. (221–223) for a detailed overview and critique of this privileging of the palate in the anthropology of the senses, with particular attention to studies of taste.

3 These discussions are based on ethnographic materials gathered during fieldwork in Moscow, Tver, and other sites in western Russia over the past two decades.

4 Neringa Klumbytė describes similar practices in Lithuania, as Lithuanian consumers and producers promoted "national" products that were intended to contain "national" qualities, even when the precise "nation" at stake was contested (Klumbytė).

5 In the early 1990s, however, before the advent of this striking "food nationalism," socialist-era food themes were also used to convey the problems of the Soviet era and the benefits of foreign capitalism for a new post-Soviet Russia. See examples of this in the discussion of socialist kitsch by Sabonis-Chafee.

6 Tura is one fascinating example of a Soviet-era parenting manual that instructed parents on such seemingly mundane matters as how far a window should be opened in order to provide the precise amount of fresh air needed or which colors should be used in a child's toys in order to encourage

intellectual development. See Haney for an account of how Hungarian social workers deployed civic hygiene standards to enforce particular parenting practices that were geared at raising socialist citizens.

7 In his ethnographic research on the Moscow Culinary Association, the nonprofit professional culinary and food services organization that sponsors the Museum of Public Catering, Stas Shectman has documented how this organization has explicitly presented itself as a protector of Russian culinary and national culture.

8 In her critical account of terroir, Amy Trubek documents how the "taste of place" typically starts at the moment of ingestion at the palate.

9 Smith also documents how ideas of "delicate" and "rough" foods played into these conceptions of national digestive systems, as French food was valued as too delicate and refined in taste and presentation and thus would be problematic because it would be too difficult to eat in moderation (67–69). Instead, sentiments of Russian superiority were evident in demands for "a certain rough quality of Russian food" (Smith 69).

References

Biltekoff, Charlotte. *Eating Right in America*: *The Cultural Politics of Food and Health*. Durham, NC: Duke University Press, 2013. Print.

Bourdieu, Pierre. *Distinction*: *A Social Critique of the Judgement of Taste*. Trans. Richard Nice. Cambridge, MA: Harvard University Press, 1984. Print.

Brillat-Savarin, Jean Anthelme. *The Physiology of Taste*; *or, Meditations on Transcendental Gastronomy*. Trans. M.F.K. Fisher. San Francisco: North Point Press, 1986. Print.

Buchli, Victor. *An Archaeology of Socialism*. Oxford: Berg, 1999. Print.

Caldwell, Melissa L. "Tasting the Worlds of Yesterday and Today: Culinary Tourism and Nostalgia Foods in Post-Soviet Russia." *Fast Food/Slow Food*: *The Cultural Economy of the Global Food System*. Ed. Richard Wilk. Lanham, MD: AltaMira Press, 2006. 97–112. Print.

————. "The Taste of Nationalism: Food Politics in Postsocialist Moscow." *Ethnos* 67.3 (2002): 295–319. Print.

Classen, Constance. *Worlds of Sense*: *Exploring the Senses in History and Across Cultures*. London: Routledge, 1993. Print.

Csordas, Thomas J. "Somatic Modes of Attention." *Cultural Anthropology* 8. 2 (1993): 135–156. Print.

De La Peña, Carolyn. *Empty Pleasures*: *The Story of Artificial Sweeteners from Saccharin to Splenda*. Chapel Hill: University of North Carolina Press, 2010. Print.

De Silva, Cara. ed. *In Memory's Kitchen*: *A Legacy from the Women of Terezín*. Trans Bianca Steiner Brown. Northvale, NJ: Jason Aronson Inc. 1996. Print.

Dunn, Elizabeth Cullen. "Postsocialist Spores: Disease, Bodies, and the State in the Republic of Georgia." *American Ethnologist* 35.2 (2008): 243–258. Print.

DuPuis, E. Melanie. *Nature's Perfect Food*: *How Milk Became America's Drink*. New York: New York University Press, 2002. Print.

Ferrero, Sylvia. "*Comida sin par*. Consumption of Mexican Food in Los Angeles: 'Foodscapes' in a Transnational Consumer Society." *Food Nations*: *Selling Taste in Consumer Societies*. Ed. Warren Belasco and Philip Scranton. New York: Routledge, 2002. 194–219. Print.

Griffith, R. Marie. *Born Again Bodies*: *Flesh and Spirit in American Christianity*. Berkeley: University of California Press, 2004. Print.

Guthman, Julie. *Weighing In*: *Obesity, Food Justice, and the Limits of Capitalism*. Berkeley: University of California Press, 2011. Print.

Guthman, Julie, and Melanie DuPuis. "Embodying Neoliberalism: Economy, Culture and the Politics of Fat." *Environment and Planning D*: *Society and Space* 24 (2006): 427–448. Web.

Haney, Lynne A. *Inventing the Needy: Gender and the Politics of Welfare in Hungary*.
    Berkeley: University of California Press, 2002. Print.

Hennion, Antoine. "Those Things that Hold Us Together: Taste and Sociology." *Cultural Sociology* 1.1
    (2007): 97–114. Web.

Herzfeld, Michael. *A Place in History: Social and Monumental Time in a Cretan Town*.
    Princeton: Princeton University Press, 1991. Print.

Howes, David. "Introduction: Empires of the Senses." *Empire of the Senses: The Sensual Culture
    Reader*. Ed. David Howes. Oxford: Berg, 2005. 1–17. Print.

Jung, Yuson. "From Canned food to Canny Consumers: Cultural Competence in the Age of Mechanical
    Reproduction." *Food and Everyday Life in the Postsocialist World*. Ed. Melissa L. Caldwell.
    Bloomington: Indiana University Press, 2009. 29–56. Print.

Jung, Yuson, Jacob A. Klein, and Melissa L. Caldwell eds. *Ethical Eating in the Postsocialist and
    Socialist World*. Berkeley: University of California Press, 2014. Print.

Klumbytė, Neringa. "The Geopolitics of Taste: The 'Euro' and 'Soviet' Sausage Industry in Lithuania."
    Food and Everyday Life in the Postsocialist World. Ed. Melissa L. Caldwell. Bloomington: Indiana
    University Press, 2009. 130–153. Print.

Korsmeyer, Caroline. "Introduction: Perspectives on Taste." *The Taste Culture Reader: Experiencing
    Food and Drink*. Ed. Caroline Korsmeyer. Oxford: Berg, 2005. 1–9. Print.

Landecker, Hannah. "Food as Exposure: Nutritional Epigenetics and the New Metabolism."
    BioSocieties 6.2 (2011): 167–194. Web.

Lappé, Frances Moore. *Diet for a Small Planet*. New York: Ballantine Books, 1982. Web.

Mann, Anna, Annemarie Mol, Priya Satalkar, Amalinda Savirani, Nasima Selim, Malini Sur, and
    Emily Yates-Doerr. "Mixing Methods, Tasting Fingers: Notes on an Ethnographic Experiment."
    HAU: Journal of Ethnographic Theory 1.1 (2011): 221–243. Web.

Mincyte, Diana. "Self-Made Women: Informal Dairy Markets in Europeanizing Lithuania." *Food and
    Everyday Life in the Postsocialist World*. Ed. Melissa L. Caldwell. Bloomington: Indiana University
    Press, 2009. 78–100. Print.

Mintz, Sidney W. *Tasting Food, Tasting Freedom: Excursions into Eating, Culture, and the Past*.
    Boston: Beacon Press, 1996. Print.

Nestle, Marion, and Malden Nesheim. *Why Calories Count: From Science to Politics*.
    Berkeley: University of Californa Press, 2012. Print.

Patico, Jennifer. "Globalization in the Postsocialist Marketplace: Consumer Readings of Difference and
    Development in Urban Russia." *Kroeber Anthropological Society Papers* 86 (2001): 1127–1142. Print.

Paxson, Heather. "Post-Pasteurian Cultures: The Microbiopolitics of Raw-Milk Cheese in the United
    States." *Cultural Anthropology* 23.1 (2008): 15–47. Web.

Petrini, Carlo. *Slow Food: The Case for Taste*. Trans William McCuaig. New York: Columbia University
    Press, 2001. Print.

Pollan, Michael. *In Defense of Food: An Eater's Manifesto*. New York: Penguin Press, 2008. Print.

Reid, Susan E. "Khrushchev's Children's Paradise: The Pioneer Palace, Moscow, 1958–1962." *Socialist
    Spaces: Sites of Everyday Life in the Eastern Bloc*. Eds. David Crowley and Susan E. Reid.
    Oxford: Berg, 2002. 141–179. Print.

Ries, Nancy. *Russian Talk: Culture & Conversation during Perestroika*. Ithaca, NY: Cornell University
    Press, 1997. Print.

Rozin, Elisabeth, and Paul Rozin. "Culinary Themes and Variations." *The Taste Culture
    Reader: Experiencing Food and Drink*. Ed. Caroline Korsmeyer. Oxford: Berg, 2005. 34–41. Print.

Sabonis-Chafee, Theresa. "Communism as Kitsch: Soviet Symbols in Post-Soviet Society." *Consuming
    Russia: Popular Culture, Sex, and Society since Gorbachev*. Ed. Adele Marie Barker. Durham,
    NC: Duke University Press, 1999. 362–382. Print.

Seremetakis, C. Nadia. "The Memory of the Senses: Historical Perception, Commensal Exchange and
    Modernity." *Visual Anthropology Review* 9.2 (1993): 2–18. Print.

Shectman, Stas. "A Celebration of *Masterstvo*: Professional Cooking, Culinary Art, and Cultural Production in Russia." *Food and Everyday Life in the Postsocialist World.* Ed. Melissa L. Caldwell. Bloomington: Indiana University Press, 2009. 154–187. Print.

Smith, Alison K. *Recipes for Russia*: *Food and Nationhood under the Tsars.* DeKalb, IL: Northern Illinois University Press, 2008. Print.

Stearns, Peter N. *Fat History*: *Bodies and Beauty in the Modern West.* New York: New York University Press, 2002. Print.

Stoller, Paul. "Embodying Colonial Memories." *American Anthropologist* 96.3 (1994): 634–648. Print.

Sutton, David E. "Food and the Senses." *Annual Review of Anthropology* 39 (2010): 209–223. Web.

————. *Remembrance of Repasts*: *An Anthropology of Food and Memory.* Oxford: Berg Publishers, 2001. Print.

Terrio, Susan. *Crafting the Culture and History of French Chocolate.* Berkeley: University of California Press, 2000. Print.

Trubek. Amy B. *Haute Cuisine*: *How the French Invented the Culinary Profession.* Philadelphia, PA: University of Pennsylvania Press, 2000. Print.

Tura, A. F. *Roditeliam o detiakh* (*To Parents about Children*). Moscow: "Meditsina" Publishers, 1978. Print.

11

Resistance is Fertile!

Anne Meneley

The practices of everyday commensality — producing, provisioning, and consuming food and drink in the West Bank of Palestine — are radically affected by the Israeli occupation. I discuss two very different Palestinian initiatives that envision production and consumption of food and drink as a nonviolent means of resisting the occupation: a craft beer called Taybeh brewed in the predominantly Christian Taybeh village close to Ramallah, and a local agriculture movement based in the Ramallah district known as Sharaka ("partnership" in Arabic). Theories of resistance in anthropology, from James Scott's (1985) conception of resistance tactics as "weapons of the weak" to Lila Abu-Lughod's (1990) idea of resistance as a "diagnostic of power," still resonate in Palestine as the Palestinians are so clearly in a position of gross inequality in relation to their Israeli occupiers, whose power is hardly disguised enough to need a diagnostic. I have found Julia Elyachar's discussion of how agency is embedded in infrastructure and infrastructure is implicated in resistance activities insightful. This is particularly salient given the peculiar status of infrastructure in the West Bank where, instead of facilitating connectivity, infrastructure is designed to impede and exclude flows — in this case, commodities of sustenance (Elyachar 2014: 460). I am primarily concerned with both Christian and Muslim Palestinians in the West Bank; while I did not have the opportunity to travel to Gaza, conditions in Gaza, including the shocking 2014 Israeli military offensive, affect political sentiments and actions in the West Bank, including resistance practices involving food, a topic I will return to briefly in the postscript of this article.

Local food and drink production and consumption have become sites of "agro-resistance." Vivien Sansour, a journalist and activist, describes 78-year-old Abu Adnan as one of Palestine's farmer revolutionaries, who "understand on an experiential level that healing for us as a community suffering from oppression and occupation requires the restoration of our sense of self — a self that is defiant but not defined by its oppressor" (Sansour 2010: 2). Dinaa Hadid cites a Palestinian farmer who, like Abu Adnan, envisions agricultural practice itself as a fertile resistance: " 'I don't throw rocks,' says farmer Khader, referring to young men who frequently hurl stones during demonstrations. He pointed to his rock-built terraces. 'I use them to build our future' " (Hadid 2012: 3). I borrow my title from that of a recent article published in *Al-Jazeera*, "Resistance Is Fertile: Palestine's Eco-War" (Brownsell 2011), itself a spinoff from the classic line by the Borg in *Star Trek*: *The Next Generation*, "Resistance is futile." Describing Palestinian "guerilla gardeners of the occupied West Bank," the author quotes Baha Hilo, then of the Joint Advocacy Initiative, responsible for planting olive trees on land that is in danger of being confiscated: "We're not a militia, our weapons are our pickaxes and shovels, our hands and our olive trees" (ibid.: 3). Baha Hilo was my guide during my five years as an intermittent "guerilla gardener" myself, as we picked olives on Palestinian land threatened by Israeli military or settlers. Here, I examine how guerrilla gardeners are part of contemporary Palestine agricultural movements and, moreover, are deployed as a new form of nonviolent resistance to the Israeli occupation.

First, the Local

Both of these movements — Taybeh craft beer and Sharaka — have in common a claim to be "local." Although the term "local" may sound familiar to food activists in North America and Europe, it has different connotations in occupied Palestine, as one might imagine. A number of themes in current Palestinian discourses about food resonate with those circulating in (middle-class) Western discourses, especially the notion that local, organic, seasonal, GMO-free, "slow" food purchased from farmers one knows is inherently superior to industrially produced, artificial, anonymous food. Don Nonini forwards a strong critique of the local food movement in the United States, suggesting that it is part of a white "ethnoracial majority" who are part of a "global cosmopolitan elite" (Nonini 2013: 274). Brad Weiss, in contrast, has a more nuanced notion of the local. He discusses how the local food movement in North Carolina is inspired by a desire to counter industrial food production, involving "efforts to combat the dire social inequities of environmental, human and animal degradation at the hands of industrialization" (Weiss 2011: 440). Weiss notes the ways in which a sense of the local is created in North Carolina craft pig production through various practices related to the rearing, production, sharing, and selling of porcine products. He also notes that the people coming to North Carolina to work in the high tech industries "take root" through a commitment to local food (Weiss 2012: 616). In Palestine, however, the question is not how individuals take root, but how they resist being uprooted in a contemporary colonial context. The literature on food and colonialism is vast, but I will draw on one example by Susanne Freidberg (2008), who describes how agricultural production is affected by colonial regimes (she uses the examples of the French in Burkina Faso and the British in Zambia), and how postcolonial relationships are inflected by concerns about food safety within the European markets. Palestine, however, has yet to face the dilemmas posed by postcolonialism, since it remains under the colonial occupation of Israel. When it comes to Palestine, the issue is more about having one's "local" disappear before one's eyes. In the words of Sari Hanafi (2009), what is going on in the Israeli occupation of the West Bank is "spaciocide" as the infrastructures of occupation — the Separation Barrier, the bypass roads, military outposts, checkpoints, and illegal Israeli settlements—continue, on a daily basis, to commandeer Palestinian land, including some of the most treasured agricultural land.

The Separation Barrier runs through several villages, thereby disrupting people's sense of "the local" and the physical space of the local itself.[1] As is so heartbreakingly presented in the 2009 documentary film *Budrus*, villagers may be separated from their own agricultural lands, and in some cases, villages themselves are split in two. Checkpoints and curfews impede the transfer of time-sensitive agricultural goods. Since the Oslo Accords in 1993, Israeli incursions into West Bank territory have escalated, land has been confiscated for settlements, and settlers destroy Palestinian olive groves almost daily.[2] Israeli industrial food products flood the West Bank markets, as do their agricultural products. Much of the latter is produced in the West Bank on Palestinian lands, particularly in the fertile Jordan Valley, which is under Israeli control. At least twenty-two illegal settlements have been built there, many of them large-scale industrial agricultural farms exploiting the water resources and fertile soil and displacing the indigenous Palestinian communities (Haddad, Erakat, and Saba 2013). Many Palestinians, displaced from their own land, have become day laborers on these agricultural settlements, which are heavily subsidized by the Israeli government and produce products that are cheaper than those produced in other parts of the West Bank.

Another enduring problem is that the Palestinian Authority does not have control over the import and export of food products (Mansour 2012a) — Israel determines what product and in what quantities the PA can import or export. Neoliberal economic theories, accelerating since the 1993 Oslo Accords, have been particularly destructive in Palestine (see LeVine 2009), a place whose legal status remains uncertain.[3] Conventional economic theories are applied to the occupied territories in expectation that Palestinian businesses will thrive by specializing in the production of goods in which they have a competitive productive advantage. According to Samer Abdelnour and Alaa Tartir, the main goal of a people under occupation should be to free their land, not to compete with free nations using economic indicators without concern for political context (Abdelnour and Tartir 2012: 2). These are the conditions under which the Taybeh Brewing Company and the guerrilla gardeners labor.

Taybeh Beer

In a recent interview, Nadim Khoury, founder of the Taybeh Brewing Company, describes the meaning of his beer:

> "This is peaceful resistance actually," Nadim says, after a momentary silence, and looks at me as I raise my eyebrows.
> "No, it is. Making beer and making business and being here. We still don't have a country, but we have a beer, and I'm proud of that" (Crowcroft 2013).

Nadim Khoury is one of the many Palestinian entrepreneurs who saw an opportunity to return to his homeland after the Oslo Accords in 1993. The "peace" part of the accords perhaps has not borne fruit, nor has the establishment of a Palestinian state come about, but Oslo did allow Khoury to establish the first Palestinian microbrewery (and the first in the Middle East) in 1994. Khoury had studied craft brewery in Boston before returning to Palestine to make it his permanent residence. Taybeh beer is interesting in its claim to represent Palestinianness and locality. The notion of craft beer production is a foreign one, and while there was local wine production in the areas around Bethlehem (the Cremisian Monastery in Bayt Jala has produced communion wine for centuries, and the anise-flavored arak of Bethlehem is famed), microbrewed beer was not a central element of the Palestinian repertoire.[4] The following excerpt from the official Taybeh website outlines Khoury's approach to brewing beer, highlighting the "naturalness" of Taybeh beer and its lack of preservatives. The beer is described as "hand crafted with state of the art equipment," as organic and prepared in small batches, all of which emphasize its distance from industrially produced beer:

Taybeh (tai-bey) in Arabic means "delicious." Our Taybeh beer is handcrafted in small batches in German traditional style using a top fermenting yeast and cold lagering. This process creates a distinctively flavored beer with a clean, crisp taste. Taybeh Golden Beer — brewed with only the finest natural ingredients: malted barley, hops, pure water, and yeast — is the fresh, flavorful alternative to imported beers. Cheers!

The Taybeh Beer Company's website indicates the strong influence of famous European beer nations such as Belgium, the Czech Republic, and Germany. The company has even imported European ingredients including hops and barley, although in the past barley was a staple crop in Palestine.

The only ingredient that guarantees "Palestinianness" is the "natural spring water" from the Ein Samia spring. This is an important point, as water in Palestine is now under serious threat, with Israelis controlling 80 percent of the water in the West Bank, and springs, like olive trees, are very much a target of Israeli settler colonialism. Manning (2012: 223), speaking of Georgian beer production, has an interesting analysis of how European beer technology insures "quality" of production, but marketing authentic Georgianness focuses on two elements: the "ethnographic" tradition of Georgia's mountain peoples, and Georgian "nature" in the form of the mountain spring water that has been renowned for centuries. In the case of Palestine, the Ein Samia water is the guarantor of Palestinian authenticity while the European ingredients and techniques are the guarantors of quality. In Taybeh's promotional material, it is not ethnography that is drawn upon but discourses about resources in Palestinian nationalism; water is as much of a concern as land. Customers are urged to "Drink Palestinian" in order to "Taste the Revolution," linking beer consumption to a wider political project of freeing Palestine from the Israeli occupation.

Taybeh provides a craft alternative to cheaper, mass-produced Israeli beer such as Maccabee and Goldstar: Taybeh's producers not only introduce a higher-quality craft product, but highlight its Palestinianness as a selling point versus the industrial beer of the occupier. This fact was persuasive to many of the "guerrilla gardener" olive picking volunteers in the West Bank, who often enjoyed drinking a cool and tasty Palestinian beer after the hot and dusty work of olive picking on endangered Palestinian land.

Food and drink in Palestine, as elsewhere, are associated with particular forms of sociality; beer production and consumption was not a central element of the traditional Palestinian repertoire, and the sociality that attends it now is a foreign one. In 2005, the Khoury family introduced the Taybeh Oktoberfest, a festival that has been held on the first week of October ever since. The two-day festival features all of Taybeh's beers, including their nonalcoholic and dark beers, local food, and all manner of locally produced Palestinian products, including Taybeh olive oil and honey. The Oktoberfest also features local Palestinian bands as well as bands from abroad: Bavaria, Italy, and Brazil, among others. The festival was popular with the Israeli left, who come in droves. It is also an event that has garnered much international attention because it is a celebratory event with drinking as a central ritual, seeming to contradict imaginaries of Palestine as a joyless place characterized only by misery and violence. In 2012, a record number of 16,000 people visited Taybeh. But by 2013, trouble was brewing from within the local: the new local council in Taybeh protested the disruption the festival caused to the everyday life of villagers, and demanded a large fee and share of the beer revenues in exchange for approval to host the Oktoberfest. An agreement was not reached and the festival was moved to the Movenpick Hotel in Ramallah (Gilbert 2013). All of this speaks to recent local discord about the Taybeh beer factory and its place in the local economy and society. Some protested the public drunkenness, saying that it offends the Muslim population which surrounds the Christian village of Taybeh. In response, Khoury notes that Taybeh also offers a nonalcoholic beer for the nondrinkers of Palestine, including pious Muslims. Those villagers opposed to Taybeh say that the company provides little employment beyond the Khoury family and no social benefit to the community. The Khourys counter that the Oktoberfest provided an opportunity for local people to sell their food, handicrafts, and agricultural products to visitors. They also argue that they supported farmers, especially during the difficult years of the Second Intifada, by using their expertise and connections to export Taybeh olive oil abroad.[5]

Khoury is not only interested in internal markets for his beer; Taybeh is exported to Japan and Belgium. The company had been in conversation with the Liquor Control Board of Ontario (Nadim Khoury, personal communication, November 2007), but it has not appeared in Ontario stores.[6] The brewery in Palestine is as active as it can be, depending on the political circumstances, but Khoury is very proud that it was the first Palestinian product to be franchised in 1997, as it is also brewed and bottled in Germany, which helps to circumvent the difficulties of exporting under the Israeli-imposed constraints on beer produced in Palestine. Although it is a product that explicitly evokes Palestinian nationalism in its promotional material, the Taybeh Beer Company does not recognize the Boycott, Divestment and Sanctions movement designed to put pressure on Israel to agree to a just peace. Taybeh is kosher certified and is sold in some establishments in Israel; my impression was that the cafes and restaurants where it was sold were relatively left-leaning. Yet Taybeh products are as vulnerable as any to the infrastructural impediments imposed by the Israeli occupation of the West Bank. If it is held up at border checkpoints, unpasteurized beer, like olive oil (Meneley 2008, 2011), can be ruined by exposure to sun. Khoury is quoted as saying: "If [our beer] gets too warm at the checkpoint, a second fermentation starts and it goes cloudy. We have to throw it away" (Philips 2001: 1). However, for Israeli beer blogger Doug Greener (*Israel Brews and Views*), it is the Khoury family's mention of politics that "clouds" their beer. He asserts that they should not mention Israeli infrastructures of control:

> The Khoury family has chosen confrontation over fermentation. Although the Taybeh website is free of politics (except for the press clippings), the Khourys never miss an opportunity to attack Israel, the "occupation," the "settlers" around Taybeh. If their company isn't growing fast enough, its [sic] the fault of the Israeli security checks and bureaucracy. If shipping their export beer takes too long, it's because Israel discriminates against them. "Anti-Israel" has become as much a part of the Taybeh Beer brand as the "pure brewing" and "building Palestine" narratives (Greener 2013).

Few in the West Bank would agree with Greener's assertion that Israel's infrastructural stranglehold over the West Bank does not have profound negative effects on perishable food items.

Yet despite the claim that one can "taste the revolution" in Taybeh beer, the Taybeh Brewing Company, and Khoury himself, do seem to fall into the category that Dana (2014) describes as "returnee capitalists," who are willing to normalize economic relationships with Israel before any political settlement has been reached about land, water, and the right of Palestinian refugees to return. Former Taybeh enthusiasts in Ramallah who were anxious to support local production have stopped consuming it, because they do not consider Taybeh's strategy of economic normalization with Israel as leading to a fertile resistance to its occupation of the West Bank.

The Sharaka Movement

While the craft beer of Taybeh has no precedent in Palestinian life, the Taybeh Beer Company has certainly brought Palestine much international attention due to its counterintuitive presence and its borrowing of the German tradition of Oktoberfest as its attendant cosmopolitan sociality. In contrast, consider the Sharaka agricultural initiative, as described in their 2013 Annual Report:

> Conceived in 2009, Sharaka is a volunteer initiative working to preserve our Palestinian agricultural heritage and bring Palestinian consumers and producers together to celebrate our seasonal harvests. We are not an NGO. We are a group of concerned Palestinian volunteers attempting to support local producers and raise awareness among our fellow Palestinians. We envision a food sovereign Palestine where Palestinians produce a sufficient food supply using traditional, seasonal, and environmentally sound farming techniques (uploaded to Sharaka's Facebook page, February 6, 2013).

The photo adorning the Sharaka — Community Supported Agriculture's public group Facebook page features a representation of the Palestinian flag made of olives, yogurt, parsley, and tomatoes.

At the heart of the Sharaka initiative is the concept of *baladi*, the Arabic word used as a translation of the English *local*. However, as a concept, *baladi* embodies much more than "local," connoting the intimate connection of the Palestinian people to their land and its agricultural products that sustain them and their homeland. Sharaka is thus more of an inward looking initiative, in contrast to Taybeh, which cultivates external markets and international attendees at its Oktoberfest. *Baladi* food invokes "authenticity" and a certain nostalgia for a life that is in danger of being lost forever. Sharaka is a nonprofit, volunteer initiative that rejects foreign aid money, opposes the neoliberal reforms of the Palestinian Authority (PA), the flooding of Palestinian food markets with Israeli products or mass-produced food products from abroad, internationally funded NGO initiatives, and fair-trade companies that focus on international markets. They are strong supporters of the Boycott, Divestment and Sanctions movement, which encourages Palestinians and global consumers to boycott, among other things, agricultural products raised in illegal Israeli settlements on the West Bank. As deployed here, the call for *baladi* products is reinventing food traditions in the sense of "rediscovering" them (Grasseni and Paxson 2014). Sharaka not only encourages individuals making different food choices, but also creates a space where local foods, once edged out, are made available. Sharaka's primary activities are the organization of a weekly farmers' market in Ramallah, providing weekly baskets of fresh produce for subscribers, and the organization of underground restaurant meals. This restaurant initiative, Al Mahjoul, is promoted and described on Sharaka's Facebook page: for a modest sum, participants enjoy a meal made of exclusively Palestinian ingredients, cooked by volunteers.

The Sharaka movement follows the idea of agriculture as resistance to the Israeli occupation, but unlike the Taybeh Beer Company, it looks inward to provide good local food for the local community. Sharaka was inspired in part by the community supported agriculture movement (CSA) in the United States, but the principles of alternative food networks take on distinctive characteristics in the Palestinian context. Aisha Mansour, Fareed Taamallah, and Carine Abu Hmeid started Sharaka in 2009 to encourage patronage of Palestinian agricultural products and farming practices. "When we refer to *baladi*, we are referring to our heirloom seeds that have been saved by our *falaheen* [peasant farmers] year after year. Unfortunately, we are losing this richness as a result of industrial GMO farming" (Aisha Mansour, personal communication, June 22, 2013). In their quest to restore *baladi* products to contemporary Palestinian markets, the organizers are embarking on a "reinvention of food" program, in the sense of striving to rediscover and "renew the foundation" of *baladi* food (Grasseni and Paxson 2014). The Israeli occupation is ever present in discussions of *baladi* food, as is evident in the following blog post on *seasonalpalestine* from May 2013, where Mansour notes the effect on agriculture of the Israeli control of the water supply in the West Bank: "I planted tomatoes for my aunt on my first spring in Palestine. But then summer encroached, with all of its side effects including increased withholding of our water resources by the Israeli occupation. No water to bathe, let alone to water the tomato plants. The tomatoes died."[7]

Sharaka supports the Boycott, Divestment and Sanctions movement by encouraging their supporters to eat Palestinian produce from local, small-scale producers who are not funded by foreign aid agencies or supplied with GMO seeds.[8] As the blurb on Aisha's blog, *seasonalpalestinian*, says: "Defy free trade. Support your health and our small-scale Palestinian producers by eating from the local and seasonal Palestinian harvest. Say no to cheap, low quality imports. And say yes to supporting a healthy community and a strong local economy."[9] The following quote indicates how the Sharaka initiative rejects the strategies of industrial agriculture, including the use of chemical pesticides and greenhouses:

My winter garden was full of flavor. Arugula, spinach and radish for wonderful winter salads. Potatoes and broccoli for soups, stews, and stir-fries. And ground and body nutrifying fava beans (foul), chickpeas, and peas. Palestinians have historically planted these three in the winter in order to build the soil for the summer garden. Our ancestors cared for our land, respecting its limits to ensure annual production. This is in stark contrast to the practices of some farmers today who use plastic green houses and chemical pesticides to produce the same two to three vegetables all year long, destroying their land in the process.[10]

Sharaka encourages people to make their own jam and pickled vegetables, sealed with olive oil, as in traditional practice. Aisha's point in pickling and preserving is not quite the same as the contemporary North American interest in preserving and pickling, which if political, tends to frame the practice as a resistance to industrial food production. Sharaka envisions it as a way of reviving practices of preserving Palestinian produce for the winter so as to be able to boycott Israeli produce. The spirit behind the preservation movement is to resurrect the *baladi* tradition of preserving spring and summer vegetables for the rainy and cold winter. But Sharaka also encourages foraging for local plants like wild cyclamen, which does not cost anything aside from time and effort.

Sharaka announces its events on Facebook and an email listserv. A recent posting notes that La Vie Café in Ramallah is sponsoring Palestinian dinners featuring produce from their rooftop gardens, "All our cakes are made with organic eggs from our very own chickens, which feed on the compost and fertilize the garden" (Sharaka, June 5, 2013). The emphasis is on organic, seasonal *baladi* produce. Perhaps the most notable contribution of the Sharaka movement is the establishment of a weekly farmers' market, Souq Akli Baladi (My Food Is Local), in Ramallah, as the following call demonstrates: "This week at the Sharaka Akli Baladi market: grapes, cucumbers, plums, apples, faquus, arugula, mloukhia, figs, free range chicken eggs, vinegar, olive oil, taboun bread, cheese, flour, spices, herbs and vegetable plants so that you can grow your own food in whatever space that you have. Shop at the market so that you too can eat baladi, seasonal, and 100% Palestinian."

The market features local musicians, along with the traditional *taboun* bread baked in a clay oven fueled by olive wood. The vegetable seedlings that they sell encourage patrons to start their own vegetable gardens in hopes of reducing local dependency on Israeli produce. Their Facebook page features fetching pictures of local produce and local producers, who are introduced by describing their troubles in holding on to their land in the face of the relentless land cooptation that attends the creeping infrastructure of the Israeli occupation:

> Meet farmer Fatima who participates weekly at the Sharaka *souq akli baladi*. Fatima comes from Beit Nuba, a Palestinian village that was evacuated due to the aggressions of the Israeli Occupation. Most of Fatima's farmland in Beit Nuba is behind the Israeli Apartheid Wall and she cannot access it. There is a small portion of the land on the other side of the Wall that she farms. She has also rented 10 dunoms of land in Betunia. Fatima produces seasonal *baladi* vegetables such as zucchini, fresh black-eyed beans, and *faquus*. She often brings a specialty dish to the market for those looking for lunch. Fatima explains that *souq akli baladi* is a helpful initiative for small-scale farmers such as herself to sell their produce to the community. She explains that some consumers are looking for the perfectly shaped fruit or vegetable. But *baladi* products are healthier and tastier than the perfectly shaped items found in the mainstream market. Stop by the Saturday market to support farmers like Fatima and feed your family good, clean, and fair food (Sharaka Facebook page).

Sharaka was delighted to be the subject of an article in *Brownbook*, a magazine about urban lifestyles in the Middle East (based in the United Arab Emirates), noting the recognition of Palestine as a place where food politics were inextricably linked to emancipatory politics (Dawson 2013).[11] Sharaka's mandate explicitly critiques the NGO model as destructive to Palestinian agriculture.[12] The foreign NGOs, funded by the United States, European Union, Kuwait, Sweden, Spain, Italy, the Netherlands, and the World Bank, have been critiqued for encouraging dependence on foreign or Israeli inputs, like genetically modified seeds, pesticides, and fertilizers. Mansour argues:

> Farmers are trained to manage their farms according to international quality management standards. And they are inspired to produce high value cash crops such as cherry tomatoes and flowers in order to earn additional income in the external market. Rather than focus on food production for subsistence, and selling the excess on the local market, the modernized Palestinian farmer produces cash crops for export, and uses the earned income to purchase food for the household. The reality is that most of these modernized Palestinian farmers find themselves in debt. Unable to export effectively under the current conditions of the Occupation as well as agribusiness intermediaries who purchase crops from these farmers at very low prices, these farmers are unable to make ends meet. The sale of their outputs is not sufficient to meet the costs of the expensive inputs, let alone household obligations (Mansour 2012a).

Sharaka was invited to the Slow Food Terre Madre meeting Convivium in Turin in October 2012 as the "Slow Food Ramallah" chapter. The Sharaka board took some time to deliberate whether their goals were compatible with those of Slow Food; they, like many, were concerned with Slow Food's elitist reputation. However, they eventually decided to join in order to heighten the profile of *baladi* Palestinian food, turning away from their inward focus. Along with Imad Asfour from

Gaza, Aisha and her colleague Fareed Tammallah were given plane tickets and a place to stay in Turin.[13] The small but vibrant Slow Food Ramallah chapter was very well received at Terre Madre, and as noted above, external recognition of the existence of Palestine as a place, a locality, with distinctive food products, is very important to the members. In the words of Fareed:

> They [Italian and foreign visitors] packed the Palestinian wing asking questions about Palestine and the Palestinian people, and they admired the products of the land of Palestine. This gave us determination and will to complete our journey to protect our mother land, not through empty slogans, but through farming and production, and to hold dear the land that provides us life and food and dignity (Taamallah 2012).

Sharaka has started an organic olive oil cooperative in Qira, whose oil is sold under the auspices of Slow Food Ramallah primarily to local residents of Ramallah and its surrounding regions, one example of developing sustainable Palestinian agricultural and herding endeavors.

Sharaka has strong links to a couple of permaculture initiatives in the West Bank, one close to Bethlehem, Bustan Qaraaqa, which teaches Palestinian and international volunteers "innovative water management and farming techniques" (Brownsell 2011: 5). Another permaculture farm has been established in the village of Marda, close to the huge Israeli settlement of Ariel, which is notorious for letting sewage seep down into the Palestinian lands below (Reidy 2013). Murad al-Kufash runs a permaculture farm that recently featured an appearance by Starhawk, self-proclaimed pagan and goddess, leading a two-week seminar which Aisha Mansour attended. According to Aisha, Starhawk was inspirational in her insistence on connecting the earth and its products with the social world, a theme that is central to Sharaka's goal of reconnecting Palestinians with their land. The permaculture initiative rejects chemical fertilizer or pesticides in favor of compost and manure; Aisha's master's thesis, which she completed at Bethlehem University, critiques both free-trade agreements and international aid that have promoted "chemically intensive industrial-style agricultural practices" (Mansour, cited in Reidy 2013: 3).

Guerrilla Gardening and Solidarity Sipping

Sharaka can be considered "guerrilla gardening," like olive tree planting and olive picking, in that its revolutionary strategies lie within the agricultural realm and has food sovereignty for Palestine as its goal. Al Kufash of the Marda Permaculture farm argues that food sovereignty is essential as a tactic for surviving under Israeli curfews or closures, which could happen at any moment. At Sharaka's annual retreat, in 2014, it was decided to pursue establishing a food coop/store to ensure year-round access to *baladi* products. As Aisha said to me, "We plan to put an action plan together and begin working, but this is a long-term thing and might take all year to implement. In the meantime, we will continue with our other activities" (personal communication, January 25, 2014). Sharaka is inward looking, in the sense that it wants to provide high-quality *baladi* food for *baladi* people, whose diets have suffered under the occupation, and to revive what Trubek (2005) calls a "taste of place" for political ends to produce a moral and ethical food economy. It invokes a return to the land, to local seeds over GMO seeds handed out by NGOs, and to envisioning resistance as an embodied, everyday act that everyone can and should perform. Sharaka is a nonprofit organization, its members envisioning themselves as brokers between producers and consumers, and educators of a tired, numb, and disenfranchised public. Jaded about peace talks and having lost whatever little faith it had in the Palestinian Authority, Sharaka envisions reclaiming local food as a means of resistance to the Israeli occupation, and the foreign aid donors who subsidize it. *Baladi* invokes a world of cultural practices that are in danger of being lost, as Palestinian land is disappearing at an astonishing rate, making a local food movement here political in a way it may not be elsewhere. In contrast to Weiss's work on the North Carolina hog producers' "place-making strategies," in Palestine this local movement embodies "place-preserving strategies." While the industrialization of food products is an issue in Palestine, it is more an issue of Israeli-industrialized food produced on co-opted Palestinian land and dumped on captive Palestinian markets. The local food movement in Palestine is fueled by the concern to retain what is left of Palestinian land and support the farmers who continue to work it, as any land that appears to be abandoned is open to confiscation by the Israeli state. They strive for food sovereignty despite the absence of political sovereignty.

Nadim Khoury's Taybeh Beer Company, in contrast, displays a completely different tactic in its cosmopolitan version of the local. Although claiming, as Sharaka does, that consuming Palestinian products produced by Palestinian family-owned businesses is a form of nonviolent resistance to the occupation, his is a corporate vision, a kind of activist-capitalism. Khoury is not producing a typical, traditional "local" product, as microbrewed beer was previously unknown in Palestine. What he did was introduce a desirable and unexpected product from a region not known for high-quality beer connoisseurship. He also introduced cosmopolitan modes of sociality in the form of the Palestinian Oktoberfest into an occupied land not imagined as a place of light-hearted revelry. These actions were highly successful in drawing attention to Palestine precisely because of the incongruous juxtaposition. Taybeh beer and the Oktoberfest proved popular with the Israeli left, but selling Palestinian beer to Israel is considered by members of Sharaka and boycott supporters to be an unfortunate economic "normalization" of the current conditions of occupation.

Postscript

Despite the Israeli infrastructures of closure that have severely restricted movement between the West Bank and Gaza since 2007, events in Gaza have a powerful haunting effect in the West Bank. The recent Israeli military onslaught in Gaza in the summer of 2014 affects food practices of individuals in the West Bank, as they read and saw images of corpses of camels and cows rotting in Gaza's streets and destroyed food factories and water purification plants (Sherwood 2014), realizing that basic food and drinking water for Gazans were in serious danger. The attacks on Gaza served to fuel the food activism of the Ramallah consumers and store owners around boycotting of Israeli food products, one of the few nonviolent means of resistance available to them. Stickers with "16%" were stuck on Israeli products in West Bank stores by volunteers. These stickers are designed to draw consumers' attention to the fact that Israel's 16% VAT taxes on their everyday food purchases are used to support the Israeli military, whose bombing produced such immediate food crises in Gaza.

The bombing campaign also had a personal dimension for participants of Sharaka, who were horrified to learn of the death of one of their colleagues in food activism, Imad Asfour, who had joined them at the Slow Food Terra Madre in Italy in 2012. Like most of the 2,200-plus victims of the Israeli 2014 bombing campaign, he was a civilian. The following appeared on Aisha's Facebook page on July 31, 2014: "Imad Asfour volunteered with us at the 2012 Slow Food/ Terre Madre event in Italy. He was killed by the Israeli Occupation attack on Gaza. RIP Imad."

Acknowledgments

I would like to thank Cristina Grasseni, Heather Paxson, and all of the participants in the Reinventing Food workshop for generative and generous exchanges about my paper and theirs. I thank Alejandro Paz for years of conversations about Taybeh beer and Israel/Palestine and Paul Manning for reading several drafts of this article at various last minutes. Baha Hilo and Kristel Leschert were fearless leaders of the olive picking program where I was initiated as a "guerrilla gardener." I met Aisha Mansour on my first olive picking expedition in 2007, and have admired not only her subsequently finished, wonderful MA thesis on Palestinian agriculture from Bethlehem University, but also her tireless energy in the Sharaka movement. Every return trip to Palestine is enlivened by a visit with her. I first visited the Taybeh beer brewery with Aisha, Peter, and Ehab in 2007, after our olive picking initiation. Thanks to them and John, Jo, Lana, Mounia, Nazaleen, and my other olive picking buddies for their conversation in the olive fields, over Taybeh beer, and over Facebook. Thanks to Vaidila Banelis for his good humor, patience, and care while this article was being written.

Notes

1   The Separation Barrier, of course, has many more implications. It has dramatically reduced wage labor opportunities for West Bank Palestinians in Israel, upon which many families had depended since Israel seized the West Bank and Gaza in 1967. Much Palestinian land has been confiscated to build the Barrier itself, which in places is 8 meters (26 feet) tall. A recent report in *Al-Jazeera* notes, "When complete, 85% of it will have been built inside the West Bank" (*Al-Jazeera* 2014). The Barrier has the effect of radically reshifting the *de facto* border known as the Green Line, the armistice agreement established in 1949 at the end of the hostilities.

2   The Oslo Accords were supposed to produce peace and self-determination for the Palestinian people; they did neither. They did, however, produce the Palestinian Authority, which has had subsequent control over its cities with the exception of East Jerusalem. Critics point out that this amounts to outsourcing the occupation to Palestinian police, who are largely funded by foreign donors. The Accords have not stopped Israeli forces from reoccupying West Bank cities. See Suad Amiry's (2006) scathing account of the Israeli occupation of Ramallah in 2002.

3   Palestine was admitted as a Member State of UNESCO in 2011 and granted "Non-Member Observer State" status in the United Nations in 2012. However, it has few properties that one associates with contemporary states; for example, the Palestinians do not control an airport, a seaport, or in any meaningful sense, their own highways. Some form of peace talks have been held since 1993, but little positive progress has been made toward defining borders. Since 2003, there has been much talk of the "two-state solution," but since Oslo, the number of illegal Israeli settlements in the West Bank has expanded dramatically, with the number of settlers now numbered at between 400,000 and 500,000, with the route of the Separation Barrier extending to encompass them on the Israeli side.

4   Arak is known in several countries in the Levant. It is similar to Turkish raki, French Pernod and Greek ouzo.

5 In this respect, Taybeh operates as Tuscan wine producers, who export olive oil through their much better developed wine exporting infrastructure.

6 A Canadian company from Prince Edward Island, Diversifield Metal Engineering Ltd., supplied and installed the brewing equipment. Yet the negotiations between the LCBO and the Taybeh brewery, as of 2008, broke down over "price and reliability of supply" (Ross 2008).

7 http://seasonalpalestinian.wordpress.com/2013/05/17/wintergarden/ (accessed 3/26/2014).

8 The Sharaka initiative does encourage Palestinians to eschew Israeli products in favor of slightly more expensive Palestinian agricultural products. And consumers have to make more of an effort to purchase local agricultural products, as opposed to the easily available Israeli agricultural products, which are sold at the main market in Ramallah

9 http://seasonalpalestinian.wordpress.com/ (accessed 3/26/2014).

10 http://seasonalpalestinian.wordpress.com/2013/05/17/wintergarden/ (accessed 3/26/2014).

11 Dawson (2013) incorrectly identifies Sharaka as a local NGO.

12 NGOs operate differently in different contexts. Mansour agrees with the arguments put forward by Arturo Escobar, who argues that development interventions constitute another form of colonization (Escobar 2005: 167, cited in Mansour 2012b: 94).

13 Slow Food had no budget for compensating Palestinians for their arduous and expensive travel to Jordan to catch a plane; Palestinians from the West Bank are not allowed to travel through Ben Gurion Airport, close to Tel Aviv.

References

Abdelnour, Samer, and Alaa Tartir. 2012. "Farming Palestine for Freedom." Al *Shabaka*, July 2. Reprinted in The Jerusalem Fund, July 9, 2012. www.thejerusalemfund.org/ht/display/Content Details/i/34992/p (accessed 7/9/2012).

Abu-Lughod, Lila. 1990. "The Romance of Resistance: Tracing Transformations of tower through Bedouin Women." *American Ethnologist* 17: 41—55.

Al-Jazeera. 2014. "Israel Says Separation Wall Will Be Border: Negotiators Tell Palestinian Officials They Will Not Get a State Based on 1967 Borders, Israeli Reports Say." December 3.

Amiry, Suad. 2006. *Sharon and My Mother-in-Law: Ramallah Diaries*. New York: Granta.

Brownsell, James. 2011. "Resistance Is Fertile: Palestine's Eco-War." *Al Jazeera Magazine*, November 1. www.aljazeera.com/indepth/ features/2011/08/2011823152713716742.html (accessed 3/27/2014).

Crowcroft, Orlando. 2013. "The Man Who Brought Beer to Palestine." *CNN Travel*, March 8.

Dana, Tariq. 2014. "The Palestinian Capitalists that Have Gone Too Far." Al-Shabaka: The Palestinian Policy Network. January Policy Brief.

Dawson, Jimmy. 2013. "Eating in Ramallah: How slow food is making an impact in the West Bank." *Brownbook Digital: An Urban Guide to the Middle East*, June 24. http://brownbook.me/eating-in-ramallah/ (accessed 3/27/2014).

Elyachar, Julia. 2014. "Upending Infrastructure: Tamarod, Resistance, and Agency after the January 25th Revolution in Egypt." *History and Anthropology* 25(4): 452–71.

Freidberg, Susanne. 2008. "Postcolonial Paradoxes: The Cultural Economy of African Export Horticulture." In *Food and Globalization: Consumption, Markets and Politics in the Modern World*, ed. Alexander Nutzenadel and Frank Trentmann, 215–33. Oxford: Bloomsbury.

Gilbert, Sam. 2013. "Oktoberfest in Palestine." *VICE Canada*, October 21. www.vice.com/read/oktoberfest-in-palestine-isnt-such-a-hit-with-the-people-of-ramallah (accessed 3/16/2014).

Grasseni, Cristina, and Heather Paxson, with Jim Bingen, Amy J. Cohen, Susanne Freidberg, and Harry G. West." 2014. Introducing a Special issue on the Reinvention of Food: Connections and Mediations." *Gastronomica* 14(4): 1–6.

Greener, Doug. 2013. "My Problem with Taybeh Beer." *Israel Brews and Views*, December 8. http://
israelbrewsandviews.blogspot.ca/2013/my-problem-with-taybeh-beer (accessed 8/8/2014).

Haddad, Bassam, Noura Erakat, and Jack Saba. 2013. "The Infrastructure of Israeli Settler Colonialism
(Part 1): The Jordan Valley." *Jadaliyya*, March 26, 1–3.

Hadid, Dinaa. 2012. "Palestinian Farmers Turn to Organic Farming in Growing Back to Land
Movement." *Associated Press*, November 9.

Hanafi, Sari. 2009. "Spacio-cide, Colonial Politics, Invisibility and Rezoning in Palestinian Territory."
Contemporary Arab Affairs 2: 106–21.

Joint Advocacy Initiative. 2008. "Taybeh Brewing: Olive Oil as School Tuition." www.jai-pal.org/content.
php?page=56 (accessed 1/27/ 2008).

Khoury, Maria 2008. "Taybeh Oktoberfest in Palestine." www. counterpunch.org/2008/09/08/taybeh-
oktoberfest-in-palestine/ (accessed 5/13/2012).

LeVine, Mark. 2009. *Impossible Peace: Israel/Palestine since 1989*. New York: Zed Press.

Manning, Paul. 2012. *Semiotics of Drink and Drinking*. London: Continuum.

Mansour, Aisha. 2012a. "Where Does Our Food Come From?" *This Week in Palestine*, June 7, 52–56.
www.thisweekinpalestine.com/details.php?id=3681&ed=205& (accessed 6/8/2012).

———. 2012b. "Impact of Post Oslo Aid Interventions on the Palestinian Agricultural Sector." Master's
thesis, International Cooperation and Development (MICAD), Bethlehem University.

Meneley, Anne. 2008. "Time in a Bottle: The Uneasy Circulation of Palestinian Olive Oil." *Middle East
Report* (Fall) 248: 18–23.

———. 2011. "Blood, Sweat and Tears in a Bottle of Palestinian Olive Oil." *Food, Culture and Society*
14(2): 275–90.

Nonini, Donald. 2013. "The Local-Food Movement and the Anthropology of Global Systems." *American
Ethnologist* 40: 267–75.

Philips, Alan. 2001. "Intifada Turns a Family Business into Small Beer." *The Telegraph*, September
8. www.telegraph.co.uk/news/worldnews/middleeast/israel/1339968/Worldwide-Intifada-turns-a-
family-business-into-small-beer.html (accessed 1/27/2008).

Reidy, Eric. 2013. "Palestinian Farmers Hungry for Change." *Al Jazeera*, October 26.

Ross, Oakland. 2008. "Family Brewery Keeps Head Up Despite Political, Religious Obstacles." *The
Star*, June 9. www.thestar.com/news/2008/06/09/family_brewer_keeps_h … (accessed 3/17/2014).

Sansour, Vivien. 2010. Palestinian Agro-Resistance. *This Week in Palestine* May(145). http://archive.
thisweekinpalestine.com/details.php?id=3114&ed=1.

Scott, James. 1985. *Weapons of the Weak: Everyday Forms of Peasant Resistance*. New Haven,
CT: Yale University Press.

Sherwood, Harriet. 2014. "Gaza Counts Cost of War as More than 360 Factories Destroyed or
Damaged." *The Guardian*, August 22. www.theguardian.com/world/2014/aug/22/gaza-economic-cos
(accessed 8/24/2014).

Taamallah, Fareed. 2012. "Palestine at the Slow Food Exhibition: A 'Partnership' in Healthy, Clean &
Just Food." Guest post from December 16 on *Noras Newsletter: The View from My Window in
Palestine*. www.noralestermurad.com/2012/12/16/guest-post-palestine-at-the-slow-food-exhibition-
a-partnership-in-healthy-clean-and-just-food-by-fareed-taamallah/ (accessed 1/19/2014).

Trubek, Amy. 2005. "Place Matters." In *The Taste Culture Reader*, ed. Carolyn Korsmeyer, 260–71.
New York: Berg.

Weiss, Brad. 2011. "Making Pigs Local: Discerning the Sensory." *Cultural Anthropology* 26: 438–61.

———. 2012. "Configuring the Value of Real Food: Farm to Fork, Snout to Tail and Local Food
Movements." *American Ethnologist* 39: 614–26.

Suggested Additional Readings

Nir Avieli. 2013. "Grilled Nationalism: Power, Masculinity, and Space in Israeli Barbecues." *Food, Culture & Society* 16(2): 301–20.

Charlotte Biltekoff. 2016. "The Politics of Food Anti-Politics." *Gastronomica* 16(4): 44–57.

Sandra Cate. 2008. " 'Breaking Bread with a Spread' in a San Francisco County Jail." *Gastronomica* 8(3): 17–24.

Michaela DeSoucey. 2010. "Gastronationalism: Food Traditions and Authenticity Politics in the European Union." *American Sociological Review* 75(3): 432–55.

Maggie Dickinson. 2017. "Free to Serve? Emergency Food and Volunteer Labor in the Urban U.S." *Gastronomica* 17(2): 16–25.

Sarah Fouts. 2018. "Re-regulating *Loncheras*, Food Trucks, and Their Clientele: Navigating Bureaucracy and Enforcement in New Orleans." *Gastronomica* 18(3): 1–13.

Susanne Freidberg. 2007. "Supermarkets and Imperial Knowledge." *Cultural Geographies* 14(3): 321–42.

Cristina Grasseni. 2014. "Re-localizing Milk and Cheese." *Gastronomica* 14(4): 34–43.

Diana Mincyte. 2014. "Raw Milk, Raw Power: States of (Mis)Trust." *Gastronomica* 14(4): 44–51.

Heather Paxson. 2008. "Post-Pasteurian Cultures: The Microbiopolitics of Raw-Milk Cheese in the United States." *Cultural Anthropology* 23(1): 15–47.

PART THREE

New Bodily Realities in a Techno-Science World

Introduction

What makes "food" is a process of transformation that turns plants, animals, and other materials into something that can be consumed, with consumption reflecting a range of activities from ritual prestation and aesthetic presentation to physical ingestion for sustenance and elimination. Domestication of plants and animals, the invention and spread of agriculture, and the development of industrial manufacturing and preservation are all processes that have created "food" as a viable and recognizable category of things. Each of these processes also reflects different moments of human intervention and creativity. Although all living beings require sustenance and nourishment, only humans have created a concept to define what counts as edible or inedible, appealing or unappealing, permitted or forbidden, and to assign values to them. "Food" itself is as much a category as it is a thing.

Paying attention to the ways in which food is a human invention not only reminds us of the humans who make "food," but it also challenges us to consider how particular foods are made by particular types of humans who live within particular constellations of culture and power. Specifically, food exists only through the work of specific types of people who are themselves made possible at different historical moments. As sustenance expands to encompass farming, cooking, manufacturing, scientific knowledge, consumption, performance, and ritual, to name just a few food-related activities, the types of persons involved in these activities transform and proliferate from being merely eaters to include growers, gatherers, farmers, farmworkers, factory workers, transporters, scientists, consumers, enthusiasts, and critics, among many others.

Innovations in science, technology, business, and governmentality over the past several decades have expanded the possibilities both for what counts as food and for what counts as a person. Notably, the interplay of new technologies, biomedical knowledge, and cultural concerns with accountability, responsibility, and safety have produced new moral regimes about ideal foods and the ideal people who engage with these foods. Attention to diet and health has also brought about new ideas about appropriate body shapes and sizes, which in turn opens up conversations about identity categories such as gender, age, race, and citizenship. Meanwhile, the commercialization of science, medicine, and policy work has illuminated the many ways in which communities make choices about who is entitled or required to prepare and consume which kinds of foods, as well as who is valued in society.

As bodies have become moralized and normalized, so, too, have the bodily experiences of the people who are presumed to inhabit those bodies. Sensory perceptions become ways for people to experience and interpret the social worlds they inhabit in very tangible, visceral ways, a reality that has inspired both chefs and food scientists to tend carefully to flavors, aromas, sounds, and textures in order to create particular experiences. Iconic sounds like the sizzle of steaks, the fizz of sodas, and the crackles of breakfast cereals reflect both commercial interests in translating sensory experiences into economic choices and the extent to which the sensory qualities of food act as mnemonic devices that evoke memories and feelings of nostalgia.

In other ways, technologies have illuminated the very different forms of labor that are involved in the production and consumption of food, which has in turn inspired critical conversations about whose bodily labors are privileged or devalued, as well as how food work is directly apparent in how people carry and experience their bodies. Migrant farmworkers, recipients of food aid programs, consumers at elite restaurants, and participants in weight loss and other health programs all have very different relationships to and experiences with their own bodies and bodily sensations. New information and media technologies further enable new modes of bodily awareness and regulation, such as through personal health monitoring devices that report data between individual bodies and health providers, commercial insurance companies, employers, and larger social networks. Scientific discoveries also change how people understand issues such as safety, taste, and pleasure, as well as provoke debates about the authenticity and legitimacy of both bodies and bodily experiences. Imitation foods, synthetic foods, and plant-based meats all represent technological innovations that challenge not only the palate but also the ways in which people interpret and experience food intellectually, ethically, and sensorially.

This section examines how new types of persons and new bodily experiences are being created through food, with particular focus on the effects of recent innovations in technology, scientific knowledge, and bureaucratic regulations. The chapters in this section cohere around a shared concern with how food practices make possible specific bodily experiences, which in turn illuminate changing values about ideal and desirable bodies. These are multifaceted relationships, as individuals use technologies to craft bodies—their own and those of others—as well as to reject body norms that are being imposed on them. Often these relationships reveal conflicts between individuals who possess very different forms of expertise and authority: children, patients, environmentalists, activists, policy makers, scientists, and health professionals. Collectively, these chapters invite critical investigation into how the entanglements of bodies, foods, information, and technologies inform ideas about the nature of appropriate bodies and how they should move through the world.

Potential Questions to Guide Reading and Discussion

How are ideal bodies and ideal persons being constructed through foods and food practices?

How do individuals experience the world through bodily sensations evoked by food?

What kinds of authorities are using food to shape particular types of persons and for what reasons?

How are different types of identity such as age, gender, class, race, and nationality constructed, imposed, or rejected through food?

How do science and technology influence how people interact with food?

What other kinds of science and technology might shape people's interactions with food?

How does food reveal categories of personhood?

How are subjectivity and a sense of self created or erased through food?

How do bodily dispositions become ways of interacting with the world?

How do systems of health, medicine, and science represent forms of power?

12

"Lose Like a Man": Gender and the Constraints of Self-Making in Weight Watchers Online

Emily Contois

"Inside every overweight woman is a woman she knows she can be."
"Really, I just want to be a better version of myself."
"It's never too late to start anew."
"Weight Watchers changed my life."

The diet industry convincingly feeds consumers not only weight loss programs and products, but also promises like the ones called out above.[1] These vows of personal transformation assure dieters that weight loss forges a path to a new and better version of oneself. Despite the near total failure rate of diets—indeed, more and more obesity research indicates that long-term weight loss is next to impossible to achieve (Gaesser 2009; Fothergill et al. 2016)—the diet industry exerts a strong hold on Americans. In a country that boasts more than 100 million dieters, the commercial diet industry churns out approximately $60 billion in revenue annually (PRWeb 2013, 2014). A nexus of discourses on food, bodies, health, and cultural ideals, dieting encapsulates the paradoxes and conflicts at the core of American identity: abundance and restriction, freedom and containment, aspirations and expectations. Indeed, anxiety about food and eating—as exemplified through dieting—has been characterized as a quintessentially American and middle-class preoccupation (Biltekoff 2013; Guthman 2014; de la Peña 2010; Stearns 2002). Furthermore, neoliberal edicts strongly promote the pillars of self-improvement and personal responsibility, elevating "good health" to a "super-value" and venerated characteristic of good citizenship (Crawford 2006). Analyzing the public faces of commercial diet programs teases apart a segment of American identity, not through what we eat, but through what we aspire so vehemently to limit and avoid.

A leading player in the commercial weight loss industry since 1963, Weight Watchers expanded its product portfolio into cyberspace with the new millennium, launching Weight Watchers Online in 2001. Featuring online tools and downloadable apps, the online program exists within the relative anonymity of the internet, divorced from the in-person weigh-ins, group meetings, and tangible resources that characterize the traditional Weight Watchers program—and the face-to-face social support credited for the program's success (Dansinger et al. 2005).

The new millennium ushered in another shift at Weight Watchers. Although 90 percent of the program's clients had historically been female, Weight Watchers expanded into the "under-tapped niche market" of male dieters (PRWeb 2013). In 2007, Weight Watchers followed Nutrisystem's lead, which began Nutrisystem for Men in 2005, and created Weight Watchers Online for Men, a program "customized just for guys" (Schultz 2011). The company reported a 28 percent increase in male subscribers between 2006 and 2007 (Newman 2008) and hungered for more. In 2011, Weight Watchers heavily promoted Weight Watchers Online for Men with a $10 million campaign, including commercials aired during the NBA and NHL playoffs that year (Schultz 2011). Invoking the spirit of sport and the cachet of celebrity, ads featured former professional basketball player Charles Barkley as a spokesman.[2]

With digital products designed to target male and female clients separately, Weight Watchers Online communicates, represents, and manipulates gender in its program pitch. Unsurprisingly, Weight Watchers upholds a strict gender binary, reinscribing traditional understandings of masculinity and femininity. Weight Watchers also attempts in specific ways to counter the cultural construction of dieting as feminine. According to the boundaries set by hegemonic masculinity (Connell 2005), male dieting is taboo and transgressive (Bentley 2005; De Souza and Ciclitira 2005; Gough 2007). As a result, Weight Watchers forcefully engages aspects of hegemonic masculinity in their men's program in order to "masculinize" and "de-feminize" dieting.

In this article, I demonstrate how Weight Watchers constructs "masculine" versus "feminine" dieting through contrasting depictions of food, the body, and technology use. For women, weight loss technologies—such as Weight Watchers points tracking apps—are intended to further the emotional, psychological, and highly internalized project of self-discipline. This discipline fuels the pursuit of idealized thinness, which purportedly transforms the body and the self. Weight Watchers portrays female dieters on a difficult but actualizing and empowering journey toward a new and better self. For men, however, Weight Watchers portrays the same dieting technology as keeping the work of weight loss at arm's length. Weight Watchers depicts male clients losing weight easily, even effortlessly, and retaining a stable and immutable masculine selfhood throughout the process. By analyzing the difference in the weight loss experiences that Weight Watchers Online promises, I argue that limited types of self are made available to women and men. This constraint upon self-making exposes how patriarchy subordinates even the men assumed to profit the most from its power, as the male weight loss promise withholds transformative potentials.

Methods: Interpreting Gender and the Foodscape

To investigate the gendered distinctions put forth by Weight Watchers Online, I conducted a side-by-side comparison of the "How Does It Work" videos for the "female" and "male" programs, which were featured on each program's website homepage.[3] Each approximately 90 seconds long and following the same overall narrative, these two short videos provide compact sources of evidence, well suited to a comparative approach. I supplemented my readings of the videos with analysis of the additional text and images featured on each of the Weight Watchers homepages. These videos distill the Weight Watchers Online program, as they summarize the plan, its attributes, and its tools, as well as the Weight Watchers promise and point of view. In these videos, Weight Watchers also constructs its own boundaries and possibilities for femininities and masculinities through depictions of food, the body, the process of weight loss, and the use of digital technologies. As Susan Bordo (1993: 110) argued in her analysis of food advertisements, these videos are cultural representations that do not just describe gender; rather, through the construction of strict binaries, they culturally reproduce gender ideology, difference, and inequality.

To interpret gender within the videos, I applied the tools of critical discourse analysis, a method that provides a multidisciplinary view of how text, verbal exchange, and other communicative events influence social structures and power relations (van Dijk 1993). I use critical discourse analysis to assess the words, tone, and style used in these videos when communicating with men and women about dieting, food, bodies, and the self. I also position these discourses within the foodscape that each video depicts and alludes to. Building from Appadurai's "scapes," the foodscape is a concept that not only depicts the material realities of the global food system, but also engages relational and dynamic networks of power (Johnson and Goodman 2015). The foodscape concept analyzes together and at once food culture, political economy, representation, mediation, space, and environment. Josée Johnston and Michael Goodman (2015: 209) argue that food media plays a significant role in both framing and mediating the foodscape:

> Foodscape mediation is, therefore, a fraught and multifaceted process. It equally contains the expressions of social resistance and acceptances. It crosses the realms of the mind, unconscious tastes, desires, and visceral embodiments with those of socially constructed ideals of fit bodies, optimal health, good taste, and responsible consumers.

In this article, I use the foodscape concept to further contextualize and extend the theoretical reach of critical discourse analysis, as the foodscape situates text, words, and language in space, in time, in culture, and within dynamic hierarchies. Using these methods, I endeavor to identify and interpret the relationships of power within Weight Watchers' gendered promises, as depicted in these online videos.

Background: The Gendering of Dieting, the Body, and Technology

This analysis engages literatures addressing gender and its intersections with dieting, the body, and technology. Taking their theoretical foundation from Michel Foucault's *Discipline and Punish: The Birth of the Prison* (1977), scholars have applied his concepts of self-surveillance, panopticonism, gaze, confession, and the potential for resistance to the study of dieting and bodies. Much of this scholarship on dieting has focused on women and femininities. Past feminist scholarship has explored how dieting enforces patriarchal power, exerts control, and conducts surveillance over women's bodies (Bartky 1990; Bordo 1993; Stinson 2001; Heyes 2006). The female dieter is simultaneously a subject and subjected in the pursuit of socially mandated thinness. In his history of diets, Hillel Schwartz draws connections between gender, fatness, and dieting, as he argues that fat men have been represented as gluttons and monsters, fat women as patients and freaks. Turn-of-the-century diet programs operationalized these conceptions in gendered terms: "Campaigns directed at men have been framed as adventures, romances that will provoke an immediate change in the world: physical prowess, political action, business success. Campaigns directed at women have been framed as rituals of watchfulness in response to external threats" (1986: 18).

These gendered constructions of dieting continue to the present day, due in part to dominant constellations of masculinity, which frame dieting as supremely feminine. "Hegemonic masculinity" is defined as the currently accepted and normative form of masculinity that secures men's dominant position, while subordinating all women and any men who are not heterosexual, white, and middle class (Connell 2005; Connell and Messerschmidt 2005: 832). In contemporary Western societies, the idealized masculine character is typically "a White, middle-class, breadwinning man" who is "strong, competent, in control, competitive, assertive (if not aggressive), rational/instrumental, and oriented toward the public rather than the private sphere" (Grindstaff and West 2011: 860). Nutrition and health knowledge, healthy eating, concern for weight, and weight loss are each considered feminine and in conflict with hegemonic masculinity (Courtenay 2000). Because of this, when commercial diet programs market their products to men, they must refute the claim that "real men don't diet" (Gough 2007).

The cultural construction of gender also affects social perception of bodies, particularly fat bodies. Fat studies scholars assert that contemporary negative assumptions about fatness—as well as fat stigma and its resulting material and ideological oppressions—are rooted in a historically specific and socially constructed view of the fat body as a social malignancy (Braziel and LeBesco 2001; Farrell 2011; Hill 2011; Kulick and Meneley 2005; LeBesco 2004; Rothblum and Solovay 2009). These forces judge women's bodies more severely than men's, based on stringent notions of ideal beauty and motherhood (Bergman 2009; Van Amsterdam 2013). In his study of men and dieting, Lee F. Monaghan complements the work of feminist fat studies scholars, arguing that fat oppression is real and that, in our current historical moment, it affects female bodies the most. It also affects fat male bodies, which are coded as feminine and emblematic of "failed manhood" (2008: 6). Based on such assumptions, male dieting is further denigrated as "an admission of that failure" (Mallyon et al. 2010).

This "failure" is due in part to shifts in the cultural construction of ideal body types for men and women, which are linked to similarly idealized notions of productive citizenship. Women have long been oppressed by the Western ideal of slimness and their bodies objectified in the media. The hegemonic ideal of a chiseled, muscular form—which emerged in the late nineteenth century (Green 1986; Schwartz 1986)—remains dominant for men, particularly the muscles frequently featured in the media, such as abdominals, pectorals, and biceps (Hoyt and Kogan 2001). Men have typically been less critical of their own bodies than women. As Susan Bordo demonstrated in *The Male Body* (1999) and others have studied (Pope, Phillips, and Olivardia 2000; Labre 2005), men's bodies are increasingly treated in similarly objectified ways. Scholarship on identity and embodiment argues that like the female body, the male body is "a new (identity) project in high/late/postmodernity," a consumerist context in which the body takes on a symbolic value (in Bourdieu's terms) for its exteriority, for what it looks like (Gill 2005). This emphasis on appearances directs an objectifying gaze that is turned upon both female and male bodies. Analyses of popular magazines from the mid- to late twentieth century indicate an increase in the number of images featuring semi-naked men, putting an ideal masculine form on display for all to see, judge, and covet (Pope et al. 2000; Stibbe 2004; Hatton and Trautner 2011).

Relatedly, male body image concerns appear to have begun increasing in the latter half of the twentieth century (Garner 1997). From Sylvester Stallone's Rambo and Rocky to former Mr. Universe and Mr. Olympia Arnold Schwarzenegger's Terminator, the "hard body" action movie hero infiltrated popular culture in the 1980s and 1990s. These films and stars linked depictions of rugged masculinity to a specific, idealized male body (Jeffords 1993), themes that still reign at the box office. In the most recent wave of superhero films, the muscular male form is front, center, and in body-centric costume. Social pressure to conform to this ideal male body type has further increased as actors like Chris Pratt and Paul Rudd have achieved them—changes characterized as "the latest bro-next-door to transform into a man of steel" (Stein 2015). Furthermore, among U.S. college-aged study subjects, men and women have been found to experience similar rates of body dissatisfaction, as high as 95 percent of both men and women (Mishkind et al. 1986).

These concerns have drawn scholarly attention, yielding new concepts, terms, and areas of study that explore men and their relationship to their bodies, such as the Adonis Complex (Pope et al. 2000), muscle dysmorphia (Baghurst 2012; Mitchell et al. 2016), and orthorexia nervosa, which is defined as "a maniacal obsession for healthy foods" (Donini et al. 2013; Brytek-Matera et al. 2015). Michael Kimmel, who is widely recognized as a leading expert on the study of men and masculinities, aptly summarizes these trends:"I don't think there's ever been a time when men have been more preoccupied with their bodies than today" (Newman 2008). Although women remain disproportionately oppressed by body ideals and social standards of physical beauty, these trends indicate that men's bodies are increasingly scrutinized as well—and that men experience, to some degree, similar dissatisfaction and distress. While dieting is culturally normative for women, "a noteworthy portion of men" also diet to combat body dissatisfaction (Markey and Markey 2005: 528).

Commercial weight loss programs have sought to profit from these shifting male body ideals and increasing discontent, but it was the emergence of an online program that facilitated Weight Watchers' attempt to garner male subscribers. Fearing men would not attend in-person meetings in significant numbers, Weight Watchers Online for Men assures subscribers that the online message boards are "men only," seeking to masculinize the Weight Watchers experience through excluding women spatially and conceptually. Weight Watchers Online also largely frames weight loss as an individualized experience mediated by digital tools. For example, the Weight Watchers Online homepage invites dieters to "Lose weight completely online," as if the work and results of weight loss occur within a suspended, cyber reality. In the Weight Watchers Online for Men video that I analyze in this article, a male dieter confesses that he thought "Weight Watchers was just for the ladies," but then he "got the trusted plan, completely online, customized just for guys." This pivot from Weight Watchers as derisively "feminine" to acceptably "masculine" depends upon the anonymity and strict gender binary that the online program endorses.

Armed with online tools and apps that can be downloaded to smartphones and tablets, Weight Watches Online subscribers engage in a relatively new system of digitized weight loss that is significantly more mobile than previous iterations. When they launched, online programs were positioned to grow and overtake more traditional diet programs; traditional program sales were flat in 2012, while online programs grew by 8 percent. Notably, Weight Watchers' 1.7 million paid subscribers led the pack, generating $504 million in revenue (PRWeb 2013). Combining aspects of its traditional in-person program and digital weight loss tools, Weight Watchers Online exists between two worlds of commercial diet programming.

Weight Watchers' foray into the online space demonstrates how technology increasingly shapes elements of everyday life. It also mirrors broader trends in digital health care and wellness. This landscape has changed significantly with the rising popularity of biometric self-tracking devices like the FitBit, which was released in 2008.[4] Deborah Lupton examines self-tracking devices and practices from various theoretical perspectives, including "concepts of technological bodily enhancement and techno-utopian visions of the perfect(ible) body, healthism and personal responsibility, visualization and bodily display and the allure and power of metrics inherent in the use of these devices" (Lupton 2013: 395). While dieting—with Weight Watchers or otherwise—has always endorsed and enhanced bodily surveillance, self-tracking devices "direct the gaze directly at the body. They privilege an intense focus on and highly detailed knowledge of the body" (Lupton 2013: 396). Employing a comparative historical approach, Kate Crawford, Jessa Lingel, and Tero Karppi explore similar phenomena. They investigate how the weight scale, which first emerged in the late nineteenth century, and twenty-first-century wearable, self-tracking devices both promise self-knowledge and require self-discipline (2015: 480). Conceptually straddling the analogue and the digital, Weight Watchers Online also demonstrates the continuity and paradox between surveillance, self-discipline, self-knowledge, and self-improvement. This expansion in voluntary self-surveillance exerts control over the shape, size, and supposed healthfulness of bodies. It also produces constructions of gender and negotiations of power.

Reading the Videos: How Does (Gender) Work?

These two "How Does It Work" videos present the success stories of Bonnie and Dan, who are presented as actual Weight Watchers Online users.... A young woman dressed fashionably in a sleeveless, V-neck, black dress and coral-colored necklace, Bonnie explains in a soft-spoken voice the Weight Watchers Online program to female consumers. With his hair shaved short on the sides in typical military style, Dan is smartly dressed in a gray sweater and dark-wash jeans as he discusses the program's components for men with confident posturing and an assertive tone. As model Weight Watchers participants, Bonnie and Dan embody a specific subjectivity that is white, middle class, heterosexual, youthful, able, and attractive. They have achieved a weight status to which viewers are expected to aspire; they exhibit a dedication to self-improvement that viewers are expected to replicate. Bonnie and Dan enact "successful" performances of both normative gender (Butler 2006) and fitness, which are ever-increasing requirements within neoliberal contexts, where bodies are read as evidence—or not—of self-sufficient and productive citizenship (Biltekoff 2013; Guthman 2011).

Both Bonnie and Dan lost significant weight on Weight Watchers; Bonnie lost forty-seven pounds, Dan sixty-seven pounds. These videos depict the meaning of weight loss differently for each of them, however. At the beginning of the video, Bonnie, a self-proclaimed "Texas girl," shares the screen with her "before" photo and attributes her weight gain to family gatherings marked by lots of fattening food.... Prompted by personal concerns for her health and weight, Bonnie signed up for Weight Watchers Online. While Bonnie engages in the self-reflective work endorsed by the Weight Watchers approach, Dan does not. Instead, he states that he was a sergeant in the military who "could have been honorably discharged [for] barely meeting the fitness requirements." Dan joined Weight Watchers not to transform himself both inside and out, as Bonnie did, but to salvage his career by changing his body. As such, Dan's motivation to lose weight is made to appear more legitimate than Bonnie's, and his "masculine" weight loss to connote enhanced importance. While the video depicts Bonnie as a woman who ate too much and then worried about the personal health consequences, Dan's weight loss is depicted as central to his career success, and as a military sergeant, to the health of the nation state as well.

Word choice reinforces the orientation of male weight loss outside of the self. Dan talks of "losing *the* weight" (italics added), while Bonnie speaks of "*my* health," "*my* weight," and "*my* weight loss" (italics added). Dan does not address his role in gaining weight; he does not adopt the mantle of personal responsibility that Weight Watchers requires. Dan does not mention, for example, wanting to be there for his children, feeling guilty, or suffering low self-esteem. Engaging the distance that "the" produces, Dan does not speak of fatness, weight, or weight loss in terms that relate to his identity and sense of self. In this way, these Weight Watchers videos articulate social beliefs that fatness diminishes selfhood and obscures gender, resulting in out-of-control women and failed, effeminate men. For dieters, weight loss is constructed as a disciplined act that "will eventually demarcate them as intelligible men and women" (Bosc 2014: 69). Within these constructions of "masculine" and "feminine" fatness and ideal bodies, Dan purposefully distances himself from his previously fat body as he adheres to hegemonic masculinity.

At the end of his video, Dan claims, "I've become an officer and a role model for my men," now that he has lost weight and is on track to run a marathon. The video again frames Dan's weight within a professional capacity, orienting his body—and its purported fat disability and thin ability—toward the masculinized, public sphere. In this space, his weight loss connotes achievement, complete with a professional promotion, accolades, self-confidence, and leadership status. On the other hand, Bonnie's weight loss is about how she feels about herself. After losing weight, Bonnie says, "Now I'm hiking, I'm biking, I'm dancing. But mostly, I'm more comfortable with myself than I've ever been." Bonnie also acknowledges her former fat self again. At the end of the video, she appears beside another "before" photo to which she says, "This used to be me. I transformed my life with Weight Watchers Online and I've never looked back and I know that you can too." … Dan never appears in the same frame as his fat body. While Dan does say, "Weight Watchers changed my life," the male program video concludes by focusing on his continual progress, embodied in his ongoing fitness journey. The final frames of the video show Dan in exercise clothes crossing a finish line. …

While Bonnie and Dan use the same digital tools, the videos depict them gaining and losing weight differently. Bonnie and Dan appear throughout the foodscape—at restaurants, in food stores, and at home—interacting with food in ways that invoke conventional definitions of gender. For example, both Bonnie and Dan use "cheat sheets," which are designed to help dieters make "point-conscious" decisions when eating out. But they use the tool in stereotypically gendered settings and to select foods that align with gender norms and expectations.

Conventional notions of gender create hierarchies of flavors, tastes, foods, and ways of eating. Masculinity maps onto spicy, hearty, and savory flavors and foods, as well as large portions consumed with gusto; while femininity marks dainty, light, and sweet flavors and foods, eaten in small portions with restraint (Kiefer, Rathmanner, and Kunze 2005; Wardle et al. 2004). Weight

Watchers Online for Men repeats such stereotypes with explicit references to foods that match "masculine" preferences and appetites. A section on the website is titled, "You can eat that. And that. And that." Alongside images of hot dogs, chicken wings, mac and cheese, ice cream sandwiches, and steak kabobs, the text assures male dieters, "Seriously—*no* food is off-limits. You can eat anything you want. You'll just learn to do it a whole lot smarter."

In the video, Dan also eats out at a stereotypically masculine location—a sports bar, filled with round, high-top tables, backless stools, and flat screen TVs. Conversely, Bonnie dines at a more formal, sit-down restaurant, with large, rectangular tables and plush booths.... Dan uses cheat sheets to order "masculine" comestibles: tacos and pizza. The video does not depict Dan making what would be considered "healthy" dietary choices. Rather, he uses the program to track what he eats and "stay on plan" in order to lose weight. The plan, these foods, and these ways of eating portray Dan maintaining an uninterrupted lifestyle and a consistent masculinity while on Weight Watchers. He curtails neither his social life nor the foods he likes to eat—Dan does not order a salad when watching the game with friends. Bonnie, on the other hand, uses cheat sheets to order more feminized and health-conscious fare: a pink-hued cocktail and a plate of whole-wheat spaghetti, lightly dressed with a red sauce and green vegetables. Her selections reinforce how Weight Watchers depicts female dieters engaged in the self-discipline of dieting, which requires altering eating habits as part of the dieting process. Following the rules of dieting and of gender normativity, Bonnie does not order a pizza.

Bonnie and Dan also use the barcode scanner on their smartphones—a tool that scans food products to determine their Weight Watchers "Points Plus" value—in gendered ways and spaces. Dan uses it to purchase a snack—in this case, a bag of chips at a convenience store—so that he "can stay on plan" while "on the go." Bonnie, however, uses the barcode scanner at the supermarket to learn the point value of a box of whole-wheat pasta. ... Again, these videos construct a gendered division between "healthy" (feminine) and "unhealthy" (masculine) food choices. Furthermore, Dan uses the barcode scanner within a public environment in which he is independent, busy, and in motion. Conversely, Bonnie uses the same tool in the supermarket, a site that since its inception has been framed as a feminized space, even "a housewife's paradise" (Deutsch 2010). Unlike Dan, who uses the tool while "on the go," Bonnie's video seamlessly transports her from the supermarket aisle to a kitchen, spatially reinforcing the enduring, feminized character of food shopping and preparation (Cairns and Johnston 2015).

Furthermore, while Bonnie discusses cooking and recipe tools in a kitchen, Dan never mentions these tools or appears in such a space. Instead, he uses the grilling cheat sheet to prepare one of his favorite foods (porterhouse steak) outdoors. ... These program videos uphold traditional gender divides between public and private spaces, as well as the feminized nature of food preparation. Cooking contains women within the kitchen, a space that men purportedly do not enter, except peripherally as Dan grills a steak outdoors. In this way, Weight Watchers reinforces the perception of cooking as "one of the most identifiable performative traits of femininity" (Parasecoli 2005: 30).

Bonnie and Dan also discuss these weight loss tools in entirely different terms. With a degree of glee, Dan says, "The tools are kind of like a video game." For men, weight loss tools are part of a game, creating distance between the work, effort, and self-discipline of weight loss. Bonnie, however, engages with these tools intensely, a connection that the video again depicts spatially. The video depicts Bonnie literally seated at a desk before a computer as if at work, actively interacting with the weight loss effort being measured, tracked, and visualized on the screen. ...

Conversely, Dan is completely off screen when the video illustrates these tools; a laptop computer screen simply animates the tools to his voiceover.

Discussion: Deconstructing Gendered Weight Loss Promises

Comparing side by side the dialogue, images, foods, and environments—as well as the ways of eating and using technology—depicted in these program videos demonstrates how Weight Watchers manipulates traditional notions of gender in order to distinguish these programs and to define the process of dieting along gender lines. These videos also reveal the different potential selves Weight Watchers promises. For women, Weight Watchers promises a transformed self and the opportunity to start life afresh in a thin body that purportedly reflects a woman's inner hopes and desires. Feminist scholars, such as Sandra Lee Bartky (1990) and Susan Bordo (1993), have written extensively on the destructive consequences of the Foucauldian surveillance and constant self-discipline that commercial weight loss programs require of women in the pursuit of a transformed self. Fat studies scholars deepen these critiques, demonstrating how weight loss promises foundationally reinforce negative portrayals and assumptions regarding fat bodies, particularly for women (Braziel and LeBesco 2001; Farrell 2011; Hill 2011; Kulick and Meneley 2005; LeBesco 2004; Rothblum and Solovay 2009). And even if weight loss yields a transformed self, it is conscribed to a particular type of potential womanhood that is subordinate; one with a curtailed autonomy and agency that is only powerful when thin.

Various scholars have argued, however, that discourses of beauty not only discipline women, but also afford female subjects agency (Peiss 2011; Cahill 2003; Brand 2000; Vester 2010). Pushing these critiques in a new direction in her article, "Foucault Goes to Weight Watchers," Cressida Heyes explores how weight loss dieting also cultivates disciplined technologies of the self that are enabling and positively productive. She argues that dieting engenders new skills and ways for mastering, knowing, and caring for the self. While she agrees with feminist analyses that the rhetoric of Weight Watchers cultivates female "docile bodies," she also argues that "the process of transformation itself invents new capacities and invites reflection on a … self that is not yet known" (2006: 141).

Weight Watchers excludes this process of transformation, this yet-to-be-imagined self, and this set of new capacities and skills from the male weight loss promise. While men keeping the therapeutic work of dieting at arm's length may prove psychologically protective, it also reveals how patriarchy traps and limits masculine selfhoods. It allows little space for the potentially empowering and actualizing effects of personal change. To embark on such a process requires destabilizing the masculine subject, conceding space for improvement, admitting vulnerability, and relinquishing power—all actions in conflict with hegemonic masculinity, as currently crystallized.

Because of this, Bonnie glows with the exhilaration of successful weight loss to and a newfound sense of self, while Dan must demonstrate how his changed body now yields productive accomplishments, such as a career promotion and new athletic abilities. The conventional boundaries of masculinity prohibit Dan from experiencing weight loss as a process in which he can work on his relationship with himself. Self-reflection, intimacy, and understanding are portrayed as off-limits. Instead, Dan must maintain his original, immutable masculinity throughout the process of losing weight and changing his body. This inflexibility reveals the ways that patriarchy not only oppresses women's bodies by idealizing thinness and scorning fat bodies, but also male selfhoods within the context of weight loss. This is due in part to socially constructed expectations for male character that devalue and discourage food and health-related knowledge and practices (Courtenay 2000; Gough 2007). In this way, the strictures of hegemonic masculinity limit the potential of gender. This study of Weight Watchers' promises demonstrates that cultural constructions of "successfully" feminine and masculine bodies are not only relational and co-constituted, but also mutually oppressive to men of all masculinities, to women, and to all those who resist gender normativity.

Conclusion: Defining Lose Like a Man

While women have long been targeted by the weight loss industry, Weight Watchers created its online men's program only a decade ago and promoted it aggressively with a multi-million-dollar campaign in recent years. As the weight loss industry expands its reach and cultural influence, these market changes incite new questions: What is suitably masculine? How do "real men" act? What is a masculine body? What are masculine ways of shaping and caring for the body? Or for mastering and knowing it? The work of weight loss engages these questions, and their answers have the potential to influence how men shape their own selfhoods within the increasingly technological landscape of American life. Engaging both food and the body, weight loss shapes definitions of masculinity and femininity, as well as gendered arrangements of power.

In their marketing, Weight Watchers Online for Men employs the tagline, "Lose like a man." The videos analyzed in this article define what "losing like a man" means. While reality weight loss TV shows like *The Biggest Loser* depict men experiencing the emotions of weight loss, Weight Watchers' men do not engage in the self-help process of reflecting upon weight gain. Dan never discusses how or why he gained weight nor shares the frame with a "before" photo of his previously fat body. Men are not expected to employ self-discipline to adopt "healthier" eating habits, as Dan eats burgers, beer, pizza, tacos, and steak—foods that also evoke masculinity, as well as unrestricted dietary choices. Men are not expected to cook, an activity deemed women's work that encroaches upon masculinity. Men do not lose weight to transform themselves or become more comfortable within the bodies that they inhabit. The work of male weight loss is external to the self—oriented around public life, professional advancement, and athletic achievement. This is the script for how Weight Watchers has extended its weight loss promise to a new "niche market." Given the diet industry's capitalist motivations and the near total failure rate of diets, weight loss promises are rarely realized (Campos 2004; Fraser 1998; Gaesser 2009). Weight Watchers' construction of "masculine" weight loss demonstrates another terrain upon which dieting fails.

Acknowledgments

Sincere thanks to the reviewers and to Melissa Caldwell for their helpful comments, as well as to Melissa Hackman and Sylvia Grove for their feedback on an earlier draft of this article. I also thank Warren Belasco and Carole Counihan for supporting my earlier research on masculinities and commercial diet programs.

Notes

1 Each of these Weight Watchers promises comes verbatim from the following Weight Watchers media: "If Not Now, When? | Oprah & Weight Watchers," *Weight Watchers YouTube Channel*, December 30, 2015, https://youtu.be/sjp57d6pL_c; Weight Watchers commercial, which ran during *The Daily Rundown* on MSNBC on February 12, 2013, archived at https://archive.org/det ails/ MSNBC_20130212_140000_The_Daily_Rundown#start/1380/end/ 1440; "A Whole New Life," *Weight Watchers Website*, www. weightwatchers.com/success/art/index.aspx?SuccessStoryId= 16491&sc=17; "Jessica Simpson for Weight Watchers," *YouTube*, https://youtu.be/29yUo6uyKw0. Dan also says, "Weight Watchers Online for Men changed my life," in the video that I analyze throughout this article.

2 For a full analysis of the Weight Watchers campaign with Charles Barkley, see Parasecoli 2016.

3 I began this study and comparison in November 2013. As of fall 2016, the Weight Watchers Online for Men "How Does It Work" video still appears on the program website (www.weightwatchers. com/men), but the "women's " version no longer appears at weightwatchers.com, as the program has been since redesigned and revitalized, as is typical for Weight Watchers, e.g., Weight Watchers Online is now Weight Watchers Online*Plus*. Interestingly, the recent changes at Weight Watchers—including Oprah Winfrey's purchase of 10 percent of the company's stock in 2015 and subsequent promotion linked to the Oprah brand—have not altered the Men's program, which appears much the same as it did in 2013 when I began this study.

4 Fitbits have also been incorporated into the newest iteration of the Weight Watchers program. Weight Watchers members can sync their tracking device data to their Weight Watchers account.

References

Baghurst, Timothy. 2012. "Muscle Dysmorphia and Male Body Image: A Personal Account." *New Male Studies* 1(3): 125—30.

Bartky, Sandra Lee. 1990. *Femininity and Domination: Studies in the Phenomenology of Oppression*. New York: Routledge.

Bentley, Amy. 2005. "Men on Atkins: Dieting, Meat, and Masculinity." In *The Atkins Diet and Philosophy*, ed. Lisa Heldke et al., 185—95. Chicago and La Salle, IL: Open Court Press.

Bergman, S. Bear. 2009. "Part-Time Fatso." In *The Fat Studies Reader*, ed. Esther Rothblum and Sondra Solovay. New York: New York University Press.

Biltekoff, Charlotte. 2013. *Eating Right in America: The Cultural Politics of Food and Health*. Durham, NC: Duke University Press.

Bordo, Susan. 1993. *Unbearable Weight: Feminism, Western Culture, and the Body*. Berkeley: University of California Press.

———. 1999. *The Male Body: A New Look at Men in Public and in Private*. New York: Farrar, Straus, and Giroux.

Bosc, Lauren. 2014. "Man, You Have Moobs! A Critical Analysis of the Fat, 'Polluted' Body in *The Biggest Loser*." *Textual Overtures* 2(1): 65–83.

Brand, Peg Zeglin, ed. 2000. *Beauty Matters*. Bloomington: Indiana University Press.

Braziel, Jana Evans, and Kathleen LeBesco, eds. 2001. *Bodies Out of Bounds: Fatness and Transgression*. Berkeley: University of California Press.

Brytek-Matera, Anna, Lorenzo Maria Donini, Magdalena Krupa, Eleonora Poggiogalle, and Phillipa Hay. 2015. "Orthorexia Nervosa and Self-Attitudinal Aspects of Body Image in Female and Male University Students." *Journal of Eating Disorders* 3(2): 1–8.

Butler, Judith. 2006. *Gender Trouble: Feminism and the Subversion of Identity*. New York: Routledge.

Cahill, Ann J. 2003. "Feminist Pleasure and Feminine Beautification." *Hypatia* 18(4): 42—64.

Cairns, Kate, and Josée Johnston. 2015. *Food and Femininity*. New York: Bloomsbury.

Campos, Paul. 2004. *The Obesity Myth: Why America's Obsession with Weight Is Hazardous to Your Health*. New York: Gotham Books.

Connell, Raewyn. 2005. *Masculinities*, 2nd ed. Berkeley: University of California Press.

——— and James Messerschmidt. 2005. "Hegemonic Masculinity: Rethinking the Concept." *Gender and Society* 19: 829—59.

Courtenay, Will H. 2000. "Engendering Health: A Social Constructionist Examination of Men's Health Beliefs and Behaviors." *Psychology of Men and Masculinity* 1(1): 4–15.

Crawford, Robert. 2006. "Health as a Meaningful Social Practice." *Health* 10(4): 401–20.

Crawford, Kate, Jessa Lingel, and Tero Karppi. 2015. "Our Metrics, Ourselves: A Hundred Years of Self-Tracking from the Weight Scale to the Wrist Wearable Device." *European Journal of Cultural Studies* 18(4–5): 479–96.

Dansinger, Michael L., Joi Augustin Gleason, John L. Griffith, Harry P. Selker, and Ernst J. Schaefer. 2005. "Comparison of the Atkins, Ornish, Weight Watchers, and Zone Diets for Weight Loss and Heart Disease Risk Reduction: A Randomized Trial." JAMA 293(1): 43–53.

de la Peña, Carolyn. 2010. *Empty Pleasures: The Story of Artificial Sweeteners from Saccharin to Splenda*. Chapel Hill: University of North Carolina Press.

De Souza, Paula, and Karen Ciclitira. 2005. "Men and Dieting: A Qualitative Analysis." *Journal of Health Psychology* 10(6): 793–804.

Deutsch, Tracey. 2010 *Building a Housewife's Paradise: Gender, Politics, and American Grocery Store in the Twentieth Century*. Chapel Hill: University of North Carolina Press.

Donini, L. M., D. Marsili, M. P. Graziani, M. Imbriale, and C. Cannella. 2013. "Orthorexia Nervosa: A Preliminary Study with a Proposal for Diagnosis and an Attempt to Measure the Dimension of the Phenomenon." *Eating and Weight Disorders: Studies on Anorexia, Bulimia and Obesity* 9(2): 151–57.

Farrell, Amy E. 2011. *Fat Shame: Stigma and the Fat Body in American Culture*. New York: New York University Press.

Fothergill, Erin, Juen Guo, Lilian Howard, Jennifer C. Kerns, Nicolas D. Knuth, Robert Brychta, Kong Y. Chen, et al. 2016. "Persistent Metabolic Adaptation 6 Years after 'The Biggest Loser' Competition." *Obesity* 24(8): 1612–19.

Foucault, Michel. 1977. *Discipline and Punish: The Birth of the Prison*. Translated by A. Sheridan. New York: Vintage.

Fraser, Laura. 1998. *Losing It: False Hopes and Fat Profits in the Diet Industry*. New York: Penguin Group.

Gaesser, Glenn. 2009. "Is 'Permanent Weight Loss' an Oxymoron? The Statistics on Weight Loss and the National Weight Control Registry." In *The Fat Studies Reader*, ed. Esther Rothblum and Sondra Solovay, 37–41. New York: New York University Press.

Gamer, David. 1997. "Survey Says: Body Image Poll Results." *Psychology Today*, February 1. www.psychologytoday.com/articles/199702/survey-says-body-image-poll-results.

Gill, R. 2005. "Body Projects and the Regulation of Normative Masculinity." *Body & Society* 11(1): 37–62.

Gough, Brendan. 2007. " 'Real Men Don't Diet': An Analysis of Contemporary Newspaper Representations of Men, Food and Health." *Social Science & Medicine* 64: 326–37.

Green, Harvey. 1986. *Fit for America: Health, Fitness, Sport, and American Society*. New York: Pantheon Books.

Grindstaff, Laura, and Emily West. 2011. "Hegemonic Masculinity on the Sidelines of Sport: Hegemonic Masculinity on the Sidelines of Sport." *Sociology Compass* 5(10): 859–81.

Guthman, Julie. 2011. *Weighing In: Obesity, Food Justice, and the Limits of Capitalism*. Berkeley: University of California Press.

———. 2014. "Introducing Critical Nutrition: A Special Issue on Dietary Advice and Its Discontents." *Gastronomica* 14(3): 1–4.

Hatton, Erin, and Mary Nell Trautner. 2011. "Equal Opportunity Objectification? The Sexualization of Men and Women on the Cover of Rolling Stone." *Sexuality & Culture* 15: 256–78.

Heyes, Cressida. 2006. "Foucault Goes to Weight Watchers." *Hypatia* 21(2): 126–49.

Hill, Susan E. 2011. *Eating to Excess: The Meaning of Gluttony and the Fat Body in the Ancient World*. Santa Barbara, CA: Praeger.

Hoyt, Wendy D., and Lori R. Kogan. 2001. "Satisfaction with Body Image and Peer Relationships for Males and Females in a College Environment." *Sex Roles* 45(3–4): 199–215.

Jeffords, Susan. 1993. *Hard Bodies: Hollywood Masculinity in the Reagan Era*. New Brunswick, NJ: Rutgers University Press.

Johnston, Josée, and Michael K. Goodman. 2015. "Spectacular Foodscapes: Food Celebrities and the Politics of Lifestyle Mediation in an Age of Inequality." *Food, Culture & Society* 18(2): 205–22.

Kiefer, Ingrid, Theres Rathmanner, and Michael Kunze. 2005. "Eating and Dieting Differences in Men and Women." *Journal of Men's Health & Gender* 2(2): 194–201.

Kulick, Don, and Anne Meneley, eds. 2005. *Fat: The Anthropology of an Obsession*. New York: Tarcher-Penguin.

Labre, Magdala Peixoto. 2005. "The Male Body Ideal: Perspectives of Readers and Non-readers of Fitness Magazines." *Journal of Men's Health & Gender* 2(2): 223–29.

LeBesco, Kathleen. 2004. *Revolting Bodies? The Struggle to Redefine Fat Identity*. Amherst: University of Massachusetts Press.

Lupton, Deborah. 2013. "Quantifying the Body: Monitoring and Measuring Health in the Age of mHealth Technologies." *Critical Public Health* 23(4): 393–403.

Mallyon, Anna, Mary Holmes, John Coveney, and Maria Zadoroznyj. 2010. "I'm Not Dieting, 'I'm Doing It for Science': Masculinities and the Experience of Dieting." *Health Sociology Review* 19(3): 330–42.

Markey, Charlotte N., and Patrick M. Markey. 2005. "Relations between Body Image and Dieting Behaviors: An Examination of Gender Differences." *Sex Roles* 53(7–8): 519–30.

Mishkind, Marc E., Judith Rodin, Lisa R. Silberstein, and Ruth H. Striegel-Moore. 1986. "The Embodiment of Masculinity: Cultural, Psychological, and Behavioral Dimensions." *American Behavioral Scientist* 29(5): 545–60.

Mitchell, Lachlan, Stuart B. Murray, Stephen Cobley, Daniel Hackett, Janelle Gifford, Louise Capling, and Helen O'Connor. 2016. "Muscle Dysmorphia Symptomatology and Associated Psychological Features in Bodybuilders and Non-Bodybuilder Resistance Trainers: A Systematic Review and Meta-Analysis." *Sports Medicine* (May): 1–27.

Monaghan, Lee F. 2008. *Men and the War on Obesity: A Sociological Study*. London and New York: Routledge.

Newman, Andrew. 2008. "The Skinny on Male 'Dieting.'" *AdWeek*, April 7. www.adweek.com/news/advertising-branding/skinny-male-dieting-95443/.

Parasecoli, Fabio. 2005. "Feeding Hard Bodies: Food and Masculinities in Men's Fitness Magazines." *Food and Foodways* 13(1–2): 17–37.

———. 2016. "Manning the Table: Masculinity and Weight Loss in US Commercials." In *Food and Media: Practices, Distinctions, and Heterotopias*, ed. Jonatan Leer and Karen Klitgaard Povlsen, 95–109. New York: Routledge.

Peiss, Kathy. 2011. *Hope in a Jar: The Making of America's Beauty Culture*. Philadelphia: University of Pennsylvania Press.

Pope, Harrison G., Katharine A. Phillips, and Roberto Olivardia. 2000. *The Adonis Complex: The Secret Crisis of Male Body Obsession*. New York: Free Press.

PRWeb. 2013. "Weight Loss Market in U.S. Up 1.7% to $61 Billion." April 16. www.prweb.com/releases/2013/4/prweb10629316.htm.

———. 2014. " U.S. Weight Loss Market: 2015 Forecasts." December 10. www.prweb.com/releases/2014/12/prweb12383477.htm

Rothblum, Esther and Sondra Solovay, eds. 2009. *Fat Studies Reader*. New York: New York University Press.

Schultz, E. J. 2011. "Weight Watchers Picks a New Target: Men." *Advertising Age*, April 22. http://adage.com/article/news/weight-watchers-picks-a-target-men/227155/.

Schwartz, Hillel. 1986. *Never Satisfied: A Cultural History of Diets, Fantasy and Fat*. New York: Anchor.

Stearns, Peter. 2002 [1997]. *Fat History: Bodies and Beauty in the Modern West*. New York: New York University Press.

Stein, Joel. 2015. "How To Get A Superhero Body." *GQ*. July 21. http://www.gq.com/story/fitness-how-to-get-chris-pratt-fit.

Stibbe, Arran. 2004. "Health and the Social Construction of Masculinity in Men's Health Magazine." *Men and Masculinities* 7(1): 31–51.

Stinson, Kandi. 2001. *Women and Dieting Culture: Inside a Commercial Weight Loss Group*. New Brunswick, NJ: Rutgers University Press.

Van Amsterdam, Noortje. 2013. "Big Fat Inequalities, Thin Privilege: An Intersectional Perspective on 'Body Size.'" *European Journal of Womens Studies* 20(2): 155–69.

van Dijk, Teun 1993. "Principles of Critical Discourse Analysis." *Discourse & Society* 4(2): 249–83.

Vester, Katharina. 2010. "Regime Change: Gender, Class, and the Invention of Dieting in Post-Bellum America." *Journal of Social History* 44(1): 39–70.

Wardle, Jane, Anne Haase, Andrew Steptoe, Maream Nillapun, Kiriboon Jonwutiwes, and France Bellisle. 2004. "Gender Differences in Food Choice: The Contribution of Health Beliefs and Dieting." *Annals of Behavioral Medicine* 27(2): 107–16.

13

Everyday Translation: Health Practitioners' Perspectives on Obesity and Metabolic Disorders in Samoa

Jessica Hardin

Introduction

To make sense of their patients' health behaviors, Samoa health practitioners contrast individually oriented *health* with socially oriented *well-being*. Samoan health practitioners frequently discuss culturally valued modes of eating and embodiment in contrast to desired health practices, including diet, physical activity, and regular primary care. They suggest food consumption fostering social well-being may also be detrimental to individual health. Apo, a Samoan physician, made this clear when he said: 'We love our food. Samoan people love to eat', minutes into an interview. He continued:

> What I am saying is, they eat those fatty foods everyday. They know they should be eating differently, but it's the *fa'asamoa* (the Samoan way). We just don't have a culture of vegetable eating. I try to counsel on the importance of prioritizing health but you know a lot of the time, they prioritize other things. If there's little money it will be for the church instead of you know going to the hospital or buying vegetables. Even though there are changes, in health and whatnot, they keep their values.

Apo focused on *fa'asamoa* as the primary barrier to lifestyle change. He used a highly objectified notion of culture to explain this disconnect between knowledge and practice.[1] According to this view, *fa'asamoa* influences food preferences and taste as well as how resources are used. He foregrounded his patients' prioritization of social obligations of church, for example, over individual health. As a result, socially oriented well-being was represented as potentially detrimental to individual health.[2]

In Samoa, where rates of metabolic disorders are very high, Samoan health practitioners focus on cultivating health priorities in order to change bodies and behaviors. They neither stigmatize patients, nor assume health is a priority, as is often the case with attitudes towards obesity in the global north (Bell, McNaughton, & Salmon, 2009; LeBesco, 2011; Monaghan, Colls, & Evans, 2013; Saguy & Riley, 2005; Solovay & Rothblum, 2009). Instead they suspend blame until their patients make health an organizing priority in their lives. They want their patients to change their lifestyle, but picture culture as problematically constraining. As a result, political and economic factors contributing to rising metabolic disorders are backgrounded. For example, health practitioners focused on changing the meaning of foods deemed unhealthy, rather than food availability. Responsibility is held in abeyance until a society-wide change in food, body, and wealth meanings occur, which positions health practitioners as mediators of cultural change.

This article explores how 'culture' comes to occupy a great deal of attention on the part of Samoan health practitioners. I refer to culture not to essentialize it as a specific set of values and practices, but to bring to light the ways my interlocutors use a highly objectified notion of culture to parse out specific practices as simultaneously cultural and metabolically risky. In exploring this topic, I employ 'everyday translation' as an analytic frame to examine how health practitioners foreground cultural over structural factors. Everyday translation refers to how Samoan health practitioners translate between knowledge systems (see Gewertz & Errington, 2010; Kingfisher, 2013; Levitt & Merry, 2009; West, 2005). Health practitioners balance biomedical knowledge, which prioritizes health as an individual project, with local cultural knowledge, which prioritizes socially oriented well-being (cf. Nading, 2013). Contrasting health and well-being makes visible health practitioners' struggles to shift from biomedical metrics, measurements, and numbers to socially significant meanings around food, body, and wealth in everyday life.

Metabolic Disorders in Samoa

The Samoas have provided a 'natural experiment' for understanding rapid epidemiological change from biocultural and evolutionary perspectives (Baker, Hanna, & Baker, 1986; McGarvey, Bausserman, Viali, & Tufa, 2005; Zimmet et al., 1981). While ethnically and genetically similar across the islands and the diaspora, integration into the global economy varies greatly between American Samoa, independent Samoa, and Samoan diaspora centers. Brewis describes this diversity as a 'meaningful gradient of exposure to the influences of modern life' (Brewis, 2011, p. 50). Thus, Samoans in Samoa have the lowest rates of metabolic disorders, while those in the diaspora have higher rates of metabolic disorders. In 2003, in Samoa nearly 30% of men and over 50% of woman were classified as obese (Keighley et al., 2007). Another striking statistic makes the rapidity of this epidemiological change apparent: between 1978 and 1991 in rural Samoa obesity increased in males by 297% and in females by 115% (Hodge et al., 1994).

Political and economic changes, including shifts in diet and physical activity – what is usually referred to as the nutrition transition – began after World War II (Keighley et al., 2007; Popkin & Adair, 2012). Scholars often point to the transition from agriculture, and related urbanization, as one of the major causes for rising rates of disease (Zimmet et al., 1981). Some scholars have posited that psychosocial stress related to the demands of kin-based reciprocity, migration, and urbanization have also contributed to rising metabolic disorders (Bergey et al., 2011; Janes, 1990). The Samoan economy is dependent on remittances from the diaspora; therefore, circular migration may play a part in increasing cash dependence, which influences notions of success based in non-agricultural labor and food consumption (cf. Kwauk, 2014; Lilomaiava-Doktor, 2009). Imported foods, including sodium and fat-dense, highly processed foods are now daily staples (DiBello et al., 2009; Galanis, McGarvey, Quested, Sio, & Afele-Fa'amuli, 1999; Gewertz & Errington, 2010). These imported foods are incorporated into everyday cultural practices as valued products. For example, a soda has come to replace a coconut during ritual gifting ceremonies.

The correlation between obesity and degrees of what biocultural anthropologists call 'modernization' has led to the theorization of the so-called thrifty gene among Polynesians (cf. Neel, 1962). This is a contested theory, but evolutionary perspectives suggest that obesity is the result of bodies adapting to shifting ecological patterns from feasting during times of abundance, to famine during times of food shortages, related to droughts or pestilence. Those who survived famine were hypothesized to be those with the thrifty gene, which favored storage of calories and increased response to insulin to ingested food, leading to increases in adipose tissue. This provided an efficient metabolism during fluctuations in food availability (McGarvey, 1994).

Cultural factors such as fat-positive attitudes have also been linked to high rates of obesity (Brewis & McGarvey, 2000), although scholars have found a downward shift in idealized body size from New Zealand to American Samoa and Samoa (Brewis, McGarvey, & Swinburn, 1998; see Brewis, 2011, pp. 92–95, cf. Becker, 2004). Recently, Brewis, Wutich, Falletta-Cowden, and Rodriguez-Soto (2011) found high degrees of fat stigma in American Samoa, suggesting fat-positive attitudes may be waning. Cultural patterns of eating are also linked to obesity. Feasts are an 'extremely visible part of Pacific Island life', and essential to social reproduction of families, villages, and churches (Pollock, 1992, p. 105). Food culture in Samoa is no exception. Consumption of high calories on Sundays and ritual events in the past were counterbalanced by physical activity on plantations. Today caloric consumption has remained the same while physical activity, especially for those in the urban area, has decreased (Pelletier, 1987).

This confluence of political and economic changes and cultural patterns of embodiment and eating can be best understood from the perspective of structural chronicities (Wiedman, 2012). Wiedman proposes a structural chronicities approach focusing 'on the social and cultural factors that structure an individual's everyday life, containing the physical body in ways that increase the three risk factors for diabetes and metabolic syndrome: (1) physical inactivity, (2) over-nutrition, and (3) chronic stress' (2012, p. 596). This approach counters the dominant focus in medical sciences on biological and genetic explanations for globally rising metabolic disorders.

Methods and Fieldwork

This research builds on nearly two years of fieldwork in the Samoan islands and diaspora between 2008 and 2012. During 14 months of fieldwork in Samoa, I participated and observed in clinical environments including hospitals, two urban clinics, and nursing home-visits. I observed clinical encounters and health education and assisted with daily administration at a diabetes clinic. I also participated in, and observed, at public health meetings and community programming, including jazzercise. I developed key interlocutor relationships with six health practitioners, who I interviewed up to 12 times.

The data for this article include 25 in-depth, semi-structured interviews with Samoan health practitioners, including physicians and nurses. Physicians all received their medical training overseas. Most nurses also received their training overseas (though younger nurses had the opportunity for local training) and were employed in government hospitals or clinics. Two physicians were in private practice and two physicians were faculty at the newly established medical school. Those working in the hospital reported usually seeing patients after a severe medical event, such as neuropathy or stroke, while those working in clinics had regular patients. The initial recruitment utilized a purposive sampling method. I first developed a list of organizations and institutions to target, and then employed the snowball method to recruit the remaining interviewees. Interviews were conducted in English or Samoan depending on the interviewee's preference. All interviews were audio recorded, transcribed, and translated by the author with the assistance of a research assistant. The author coded transcripts, using NVivo software, to compare thematic convergences and divergences.

Health and Well-Being

Health practitioners expressed ambivalence about helping their patients change their health behaviors because changing these health behaviors may challenge socially grounded well-being. This ambivalence reflects diverse understandings of health and well-being, which are culturally located ideas, signifying practices, and ideological constructs about the body and disease (Adelson, 1998; Crawford, 2006). Commonly in medical practice and popular imagination, health is limited to measure-based assessments of the body, suggesting individual responsibility: BMI, blood sugar, blood pressure, and weight (McCullough & Hardin, 2013). In Samoa, health is a meaningful, perhaps novel, way of being-in-the-world. One physician was in the process of pitching a 'Know Your Numbers' campaign. He asked his patients 'do you know your phone number? How about your pin? What about your blood sugar? Blood pressure? Cholesterol? Waist circumference? You should'. The physician identified a lack of numerical knowledge as evidence of his patients' lack of orientation to health metrics. Well-being, on the other hand, refers to 'the optimal state for an individual, community, society and the world as a whole' (Matthews & Izquierdo, 2009, p. 5). Well-being in Samoa is focused on 'living well' more than on 'bodily vigilance' (Smith-Morris, 2006, p. 6; cf. Agee, McIntosh, Culbertson, & Makasiale, 2013; Capstick, Norris, Sopoaga, & Tobata, 2009; Carlisle & Hanlon, 2007, 2008), including placing social priorities over individual health. Health practitioners grapple with these differences by asking: 'How can you reduce sugar intake when tea is made in one pot for the household?' and 'how can you reduce sodium intake when the family meal is prepared in one pot?' If health was a priority, their patients would not drink tea or they might request alternative foods. However, most patients, they felt, privilege the family over individual health. Patients eat the food and drink the tea in order to avoid disrupting the family unit, which promotes well-being but also reveals the 'problem of *fa'asamoa*'.

The Problem of Fa'asamoa

At the annual health forum, in a large conference hall with windows peeking out to the blue Pacific Ocean, Samoan health practitioners gathered to discuss current health care issues. 'Food is life, food is our culture', a nurse whispered to me during the session dedicated to nutrition. The session speaker started:

> Food is very important to us Samoans. With the no more convincing fact than half of us are on our way to being obese. Remember the way to a man's heart is through his stomach, so if you really love your husband and you also want your husband to die early, give him all the fatty food, very salty food.

These comments met voracious laughter in part because speaking of bodies is generally humorous in Samoa. More markedly though, the humor reflected the imponderability of the current epidemiological context, which these health practitioners positioned as resulting from the inextricable connections between food, love, and *fa'asamoa* practiced in everyday life (see Alexeyeff, 2004 for comparative material from the Cook Islands). Food, eating, and feeding are expressions of *fa'asamoa*, yet the ways Samoans currently eat, feed, and share resources was also associated with metabolic disorders.

Many of my interlocutors felt that *fa'asamoa* influenced various health behaviors, including primary care, pharmaceutical use, physical activity, and diet. This became clear to me one morning as I drove two hours to a rural clinic with Iona, a physician, who worked there once a week. He said, 'Unless the *fa'asamoa* changes, the NCDs (non-communicable diseases) will never change. The attitudes need to change but it is difficult because it is the culture. It's the whole way of life'. Lupe, a nurse at this clinic, confirmed Iona's perspective:

> We see patients coming back with even more problems because they don't take their prescribed medicines. So when they come for their follow-up checks, their condition is worse, their blood sugar levels or blood pressure have not dropped to a stable level. It shows that they are not taking their medication.

She continued, 'to me the number one problem is no sense of value, they do not value a healthy lifestyle. They would prefer to worry about cultural things, the *fa'asamoa*'. Neither Iona nor Lupe pointed to primary care insufficiencies where medications were often only available once a week when the physician visited, which created long waits for brief appointments.[3] Iona and Lupe suggested if their patients valued health they would change their priorities.

Another physician, Philip, said, 'Samoans are a cheeky population, eh?' After diagnosis, Philip explained, patients will continue to eat the same foods and will not keep up with their medicines. He called this 'the problem of *fa'asamoa*'. Philip used the term 'cheekiness' to point to the mismatch of knowledge and behavior. This mismatch reflects local ideas of selfhood: Samoans tend to privilege social context in determining self-identity and action (Shore, 1982). Duranti writes, Samoans are not concerned with knowing intentions but with 'the implications of [a] speaker's actions/words for the web of relationships in which … life is woven' (1992, p. 42). In other words, Samoans tend to prioritize adhering to a role and role expectations over individual expression. For Philip, cheekiness referred to this prioritization of role over individual need.

Lea, a nurse, explained a similar prioritization regarding ubiquitous social gatherings, associated with *fa'asamoa*, as the 'biggest barrier to health'. Even in health care contexts, morning tea was served with copious amounts of sugar and *pankeke* (fried bread). Often, morning tea or lunch is orchestrated by groups at the workplace, where those who provide are socially evaluated based on how much food they serve. The best foods to serve are *mea'ai lelei*, (good food), which are associated with expense, sweetness, fattiness, or saltiness. *Mea'ai lelei* are almost never *mea'ai paleni* (balanced/healthy food), including fruits and vegetables (cf. Pollock, 2011). Lea specifically explained:

> At church gatherings there are so many foods that you can't control. I had one experience last week. Our church had a camp for the youth and because my husband is in leadership we were told to prepare the tea for after the activity. We had a meeting about the tea with a few other church ladies. And I said, look that time of the night we don't want much to eat. And then I said we should eat healthy and they all laughed. I said we should provide a small amount but even if we provide a huge amount we need to consider the balance and provide healthy foods. And then, one of the women said, 'yea that's nice, eating healthy is good but we need to do the best thing we can do.' And the best thing they think of is a lot of food on the table.

Abundant, rather than healthy, food was the best option according to Lea's interlocutors, and her attempts to create change in her own community were met with resistance and derision. Even as a health practitioner, Lea could not make change in her own community because, in her words, 'the *fa'asamoa* is so strong'. As we wrapped up our interview, Lea added:

> One of the things that we need to stress to the people is that they need to have annual checks. They don't unless they're sick, then they come. So it's, it's really hard. It's the behavior of the people that we need to change. But it takes time. And it's really, really difficult.

Chronic metabolic disorders require everyday health management, whereas in traditional approaches to disease healing is event-based, with problems seen to result from isolatable social, spiritual, or physical causes, to which healing is sought in singular ways (cf. Macpherson & Macpherson, 1990). Health practitioners actively worked against this model to encourage patients to see their health as something to be cared for everyday.

Similarly, many health practitioners and patients mentioned that adopting a daily pharmaceutical regiment requires cash for travel and medications, which can be a hardship. They also mentioned how changing how one eats also influences the family by necessitating different purchasing and preparation choices, for example, cutting fat off meat, preparing meals without salt, or buying vegetables over other foods. One patient said, 'I eat whatever [my family] gives me'. Daily changes like these, health practitioners reported, could affect the family's overall sense of well-being by placing the needs of one individual above the family unit, by drawing attention to the individual who may be sick, or by developing what is perceived to be a dependency on medication (cf. Elstad, Corabelle, Rosen, & McGarvey, 2008; Rosen, DePue, & McGarvey, 2008).

Fa'asamoa also influences physical activity. Stillness is an embodied mode of wellness that indicates status. As Samoan people age they engage in less physical activity, encouraging those beneath them to do the chores and agricultural labor. Health practitioners also indicated that physical activity is gendered; they explained that once child rearing begins men become inactive because they no longer engage in as much physical activity, including plantation labor and leisure activities of rugby. Likewise, after women have had children they do less-demanding chores. Others noted that walking, jogging, or running are seen as a disruption to village life. For many, walking is stigmatized, suggesting the inability to buy a car or petrol. Physical activity, especially for non-youth, also has the potential to elicit 'fear of ridicule and shame' because this activity challenges 'dignified and controlled comportment' (Besnier, 2011, p. 218).

Conversely, participation in *fa'asamoa* is generally linked to wellness. According to Macpherson and Macpherson:

> At the center of the general [Samoan] model of wellness and illness is a set of beliefs about the lifestyle and conduct which, if followed ensure a balanced life and good health and that which will disturb this balance and will cause illness. The lifestyle which ensures general well-being is achieved and maintained by accepting a Samoan view of the world and living by those customs, *o le aganu'u samoa* [Samoan culture],[4] which support it. Conversely, the rejection of the worldview, and the customs which underpin it, can lead to the imbalance which results in illness. (1990, p. 157)

Well-being is, thus, wrapped up with the participation in *fa'asamoa*. Health practitioners struggled to interpret cultural practices as potentially detrimental health behaviors, for example, preference for stillness or silence about health needs, because in other contexts these are valued expressions of *fa'asamoa*.

When translating between biomedical imperatives for individualized health management and cultural imperatives for socially oriented wellness, health practitioners tended to emphasize how culture limited individual choice, which influenced medication practices, eating habits, and physical activity patterns, over structural influences. For example, access to primary care in rural villages was not highlighted. Instead, patients were presented as unwilling participants in their own health care because of culture. Health practitioners did not expect their patients to align behavior with new health knowledge because they expected patients to make choices based on *fa'asamoa*, not individual health needs. When risk was linked to *fa'asamoa*, health practitioners were left to question how they could assist individuals in making better health choices without challenging *fa'asamoa*.

Mentalities and Health Priorities

'What makes it so hard for your patients to manage their diabetes, high blood pressure, or weight?' I asked in all my interviews. 'It goes back to their own mentalities', one physician said. He continued: 'many patients need daily self-care, but then they go home and a relative will ... say 'just leave that stuff' [medications]. So again it goes by the health mentalities'. The physician explained that family members of patients sometimes encourage patients to stop taking medications, or to seek traditional healers. He felt that his patients often listened to their families over his medical advice. Another nurse said, the 'mentality of the people is that health is not a priority'. Samoan health practitioners talked about 'mentalities' as a way to discuss how culture shapes health priorities. Ideally, they wanted their patients to privilege health needs over social needs that might contribute to well-being, but not health. Social priorities were illustrated by examples: a family elder saving money for ritual exchange obligations instead of bringing his feverish grandson to the hospital or caring for a sore. Health practitioners suspended individual blame and focused on priorities by drawing attention to *fa'asamoa*, while striving to change those priorities so individuals could be held responsible for their health.

One physician said,

> The worst thing you can do is attack their culture. So you've got to be proactive and then you can educate about the good practices and discourage them from the bad practices but not discourage them from their beliefs. *Fa'asamoa* is a big part of the Samoan people.

This physician suggested that medical practitioners needed to carefully encourage their patients to selectively draw from culture in positive ways. Another explained:

> I think creating a whole shift in mentality about our relationship with food and what our definition of wealth and beautiful is. Our definition of wealth does not necessarily have to be, we don't necessarily have to demonstrate wealth through having so much food.

Health practitioners hoped individuals would make better health choices if they saw body size as an indicator of health not wealth. However, they also viewed their patients as maintaining an outdated linkage between body size and wealth. With a joking tone, one physician said: 'you know the people they think if you are fat, you are wealthy'. This joking also drew attention to *fa'asamoa*.

Speaking about mentalities, thus, permitted health practitioners to suggest instituting cultural change without directly criticizing *fa'asamoa*. Health practitioners were uneasy about their problematization of the cultural priorities their patients held. This was evident in the substantial efforts they made to contextualize socially oriented well-being. 'But this is the culture', one nurse said, 'So I don't think we need to change that but we do need to change the priorities'. Most interviewees also felt pressure to privilege the obligations of exchange networks over their own individual health. A few health practitioners expressed their struggles to provide financial support for their elders knowing the money would be used for cultural obligations over, for example, expanding the budget for healthier daily meals. Apo, who mentioned a love of food, started to refuse food gifts from his family to make healthier dietary choices. He refused fatty tinned meats, pork, and salt-preserved beef. This also unburdened his family from the expense, which he hoped would provide them more resources to spend on health. However, his refusal led his family to call him *fiapoto* (wanting to be smart). *Fiapoto* insultingly suggests one is not acting appropriately to cultural expectations and implicitly questions Samoanness (Gershon, 2012, p. 146). Apo implicitly acted against role expectations (i.e. to participate in gifting is to be a good family member). He also explicitly criticized *fa'asamoa* by not accepting gifts. Apo offered this example to make the point that to prioritize health one must make public changes to how one practices culture, which can place that person's Samoanness in question.

When health practitioners spoke of mentalities, culture was highlighted as constraining individual choice, which suspended individual blame. One physician said:

> All these things are fatty. They're okay in moderation but maybe our biggest challenge is to change our mentalities about what we can eat that's still festive. And the amounts that we eat. Food is tied in a big way to festivities and celebration and offering hospitality. I don't think we need to change that. I think it's just a matter of food choices they make, and the amount we consume.

The physician interpreted food choice as primarily cultural, thereby rendering invisible the structural influences on the food environment. Today, foods associated with festivity are primarily imported products, including rice, tinned fish and corned beef, and frozen meats, such as chicken, turkey tails, and mutton flaps. In both everyday diet and food presentations, imported fried chicken, sausages, snack foods, ice cream, and cakes have all come to stand in for local foods, like fish, pork, local lean chickens, and starchy root vegetables. These prestige foods have become essential to sustaining extended family networks; however, they have also been identified as contributors to rising metabolic disorders. Health practitioners held communities and individuals responsible for choosing healthier alternatives when they focused on cultural influences on diet and not on changing foods. This in turn obscures the inequities of global food trade.

Changing Meaning, Changing Leadership

Health practitioners faulted leadership as ineffective agents of change, instead of considering the political and economic influences on culture and health. According to one physician, pastors and chiefs 'are the problem'. Samoan society can be characterized as a dynamic titled-based hierarchy, where respect is given to elders and those with ranked status (Duranti, 1994; Shore, 1982). Because chiefs, pastors, and their wives traditionally demonstrated authority in body size and food displays (Shore, 1989), health practitioners emphasized that leaders needed to change their eating habits and physical activity levels in order to change community orientations to health. Once leaders were publicly engaged in their health by exercising or walking society-wide change would follow, they felt. One suggested the Prime Minister should have his numbers checked on television, following the success of the locally produced Samoa Challenge, a weight-loss competition reality TV show.

Health practitioners recognized that they were also implicated in the needed community-wide change. Health practitioners are held in high esteem because they have achieved scholarship-dependent overseas education. As role models and respected community leaders, health practitioners' bodies and health are publicly visible (cf. Wendland, 2010). Most health practitioners reported struggling with their weight; they shyly laughed about how they shared these problems with their patients. 'Look at me!' said four of the interviewees. They often framed themselves as hypocrites, which they felt made it difficult to advise patients about weight loss. They explained, in jest, their personal paradox: how could they advise patients when they themselves could not lose weight? Aligning health advice with health behaviors was critical for health practitioners, as they felt they could not advise their patients without making changes in their own lives. One nurse explained:

> I was unfit and I said to myself, I am a healthcare worker. I need to walk the talk. I want to live longer and have a better quality of life. It was hard, the first year was very hard. You have to make … you have to change your whole mind and change your behavior.

She explained the difficulties she faced in adopting an exercise routine and changing her diet. She was criticized for bringing vegetable platters or salads to family meals, many dismissed her as *fiapalagi* (wanting to be like a white person). As with Apo, changing food practices was difficult, even for health practitioners, because accusations of *fiapotu or fiapalagi* implicitly questioned their Samoanness.

Health practitioners also suggested that leaders must publicly engage in their own health to affect society-wide change. Some had heard of pastors in the diaspora limiting food at church events to fruits and vegetables (cf. Bell, Swinburn, Amosa, & Scragg, 2001; Simmons, 1998, Simmons, Voyle, Fout, Feot, & Leakehet, 2004). They considered this desirable because: (1) leadership demonstrated health priorities, (2) congregants could offer these healthier options without fear of reproach, and (3) the community rallied around health. In this example, leadership exhibited a change in orientation towards health, encouraging the meanings associated with body size and food to also change. They felt that if leadership publicly ate and accepted food gifts differently, then perhaps food meanings could change, without challenging culturally relevant notions of love, respect, and service.

In these examples, health practitioners suggested that leaders needed to change their health behaviors, which in turn would promote health, and encourage communities to change their orientations toward health. In doing so, health practitioners posited that metabolic disorders were a problem of individual control, but their patients could not change their orientations towards health until leadership-driven cultural change occurred. Responsibility for health is thus diffused to leaders to create change, which would enable individuals to become responsible for their health.

Conclusion

In this paper, I have argued that health practitioners avoid blaming individuals for their metabolic disorders by focusing on 'culture'. They focus on cultural change as necessary for health to become a priority for their patients, which implicates community leaders, including health practitioners themselves, who must become responsible for the change. This only suspends blame and responsibility until culture changes. In their narratives, the meanings of health and well-being emerge and reveal health care as a space of cultural change. Samoan health practitioners and their patients are 'embedded in ... simultaneously opposed and conspiring worlds' (Garcia, 2008, p. 720). Within clinics and hospitals, Samoan patients are expected to participate in their health management through diet, physical activity, and medication. However, Samoan patients are also family members and caretakers in their homes, where the expectations are to serve others, which often means sharing a single family meal, avoiding physical activity, and assigning the cash needed for medications to other family obligations.

Public health focused on obesity and metabolic disorders is increasingly concerned with ways to address food environments and broader structural inequalities (Benson, 2012; Stuckler & Nestle, 2012; Swinburn et al., 2011). Health practitioners do not foreground global trends, including increasing transnationalism, dependence on the cash economy, a move away from customary agriculture, and the incorporation of foreign imported foods as prestige foods. Despite health practitioners' efforts to suspend blame on individuals, when they focus on culture they inadvertently reproduce the invisibility of structural influences on health that have contributed to rising rates of metabolic disorders. Farmer (2003) discusses a similar conflation on the part of anthropologists to see 'culture' as a source of inequality, rather than structural violence. In this case, health practitioners invoke 'culture' as a way to explain metabolic disorders, and in doing so they negate structural factors. When health practitioners focus on culture, they make structural inequalities difficult to see and, therefore, alleviate. As a result, responsibility is placed on the community and its leaders to change meaning and priorities. This suggests that if meaning changed, then individuals could and would make different health choices. Thus, when health practitioners focus on culture, even though they suspend individual blame, they still posit that metabolic disorders can be addressed through individual choice and responsibility.

Exploring health practitioners' dilemmas reveals how responsibility discourses are reproduced, even as they are resisted, in everyday clinical practice. Considering how health practitioners obscure structural factors is essential to developing ways to systemically address those factors. Unlinking culture from risk will not only make structural factors more visible but will also alleviate some of the unease of health practitioners as they act as mediators of cultural change. In order to imagine public health initiatives that can reduce the burden of metabolic disorders, health practitioners and scholars must find bridging approaches between health-centric and well-being-centric orientations.

Acknowledgements

I am grateful to those health practitioners who were generous with their time while in Samoa and to the Ministry of Health for their assistance. This paper was originally presented at a panel on obesity organized by Nancy Pollock and Aunchalee Palmquist at the Association for Social Anthropology in Oceania. I am grateful for their feedback. I would like to thank Sarah Lamb, Megan McCullough, and Stephen McGarvey, as well as Annie Claus, Casey Golomski, Anna Jaysane-Darr, Laura John, Christina Kwauk, Ram Natarajan, and Allison Taylor for helpful comments on earlier drafts. A special thanks also to Greg Hayes for meticulously reading many drafts.

Funding

The research for this paper was funded by a Wenner-Gren Foundation Dissertation Fieldwork Grant for 2011–2012.

Notes

1   Ethnographers of Samoa have noted 'their interlocutors' comfortable willingness to be explicit about Samoan culture and values' (Gershon, 2012, p. 14).

2   *Fa'asamoa* is associated with values of *tautua* (service), *alofa* (love), and *fa'aaloalo*, (respect). These values are expressed in participation in *fa'alavelave*, ritual exchange events organized around major life transitions including weddings, funerals, and title-bestowals. *Fa'asamoa* is also associated with commitments to church, which require participation in church-based exchange including weekly offerings and other project-based obligations (see Macpherson & Macpherson, 2011 for an overview of church-based exchange).

3   In everyday clinical practice and conversation, obesity is rarely referred to but *ma'i suka* (diabetes) and *toto maualuga* (high blood pressure) are discussed. Focusing on non-communicable diseases,

as is common in Samoa, 'fix[es] these afflictions within individual bodies where they are best managed by individual choices' (Ferzacca, 2000; Rock, 2003; Yates-Doerr, 2012, p. 136). Diet and physical activity are discussed as the means to lowering risk for these metabolic disorders rather than a focus on weight loss. As a result, I opt to refer to metabolic disorders, the clustering of disorders to more closely reflect Samoan discourses and experiences of disease.

4   Roughly, a*ganu'u* refers to the culture and traditions specific to particular villages while *fa'asamoa* refers broadly to Samoan culture.

References

Adelson, N. (1998). Health beliefs and the politics of Cree well-being. *Health*, 2, 5–22.

Agee, M. N., McIntosh, T., Culbertson, P., & Makasiale, C. O. (Eds.). (2013). *Pacific identities and well-being*. New York, NY: Routledge.

Alexeyeff, K. (2004). Love food: Exchange and sustenance in the Cook Islands diaspora. *The Australian Journal of Anthropology*, 15, 68–79.

Baker, P. T., Hanna, J. M., & Baker, T. S. (Eds.). (1986). *The changing Samoans: Behavior and health in transition*. New York, NY: Oxford University Press.

Becker, Anne E. (2004). Television, disordered eating, and young women in Fiji: Negotiating body image and identity during rapid social change. *Culture, Medicine and Psychiatry*, 28, 533–559.

Bell, K., McNaughton, D., & Salmon, A. (2009). Medicine, morality and mothering: Public health discourses on foetal alcohol exposure, smoking around children and childhood overnutrition. *Critical Public Health*, 19, 155–170.

Bell, A. C., Swinburn, B. A., Amosa, H., & Scragg, R. K. R. (2001). A nutrition and exercise intervention program for controlling weight in Samoan communities in New Zealand. *International Journal of Obesity*, 25, 920–927.

Benson, P. (2012). Commentary: Biopolitical injustice and contemporary capitalism. *American Ethnologist*, 39, 488–490.

Bergey, M. R., Steele, M., Bereiter, D. A., Viali, S., & McGarvey, S. (2011). Behavioral and perceived stressor effects on urinary catecholamine excretion in adult Samoans. *American Journal of Human Biology*, 23, 693–702.

Besnier, N. (2011). *On the edge of the global: Modern anxieties in a Pacific Island nation*. Stanford: Stanford University Press.

Brewis, A. (2011). *Obesity: Cultural and biocultural perspectives*. New Brunswick, NJ: Rutgers University Press.

Brewis, A. A., & McGarvey, S. T. (2000). Body image, body size, and Samoan ecological and individual modernization. *Ecology of Food and Nutrition*, 39, 105–120.

Brewis, A. A., McGarvey, S. T., & Swinburn, B. A. (1998). Perceptions of body size in Pacific Islanders. *International Journal of Obesity*, 22, 185–189.

Brewis, A., Wutich, A., Falletta-Cowden, A., & Rodriguez-Soto, I. (2011). Body norms and fat stigma in global perspective. *Current Anthropology*, 52, 269–276.

Capstick, S., Norris, P., Sopoaga, F., & Tobata, W. (2009). Relationships between health and culture in Polynesia – A review. *Social Science & Medicine*, 68, 1341–1348.

Carlisle, S., & Hanlon, P. (2007). The complex territory of well-being: Contestable evidence, contentious theories and speculative conclusions. *Journal of Public Mental Health*, 6, 8–13.

Carlisle, S., & Hanlon, P. (2008). 'Well-being' as a focus for public health? A critique and defence. *Critical Public Health*, 18, 263–270.

Crawford, R. (2006). Health as a meaningful social practice. *Health: An Interdisciplinary Journal for the Social Study of Health, Illness, and Medicine*, 10, 401–420.

DiBello, J. R., McGarvey, S., Kraft, P., Goldberg, R., Campos, H., Quested, C., Laumoli, T. S., & Baylin, A. (2009). Dietary patterns are associated with metabolic syndrome in adult Samoans. *Journal of Nutrition*, 1933–1943.

Duranti, A. (1992). Intentions, self, and responsibility: An essay in Samoan ethnopragmatics. In J. Hill & J. T. Irvine (Eds.), *Responsibility and evidence in oral discourse* (pp. 24–47). Cambridge: Cambridge University Press.

Duranti, A. (1994). *From grammar to politics*: Linguistic anthropology in a Western Samoa village. Berkeley: University of California Press.

Elstad, E., Corabelle, T., Rosen, R., & McGarvey, S. (2008). Living with Ma'i Suka: Individual, familial, cultural, and environmental stress among patients with Type 2 diabetes mellitus and their caregivers in American Samoa. *Preventing Chronic Disease*, 5(3), 1–10.

Errington, F., & Gewertz, D. (2001). On the gentrification of culture: From blow fish to Melanesian. *Journal of the Royal Anthropological Institute*, 7, 509–525.

Farmer, P. (2003). *Pathologies of power*: Health, human rights, and the new war on the poor. Berkeley: University of California Press.

Ferzacca, S. (2000). 'Actually, I Don't Feel That Bad': Managing diabetes and the clinical encounter. *Medical Anthropology Quarterly*, 14, 28–50.

Galanis, D. J., McGarvey, S., Quested, C., Sio, B., & Afele-Fa'amuli, S. (1999). Dietary intake of modernizing Samoans. *Journal of the American Dietetic Association*, 99, 184–190.

Garcia, A. (2008). The elegiac addict: history, chronicity, and the melancholic subject. *Cultural Anthropology*, 23, 718–746.

Gershon, I. (2012). *No family is an island*: Cultural expertise among Samoans in Diaspora. Ithaca, NY: Cornell University Press.

Gewertz, D., & Errington, F. (2010). *Cheap meat*: Flap food nations in the Pacific Islands. Berkeley: University of California Press.

Hodge, A. M., Dowse, G. K., Toelupe, P., Collins, V. R., Imo, T., & Zimmet, P. Z. (1994). Dramatic increase in the prevalence of obesity in Western Samoa over the 13 year period 1978–1991. *International Journal of Obesity*, 18, 419–428.

Jackson, M. (2011). *Life within limits*. Durham, NC: Duke University Press.

Janes, C. R. (1990). *Migration, social change and health*: A Samoan community in urban California. Stanford, CA: Stanford University Press.

Keighley, E. D., McGarvey, S., Quested, C., McCuddin, C., Viali, S., & Maga, U. O. A. (2007). Nutrition and health in modernizing Samoans: Temporal trends and adaptive perspectives. In R. Ohtsuka & S. J. Ulijaszek (Eds.), *Health change in the Asia-Pacific region* (pp. 147–191). Cambridge: Cambridge University Press.

Kingfisher, C. (2013). *A policy travelogue*: Tracing welfare reform in Aotearoa/New Zealand and Alberta, Canada. New York, NY: Berghahn.

Kwauk, C. T. (2014). *Navigating development futures*: Sport and the production of healthy bodies in Samoa (PhD dissertation). Department of Comparative and International Development Education, University of Minnesota.

LeBesco, K. (2011). Neoliberalism, public health, and the moral perils of fatness. *Critical Public Health*, 21, 153–164.

Levitt, P., & Merry, S. (2009). Vernacularization on the ground: local uses of global women's rights in Peru, China, India and the United States. *Global Networks*, 9, 441–461.

Lilomaiava-Doktor, S. (2009). Beyond "Migration": Samoan population movement (Malaga) and the geography of social space (Va). *The Contemporary Pacific*, 21,1–32.

Macpherson, C., & Macpherson, L. (1990). *Samoan medical belief and practice*. Honolulu: University of Hawaii Press.

Macpherson, C., & Macpherson, L. (2011). Churches and the economy of samoa. *The Contemporary Pacific*, 23, 304–337.

Matthews, G., & Izquierdo, C. (Eds.). (2009). *Pursuits of happiness*: Well-being in anthropological perspective. New York, NY: Berghahn Books.

McCullough, M., & Hardin, J. (Eds.). (2013). *Reconstructing obesity research: The measures of meaning, the meaning of measures*. New York, NY: Berghahn Books.

McGarvey, S. (1994). The thrifty gene concept and adiposite studies in biological anthropology. *Journal of the Polynesian Society*, 103, 29–42.

McGarvey, S., Bausserman, L., Viali, S., & Tufa, J. (2005). Prevalence of the metabolic syndrome in Samoans. *American Journal of Physical Anthropology*, 40, 14–15.

Monaghan, L. F., Colls, R., & Evans, B. (2013). Obesity discourse and fat politics: Research, critique and interventions. *Critical Public Health*, 23, 249–262.

Nading, A. M. (2013). Love Isn't there in your stomach. *Medical Anthropology Quarterly*, 27, 84–102.

Neel, J. V. (1962). Diabetes mellitus: A 'Thrifty' genotypes rendered detrimental by 'progress'? *The American Journal of Human Genetics*, 14, 353–362.

Pelletier, D. (1987). The relationship of energy intake and expenditure to body fatness in Western Samoan men. *Ecology of Food and Nutrition*, 19, 185–199.

Pollock, N. (1992). *These roots remain: Food habits in islands of the Central and Eastern Pacific since Western contact*. Laie, HI: The Institute for Polynesian Studies.

Pollock, N. (2011). *The language of food*, Vol. Oxford. New York, NY: University Press, The Oxford Handbook of Linguistic Fieldwork.

Popkin, B. M., & Adair, L. S. (2012). Global nutrition transition and the pandemic of obesity in developing countries. *Nutrition Reviews*, 70, 3–21.

Rock, M. (2003). Sweet blood and social suffering: Rethinking cause-effect relationships in diabetes, distress, and duress. *Medical Anthropology*, 22, 131–174.

Rosen, R. K., DePue, J., & McGarvey, S. (2008). Overweight and diabetes in American Samoa: The cultural translation of research into health care practice. *Medicine and Health/Rhode Island*, 91, 372–377.

Saguy, A. C., & Riley, K. (2005). Weighing both sides: Morality, mortality, and framing contests over obesity. *Journal of Health Politics, Policy and Law*, 30, 869–923.

Shore, B. (1982). *Sala'ilua: A Samoan mystery*. New York, NY: Columbia University Press.

Shore, B. (1989). Mana and Tapu. In A. Howard & R. Borofsky (Eds.), *Developments in Polynesian ethnology* (pp. 137–173). Honolulu: University of Hawaii Press.

Simmons, D. (1998). A pilot urban church-based programme to reduce risk factors for diabetes among Western Samoans in New Zealand. *Diabetic Medicine*, 15, 136–142.

Simmons, D., Voyle, J. A., Fout, F., Feot, S., & Leakehet, L. (2004). Tale of two churches: Differential impact of a church-based diabetes control programme among Pacific Islands people in New Zealand. *Diabetic Medicine*, 21, 122–128.

Smith-Morris, C. (2006). *Diabetes among the Pima: Stories of survival*. Tucson: University of Arizona Press.

Solovay, S., & Rothblum, E. (Eds.). (2009). *The fat studies reader*. New York, NY: New York University Press.

Stuckler, D., & Nestle, M. (2012). Big food, food systems, and global health. *PLoS Med*, 9(6), 1–4.

Swinburn, B. A., Sacks, G., Hall, K., McPerson, K., Finegood, D., Moodie, M., & Gortmaker, S. (2011). The global obesity pandemic: Shaped by global drivers and local environments. *The Lancet*, 378, 804–814.

Wendland, C. L. (2010). *A heart for the work*. Chicago, IL: University of Chicago Press.

West, P. (2005). Translation, value, and space: Theorizing an ethnographic and engaged environmental anthropology. *American Anthropologist*, 107, 632–642.

Wiedman, D. (2012). Native American embodiment of the chronicities of modernity reservation food, diabetes, and the metabolic syndrome among the Kiowa, Comanche, and Apache. *Medical Anthropology Quarterly*, 26, 95–612.

Yates-Doerr, E. (2012). The weight of the self: Care and compassion in Guatemalan dietary choices. *Medical Anthropology Quarterly*, 26, 136–158.

Zimmet, P. Z., Faaiuso, S., Ainuu, J., Whitehouse, S., Milne, B., & DeBoer, W. (1981). The prevalence of diabetes in the rural and urban Polynesian population of Western Samoa. *Diabetes*, 30, 45–51.

14

Sensorial Pedagogies, Hungry Fat Cells and the Limits of Nutritional Health Education

Emilia Sanabria

Introduction

Valérie, 48, has gone on and off diets for over 30 years and has what she describes as a terrible relationship to her body. She recently calculated her body mass index (BMI) using an online calculator (www.imc.fr). At 79 kg for 1.77 m she has a BMI of 28 and is classified as overweight. When she entered her measurements, a flashing red dialogue box appeared on her screen, warning her, "ATTENTION: you are OVERWEIGHT. Consult your doctor or a nutritionist immediately to determine the causes. You must lose weight." Valérie has consulted innumerable doctors about her weight and tried most of the mainstream weight loss diets. Whatever weight she has lost, she has always gained back, sometimes in excess. As summer approaches, she makes an appointment at her local hospital's endocrinology service and a few tests later meets with an endocrinologist who enters her into an 'eating rehab' programme. "You have a slow metabolism", he tells her. "You're unlucky, you gain weight just by looking at food. It's not fair, but it's your reality. Your ancestors were famine survivors and have passed on these genes to you. It's not your fault. But you'll need to change the way you eat if you want to lose weight durably."

This article is based on ethnographic work with nutritionists who believe that long-term effective weight loss is only possible if you eat 'to feed pleasure'. This group of practitioners does not forbid any kind of food – not even greasy chips or chocolate mousse – and even teaches patients the art of food *dégustation*. Patients who have endured decades of restrictive diets are invited to taste and savour *with* their dietician the very foods that have been proscribed and banished but which they feel they irremediably succumb to. The GROS (literally fat/big), or Research Group on Overweight and Obesity, is an association of health professionals comprising nutritionists, dieticians, psychiatrists and psychologists working with overweight and obese patients in reference centres or private practices across France. The network counts nearly

200 specialists across France trained in the GROS method and organises a yearly conference and training programme (which I have partially undertaken). The GROS method is founded on a programme of therapeutic education that is centred on the eater's bodily sensations. Pleasure is a leitmotif.[1] The GROS approach takes as its starting point the idea that food intake is regulated by complex sensorial mechanisms that signal to the eater when to initiate or end a meal. GROS practitioners consider that all dietary recommendations, including those promoted by the French National Program for Nutrition and Heath (PNNS), encourage eaters to "eat with their head rather than with their sensations," as GROS co-founder Gerard Apfeldorfer summarised in an interview. The GROS' explicit goal is to reunite eaters with the pleasure and the sensations of eating. Rather than 'cognitive messages' or dietary advice, the GROS considers that 'sensations' should guide eating. The GROS website's "regulating alimentary behaviour" information pages asks, "Why tell the French population how they should eat, when every human being is naturally equipped with a system of sensorial regulation that enables him or her to eat adequately?"

As in most European nations, vast public health initiatives were launched in France to tackle non-communicable, chronic disease associated with high BMIs. While the causes, mechanisms and means of calculating the rising rates of obesity are contested and uncertain, emphasis is recurrently placed on the shift between energy intake and expenditure in societies where energy-dense foods have become widely available and aggressively advertised. Given this context of uncertainty concerning how to qualify and circumscribe the 'problem', let alone define its aetiology, developing effective public health responses presents considerable challenges. This article traces some of the shifts in the epistemological understanding of appetite regulation and examines how these are mobilised to different care or policy ends. It aims to contrast two positions and map an emergent transformation in understandings of obesity and its prevention. The first centres on informing eaters about nutrients and on proscribing certain calorie-rich foods. The second, more emergent, is the position developed by practitioners such as those trained in the GROS method and builds on scientific understandings of the role of sensorial processes in appetite regulation. It constructs its rationale on an explicit rejection of dieting practices, noting that diets ultimately fail to bring about weight reduction and lead to overall weight gain or disordered eating in the long term.[2]

I examine the uncertain materialities these sensorial pedagogies bring to life and trace the boundaries where foods and eaters, and matter and subjects, merge and transform one another. By considering how the appetite control systems of eaters are conceptualised and presented as undermined by a contemporary environment of irresistible highly palatable foods, my aim is to examine how the promotion of conscious and intimate sensory engagements with foods is understood by practitioners such as those working with the GROS method to provide an alternative response. In so doing, I examine the ways in which scientific evidence concerning appetite regulation, taste, pleasure and sensoriality is mobilised to explain the purportedly epidemic rise in obesity. What emerges is the idea of a misfit or maladaptation between the plethoric environment in which 'we' live today and the body 'we' are said to have inherited from a distant Palaeolithic past whose regulation system is geared towards defending its fat stores.

The analysis of how sensorial mechanisms are studied (in scientific practice) and used to treat patients or to promote health (in clinical practice or health education) provides an interesting vantage point into the ways the materialities of foods and bodies mutually transform each other. The sensorial systems that regulate food intake are triggered, at one end, by materials (foods), information about which is gathered through olfaction and sight and through taste and somesthesia,[3] once the food has entered the eater's mouth (although olfaction continues and somesthesia may begin earlier).[4] Bodies and foods become so profoundly enfolded into each other that it is impossible to determine where one begins and the other ends. The cascade of metabolic processes that takes place in bodies once food has triggered taste and olfaction, and the complex hormonal feedback mechanisms that follow, leads across a threshold of sorts. As endocrine processes spark off neurological responses, the tangibility and materiality of the process becomes more uncertain. The relation between the body's sensorial apparatus, the environment, and the relative importance of cognitive and automatic processes in food intake regulation forms an important area of research in 'obesity science'. The findings developed in this area feed a host of popular science books and media coverage on topics such as food addiction, willpower, dieting and overeating. They are in turn picked up by actors in the field of food health promotion such as those I have been working with. The questions that are being formulated by clinical and biomedical research around the topic of the sensorial concern the biological mechanisms that are driving people worldwide to eat more, and more of certain kinds of foods.

My aim is to attend to the way the category of the sensorial is used in the practices put in place by the GROS (and similar groups outside France). I start by contextualising their approach in a public health landscape dominated by health information and education. I then analyse two key areas of scientific research that the GROS draws on to found its rationale: the analysis of the active endocrine role of fat tissue in the regulation of appetite, and debates surrounding the feedback models that regulate energy in the body. Here, I draw on the distinction between first- and second-order cybernetics to examine the way in which homoeostatic regulation is repeatedly set against hedonism in discussions of obesity. Are the hedonic processes that are said to be disrupting homoeostatic regulation of appetite merely a dis-regulation in a closed loop system or a different kind of system altogether? How might these conceptual differences map onto the debates taking place around regulation in obesity science? The complex models of homoeostasis and analyses of the mechanisms of its contemporary dis-regulation that circulate in this field open up important questions for public intervention and the individualisation of responsibility for health, and invite us to reconsider the ways in which nutritional recommendations cast specific relationships between eaters and the foods they consume.

Beyond Informing: Forging the Domain of the Sensorial

Mol (2012, p. 379) notes that "the overriding message of most dieting advice is that a person who wants to lose weight needs to overrule the desires of her craving body." The fact that people are taught to relate to food in a calculative way suggests, she argues, a particular enactment of a mind-body distinction according to which without information, bodies would overeat, indulging in pleasure. The "ontonorms" at play in the Dutch dieting advice she analyses construct the natural homoeostatic capacities of bodies as an ideal and "hedonistic enjoyment" as a danger (Mol, 2012, p. 383). Information on calories, nutritional content of foods and the importance of a balanced diet is presumed in the dietary advice provided through public health nutrition programmes to enable "the rational mind to take control of the pleasure seeking body," Mol notes. The GROS explicitly posit that information and rational (or "cognitive," in their terms) control not only fail to bring about durable weight loss but actually impair eaters' natural bodily capacities to regulate weight. Like the practitioners on the margins of Dutch dieting that Mol describes, the GROS – who have developed a more structured and centralised approach than their Dutch colleagues, encourage people to taste, savour and *enjoy* their food.

Much of the debate in the obesity arena concerns the relative importance of willpower and biological factors in the development of adiposity and its control. This debate goes back to the early part of the twentieth century and to the shifting influence that endocrinologists and psychiatrists had in defining the aetiology and outlining treatment for obesity. Rasmussen (2012) traces the shift in the United States from an endocrinologically oriented approach that centred on glandular disorders to a psychiatrically oriented one that focused on the neural determinants of excess appetite. Obesity was framed as an addiction and constructed as a disorder of willpower (Rasmussen, 2012, p. 890). Interestingly, a new current in obesity research is attempting to re-qualify overeating as a form of addiction. However, this can be seen as an attempt to map public policy responses to BigFood on those that have been carried out against BigTobacco (see in particular Brownell and Gold, 2012). So while food addiction is gaining renewed attention, the rationale behind this is to shift the blame from individuals to industry-related activities that deliberately harm health through what the Lancet Non-Communicable Disease Action Group refer to as "corporate disease vectors" (Moodie *et al*, 2013). It is beyond the scope of the current article to examine why educating eaters and conveying information about nutritional and calorific content of foods emerged as a key domain of intervention in nutrition. Suffice it to say that nutritional health education is increasingly deemed to be at best a weak strategy in the face of the strong biological drive inscribed in our hardwiring to seek out calorie-dense foods and at worst a harmful or counterproductive one, shifting blame onto individuals (James, 2007; Herrick, 2009; Guthman, 2011). Part of the problem lies in the fact that the epidemiological patterns of obesity are contested (Gard, 2011), as are the causes and mechanisms that lead to the widely denounced gain in girth. In the absence of effective, population-wide interventions (such as pharmaceutical magic bullets or surgical solutions), information-education-communication models of behaviour change have thus been favoured.

The PNNS, French National Program for Nutrition and Heath (Ministère de la santé, 2011, p. 10), adopts a broad definition of 'nutrition' that includes physical activity and recognition that nutrition includes "nutrients, foods, social determinants, cultural, economic, sensorial and cognitive" aspects of food behaviours. Nevertheless, the PNNS identifies information, communication and education to shape food behaviours and physical activity as its main 'strategic lever'. The idea that obesity would be solved if people ate balanced meals and were less sedentary remains a tacitly shared one – largely reinforced by the tenor of health promotion messages. One implication of such a view is that if people are informed and fail to change their behaviour they are seen to be individually responsible for any ill health that may ensue. The relationship between access to information and 'positive' health behaviours has been problematized in a number of ways in public health, notably through greater attention to the social determinants of health (CSDH, 2008) or to the complex interplay of environmental, urban and metabolic factors in obesity. The Foresight Report on obesity put forward the notion of "passive obesity" to suggest that default choices posed by the social and built environment mean that combatting weight gain requires active strategies.

People in the UK today don't have less willpower and are not more gluttonous than previous generations. Nor is their biology significantly different to that of their forefathers. Society, however, has radically altered over the past five decades, with major changes in work patterns, transport, food production and food sales. These changes have exposed an underlying biological tendency, possessed by many people, to both put on weight and retain it. (Butland *et al*, 2007, p. 5)

At a recent conference on the social determinants of health held in France, one economist even suggested that health education had deepened health inequalities as more educated segments of the population had benefited disproportionally, deepening the gap in health outcomes across the social economic gradient. The relationship between providing information through public health campaigns and changed behaviour has also been problematized by behavioural economists who are paying increasing attention to the 'non-rational' processes that shape health decision making. The concept of nudging (Thaler and Sunstein, 2008), itself closely tied to social marketing, draws on a distinction between reflective and impulsive decision-making processes. Nudging opposes rational, reflective or cognitive processes to 'automatic, affective' reactions and 'feelings' that are triggered by environmental cues and driven by the lure of pleasure. In the context of a generalised moral panic surrounding rising rates of obesity, disparate approaches such as those appropriated by some eating disorder specialists adopting cognitive behavioural or mindfulness therapies (for example, Kristeller and Wolever, 2011) or organisations such as SlowFood that have taken up taste education (Barzanò and Fossi, 2010) have coalesced around the questioning of nutritional interventions that address overeating through abstract, disembodied information.[5] The rational, autonomous individual who has been the target of public health initiatives is attacked, so to speak, on two fronts by the emergence of a critique of health information and communication (Gastaldo, 1997; Evans *et al*, 2008; Whithead and Irvine, 2011; Ayo, 2012; Fitzpatrick and Tinning, 2014). On the first, she is seen to be fighting against an obesogenic environment and structural forces that determine she will have disproportionally worse health outcomes if she is female and of low social economic status (in France, and where obesity is concerned). On the second, she is seen as driven by unconscious, affective and automatic – largely biologised – forces that determine her behaviour and actions against her will or rational intentions (Thaler and Sunstein, 2008; Rice, 2013).

The GROS, for its part, draws a fairly radical distinction between what they refer to as "cognitive" or informational approaches and those, such as theirs, that centre on *les sensations alimentaires* (alimentary sensations). The 'sensorial' emerges as a central category in their practices. While there is an important literature on the anthropology of the senses (Serres, 1985; Classen, 1993; Seremetakis, 1994; Korsemeyer, 2002; Howes, 2003, 2005) and on the importance of attending to the senses in the study of health and illness or eating (Hinton *et al*, 2008; Nichter, 2008; Sutton, 2010), less has been written on how the sensorial may itself be rendered a therapeutic tool. The GROS practices I examine participate in what Seremetakis (1994, p. 123)[6] has referred to as a modern concern with "sensory loss." These practices aim to "re-sensitise" eaters who have become "divorced" from their sensations. They aim to bring heightened attention to the senses and the differences in sensory input (differentiating textures, olfactory, gustative or visual stimuli) and the importance of sensorial blending (sensations that are produced by the interaction of multiple sensory inputs). Nichter (2008) notes that meaning and experience of sensation are shifting and deeply biosocial (p. 186). He draws links between the increasing medicalisation and pharmaceuticalization of bodily sensations and the decreasing tolerance to discomfort and sensation. Sensations are so numerous in our daily lives that only some of them are cognitively processed and given meaning. They are typical hybrids and as such provide a zone through which biologies are encultured. As certain sensations become more salient through being stimulated or made culturally meaningful, certain neural pathways are reinforced, thus increasing the "inducibility" of the sensation, a process that Hinton *et al* (2008) refer to as the kindling of sensation.

Kindling aptly describes the industrial processing of "hyperpalatable foods", or foods that GROS practitioners refer to as "highly sensorial." Palatability is the fine-tuning of foods to enthral the senses, stimulate appetites, drive wanting, override satiety and motivate eaters to pursue more of that taste. In *The End of Overeating; Taking Control of Our Insatiable Appetite*, ex-FDA commissioner, paediatrician and Dean of Yale medical school Kessler (2009) argues that the multisensory dimensions of hyperpalatable foods reinforce reward (p. 49) and are drivers in overeating (p. 98). "Mixture is where the magic happens," a food industry consultant told Kessler (2009, p. 100). Industry, Kessler tells us, is shifting towards greater complexity, combining optimal amounts of sugar and fat to attain a "bliss point" and developing a versatile range of "inclusion products" to add crunch, blasts of flavour, and dynamic contrasts in flavour or colour, and to enhance the sensory properties of foods that drive desires. Processing makes chewing increasingly unnecessary, facilitating swallowing and reducing the time food spends in the mouth, thereby undermining satiety mechanisms that arise when food is savoured and not just gobbled down. In what follows I attend to the way the deeply encultured category of 'the sensorial' is increasingly being mobilised across a range of care and prevention practices in the field of nutrition. I present some of the scientific evidence that is drawn upon in this context with specific reference to the practices deployed by the GROS, and the relations that they draw between sensorial overriding and overeating.

Returning to Alimentary Sensations

Cognitive restriction is a central concept for GROS practitioners. Initially developed in 1975, the term is reworked by Polivy and Herman (1991) to refer to eating that ceases to be controlled by internal factors and alimentary sensations and that becomes controlled and planned according to cognitive factors such as dietary prescriptions. Many of the obese patients that GROS practitioners treat in their private practices have been through years of diets that GROS practitioners feel have led them to lose touch with their bodily sensations. The aim of treatment is to shift from a mode of eating that is cognitively determined (that is, by external injunctions and beliefs) to one that is "intuitive and *sensorial*, governed by an attention to and a respect of alimentary sensations and emotions" (Zermati and Apfeldorfer, 2010, p. 154, my translation).

During a GROS training session I attended in Spring 2012 along with two dozen psychiatrists and dieticians from across France, GROS co-founder Zermati spoke of a diet as any form of "deliberate control of food intake on the basis of external, cognitive factors that take precedence over internal signals such as those that ensure our energetic homeostasis". He then provided a detailed explanation of why, on the basis of the scientific evidence we have on adipose tissue hyperplasia and negative feedback, people cannot lose weight efficiently or durably, let alone happily, when they use cognitive restraint "against" their bodies. Apfeldorfer, Zermati's colleague and co-founder of the GROS, explained the GROS method to me in the following terms:

Our neurophysiological needs impose themselves upon us through a series of sensorial mechanisms. Breathing is vital and independent of our control. It is an automatically regulated processes. Eating like sleeping is a semi-automaticaily regulated behaviour. If we are tired we can resist sleep, but the more we stray from our sensations, the stronger the backlash. Because food was not always available in our past, we have developed mechanisms to tell us when to seek out and end meals as well as to stock calories. Sometimes we have to make do with the sensation of hunger, and at others to eat without hunger. Pleasure was once the regulator, but because our pleasure centres are overstimulated by hypersensorial foods, we have lost track of our internal messaging system. The GROS defends an approach based on the attention to and the respect of bodily sensations through work on the events that impede us from respecting these sensations and which leads to addiction-type processes.

The GROS method is put to work in a range of therapeutic settings, from private dietetic practices to clinics specialising in the treatment of obese patients. Founded in 1997, the GROS counts nearly 200 practicing members across France who have received certification. The typical GROS patient is female, has been on restrictive diets all her life and consults in a private practice through the liberal system of 'town' (as opposed to hospital) medicine. However, a growing number of specialised services across public hospitals and private clinics are training their staff in the GROS method and integrating aspects of the sensorial approach into the care practices they offer their patients. The method itself centres on a series of practical exercises and techniques that include experiments with taste. Many practitioners begin with a *dégustation* of a 'problem food'. Patients are invited to bring in a food that they cannot resist and that they readily overeat. This invitation to explore and consume a taboo food with a dietician is also a means of building trust with the patient and is used by GROS practitioners to demarcate their approach from all the 'restrictive' injunctions patients have often endured previously. Drawing on the model of a wine tasting, patients are invited to consciously examine the food item they have chosen, its shape, texture or smell, before beginning the *dégustation*. Each mouthful is taken 'in full consciousness' of the cascade of sensations that unfold as the dietician explains the molecular and physiological processes that produce a taste and through which the organoleptic properties of the food being consumed are relayed into a mental image and a sensation of pleasure. As the *dégustation* proceeds, the patient is invited to note changes in texture and sensation. Is the pleasure experienced in the same way? Does it peak or drop? Does the food item taste the same after the *nth* bite? Such an experience is expected to bring awareness to the natural internal signalling mechanisms that the 'disregulated' eaters 'we' have become fail to attend to. The objective is to find the point of *rassasiement*[7] at which the food no longer has the same taste and at which both the wanting and liking of it decrease. Although the awareness that is sought through the body is set against that derived from rational, mind-driven control, it is interesting to note the way terms such as 'mental images' or 'full consciousness' creep back in.

The GROS training introduces practitioners to an explicitly cybernetic understanding of appetite regulation. As Zermati explained during a training session, when the homoeostatic system is internally unbalanced, a biological value (such as a drop in blood sugar) is transformed into a specific sensorial message. When this message is transformed into a sensation, it activates a behaviour such as the initiation of a meal or a desire for a specific food. When the need has been satisfied, a sensorial message in the form of the feeling of satiety is returned to end the meal.

Negative feedback characterises a balanced homeostatically regulated system, where the need diminishes with the behaviour. In a 'dis-regulated' system, the need (hunger) augments with the activity: there is positive feedback. Satiety cannot be experienced if eating takes place too fast, or while focusing attention on another activity simultaneously. When foods are enjoyed and not just gulped down, chemically induced gustative modifications occur, triggering sensory-specific satiety. Zermati and Apfeldorfer (2010) ask how one can understand one's hunger and sensations if one is plugged into the outside world, eating unconsciously and without truly stopping to feel one's internal sensations.

GROS-led experiences also include work on the emotional aspects of hunger. During their training, dieticians and health professionals seeking GROS certification are themselves invited to experiment with the sensations and emotions raised by hunger through exercises that include skipping meals and recording the physical and emotional sensations this gives rise to. Ensuing discussions during training provide a platform from which to introduce the scientific literature on which the GROS founds its rationale. Hunger is graduated and the emotions it gives rise to (such as anxiety, fear, anger, sadness) identified. The experiment aims to rid the sensation of hunger of any anxiogenic emotions it may carry and return it to its primary physiological function of indicating a need to feed. Patients may also be invited to keep a *carnet des sensations* (sensations notebook) where all foods consumed in a week are noted to bring attention to the temporal and emotional contexts of eating. This teaches patients to differentiate eating that is triggered by hunger from eating that is triggered by emotional states. It leads them to identify the emotional states that lead to a desire to eat. As Zermati and Apfeldorfer note (2010, p. 138), contrary to common understandings, it is not hunger that makes us eat but the motivation to seek out food that results from hunger. This may also result from other factors such as emotional states. One of the fundamental issues in GROS therapeutic practice is learning to distinguish between desire to eat that is triggered by hunger and one that is triggered by an emotion. Blame and guilt that result from a failure to follow dietary recommendations are seen by GROS practitioners – and by others approaching eating in a similar vein – as having an embodied effect and increasing the feelings of hunger, decreasing the feeling of satiety and satisfaction, and putting the body in 'starvation' mode, hence increasing the likelihood of stocking the calories ingested. The sensorial thus becomes an interface between processes that are classified on either side of body/mind or biological/social distinctions. Satiety, in this model, and the stabilising of the energy balance are dependent on guilt-free pleasure.

Zermati and Apfeldorfer (2010, p. 137) note that obesity is due to two consecutive dis-regulations. The first is a dis-regulation of the system of homoeostatic regulation that leads eaters to consume more than their calorific needs, due to the fact that they are no longer sensitive to the natural sensorial mechanisms that signal satiety. The second is linked to what they refer to as the "set point", which is a function of adipose tissue signalling and which is determined by the quantity of adipocytes in the body. As these multiply they raise the set point, making weight loss beyond a certain threshold practically impossible. For these reasons, dieting cannot lead to durable weight loss because the augmentation in adipose tissue is sometimes not reversible, and mental control over alimentary behaviour cannot be maintained in the long run. In the remainder of the article, I thus draw on two key issues that arise from the scientific debate that the scientific committee of GROS draws on: the shift from homoeostasis to hedonism and the role of adipose tissue in the regulation of appetite.

The Agency of Fat: Adiposity and Negative Feedback in Plethoric Environments

This section focuses on some of the scientific work being done in the area of food intake regulation and examines the disquieting effects foods are presented as having on eaters in some of this literature. This raises specific questions for the issues I opened with concerning preventative or educational strategies. If foods exert their influence on eaters in ways that bypass or circumvent eaters' wills, what is the effect of educating eaters about food groups, or the importance of eating five fruit and vegetables? The regulation of human appetite is controlled by complex feedback mechanisms involving a range of hormones that connect the different sensory organs such as the tongue, taste buds and gut to nodes in the central nervous system such as the hypothalamus. These elaborate pathways are still being explored as new hormones and receptors are discovered and their functioning explained. In 1994, the hormone leptin was discovered and shown to have a central role in appetite regulation. Leptin is produced in the adipose tissue and plays a key role in the regulation of hunger. Two key mechanisms are at play in appetite control and food intake regulation: a homoeostatic mechanism and a hedonic one. Much of the current work being carried out in this area points to the increased role of the latter in the contemporary food-rich environment to which we are increasingly exposed. The argument is that the marketing by BigFood of energy-dense hyperpalatable foods stimulates the hedonic system, driving wanting and exciting pleasure, thus overriding homoeostatic control mechanisms (Kessler, 2009; Gearhardt *et al*, 2011; Brownell and Gold, 2012).

But first let us briefly consider how the homoeostatic system is said to function. Energy homoeostasis works to maintain the stability of body fat stores by regulating both food intake (the motivation to initiate and end meals) and energy expenditure (the rate at which calories are burnt). In their conclusion to a review on central nervous system food intake control published in *Nature*, Morton *et al*, 2006, note that there is no consensus on the fundamental aspects of obesity parthogenesis. The review examines evidence concerning the molecular and behavioural mechanisms that link modulations in body fat to the regulation of food intake through mechanisms such as satiation and motivation to initiate meals. It shows that central nervous system-controlled energy homoeostasis responds to changes in body fat stores. As these stores diminish (as weight is lost) "the motivation to find food and the size of individual meals tend to increase until energy stores are replenished" (Morton *et al*, 2006, p. 289). Adipose negativity feedback signalling posits that signals inform the brain of changes in body fat stores, leading to adaptive adjustments that aim to stabilise fat stores by acting on the regulation of satiety perception and brain reward circuitry. The authors thus make a claim that goes against commonly held assumptions about weight gain, proposing that "obesity involves the *defence* of an elevated body weight, rather than the absence of regulation", and that the "global obesity pandemic" (*sic.*) is the product of "deleterious interactions between obesity-promoting environmental factors and homeostatic control systems". This to say that the homoeostatic regulatory mechanism is driven to defend against fat loss rather than to prevent weight gain. This is often explained by reference to our palaeontological past, in which periods of feast and famine were common and where the capacity to maintain fat stores would have been an evolutionary advantage. In this sense, the 'natural' body 'we' are said to have inherited from this collective past has mechanisms that motivate eaters to seek out energy-dense foods, a hardwiring that is maladaptive in today's plethoric environment. The adaptations that are imagined to have favoured the survival of our ancestors, such as mechanisms to maintain fat stores in prevision of periods of famine, are understood to be our modern plagues, leading to the increase of cardiovascular disease and type-2 diabetes.

Kessler (2009) argues that the homoeostatic regulation system described above is often overridden by another mechanism with different brain circuitry. "This is known as the reward system. And […] in the fight between energy balance and reward, the reward system is winning". The reward system reinforces motivation to seek out certain desirable foods. It is based on a feedback system that teaches eaters to associate specific caloric intake with particular tastes and foods. This is an acquired process, built up over time and one that is reinforced by the increasing presence of hyperpalatable foods in global foodscapes. In a sense it can be argued that the turn to the sensorial dimensions of appetite regulation in obesity prevention circles arises subsequent to the close attention given by the food industry to tailored modifications in the sensorial qualities of processed foods. Guyenet and Schwartz (2012) define reward as "the process whereby certain behaviours are reinforced in response to specific environmental stimuli." Palatability, they argue, has been consistently shown to influence meal size in humans. As Guyenet (2012) notes in a blog post, alluding once more to an evolutionary explanation:

> Our brains are highly attuned to these qualities because they're all elements of nutritious, calorie-dense foods that would have sustained our ancestors in a natural environment, but today, the exaggerated combinations of these qualities used by processed food manufacturers […] overstimulate our natural reward pathways. Commercial foods are professionally designed to maximize reward, because reward is precisely what keeps you coming back for more.

These developments, and the shifts in language that are required to communicate them, are interesting in that they give adipocytes substantial agency. These cells are said to actively defend the fat stores in bodies through a range of metabolic, neurologic and endocrine processes. They are, as it were, hungry, and in turn make eaters hungry. Eaters' capacities to make rational choices are subverted by these hungry fat cells. They decide for them, or interfere with their decision-making capabilities. What does it imply to say that it is the fat that is hungry, rather than the eater?

In its training programme the GROS gives considerable attention to recent findings on the mechanisms of adipose tissue growth. They regularly refer to the fact that there are two mechanisms of adipose tissue development: adipocyte hypertrophy and adipocyte hyperplasia. In the first case, fat cells *increase* in size as they stock excess energy. This mechanism of weight gain is easier to fight as weight is lost through the 'emptying out' of adipocytes. However, recent attention has turned to a second process of fat accumulation that consists in the multiplication of fat cells (Jo *et al*, 2009). There is debate concerning whether or not adipocyte hyperplasia occurs after the age of 20 (Tchoukalova *et al*, 2010). What is significant for the present purposes is that the adipose tissue has come to be portrayed in such literature as having an active endocrine function. It is now conceived of as "an organ in and of itself, like the pancreas or liver," as one nutritionist put it to me during the 2012 GROS congress. Attention is being given to the role of fat cell progenitors from different parts of the body in generating adipose tissue with different inflammatory or 'dis-regulatory' impacts. While hypertrophied adipocytes can be expunged, their multiplication at a young age implies that the future adult will have a much greater susceptibility to weight gain due to the fact that the set point defended by negative feedback is higher.

The relation between fat and appetite as it is described in scientific investigations into the endocrine functions of adipose tissues and the active role fat tissue plays in the regulation of appetites is a classic case of what Leslie Aiello, President of the Wenner-Gren Foundation for Anthropological Research, has termed a "paleofantasy". Paleofantasies are stories about human behaviour that are constructed upon evolutionary narratives based on limited fossil evidence. In an essay citing Aiello, evolutionary biologist Zuk (2009) notes that "The notion that there was a time of perfect adaptation, from which we've now deviated, is a caricature of the way evolution works." The idea of a mismatch between the body we have inherited and the environment we now live in is so recurrent it appears self-evident. The recursive nature of the argument gives weight to the idea that the complex molecular pathways that regulate our appetite have developed in response to a poor, famine-ridden environment. It is as if the environment we evolved in during the Pleistone were now irremediably enfolded in our molecular make-up. This "primordial gluttony", as Kluger (2007) puts it in his review *The Science of Appetite*, arises from a prehistoric time when we were "programmed" to overeat. In this imagined race for survival, those who did not lose their appetite immediately put on more weight and survived the next famine, passing on the genes.[8] Yet, along with many public heath nutritionists, I would like to suggest that this mismatch may not be so accidental, as it were. The shape urban environments are taking worldwide, interspersed as they increasingly are with a dense network of outlets for highly processed and highly palatable foods available at all hours of the day and night at prices defying competition, are the product of specific forces that have tailored their marketing strategies to certain features of 'our' inherited hardwiring (Hawkes and Buse, 2011; Monteiro *et al*, 2011; Kleiman *et al*, 2012; Stuckler and Nestle, 2012; Stuckler *et al*, 2012).

Hedonic and homoeostatic mechanisms are deeply intermingled. As excessively rewarding foods are consumed, body fat stores increase, and with them, the level of body fat that is 'defended' by homoeostatic feedback mechanisms. This raises important questions concerning the burden of responsibility that is placed upon eaters, particularly overweight or obese eaters. What are the implications of recognising that adipose tissue stimulates appetites? Can this move us beyond the responsibility placed on individuals to care for their own health despite living in environments widely recognised to be deleterious to health? Or does this on the contrary further render overweight people targets of specific risk reduction action? As far as the GROS approach is concerned, the objective is explicitly to *déculpabiliser* (de-blame) overweight people and to demystify commonly held ideas concerning the fact that they eat more (which may not be true) by demonstrating that their bodies are defending a larger body fat store (which does not necessarily imply higher food intake). The objective of training practitioners on topics such as adipose tissue negative feedback or adipose hyperplasia is not so much to biologise behaviour as to reveal that the standard treatment – cognitive dietary restraint – is inefficient and profoundly damaging for many patients. If we consider, as the GROS suggests, that the body naturally strives to get back to its set point, as defined in part by levels of adiposity, and that this set point cannot be modified (without surgical intervention, but even then there is controversy), then dietary restraint is a very limited response.

Feedback Models and Complex Systems in Changing Environments

Set point, negative feedback and homoeostasis are all terms that have been borrowed from cybernetics and the science of complex systems regulation. As we have seen, there is an extensive scientific literature that examines the way hunger and satiety are regulated. Such processes are described as being regulated by complex neuroendocrine processes that involve a number of brain centres (some of which are even being located in the digestive system), sensory receptors throughout the body and a list of hormones that continues to expand. Body weight is modulated by interrelated systems that function on different temporalities, a shorter one modulating blood sugar levels and a slower one modulating adiposity. Feedback mechanisms maintain stability in changing environments, and are thus seen as playing a vital evolutionary role as we have seen here. However, as we have seen here, a growing number of obesity researchers are calling attention to the fact that environmental conditions have shifted so drastically with the widespread availability of calorie-dense foods that negative feedback mechanisms are failing, generating pathology.

The sensorial approach defended by GROS raises important questions concerning the complex feedback relations between the commensal, social and environmental dimensions of eating that shape the sensorial mechanisms through which people gauge hunger and satiety.[9] Social norms concerning appropriate meal frequency, or portion size and environmental factors concerning availability of foods in the various environments people circulate through, become enfolded in the molecular processes that control appetites. For example, hunger signals are known to occur at regular intervals in accordance with habitual meal schedules. Nichter (2008, p. 173) notes that the rural agriculturalists he worked with in India literally told the time of day by their rumbling bellies. The sensorial domain is thus socially modulated in complex ways. Although advocates of sensorial education make a strong distinction between 'external' eating cues and 'internal' sensations, the demarcation is not so clear if we consider the extent to which internal sensations respond according to these elaborate feedback mechanisms to external, societal, conditions. How, then, can we effectively return to our bodily signals in a context where these are always already shaped by the social context that is understood to disrupt our natural capacity to self-regulate? There is a reflexive loop here that poses considerable difficulties to practitioners and patients alike, as attested by the centrality of the task of learning how to differentiate between 'real' physiological hunger and 'emotional' or 'triggered' hunger. Such issues, for example, took on a particular difficulty in the context of discussions in the GROS training sessions I attended and in debates following GROS method presentations at conferences, concerning child feeding. While children are often taken as a prime example of our innate capacity to eat in accordance with our energetic needs (and not with emotions or as driven by hedonic processes), the importance of socialising children's senses is emphasised as, without guidance, it is suggested they would eat only sweet and calorie-dense foods. These contradictions point to the subtle and fragile nature of the feedback mechanisms that regulate appetite. I would like to suggest that the conceptual difficulties raised through such discussions point to the ways in which bodies and their environments are tacitly classified on different ends of a polarity. The sensorial mechanisms these different practices seek to engage are interesting precisely in that they straddle these conceptual divides between the inside and the outside of bodies, between matter and subjects, between conditioned and inherited processes.

Feedback models are central to the way endocrinologists are trained to think about the regulation of the energy balance. Complex systems-thinking is increasingly important to analyses of obesity policy (Ulijaszek, 2015). However, systems thinking is itself a complex and evolving field. I briefly turn to some important distinctions between models of complexity and consider their implications for the ways in which the complexity of obesity is conceptualised on the one hand, and for the practices promoted by the GROS on the other. Different models to analyse and predict the behaviour of complex systems are more or less able to accommodate internal complexity and the regulation of variation in input from outside the regulated system. This lead to a break between what has been referred to as first- and second- order cybernetics. First-order cybernetics, of the kind associated with Bateson (1972), sought to describe the total patterns that connect the elements of a system through loops of negative and positive feedback. It adopted a putative distinction between the inside and the outside of the system and aimed to provide an overarching, integrated perspective that assumed the totality or wholeness of the system. By contrast, theorists of second-order cybernetics, most notably Maturana and Varela (1992), aimed to bypass the "geography of inner versus outer" (p. 172), For Maturana and Varela, the looping that occurs in complex systems is always contingent on the observer. While first-order cybernetic systems are conceptualised as closed, total systems, second-order cybernetics posits a circular looping system more aptly represented by the image of the Mobius strip. Maturana and Varela (1992) propose to think the distinction between first- and second-order cybernetics in terms of a contrast between an integrated totality regulating the smaller parts and "an unruly conversational interaction: the very presence of this unruliness allows a cognitive moment to come into being according to the system's constitution and history" (p. 336). In such systems, referred to as 'autopoeitic', the relationship between an organisation (or system) and its elements (or structure) is open-ended but not random. The elements in the system are neither just analytical constructs nor ontological: their existence is a factor of the reference point from which they are described. So while first-order cybernetics placed an emphasis on systemic homoeostasis, second-order cybernetics is based on the idea that it is not possible to see the totality from any particular point of view.

To which order of cybernetics do the feedback mechanisms mobilised in the obesity literature belong? Clearly, there are important differences within the scientific fields engaged in these debates. Most of the literature reviewed for this article provides a fairly closed and integrated model of regulation in which the biological system analysed (in rats or humans) and its – for the most part lab – environment are presented as ontologically distinct. Nevertheless, in their analysis of the cybernetics of body weight regulation, Fricke *et al* (2006) examine the role of systems thinking in analysing the molecular aspects of homoeostatic control of food intake. Their conclusion is worth citing at length for it marks a clear break with the tenor of much of the literature on homoeostatic regulation:

> The attribution of control elements to biological structures always contains the problem of semantic simplification, because the biological structure is reduced to a singular meaning. The same biological structure can be a controlled variable in a certain feedback loop and a manipulated variable in a different loop. Therefore, feedback loops might be organized in chains, where elements are parts of different loops in different functions.
>
> (Fricke *et al*, 2006, p. 171)

An important question for future work in this area – both for scientific research and the examination of its policy implications – concerns the kinds of models that are put to work to conceptualise shifts in the way environments and bodies interact through 'the sensorial." Does the rise of 'hedonism' and renewed attention to 'addiction' in obesity science simply signal a historic shift in the food system, or does it also reflect a shift in epistemological understandings of the processes of appetite regulation? To what extent do first- or second-order cybernetic models actually influence the way research is carried out in this field? What are the genealogies of the models used in the different domains of obesity science and how do they come to impose themselves in the academic practices of different scientific communities? What political and conceptual implications do these different models have for the way we think about eating, treat its disorders and regulate the food system? In practice, the GROS method is messy. The interactions between sensations, food cues, desires, fears, habits and so on that it re-sensitizes eaters to are not neatly classifiable according to a topology of inside or outside, input or output. The method that has been drawn up experimentally from work with patients aims to return eaters to liking, rather than being driven by wanting (see Finlayson and Dalton, 2012).

Conclusion

If obesity involves the biological defence of an elevated level of body fat, as current evidence suggests, advice to simply "eat less, move more" cannot be expected to remedy the problem. This is because interventions that reduce body fat stores without a corresponding decrease in the defended level of fat mass elicit compensatory responses that promote the recovery of lost fat and are difficult to consciously override. (Guyenet and Schwartz, 2012)

Public health initiatives aiming to curb the rising rates of obesity are often still implicitly based on the idea that controlling weight is a matter of willpower and choice. In this model, people are given information and are expected to understand it and change their behaviour in accord. Little recognition is given to the fact that there are a series of factors, ranging from the structural to the neurophysiological (themselves intrinsically tied up with global economic factors), that intercede in the neat progression that would lead from the provision of health information to changed eating behaviour.

In this article, I have mobilised scientific literature on the question of appetite regulation in order to reveal the models that are used to think about the complex interplay between foods, bodies and their environments. What has captured my attention is the way in which the different findings emerging from the fields of adiposity research or the science of appetite reconfigure the relative balance of agency between foods and eaters. Here foods are seen to subvert eaters' will by exerting certain influences on them that are beyond the realm of rational control. The intimate encounter between foods and eaters is not accidental or incidental but the product of fine-tuning between food production and homoeostatic and hedonic pathways of food intake regulation. This opens the question of the implications, for public health, of recognising the ways in which food may have agency over eaters. While industry has long understood and capitalised upon this, public health has been slower to do so.

I have grappled with two rather different sets of material effects in this article. The first concerns the material effects of foods (or fat, as stocked in adipose tissue) on eaters. The second concerns a political economy notion of materialism as it relates to the role of the food industry in both driving the first set of material effects and subsidising efforts to seek out solutions to the problems generated. Examining the way the science of sensoriality, food intake regulation and appetite control is mobilised in public health strategies targeting *le comportement alimentaire* (alimentary health behaviours) provides a vantage point onto some of the ways politics and metabolism collide and into the complex effects of scale that eating engages. What is striking is the recurrent play on a balance between reflective, information-based approaches understood to relate directly to people's will and agency and a growing consensus around the idea that food choices are in fact largely guided by affective, physiological, endocrine or otherwise unconscious mechanisms. This raises questions as to the kinds of initiatives that can be effectively mobilised to target what – notwithstanding the controversy surrounding the epidemiological claims regarding 'overnutrition' – continues to be presented as a major public health priority.

Notes

1 There is much to be said about the way industry has seized this notion of 'pleasure' and the anti-dieting sentiment (notably through the industry support groups such as GROS receive). To give but one example, France's Weight Watchers launched a shock campaign provocatively titled "Stop Dieting! Relearn how to eat!" In January 2011 onwards, huge billboards appeared across France with provocative and highly sexualised images of voracious women's mouths bursting with all sorts of foods, from fries to sweets to broccoli.

2 This was corroborated by a report by the French National Agency of Food Security, Enviroment and Work (ANSES, 2010) on the physical and psychological risks of weight-loss dietary practices. The 10 most practised diets were evaluated for their risks for vital organ functioning, nutrient deficiencies and impact on food intake regulation mechanisms. The most damning aspect of the report concerns weight regain, estimated at 80 per cent of subjects at 1 year and higher beyond. This idea is not new to GROS, who has built its action around an anti-diet stance for over 10 years. However, the publication of the report lent support to a more diffuse anti-dieting sentiment arising from uncertainty about both the efficiency of diets and their long-term effects on health.

3 This faculty of bodily perception includes skin senses and proprioception of the internal organs.

4 On this topic, see Mann *et al* (201 1).

5 This distinction between rational, will-governed behaviour and emotional, irrational or pleasure-driven behaviour finds parallels in public health approaches to the consumption of harmful substances that I do not address here but that would merit greater attention (see, for example, Greco, 1993, or Valverde, 1997),

6 Although she is referring to a discursive production concerning the loss of senses for 'us' and a turn to the sensoriality of the 'Other' in anthropology.

7 French distinguishes between 'rassasiement' and 'satiété'. The first concerns the decrease in hunger signals during a meal; it takes place roughly 15–20 min after meal initiation. The second occurs just after the first and is the period during which hunger is no longer experienced.

8 While not denying the complex processes of evolution that link the metabolic process at work in human bodies today to those of their prehistoric predecessors, my point is simply that such self-evident conclusions appear repeatedly in neurobiology or endocrinology articles without any reference to published research on these questions. Past environments are presented as homogenously poor in nutriments without any recognition of the vast diversity of environments in which humans have lived, thrived and evolved.

9 Fischler (2011) proposes that the French have been "protected" against obesity because they spend more time eating, and eating together, than the British or Americans, a fact that increases the chances of pleasure and satiety.

References

ANSES (2010) *Évaluation des risques liés aux pratiques alimentaires d'amaigrissement*. Rapport d'expertise collective. Agence nationale de sécurité de l'alimentation, de i'environnement et du travail.

Ayo, N, (2012) Understanding health promotion in a neoliberal climate and the making of health conscious citizens. *Critical Public Health* 22(1): 99–105.

Barzanò, C. and Fossi, M. (2010) *In What Sense? A Short Guide to Sensory Education*. Bra, Italy: Slow Food®.

Bateson, G. (1972) *Steps to an Ecology of Mind: Collected Essays in Anthropology, Psychiatry, Evolution, and Epistemology*. Chicago, IL: University of Chicago Press.

Brownell, K. and Gold, M. (2012) *Food and Addiction: A Comprehensive Handbook*. Oxford: Oxford University Press.

Butland, B. *et al* (2007) *Foresight: Tackling Obesities: Future Choices Project Report*. London: Government Office for Science.

Classen, C. (1993) *Worlds of Sense: Exploring the Senses in History and Across Cultures*. London and New York: Routledge.

Commission on Social Determinants of Health (CSDH) (2008) Closing the gap in a generation: health equity through action on the social determinants of health. Final Report of the Commission on Social Determinants of Health. Geneva, World Health Organization.

Evans, J., Rich, E., Davies, B. and Allwood, R. (2008) *Education, Disordered Eating and Obesity Discourse: Fat Fabrications*. Abingdon, UK: Routledge.

Finlayson, G. and Dalton, M. (2012) Current progress in the assessment of 'liking' vs. 'wanting' food in human appetite. Comment *Appetite* 58(1):.373–378.

Fischler, C. (2011) Commensality, society, and culture. *Social Science Information* 50(3–4): 528–548.

Fitzpatrick, K. and Tinning, R. (2014) *Health Education: Critical Perspectives*. London: Routledge.

Fricke, O., Lehmkuhl, G. and Pfaff, D.W. (2006) Cybernetic principles in the systematic concept of hypothalamic feeding control. *European Journal of Endocrinology* 154: 167–173.

Gard, M. (2011) *The End of the Obesity Epidemic*. London: Routledge.

Gastaldo, D. (1997) Is health education good for you? Rethinking the concept of health education through the concept of biopower. In: R. Bunton and A. Peterson (eds.) *Foucault, Health and Medicine*. London: Routledge, pp. 113–133.

Gearhardt, A.N., Yokum, S., Orr, P.T., Stice, F., Corbin, W.R. and Brownell, K.D. (2011) Neural correlates of food addiction. *Archives of General Psychiatry* 68(8): 808–816.

Greco, M. (1993) Psychosomatic subjects and the 'duty to be well': Personal agency within. *Economy and Society* 22(3): 357–372.

Guthman, J. (2011) *Weighing In: Obesity, Food Justice and the Limits of Capitalism*. Berkeley, Los Angeles, London: University of California Press.

Guyener, S.J. (2012) Seduced by food: Obesity and the human brain, blog post, 9 March, http://boingboing.net/ 2012/03/09/seduced-by-food-obesity-and-t.html#disqus_thread, accessed 29 June 2012.

Guyenet, S.J. and Schwartz, M.W. (2012) Regulation of food intake, energy balance, and body fat mass: Implications for the pathogenesis and treatment of obesity. *Journal of Clinical Endocrinology and Metabolism* 97(3): 745–756.

Hawkes, C. and Buse, K, (2011) Public health sector and food industry interaction: It's time to clarify the term "partnership" and be honest about underlying interests. *The European Journal of Public Health* 21(4): 400–401.

Herrick, C. (2009) Shifting blame/selling health: Corporate social responsibility in the age of obesity. *Sociology of Health & Illness* 31(1): 51–65.

Hinton, D., Howes, D. and Kirmayer, L. (2008) Toward a medical anthropology of sensations: Definitions and research agenda. *Transcultural Psychiatry* 45(2): 142–162.

Howes, D. (2003) *Sensual Relations*: *Engaging the Senses in Culture and Social Theory*. Ann Arbor, MI: University of Michigan Press.

Howes, D. (ed.) (2005) *Empire of the Senses*: *The Sensual Culture Reader*. Oxford and New York: Berg.

James, P. (2007) Developing national obesity prevention policies: An international perspective. *Obes* 2(1): 122–132.

Jo, J. *et al* (2009) Hypertrophy and/or hyperplasia: Dynamics of adipose tissue growth. in *PLoS Computational Biology* 5(3): el000324.

Kessler, D. (2009) *The End of Overeating*: *Taking Control of our Insatiable Appetite*. London: Penguin Books.

Kleiman, S., Ng, S.W. and Popkin, P. (2012) Drinking to our health: Can beverage companies cut calories while maintaining profits? *Obesity Reviews* 13(3): 258–274.

Kluger, J. (2007) The science of appetite. *Time* 31 May.

Korsmeyer, C. (2002) *Making Sense of Taste*: *Taste, Food, and Philosophy*. Ithaca: Cornell University Press.

Kristeller, J.L. and Wolever, R.Q. (2011) Mindfulness-based eating awareness training for treating binge eating disorder: The conceptual foundation. *Eating Disorders* 19(1): 49–61.

Mann, A. *et al* (2011) Mixing methods, tasting fingers Notes on an ethnographic experiment. *HAU*: *Journal of Ethnographic Theory* 1 (1): 221–243.

Maturana, H. and Varela, F. (1992) *The Tree of Knowledge*: *The Biological Roots of Human Understanding*. Rev. ed. Boston, MA: Shambhala.

Ministère du Travail, de l'Emploi et de la Santé (2011) *Programme national nutrition santé 2011–2015*, http:// www.sante.gouv.fr, acessed 18 March 2014.

Mol, A. (2012) Mind your plate! The ontonorms of Dutch dieting. *Social Studies of Science* 43(3): 379–396,

Monteiro, C.A., Levy, R.B., Claro, R.M., Castro, I.R.R. and Cannon, G. (2011) Increasing consumption of ultra-processed foods and likely impact on human health: Evidence from Brazil. *Public Health Nutrition* 14(1): 5–13.

Moodie, R. *et al* (2013) Profits and pandemics: Prevention of harmful effects of tobacco, alcohol, and ultra- processed food and drink industries. *The Lancet* 381 (9867): 670–9.

Morton, G.J., Cummings, D.E., Baskin, D.G., Barsh, G.S. and Schwartz, M.W. (2006) Central nervous system of control of food intake and body weight. *Nature* 443(7109): 289–295.

Nichter, M. (2008) Coming to our senses: Appreciating the sensorial in medical anthropology. *Transcultural Pyschiatry* 45(2): 163–197.

Polivy, J. and Herman, H. (1991) Good and bad dieters. Self-perception and reaction to a dietary challenge. *International Journal of Eating Disorders* 10(1): 91–99.

Rasmussen, N. (2012) "Weight stigma, addiction, science, and the medication of fatness in mid-twentieth century America. *Sociology of Health & Illness* 34(6): 880–895.

Rice, T. (2013) The behavioral economics of health and health care. *Annual Review of Public Health* 34: 431–47.

Seremetakis, N. (ed.) (1994) *The Senses Still*. Chicago, IL: University of Chicago Press.

Serres, M. (1985) *Les cinq sens. Philosophie des corps mêlés 1*. Paris, France: Grasset.

Stuckler, D,, McKee, M., Ebrahim, S. and Basu, S. (2012) Manufacturing epidemics: The role of global producers in increased consumption of unhealthy commodities including processed foods, alcohol, and tobacco. *PLoS Medicine* 9(6): el 001235.

Stuckler, D. and Nestle, M. (2012) Big food, food systems, and global health, *PLoS Medicine* 9(6): el001242.

Sutton, D.E. (2010) Food and the senses. *Annual Review of Anthropolology* 39: 209–23.

Tchoukalova, Y. *et al* (2010) Regional differences in cellular mechanisms of adipose tissue gain with overfeeding. *Proceedings of the National Academy of Sciences* 107(42): 18226–18231.

Thaler, R. and Sunstein, C. (2008) *Nudge*: *Improving Decisions about Health, Wealth and* Happiness. New Haven, CT: Yale University Press.

Ulijaszek, S. 2015. With the benefit of Foresight: obesity, complexity and joined-up government. *BioSocieties* 10: 213–228.

Valverde, M. (1997) Slavery from within: The invention of alcoholism and the question of free will. *Social History* 22(3): 251–268.

Whithead, D. and Irvine, E. (2011) Ottawa 25+ 'all aboard the dazzling bandwagon' – developing personal skills: What remains for the future? *Health Promotion International* 26(S2):pp. ii245–ii252.

Zermati, J.P. and Apfeldorfer, G. (2010) Vers une nouvelle théorie de l'obésité. In: J.P. Zermati, G. Apfeldorfer and B. Waysfeld (eds.), *Traiter l' obésité et le surpoids*. Paris: Odile Jacob.

Zuk, M. (2009) The evolutionary search for our perfect past. *The New York Times* 20 January.

15

The Environmental Account of Obesity: A Case for Feminist Skepticism

Anna Kirkland

It has become common in progressive circles to lament that poor people are fatter than affluent people because they do not have access to fresh fruits and vegetables or safe outdoor spaces for exercise. Feminist scholars have recently echoed the public health perspective on obesity, in which a heavier population is a serious problem that must be broadly addressed through taxation, agricultural policy, food labeling and advertising, wellness programs, and urban planning (Yancey, Leslie, and Abel 2006; Berlant 2007; Probyn 2008).[1] Feminist enthusiasm for tackling the so-called obesogenic environment arises from an interest in helping poor minority populations, particularly the women and children of those groups.[2] In presenting my research on fat rights to feminist audiences in recent years, I've been told explicitly that to oppose obesity reduction efforts is racist and sexist because they are needed to help poor minorities, particularly women.

There is no doubt that food environments have changed, that intolerable health disparities exist along lines of race and class, that there are some weight differences by race and class, and that, while the link between body fat and health is often misstated and exaggerated, there are correlations between weight and some chronic diseases (Murray et al. 2006; Kolata 2007a; Wildman et al. 2008). So why balk at the environmental account of obesity, particularly when it aims to ease the suffering and expand the choices of low-income minority women? I argue that this environmental approach to obesity has been sold as a progressive, structurally focused alternative to stigmatization, but it actually embeds and reproduces a persistent tension in feminist approaches to social problems: well-meant efforts to improve poor women's living conditions at a collective level often end up as intrusive, moralizing, and punitive direction of their lives. In this case, the environmental argument seems structural, but it ultimately redounds to a micropolitics of food choice dominated by elite norms of consumption and movement. ...

My aim here is to create a feminist debate over obesity policy by dissenting from feminist affirmations of the environmental account of obesity and showing how we could raise new questions and complicate things a bit. I hope to trouble the recent feminist embrace of the environmental account of obesity from several directions: empirical, theoretical, political, ethical, and practical. Specifically, I argue, first, that some of the baseline empirical assumptions of the environmental account are wrong or at least not sufficiently well established; second, that the popularity of this account depends on unacknowledged moralism; and, third, that policies based on the environmental account will end up being punitive, ineffective, and patronizing and will come with burdensome unintended consequences that will hurt the groups feminists claim to most want to help. In the sections that follow, I explain the rise of the environmental account of obesity among progressive policy elites and show how it is not really what it seems at first. I conclude by noting that the enthusiastic embrace of the environmental view has been a lost opportunity for feminist scholarship to enliven this public issue with new perspectives, fresh data, and theoretical frameworks not overly determined by the health sciences, and I suggest both alternative paths for feminist inquiry and some fixes to the problems I describe.

The Progressive Embrace of the Environmental Account

As British Health Secretary Alan Johnson recently told Parliament, "The chilling reality is that modern life makes us overweight [and] solutions will not be found in exhortations for greater individual responsibility" (Johnson 2007, col. 826). The response to obesity, advocates argue, must be preventative, broad based, forward looking, and suffused throughout the built environment, across the life span, and into both public and private spheres (Hill and Peters 1998). In Foucauldian terms, the environmental approach is paradigmatically biopolitical, acting at the population level to improve health (Foucault 1991). In the United Kingdom, this environmental account of obesity has been widely embraced, with policies such as weighing schoolchildren, designing "fit towns" (Wintour 2007), mandating cooking classes in public schools, and closely monitoring pregnant women. The Scottish government has recently targeted pregnant women and children under age five in a £40 million campaign to provide fruit and vegetable vouchers, as well as to promote walking and jogging and to pay for a cooking bus to tour the country with chefs demonstrating healthy eating techniques (Davidson 2008).

In the United States there is less enthusiasm for the most far-reaching measures, but many of the same proposals have been offered in state legislatures and in Congress (Campos 2006). The city of Los Angeles recently banned new fast food restaurants from a swath of lower-income areas in an effort to improve residents' food choices (Severson 2008). Other policy suggestions include banning advertising of fatty and sugary foods to children; reinstating or extending physical education programs in schools; instituting healthy eating incentives in places the government controls, such as military installations and federal workplaces; requiring more calorie labeling on foods; increasing food stamp purchasing power for fruits, vegetables, and whole grains; funding more bike paths, recreation centers, swimming pools, parks, and sidewalks; zoning for pedestrian malls and greater walkability; taxing soft drinks and other high-fat, high- sugar foods; subsidizing low-calorie foods; and providing incentives for purchases of exercise equipment and enrollment in weight-loss programs (Nestle and Jacobson 2000). As Rogan Kersh and James Morone (2002) explain, obesity regulation is currently driven by outrage at corporate misbehavior (fast food companies and agribusiness primarily), though there will have to be more organized interest group action and mass protest to spark reform beyond the easily reachable areas of school lunches and soft drink access for children during the school day.

The first step in the way progressives currently deploy the environmental account is to remove moral blame from individuals for getting fat and to place it on social and economic factors like the proliferation of high-fructose corn syrup in our food supply accompanied by decreased physical activity at work and increased reliance on cars. The second step is to note that some demographic segments of the population (lower-income people, racial and ethnic minorities, poor rural populations, children) are much more at risk in this environment than others (affluent urban whites). That is, there are multiple environments, and elites have the means to evade the fattening ones while the poor do not. The environmental mode of intervention aims to shift the ground beneath the most basic habits and choices during daily life, with the aim of making poor environments more like elite ones. Food taxes and changes to agricultural subsidies will change the prices and availability of foods so that consumers will be more inclined to buy fruits and vegetables instead of hamburgers. If there are more parks, bicycle paths, and recess times during the school day, people will just start to use them without having to be motivated to go out and exercise. These interventions are supposed to operate in the background of our consciousness so that consumers do not have the sensation of being forced to exercise or kept from delectable foods, just gently rerouted into healthier choices that become natural to make.

There are actually two distinct working parts within the environmental account. They look like political opposites or perhaps distortions, but they are actually closely intertwined. That is precisely the problem: that these two undercurrents constitute what is called an environmental approach and thus fatally undermine it. The first part is responsibilization, or the notion that each individual must act to take care of herself so that she does not become a burden on society—by smoking, by failing to be careful during pregnancy, or by getting fat, for example (Rose 1999). A responsibilizing version of the environmental account would stress the need to give people more information to make better decisions about self-care: calorie labeling, cooking classes, incentives to join gyms, and so on. These policies remake the environment in ways that supply more choices and information to citizens modeled as consumers (Morone 2000; Guthman and DuPuis 2006). Environmental refashioning, such as the construction of more bike paths, often depends on personal responsibility because people must choose to use them. The second part is what I will term "collectivism," or the notion that our bodies, our fellow citizens' bodies, and the environment constitute an interrelationship that is best understood as a whole if we want to create a healthier society. On this view, the individual cannot necessarily act on her own to remove pollutants from the food supply or to make a safe route for biking to work, and she should not be asked to do so. These are collective problems that must be structurally addressed with redistributionist policies. Collectivist solutions are not focused on the citizen as consumer only but on a subject whose freedom depends on things only collective action can provide, things like public transportation, universal health care, and safe food, water, and air.

The environmental approach to fighting obesity is supposed to be collective, not responsibilizing. Responsibilizing individuals is not really environmental in the obvious sense of the word, after all. But because the animating problem is that poor people are fat, the focus on weight loss becomes the metric of success. The aim, then, is to get the poor and the fat to make virtuous personal choices to combat a contaminated world. As Julie Guthman puts it, "food politics has become a progenitor of a neoliberal anti-politics that devolves regulatory responsibility to consumers via their dietary choices" (2007, 264). The environmental account of obesity depends on an account of political subjects as duped by capitalist forces (Big Food), on the one hand, and entirely self-determining (thin because of healthy eating), on the other hand, and neither is satisfactory.[3] Once we see how creating contexts for virtuous personal consumer choices has become the primary work of the environmental approach, it will be easier to parse out the problems with embracing it as feminism's answer to the so-called obesity epidemic. These problems are clear in the three most recent feminist endorsements of environmental approaches to obesity.

Feminism and Fat

In 2006, Antronette Yancey, Joanne Leslie, and Emily Abel argued … that feminists in particular should embrace the environmental view of antiobesity policy on antiracist and antisexist grounds. They argue that feminists should look to the health consequences and socioeconomic inequities of obesity that place women, particularly lower-income and minority women, in positions of risk. "Advocacy and scientific endeavor promoting environmental approaches to healthy eating and active living are quintessentially feminist," they conclude (Yancey, Leslie, and Abel 2006, 438). Their account exemplifies the basic two-part view: the turn to the environment rather than individual behavior, then the observation that some people's wealth and living conditions enable them to evade that environment while others are more entrapped in it. Yancey, Leslie, and Abel assume that the dominant public health account of the dangers of obesity is correct, but they amplify the case for focusing on the situation of lower-income minority women. They support the standard reforms (more fruits and vegetables in poor neighborhoods, more exercise opportunities, less television viewing, less advertising of food to children, and more public transit) and assume that if more consumer choices are available, the poor will adopt healthy lifestyles. "A focus on environmental causes may be particularly beneficial in reducing overweight and obesity among the demographic segments of the population that are at highest risk," they note (432). In other words, they assume that getting poor women to serve and consume different foods, get out and exercise, and turn off the television should be carried out at the environmental level rather than the personal level, and they also assume that these reforms will help poor minority women lose weight.

Their argument restates some significantly misleading reports, however, such as the "conservative estimate" that three hundred thousand deaths per year are attributable to obesity, inactivity, and poor diet (Yancey, Leslie, and Abel 2006, 427), a number that had been debunked by Centers for Disease Control (CDC) scientists well before their article's publication (Kolata 2004). Oddly, they cite a 2005 study by Katherine Flegal and others that significantly downgraded those estimates (Flegal et al. 2005) though only to complain that the 2005 study's data "creat[ed] a mistaken impression of scientific uncertainty about the epidemic's severity" (Yancey, Leslie, and Abel 2006, 427). It is also widely accepted that obesity has caused greatly increased rates of type 2 diabetes in children, a trend Yancey and her colleagues cite to quell criticism of the notion of an epidemic. Their evidence, however, comes from a small study of high-risk children. Follow-up studies using a broad representative sample of young people (including an oversampling of minority children) have found that "rates of type 2 diabetes among adolescents remained relatively stable" from 1988 to 2000, which is as far back as we have any data (Lee 2008, 683). As other skeptics of fat panic have pointed out, much of the evidence about diabetes in children has been anecdotally reported ("You didn't used to see that in children, and now we do") while the wave of cases has been difficult to find (Gibbs 2005). There is no acknowledgment of the critical literature available at the time (e.g., Campos 2004; Gard and Wright 2005; Saguy and Riley 2005); instead, Yancey, Leslie, and Abel incorrectly characterize dissenters as merely "food industry critics" (2006, 427).

Lauren Berlant (2007) has also made a version of the environmental argument about obesity in a recent piece reflecting upon the drudgery of ordinary life in the U.S. economy, using the figure of the working-class fat person to rethink conceptions of sovereignty in an age of dull repetition, mind-numbing labor, and eating to pass the time. She begins at the register of the structural and the environmental, arguing that "agricultural policy and the development of tax and zoning codes … have diminished the health of the U.S. wage and low-salaried worker mainly through indirect means" (Berlant 2007, 772). Berlant proposes that we think of "eating as a kind of self-medication through self-interruption, … a fitting response to a stressful environment" (777). The bodies of those workers, she argues, "will be more fatigued, in more pain, less capable of ordinary breathing and working, and die earlier than the average for higher-income workers, who are also getting fatter, but at a slower rate and with relatively more opportunity for exercise" (775). Her account weaves the individual's capacity for self-care into the material conditions of life in a theoretically sophisticated presentation of the environmental view. Her argument nonetheless runs into some of the same tensions that Yancey, Leslie, and Abel's does. Berlant assumes the truth of a long string of empirical claims, such as that poor people have eating habits not shared by the rest of us, that their eating conditions are determined by agricultural and environmental policy, that they eat in response to dreary lives, and that they are fat because of that eating rather than because of something else. The essay does nothing to raise our curiosity about these crucial assumptions, instead inviting us to sigh with each other (that "we" again) at all those miserable, poor, fat people. Her rich account of human misery under capitalism suggests a collective environmental response, but her focus on fat people and their eating habits would pull a sympathetic policy maker back toward asking how to make workers take better care of themselves.

Other feminists are more directly opposed to fat acceptance messages. Elspeth Probyn, an Australian feminist theorist, criticizes feminist body image studies that aim to advance fat acceptance (2008). Probyn is concerned that feminist critiques of the demand for thinness have led us to be dangerously and naively sympathetic to fat people. My argument here is precisely the opposite: that feminist critiques of obesity have made us dangerously and naively sympathetic to public health moralism. Her target is feminist celebration of transgressive fat bodies while "people are increasingly terrorized and seriously damaged by what they eat" (Probyn 2008, 402). In other words, we can defy body norms all we want, but the material realities of food and eating are plain public health threats, more like viruses than culturally contingent practices. She argues that embracing fat acceptance as a feminist cause is "painfully limited and can have quite disastrous political consequences" (403). Although she does not spell out those consequences, it seems clear that she means that an overly hasty rush to celebrate and defend fatness would make feminists complicit in the degradation of health that obesity signifies. Probyn's argument is a perfect example of how the environmental account would be more collectivist in subsidizing different kinds of food production but more responsibilized as it confronts the fact that many people probably like to "terrorize" themselves with the food they eat. Her essay also perfectly exemplifies how this feminist trajectory sets itself up for moralized interventions into women's lives. Feminists defended the Welfare Queen, but what about the Diabetes Time Bomb (Kirkland 2008)? What will we do about someone who intentionally "terrorizes" and damages herself? What kind of a citizen would do that? What kind of mother would do that to her children?

Troubling the Environmental Account

Erroneous or Lopsided Assumptions

For the environmental policy approach to obesity to be efficacious and necessary, it must be the case that increased body weights in the population are the cause of widespread ill health, that body weights are increasing because of people's consumption of bad food and lack of exercise, and that the proposed changes are likely to reverse those habits, bring about weight loss, and increase health and well-being. As I explain in this section, there are compelling reasons to doubt some of the crucial empirical assumptions behind the public health approach to fighting obesity. At the very least, we should be aware that the information environment from which we draw our understandings of obesity as a social problem promotes misleading and alarmist views of fatness …

First and foremost, feminist scholars must recognize that panicky claims about something increasing are based on numbers that have a history. The body mass index (BMI) is the number in question here, and it turns out that standards for "overweight" and "obese" were lowered in 1998, creating millions of new fat people simply by definitional fiat (Campos et al. 2006; Oliver 2006). There had been widespread moderate weight gain (on the order of seven to twelve pounds on average per person in two decades), and so millions of people shifted up one category into the new stricter "overweight" (BMI 25 or above) and "obese" (30 or above) categories. Nor were decisions about BMI cutoffs made in a scientifically disinterested fashion: the decision-making organizations are funded by drug companies for whom pathologizing fat will be enormously profitable (Moynihan 2006). While BMI categories supposedly mark off clear points at which health problems increase, as I noted above, the CDC found that mortality levels are actually the lowest for those in the "overweight" BMI category and do not enter the range of statistical significance for possible harm until BMIs reach 35 or above, which includes less than 8.3 percent of the population (Flegal et al. 2005). (These are the data that Yancey, Leslie, and Abel dismiss as creating false debate about the dangerousness of fat.) The yearly death estimate dropped to twenty-six thousand after this correction (for perspective, at least forty thousand Americans die on the roads each year). Another recent study found that one in four people with BMI ranges of "healthy" had cardiac risk factors normally associated with obesity while half of overweight and one third of obese people had healthy metabolic profiles (Wildman et al. 2008). The BMI categories are absolutely crucial for describing the high rates of overweight and obesity we keep hearing about; there is no epidemic without them drawn as they are. But they do not deserve the status they currently enjoy as proxies for health.

In this context of panicky misinformation, I wonder how much we really know about what poor black and Latina women actually eat, why and how they move about the world, how public policy might alter these habits, and what the effects might be. A recently released nationally representative study of what Americans eat did not bear out a picture of poor minorities consuming lots of high-calorie food while wealthy whites nibble salads: adult whites averaged 2,198 calories per day, African Americans 2,095, and Mexican Americans 2,109; those with incomes of less than $25,000 per year averaged 2,104 calories a day and those making over $75,000 a year consumed 2,238 (U.S. Department of Agriculture et al. 2008, table 3). Much larger estimates of 3,900 calories per day describe how much food is produced per person in the United States, not how much is eaten (Nestle 2007, 13). This study's methodology is quite careful about getting accurate reports, with extensive follow-ups and reminders of what the person might have eaten in the previous 24 hours, though of course there could still be understatement of intake. Nonetheless, it is likely that distortion would be relatively even across groups, and it is notable that whites and wealthy people consumed more yet all the amounts clustered around the recommended 2,000 calorie standard. The most recent survey of Americans' fast food habits revealed high-frequency customers (the 14 percent of the population that accounts for half of sales) to be men below middle age with incomes averaging $67,575 ("Study Says" 2008). I have yet to see upper-middle-class men discussed as a subpopulation of concern for obesity researchers. Americans are actually more physically active today than in past decades (Kolata 2007b, 194). It would seem that this would make us thinner, except that it turns out that exercise cannot be shown to necessarily produce weight loss (Taubes 2007). Walking (which many urban residents of all income levels presumably do a lot of) can have health benefits, but people participating in walking programs only lose about two pounds on average (Richardson et al. 2008). We make a long chain of assumptions about causal relationships in antiobesity policy, and the rhetoric in which they are presented rarely represents them as contested, uncertain, or incomplete.

Inaccurate perceptions can promote ordinary people's weight anxieties for themselves, for their children, and for the population. A recent University of Michigan survey of parents nationwide revealed that they considered child obesity the number 1 health concern for their children for the first time this year, topping smoking, drug abuse, and neglect (C.S. Mott Children's Hospital 2008). The more affluent the household, the more concern there was about obesity. The poorest families worried most about drug abuse, smoking, and teen pregnancy (in that order). Black parents rated teen pregnancy as the most pressing health problem for youth, while Latino parents' first-rated worry was smoking and tobacco use. The authors of the report were then concerned that minority parents were not concerned about fat. And yet children's obesity levels actually have not increased over the past decade—hardly the soaring rates we hear about constantly (Ogden, Carroll, and Flegal 2008). David B. Allison, the researcher behind another oft-heard claim—that this generation of children will be the first not to live as long as their parents—had to admit that statement was a back-of-the-envelope calculation without credible support (Gibbs 2005).

Why are we fatter, then, and can we get thinner? Large-scale studies of twins reared apart and of adopted children suggest that about 80 percent of what we weigh is inherited and that, for most people, moving out of about a twenty-pound weight range is very difficult (Kolata 2007b). Decades and decades of diet research shows that while most any calorie restriction will initially cause weight loss, over the longer term even more weight comes back (Garner and Wooley 1991). One evaluation of a comprehensive school-based nutrition and exercise program targeting Native American children found that even though the children ate leaner food at school, were more active, and learned about good nutrition, they were not on average any thinner after the program than students who had not been included (Stone et al. 2003). However, nearly every obesogenic-environment account emphasizes weight differentials by race and income, then points out that it is harder for poor people and minorities to obtain affordable low-calorie food and to get exercise, and concludes by urging policy changes to provide those things so that the weight disparities will equalize (through weight loss in poor populations). Yet evidence suggests that major changes in population weights seem unlikely to occur even if environmentally focused programs bring more affordable low-calorie food and more accessible spaces for physical activity to poor areas (assuming, of course, that those things are not already there). ...

Why, given all this, is there still so much hype? Genuine concern is clearly one reason. The hype over increasing weights also keeps grants flowing to public health researchers, insures profits for the diet industry (with annual spending valued at $50 billion), and creates a market for bariatric surgery and prescription weight loss drugs (Oliver 2006; Weintraub 2008). Journalists have a steady supply of alarming headlines to report to an anxious public. The larger context is a world in which contagious diseases of the past have largely been fought back, leaving the persistent problems of chronic conditions in an aging population. Perhaps we also fear fat because of its signification of downward mobility; the hatred of fat as an aesthetic matter, particularly in women; the century-old use of diet and weight to demarcate those who can be virtuous in the face of postindustrial abundance from those who cannot; and displacement of our anxieties about American over-consumption and imperialism (Stearns 1997; Campos 2004; Oliver 2006). The environmental account of obesity has no place for this rich historical, economic, and cultural context for our fat hatred.

Unacknowledged Moralism

Abigail C. Saguy and Rene Almeling's (2008) study of media coverage of obesity found that coverage was more likely to highlight bad food choices and sedentary lifestyle as causes for obesity when discussing minorities and poor people than when those groups were not discussed. The turn to the environment and away from personal choice is supposed to be a way to avoid that kind of racialized stigma. But what if it is the case that many elites find the terms of the environmental account to be simply a more palatable way to express their disgust at fat people, the tacky, low-class foods they eat, and the indolent ways they spend their time? Proper practices of food, eating, and exercise have been raised to the status of absolutely correct rules for good health rather than simple features of human cultural variety. There is a highly specific and evolved set of social rules governing the hierarchy of foods. A baguette is not junk food, but sliced white bread is; the sugar in honey and fruits is healthy while white granular sugar is junk. Modes and moments of consumption are also hierarchically arranged: growing or obtaining local fresh produce is the best way to eat, while eating outside the home and on the move is the worst. Why not exhort inner-city mothers to consume canned or frozen vegetables, presumably much easier to provide than access to farmer's markets? One is hard pressed to find antiobesity recommendations that do not include "fresh" modifying "fruits and vegetables," after all. Could it be that shopping at farmer's markets is simply the most virtuous mode of food consumption for the upper classes at this moment in history (Guthman 2003; Pollan 2006)? Perhaps one reason that feminists have either embraced the environmental account or shied away from fat acceptance is that many of them belong to the cultural subgroup that is most highly invested in both the personal appearance norms (mostly being thin or at least not fat) and cultural practices (lots of veggies, yoga, farmer's markets) that mark elite status and promise to keep age and disability away. ...

The ideological formations that currently organize the healthy lifestyle and dieting practices of American elites are fat negativity, the lack of a counter discourse to healthism (my reformulation of Rubin's fallacy of the misplaced scale), the hierarchical valuation of foods and activities described above, the time bomb theory of obesity present in media accounts (akin to Rubin's domino theory), and the lack of a concept of benign variation in body sizes and eating habits. I have not included something like fat essentialism because the ideology actually views fat not as a natural and enduring part of many people's bodies but as something that proper effort can dissolve away. Most elites recognize that fat has not always had the negative valence it has today and would agree that it carries cultural meanings that have changed across time and place. Often the next move after acknowledging the Venus of Willendorf is to say approvingly something like "In the African American community, they have a much broader appreciation for women's bodies," or perhaps something about the Pima Indians who just cannot help being fat because of their genetic isolation. I've always suspected these comments of constituting something like fat orientalism, as in, "It's nice that those more natural, communal, and embodied people can be content with fatness, but it's not okay for me to be fat."

Psychologists have found fat negativity in subjects of all ages for decades (Crandall and Biernat 1990). Being fat is associated with lower incomes, especially for white women, with fat highly educated white women making about 30 percent less money than their thinner counterparts (Brownell et al. 2005). Studies of doctors' and nurses' attitudes toward fat patients over many decades have consistently shown that fat people are considered repellant and noncompliant (Brownell et al. 2005). The lack of a counter discourse to healthism (exhortations to diet and exercise, diet talk, fat-hating talk, designating "good" and "bad" foods, etc.) means that it is not considered rude to talk about getting fat or the bad qualities of the food while dining with others, for example. These practices are assisted by the individualism of health discourses: "I can accept that other people's bodies are different, but it's not okay for me to gain weight because I would feel bad about myself" (akin to the unassailability of "I don't like looking over the ledge because I'm afraid of heights"). This is how fat anxiety is not heard as hatred of a status shared by a group but as a completely internal, idiosyncratic, apolitical, and individualized account of that particular woman's feelings of well-being.

There is nothing inherently wrong with morality as part of social control. My point is that in this case the moralism is dangerously unacknowledged because it runs under an environmental account that starts off trying to avoid personal blame. My goal here is to draw out this latent moralism and make it grounds for explicit political contestation. It would be better to discuss sustainability, food production, poverty, and environmental justice in terms that make clear the distinctions between normative commitments to views of the good life and the stakes involved in policy implementation, including things like how much it will cost and how the people being affected can have some say. All too often health-conscious elites regard correct lifestyle practices as obvious if only one were properly educated, when it would be both more humble and more politically savvy to regard these as sites of power that must be justified and may be overbearing.

There is one final crucial point about the hidden moralism of the environmental account. It suggests that some people are impervious to bad environments (the elites, who still manage their bodies properly) while others are more fully constructed by their environments (poor fat people). Members of one group move powerfully through the world determining their body sizes and health statuses; others are pitiably stuck within and determined by the environment. Progressives usually insist that it is just literally impossible for fat poor people to be physically active and eat well without environmental transformation. If we grant that there are many overlapping environments, the account gets more complex, but it is still hard to evade the conclusion that the poor are simply stuck (though if environments do overlap, as in cities, why aren't the poor making the effort to use the parks that are already there?). This view is necessary to avoid the awkward possibility that the poor and the fat could actually move more and eat more vegetables if they wanted to—or that they already do and are fat anyway. (Recall my discussion of how much we do not know about what people are actually doing and how much we do know about how standard recommended interventions fail to make people thin.)

It will to be hard to banish the moralism of the environmental account because it draws on a deep reservoir of ideological formations and contains such a belittling view of poor fat people's agency. That stunted account of agency is necessary to keep at bay the other possibility, which is that poor people are already full agents and would not readily adopt elite eating practices without a lot of pressure. The cost argument (pointing out that lower-fat, lower-sugar foods are more expensive) assumes that lack of funds constrains poor shoppers' agency rather than food preferences, or perhaps that funds, preferences, and availability are interwoven. Subsidization is a carrot, not a stick. If the lack-of-agency problem is really just about lack of funds, then we would expect to see poor people adopting more elite diets if those diets were sufficiently subsidized. I have argued, though, that what looks like a benign collective intervention into environmental conditions is more like a micropolitics of food choice dominated by elite norms of consumption and movement. Collective norms determine what environmental changes will be enacted into policy, and those norms are, as I have argued in this section, the highly specific cultural preferences of elite consumers. If we see it this way, it is easy to anticipate that poor shoppers may be harder to mold into healthy lifestyle practitioners than advocates think. That is where the stick part comes in.

Backlash and Unintended Consequences

My next concern about the feminist embrace of the environmental account is that policies based on it will end up being punitive, ineffective, and patronizing and will entail burdensome unintended consequences that will hurt the groups feminists claim to most want to help. To tease out the possibilities, it is first necessary to understand how antiobesity policy sits within neoliberal governance policies. As Wendy Brown explains, neoliberalism's primary features are its imposition and nurturance of a market rationale for decision making in multiple arenas of social life and its account of the citizen-subjects of this order, who are "individual entrepreneurs and consumers whose moral autonomy is measured by their capacity for 'self-care'" (2006, 694). Because neoliberalism disavows redistributive ideals, it charges the citizen with responsibility for ensuring the security of herself and her own family rather than depending on the state (now seen as robbing people of dignity and opportunities for accomplishment). Nikolas Rose (1999) argues that this "ethics of lifestyle maximization … generates a relentless imperative of risk management … through daily lifestyle management, choices of where to live and shop, what to eat and drink, stress management, exercise, and so forth" (160). This responsibilization of the citizen generates particular anxiety about "the uneducated dietary habits of children and the poor" (Rose 1999, 160). Crucially, responsibilization creates a swath of new areas in which a citizen can fail to live up to expectations.

A primary reason the dangers of backlash and restigmatization loom is very simple: when we try to make people thinner, it does not work. And just making them thinner does not necessarily make them healthier. Add that to the concern discussed above that poor people may not want to eat what elites think they should eat (even after being educated and shown the way), and we have widespread noncompliance and policy failure in a neoliberal governance context. It will be difficult to contain punitive and invasive impulses if the policy has roots in a dramatized account of how desperately poor people's habits need to change. Moreover, we will have been distracted into chasing an effect or a symbol (of many things, not all well understood) while much more difficult problems of inequality remain.

We must squarely face the alternate paths down which environmental antiobesity measures aimed at poor minorities may go: more like welfare surveillance (Schram 2006), child protective services interventions (Roberts 2002), mandatory arrest for domestic violence (Richie 2005), and population control policies in development aid (McIntosh and Finkle 1995; Ewig 2006). As Dorothy Roberts documents in her study of race and child protection, many families are drawn into a supervisory relationship with the state initially because of poverty: children crowded into a dirty apartment, for example (2002, 35–40). Increased state surveillance means increased opportunities for detecting failure and for triggering a second-order set of rules that punishes nonresponse to the state's orders. This second-order bureaucratic system is currently run in a fairly punitive and politically invisible manner. That is, dealing with the watchful and punitive state becomes part of the ordinary struggle of getting by for poor women but is rarely grounds for reconsidering a policy. If a social worker intervenes because a child is fat, will the child lose weight while in the home or continue to be fat? If the child is still fat a few months later, will the next step be removal from the home, as Australian antiobesity advocates have recently argued is the proper response (Alexander et al. 2009)? Mandatory arrest policies for domestic violence offences, championed early on by feminist activists, have resulted in minority women's criminalization (so-called dual arrest) and brutalization by police, yet they remain widely popular (Richie 2005). Trying to get women to have fewer children has seemed like a tidy solution to global poverty and environmental degradation, but it has often meant framing empowerment as enhanced consumer choice and access to contraceptives rather than addressing the roots of third-world poverty.[4] The comparison between these regimes and the antiobesity discourse suggests that the embrace of an environmental strategy is not necessarily racially benevolent. Even though well-meaning antiobesity campaigners may be thinking of parks and bicycle paths and not visits from social workers, it would be naive to think these state apparatuses would not be triggered by the types of policies being considered in the United States, the United Kingdom, and Australia.

Conclusion: Missed Opportunities, New Directions

There is an obvious right-wing direction that antiobesity efforts could take. A straightforwardly neoliberal account of fat simply demands more personal responsibility from fat people without any environmental or collective efforts at all: charging them more for goods and services, incentivizing weight loss, building in more and more diagnostic moments meant to record and predict who is fat or getting fatter, and, inevitably, avoiding hiring fat employees in the first place. Removing food outlets in Los Angeles without providing any new grocery stores is an example of punitiveness without provision. The fact that many antiobesity policies are being implemented in the workplace underscores the fact that right now free market priorities tie health care, health insurance, and rewarded statuses and behaviors tightly together (Egan 2006). This account keeps the focus on fat's costs and burdens to society and emphasizes personal responsibility for one's own body. The most immediate danger may not be a hastily adopted environmental approach, then, but a full-scale campaign of personal blaming of fat people for overburdening our health care system with only dieting and bariatric surgery as the solutions. The best way to prepare to engage such a campaign would be to take stock of the assumptions that even supposedly benign variants of antiobesity campaigns share with this nastier version. I have argued that the environmental account—the leading progressive account—may begin as a structural program for better health but quickly narrows to teaching correct consumption and lifestyle practices to the poor to make them less fat. Panicky thinking, misinformation, pity and disgust, and risk factor-focused interventions combine with genuine concern to make the environmental account rife with pitfalls.

Beyond avoiding policy pitfalls, what political and intellectual opportunities are we missing as scholars? The ways fat operates in cultures around the world right now are endlessly fascinating and offer a wide range of entry points for illuminating long-standing feminist puzzles. We should reflect deeply on the contingencies of health and the place of its pursuit in our lives; the inevitable developments of aging, dependence, and death; the near impossibility of success in fighting marketization in so many areas of life; the globalization of fat and fat panic; and the ways that individualism and a chirpy consumer ethic lead us away from political solutions that could begin to address some of the misery that many citizens face, to name just a few. After all, the pretense that the elites are thriving because of their lifestyles while the poor are miserable because they are fat lets elites pretend we can control our bodies like well-oiled machines if we just try hard enough. Feminists ought to think very hard about what a just and happy world for millions of aging citizens, most of them women, ought to look like in coming decades. Wrangling with inevitable and intertwined vulnerabilities will be a necessary first step to doing just that, as Martha Fineman (2008) suggests.

My hope here is that feminist scholars will draw on past disobedience to social norms about health and appearance as well as interrogate our ignorance, particularly about the lived experiences of the women who would be targeted under antiobesity policy. The framework for such research should not be that of the intervention (how to design it, how to make it more palatable). We need not copy the epidemiological thinking of health researchers. Adding a feminist gloss to the public health view does not add any new theoretical depth, raise new ethical questions, or draw on the wealth of past feminist engagements with similar social problems. Berlant's essay powerfully captures the dreary drudgery of work for many people in a project that, but for its turn to obesity, would be a classic complaint about how capitalism can make many lives fairly grim. If the emphasis of these projects were shifted from concern about fatness, we could make a very rich array of observations about human misery that would not be so overinclusive (because many fat people are not miserable, unhealthy, and eating to escape it all) and underinclusive (because conditions of suffering may have little to do with fat).

One immediate practical step in both research and policy is to end the focus on weight and weight loss. We should not frame poverty in terms of fat so that helping the poor comes to mean addressing their fat. Luckily there is already a well-established approach called "health at every size" (Bacon 2008) that we can call upon to break up the overstated connection between health and weight, and luckily there are plenty of other reasons to promote public transit and farmer's markets, like sustainability, emissions control, and pleasure. Another step is to enact broad antidiscrimination measures in employment, insurance, and public accommodations so that what citizens weigh becomes less and less meaningful for life opportunities. As I have explained in detail elsewhere, antidiscrimination measures have significant limitations but are so highly resonant that without them, it is hard to describe fat people as deserving citizens (Kirkland 2008).

… A final suggestion is therefore more aspirational: to reorient ourselves toward what we really want—poverty reduction, for instance, universal health care, or better public transportation—and to make political arguments for those goals. Much of the environmental account is buoyed along by elite ethnocentrism about the superiority of our own habits, but the undercurrent is real concern for the suffering, deprivation, and dangers that bedevil poor people in our societies and around the world. It is unethical and self-defeating to ride anxiety about fatness to fulfill political goals that actually call for a sustained commitment to economic redistribution for their long-term success. Asking for what we really want—all the different formulations that sophisticated feminist analyses can surely devise—will be harder and less popular, and it will not get a boost from riding along on a wave of moral panic. But if feminist scholars have any special role in political debates, this is surely it.

Acknowledgments

This essay has benefited greatly from feedback from audiences at the Centre for Law, Gender, and Sexuality (Universities of Keele, Kent, and Westminster) and the Feminist Legal Theory Project at Emory University School of Law, especially Davina Cooper, Martha Fineman, and Didi Herman; from Marc Spindelman and his students at the University of Michigan Law School; from exchanges at the American Political Science Association meetings, especially with Sanford Schram, Rogan Kersh, Eric Oliver, Jeffery Sobal, and Jim Morone; from anonymous *Signs* reviewers; and from colleagues and graduate students in the University of Michigan Women's Studies Works-in-Progress seminar and the Theory Seminar in the University of Michigan Political Science department, especially Naomi André, Lisa Disch, Jane Hassinger, Don Herzog, Carla Keirns, Deborah Keller-Cohen, Mika LaVaque-Manty, Anne Manuel, Michelle Segar, Ruth Tsoffar, Liz Wingrove, and Mariah Zeisberg. Correspondence with Charlotte Cooper, Julie Guthman, and Abigail Saguy considerably improved previous drafts. I am very grateful for travel funds from the Institute for Research on Women and Gender at the University of Michigan.

Notes

1 I use "obesity" to refer to the medicalized and popularized account of fat governed in these policies. The term "fat" is an alternative meant to deny these conceptions and to render fat ordinary and open to many meanings. Because this essay confronts a construction of obesity discourses, not fat discourses, I use the term "obesity" for the sake of accuracy. I use "fat" when I am not referencing contemporary obesity discourses per se.

2 The new *Fat Studies Reader* is edited by feminist scholars Esther Rothblum and Sondra Solovay (2009), and researchers such as Kathleen LeBesco (2004) and Rosemarie Garland-Thomson (2005) have made explicit connections with feminism. Feminism has not entirely given up on interrogating fat, but feminist scholars overall are eclipsed by scholars from the social sciences in raising a critical response to obesity panic.

3 I thank Julie Guthman for clarifying this observation.

4 I thank Lisa Disch for pointing me toward these connections.

References

Alexander, Shirley M., Louise L. Baur, Roger Magnusson, and Bernadette Tobin. 2009. "When Does Severe Childhood Obesity Become a Child Protection Issue?" *Medical Journal of Australia* 190(3):136–39.

Bacon, Linda. 2008. *Health at Every Size: The Surprising Truth about Your Weight.* Dallas: BenBella.

Berlant, Lauren. 2007. "Slow Death (Sovereignty, Obesity, Lateral Agency)." *Critical Inquiry* 33(4):754–80.

Brown, Wendy. 2006. "American Nightmare: Neoliberalism, Neoconservatism, and De-democratization." *Political Theory* 34(6):690–714.

Brownell, Kelly D., Rebecca M. Puhl, Marlene B. Schwartz, and Leslie Rudd, eds. *Weight Bias: Nature, Consequences, and Remedies.* New York: Guilford.

C. S. Mott Children's Hospital. 2008. "Obesity Tops List of Biggest Health Problems for Kids in 2008." *National Poll on Children's Health* 4(2):1–2.

Campos, Paul F. 2004. *The Obesity Myth: Why America's Obsession with Weight Is Hazardous to Your Health.* New York: Gotham.

———. 2006. "The Legalization of Fat: Law, Science, and the Construction of a Moral Panic." Working paper no. 1046. Bepress Legal Series, Berkeley, CA. http://law.bepress.com/expresso/eps/1046/.

Campos, Paul, Abigail Saguy, Paul Ernsberger, Eric Oliver, and Glenn Gaesser. "The Epidemiology of Overweight and Obesity: Public Health Crisis or Moral Panic?" *International Journal of Epidemiology* 35(1):55–60.

Crandall, Christian, and Monica Biernat. 1990. "The Ideology of Anti-fat Attitudes." *Journal of Applied Social Psychology* 20(3):227–43.

Davidson, Lorraine. 2008. "Women and Children Are Focus of Anti-obesity Drive." *Times* (London), June 22. http://www.timesonline.co.uk/tol/news/uk/scotland/article4193635.ece.

Egan, Paul. 2006. "Bosses Want a Say in What We Weigh: Michigan Law Banning Discrimination Worries Employers Who Want to Curb Unhealthy Behavior." *Detroit News*, October 9, 1A.

Engber, Daniel. 2010. "Fat Kids: Get Ready for a New Front in the War on Obesity." *Slate*, March 9. http://www.slate.com/id/2247038/.

Ewig, Christina. 2006. "Hijacking Global Feminism: Feminists, the Catholic Church, and the Family Planning Debacle in Peru." *Feminist Studies* 32(3): 632–59.

Fineman, Martha Albertson. 2008. "The Vulnerable Subject: Anchoring Equality in the Human Condition." *Yale Journal of Law and Feminism* 20(1):1–23.

Flegal, Katherine M., Barry I. Graubard, David F. Williamson, and Mitchell H. Gail. 2005. "Excess Deaths Associated with Underweight, Overweight, and Obesity." *Journal of the American Medical Association* 293(15):1861–67.

Flynn, Kristin J., and Marian Fitzgibbon. 1998. "Body Images and Obesity Risk among Black Females: A Review of the Literature." *Annals of Behavioral Medicine* 20(1):13–24.

Foucault, Michel. 1991. "Governmentality." In *The Foucault Effect: Studies in Governmentality*, ed. Graham Burchell, Colin Gordon, and Peter Miller, 87–104. Chicago: University of Chicago Press.

Gard, Michael, and Jan Wright. 2005. *The Obesity Epidemic: Science, Morality, and Ideology.* New York: Routledge.

Garland-Thomson, Rosemarie. 2005. "Feminist Disability Studies." *Signs: Journal of Women in Culture and Society* 30(2):1557–87.

Garner, David M., and Susan C. Wooley. 1991. "Confronting the Failure of Behavioral and Dietary Treatments for Obesity." *Clinical Psychology Review* 11(6): 729–80.

Gibbs, W. Wayt. 2005. "Obesity: An Overblown Epidemic?" *Scientific American* 292(6):70–77.

Goode, Erica. 1999. "For Good Health, It Helps to Be Rich and Important." *New York Times*, June 1, F1.

Guthman, Julie. 2003. "Fast Food/Organic Food: Reflexive Tastes and the Making of 'Yuppie Chow.'" *Social and Cultural Geography* 4(1):45–58.

———. 2007. "Commentary on Teaching Food: Why I Am Fed Up with Michael Pollan Et Al." *Agriculture and Human Values* 24(2):261–64.

Guthman, Julie, and Melanie DuPuis. 2006. "Embodying Neoliberalism: Economy, Culture, and the Politics of Fat." *Environment and Planning D* 24(3): 427–48.

Hill, James O., and John C. Peters. 1998. "Environmental Contributions to the Obesity Epidemic." *Science* 280(5368):1371–74.

Johnson, Alan. 2007. Speech to the House of Commons, October 17. *Parliamentary Debates*, Commons, 6th ser., vol. 464, col. 825–27.

Kersh, Rogan, and James Morone. 2002. "The Politics of Obesity: Seven Steps to Government Action." *Health Affairs* 21(6):142–53.

Kirkland, Anna. 2008. *Fat Rights*: *Dilemmas of Difference and Personhood*. New York: New York University Press.

Kolata, Gina. 2004. "Data on Deaths from Obesity Is Inflated, U.S. Agency Says." *New York Times*, November 24, A16.

———. 2007a. "Causes of Death Are Linked to a Person's Weight." *New York Times*, November 7, A27.

———. 2007b. *Rethinking Thin*: *The New Science of Weight Loss—and the Myths and Realities of Dieting*. New York: Farrar, Straus & Giroux.

LeBesco, Kathleen. 2004. *Revolting Bodies? The Struggle to Redefine Fat Identity*. Amherst: University of Massachusetts Press.

Lee, Joyce M. 2008. "Why Young Adults Hold the Key to Assessing the Obesity Epidemic in Children." *Archives of Pediatrics and Adolescent Medicine* 162(7): 682–87.

McIntosh, C. Alison, and Jason L. Finkle. 1995. "The Cairo Conference on Population and Development: A New Paradigm?" *Population and Development Review* 21(2):223–60.

Mink, Gwendolyn. 2002. "From Welfare to Wedlock: Marriage Promotion and Poor Mothers' Inequality." *Good Society* 11(3):68–73.

Morone, James. 2000. "Citizens or Shoppers? Solidarity under Siege." *Journal of Health Politics, Policy and Law* 25(5):959–68.

Moynihan, Ray. 2006. "Obesity Task Force Linked to WHO Takes 'Millions' from Drug Firms." *British Medical Journal* 332(7555):1412.

Murray, Christopher J. L., Sandeep C. Kulkarni, Catherine Michaud, Niels Tomijima, Maria T. Bulzacchelli, Terrell J. Iandiorio, and Majid Ezzati. 2006. "Eight Americas: Investigating Mortality Disparities across Races, Counties, and Race-Counties in the United States." *PLoS Medicine* 3(9):1513–24. http://www.plosmedicine.org/article/info:doi/10.1371/journal.pmed.0030260.

Nestle, Marion. 2007. *Food Politics*: *How the Food Industry Influences Nutrition and Health*. Rev. ed. Berkeley: University of California Press.

Nestle, Marion, and Michael F. Jacobson. 2000. "Halting the Obesity Epidemic: A Public Health Policy Approach." *Public Health Reports* 115(1):12–24.

Ogden, Cynthia L., Margaret D. Carroll, and Katherine M. Flegal. 2008. "High Body Mass Index for Age among US Children and Adolescents, 2003–2006." *Journal of the American Medical Association* 299(20):2401–5.

Oliver, J. Eric. 2006. *Fat Politics*: *The Real Story behind America's Obesity Epidemic*. New York: Oxford University Press.

Pollan, Michael. 2006. *The Omnivore's Dilemma*: *A Natural History of Four Meals*. New York: Penguin.

Probyn, Elspeth. 2008. "Silences behind the Mantra: Critiquing Feminist Fat." *Feminism and Psychology* 18(3):401–4.

Richardson, Caroline R., Tiffany L. Newton, Jobby J. Abraham, Ananda Sen, Masabito Jimbo, and Ann M. Swartz. 2008. "A Meta-analysis of Pedometer Based Walking Interventions and Weight Loss." *Annals of Family Medicine* 6(1):69–77.

Richie, Beth E. 2005. "A Black Feminist Reflection on the Antiviolence Movement." In *Domestic Violence at the Margins*: *Readings on Race*, *Class*, *Gender*, *and Culture*, ed. Natalie J. Sokoloff with Christina Pratt, 50–55. New Brunswick, NJ: Rutgers University Press.

Roberts, Dorothy. 2002. *Shattered Bonds*: *The Color of Child Welfare*. New York: Basic.

Rose, Nikolas. 1999. *Powers of Freedom*: *Reframing Political Thought*. New York: Cambridge University Press.

Rothblum, Esther, and Sondra Solovay, eds. 2009. *The Fat Studies Reader*. New York: New York University Press.

Rubin, Gayle S. 1993. "Thinking Sex: Notes for a Radical Theory of the Politics of Sexuality." In *The Gay and Lesbian Studies Reader*, ed. Henry Abelove, Michéle Aina Barale, and David M. Halperin, 3–44. New York: Routledge.

Saguy, Abigail C., and Rene Almeling. 2008. "Fat in the Fire? Science, the News Media, and the 'Obesity Epidemic.'" *Sociological Forum* 23(1):53–83.

Saguy, Abigail C., and Kevin W. Riley. 2005. "Weighing Both Sides: Morality, Mortality, and Framing Contests over Obesity." *Journal of Heath Politics*, *Policy and Law* 30(5):869–921.

Schram, Sanford F. 2006. *Welfare Discipline*: *Discourse*, *Governance*, *and Globalization*. Philadelphia: Temple University Press.

Severson, Kim. 2008. "Los Angeles Stages a Fast Food Intervention." *New York Times*, August 13, F1.

Stearns, Peter N. 1997. *Fat History*: *Bodies and Beauty in the Modern West*. New York: New York University Press.

Stone, Elaine J., James E. Norman, Sally M. Davis, Dawn Stewart, Theresa E. Clay, Ben Caballero, Timothy G. Lohman, and David M. Murray. 2003. "Design, Implementation, and Quality Control in the Pathways American-Indian Multicenter Trial." *Preventive Medicine* 37 (suppl. 1): S13-S23.

"Study Says Fast Food Remains Popular." 2008. *QSR Magazine*, June 20. http://www.qsrmagazine.com/articles/news/story.phtml?idp6789&micrositepfood_beverage.

Taubes, Gary. 2007. "The Scientist and the Stairmaster." *New York Magazine*, September 24, 44–50.

U.S. Department of Agriculture, Agricultural Research Service, Beltsville Human Nutrition Research Center, Food Surveys Research Group, U.S. Department of Health and Human Services, Centers for Disease Control and Prevention, and National Center for Health Statistics. 2008. "What We Eat in America, NHANES 2005–2006." Beltsville, MD. http://www.ars.usda.gov/Services/ docs. htm?docidp18349.

Waite, Linda J., and Maggie Gallagher. 2000. *The Case for Marriage*: *Why Married People Are Happier*, *Healthier*, *and Better Off Financially*. New York: Doubleday.

Weintraub, Arlene. 2008. "Inside Drugmakers' War on Fat." *Business Week*, March 17, 40–45.

Wildman, Rachel P., Paul Muntner, Kristi Reynolds, Aileen P. McGinn, Swapnil Rajpathak, Judith Wylie-Rosett, and MaryFran R. Sowers. 2008. "The Obese without Cardiometabolic Risk Factor Clustering and the Normal Weight with Cardiometabolic Risk Factor Clustering: Prevalence and Correlates of 2 Phenotypes among the US Population (NHANES 1999–2004)." *Archives of Internal Medicine* 168(15):1617–24.

Wintour, Patrick. 2007. "'Fit Towns' Plan to Tackle Child Obesity." *Guardian* (London), November 1, 1.

Yancey, Antronette K., Joanne Leslie, and Emily K. Abel. 2006. "Obesity at the Crossroads: Feminist and Public Health Perspectives." *Signs* 31(2):425–43.

16

Who Defines Babies' "Needs"?: The Scientization of Baby Food in Indonesia

Aya Hirata Kimura

Introduction

Recently, there has been a broad shift in the discourse of the Third World food problem from food quantity to food *quality*, from hunger to "hidden hunger," and from famine to micronutrient deficiencies. In this new framing, Third World countries might have enough food, but they do not have "quality" food, where quality is signified by the amount of micronutrients. Micronutrients refer to vitamins and minerals that are essential for physiological functions, such as vitamin A, iron, and iodine. Micronutrient deficiencies, often called "hidden hunger," refer to the lack of those micronutrients. Infants and pregnant and lactating women are particularly vulnerable to micronutrient deficiencies. In particular, vitamin A deficiency (VAD), iron deficiency anemia (IDA), and iodine deficiency disorder (IDD) among the "vulnerable populations" have become major concerns (Uvin 1999).

To combat these micronutrient deficiencies, an increasingly popular tool, promoted by development experts, is the fortification of baby food with micronutrients. Fortification refers to the process of adding micronutrients, typically at the site of production. Fortifying various types of food for babies, such as formulas, snacks, and porridges, became an attractive health intervention in many developing countries. The recent rise of fortification as an ideal solution to the Third World food problem poses an intriguing puzzle, however. Although development professionals' enthusiasm for micronutrients might give the impression that the science of micronutrients is new, we have long known about the existence of micronutrients in food and the impacts of a lack thereof. A technology for fortification is also not particularly novel. Developed countries have fortified various products from milk to wheat flour for decades (Carpenter 1994). Furthermore, fortification is not the only available option for combating micronutrient deficiencies. In the 1970s, for instance, micronutrient concerns prompted governments to distribute supplements to its more vulnerable populations (Allen 2000). Other policy options are also available, such as nutrition education and home gardening. Enabling people to produce such micronutrient-rich vegetables in their yards is one option for policy planners who are concerned with micronutrient deficiencies, and some countries have implemented gardening projects and educated mothers about providing these micronutrient-rich vegetables when weaning their babies (Underwood 1998). Yet in the 1990s, fortification became the popular means for combating micronutrient deficiencies. Why did fortifying baby food come to be considered the ideal solution to infant "hidden hunger"? I explore this puzzle through a case study on Indonesian baby food.

Theoretically, this article locates the recent micronutrient-emphasis of baby food in the historical context of the scientization of motherhood: a changing understanding of mothering increasingly based on scientific reasoning. In other words, the meaning of what it is to be a good mother has profoundly changed in the modern era. Pregnancy, birthing, and child rearing have become subject to intense scrutiny from scientific and professional communities, and babies' feeding has been no exception. Experts started to confer "scientific" advice on mothers about when, how, and what to feed their babies and many felt obliged to abide by this information. The literature on scientized motherhood has emphasized the rise of childrearing experts, medical professionals, and scientists as the motor powering scientized motherhood. Yet the recent popularity of fortified baby food cannot be explained as simply a result of the accumulation of scientific wisdom, since the science of micronutrients and fortification technology had long been available before their popularity in the 1990s. It is not the case that the motherhood ideal changed simply in response to scientific "facts."

Instead of searching for the phenomenon's ultimate driver in the truth power of science, this article analyzes scientific knowledge as a social construct and adds nuance to our understanding of the scientization of motherhood by situating infant nutritional knowledge at the intersecting historical processes of development discourse, global capitalism, and transnational knowledge circulation. It analyzes science's impact on the institution of motherhood, but the content of science itself is not taken as predetermined. This is critically important to understand power and politics behind what might seem like an unproblematic instance of a public health initiative. It should be noted here that this article does not discuss the merits of scientization, as that deserves a full analysis of its own. Whether this current phase of the scientization of baby feeding is harmful or beneficial will be addressed in another paper based on interviews with poor women in Indonesia. Instead, this article focuses on the processes and driving forces of scientization.

Through the analysis of the Indonesian case, I identify multiple factors that enabled fortified baby food to ascend as the solution to micronutrient deficiencies in the global South; the shift in the broader discourse of the Third World food problem, from hunger to "hidden hunger"; the construction of infant feeding primarily as a biochemical issue by nutritional science and international development professionals; the business community's marketing operative to functionalize baby food; a general policy move toward market-based health programs; and bureaucratic and professional preferences for quantifiable development projects. Furthermore, fortified baby food's potential to bypass mothers as the gatekeeper of babies' health is attractive to development professionals, scientists, and policy-makers. …

The Scientization of Motherhood

… Since the eighteenth century, medical professionals started to see motherhood as a site requiring education and intervention through rationalized and science-based regimens (Badinter

1981). "Scientific motherhood" was an instance of technical rationality extending into a formerly nonscientific arena, specifically the area of the household and family. Family reproduction issues like contraception, pregnancy, and childbirth became subject to professional controls (Ehrenreich and English 1978; Margolis 1984). Children were increasingly considered to be in need of rigid scheduling and expert instructions in order to be properly civilized (Ladd-Taylor 1994). Experts urged mothers to seek advice on child-rearing issues and child development from them. The idealized mother image in such discourse was implicitly one from the white upper class who had resources to invest in such a task (Ladd-Taylor 1994). Immigrant communities and minority groups sometimes partook in the hegemonic ideal of scientific mothering as a path to social respectability (Litt 2000). Apple (2006) suggests that we might have passed the worst of scientization: in the United States, social movements such as the natural childbirth movement, the La Leche League, and the women's heath movements in the past several decades are partly countering the oppressive effects of scientization, urging mothers not to be a passive recipient of expert advice but rather to partner with them. Analyses of contemporary motherhood discourses suggest, however, that the importance of turning to expert advice still continues in the contemporary ideologies of "intensive mothering" (Hays 1996) and "sacrificial motherhood" (O'Reilly 2004) that powerfully structure the institution of motherhood. Familiarity with scientific assessments of all sorts of parenting practices still counts as an important requirement of being a "good" mother today.

To be sure, the expanding role of science in daily life is not unique to the area of motherhood. An important intervention by feminist scholars has been to point out that the scientization of culture has had gendered effects. Gender itself was an object of ever-increasing scientific scrutiny. Science was used to legitimate and solidify the notion of dichotomous sexes and pathologize homosexuality (Fausto-Sterling 2000). Scientization was also profoundly gendered in that science tended to provide justifications for existing discrimination and prejudices against women, and to further perpetuate them by providing "scientific" backing. Martin (1987) finds that the increasing role of the modern scientific establishment in defining female bodies was linked to a societal unease with women's entrance into higher education and the labor market. Historically, scientists and technical experts tended to be male and consequently, scientization has often implied a loss of women's authority and power. For instance, the scientization of birth and child delivery meant a transfer of power from midwives to predominantly male physicians (Rooks 1997). Researchers have also found that the scientization of motherhood decreased women's autonomy in many instances by setting up increasingly higher standards for perfect motherhood and reinforcing the patriarchal ideology of society (Douglas and Michaels 2004). It also tended to underpin mothers' sense of dependency and inadequacy (Fox and Worts 1999). The "good" mothers depicted in professional discourses often imply heterosexual, married, white, middle-class, and stay-at-home mothers (Malacrida 2002), marginalizing women that do not fit this category. A scientized discourse also emphasizes individual responsibility, obfuscating material realities and cultural factors that prevent women from becoming "perfect" as prescribed by the experts (Carter 1995; Blum 1999).

While a rich account of the scientization of mothering in the West, particularly its historical contexts and outcomes, has been accumulated, the situation in contemporary developing countries has been much less analyzed by feminist scholars. Pertinent to this topic are works on scientization in developing countries by scholars studying international relations. With an increasing attention to a variety of forms of transnational governance by nonstate actors (Djelic and Sahlin-Andersson 2006), some scholars have started to theorize the growing role of science in social control around the world.

In particular, neo-institutionalist scholars have highlighted the role of scientists and experts, or what is called "epistemic community," in diffusing global norms to different countries (Dori et al. 2003). They argue that scientists have come to bear a significant cultural authority in modern times, by creating and channeling "international norms" to many states and shaping their domestic institutions and policies. In their view, it is science's authoritative status that influences countries to adopt similar sets of institutions and policies (Dori et al. 2003). Health issues are no exception. Third World health became a field inhabited by a growing number of international and nongovernmental organizations that increasingly adopted science as the basis of their projects (Inoue and Dori 2006)....

In asking what drives the scientization of infant feeding, the task of this article becomes twofold. It first considers knowledge of infant nutrition as a social and historical product and then how a particular knowledge gets privileged. We need to ask how different forces propel a particular vision of "good feeding" and the "nutritional needs" of babies. To understand the context in which the "need" for micronutrients became the "need" for fortified baby food, Nancy Fraser's notion of "politics of needs interpretation" is instructive. Fraser (1989) points out that although the policy debate tends to focus on the ways of fulfilling the "needs" of the socially marginalized, it is crucially important to realize how "needs" themselves are constructed in the first place. By revealing that "needs" interpretation is profoundly political, her concept of "politics of needs interpretation" unmasks the social construction of "needs" as a scientific and bureaucratic pretense of neutrality. Haney (2002) used this concept to analyze welfare politics in Hungary, pointing out that the particular needs interpretation significantly impacted women's lives by altering the structure of the system. These scholars have usefully suggested that any definition of "needs" is negotiated and thus never to be taken for granted.

This insight becomes particularly noteworthy when "needs" are presented as natural and factual, as in the case of nutritional needs. Nutritional "needs" have the aura of "science" and "expertise." The changing understanding of baby food is often portrayed as merely a response to the accumulation of greater knowledge and better science. The notion of "politics of needs interpretation" helps us unpack the processes constructing babies' "needs" by pointing to the arbitrariness of any "needs" definition. My analysis of Indonesian baby food, therefore, explores a particular way that infant nutritional "needs" are constructed and how "solutions" are naturalized at a specific historical moment....

From Hunger to "Hidden Hunger"

In the 1990s, "hidden hunger," rather than hunger and famine, became the signature problem of the global South and fortification arose as its solution (Uvin 1999). The problem is now seen as a lack of good food rather than a simple lack of food. *The Economist*, for instance, underscored this shift from quantity to quality, or from hunger to "hidden hunger" in the discourse of the Third World food problem when it says, "Obviously, what hungry people need first and foremost is more food. But they also need better food" (Economist, 31 July 2004). And here, food quality is measured by micronutrients. This is a dramatic shift in the framing of "problem," "solution," and "needs" associated with food in developing countries. This plays out as hunger versus hidden hunger, needs for food versus needs for quality food, and food production and population control versus micronutrient strategies as solutions.

It is only recently that vitamins and minerals began to be grouped together as "micronutrients," and the international development community started to see a deficiency thereof as the signature problem of Third World food. A number of international agreements started to approach micronutrient deficiency as the major problematic of Third World food. The first major agreement was the 1990 World Summit for Children followed by the 1991 Montreal meeting aptly entitled "Ending Hidden Hunger" and the 1992 International Conference on Nutrition, and finally the 1996 World Food Summit (Underwood and Smitasiri 1999). These conferences called for global efforts to eliminate micronutrient deficiencies. Thus the World Declaration on Nutrition pledged "to make all efforts to eliminate before the end of this decade … iodine and vitamin A deficiencies … and other important micronutrient deficiencies, including iron" (FAO and WHO 1992). Another important indication of rising micronutrient popularity was the establishment of the Millennium Development Goals (MDG), agreed to by all the member states of the United Nations in 2000. The MDG set specific goals for the global society to aspire to by 2010. In order to make concrete benchmarks for the global development efforts, the number of indicators was consciously limited, but micronutrient deficiency was addressed in the MDG and a reduction in micronutrient deficiencies included in the list of goals to be achieved by 2010. International organizations such as the World Bank, USAID, and the Asian Development Bank (ADB) started "hidden hunger" projects around the world. Among them are Opportunities for Micronutrient Interventions Project (OMNI), the Micronutrient Initiative, the Global Alliance for Improved Nutrition (GAIN), and the Business Alliance for Food Fortification (BAFF).

In the 1990s, not only did micronutrient deficiencies gain greater attention, but the preferred prescription for hidden hunger also changed. In the 1970s, although micronutrient deficiencies were not yet a signature problem of Third World food, the typical expert recommendation was vitamin supplement distribution. For instance, governments of many developing countries distributed vitamin A tablets to their citizens. Governments also distributed iron capsules to pregnant women and iodine tablets in the 1970s (Hartini et al. 2003). In contrast to such prior "supplement approaches," fortification more recently emerged as the popular policy prescription. Advocates of fortification argue that we now must move on to food-based approach to hidden hunger, as opposed to "medicalized" approaches like supplements.

These trends—the general rise of interest in micronutrient deficiencies and fortification's popularity as the solution in the development circle—manifest strongly in baby food. As interest in hidden hunger grew, scientists started to take a closer look at the adequacy of micronutrients in food for what they consider "the most vulnerable groups of society." Here, mothers come into the picture to some extent because their nutritional status influences the nutritional status of their fetus and infants. Globally, scientists estimate that 127 million preschool-aged children under five years of age are Vitamin A deficient (West 2002), and IDA affects 45.8% of children under five years of age in Asia and 40.4% in Africa (UN/SCN 1998).

There are various causes for babies' hidden hunger, but it is food quality that is currently getting attention as the culprit, while the solution is seen as fortification. In particular, what nutrition experts term "complementary food" (CF: additional food provided to infants and young children, 6–24 months, to complement breastfeeding) and supplementary food (SF: food provided to children or pregnant women in addition to their regular daily food consumed) became a target of intense scientific analysis. Many parts of the world depend on home-made CF and SF, but a number of studies have found that many of these are not up to standard from the perspective of micronutrients. Scientists increasingly doubt that home-made baby foods are nutritious enough to fulfill babies' daily nutritional requirement. Therefore, commercial baby food became an attractive option in the eyes of experts.

Of course, there was considerable tension among nutrition experts regarding recommending commercial fortified foods in the Third world. Expert recommendations often carefully include fresh fruits, meat, vegetables, and commercial fortified food as possibilities. Nevertheless the suboptimal micronutrient level of many traditional baby foods in developing countries has resulted in an emphasis on commercial alternatives. This is exemplified in the following quotes by WHO:

> It appears that it is practically impossible to supply enough iron from unfortified complementary foods to meet the iron requirements of infants. … The situation appears to be similar for zinc at 6–8 month. (1998)

> Rapid urbanization and changing social networks affect caregivers' ability to use freshly prepared home-grown foods. Centrally processed fortified foods, which can play an important role in ensuring adequate complementary diets, have been successfully promoted in various settings. Public-private partnerships can play an important role in making available nutritionally adequate low-cost processed foods. (2001)

Such an international trend is strongly reflected in Indonesia. Since its independence, the Indonesian government equated food problem with lack of rice, Indonesia's staple crop. The former president Soeharto famously declared "rice self-sufficiency at any cost" (Arifin 1993; Thorbecke and van der Pluijm 1993). The government sought a "solution" to this food problem through the intensification and modernization of agriculture and through avid population control policies (Hull and Hull 2005). Now, however, the country's food problem is increasingly translated into nutritional vocabularies. Nutrition and health experts now talk more about the invisible threat of "hidden hunger."

Not only is there a shift from macronutrients, or from calorie and quantity of food, to micronutrients, but the government nutrition program now also emphasizes fortification. The earlier government policies toward vitamin deficiencies tended to take a different approach from fortification. For instance, the Indonesian government started to distribute vitamin A supplements to children under five in the 1970s (Soekirman et al. 2005). In fact, this vitamin A supplement program was so successful that it received an award from Helen Keller International for its achievement. Nutrition education for the poor was also conducted (Shaw and Green 1996). In contrast, in recent years what is showcased is fortification. For instance, the Indonesian government initiated the first mandatory fortification program with wheat flour in 1998. The new regulation required that *all* wheat flour that is sold in Indonesia—imported or domestic—be fortified with iron, zinc, folic acid, vitamin Bs, according to the Indonesian National Standard (SNI).

As a part of a broader push toward "healthy babies," the government and international organizations also started fortification projects focused on children under five years of age and their mothers. For instance, the World Food Program, in collaboration with the government, started targeting mothers and infants in the distribution of fortified biscuits and instant noodles. These are fortified with micronutrients, such as iron, zinc, calcium, magnesium, phosphorus, potassium, vitamin A, D, E, K, B1, B2, B6, B12, and folic acid. Other organizations are also involved in distributing fortified products to infants, mothers, and children. International Relief and

Development (IRD), Land O'Lake and USDA, Helen Keller International, and UNICEF work with the Indonesian government to distribute fortified food for children and mothers.

The government also started a nutrition program called MP-ASI, the Indonesian abbreviation for "complementary food to breast milk," using an instant baby porridge fortified with micronutrients. MP-ASI is fortified with Vitamin A, D, E, K, B12, B6, C, iron, calcium, zinc, iodine, thiamin, Riboflavin, and niacin among others. In 1999–2000, the government spent Rp 30.9 billions, about US \$3.4 million, for MP-ASI. It increased this to Rp 102 billion, about US \$11.3 million, in 2000–2003, and Rp120 billion, US \$13.3 million, in 2003–2004 (Soekirman et al. 2005). Behind this shift to micronutrients were the international organizations and experts who vigorously marketed the importance of micronutrients and the use of fortification. They were instrumental in creating and extending a network of Indonesian organizations and individuals that advocated for fortification through conferences, workshops, seminars, and grants. For instance, the group of nutritional experts under the Indonesian Fortification Coalition (*Koalisi Fortifikasi Indonesia*) was active in calling for government fortification policies. This coalition was established in the late 1990s by policy-makers and leading nutritional scientists in Indonesia who had close ties with international funding agencies and international development professionals such as UNICEF and WHO.

Indonesian scientists started to scrutinize the value of traditional methods of feeding babies and to evaluate them in terms of micronutrient make-up. Traditionally, Indonesian mothers feed babies a porridge made from rice and rice flour, banana, papaya, beans, and vegetables (Komari 2000). Nutrition scientists conducted studies and found that the quality of these home-made foods for infants was below micronutrient requirements (Departmen Kesehatan 1999; Komari 2000). Nutrition scientists and development experts working in the country, therefore, began turning an increasingly skeptical eye toward women's ability to prepare "good" baby food at home. For instance, an Indonesia nutrition expert suggests the following:

Only in late 1990s scientific evidence demonstrated that traditional-home-made, whatever the cost, could not meet infant and young children's micronutrient requirement, especially iron and vitamin A. In order to meet infant and young child requirement, they need fortified complementary food that are only available commercially. (Soekirman et al. 2005)

Nutritional science experts increasingly view commercial baby foods as superior to home-made ones, as the former is fortified to satisfy scientifically determined micronutrients standards. The following quote from Indonesia's leading nutrition experts summarizes the new-found virtue of commercial baby food and experts' call for a "new paradigm" of baby food:

The new paradigm affects the common or existing concept of complementary food for infants and young children. The old paradigm stated that there was no difference between homemade complementary foods and commercial or factory-made complementary food. The new concept reveals the significant difference between the two complementary foods, especially in terms of micronutrient content and bioavailability. (Soekirman et al. 2005)

The new gospel of micronutrients is not restricted to doctors and bureaucrats. Experts are now using the micronutrient language when giving feeding advice to mothers. For instance, a doctor from the Indonesian Pediatrician Association advised at a seminar that "mothers can purchase various kinds of baby food, which is more practical, hygienic and nutritious, or prepare multimixed weaning foods that include four food components" (Jakarta Post 2001). Mothers are also hearing more about the need for micronutrients and the virtue of fortified baby food from the commercial sector. This will be examined in the following section.

Propelling the Scientization of Baby Food: The Role of the Market

There is no doubt that the public advocacy of fortified baby food is a welcome one for the baby food industry. As science emphasizes micronutrients as the signifier of "good" baby food, the industry positions itself as the superior provider of this. As a business, commercial baby food presents a huge market. This is the case in many other developing countries too. Indonesia's precise market size is unknown, but it was estimated in 2001 to be 36 million dollars in annual sales. Between 1997 and 2004, the market is said to have grown by approximately 90% ... (also see Indofood 2003; INSTATE Pty Ltd 2003). Major global corporations such as Nestle and Nutricia compete in this market.... Indonesia is an attractive market for these companies due to the large population of babies and mothers (Madden 2003). As one of the businessmen I interviewed told me, it is a market of four million babies per year.

There are a variety of products in the Indonesian baby food market, but the market mainly consists of starter formula (0-6 months old), follow-on formula (6–12 months), growing-up milk (1–10 years), pregnant and lactating mothers' milk, cereals/porridges, and special products for lactose low/free and products for babies with low birth weight.... In this Article, the term "baby food products" is used to refer to these product lines.

Given that the commercial sector has such a large presence, its power to shape the meaning and interpretation of baby food should not be neglected. How does the industry construct and communicate a particular image of ideal motherhood and feeding? How has it changed over time, and what are the characteristics of the current marketing? To answer these questions, I conduct a content analysis of advertisements for baby food products in a parent magazine in Indonesia. The advertisements' content analysis shows that there have been significant changes in the marketing strategy for baby food products. Contrary to my initial expectation, older advertisements were not silent on vitamins and minerals. Many of them mentioned vitamins and minerals in addition to proteins and calories. There are, however, major differences between the earlier advertisements and the current ones. While the overall message of the older advertisements focuses on the child's growth and development, the current advertisements focus on nutritional components and their benefits, and on the complex engineering that is required to obtain optimal nutrition for babies.

In the older advertisements, growth is the featured message.... The image of a growing baby appears in various parts of the advertisements, but figures most strongly in the main text: "healthy and happy growth" (Morinaga baby formula 1979), "important for baby's healthy growth" (Vita rice flour 1982), "nutrition for the growth of your children" (Proteina 1984), "healthy growth, growth to win" (Bendera formula 1984), "Mil porridge for good growth" (Nestle porridge 1985), "Milna always cares about our babies' growth" (Milna porridge 1986), "help baby's healthy and complete growth" (Farley porridge 1986), "milk for our baby's growth and development" (Promil formula 1986). The images in the advertisements reinforce this message. In addition to babies that are being fed, images of strong and active children are prevalent, including children holding giant stuffed animals (Nutrima 1989), holding up training weights (Farley's 1981), or being active in sports (Sustagen 1979; Bendera milk 1984). The older marketing also emphasizes additional benefits such as convenience, taste, and flavors. Texts say, "Ballita is instant, practical and easy to prepare" (Ballita flour 1984), "Nasi tim for baby, high quality, practical" (Milna porridge 1986), "Nestum instant, just needs to be mixed with milk" (Nestum porridge 1986), "PRENAGEN is easy and quick to prepare" (Prenagen mother's milk 1989), emphasizing that the products are practical.

The current advertisements have major contrasting characteristics.... Most notable is their emphasis on the benefits linked with a particular nutritional element. The most prevalent benefit is the child's intellectual development rather than merely the physical growth of the body, as in the older [advertisements]. Few products fail to mention that nutrients are supposed to help the brain development of children. The main texts of ads emphasize intelligence as the biggest benefits of using the products. Examples include "The EYE Q System of Nutrients" (Gain Plus 2005), "Development of left and right brains are both important" (Enfagrow), "Proud … See My Kid More and More Brilliant" (Chil-kid 2005), and "Building blocks for your child's intelligence" (Enfagrow 2005). Images in the ads strongly emphasize the intellectual benefits by featuring children with activities that seem to require brain power. Unlike older ones, there are few images of babies simply being fed or playing with regular toys. The current images feature children with objects associated with intelligence—complex toys (Dancow 2005; Nutricia 2005), computers (Procal Gold 2005), and artifacts presumably made by children themselves (Chil-kid 2005; Enfagrow 2005; Nutrilon 2005). These images reinforce the message that the product enhances the intelligence of children.

In addition to the message of more specific health benefits associated with the use of the products, the current ads tend to have a specific nutrient associated with each health benefit. Many establish causality between a particular nutrient and a particular health benefit. For instance, the Milna biscuit claims three distinct health benefits from specific nutrients. DHA (docosahexaenoic acid) is "to help brain development," Prebiotic "to increase body defense," and calcium for "the development of strong bones and teeth." Similarly, Procal Gold says DHA for "brain growth," αβγ carotene for "body immunity," and vegetable oil to "protect healthy heart." Gain Plus claims "three prime benefits" that include: (1) brain development by DHA, GLA, Taurin; (2) bone and bone density by non-palm oil and calcium; and (3) body resilience by sinbiotic. Triple Care similarly touts three benefits including: (1) brain development by Omega 3, 6, and 9; (2) body resilience with beta carotene, vitamin C, E, B6, and zinc; and (3) improved digestion by fiber. This claim to a specific benefit from a particular nutrient marks a strong contrast with the older ads which tended to portray all-purpose and unspecified benefits from the product. This tight linkage also emphasizes the highly technical nature of the products.

This interpretation is supported by a comparison of the same products from the same manufacturer over time. Ads for Nestlé's Dancow milk in 1981 and 2005 reveal striking differences in their message over time. The ads in 1981 only talked about convenience and taste:

Now Dancow Instant- delicious, from pure and fresh milk. … Quickly. Yes, only 4 seconds and Dancow Instant rich in vitamins can dissolve in cold water. Moreover, taste soft, white as snow.

Soft, fresh, your children and family certainly will like it. No clumps no waste. Dancow Instant, milk in 4 seconds.

In 2005, the advertisement for the same product emphasized the components and their specific health benefits:

DANCOW 1 +, now more complete with DHA. DANCOW 1 + is now not only giving protection with Prebio 1 which helps to protect digestive system, but also complete with DHA that is important for brain. DHA in DANCOW contains one of the highest among other growth milk products.

This advertisement in 2005 shows a picture of a girl whose brain is glowing as she plays with a complicated toy. The package of Dancow now emphasizes nutrient components (DHA, Prebio1, LA, ALA, and twenty-six vitamin and minerals), each with a specific composition. Each nutrient is checked with a √ symbol, inviting consumers to feel that all the necessary nutrients in right amount are in the product. The text of the ad links a particular nutrient with a particular health benefits, Prebio for digestion, DHA for brain development.

Thus nutritional make-up and its efficacy play an increasingly important role in the marketplace as well. The current marketing portrays the food for mothers' and children's needs as having a variety of nutrient components, each of which is specifically linked to a particular health benefit. The appeal to consumers is based on the specific nutrient needs for the specific health benefits, rather than the general "growth and health" appeal of the older advertisements. Another important point is that the nutritionalized marketing messages construct "needs" of babies as a complex amalgam of micronutrients that require engineering by experts. Therefore, it positions professionals and experts, presumably at the corporate laboratories, as superior providers of nutrition. Mothers are then framed as responsible for buying those products, in order to be "good" mothers. Thus advertisement for EnfaMama highlights mothers' responsibility by saying, "For a new baby, I don't compromise. A healthy and smart baby is not just born. Mothers don't want to compromise during pregnancy and breastfeeding, because they play an important role. EnfaMama is complete with 65 mg of DHA and Omega 6, and DHA that is clinically proven to help a fetus's brain development. Your sweetheart starts smart since birth, you don't want to compromise."

In summary, the content analysis shows that baby food marketing increasingly emphasizes micronutrient make-up and its benefits. Similar to the shifting focus in science and policy, nutritional make-up and its engineered efficacy are playing an increasingly important role in the marketplace.

Why Fortification as the Solution?

Scientization has been seen as rooted in modern scientific knowledge with its perceived power as being the beholder of truth. The scientization of motherhood has similarly been linked to the growing role accorded scientists and child-rearing experts in the past two centuries. Medical professionals, teachers, and child domestic development specialists have been seen as the primary proponents of the doctrine of scientific motherhood. Yet the infant feeding case in Indonesia examined in this article shows the complex ways that baby food has become increasingly couched in terms of the needs for micronutrients *and* commercial products.

Although the need for fortified baby food might seem to naturally stem from scientific findings about micronutrient deficiencies, this is not the only logical answer. Micronutrient deficiencies can be tackled by other means such as preventing infection and parasite infestation. Even the dominant discourse that privileges dietary deficiency as the primary culprit in malnutrition prevails, this does not necessarily warrant the promotion of fortification. Indeed, understanding the importance of micronutrients and micronutrient deficiencies did not lead to the promotion of fortification in the 1970s. Some nutrition experts still favor home gardening and nutrition education as better options for improving the population's micronutrient status (Underwood 1998). Therefore, the question arises of how a particular infant nutritional need became championed above others.

The shift in international norms played an important role. The 1990s saw the growth of international agreements and consensus on micronutrients and hidden hunger. New forums for micronutrient experts were created which issued recommendations for Third World governments which typically included fortification in its list of policy options. Indonesian nutritionists and health bureaucrats participated in this transnational network. The recognition of the influence of the international community must not be equated with the simple diffusion model, however. Of critical importance is how a particular knowledge became globally dominant and disseminated widely. This is where Fraser's concept of "needs interpretation" is useful. It might seem like infant nutritional needs were simply discovered and then acted upon by professionals. Yet, what became dominant was actually a very particular discourse of "needs" which limits nutritional to biochemical ones. This discourse constructs food as an amalgam of identified nutrients and evaluates goodness of diet against a checklist of nutrients. Diet is about delivering an optimal variety and amount of nutrients. The "needs" of babies is the gap between the two measurements—the status quo and the standard levels of nutrients. Description and prescription of the food problem is provided in relation to such narrow "needs."

This compartmentalized view of the "needs" of babies in science translates well into the market. The analysis of advertisements shows that the baby food industry echoes the micronutrient-based understanding of feeding. Their marketing presents baby food as an amalgam of micronutrients. It portrays baby food as a highly technical product that needs to be manufactured by experts in modern facilities. The market presents itself as well-equipped to serve those "needs." Sometimes it implies that their products are better equipped to fulfill babies' "needs" than mothers' breast milk. As the marketing messages construct the "needs" of babies as a complex amalgam of micronutrients that require engineering by experts, they position professionals and experts at the corporate laboratories as superior providers of nutrition. Mothers then are portrayed as responsible for buying those products in order to be "good" mothers.

For the state, such reductionist "needs" construction helps legitimize the currently prevalent neoliberal model of social policies. In contrast to other policy tools such as nutrition education and supplement distribution, commercial fortified baby food takes the burden off the shoulder of the government. This resonates well with neoliberal ideal of small government. That fortification is cost-effective means to improve food security was emphasized by international organizations such as the World Bank and the ADB. The World Bank's *Enriching Lives* (1994), the booklet that advocated the importance of "hidden hunger," appealed micronutrient strategies' cost-efficiency as the primary advantage. The ADB similarly argued that "food fortification could also be the most assured and least-costly strategy to correct iodine, vitamin A, and iron deficiencies" (ADB 2000, 9). We can also see the same logic in the BAFF, a network of World Bank and other organizations with multinational companies including Nestle, Heinz, and Ajinomoto, Danone, Unilever, and Coca-Cola to promote fortification in the Third World (GAIN 2005).

Indonesia did not escape the market triumphalism of the late twentieth century, and its development paradigm shifted to a more neoliberal one (Wie 2002). State intervention was increasingly considered to be problematic and in need of replacement by the well-functioning market, and food and nutrition policy was not an exception. Publicly financed food and nutrition programs, such as supplement and agricultural intensification programs, fell out of vogue. The necessary transition from such a state-heavy approach was envisioned as being "from Green Revolution to 'Market Revolution,'" in the words of the head of Department of Food Affairs and Food Logistics Agency (Hasan 1993). Market triumphalism was another reason for the fortification campaign, as it was seen as the most obvious "market revolution" in the nutritional field. Positioning the food industry as a partner for solving the newly redefined food problem, fortification was a perfect example of private-public partnership, the use of the market approach, and cost-benefit efficient public policy. The Indonesian Fortification Coalition appealed to this neoliberal mode of public policy when they made an argument for fortified baby food. They argued that commercial fortified baby food could shift the primary role of the government toward "assist[ing] market forces" (Soekirman et al. 2005). With fortification, the solution to the micronutrient problem could come from the market rather than the state. Because "needs" is redefined to micronutrients rather than the general health and well-being of the people, the market emerges as a more efficient provider. This framing reduces the role and responsibility of the state and it becomes the consumers' responsibility to tap the wealth of offerings by the industry.

In the eyes of bureaucrats, professionals at international organizations, and the scientists who work with them, another appeal of fortified food is its quantifiability. Not only does it satisfy the scientists' preference for hard data but it also enables experts to fulfill their reporting and monitoring requirements. Experts at international organizations particularly expressed this advantage. With fortification, it is easy to report that X mg of vitamin A and iron were delivered. Contrast this to the much messier picture of nutrition education; one needs to conduct at least a twenty-four hour recall of food consumption survey which is notorious for its inaccuracy, measure the amount of micronutrients in different kinds of local food stuffs, calculate the loss of nutrients during processing and cooking, and monitor the changes in behavior over time. Fortification's quantifiability is even more appealing in the current environment of greater demand for evidence-based decision-making in international development (Graham 2002).

What gets hidden in this needs construction, however, is a more holistic way of understanding babies' nutrition and health. Broader—and perhaps more political—"needs" of babies such as a decent living environment, access to clean water, eradication of poverty, basic medical services, and so on get lost in such a construction of "needs." It is not that nutrition scientists do not recognize that broader structural issues are critical for combating micronutrient deficiencies. Any international nutrition expert would be quick to agree that these things do matter. Yet the way "needs" are constructed currently focuses attention more on diet and individual food habits, and consequently on "bad" baby food that lack micronutrients. Poverty and lack of access to medical care, water, and hygienic living condition become a mere background for "bad food." This depoliticization is a frequently observed dynamic in the medicalization of women's health (for instance, see Ratcliff 2002)....

That micronutrient deficiencies are "hidden" as its nickname suggests makes it even more difficult to convince mothers of the need to change their behavior. If their babies seem healthy on the surface, why take the vitamin A pill? Why cook more spinach? The steps toward convincing mothers, assuring compliance, and monitoring their behavioral change are tedious and often frustrating steps for experts and policy-makers. Fortification is attractive because nutrients can be added to whatever mothers are already buying without involving them. Policy planners and project officers do not have to deal with individual mothers. Instead, their nutritional objective is achieved by increasing the total amount of nutrients circulating in the food system.

This is consistent with literature that has found that the scientization of motherhood was propelled partly by social distrust of mothers' ability. In her study of medicalization of child birth, Ann Oakley found that distrust in women's ability to accurately observe, report, and make rational decisions was the impetus behind the increasing use of machines to monitor birthing process (Oakley 1986). In the discourse of scientized motherhood, women tend to be displaced as the subject—they are surrogates for the more important fetus and infants. Women matter to the extent that they are carriers of fetus or feeders of infants. Women's welfare is not the end—it is a means for the experts. It is for the sake of their children that proper management by mothers is necessitated, rending women's needs and wants further obfuscated. This echoes the critique of the increasingly popular Mother and Child Health (MCH) programs in which women are instrumentalized as a way to achieve national development (Beall 1997; Kumar 2003). In this discourse, women are a mere conduit to achieve the bigger objective of healthier and ultimately more economically productive population. Women's agency is then an obstacle to national development, rather than a goal in itself.

There is a profound dilemma. Under current scientization, many mothers are neither informed of the causes of micronutrient deficiencies nor of other alternative cures. Instead, they are flooded with information on what to buy via advertisements. These tell mothers what they should do, to purchase, but not why their babies are sick. The particular construction of "needs" being additional micronutrients is useful in forging an alliance among certain scientists, the private industry, and the state. It facilitates the agreement among these powerful actors on what ideal baby food is and how best to deliver it. Simultaneously, however, it makes it seem that it is not necessary to open a participatory process in food and nutrition policy-making. The presumed beneficiaries—mothers and babies—are no longer the legitimate voice in defining their own "needs."

By showing the interconnection of global and domestic development discourses, state policies, market dynamics, and gender ideology, the case study underscores my argument that the scientization of motherhood is not a simple intrusion by science and experts in a previously nonscientific area, but rather the result of interacting social forces that give prominence to a certain kind of scientific talk about ideal mothering. Understanding the complex nature of scientization of motherhood in contemporary developing world begs the question as to its implication for women's autonomy and participation in development practices.

References

Allen, Lindsay H. 2000. *Ending Hidden Hunger: The History of Micronutrient Deficiency Control: Background Analysis for the World Bank-UNICEF Nutrition Assessment Project.* Washington, DC: The World Bank.

Apple, Rima D. 1987. *Mothers and Medicine: A Social History of Infant Feeding, 1890–1950.* Maddison, WI: University of Wisconsin Press.

————. 1996. *Vitamania: Vitamins in American Culture*. New Brunswick, NJ: Rutgers University Press.

————. 2006. *Perfect Motherhood: Science and Childrearing in America*. New Brunswick, NJ: Rutgers University Press.

Arifin, Bustanil. 1993. *Pangan Dalam Orde Baru*. Jakarta, Indonesia: Koperasi Jasa Informasi.

Asian Development Bank (ADB). 2000. *Nutrition and Development Series: Manila Forum 2000: Strategies to Fortify Essential Foods in Asia and the Pacific*. Manila, Philippines: Asian Development Bank.

Badinter, Elisabeth. 1981. *The Myth of Motherhood: An Historical View of the Maternal Instinct*. London: Souvenir Press.

Beall, J. 1997. " 'In Sickness and in Health' Gender Issues in Health Policy and Their Implications for Development in the 1990s." In *Searching for Security: Women's Responses to Economic Transformation*, eds. I. Baud and I. Smyth, 67–95. London: Routledge.

Blum, L. M. 1999. *At the Breast: Ideologies of Breastfeeding and Motherhood in the Contemporary United States*. Boston, MA: Beacon.

Carpenter, Kenneth J. 1994. *Protein and Energy: A Study of Changing Ideas in Nutrition*. New York: Cambridge University Press.

Carter, Pam. 1995. *Feminism, Breasts and Breast Feeding*. New York: St. Martin's Press.

Departmen Kesehatan. 1999. *Strategi Nasional PP-ASI*. Jakarta, Indonesia.

Djelic, Laure, and Kerstin Sahlin-Andersson. 2006. *Transnational Governance: Institutional Dynamics of Regulation*. Cambridge, UK: Cambridge University Press.

Dori, S. Gili John, W. Meyer, Francisco O. Ramirez, and Evan Schofer. 2003. *Science in the Modern World Polity: Institutionalization and Globalization*. Stanford, CA: Stanford University Press.

Douglas, Susan J., and Meredith W. Michaels. 2004. *The Mommy Myth the Idealization of Motherhood and How It Has Undermined Women*. New York: Free Press.

Economist. 2004. "Food for Thought." *Economist*, July 31, no. 372: 71.

Ehrenreich, Barbara, and Deirdre English. 1978. *For Her Own Good 150 Years of the Experts' Advice to Women*. Garden City, NY: Anchor Books.

FAO and WHO. 1992. "International Conference on Nutrition, World Declaration and Plan of Action." ICN/92/2.

Fausto-Sterling, Anne. 2000. *Sexing the Body: Gender Politics and the Construction of Sexuality*. New York: Basic Books.

Fox, Bonnie, and Diana Worts. 1999. "Revisiting the Critique of Medicalized Childbirth: A Contribution to the Sociology of Birth." *Gender and Society* 13 (3): 326–46.

Fraser, Nancy. 1989. *Unruly Practices Power, Discourse and Gender in Contemporary Social Theory*. Cambridge, UK: Polity Press.

GAIN. 2005. "The Business Alliance for Food Fortification (BAFF)." http://www.gainhealth.org/gain/ch/en-en/index.cfm?page=/gain/home/activities/business_consumer_programs/business_action_network (accessed 16 May 2006).

Graham, Wendy. 2002. "Now or Never: the Case for Measuring Maternal Mortality." *The Lancet* 359 (9307): 701–4.

Haney, L. 2002. *Inventing the Needy: Gender and the Politics of Welfare in Hungary*. Berkeley: University of California Press.

Hartini, S., A. Winkvist, L. Lindholm, H. Stenlund, V. Persson, D. S. Nurdiati, and A. Surjono. 2003. "Nutrient Intake and Iron Status of Urban Poor and Rural Poor Without Access to Rice Fields Are Affected by the Emerging Economic Crisis: The Case of Pregnant Indonesian Women." *European Journal of Clinical Nutrition* 57:654–66.

Hasan, Ibrahim. 1993. "Sambutan Pengarahan Menteri Negara Urusan Pangan/Ketua BULOG Widyakarya Nasional Pangan Dan Gizi V, Jakarta, 20 April 1993." In *Widyakarya Pangan Dan Gizi V*, eds. Mien A. Rifai, A. Nontji, Erwindodo, F. Jalal, D. Fardiaz, and T. Fallah. Jakarta: Lembaga Ilmu Pengetahuan Indonesia.

Hays, Sharon. 1996. *The Cultural Contradictions of Motherhood*. New Haven, CT: Yale University Press.

Hull, Terence H., and Valerie J. Hull. 2005. "From Family Planning to Reproductive Health Care: A Brief History." In *People, Population, and Policy in Indonesia*, ed. Terence H. Hull, 1 -70. Jakarta, Indonesia: Equinox Publishing.

Indofood. 2003. *Annual Report 2003: Facing the Future*. Jakarta, Indonesia: Indofood.

Inoue, Keiko, and Gili S. Dori. 2006. "The Global Institutionalization of Health as a Social Concern: Organizational and Discursive Trends." *International Sociology* 21:199–219.

INSTATE Pty Ltd. 2003. *Food Exporters' Guide to Indonesia: A Report Prepared for the Australian Government Department of Agriculture, Fisheries and Forestry*. www.daff.gov.au/foodinfo.

Jakarta Post. 2001. "Averting 'Lost Generation' Through Nutrition Plan." *Jakarta Post*, July 22.

Jasanoff, S., ed. 2004. *States of Knowledge: The Co-Production of Science and Social Order*. London: Routledge.

Komari. 2000. "Makanan Pendamping Asi (MP-ASI) Sebagai Teknologi Intervensi Gizi." In *Kumpulan Makalah Diskusi Pakan Bidang Gizi Tentang ASI-MP ASI*. Persatuan Ahli Gizi Indonesia. Jakarta, Indonesia: LIPI, UNICEF.

Kumar, Rachel Simon. 2003. "Claiming the State: Women's Reproductive Identity and Indian Development." In *Feminist Futures: Re-Imagining Women, Culture and Development*, eds. Kum Kum Bhavnani, John Foran, and Priya Kurian, 74–88. London: Zed Books.

Ladd-Taylor, Molly. 2004. "Mother-Worship/Mother Blame: Politics and Welfare in an Uncertain Age." *Journal of the Association for Research on Mothering* 6 (1): 7–15.

Litt, Jacquelyn S. 2000. *Medicalized Motherhood: Perspectives from the Lives of African-American and Jewish Women*. New Brunswick, NJ: Rutgers University Press.

Madden, Normandy. 2003. "Formula Marketer Busts Myths." *Advertising Age* 74 (41): 4.

Malacrida, Claudia. 2002. "Alternative Therapies and Attention Deficit Disorder: Discourses of Maternal Responsibility and Risk." *Gender & Society* 16 (3): 366–85.

Margolis, Maxine L. 1984. *Mothers and Such Views of American Women and Why They Changed*. Berkeley: University of California Press.

Martin, Emily. 1987. *The Woman in the Body: A Cultural Analysis of Reproduction*. Boston, MA: Beacon Press.

Nestle, Marion. 2002. *Food Politics: How the Food Industry Influences Nutrition and Health*. Berkeley: University of California Press.

O'Reilly, Andrea. 2004. "Introduction." In *Mother Matters: Motherhood as Discourse and Practice*, ed. Andrea O'Reilly, 11–28. Toronto, ON, Canada: Association for Research on Mothering.

Oakley, Ann. 1986. "Feminism, Motherhood and Medicine-Who Cares?" *What Is Feminism?*, eds. Juliet Mitchell and Ann Oakley, 127–50. Oxford, UK: Basil Blackwell.

Ratcliff, Katherine Strother. 2002. *Women and Health: Power, Technology, Inequality, and Conflict in a Gendered World*. Boston, MA: Allyn and Bacon.

Rooks, Judith Pence. 1997. *Midwifery and Childbirth in America*. Philadelphia, PA: Temple University Press.

Shaw, W. D., and C. P. Green. 1996. "Vitamin A Promotion in Indonesia: Scaling Up and Targeting Special Needs." In *Strategies for Promoting Vitamin A Production, Consumption, and Supplementation: Four Case Studies*. Washington, DC: The Academy for Educational Development.

Soekirman, Atmarita, B. Abas, Sanjaya Jahari, and Drajat Martianto. 2005. "Review of Nutrition Situation, Conceptual Framework and Strategy for Nutrition Interventions in Indonesia: With Emphasis on Micronutrient Deficiencies," (draft, as of January 2005). Jakarta, Indonesia: The Indonesian Coalition for Fortification.

Thorbecke, Erik, and Theodore van der Pluijm. 1993. *Rural Indonesia: Socio-Economic Development in a Changing Environment*. New York: New York University Press.

UN/SCN. 1998. "Full Report of the Meeting of the Working Group on Iron Deficiency." *Report of the Sub-Committee on Nutrition at Its Twenty-Fifth Session, 30 March-2 April 1998*. Administrative Committee on Coordination, (UN) B04, Oslo, Norway.

Underwood, Barbara A. 1998. "Prevention of Vitamin A Deficiency." In *Prevention of Micronutrient Deficiencies: Tools for Policymakers and Public Health Workers*, 103–65. Institute of Medicine. Washington, DC: National Academy Press.

Underwood, Barbara A., and Suttilak Smitasiri. 1999. "Micronutrient Malnutrition: Policies and Programs for Control and Their Implications." *Annual Review of Nutrition* 19:303–24.

Uvin, Peter. 1999. "Eliminating Hunger after the End of the Cold War: Progress and Constraints." In *Scaling Up, Scaling Down: Overcoming Malnutrition in Developing Countries*, ed. Thomas J. Marchione, 1–22. New York: Gordon and Breach.

West, Keith P., Jr. 2002. "Extent of Vitamin A Deficiency Among Preschool Children and Women of Reproductive Age." *The Journal of Nutrition* 132 (9): 2857S-66S.

World Health Organization. 1998. *Complementary Feeding of Young Children in Developing Countries: A Review of Current Scientific Knowledge*. Geneva, Switzerland: World Health Organization.

———. 2001. *Iron Deficiency Anemia Assessment, Prevention and Control: A Guide for Programme Managers*. Geneva, Switzerland: World Health Organization.

Wie, T. K. 2002. "The Soeharto Era and After: Stability, Development and Crisis, 1966–2000." In *The Emergence of a National Economy in Indonesia, 1800–2000*, eds. H. W. Dick, V. J. H. Houben, J. T. Lindblad, and Thee Kian Wie, 194–243. Sydney, Australia: Allen & Unwin.

World Bank. 1994. *Enriching Lives: Overcoming Vitamin and Mineral Malnutrition in Developing Countries*. Development in Practice Series. Washington, DC: World Bank Publications.

Suggested Additional Readings

Megan A. Carney. 2013. "Border Meals: Detention Center Feeding Practices, Migrant Subjectivity, and Questions on Trauma." *Gastronomica* 13(4): 32–46.

Frederick Errington, Tatsuro Fujikura, and Deborah Gewertz. 2012. "Instant Noodles as an Antifriction Device: Making the BOP with PPP in PNG." *American Anthropologist* 114(1): 19–31.

Anna Harris. 2015. "The Hollow Knock and Other Sounds in Recipes." *Gastronomica* 15(4): 14–17.

Lewis Holloway, Christopher Bear, and Katy Wilkinson. 2014. "Robotic Milking Technologies and Renegotiating Situated Ethical Relationships on UK Dairy Farms." *Agriculture and Human Values* 31: 185–99.

Seth M. Holmes. 2007. " 'Oaxacans Like to Work Bent Over': The Naturalization of Social Suffering among Berry Farm Workers." *International Migration* 45(3): 39–68.

Hannah Landecker. 2013. "Postindustrial Metabolism: Fat Knowledge." *Public Culture* 25(3): 495–522.

Anna Mann, Annemarie Mol, Priya Satalkar, Amalinda Savirani, Nasima Selim, Malini Sur, and Emily Yates-Doerr. 2011. "Mixing Methods, Tasting Fingers: Notes on an Ethnographic Experiment." *HAU: Journal of Ethnographic Theory* 1(1): 221–43.

David E. Sutton. 2010. "Food and the Senses." *Annual Review of Anthropology* 39: 209–23.

Emily Yates-Doerr. 2012. "The Weight of the Self: Care and Compassion in Guatemalan Dietary Choices." *Medical Anthropology Quarterly* 26(1): 136–58.

PART FOUR

More than Human, More than Food

Introduction

Despite the centrality and ubiquity of food, in many respects food has always been an elusive object. Because what counts as food is ambiguous, food always exceeds and complicates the categories and expectations placed on it, morphing into something that is more than food. Yet at the same time, food always retains its significance as something at the core of human life. It is something that matters, and matters profoundly, given that the survival of humans and other biological beings depends on it. Ultimately, critical studies of food take seriously the very essence of food by seeking to understand not just the nature of food but also how food is completely and thoroughly enmeshed in every aspect of people's lives so that it can be difficult to identify with any certainty what food is and what it is not. When viewed dynamically through time and across regions, what people have identified as food has changed dramatically, further revealing the simultaneous stability and instability of food.

Recent directions in social theory inspired by multispecies ethnographies, animal-human relations, more-than-human approaches, and critical design studies, among others, have offered possibilities for making sense of food's many different manifestations and realities. Studies from the humanistic and behavioral sciences that have sought to deprivilege and decenter the human have also reframed people's social worlds as belonging to larger or more extended ecosystems that include nonhuman actors such as plants, animals, and even nonliving entities such as robots or algorithms. Coinciding with these conversations are new approaches in art, design, and science and technology studies that reveal the ephemerality and alternativity of any singular reality, while situating the here and now in multiple spaces and temporalities. When these conversations come together, they create opportunities for examining food beyond its current or expected presentation or form. Specifically, these conversations inspire provocative debates about food and food experiences in terms of their potentialities and futures. What could food be? What more could food be than what it already is?

Studying food in terms of "something more" shifts both our awareness of what food is and could be as well as our recognition of where food and food practices fit within the range of human and nonhuman experiences. This helps us ask different questions about how food and its users and consumers extend beyond people and include nonhuman actors. Animals, bacteria, and microflora are not only eaters with unique preferences but also laborers that produce the foods that others consume. How does this realization alter our assumptions about whose taste preferences matter and under what circumstances? The increasing porosity of boundaries between art and science has revealed that food travels across many spheres, so that the emergent qualities of foodstuffs transform them into musical instruments, clothing, and protest weapons, among other things. Above all, food has the power to disrupt our expectations at the same time that we disrupt the nature and potentiality of food itself.

This final section explores this more-than quality in order to think about food beyond food. By engaging with diverse methods and theories from multispecies, more-than-human, and critical design studies, the chapters in this section confront and disrupt our expectations about food and offer possibilities for different conversations and questions. In this section, person-centric and consumption-focused studies are displaced by investigations that look at food's life cycles beyond production and consumption or the ways in which taste preferences move beyond a single individual and encompass imagined experiences between different species. Both the nature of food and the nature of humanness are unbounded and become flexible in ways that highlight how they are multiply and mutually entangled. Above all, by showing how humans are not the only beings that eat and use food, these chapters prompt us to think seriously and carefully about the materiality of food and whether food's materiality matters. In that way, these chapters open up new possibilities and futures for food and food studies, even while affirming that these new directions are themselves emergent from the debates and approaches that initiated this volume.

Potential Questions to Guide Reading and Discussion

What are the possibilities, potentialities, and limits of food?

How does food offer new possibilities for rethinking the presumed differences and boundaries between art and science?

What insights emerge by resituating food within different social relationships, such as between human and nonhuman actors?

What do we understand differently when we take seriously that foods have their own life cycles and fit within their own communities?

How do scientific and technological innovations denature food and food experiences and transform them into something else?

How does food move across different states of being, and why does that movement matter and for whom?

How does the denaturing of food affect important cultural phenomena such as heritage, tradition, and authenticity?

How might scientific and technological innovations offer new possibilities for resolving enduring problems such as food shortages, food safety, access, and affordability?

How do scientific and technological innovations reveal important ethical questions?

What is the future of food?

17

Waste, Incorporated

Chika Watanabe

Taking a deep breath in the lush vegetable fields of a Japanese agricultural training center in Myanmar fills my body with a distinct smell of excrement. Jolted by the stench, I nevertheless try to breathe normally in front of my Burmese co-workers and trainees. We squat down close to the ground, digging into the moistness of the earth to uproot the weeds that will eventually be fed to the animals and cooked for our dinner. Where is the smell coming from? I squint toward the plot of freshly planted tomatoes that are struggling in the intense heat of central Myanmar. To our left stands the staff living quarters, and I wonder if the outdoor sinks are the culprits, although they always seem spotless. To our right lies the waste treatment infrastructure consisting of what look like a sedimentation tank and small stabilization ponds for the wastewater. Surely, I glance hopefully at the concrete structures, they are the source of the smell. Even so, I cannot bring myself to look at the mud caked around my fingers because I know, deep down, that the stink is rising from underneath me.

It did not take long for me to realize that the soil in the paddies and fields of this training center did, indeed, include waste matter, such as our bodily wastes. Wai Aung, one of the staffers at the training center, had shown me how to help the trainees take care of the pigs, and after touring the pigpens and discussing the different types of pigs, he explained that they used an effective microorganism (EM) solution to disinfect the pig manure. "It doesn't smell, right?" he smiled proudly. Two pigs shared each of the rectangular spaces made of concrete flooring, and there was a trough toward the back into which trainees were shoveling the pigs' excrement. They mixed the manure with rice husks and took it out of the pigpen every six months in order to use it as an ingredient for the organic fertilizer in the rice paddies and vegetable fields. I inhaled the air in the direction of the manure-filled troughs and nodded in agreement. Wai Aung continued, "Actually, human excrement is the best, and so the training center also uses the wastewater from the living quarters for agriculture."

So there it was. We were eating the products of our own feces, in addition to animal manure. In this article, I argue that the circulation of waste in the training center created intimate relations among human and nonhuman beings, a process that I call "circulatory sociality." What we had distanced from ourselves suddenly reappeared in the closest form possible, that is, in the food that we consumed. To be even more precise, we were ingesting other people's waste matter. If living side by side with others in this small-scale environment, as well as with the pigs and chicken, surrounded by rice paddies and vegetable fields, created a tightknit community, the circulatory processes through which waste was transformed and passed through our own bodies wove us into an even more intimate relationship with the environment and with each other. There was little that we did not see, hear, smell, touch, and in some form, eat. And, as I show in the course of this article, discipline was key to these intimacies.

*   *   *

The Japanese organization running the training center, the Organization for Industrial, Spiritual and Cultural Advancement (OISCA), is one of the oldest international NGOs in Japan, established in 1961, and it derives from a Shinto-based new religion called Ananaikyō.[1] It focuses on sustainable development and environmental education activities through long-term trainings in organic agriculture around Asia, among other projects. The organizational mission is founded on a principle of human-nature coexistence, which in part states that "all life-forms are closely interconnected and that their source is in the universe" (OISCA n.d.). OISCA's projects in Myanmar take place in a region called the Dry Zone, where temperatures can rise to as high as fifty degrees Celsius. Despite the difficult climate, OISCA's Japanese director, the forty Burmese staff members, and the twenty trainees have been successfully cultivating organic rice and vegetables, and raising chicken and pigs in environmentally sustainable ways. Over the course of fifteen years, in an area stretching to almost nineteen acres, Japanese and Burmese aid workers and trainees have transformed an arid land into a compound of fertile rice paddies and bustling agricultural activities. Hundreds of young people have passed through the place, learning about organic agriculture, and dozens have joined the staff ranks.

The training programs last for a year, during which time trainees, Burmese staffers, and the Japanese director live together in a communal lifestyle that emphasizes discipline and collective harmony. Japanese staff members described their work as *hitozukuri* (literally "making persons"), a form of Japanese aid that focuses on human resource development. But this *hitozukuri* aid goes beyond a simple transfer of skills. OISCA staffers in Japan told me that the ethos of communal living was perhaps more important than the teaching of agricultural techniques. According to them, the trainees come from farming families and might already know about agriculture, but they are less likely to know what it means to be disciplined, punctual, and in harmony with the collective. Hence, life at the training center in Myanmar was rigorous: everyone woke up at five in the morning to clean the grounds together and engage in prescribed physical exercises, followed by a day of hard agricultural labor. We worked even through the hottest times of day in the afternoon, when local farmers tended to rest. There was little or no privacy, and each of our activities contributed to a collective task: cleaning the chicken coops, weeding the vegetable fields, cooking everybody's meals, feeding the pigs.

In the training center, the circulation of waste foregrounded a suspension of one's self amidst intimate connections with others. Everyone had a role to play in the scheme of the training center. Even the chickens and the pigs participated in the sociality of the training center in their own ways. In this submersive involvement, we felt that we were part of a totalizing system and that each of us as individuals did not and could not matter much. Personally, I also developed an acute awareness of my surroundings: the clucking from the chicken coops echoing in the walls of my bedroom, the sandy ground never staying put as people shuffled busily across the courtyard. These sensations pushed against the boundaries of my body. The sweat, the smell, and the heat clung to my skin and my interactions with others. The young female trainees were especially affectionate, and whenever they held my hand or passed their arms through mine on our walk to the rice paddies, I was particularly aware of the sweaty indistinction between their bodies and mine.

The use of waste matter for agriculture made sense given OISCA's focus on sustainable and organic agriculture. But what I want to argue in this article is how the circulation of waste created not only a particular agricultural system, but also an environment in which intimate sensations and relations cultivated specific kinds of persons. In what follows, I offer a brief exploration into the ways that waste was incorporated into the environment of the training center under the organizational aim to "make persons" who can usher in a sustainable future. Specifically, Japanese aid workers described the training center as *junkangata shakai*, which I translate as "circulatory sociality." Using this idiosyncratic translation, I hope to offer a framework for understanding how the movement and transformation of waste through the environment produced particular forms of persons based on intimate relations with one's environment and with others.

Junkangata shakai is a phrase used among Japanese actors engaged in environmental sustainability policies and practices, officially translated as "material-cycle society" by the government. No doubt that OISCA's Japanese aid workers used the term *junkangata shakai* to make their work relevant in light of these wider discourses. In many ways, the ideas about *junkan* ("circulation" or "cycle") expressed in the Basic Environment Plan (*kankyō kihon keikaku*) of 1994 resonates with OISCA's philosophies about human-nature coexistence: for instance, in the section about "long-term goals," the policy states that "the environment is founded upon a circulation (*junkan*) of materials (*busshitsu*) between air, water, soil, and life forms, and the maintenance of an intricate balance of the ecosystem" (Ministry of the Environment 1994). But contrary to these wider and more abstract conceptualizations of *junkangata shakai*, the actual Fundamental Plan for Establishing a Sound Material-Cycle Society (*junkangata shakai keisei suishin kihonhō*) defines the term narrowly in terms of waste management and recyclable resources, such as through the 3Rs of waste (reduce, reuse, recycle) (Ministry of the Environment 2000). Unlike this policy framework, what I translate as circulatory sociality in OISCA did not simply point to a system of waste management. I suggest that the circulatory sociality in the training center sprung from and aimed at a different kind of worldview. In short, it was a perspective framed by OISCA's roots in a Shinto-based new religion.

The man who created OISCA, Nakano Yonosuke, was also the founder of a religious group called Ananaikyō, which he established in 1949. Despite its religious roots, most of OISCA's Japanese aid workers today stress that their organization is neither religious nor secular, but rather, inspired by a nonreligious, "Shinto" ecological worldview (Watanabe 2015).[2] Therefore, a Shinto-derived philosophy of ecological harmony framed OISCA's activities around the Asia-Pacific. In the early years of the organization, Nakano (1963: 42) wrote:

All life forms, including humans, live in the womb of the Great Life of the Universe. Even after being born on earth through the power of Great Nature, we are connected to the universe by an invisible lifeline and protected by it, bathing in the great virtues of the earth, and breathing the air of the great skies. … When we sense the pulse of life running through our flesh and the honorable will of Great Nature residing there, that is, the flow of the Great Spirit of the

Universe, our hearts tremble at the precious existence of humanity, and we cannot but be grateful for the Great Nature of the Universe.

This philosophy promotes an awareness of oneness among humans, nature, and all living beings under the Great Spirit of the Universe. Accordingly, Nakano's mission, and thereby that of OISCA, has focused on activities that are considered to be in line with nature, the most important form of labor being agriculture. It is worth noting that this idea of oneness with nature does not derive from a concept of a pristine nature or the banishment of waste, but a transformation of both. As scholars have pointed out, nature as pristine and unmanned wilderness does not possess a positive quality in Japan. Nature's virtue emerges in being associated with supernatural forces but also tamed in particular ways on a continuum with human activity, consequently often leading to ambiguous and contradictory relationships between humans and their environments (Kalland and Asquith 1997; Kirby 2011; Knight 1996; Thornber 2013). Similarly, just as waste was incorporated into nature, OISCA's aid actors aimed to alter natural environments for specific practices of agriculture and visions of sustainability. The environmental goal lay in a co-transformation and coexistence of humans and nature, not in the former's submission to the latter.

Although Nakano's philosophies were rarely articulated directly in practice, they trickled into Japanese staffers' views of their work. One senior staff member in Japan summed up the organization's approach to sustainable agriculture and development as focused on the soil (*tsuchi*)—the foundation of circulation (*junkan*) and the basis of life. Drawing scenes in the air with animated hands, he explained that there are trees on the mountain, fruits on those trees, animals that eat those fruits, and their feces that go back to the soil, which then nourishes the trees. So on and so forth. "All life is connected," he said. In this sense, the *junkangata shakai* in OISCA aid workers' imaginations went beyond the ordinary use of the term in Japanese government policies around technologies of waste management and recycling. The circulation of waste matter such as excrement was one link in the connections of life and the oneness of the Great Spirit of the Universe.

In thinking about the circulation of waste as a process that connects different life forms, I find useful the perspective of scholars who have proposed that we take waste as an analytical object and process. Sociologist Gay Hawkins (2006: 11) argued that we open ourselves to "the possibility of having different relations with things that we frame as ontologically other," such as waste. Her approach sees waste not as excess (Bataille 1991) or "matter out of place" (Douglas 2002), but as an actor with material presence and social productivity (see also Evans et al. 2013; Hetherington 2004; O'Brien 1999). Hence, while many historians, anthropologists, and philosophers have analyzed how waste and its symbolic pollution feeds into the politics of exclusion such as in colonialism and postcoloniality, projects of modernity, and government (Anderson 1995, 2010; Chakrabarty 1991; Esty 1999; McFarlane 2008; Scanlan 2005), the perspectives of Hawkins and others treat waste as a material reality that embodies and shapes social order and relations. In other words, waste does not simply exist outside of the order of things, nor does it solely symbolize negative values. If we paid attention to its material presence, we would see that it also generates new forms of sociality and values—that is, we would see that waste is a process (see Hetherington 2004; Lathers 2006; Reno 2014).[3] This view challenges my own initial reactions to the presence of waste matter in the soil at the training center. Waste such as excrement, leftover food, and weeds in OISCA were not simply polluting and repulsive remainders. The most important aspect of waste matter was that it was transformed *and* was transformative in its circular movement. It is not that trainees and staffers did not comment on the unpleasant smells of waste and organic fertilizer around the training center. Rather, despite these reactions, the ways that the training center operated turned people's attention to waste as something other than refuse, and even as something beneficial, once it was changed into fertilizer or food. Most notably, I suggest that waste as process made visible particular actors, social relations, and ways of being.

An important aspect of the circular movement of waste in the training center was the presence of different actors who facilitated this flow, human and nonhuman. In this sense, we can see waste as a medium through which one life becomes another—or, to see waste as a sign of life, rather than of decay, disorder, and death (Reno 2014). One instance of this character of waste as life appeared in the ecosystem of microorganisms that participated in the circulation of manure and excrement. When the trainees and staff members pushed the pig manure into the trough, they mixed it with rice husks and a liquid EM solution. Effective microorganisms, or *akyo:pyú thekshí anúziwá* in Burmese (literally meaning "micro life form with benefits"), "consists of a wide variety of effective, beneficial and non-pathogenic microorganisms produced through a natural process and not chemically synthesized or genetically engineered," according to the EM Research Organization (EMRO) in Japan. EMRO, affiliated with the professor who developed EM technology, Higa Teruo, explains on its website that there are three kinds of EM: lactic acid bacteria, yeast, and phototrophic bacteria. They are all microorganisms that exist in nature and are cultivated through fermentation. The EM solution that is used in agriculture and wastewater treatment, as in OISCA's case, contains mostly the third of these types, and can be reproduced by "feeding" the microorganisms with organic matter such as rice bran or bone meal, molasses, and water.

The particular EM solution used in the Myanmar training center during my time there was an amber-colored liquid stored in plastic water bottles in the Japanese director's room. Taking the bottles out of the cabinets to show me, Sakurai confessed that he had inadvertently destroyed the original EM solution from Japan that the previous director had been propagating. This original solution had come from a small amateur laboratory run by a veterinarian in Japan. This EM enthusiast had created the solution using soil from local rice paddies (Satō Kenkyūjo n.d.).[4] Sakurai was a young man in his thirties with much less agricultural experience and knowledge than his predecessor, and his failure derived from a miscalculation of the heat of central Myanmar in April, when temperatures rise far above the required thirty degrees Celsius for reproducing the EM solution. When the original bacteria died, Sakurai turned to what he called his bible, the Japanese agricultural magazine, *Gendai Nōgyō* (*Modern Agriculture*), and found a recipe for making EM solution using one's own paddy soil. After several experiments fermenting mud from the paddies in the training center, he succeeded in making the amber liquid that was now helping turn excrement into food. Sakurai believed in giving back to the land what one takes from it. Coaxing beneficial bacteria from local soil to facilitate this kind of return and circulation was precisely what his vision was about.

There is nothing new in using animal manure or microorganisms to reduce the use of chemicals in agriculture and re-relate ourselves to waste. The circulation of human waste for agricultural usage has also been practiced for centuries around the world, although currently only 10 percent of human excreta is used in agriculture or aquaculture (Cordell et al. 2009; Goddard 1996; Jewitt 2011). Scholars have turned especially to the histories of China and Japan to examine systematic uses of the euphemistically called "night soil" (Ferguson 2014; Hanley 1997; Howell 2013; Walthall

1988). These studies show that since at least the sixteenth century, urban and rural citizens, as well as municipal and national governments in these places, saw human feces and urine as useful for agriculture, and even profitable. For instance, for landlords in eighteenth-century urban Japan, the income from human excrement sometimes exceeded that from rent (Howell 2013: 144). The use and circulation of night soil constituted a valuable part of the economy, agriculture, and health conditions in these countries even until the early twentieth century. David Howell (2013) argues that, although people saw human excrement as "yucky," they did not see it as "pollution" in symbolic and categorical terms, and the people who handled the waste did not become social outcasts (146). As he evocatively states, "even useful shit is still yucky; but its utility trumps its yuckiness" (138).

As this statement points out, the value of night soil in places such as Japan and China in previous centuries derived from its utility; it was not for environmental reasons (Howell 2013: 147–48; Iwabuchi 2004). As times changed, the usefulness and efficiency of night soil application decreased, and as of 2014, Japan was hardly reusing the organic waste in its sewage (JSWA n.d.). But there is momentum again in Japan and elsewhere to try to make use of human waste matter, this time for "green" causes. With climate change and the depletion of natural resources, actors such as international agencies, corporations, and governments are investing increasing energy into developing waste circulation systems such as ecological sanitation (ecosan) toilets that turn night soil into fertilizer, technologies that create biomass energy out of sewage sludge, and other initiatives—including a Danish music festival where the urine of festivalgoers will be used to fertilize the barley that will make the beer for future guests (Fraunhofer 2012; NEDO 2011; Russell 2015; WHO n.d.).[5] While the use of human and other waste is not a new phenomenon, its re-emergence today appears in an era of environmental concerns. It is in this context, in addition to Ananaikyō framings, that OISCA's activities can be understood.

A leading proponent of ecosan initiatives, Steven A. Esrey (2002: 1), argued that ecosan is "about a way of life, and how we should live on this planet, not just about how toilets should be different." His view resonates with the mission voiced by OISCA's founder and aid workers: that the importance of the circulation of waste lies in particular values and ways of living that can usher in a sustainable future. One component in Esrey's formulation is particularly relevant in looking at OISCA. He explains that "ecosan is a closed-loop ecosystem approach," in which there are no external inputs or outputs to the system (ibid.: 2). In other words, the ideal environment here is one that is enclosed and controlled—therefore, as I suggest, one that requires discipline. To ensure that no input or output is required, life in this system would need to adhere to particular rules about production, consumption, and waste treatment. If we consider this requirement for a successful circulation of waste, we can see why some scholars believe that the widespread use of night soil today is nearly impossible, since no society can ensure that communities and individuals do not dump toxic materials down the drains (Rockefeller 1998: 18). To state the point in another way: small-scale environments in which discipline could be demanded from all its members might be where the circulation of waste as a technology and a way of life could, perhaps, be achieved.

In this sense, it seems to me that what makes the movement of waste in OISCA a kind of sociality rather than just a form of waste management is the small scale in which it is impossible to avoid the bodily sense and importance of discipline in consuming the products of our waste. In contrast to forms of anonymous "mass waste" whose connections to the beings that produced them are obscured (Reno 2014: 17), small-scale environments confront us with the fact that waste matter shapes persons and relations in intimate ways (see also Parreñas 2016). Arun Agrawal's (2005) concept of environmentality is relevant here, as it shows how regimes of environmental management mobilize not only technologies of rule and politics by other means, but also forms of "intimate government" in which people's subjectivities are molded through everyday practices (see also Hawkins 2006; cf. Blaser 2009; Brosius 1999; Escobar 1995). One difference is that Agrawal's theory derives from a Foucauldian analysis of (neo)liberal government and self-governance, whereas in OISCA the making of persons is not framed by liberal traditions, but rather, in nonliberal and spiritual terms (Watanabe 2014). Yet, for the purposes of this article, environmentality's dual focus on intimacies and the regulation of people's actions speaks to what I aim to evoke in the circulatory sociality in the OISCA training center—namely, the primacy of intimate relations that become possible only through a collective discipline around the circulation of waste.

The awareness of waste transformed into fertilizer, and then food, created a sensation of proximity with other people, the animals, and the environment itself. Yet intimacy can be a suffocating thing. The lack of interpersonal distance that this environment created meant that it was impossible to have nonconforming spaces. Critiques of the organization and lifestyle were difficult because there was no room for external perspectives. To make a circulatory sociality possible, it was not necessary to reduce waste, but we did have to control what kind of waste was produced and how we lived with it. Discipline became paramount and this was not just a form of behavioral regulation, but an affective condition. Watching what we ate—only products from our fields—and how we disposed of the remains stirred feelings of constraint. Pigpens and chicken coops had to be cleaned thoroughly and regularly to avoid excrement from becoming sources of disease, an exhausting task. The interpersonal, environmental, and collective intimacy of the circulatory sociality of waste went hand in hand with a disciplinary lifestyle—the pleasures of intimacy were possible because of the discipline, and most likely, vice versa. The strict rules of communal and sustainable living were acceptable because we also felt that we belonged together. "We are like family," many of the trainees and staffers told me repeatedly. In such an environment, it was difficult to challenge the system, given that it was what made us close. It was also risky to deviate from the discipline because it was what kept waste circulating, intimately, instead of putrefying in place. We were cogs in the machine of the movement of waste, embodying the possibilities of a sustainable future.

* * *

And so, I hold my breath and continue to weed with the Burmese staff members, trying to keep in my mind the vision of waste becoming our food, the vision of a sustainable world as intimately connected as we are in this training center.

Acknowledgments

I am grateful to the trainees and staffers at OISCA, especially those in the Myanmar training center, for making this project possible. The research was funded by the Social Science Research Council and Cornell University. Feedback on earler drafts from Sarah Grant and Gökçe Günel helped strengthen the article. I also thank the reviewers, Peter Kirby and Annie Claus, as well as Melissa Caldwell, whose incisive comments were critical in sharpening my arguments.

Notes

1 Scholars of religion in Japan have often defined "new religions" (*shinshūkyō*) as those that were established between the early 19th century to the early 1950s. Ananaikyō was established in 1948, and would thus fall under this category. Shimazono (1992) calls religious groups that were established or rose to prominence after the 1970s and 1980s "new new religions" (*shin-shinshūkyō*).

2 I put "Shinto" in quotation marks because, as scholars have shown, Shinto as a religion or nonreligion, and as an ecological tradition, is a historical and political product (see, e.g., Hardacre 1989; Josephson 2012; Kuroda 1981; Thomas 2001).

3 Marie Lathers (2006) makes an interesting argument in her analysis of women primatologists' relationship with nonhuman waste, stating that these primatologists engage positively with primate excrement, making possible a shared sociality between humans and nonhumans, and thereby the potential for a posthumanist future. Reno (2014) makes a similar argument.

4 In Japan, people make a distinction between EM and *dochakukin* ("indigenous bacteria"), the former referring specifically to the formula produced in EMRO and the latter taken from local environments. In this analysis I do not make a distinction since the people at the Myanmar training center did not differentiate between the two terms.

5 Japanese NGOs are also promoting organized and hygienic night soil use among farmers in Myanmar, where individuals have been using human and animal waste for agricultural purposes but often without proper treatment (e.g., NICCO 2015). Although little reliable information exists on this topic, documents from international agencies as well as my own observations in rural central Myanmar indicate that night soil and animal manure have not been used systematically in agriculture in Myanmar (e.g., FAO n.d.; Myint 1989). Chemical fertilizers have been the norm so far.

References

Agrawal, Arun. 2005. *Environmentality: Technologies of Government and the Making of Subjects.* Durham, NC: Duke University Press.

Anderson, Warwick. 1995. "Excremental Colonialism: Public Health and the Poetics of Pollution." *Critical Inquiry* 21(3): 640–69.

———. 2010. "Crap on the Map, or Postcolonial Waste." *Postcolonial Studies* 13(2): 169–78.

Bataille, Georges. 1991[1967]. The Accursed Share, vol. 1. *New York: Zone Books.*

Blaser, Mario. 2009. "The Threat of the Yrmo: The Political Ontology of a Sustainable Hunting Program." *American Anthropologist* 111(1): 10–20.

Brosius, J. Peter. 1999. "Green Dots, Pink Hearts: Displacing Politics from the Malaysian Rain Forest." *American Anthropologist* 101(1): 36–57.

Chakrabarty, Dipesh. 1991. "Open Space/Public Space: Garbage, Modernity and India." *South Asia* 14(1): 15–31.

Cordell, Dana, Jan-Olof Drangert, and Stuart White. 2009. "The Story of Phosphorus: Global Food Security and Food for Thought." *Global Environmental Change* 19: 292–305.

Douglas, Mary. 2002[1966]. *Purity and Danger.* New York: Routledge.

Escobar, Arturo. 1995. *Encountering Development: The Making and Unmaking of the Third World.* Princeton, NJ: Princeton University Press.

Esrey, Steven A. 2002. "Ecosan: The Big Picture." Paper presented at the first International Conference on Ecological Sanitation, Nanning, China, November 5–8, 2001. www.ecosanres.org/.../ Esrey%20Ecosan%20the%20Big%20Picture.pdf (accessed 6/25/2015).

Esty, Joshua. 1999. "Excremental Postcolonialism." *Contemporary Literature* 40(1): 22–59.

Evans, David, Hugh Campbell, and Anne Murcott. 2013. *Waste Matters: New Perspectives on Food and Society*. Oxford: Blackwell-Wiley.

Ferguson, Dean T. 2014. "Nightsoil and the 'Great Divergence': Human Waste, the Urban Economy, and Economic Productivity, 1500–1900." *Journal of Global History* 9(3): 379–402.

Fraunhofer. 2012. "Using Wastewater as Fertilizer." *Research News*. August 1. www.fraunhofer.de/en/ press/research-news/2012/august/ using-wastewater-as-fertilizer.html (accessed 9/3/2014).

Food and Agriculture Organization (FAO). N.d. *Report on the Formulation of a National Water Vision to Action in the Union of Myanmar*. Prepared by a Special Working Team established by the Ministry of Agriculture and Irrigation and related agencies of the Government of the Union of Myanmar, in cooperation with Le Huu Ti and Thierry Facon. www.fao.org/docrep/008/ae546e/ ae546e04.htm (accessed 6/25/2015).

Goddard, Nicholas. 1996. " 'A Mine of Wealth'? The Victorians and the Agricultural Value of Sewage." *Journal of Historical Geography* 22(3): 274–90.

Hanley, Susan B. 1997. *Everyday Things in Premodern Japan: The Hidden Legacy of Material Culture*. Berkeley: University of California Press.

Hardacre, Helen. 1989. *Shinto and the State, 1868–1988*. Princeton, NJ: Princeton University Press.

Hawkins, Gay. 2006. *The Ethics of Waste: How We Relate to Rubbish*. Lanham, MD: Rowman & Littlefield.

Hetherington, Kevin. 2004. "Secondhandedness: Consumption, Disposal, and Absent Presence." *Environment and Planning D: Society and Space* 22: 157–73.

Howell, David. 2013. "Fecal Matters: Prolegomenon to a History of Shit in Japan." In *Japan at Nature's Edge: The Environmental Context of a Global Power*, ed. Ian Jared Miller, Julia Adeney Thomas, and Brett L. Walker, 137–51. Honolulu: University of Hawai'i Press.

Iwabuchi Reiji. 2004. "Edo no gomi shori saikō: 'Risaikuru toshi,' 'seiketsu toshi' zō o koete" [Rethinking Waste Disposal in Edo: Beyond Images of "the Recycling City" and "the Hygienic City"]. *Kokuritsu Rekishi Minzoku Hakubutsukan kenkyū kiyō* 118: 301–36.

Japan Sewage Works Association (JSWA). N.d. "*Statistical Data*." www.jswa.jp/data-room/data.html (accessed 8/27/2014).

Jewitt, Sarah. 2011. "Geographies of Shit: Spatial and Temporal Variations in Attitudes towards Human Waste." *Progress in Human Geography* 35(5): 608–26.

Josephson, Jason A. 2012. *The Invention of Religion in Japan*. Chicago: University of Chicago Press.

Kalland, Arne, and Pamela J. Asquith. 1997. "Japanese Perceptions of Nature: Ideals and Illusions." In *Japanese Images of Nature: Cultural Perspectives*, ed. Pamela J. Asquith and Arne Kalland, 1–35. Surrey, UK: Curzon.

Kirby, Peter Wynn. 2011. *Troubled Natures: Waste, Environment, Japan*. Honolulu: University of Hawai'i Press.

Knight, John. 1996. "When Timber Grows Wild: The Desocialisation of Japanese Mountain Forests." In *Nature and Society: Anthropological Perspectives*, ed. Philippe Descola and Gísli Pálsson, 221–39. London: Routledge.

Kuroda, Toshio. 1981. "Shinto in the History of Japanese Religion." *Japanese Journal of Religious Studies* 7(1): 1–21.

Lathers, Marie. 2006. "Toward an Excremental Posthumanism: Primatology, Women, and Waste." *Society & Animals* 14(4): 417–36.

McFarlane, C. 2008. "Governing the Contaminated City: Infrastructure and Sanitation in Colonial and Postcolonial Bombay." *International Journal of Urban and Regional Research* 32(2): 415–35.

Ministry of the Environment. 1994. *Kankyō Kihon Keikaku* [Basic Environment Plan]. www.env.go.jp/ policy/kihon_keikaku/plan/ main.html (accessed 6/16/2015).

———. 2000. *Junkangata Shakai Keisei Suishin Kihonhō* [Fundamental Plan for Establishing a Sound Material-Cycle Society]. www.env.go. jp/recycle/circul/kihonho/law.html (accessed 6/16/2015).

Myint, Cho Cho. 1989. "Nature Farming in Myanmar." Paper presented at the First International Conference on Kyusei Nature Farming, October 17–19, 1989. International Nature Farming

Research Center. www.infrc.or.jp/english/KNF_Data_Base_Web/PDF%20KNF%20Conf%20Data/C1–3–005.pdf (accessed 6/25/2015).

Nakano, Yonosuke. 1963. Sangyō no Shūkyō [The Religion of Industry]. Tokyo: Bunkasha.

New Energy and Industrial Technology Development Organization (NEDO). 2011. *Gesui odei kara nenryō gas wo kaishū/hatsuden: Sekaihatsu no gesui odei gas ka hatsuden shisetsu* [Collecting Fuel Gas and Creating Energy from Sewage Sludge: The World's First Sludge Gas Energy Facility]. October 2011. www.nedo.go.jp/hyoukabu/articles/201103metawater/index.html (accessed 6/23/2015).

NICCO. 2015. "Myanmar shōsūminzoku shien: Ecosan toire kengakukai" [Assistance for Myanmar Ethnic Minorities: Training in Ecosan Toilets]. *NICCO blog,* Feburary 17. http://kyoto-nicco. seesaa. net/article/414200441.html (accessed 6/24/2015).

O'Brien, Martin. 1999. "Rubbish Values: Reflections on the Political Economy of Waste." *Science as Culture* 8(3): 269–95.

Organization for Industrial, Spiritual and Cultural Advancement (OISCA). N.d. "OISCA ga mezasu mono" [What OISCA Aims For]. www.oisca.org/about/ (accessed 7/1/2015).

Parreñas, Juno Salazar. 2016. "The Materiality of Intimacy in Wildlife Rehabilitation: Rethinking Ethical Capitalism through Embodied Encounters with Animals in Southeast Asia." *positions: asia critique* 24(1): 97–127

Reno, Joshua Ozias. 2014. "Toward a New Theory of Waste: From 'Matter Out of Place' to Signs of Life." *Theory, Culture & Society* 31(6): 3–27.

Rockefeller, Abby A. 1998. "Civilization and Sludge: Notes on the History of the Management of Human Excreta." *Capitalism, Nature, Socialism* 9(3): 3–18.

Russell, Helen. 2015. "Out on the Piss? Danish Festival Recycles Urine to Make Beer." *The Guardian.* July 2. http://gu.com/p/4aa8g/sbl (accessed 7/3/2015).

Satō Kenkyūjo. N.d. "Mikawa Kankyō Biseibutsu" [Mikawa Environmental Microorganisms]. www10. ocn.ne.jp/~tamagoya/ satou_labo.htm#aisatsu (accessed 9/3/2014).

Scanlan, John. 2005. *On Garbage.* London: Reaktion Books.

Shimazono, Susumu. 1992. *Shin-shinshūkyō to shūkyō būmu* [New-new religions and the rise of Religions]. Tokyo: Iwanami Shoten.

Thomas, Julia A. 2001. *Reconfiguring Modernity: Concepts of Nature in Japanese Political Ideology.* Berkeley: University of California Press.

Thornber, Karen. 2013. "Japanese Literature and Environmental Crises." In *Japan at Nature's Edge: The Environmental Context of a Global Power*, ed. Ian Jared Miller, Julia Adeney Thomas, and Brett L. Walker, 207–21. Honolulu: University of Hawai'i Press.

Walthall, Anne. 1988. "Village Networks: *Sōdai* and the Sale of Edo Nightsoil." *Monumenta Nipponica* 43(3): 279–303.

Watanabe, Chika. 2014. "Muddy Labor: A Japanese Aid Ethic of Collective Intimacy in Myanmar." *Cultural Anthropology* 29(4): 648–71.

———. 2015. "The Politics of Nonreligious Aid: A Japanese Environmental Ethic in Myanmar." In *Religion and the Politics of Development*, ed. Robin Bush, Michael Feener, and Philip Fountain, 225–42. London: Palgrave Macmillan.

World Health Organization (WHO). N.d. "Wastewater Use: Safe Use of Wastewater, Excreta and Greywater." www.who.int/water_sanitation_health/wastewater/en/ (accessed 9/3/2014).

18

Arts of Inclusion, or How to Love a Mushroom

Anna Tsing

Next time you walk through a forest, look down. A city lies under your feet. If you were somehow to descend into the earth, you would find yourself surrounded by the city's architecture of webs and filaments. Fungi make those webs as they interact with the roots of trees, forming joint structures of fungus and root called mycorrhiza. Mycorrhizal webs connect not just root and fungus, but also—by way of fungal filaments—tree and tree, in forest entanglements. This city is a lively scene of action and interaction. There are many ways here to eat and to share food. There are recognizable forms of hunting. For example, some fungi lasso little soil worms called nematodes for dinner. But this is one of the crudest ways to enjoy a meal. Experts in refinement, the mycorrhizal fungi siphon energy-giving sugars from trees. Some of those sugars are redistributed through the fungal network from tree to tree. Others support dependent plants, such as mushroom-loving mycophiles that tap the network to send out pale or colorful stems of flowers (e.g., Indian pipes, coral-root orchids). Meanwhile, like an inside-out stomach, fungi secrete enzymes into the soil around them, digesting organic material—and even rocks—and absorbing nutrients that are released in the process. These nutrients are also available for trees and other plants, which use them to produce more sugar for themselves—and for the network.

Throughout this process, there is a whole lot of smelling going on, as plants, animals, and fungi sniff out not just good meals but also good partners. And what wonderful smells, even for an animal nose, like mine! (Some fungi, such as truffles, depend on animals to smell out their reproductive bodies, to spread around their spores.) Reach down and smell a clot of forest earth; it smells like the underground city of fungi.

As with human cities, this underground city is a site of cosmopolitan transactions. Unfortunately, humans have mainly ignored this lively cosmopolitanism. We have built our human cities through destruction and simplification, chopping down forests and replacing them with food-growing plantations while we live on asphalt and concrete. In agribusiness plantations, we coerce plants to grow without the assistance of other beings, including fungi in the soil. We replace fungally supplied nutrients with fertilizers obtained from the mining and chemical industries, with their trails of pollution and exploitation. We breed our crops by isolating them in chemical stews, crippling them, like caged and beakless chickens. We maim and simplify crop plants until they no longer know how to participate in multispecies worlds. One of the many extinctions that result from all this planning is the cosmopolitanism of the underground city. And almost no one notices, because so few humans even know of the existence of that city.

Yet a good many of those few who do notice fungi love them with a breathless passion. Gourmets, herbalists, and those who would remediate world ecology often become devotees of the fungal world. Wild mushroom foragers praise their unexpected bounty, their colors, tastes, and smells, and their promise of a livelihood from the woods. How many times have foragers told me of the heat of "mushroom fever," which drives them to dodge their other obligations to take up the wild thrill of the chase? Even commercial agents are giddy with the unpredictability of deals involving a capricious commodity. Scientists who study fungi rave about them in a manner quite dissimilar to scholars of fruit flies or HeLa cells. And, while some fungal devotees are content with personal association with fungi, others long to share their passion with the world.

How do lovers of fungi practice *arts of inclusion* that call to others? In these times of extinction, when even slight acquaintance can make the difference between preservation and callous disregard, we might want to know.

Noticing

Henning Knudsen, curator of fungi at Copenhagen University's Botanical Museum, shows me around the fungi collection at the herbarium in April 2008. At first the aisles seem neat and impersonal. Then we open the folded envelopes and expose dried specimens, each named and labeled by its collector. Hiding in their dust lie the shriveled but still talking mushrooms, carrying their names and the names of their collectors into the story of life on earth.

Taxonomy is not very popular these days; indeed, detractors think of it as dry classification that spoils all enjoyment. But handling the specimens at the herbarium, it is easy to feel the pleasure of naming. Here, through naming, we *notice* the diversity of life. Taxonomy was once closely allied with drawing, another art of noticing. (See page 193, left.)[1]

Northern Europe, including Britain, is the homeground of amateur as well as scientific botanizing, the collecting and naming of plants. Still, noticing fungi did not come easily, Dr. Knudsen explains, because northern Europeans have despised mushrooms—perhaps a reminder of their pagan past. It took a nineteenth-century French-born monarch of Sweden, Karl Johan, to bring even the prized king bolete (also, cep or porcini) to the attention of Scandinavians—and the mushroom is still known by his name. Besides, fungi are difficult to collect and identify because their bodies tend to be underground. Only their reproductive organs—the mushrooms—come up into the air, and those only sporadically, sometimes in intervals of many years.

Dr. Knudsen tells me about Elias Fries (1794–1878), the father of modern systematic mycology. Like Linneas, Fries was a Swede and a lover of plants; Fries extended Linnean botany to the world of fungi. His work was made possible through a combination of his extraordinary memory and extraordinary passion. He recognized five thousand species, remembering them from year to year across the mushroom-empty times. Many of the specimens he collected were from near the village where he was born and first learned to love mushrooms. Dr. Knudsen remembers Fries' account of his early, persistent love. When, as a boy, he found an enormous specimen of the species *Tricholoma collosum,* he was thrilled: "I love my sister, I love my father, but this is better." Dr. Knudsen gives me a copy of Fries' memoir, which has been translated from Latin to English. Equally passionate love stories jump from the page:

> To this day, more than half a century later, I remember with gratitude the admiration that seized me when in 1806 I went with my mother to a burnt-down forest to pick strawberries and there I succeeded in finding an unusually large specimen of Hydnum coralloides, which was the first thing that induced me to study fungi. (Fries 1955: 140–141)

Afterwards, Fries *noticed* fungi everywhere and, indeed, devoted his life to noticing them. Through his taxonomy, Fries brought fungi to public attention. His enthusiasm encouraged the founding of a line of systematic mycologists, to which Dr. Knudsen—mushroom sociologist and coeditor of *Nordic Macromycetes*—is an heir.[2]

The line of mycologists stretches far beyond northern Europe. Consider the polymath naturalist Minakata Kumagusu (1867–1941), remembered for offering the Emperor of Japan a box of horse manure—containing interesting species of slime mold.[3] Minakata's watercolors bring together art and taxonomy. They guide our attention. The colors swirl; the fungi pose; the herbarium is alive. (See page 193, right.)[4]

Noticing inspires artists as well as naturalists. American composer John Cage (1912–1992) was a mushroom hunter who believed noticing mushrooms and noticing sounds in music were related skills. In contrast to other musicians, Cage wanted a music that forced listeners to attend to *all* the sounds around them, whether composed or incidental. Teaching and writing about mushrooms helped him explain how to practice an open yet focused attention. In one of his compositions, *Indeterminacy,* one-minute-long paragraphs, thoughts, and anecdotes are read aloud in random order—sometimes to the accompaniment of dance or music. Indeterminacy is exemplified in many levels of open-endedness. Many of the stories are about people's interactions with mushrooms. Mushrooms, too, are unpredictable; they help one listen and pay attention. In his entry #113, Cage is explicit:[5]

> Music   and   mushrooms:
>   two words next to one
> another   in   many   dictionaries.
>   Where   did   he
>   write   *The   Three-Penny   Opera*?
>   Now   he's
>   buried below the grass at the
>   foot   of   High   Tor.
>   Once   the   season   changes
>   from   summer   to   fall,
>   given   sufficient   rain,
>   or   just   the
>   mysterious   dampness   that's   in   the
>   earth,   mushrooms
>   grow   there,

carrying   on,   I
   am   sure,   his
   business   of   working   with
sounds.
                        That   we
   have   no   ears   to   hear   the
     music   the   spores   shot   off
     from   basidia   make   obliges   us
     to   busy   ourselves   microphonically.

Basidia are part of mushroom reproductive organs; from basidia, spores are "shot off" into the air. One mushroom, called the "cannonball fungus" (*Sphaerobolus stellatus*), throws out its spore mass (but not from basidia) with a sometimes-audible pop. For most mushrooms, however, the shooting off of spores cannot be heard by human ears. Even in the sounds we miss, Cage wants us to find inspiration for music.

The parsed, anecdotal style of *Indeterminacy* is reminiscent of other formal poetics, such as haiku. Noticing mushrooms—especially those aromatic delights Japanese call matsutake—has not escaped haiku poets as a subject. Recognition of indeterminacy similarly guides the haiku, as in this poem by Kyorai Mukai (1651–1704):[6]

Matsutake yo hito
Ni toraruru hana no saki

Matsutake;
Taken by someone else
Right in front of my nose.

Matsutake (*Tricholoma matsutake* and allies) are much-loved mushrooms in Japan. They cannot be cultivated, so they draw mushroom lovers into the forest to search for them. Matsutake are difficult to spot. Always it seems that the matsutake we are about to find has been taken by another. We must look more carefully.

The poem's phrasing and sound draw us into a world where we are able to notice. Even this one valued species group, matsutake, can inspire cosmopolitan worlds of mushroom loving. Kyorai's poem can spur us to consider matsutake worlds—and their arts of inclusion.

Conjuring Matsutake Worlds: Toward a Democratic Science

Under the name of Matsiman (Americans sometimes call matsutake *matsi*), Andy Moore has dedicated his life to producing and spreading knowledge about matsutake mushrooms. Moore is not a commercial producer; matsutake cannot be cultivated. He is not a gourmet cook; he doesn't even like the taste and smell of matsutake. He is not a trained scientist, although he participates in matsutake-oriented science. Rather, his goal is to make knowledge accessible. He wants a democratic, inclusive science. Through attention to matsutake, he spreads knowledge—and his vision of democratic science. On his website, Matsiman.com, Moore posts everything he can find about matsutake and prompts discussions about mushroom worlds.

Matsutake inhabit northern hemisphere forests, associating particularly with conifers such as pine. It's a wide-ranging species group, with populations stretching across Eurasia, down through North Africa, and across the Atlantic into Canada, the United States, and Mexico. In most of the places where the mushrooms grow, people do not enjoy them as a food. Europeans first called them *Tricholoma nauseosum* to indicate their dislike of the smell. (U.S. mushroomer David Aurora [1986:191] describes the smell as "a provocative compromise between 'red hots' and dirty socks.") But for many Japanese, the smell is enticing. Grilled or cooked in soup, matsutake are an expensive gourmet treat as well as a reminder of the beauty of the autumn season.

Until the 1970s, Japanese pine forests produced a rich complement of matsutake. But pine forests, associated with village life, declined after World War II. In this same period, Japanese incomes rose. In the 1980s, Japan began importing matsutake from around the world. The prices were high; mushroom entrepreneurs rushed to enter the fray. At first, Japanese in the diaspora who had found mushrooms for their own use abroad guided Japan's imports. But soon enough, all kinds of people were picking matsutake—whether or not they enjoyed the mushroom for their own use.

Andy Moore was one of these people. Originally from Louisiana, he found his way into the Oregon woods during the U.S. war in Vietnam. Having enlisted as a soldier, he was disillusioned by what he saw and experienced there. He felt lucky when he managed to aggravate a childhood injury and was sent home. Based in the U.S., he drove a jeep at a marine base. But one day he received word that he was to be sent back to Southeast Asia. He was not willing to go. With pride, he recounts how he returned the jeep, walked out of the gates, and declared himself AWOL ("absent without leave"). To avoid capture, he ran to the mountains, where he made a living in various kinds of forest work, such as cutting firewood. He loved the forest. The experience gave him a new goal: "To live in the woods and never pay rent."

At the very end of the 1980s, matsutake madness came to the U.S. Pacific Northwest. The woods filled with pickers. Matsutake buyers set up tents by the side of the road, eager to export the mushrooms to Japan. Japan at that time was still wealthy from the boom economy; prices were very good; and pickers hoped to strike it rich with "white gold." Moore tried picking and found it very much to his liking.

Moore had an ideal situation for picking—and studying—the mushrooms. He had obtained a position as the caretaker for a large private forest. He lived in a small cabin at the top of the property, and his job allowed him plenty of time and opportunity to explore. He discovered matsutake on his property just waiting to be picked. Because matsutake has a long-term relationship with particular trees, the best way to pick is to go to the same trees every year to see if there are mushrooms. But most pickers in the U.S. Pacific Northwest pick on national forests with open access; they go back to the same trees, but, often enough, other pickers have beat them to the harvest. ("Matsutake / Taken by someone else / Right in front of my nose"!) Moore's situation was unique: he had a large forest area to harvest, and a locked gate to keep out other harvesters.

The situation awakened his curiosity about the mushrooms. When the fungus is not fruiting, the area around even the most heavily mycorrhizal trees is empty and unpromising; suddenly and unexpectedly mushrooms spring up. What factors control when mushrooms appear? Moore knew various contradictory rumors about this question, but there seemed to be no solid, experimental knowledge. So he decided to start his own experiment. Because other pickers did not intrude on his haven, he was able to mark all the spots where matsutake appeared. Then he was able to keep records of exactly when they appeared, how many, what weight, and their price. These records could be correlated with rainfall, temperature, and other factors.

Moore did not have either training or mentoring for his experiments. He simply started doing them. Later, he worked with U.S. Forest Service researchers on their projects and became a coauthor of several papers. But in those circumstances he was an assistant, without the ability to frame questions or suggest methods. On his own, he was forced to invent science using his own means. Obscure terminology, standardized scales, and sophisticated testing procedures hardly seemed necessary to him. Instead, he started with the questions pickers want to know: when and where do the mushrooms appear?

With some startling results in hand (his mushrooms responded to temperature not rainfall), Moore decided to make his results public. In 1998, Moore opened the Matsiman.com website. The site was not, however, designed to be Moore's personal blog; instead, he facilitated the making and exchange of knowledge. Everyone, the site suggests, can do research; all it takes is curiosity. The site poses the question, "Who is Matsiman?"

Anyone who loves hunting, learning, understanding, protecting, educating others, and respects matsutake mushroom and its habitat is matsiman. Those of us who can't get enough understanding, constantly trying to determine what caused this or that to happen, or not happen. We are not limited to nationality, gender, education, or age group. Anyone can be a matsiman. There is at least one in every picking community.

To appreciate the extraordinary nature of this public knowledge, it is important to allow Moore his eccentricities. His forest-caretaker position has ended, but he has found a job as a campground host, which allows him to live year-round in a motor home as a steward of public lands. To live in the woods and never pay rent!

He tries out various mushroom-based commodities, such as smoked mushroom seasoning and dried mushroom snacks. It seems unlikely that such experiments generate much of an income, but they keep Moore's exuberance for mushrooms high. Meanwhile, there is nothing proprietary about any of the many ideas he generates. He believes that all knowledge should be accessible; the Matsiman site builds a community of knowledge. Moore loves nothing better than to introduce new people to the world of matsutake, whether through his site or as a visitor to the forests he knows well. I spent a very happy time learning about Moore's matsutake under tanoak, Shasta red fir, and pine.

Conjuring Matsutake Worlds: Toward More Inclusive Modes of Well-being

Now consider a different mushroom-based project of inclusion: an appeal to matsutake to help us build models of well-being in which humans and nonhumans alike might thrive. The charismatic and energetic organizer Fumihiko Yoshimura has been studying and working with matsutake for most of his life. As a scientist, Dr. Yoshimura conducts some of his work in laboratories and forest field sites. But he is also founder of the Matsutake Crusaders, a Kyoto-based citizens' initiative to revitalize Japan's matsutake forests. The Matsutake Crusaders are volunteers; their job is sculpting the forest to bring back the health of red pine with its associate, matsutake. Matsutake here is not just a delicious food; it is also a valued participant in a world of ecological well-being. The Crusaders' motto is "Let's revitalize the forest so we can all eat *sukiyaki*." *Sukiyaki* (a meat and vegetable stew best made with matsutake) is a popular and traditional food. Sometimes *sukiyaki* is eaten on festive occasions and sometimes during outings in which urbanites enjoy the fresh air. Eating together in appreciation of the natural world, people revitalize their selves as well as their forests. Dr. Yoshimura's movement brings participants into the countryside to offer new vitality to the world.

Dr. Yoshimura draws on a long legacy of applied matsutake science in Japan. Minoru Hamada deserves credit for making matsutake an object of modern science in the twentieth century. Dr. Hamada designed matsutake research to address basic biological questions while simultaneously promoting the production of a valued economic product. After World War II, Dr. Hamada trained a cohort of matsutake researchers who in turn trained many of today's researchers. Makoto Ogawa, one of Dr. Hamada's students, was particularly effective in spreading matsutake research by convincing the government to send matsutake researchers to every prefectural forestry station.[7] Dr. Yoshimura spent most of his career in Iwate prefecture conducting matsutake research and promoting matsutake.

While researchers have successfully grown matsutake mycelia and even matsutake-pine mycorrhiza in laboratories, no one has succeeded in getting these cultivated stocks to produce a mushroom. The focus in promoting matsutake, therefore, has been to make the kind of forest where matsutake likes to live. In Japan, matsutake associates with red pine, *Pinus densiflora*, a pioneer species of disturbed areas. For many centuries, villagers in Japan have created disturbed forests by shifting cultivation and selective harvesting of broadleaf trees that are used for firewood and charcoal. Villagers have traditionally also collected herbs and grass, and raked leaves for green fertilizer. These practices left bright, open hillsides of exposed soils—the conditions preferred by red pine and its partner, matsutake.

All this changed after World War II. Villagers started to use fossil fuels for heating and tractors instead of oxen for plowing. People no longer collected firewood to make charcoal, or gathered leaves and grass. Young people moved to the city, and village forests were neglected. Broadleaf trees grew back with a vengeance, shading out pines; furthermore, pines were weakened by a wilt disease spread by an imported nematode. In the deep shade of the neglected broadleaf forests, pines died. Without their hosts, matsutake also expired. Many matsutake lovers described hillsides they had seen white with mushrooms when they were children, now without a single host pine.

By the 1970s, urbanites became nostalgic for the village forests of their youth—places to see wildflowers in spring, fireflies in summer, and the leaves changing in autumn.[8] Citizens' movements emerged to address the impoverished environment of modern Japan. Unlike wilderness advocates in the United States, many Japanese focused on the lively ecologies of sites that had long experienced human disturbance: the verges of roads, the flood plains of rivers, village irrigation networks and rice paddies—and the open village forest. In these disturbed sites, something that might be called a sustainable relationship between humans and nonhumans could be imagined. Preservation came to mean not human withdrawal from nature but rather guided disturbance. In the process of studying ancient methods of disturbance, modern citizens educated themselves about being in nature.

It was from this milieu that Dr. Yoshimura's Matsutake Crusaders emerged. The name of the group is derived from the popular mobilization effort of the 1980s, known as the Woodland Maintenance Crusaders, in which student volunteers removed grass and weeds that were choking the forest.[9] Dr. Yoshimura's group has the added excitement of not just fixing the forest but also, possibly, producing tasty mushrooms. His methods are to promote the growth of pine by removing evergreen broadleaves completely, thus opening hillsides to light. As the pines come back, the hillsides become open forests where wildflowers, rabbits, and hawks can find niches. But no one can guarantee mushrooms. The volunteers must do the work for the love of nature, not just for matsutake.

All of this leads me to a Saturday in June 2006, when my research collaborator Shiho Satsuka and I joined the Crusaders for a day of forest work and play. The site was a steep hillside that had become choked with young evergreen broadleaves. The many slender trees were so close together that a person could not peer very far into the forest, much less walk through it. Our task, Dr. Yoshimura explained, was to clear the land so that only red pine would grow. When Dr. Satsuka and I arrived, a group of men were busy removing trees and shrubs. Surprisingly, to me, they were even digging out the roots of the broadleaf trees. It was labor-intensive work, all done with hand tools, and I realized it would take years to clear even this one mountain. Still, everyone there was cheerful and full of enthusiasm.

Dr. Yoshimura showed us the adjoining hillside, which after much work was open, bright, and green with pine. "This is what our hillside might have looked like in earlier days," he explained. Animals and birds had settled in—and there was hope for mushrooms. Meanwhile, other projects were underway: a garden; a charcoal-making kiln; and a beetle-breeding mound for hobbyists. At the base of the hill was a place to eat, relax, and talk. At lunchtime, the workers sweating on the hill came down. Their colleagues had been constructing a long bamboo aqueduct for serving a special summer dish: noodles in the stream (or "flowing somen"). At the high end of the aqueduct, we poured hot steaming noodles into the cool running water. Everyone gathered around the bamboo "stream" and grabbed the flowing noodles with their chopsticks, mixing them with sauces in ready bowls. There was much joking and laughter. I met rural landowners and urban housewives, and even an anthropology graduate student. Someone offered an amusing haiku about coming from America. Someone else showed off the ingeniously handcrafted crabs he had made. A landowner showed pictures of his property, which he hoped to revitalize using Crusader techniques. We lingered long together before going back to work. This was a revitalization not just of the hillside but of our senses.

Loving in a Time of Extinction

The forms of love I have called up in this paper are diverse, even contradictory. Despite the fact that Andy Moore and Dr. Yoshimura are both concerned with matsutake mushrooms, they might find each other's practices strange. The sciences—and the social and natural ecologies in which they participate—are linked but not continuous in any simple way. I have written elsewhere about the glancing relationship between "forest ecologies" as observed and interpreted in Oregon and Kyoto (Tsing and Satsuka 2008; Tsing 2010). Here, I introduce these separate regions only to the extent that they inform our appreciation of each creative intervention. For Moore, the wild mushroom economy, with its encouragement of participation by people who love the woods, creates the possibilities for vernacular science. He works to free knowledge production from the rule of experts; anyone with a passionate curiosity can contribute. For Dr. Yoshimura, citizens' interest in environmental remediation offers the chance to build connections between human and nonhuman well-being. For him, efforts to re-sculpt forest landscapes make the volunteers happier and healthier, as they work for a more hospitable multispecies environment.

Both interventions contrast with the hegemonic, extinction-oriented practice of what might be called "plantation science." Plantation science teaches us to strive for control of human and nonhuman landscapes. For those who love wild mushrooms, full mastery is not the goal; *indeterminacy* is part of the point. Wherever volunteers gather to promote disturbance forests, or matsutake pickers stop to ponder why the mushrooms come up, plantation science loses a little authority.

In plantation science, managers and specialists make decisions; harvesters are never consulted about the crops. In plantation science, well-being is a formula defined at the top, and no one stops to ask, "Well-being for whom?" In plantation science, experts and their objects of expertise are separated by the will to power; love does not flow between expert and knowledge-object. In contrast, my stories describe how advocacy for mushrooms can lead to projects for building democratic science and publicly inclusive well-being. It's the passion for the mushroom—in all the details of its social-natural ecology—that makes these projects possible.

At the intersection between the sciences of nature and the sciences of culture, a new model is afoot, the key characteristic of which is multispecies love. Unlike earlier cultural studies of science, its raison d'être is not, mainly, the critique of science, although it can be critical. Instead, it encourages a new, passionate immersion in the lives of the nonhuman subjects being studied. Once, such immersion was allowed only to natural scientists, and mainly on the condition that the love didn't show. The critical intervention of this new form of science is that it encourages learnedness in natural science *along with* all the tools of the humanities and the arts. The objectives of those of us in this field are to open the public imagination to make new ways of relating to nature possible. For this, we need to summon the unexpected talents others—whether scientists or nonscientists—have brought to this task. My stories of mushroom lovers and their projects are a small contribution.

Notes

1   Jacob E. Lange, *Flora agaricina danica,* Volume 1, plate 7A,C. Published under the auspices of the Society for the Advancement of Mycology in Denmark and the Danish Botanical Society, Copenhagen, 1935–1940.

2   Lise Hansen and Henning Knudsen are coeditors of the three-volume *Nordic Macromycetes* (1992, 1997, 2000).

3   Alan Christy, personal communication 2008. See Blacker (2000).

4   Minakata Kumagusu, in *Minakata Kumagusu Kinrui Zufu: Colored Illustrations of Fungi.* Watariumu Bijiutsukan and Hiromitsu Hagiwara, eds. Tokyo, Shinchōsa, 2007, p. 76 (original 1921).

5   Mushroom-related sections of *Indeterminacy* can be found by going to www.mundusloci.org/ fungus/culture/cage2.htm. Also see the site www.lcdf.org/indeterminacy/index.cgi by Eddie Kohler. Since the stories are gathered from various Cage books and performances, put back together in new performances, they thwart the determinacy of standard citation practices.

6   Translated and published by Reginald Blyth (1973). For Cage performing a different matsutake haiku, see www.youtube.com/watch?v=XNzVQ8wRCB0.

7 See Tsing and Satsuka (2008) for citations and fuller treatment of this history.

8 The distinction between two kinds of broadleaf trees—deciduous and evergreen—is important in central Japan. Deciduous broadleaves are preferred for firewood and charcoal. Villagers selectively weeded out the evergreen broadleaves. Meanwhile, the deciduous broadleaves grew back from coppice shoots after harvesting, thus establishing their dominance in the forest architecture. This helped to keep forests bright and open. In the late twentieth century when no forest management was being done in many areas, evergreen broadleaves, no longer cut back, became the dominant forest vegetation. Besides discouraging pine and its associates, these new dark forests do not allow the familiar wildflowers, birds, and insects associated with earlier village forests. They also do not offer autumn colors.

9 See Nakagawa (2003, 114) for a discussion of these earlier Crusaders.

References

Arora, David. 1986. *Mushrooms Demystified: A Comprehensive Guide to the Fleshy Fungi.* Berkeley: Ten Speed Press.

Blacker, Carmen. 2000. "Minakata Kumagusu, 1867–1941: A Genius Now Recognized." In *Collected Writings*, 235–247. New York: Routledge.

Blyth, Reginald H. 1973. "Mushrooms in Japanese Verse." In *Transactions of the Asiatic Society of Japan*, Third series, 11(December):93–106.

Fries, Elias. 1955 [1857]. "A Short Account of My Mycological Study." Translated by Ib Magnussen and Annie Fausboll. *Friesia* 5(2):135–160.

Hansen, Lise, and Henning Knudsen, eds. 1992, 1997, 2000. *Nordic Macromycetes*, vols. 1, 2, and 3. Copenhagen: Nordsvamp.

Nakagawa, S. 2003. "Nationwide Partnerships for Satoyama Conservation." In *Satoyama: The Traditional Rural Landscape of Japan*, edited by K. Takeuchi, R.D. Brown, I. Washitani, A. Tsunekawa, and M. Yokohari, 111–119. Tokyo: Springer.

Tsing, Anna. 2010. "Worlding the Matsutake Diaspora, or, Can Actor-network Theory Experiment with Holism?" In *Experiments in Holism: Theory and Practice in Contemporary Anthropology*, edited by Ton Otto and Nils Bubandt, 53–76. Oxford: Wiley-Blackwell.

Tsing, Anna, and Shiho Satsuka. 2008. "Diverging Understandings of Forest Management in Matsutake Science." *Economic Botany* 62(3):244–256.

"Who Is Matsiman?" n.d. Accessed September 20, 2010. www.matsiman.com/ matsiman.htm.

19

How to Taste Like a Cow: Cultivating Shared Sense in Wisconsin Dairy Worlds

Katy Overstreet

Introduction

After the hay sale, Margie, her son Steve, and I sat down to drink tall frosty glasses of rootbeer. The weekly auction-style sale takes place in the parking lot of a gas station in rural southern Wisconsin. Half the gas station convenience store is dedicated to a fast food restaurant, which offers sodas, hot dogs, and hamburgers. Margie and Steve attend the hay sale every week to scout for bargains on hay bales for their approximately sixty-cow dairy herd. Margie gossiped with two of the auctioneers at the table next to ours as they ate hot dogs. Steve and I continued our conversation about how he chooses particular bales of hay to buy at the auction. Steve leans forward and says, "The best way to do that is find something that you would want to eat if you were a cow. You gotta think like a cow. Is this something you're gonna want to eat? Because if you're going to be willing to eat it then the cows will eat it. That's the way I do it."

Before the hay sale each week, Steve and the other buyers walk through the gas station parking lot, carefully assessing the qualities of the various hay bales. Several times I followed along with Steve as he examined the hay by sight, smell, touch, taste, and more. Through sensory cues he evaluated hays for nutritional value, freshness, digestibility, and palatability. While Steve references formalized knowledge such as research documents publicly available through University Extension as he considers nutritional values, Steve claims to assess palatability through "thinking like a cow." But what exactly does he mean by this? Certainly there is a sense of "cow" as a sentient and perhaps thinking "other" in Steve's description. But when Steve told me to "think like a cow," we were discussing feed specifically, rather than the general cognitive abilities of cows. Therefore, Steve means something along the lines of "thinking through the senses" (Classen 1993) and thus I will pose the question instead as: what does it mean to taste like a cow?

While many studies of animal agriculture argue that animal others are rendered as objects through their use for producing profit, I found through research among Wisconsin dairy farmers that even on farms of 500 or more cows, commodification was never complete; it was one among many ways of relating between humans and cows. Even during routine handling or painful interventions, cows were still understood to be subjects and on most dairy farm visits I found that at least some cows were known as individuals, pets, or family members. Over the course of almost two years of fieldwork with dairy farmers and dairy experts in primarily south-central Wisconsin, I participated in milking and chores on five farms and visited over 100 farms of varying sizes. I also rode along with experts important to many aspects of cow care including veterinarians, dairy nutritionists, extension agents, and siring specialists. I came to see how the "ontological choreography" or the coordination of various ontological orders legal, medical, religious, and otherwise (Thompson 2005) through which cows and humans are kept separate, at times becomes very messy. In other words, it was not always clear where cows ended and humans began. Traditionally, phenomenological and social science accounts of sensory experience, while at times engaging questions of intersubjectivity, or the social relations between beings that recognize each other as subjects, continue to confine sensory experience to individual bodies even while they show that senses are shaped through cultural values and culturally informed "modes of attention" (see for example Csordas 1993 and Grasseni 2009). Through examination of how farmers, dairy nutritionists, and cows select feed, I aim to show how senses, in this case a sense of taste, might be understood as something that transcends the assumed edges of individual species-bodies. As Steve tastes hay or as dairy nutritionists sample feed, they are working to taste not for *themselves* but for *others*. And thus they extend their sensorium towards that of cows. They do so through sedimented experience and skilled practice.

At the same time, cows, too, learn to taste. Cows on dairy farms in Wisconsin, also known as America's Dairyland, commonly eat substances that might have been unimaginable as a food for cows 100 years ago. Further, their diets are based heavily on grain in order to support high levels of milk production. In other words, they too have learned to eat cow feed. Therefore, the taste for cow feed is not-quite-human and not-quite-cow. It is heterogenous and recursive. Taste emerges recursively as humans observe what and how cows eat while cows eat feeds shaped by available industrial byproducts, ideas about the productive modern dairy cow, and local proclivities towards particular flavors. Through the circling kinds of eating and observations of others eating, taste moves through and across bodies: it is *transcorporeal*. Through an examination of how taste for cow feed emerges through practices of care, noticing, biopolitical control, and resistance, I aim to push for a sensory model that moves beyond phenomenological preoccupations with separable individual bodies as the base unit for sensory experience.

Cow Sense

As Steve walks through the hay sale, he attends to the qualities of hay bales through multiple forms of sensing. He examines hay bales visually before he approaches them, which enables him to skip a further assessment if he finds the bales on a particular trailer to be undesirable. Indeed the qualities of the bales are various although this is not always obvious from afar. The trailers are a hodge-podge ranging from those that lean and creak, revealing their age through rusty rails and cracked wood to ones that look almost new. The hay bales themselves range from large cylindrical "round bales" held together with plastic sheeting or twine to cuboid "square bales." Some bales are tightly packed while others seem to resemble almost a pile. They come in shades of yellow, green, and brown, some dry and pale from sun exposure and others holding richer colors.

As I tagged along with Steve, he walked right past hay that to my untrained eye looked just like the previous batch. When I asked Steve why these bales did not appeal to him, he led me closer to the bales and pulled a handful out of the middle of the large round bale. "This is first crop hay here," he told me as he held the sample out to me. Farmers often cut "hay," which is a mixture of grasses and forbs, several times throughout the growing season. Steve pointed out that the stems of first crop hay are often much thicker than the stems in later cuttings and I could easily see that, compared to the last bale of "third crop hay" or "third cutting", these stems were much sturdier and thicker. Steve said that while he is not opposed to feeding his cows first crop hay, it can be too "pokey" for them, making the hay less palatable and more likely to cause jaw abscesses. It would certainly be too coarse for the sensitive mouths of his young heifers.

As he described the difficult texture of first crop hay, he poked the tips of some of the stems into his hand as if to emphasize the way he, too, found the texture unpleasant and that his hands could be sensitive to the coarse stems in a way that might tell him something about the experience that cows might have when eating the hay. His hands could tolerate the rough stems and at the same time discern that the degree of coarseness would be uncomfortable and potentially even harmful for the sensitive mouth interiors (palate, gums, and cheeks) of his cows and the young heifers in particular. His hands thus imagine themselves to be the chewing mouths of cows as they rub the hay sample between the fingers. They discern the softer textures of later crops of hay as something more palatable to Steve's heifers. In this way, Steve's hands might be understood to "taste forward" or anticipate the potential eating experience of a bovine other. Steve's use of his hands to anticipate the palatability of hay for his family's dairy cows and heifers raises an important question of where taste happens.

In an experiment aimed at testing the remark of one participant that food tastes better when eaten with the hands, Mann et al. (2011) prepared and ate a dinner with a variety of flavors and textures, which they consumed using their fingers and hands. As they mashed, rolled, and mixed food before bringing it to the mouth, they found that their fingers and hands anticipated how food might feel in the mouth in terms of texture and flavor and thus participated in the sensory experience of taste (Mann et al. 2011; see also Janeja 2010). In a similar way, Steve's hands take part in the tasting of hay and the anticipation of mouth feel. Thus taste extends beyond the mouth and the moment of tasting is initiated before food enters the mouth.

Continuing our survey of the hay bales that would be auctioned off, Steve and I approached some cuboid bales. He used these bales, which were loosely held together by twine to show me that sometimes a bale can appear to be in fine shape but that the interior can hide something different. "You want to make sure that the bales are tight," Steve said. "If they aren't tight then they fall apart when you move 'em around. And they might go bad inside too." He pulled out a handful of hay and smelled it. "Put your hand in there," he said to me. The hay bale was wet on the inside despite the dry appearance on the outside. Then he held out the sample for me to smell. "Smell that sweaty sweet smell? 'That means it's too wet. Yeah that'll have to get fed up right away," Steve said as he stuffed the sample back into the bale. We moved on to the next trailer.

Steve had purchased hay that was too wet before and he said that it had been a waste of money because they had not been able to use it all before it molded. Cows, he told me, will tolerate a little bit of mold but it could make them sick. Thus, as Steve assesses the hay at the hay sale, he draws on memories of sick cows as well as local commonly held knowledge of what could make cows sick, in addition to information distributed by the local University Extension agents about the possible perils of hay such as nitrate poisoning, mold, or inadequate nutritional content for lactating cows in particular. As Lévi-Strauss showed, Steve's discernment between rotten and fresh feed is shaped through shared cultural understandings of these qualities as well (1997).

Steve brings his body, through the work of his senses to the task of selecting feed. This is what he means by, "You gotta think like a cow." Steve is thinking like a cow by sensing according to a cow-ness as he has come to understand it through working with many different cows. Much of what he's learned has been from being with his family's cows as they eat, as they get sick, and so forth. And so he has become sensitive to the bodily needs and vulnerabilities of cows in different life stages. Steve has trained his senses towards an attunement with what constitutes palatability through aroma, texture, and flavor for a cow. In other words he has developed a skilled sensorium (Grasseni 2007, 2009) by honing his attention to particular discernible characteristics of feed and through bringing multiple senses to the anticipation of taste. David Sutton describes the ways that senses come together as synesthesia (2001, 2010) inspired by the tendency of Kalymnian islanders to describe the sound of a smell. Steve's sensory assessment of the hay is thus constituted through memory, through synesthetic attention to and experience with cows, and through institutional knowledge.

Through feeding cows, Steve and his family seek to provide sustenance as well as to prevent harm through sickness or injury. Feeding cows is a form of care at the same time as it is a necessary part of milk production. In order to prevent harm, Steve draws on transcorporeal taste, or that which is trained through experience being with cows in order to assess everything from aroma to texture to the digestive effects that different feeds may have. For instance we examined a trailer piled high with alfalfa hay and Steve thought that while this might be good in a mix, it might give his cows diarrhea if fed alone. As farmers and nutritionists consider digestive effects alongside palatability, they demonstrate how cultural studies of taste have perhaps been too limited in considering only the sensations of the mouth rather than what happens throughout the gut (Caldwell 2014). This is a key aspect of transcorporeal taste: humans who develop cow sense are able to discern the potential for particular digestive effects of feed for cow others even while human and cow digestion differ significantly. While the qualities of the hay may not effect Steve's body in the same way as that of cows, his senses extend towards potential futures of eating and digesting of bovine others.

Margie and Steve have a small farm and are responsible for all the feeding of their cows through a combination of growing feed crops, grazing cows in their wood lot, and purchasing feed through hay sales and feed dealers. They cobble together different sources of feed in order to make an affordable and nutritious diet and they remain "self-taught" in that they draw on their own experience, accrued family knowledge through multiple generations of dairy farming, vernacular knowledge through talking with neighbors and friends, and their own research into formalized knowledge through publicly available resources largely through University Extension. Margie and Steve's strategy is exemplary of that of many smaller-scale farms in the area. On the other hand, larger farms have come to more heavily rely on professional dairy nutritionists to design diets and evaluate the nutritional content and the costs of different feeds and supplements.

During my field research in Wisconsin, I interviewed and followed several dairy nutritionists as they evaluated cattle and feed on farms and designed diets. Through this research, I saw that dairy nutritionists, like farmers, cobbled together information in order to design diets. They were more likely to rely on formalized knowledge in the sense that they followed university-based research on dairy nutrition, they sometimes had a Masters degree or other kind of certification in dairy nutrition and they also drew on information on feed and cows from their companies be they private corporations or member-owned cooperatives. While these sources figured in significant ways that shaped the diets they produced, dairy nutritionists also drew on transcorporeal taste in ways similar to farmers. I did not meet a single dairy nutritionist in my time in the field who had not spent significant time with dairy cows while growing up. I met one who did not grow up on a farm, but she had spent a great deal of her childhood on a neighbor's farm. She worked on this dairy farm throughout high school and college and is now their dairy nutritionist. In Mathew Desmond's study on wildland firefighters, he examines how many of the firefighters embody a self-described "country boy" *habitus,* or embodied way of being in the world, which translates well into their work as firefighters (Desmond 2006). In a similar way, the dairy nutrition profession is largely made up of people who have developed cow sense or a sensory attunement to cow ways of being. And so, the kind of sedimented sensory experience that enables farmers to imagine how feed might taste to a cow, also figures in the work of more formalized nutritional planning. Consider the following example.

While attending the World Dairy Expo (WDE) in 2014, I met an animal nutritionist who worked specifically with dairy farms that use robots to milk their cows. Many milking robot companies and owners claim that cows like robots because they can decide when to get milked. It is common practice to provide an "added incentive" for the cows to come to the robots in the form of pellets that drop down for the cow when she is getting milked. Brian, a dairy nutritionist who works specifically with robot farms, spoke at WDE about how he designs pellets for robot farms. He said that he designs pellets based on what cows like to taste by tasting them himself. They need to taste good to him in order for the cows to find them palatable as well. Later, during a phone interview, I asked Brian how he knows what will taste good to a cow.

"Very simple. Back when I was a kid, and we were feeding roasted beans, we kids would eat them too. They sort of taste like a peanut. So you develop taste." In addition to tasting the feed that cows are eating, Brian described watching what cows eat and what they seem to prefer. He described how sometimes developing pellets required trial-and-error in order to see what cows like best. Taste, then, for dairy nutritionists is something separate from that which is learned through formalized courses in dairy nutrition or scientific research. It is something accrued through long-term relations with cows on dairy farms as well as careful observations of cow preferences. In order to develop taste, humans must pay attention to what cows will eat and how they eat.

Nutritionists often described to me how important it was to "listen to cows." John, a dairy nutritionist who generously let me ride along several times with him as he visited farms and assessed the feed and the diet-related condition of cows, told me that the "cows will tell you what you need to know" if only one pays attention. He told me stories of visiting farms where he saw cows drinking urine or "consuming hillsides" (i.e. eating soil), which he read as a sign that the cows' diets were deficient in important minerals. Lyndsey, a farmer that I worked with frequently throughout my fieldwork, has one cow named Iodine because they give her a squirt of iodine in her nose and mouth every feeding, a practice that she started after Iodine regularly sucked on "cow towels" leftover from cleaning teats with iodine. Now Iodine "asks" for iodine at each milking through turning back to the person milking her, and licking them until she gets her squirt. Farmers and nutritionists also try to watch out for how the social dynamics among cows affect eating.

Some cows tend to "boss" others by pushing them away from feed. Farmers and nutritionists pay attention to these types of behaviors and sometimes address the issues that arise for particular cows through grouping cows differently or changing how they offer feed.

Transcorporeal taste emerges through these careful practices of noticing and copresence, a term that Barbara Smuts uses to describe the experience of singular awareness with another, and in particular a member of another species (2001). Barbara Smuts and Donna Haraway both describe experiences of "deep intersubjectivity" that have arisen out of long-term relationship and being with their dogs. As Barbara Smuts argues, this shared awareness can only arise through "pureness of motives" (2001: 308) meaning not that the relationship is free from all utilitarian benefits but that the experience "cannot be coerced but must, by definition, reflect independent agency by each animal" (308). It would seem that Smuts' definition of this shared awareness would preclude the relationships of humans and livestock animals in production agriculture, even while she does not seem to fully account for the disparity in power between her and her dog, Safi. It would certainly be erroneous to describe dairy cows as having independent agency when they are subject to deep forms of biopolitical control on a daily basis not to mention frequent and sometimes painful bodily modifications. Yet even these forms of control open possibilities for being with, such as the kinds of "shared suffering" that workers and pigs experience through the course of working together on industrial pig farms (Porcher 2011).

Donna Haraway makes theoretical space for deep intersubjectivity in spaces where animals are involved in relations of use that are highly controlled by humans and that may involve suffering or death on the part of the animals (2008; also see Hayward 2010). In the case of dairy cows and farmers, the unequal power relations mean that not everyone comes to the relationship entirely by choice. Cows do not decide to work in dairy. Yet, dairy farming relies on the kinds of everyday willingness of cows to participate in work (Porcher 2012) which becomes unavoidably clear when cows refuse to do what is expected of them as workers (Porcher 2012; Despret 2016). I would argue that transcorporeal taste speaks to a depth and a kind of shared bodily attunement that is related to Smuts' conception of copresence. As farmers and nutritionists learn to taste like cows, they are shaping their awareness towards that of another. And this awareness, or what we could call "cow sense" only becomes possible through long-term being with. This is not to say that every person who worked frequently with cows that I encountered in the field had what I am describing as "cow sense."

On one of the farms I frequented throughout my research, Diane and Bill Brown split the farm work; Bill did the cropping while Diane managed the cows. Bill grew up on a dairy farm and generally liked the work but he would easily get frustrated with the cows. He would shout in the milking barn or be quick to strike them on their flanks or to twist their tails. Diane told me that the cows were always jumpier when she returned from a trip because of her husband's impatience with them. Thus, cow sense also requires an interest in noticing cows that not all dairy people engage.

As numerous social science scholars have shown, food often becomes a medium through which social relations are enacted. Foods and food sharing create and sustain social networks. Foods inflect memories. Foods are political and laden with meaning and histories. Like Mauss' description of gifts, food can be thought of as a "total social fact" (Mauss 2000). Generally anthropological accounts of food as a social medium are confined to sharing between humans. In this case, the consumers are cows. But this does not mean that acts of feeding become devoid of social meaning for either humans or cows. Rather, farmers describe feeding their cows as a form of "care" often inflecting both their sense of responsibility to the cows from whom they make a living and their felt affection for their cows. Feeding cows might involve empathetic and compassionate registers, but it is also done in the name of production. Cows are fed rations that are geared towards producing the most milk in the smallest amount of time at the least cost. Feeding for production can lead to many issues for cows including acidosis, laminitis, and liver abscesses. The feeds and practices of feeding in dairy are also shaped through trends in nutritional science, seed technologies, milk prices, state and federal legislation, consumer desires, and more.

Feed therefore takes on many meanings at once. It becomes a technology for milk production as well as a form of intimacy and care between farmer and cow. Feed and feeding practices can also be a marker of a farmer's skill as a manager. Many times I heard farmers or veterinarians remark on the skill of a farmer based on the state of their cows. If the cows were deemed too skinny then the farmer was by implication a poor manager. Cows with luster to their coats and who come through the winter without losing too much weight are described as a sign that a farmer "knows what they're doing." In this way the ability to "taste like a cow" matters for both human-cow as well as human-human relations.

Cultivating Taste

Feeding cows on dairy farms involves affective registers of responsibility and nurturing through food provision. Yet the relations between humans and cows in dairy barns are oriented towards production and thus are not necessarily about providing the kinds of foods that are the most health-giving for cattle. Instead these diets are about increasing milk production and sustaining cow bodies enough to carry on in the work of producing milk, an attitude towards animal welfare in livestock agriculture that Donna Haraway describes as "just healthy enough" (2008). While most farmers grow at least some portion of their feed, feed costs average around 30 percent of input costs for dairy farmers and have at times threatened to put farmers out of business. For example, the drought of 2012–2013, largely through the spike in feed prices alongside crop failures, meant that many dairy farmers "paid to produce milk" as they put it. Most farms survived the drought but many did not. Feed, while a source of risk, is also a key means through which dairy farmers have sought to improve their herd productivity. It is considered common sense in the dairy industry that improved feeding practices have enabled the unprecedented levels of milk production per cow that we see today. Dairy farmers seek to make a profit, which motivates farmers to find ways to meet particular energy and nutritional requirements through inexpensive materials. And this requires training cows to develop tastes for particular kinds of feedstuff's and using products to make what would normally be unpalatable to cows more appetizing.

During my fieldwork, I spent time milking and doing chores on five different farms. Usually I was given "calf chores," which involves weaning calves from milk to solid feed. There is of course a lot of variation in caring for calves but it is possible to describe a pattern based on my experience doing a lot of calf chores and observing calf chores on many farms. During the first days of their lives, calves are given colostrum from their mother or another cow who recently "freshened" or calved. Then calves are switched to bottles of milk or a sweet-tasting "milk replacer." Calves then learn to drink from buckets. I learned to train a calf to drink from a bucket by letting the calf suck my fingers while slowly pulling my hand down into a bucket of milk and then repeating this until the calf learns to slurp up the milk. After the calves finish their buckets of milk, I was taught to mix a bit of "calf starter" into the remaining milk at the bottom of the bucket and then to offer that to the calves. Additionally, between milk feedings, calves are usually left with a bucket of water and a bucket of calf starter with the assumption that they will eventually figure out how to eat and drink them on their own. Calf starter is usually grain-based pellets or rolled feed. Calves must learn to eat grain because this is the basis for a production-oriented diet.

Since the 1950s, American dairy farmers have largely switched to a feeding technology known as a Total Mixed Ration (TMR). TMR has gained a lot of traction as a means to standardize dairy cow diets in order to allow farmers and nutritionists to design diets according to nutritional science recommendations for amounts and percentages of particular vitamins, minerals, carbohydrates, proteins, and more. A key driver for adoption of TMR diets has been the desire to incorporate cheap industrial byproducts from milling, manufacturing, and agriculture into cattle feed. In order to do so, these byproducts are measured according to characteristics such as digestible protein or vitamin content. Through evaluating byproducts as inputs of protein, vitamins, or carbohydrates, cows have come to eat the otherwise unimaginable; today dairy cattle on TMR diets frequently consume chicken litter, cottonseed, candy and chocolate, fish meal, and pork blood. These foods are only made appropriate as cattle feed through translation (Callon 1984) into nutritional components. Such incorporation of industrial byproduct is not new. In the 1980s and 1990s researchers attributed an epidemic of bovine spongiform encephalopathy or mad cow disease to the incorporation of cow bone and meat meal, the byproducts of slaughterhouses, into cattle feed.

A TMR is designed to be a complete balanced diet for cattle. And it is designed with the idea that every bite will provide balanced nutrition. In order to achieve this, TMRs are blended to a homogenous consistency from various materials. Depending on the farm, either the farmers or their nutritionists will design TMR diets through assessing the nutritional content of crops and stored feeds and through adding supplements to help the diet meet industry standards for nutritional content. Some farms mix their own TMR while others purchase mixed feed through dairy service cooperatives. It is worth mentioning that Steve and his mother Margie do not use a TMR. Like many small farms, they do not have the financial capital that it requires to either pay for mixed feed or to purchase the equipment necessary to make their own. Therefore it is a technology that is more accessible for farmers who are able to take advantage of economies of scale.

As I rode around with animal nutritionists and discussed feed with farmers, a frequent concern about TMR feeding emerged: feed sorting. TMR diets are designed to deliver an optimally balanced nutritional package in every bite. But cows might not always agree with this optimized kind of eating. Instead, the cows often push the feed around with their noses in order to eat the pieces of feed that they prefer, undermining the careful design of the blend by farmers and nutritionists. This places the humans in a bit of a dilemma: blending and chopping the TMR too much will reduce particle size which can lead to digestive issues for cows while too little blending enables cows to choose what to eat, which can mean deficiencies or overeating of feed components. When cows sort for too much grain or components, they risk acidosis or other metabolic and digestive issues. When they sort for too much forage, they may not make the energy requirements of high-milk production.

In addition to problems with feed sorting, cows may refuse feed altogether. Angela, a dairy nutritionist that I rode along with several times, described how cows often refuse TMR feed when diets are not properly designed to mask the bitter flavors of added vitamins and minerals or when industrial byproducts vary in flavor or texture. As she designs diets for clients, she often includes feed flavorings in order to make the feed more palatable and to limit stress for cows when feed components change by maintaining aroma and flavor in the feed. Angela showed me a brochure from a company called QualiTech™ for dairy feed flavor enhancers with names such as "Caramel Delight," "Accelerate Berry," and "Butterscotch Savour". At the time, I was surprised that cattle feed enhancers sounded more like ice cream or candy flavors. But these flavors point to similarities in cultural perceptions around food provisioning as well as localized tastes for sweet foods.

A major challenge for many anthropologists is the adjustment to local eating practices. Before fieldwork, I spent many years participating in the "health food" worlds of California through working at farms, non-profit organizations, and cafés. In these eating arenas, sugar is not entirely absent but there is a propensity towards limiting or completely abstaining from processed white sugars. Like most Wisconsinites, my hosts had strong proclivities towards sweet foods, often purchasing ready-made sweets and baking desserts in the evenings and on weekends. Unlike California health worlds' vilification of sugar and sometimes sweets more generally, my host families considered sweets to be part of a healthy diet as long as they are consumed in moderation. To my sensibilities, Wisconsin foods were ubiquitously sweet. When offered a glass of wine for example, the options might be "chocolate wine" or "cherry wine" both of which would be syrupy sweet. Dinners at the houses of acquaintances and friends in Wisconsin might include such side salads as Jell-O or whipped cream salad as part of the dinner plate. Restaurants, gas stations, and farmers usually offered coffee accompanied by sweetened and flavored creamers. While living with Barbara, a nurse who grew up on a farm in the area, I once had a visitor who stayed with us who did not enjoy sweet foods. Before my friend's arrival, Barbara had generously baked a loaf of banana bread, a tray of chocolate bars, and another of Rice Krispies treats ™. This was a common activity for Barbara who usually baked at least one sweet treat but usually more on her days off. My visitor left without partaking of any of Barbara's home-baked goods. Barbara was upset and tearfully explained to me the rejection she felt after providing these foods that went un-eaten by my guest and myself. "Food is how I show love," she told me after my guest left. It is not surprising that food and food provisioning is imbued with affect and the kinds of relationship building spirit that giving material goods entails (Mauss 2000). What is interesting here, however, is that this sense of caring through food is extended to cows and that cultural proclivities toward sweetness (Mintz 1996) inform efforts to select feed and to make cattle feed palatable.

Sweetness and sweet foods are understood to be a basic pleasurable good. It is perhaps unsurprising then that in an effort to make cattle feed more palatable, farmers and nutritionists would do so through making the feed sweeter and more like a fruit or dessert. Farmers and nutritionists often told me that cows enjoy sweet flavors, much like humans. For example, Jessica, a young farmer who had recently taken over her parents' farm, described how her cows sort through the hay that Jessica's husband cuts from their field: "I've seen cows go through and pick out the clover flowers. It's sweet. Cows would go through and pick out all these flowers and then they'd go through all the rest. It tastes just like honey. I like it. So … cows'll like it. I've seen them do it." There is an assumption here that cows prefer sweet foods. But rather than refer to some kind of predetermined biological bovine taste preference, I would argue that dairy cows, like their humans, are cultural eaters. They learn as calves to eat grains and calf starter, which usually contain molasses. Therefore it seems unsurprising that they might often sort for these kinds of foods or prefer sweetened feeds.

Wisconsin dairy cows then are learning to eat foods that have cultural relevance and value as "good" in the sense that sweetness is understood to be a basic pleasure in life. But, like humans, cows also prefer some flavors over others, and they do not necessarily eat in standardized ways. Despite the dream of a standardized eating that imbues the TMR philosophy of feeding cattle, on a daily basis cows are frequently resisting an approach that treats them as homogenous eaters. If Steve and Margie's abilities to anticipate the tastes of their cows constitutes transcorporeal taste wherein both cow and human senses are shaped through close intersubjective encounters, then cows refusing to eat TMR mixtures or sorting the feed constitute the failures of anticipatory taste. As opposed to empathetic encounters wherein understanding occurs, this resembles what Douglas Hollan (2008) calls "projection" wherein the experience of the empathizer and that of the empathizee do not match up. This failure has been observed in numerous contexts when expert-others create meals or diet plans based on nutritional planning or other interests but which the eaters themselves, be they children or food aid recipients refuse. Micah M. Trapp shows how Liberian refugees undermine the biopolitics of humanitarian food aid through refusing particular foodstuffs and through upending the logic of the "taste of necessity" by invoking the necessity of taste through sophisticated culinary transformations of humanitarian food aid as well as through using food to critique their positionality (Trapp 2016). Refugees thus resist the top-down and paternalistic food aid regime that would render them passive recipients. My point here is that nutritional planning has become a common form of biopolitical control across vastly different contexts. Many kinds of eaters refuse the standardization of eating by expressing taste preferences or refusing food altogether.

Through TMR feeding, dairy nutritionists seek to render cows as passive recipients of standardized feed in a form of dietary biopolitical control. Cows undermine the politics of particular nutritional models of diet through expression of particular tastes and through food refusals. Indeed the enormous amount of research on how to make food palatable and the numerous businesses that market solutions certainly seem to upend the logic of cows as passive subjects. Instead cows become the consumers and enormous amounts of effort go into figuring out what they will eat. In addition, they are cultural eaters, what and how they eat is shaped through idiosyncratic preferences but also through Midwestern proclivities towards sweet foods.

Extending Taste

Research in the dairy worlds of Wisconsin reveals how senses, and taste in particular, exceed species-bodies. Taste for cow feed is not reducible either to the tasting bodies of humans or cows but instead is a sense that develops across bodies through a long-term co-presence that enables cow preferences to be understood and that extends cultural associations between care and food provisioning towards cows. As farmers and dairy nutritionists attend to what and how cows eat through observing, tasting, smelling, and touching, they learn transcorporeal taste.

Cows, too, develop taste through learning to eat particular foods and feedstuffs. But they are not passive recipients of feed, despite the biopolitical organization of eating represented by TMR feeding technologies. Cows sort and refuse feed according to personal preferences, social dynamics, and distaste for the flavors and textures of feed components and additives. In this way, taste for cow feed is not at all static, but a continuously evolving transcorporeal form of sensing.

Transcorporeal taste contributes to a growing literature that questions the five-sense model. This model presumes a universal individualized body with distinct and separable sensing capacities. When taste is transcorporeal, it emerges through social interactions not only among humans but among other co-present bodies. It is not a kind of taste that anyone is born with but instead is shaped through encounter. Further, it is not a kind of taste that can be understood through looking only at taste cells in the mouth. Trancorporeal taste extends beyond the mouth and beyond what might seem to be the boundaries of bodies. It brings attention to the locations of taste, the extension of where taste begins, and the co-species training of sensory attention.

Acknowledgments

This material is based upon work supported by the National Science Foundation under Grant No. 1256532; the Danish National Research Foundation and Aarhus University Research on the Anthropocene (AURA); the University of California Santa Cruz (UCSC) Department of Anthropology; and the UCSC Center for Agroecology and Sustainable Food Systems (CASFS). Special thanks also go to Melissa Caldwell, Carole Counihan, Natalie Forssman, Spencer Orey, Jessica Partington, Susanne Højlund Pedersen, Pierre du Plessis, Anna Tsing, and Michael Vine.

References

Caldwell, M.L. (2014). "Digestive Politics in Russia: Feeling the Sensorium beyond the Palate." *Food and Foodways*, 22 (1–2): 112–135.

Callon, M. (1984). "Some Elements of a Sociology of Translation: Domestication of the Scallops and the Fishermen of St Brieuc Bay." *The Sociological Review*, 32 (1_suppl): 196–233.

Classen, C. (1993). *Worlds of Sense: Exploring the Senses in History and Across Cultures*. London: Routledge.

Csordas, T.J. (1993). "Somatic Modes of Attention." *Cultural Anthropology*, 8(2): 135–156.

Desmond, M. (2006). "Becoming a Firefighter." *Ethnography*, 7(4): 387–421.

Despret, V. and B. Buchanan (2016). *What Would Animals Say if We Asked the Right Questions?* University of Minnesota Press.

Grasseni, C. (2007). "Good Looking: Learning to be a Cattle Breeder," in C. Grasseni, ed., *Skilled Visions: Between Apprenticeship and Standards*. 47–66. New York: Berghahn Books.

Grasseni, C.(2009). *Developing Skill, Developing Vision: Practices of Locality at the Foot of the Alps*. New York: Berghahn Books.

Haraway, D.J. (2008). *When Species Meet*. Minneapolis: University of Minnesota Press.

Hayward, E. (2010). "Fingeryeyes: Impressions of Cup Corals." *Cultural Anthropology*, 25(4): 577–599.

Hollan, D. (2008). "Being There: On the Imaginative Aspects of Understanding Others and Being Understood." *Ethos*, 36(4):475–489.

Janeja, M.K. (2010). *Transactions in Taste: The Collaborative Lives of Everyday Bengali Food*. London: Routledge.

Lévi-Strauss, C. (1997). "The Culinary Triangle", in C. Counihan and P. Van Esterik, eds., *Food and Culture: A Reader*, 28–35. London: Routledge.

Mann, A.M., et al. (2011). "Mixing Methods, Tasting Fingers: Notes on an Ethnographic Experiment." *HAU: Journal of Ethnographic Theory*, 1(1): 221–243.

Mauss, M. (2000). *The Gift: The Form and Reason for Exchange in Archaic Societies*. WW Norton & Company.

Mintz, S.W. (1996). *Tasting Food, Tasting Freedom: Excursions into Eating, Culture, and the Past.* Boston: Beacon Press.

Porcher, J. (2011). "The Relationship between Workers and Animals in the Pork Industry: A Shared Suffering." *Journal of Agricultural and Environmental Ethics*, 24 (1): 3–17.

Porcher, J. and T. Schmitt (2012). "Dairy Cows: Workers in the Shadows?" *Society & Animals*, 20(1): 39–60.

Smuts, B. (2001). "Encounters with Animal Minds." *Journal of Consciousness Studies*, 8 (5–6): 293–309.

Thompson, C. (2005). *Making Parents: The Ontological Choreography of Reproductive Technologies.* Cambridge: MIT Press.

Trapp, M.M. (2016). "You-Will-Kill-Me-Beans: Taste and the Politics of Necessity in Humanitarian Aid." *Cultural Anthropology*, 31(3): 412–437.

FCJ-142 Spectacles and Tropes: Speculative Design and Contemporary Food Cultures

Carl DiSalvo

Introduction

Speculative design is a practice of creating imaginative projections of alternate presents and possible futures using design representations and objects. At times critical and at other times whimsical, it is a distinctive, if loose, grouping of projects. Using the term broadly, speculative design covers a range of work across disciplines, fields, and historical and contemporary movements. For example, much of the work of the Futurists and Constructivists in the early Twentieth Century, which blended machines, politics, and everyday life, is suggestive of speculative design as it is practiced today. Collectives such as Archigram and Superstudio in the 1960s and 70s produced now iconic graphic representations of future cities, which stylistically and thematically inspired generations of architects and designers. In the late 1990s Tony Dunne and Fiona Raby coined the term 'Critical Design' to label product and interaction design that sought to 'challenge narrow assumptions, preconceptions and givens about the role products play in everyday life.' (2007) More recently, the term 'Design Fiction' has been used to characterize the 'use of diegetic prototypes to suspend disbelief about change.' (Sterling, 2012, see also Bleeker, 2009) All of these, I maintain, can broadly be considered as kinds of speculative design because what is common across this work is the use of designerly means to express foresight in compelling, often provocative ways, which are intended to engage audiences in considerations of what might be.

As Anne Balsamo points out, design is not only inventive, it also reproduces culture: 'Through the practices of designing, cultural beliefs are materially reproduced, identities are established, and social relations are codified. In this way culture is both a resource and an outcome of the designing process.' (2010, 3) This notion of design reproducing culture is certainly as true for speculative design as it is for any other form of design. Even though we often think of speculative design as being particularly inventive, at times fantastic, like any design it is grounded in the present. Even as speculative design expresses alternatives it references, often mimicking, the status quo and replicates the various styles and themes of the moment. Because of this, close examinations of speculative design projects offer us a view of the present reinterpreted and in relief.

As speculative design continues to develop as a practice, it is incumbent upon critics to provide ways of analyzing its construction and the work that it is, and is not, doing. Although speculative design projects offer promise as a way of using design to comment upon culture, there are also limits to speculative design. I begin this essay by tracing the ways two recent speculative design projects reproduce aspects of contemporary food cultures. I will then draw out from these projects two general strategies of speculative design, by which these designs work to lure us into a consideration of what might be. I will also take a critical view of these strategies, to discuss their limits as well as their potential. The intention of this is not to level critiques specifically against these projects, but rather, to contribute to the ways in which we might analyze speculative design, its ways of working and effects.

Food Culture and Design

Although public interest in food is not new, there seems to be a reinvigorated attentiveness to food in contemporary society. Multiple factors are at play in this. In part this reinvigorated attentiveness to food stems from an increasing awareness of the connection between kinds of food, modes of food production, and health. In part it stems from the topic of sustainability and the realization that changes in agricultural practices could help foster a more sustainable society. For some, this attention to food is as an act against previous paradigms of domestic convenience. And, in part this reinvigorated attentiveness to food stems from access to a greater diversity of food and thereby an ability to experiment with different foodstuffs and cuisines. From the confluence of these factors, there is a blossoming of 'food cultures,' by which I mean communities of practice and interest that are defined by their relation to the production, preparation, and consumption of food. One need only look at popular media to see evidence of this, from the *Food Network* channel to CNN's Eatocracy series, to the stardom of food advocates such as Jamie Oliver and Michael Pollan, and in changing consumer habits and public policy, from the increase in farmer's markets and the farm to table movement (see Sonnino and Mardsen 2006 and Martinez et al. 2010), to the recent re-design of the so-called food pyramid by the United States Food and Drug administration. This blossoming of food cultures is reflected throughout design research and practice, even prompting the formation of new design communities. For instance, there is now an International Food Design Society and in 2010 the first Food Experience Design conference was hosted in London, England. More and more, designers are exploring the relations between food, science, and technology. The 2012 exhibition *Edible: The Taste of Things to Come* at the Science Gallery in Dublin, which featured over a dozen projects, many of them speculative in nature, is one example of how designers and artists are engaging cuisine and food consumption as both themes for investigation and mediums of expression. Other designers are working to develop systems to support new forms and practices of agriculture. The collective of designers involved with the *Re:farm the City* project (2008-present) are working to create both hardware and data sharing platforms for urban farming and gardening. This loose organization provides online information resources, hands-on workshops, and software for designing and using environmental sensing technologies and computational visualizations to assist small-scale sustainable agriculture. This work is exemplary of another pragmatic way that design, and in particular interaction design, is engaging with food cultures through the making of new agricultural technologies.

To use Balsamo's framing of design, food cultures are lively sites of both the invention and reproduction of culture through design. And as design concomitantly invents and reproduces culture, speculative design does so in a distinctive manner. Speculative design works by isolating facets of culture and recasting those facets in ways that alter their meaning in order to produce new images — new imaginative instantiations — of what might be. So, how is this occurring with regards to food cultures? What is it that speculative design is reproducing and recasting and to what effects, or lack of effects?

The Reproduction of Food Cultures in Speculative Design

In 2009 Design Indaba (an organization that sponsors design programs in South Africa) commissioned five designers to produce visions of the future of farming, under the program title *Protofarm 2050*. The designers selected were all known for their speculative approaches: Futurefarmers, 5.5 Designers, Dunne & Raby, Revital Cohen, and Frank Tjepkema. As with many such projects, the motivation was grounded in issues of sustainability, specifically conditions seen as contrary to sustainability including population growth and other strains put on the food system, such as climate change and increased meat consumption. The collection of concepts in *Protofarm 2050* were thus intended to explore possible futures of agriculture with respect to these conditions now and how they might be in the year 2050. In considering what it is that speculative design does, it is worth noting that the projects of *Protofarm 2050* were framed as 'looking beyond the possibilities and predictions currently in the public domain.' Of the five proposals, I will discuss one of them here.

For *Protofarm 2050* the French design firm 5.5 Designers produced a project titled *Guide to Free Farming* (2009). The project consists of a series of print booklets for different cities and the Paris booklet is presented in the video documentation. (http://www.designindaba.com/video/protofarm-2050-guide-free-farming) The Paris booklet begins with a map of the city, and then goes into page spreads with pictures of the edible flora and fauna of the city. Immediately, a hint of dark humour foreshadows content yet to come, as a poodle is pictured along with the other edible fauna. What follows throughout are a series of hunting and gathering tactics for the city of Paris, along with recipes for the hunted and gathered, and prototype tools to assist in the process.

The first concept presented is hunting pigeon and the page spreads include an image of a person in a camouflaged cloak, designed to blend in with a cobblestone street, stalking a pigeon for the kill. The following page spread then shows how to dress and grill the pigeon to be served on a stick. The rest of this section, titled *Specialties*, includes similarly extreme forms of hunting and preparation, such as methods of trapping starlings and using them for pâté or trapping rats for grilling, as well as more tame practices of gathering dandelions. The next section, *Addresses*, provides site-specific food gathering activities, such as fishing the river Seine using a modified cane or gleaning fruit left over from Parisian street markets with the help of a special gleaning bag. Diverging from food, the section even covers scenarios of gathering hair from sheared dogs to be used for making clothes. The final section of the book, titled *Farm Tools*, provides photographic documentation of the various design products used throughout the book for the featured activities, such as the camouflage cloak for pigeon hunting, the starling trap, the rat trap, the cane for fishing, etc. Each of these objects is simply styled: most all are grey or white with clean geometries.

Guide to Free Farming may at first appear outrageous, but it is not so far from reality, at least in regards to the notion of seeing the city as an environment for hunting and gathering. In considering *Guide to Free Farming* as a speculation on the future of farming, what we find is a reproduction of the contemporary practice of foraging. Foraging — the opportunistic gathering of foodstuffs as they grow wild — is a practice that predates modern agriculture for the collection of edible plants. It is also a practice that has seen resurgence. We can conjecture reasons why: it is hyper-local, sustainable, and often provides novel food varieties. Indeed, it is common to find foraged greens and edible flowers for sale at farmers markets and for some chefs to use foraged foods on their menus. The notion of hunting in the city, though, is a bit different. Fishing in cities is certainly common enough. Hunting of pigeons and trapping of starlings and rats for human consumption is not unheard of, but it is uncommon. Moreover, it is usually associated with poverty. But its presentation within *Guide to Free Farming* casts such hunting and trapping as seemingly reasonable, perhaps even desirable endeavours for all to engage in, resulting in foods that appear appealing.

This reproduction of foraging is also an interpretation of foraging, a new imaginative instantiation of what might be. The project leverages contemporary cultural imaginaries and practices of foraging, extending them to the notion of hunting. As if taking lessons directly from Barthes 'Rhetoric of the Image' (1977) the designers employ the visual styles of high-end product photography to document both the process and the product of urban hunting and gathering, expressing it in a way that draws a set of associations with consumer goods of a certain class. The photography would not be out of place in an IKEA catalogue or an issue of Dwell magazine. In so constructing these images, the designers constructs connections to an even broader trend of food cultures: the aestheticisation of food production and consumption, which finds its apogee in the notion of the artisanal.

From clothing to beers to cheeses and chocolates, the artisanal is a cultural trend of the early 2000s and 2010s. In the common use of the term, 'artisanal' refers to goods that are hand-made, usually in small-batches. Indeed, one way to characterise artisanal goods is as that which is small-scale. And even more than being small-scale, artisanal goods have a peculiar relationship to scale in that they do not scale, or at least, they do not profit from scale: 'Artisanal products are labor-intensive rather than capital-intensive and therefore cannot benefit from economies of scale.' (Barjolle and Chappuis, 2000, 1) With artisanal goods, be it cheese or clothing, there is a great attention to the craft and materials of production, which in turn, results in a product that is considered to be of unique character and quality. Artisanal goods have become popularised because of their exclusivity and a cultural embrace of the bespoke. In part this may be due to a search for greater quality and value in times of economic downturn, but more likely, it is an expression of nostalgia and some notion of authenticity as style. This is not to diminish the artisanal in any way, but rather to acknowledge that the artisanal is currently as much a marketing phenomena as it is a commitment to craft.

An unusual take on the artisanal is found in *Family Whiskey* (2010) (http://www.jamesgilpin.com/ Diabetesengage.html), a speculative design project by James Gilpin in which he proposes that the urine from diabetics might be used in the production of custom whiskeys. These whiskeys could then be marketed as having distinctive family origins. Unlike the family origin of most whiskeys that trace to a family recipe or locale, these could ostensibly be traced, or at least claim association with, a family's physiology: each whiskey would be distinct by the qualities of the urine produced by that family. According to Gilpin the motivation for the project is a reflection on and exploration of 'the consequences of using science to alter our bodies' abilities.' (2010) This reflection is grounded in the lived experience of Gilpin, who is himself a Type 1 diabetic. One result of diabetes is that diabetics produce urine with extremely high sugar content. In Gilpin's proposal, this sugar would be extracted from the urine and then combined with mash used in the production of whiskey, in order to accelerate the fermentation process and produce distinctive flavour profiles. The project is expressed through multiple formats, including a series of flasks filled with various whiskeys produced through this process and staged photographs of home distillation equipment. These items are brought together in an installation and performance of sorts in which Gilpin serves the whiskey.

In *Family Whiskey*, Gilpin is clearly reproducing trends of artisanal goods. So-called bespoke beverages are one such domain of production and consumption. For instance, there is a niche of consumers reverse-engineering mineral waters using home carbonation systems and base elements ordered from online retailers (see Twilly 2012). Closer even to Gilpin's project, *WhiskeyBlender* (www.whiskyblender.com/) allows users to experiment in a online laboratory of sorts, mixing blends (with names such as 'Burnt Puddin'' and 'Smoke on the Water') to produce new taste profiles and custom single bottle batches of scotch. The concept of *Family Whiskey* fits right within these artisanal goods and practice—it is not the notion of the bespoke beverage that is odd, just the ingredients for this beverage. In addition to reproducing the notion of the bespoke beverage, the design of *Family Whiskey* also reproduces the visual and material cultures of artisanal goods. The various parts of the installation—the glass flasks and their mounting hardware, the labels on the whiskeys, the still, even the objects in the staged photographs—exhibit an artisan-like attention to construction and presentation. At one and the same time they reference the object aesthetics of a modern laboratory and those of a traditional bar.

There are strong aesthetic and conceptual connections between these two projects. Both trade upon an aestheticisation of food production and consumption. And even more than an aestheticisation, we might describe the treatment of foraging and distilling in these projects as a fetishising of food production and consumption. There is, in both *Guide to Free Farming* and *Family Whiskey* an intimacy, a closeness, brought to food goods and their making, which reproduces and aligns it with trends in food culture.

Most generally, we can read *Guide to Free Farming* and *Family Whiskey* as reproducing practices and discourses of small-scale agriculture. Although there is no strict definition, small-scale agriculture can easily encapsulate foraging and artisanal foodstuffs and also include all manner of growing, harvesting, selling, and making foodstuffs on smaller farms, slaughterhouses, and production facilities. The design of *Guide to Free Farming* hones in on the trend of urban farming and the notions of do-it-yourself sufficiency that often accompany discussions of urban farming. Likewise with *Family Whiskey*, Gilpin's project leverages the trend of small-batch whiskey, which is a trend regularly positioned as being counter to corporatized distilleries. By being expressive of this general trend away from industrialized agriculture and foodstuffs, these projects can be seen as imaginative projections along current vectors in food culture. They are extreme to be sure, but still situated and identifiable within a constellation of contemporary theories, beliefs, and values concerning the future of food. By aligning with notions of small-scale agriculture, these speculative designs also position themselves as distinct from earlier visions of the future of farming and food, which more often explored concepts of technological automation and monitoring or the reduction of cuisine to pills or simulated food products.

Through their interpretation and recasting of food cultures, *Guide to Free Farming* and *Family Whiskey* offer us provocative images for consideration. The notion that the images and objects can spark meaningful reflection or dialogue is the potential of speculative design. But it is also the aspect of speculative design that is most problematic because it has been the least well documented, is the most difficult to ascertain, and seemingly too often, simply does not come to fruition. A critical and yet still appreciative voice towards these speculative designs is appropriate. How do these images and objects provide, or fail to provide, opportunities for dialogue and reflective considerations of what might be?

Spectacles and Tropes

These two speculative design projects — *Guide to Free Farming* and *Family Whiskey* — exemplify two ways of engaging audiences in a consideration of what might be. The strategies for constructing and communicating imaginative instantiations in each of these projects are, however, quite different. This difference in strategy also reflects a difference in how the projects structure the audiences' engagement with food as a subject matter, and reveals the designer's commitments to food cultures and other topics.

With *Guide to Free Farming* what we are presented with is speculation in the form of spectacle. The practice of foraging is commoditised in the production of fictional implements. The designerly representations of the activities of urban hunting and gathering cast those activities as dramatic events. At first, it is unclear whether and to what extent this work is intended to be ironic or perhaps a kind of classical détournement — the use of spectacle and the images of capitalism as a disruption to the system of spectacle and consumerism (Debord and Wolman 2006). The skillful and clever use of spectacle *can* serve a critical purpose. This is part of the intent of the détournement as developed by the Situationists. But that is not what we encounter with *Guide to Free Farming*. On the back of the book the designers provide some insight into the motivation and desired outcome of the project. It states:

> The Guide to Free Farming project was presented in the form of a book that aimed to restore a close relation between consumers and the natural environment, creating a shorter link to guide people who live in cities to take on the role of farmers in their urban environment. It is about farming in the city and encourages readers to discover the unsuspecting resources hidden in our towns. (2009)

This statement demonstrates how designers attempt to make use of alluring images and objects as props for ideas, as gateways for discourse or other forms of action. The suggestion is that the content of the book might have some sort of effect in initiating change. But, upon scrutiny, it is unclear what that effect or change might really be. The implicit claim being made is that in order to shorten the link between consumers, food, and the urban environment, what is needed are more products (camouflage cloaks, window box traps, etc.). This claim is problematic—it seems dubious. And with little more than the catalog-like displays to examine, we, as audiences to be prompted into reflection, are left without much support for further exploration of these activities and the broader issues they might engage.

Indeed, upon consideration one of the most striking aspects of the *Guide to Free Farming* is how little it seems connected to the practice of foraging or food cultures more generally. Although the project reproduces the practice of foraging and thereby draws associations with food culture, its reproduction of foraging is only a surface reflection. The activities, values, techniques, histories, traditions, and controversies of foraging are nowhere to be found, or even alluded to in this work. What, then, is it that we are supposed to glean from *Guide to Free Farming*? It would seem as if the project is reductively spectacular: pragmatic information and critical perspectives have been exchanged for extraordinary images. The problem with this is *not* that the speculation is unrealistic or exaggerated. The problem is that the speculation seems disconnected from the very practices and issues it purports to be commenting on, and the reinterpretation of foraging is reduced to a re-styling of foraging.

Gilpin's *Family Whiskey* also trades upon spectacle, but it is not really the intent of *Family Whiskey* to engage us in a consideration of food cultures. Gilpin states that the purpose of *Family Whiskey* is to explore 'the consequences of using science to alter our bodies' abilities.' (2010) Thus, in this project food and food cultures are not a topic, they are a trope. Within literature, tropes are figurative language such as metaphor, irony, or hyperbole. They work to convey an idea through terms and structures that are not literal, but rather symbolic. Design too can employ such figurative turns and expressions in the making and interpretation of objects. Tropes simply are tools for crafting meaning. They enable the creative manipulation of material and form so that we can make one thing mean another thing. In *Family Whiskey*, food and food culture is used as a figurative means of investigating and expressing issues concerning science and bodies. More specifically, the culture and practices of small-batch whiskey function as a metaphor for Gilpin's topics of science and bodies: a way of engaging the topic through an association of food to science and an exploration of the transfer of qualities across these categorical things. As Lakoff and Johnson state "The essence of metaphor is understanding *and experiencing* one kind of thing in terms of another." (1980, 5) Gilpin's *Family Whiskey* allows us to understand and experience science and food and food as science.

It is useful to consider how this metaphor is constructed and the work it does. Tracing the relations within the metaphor gives insight into how tropes can function to scaffold meaning. There is an inherent relationship between food and science. Before the human hand enters in to pluck the fruit from the tree, even the most organic of foodstuffs is the product of a series of biological and chemical interactions and reactions. Contemporary foodstuffs are very much products of science, with 'food science' being an established field. Moreover, the relationship between artisanal foods and science is enticingly complex. On the one hand the artisanal is defined by being distinct from industrial modes of food production and food products that tend to rely on food science. On the other hand, many craftspeople involved in artisanal goods rely upon a deep understanding of the science of production, from the biological processes and transformation of cheese to the chemical processes of baking bread. What a close reading of *Family Whiskey* does is bring to the fore how food and foodstuffs operate as figurative instantiations of science.

What is missing still from *Family Whiskey* though, is a substantive explanation of those relationships between food and science: between diabetes and the production of sugar and the fermentation of whiskey. It is unclear how the flavour of whiskey is affected by this sugar drawn from urine. Does it add a peaty richness or briny bite? Does it round out gaps in an otherwise incomplete taste profile? Or doesn't it matter? Perhaps it is less about the culinary experience of the product and more about an appreciation of the ways in which the process creatively intermingles the corporeal, technical, and everyday? In *Family Whiskey* the groundwork of identifying the relations and a set of factors between science and food culture has been done. But whilst this provides us with a starting point for further consideration it leaves us hungry for more critical engagement.

From Provocation to What?

Both *Guide for Free Farming* and *Family Whiskey* present us with enticing images for consideration of what might be. We are initially taken aback and pause to think through the scenarios of use that we are witness to in these works. As a means for provocative expression, spectacles works well — they arrest us and pique our interest. But without connection to actual practices or issues, spectacles can quickly disappoint. Reflecting on the images of spectacle, too often we are left wanting for meaning and significance. The construction of tropes, particularly well-crafted tropes, can further the effect of spectacle by providing a scaffolding of sorts for reflection or inquiry. This scaffolding must be apparent and accessible and connect to the social contexts of the present or the presumed social contexts of the future.

Engaging with politics and the political is one way to construct such scaffolding. But too often, speculative design seems to skirt these themes. For instance, politics and the political issues that embroil food cultures in contemporary society are absent from *Family Whiskey* and *Guide to Free Farming*. This is surprising given that food is a highly contested domain, governed by a host of disputed regulations and codes. This is particularly true of artisanal food production. For instance, in the United States cheese production is highly regulated and raw milk, a staple of artisanal cheese production, is a contested animal product, all but made illegal. Certainly, using urine for whiskey or hunting in Paris would be mired in health codes and regulatory conundrums. Many of these codes and regulations are in fact expressions of values that are operationalised along political registers in the form of laws and ordinances.

Not all speculative design must be political, but to not address politics in social contexts where they are usually present is a striking omission. It is also a missed opportunity. If one purpose of speculative design is to prompt reflection on contemporary issues and the possible consequences of science and technology, then engaging with politics and the political could lend speculative design projects tractability and fodder for dialogue and debate. For instance, in regards to *Guide for Free Farming*, one might ask, is the hunting of pigeons currently legal or illegal? If it were legalised would one need a hunting license? If it were illegal, would people go to jail over this crime? Where is line between foraging and poaching? Would there be city game wardens that would police and protect the pigeon, rat, and starling populations? Or with *Family Whiskey* one could ask, what are the regulations that structure the production of spirits and the disposal of human bio-waste? Is whiskey made from urine like any other animal-based product, or does the introduction of human materials place it in a new category of foodstuffs? Attention to questions such as these, which immediately engage the politics of farming and food production through a speculative lens, would provide depth to the projects.

One limit of speculative design, then, is the extent to which it foments or supports substantive reflection on alternate presents and possible futures. This limit is not determined by any one strategy, but rather by the efforts of the designers employing the strategy. So, it is not that spectacle is without value. There *is* value in base provocation as it can serve to jolt us from assuredness and complacency, if only momentarily. It can spark a curiosity that might be pursued, but to be truly provocative is to rouse to action. If an object of speculative design does not provide access to a breadth or depth of subject matter, then we should be careful about making claims for its capacity to foment or support substantive reflection. It is difficult to meaningfully consider what we are uninformed about. The challenge and responsibility for the designer, then, is to provide that information, those scaffolds, in compelling and productive form.

It is useful to ask how speculative design could be used for more than provocation, to enable more meaningful engagement with the substance of an issue. In order for engagement to occur what is needed is articulation of both the components and potential consequences of a situation, such that an audience might be able to appreciate that situation. Or, put another way, what is needed is to express the situation of an alternate present or possible future as an issue: a situation that is contestable. As a way of sculpting meaning, the trope lends itself to this. In the making and expression of a trope, relationships are constructed between ideas and objects, and these relationships can be interrogated and challenged. For example, with *Family Whiskey*, the (literally) fluid transfer between science and foodstuffs, between what the body produces and what the body consumes, and the transformation of the effect of a disease into a quality of product are new pathways along which to explore Gilpin's issue of concern: 'the consequences of using science to alter our bodies' abilities.'

Gilplin's project *Family Whiskey* also points to the performative possibilities of speculative design: the events at which he attempts to serve the whiskey become further opportunities for engagement. Some designers are beginning to explicitly explore the performative and eventful potentials of speculative design. The *Material Beliefs* (http://www.materialbeliefs.com/) project is exemplary in this regard. Over the course of several years the designers and researchers from the project staged a series of events that made use of the products and processes of speculative design to bring together various publics to consider possible futures of biotechnology. The *Center for Genomic Gastronomy* (http://www.genomicgastronomy. com/) provides another example of using workshops as a design form, with an emphasis on exploring the relationships between biotechnology and food. Images and objects still exist in such projects, but it is the performative and eventful qualities that are fundamental to this design work. In addition to providing a novel form for engaging in speculation, "the event" also provides a novel form for engaging politics and the political.

As designers explore new forms and purposes of speculative design, the design critic must also develop new ways to make sense of those forms and purposes, working in tandem to articulate the possibilities and limits of speculative design. Too often, speculative design is spectacle alone, devoid of the content and grounding necessary to make productive critical statements or to be an instigator of public debate. This is particularly the case with regard to politics and the political. If design reproduces culture, what politics are being reproduced in speculative design? If speculative design turns from objects to events, how do we appreciate and critique the political qualities of these performative experiences? Spectacles and tropes are two constructs for describing and analysing speculative design. More constructs need to be elucidated and experimented with. Given the opportunity to prompt reflection on contemporary conditions and express the possible implications of current trends in science and technology, there is much more speculative design, and speculative design criticism, yet to be done.

References

5.5 Design, *Guide to Free Farming* (2009). http://www.designindaba.com/video/protofarm-2050-guide-free-farming.

Balsamo, Anne. 'Design', International Journal of Media and Learning 1 (4, 2010): 1–10.

Barjolle D & JM Chappuis. 'Transaction Costs and Artisanal Food Products' Proceedings of the Annual Conference of ISNIE (International Society for New Institutional Economics), Tuebingen (D) 22–24 September, 2000 (2000): 1–21.

Barthes, Roland. 'Rhetoric of the Image.' Image, Music, Text. (ed. and trans. Stephen Heath) (New York: Hill and Wang, 1977): 32–51.

Bleeker, Julian, *Design Fiction: A short essay on design, science, fact and fiction.* (2009). http://www.nearfuturelaboratory.com/2009/03/17/design-fiction-a-short-essay-on-design-science-fact-and-fiction/.

Binder Thomas, Pelle Ehn, Giorgio De Michelis, Giulio Jacucci, Per Linde, and Ina Wagner. Design Things. (Cambridge: MIT Press, 2011).

The Center for Genomic Gastronomy (2012). www.genomicgastronomy.com/

Debord, Guy and Gil J. Wolman. 'Mode d'emploi du détournement.' Originally appeared in the Belgian surrealist journal Les Lèvres Nues #8 (May 1956). Translation by Ken Knabb from the Situationist International Anthology (Bureau of Public Secrets: Revised and Expanded Edition, 2006). No copyright.

Dunne, Anthony. *Hertzian Tales* (Cambridge: MIT Press, 2006).

Dunne, Anthony and Fiona Raby. *Critical Design FAQ.* 2007. http://www.dunneandraby.co.uk/con-tent/bydandr/13/0. Accessed March 19, 2012.

Dunne, Anthony and Fiona Raby. *Design Noir* (Basel: Birkhäuser, 2001).

Gilpin, James, *Family Whiskey* (2010). http://www.jamesgilpin.com/Diabetesengage.html

Lakoff, George and Mark Johnson. *Metaphors We Live By.*(Chicago: University of Chicago Press, 1980).

Marinetti, Filippo Tommaso, and Fillia, *La Cucina Futurista*, (ed. Pietro Frassica) (Milan: Vienne-pierre Edizioni, 2009).

Martinez, Steve & Michael Hand, Michelle Da Pra, Susan Pollack, Katherine Ralston, Travis Smith, Stephen Vogel, Shelley Clarke,Luanne Lohr, Sarah Low, Constance Newman. 'Local food systems: concepts, impacts, and issues', MPRA Paper 24313, University Library of Munich, Germany (2010).

Material Beliefs (2012). http://www.materialbeliefs.com/

Michael, Mike. 'What are We Busy Doing': Engaging the Idiot. Science, Technology, and Human Values. Online preprint (2011): 1–27.

ProtoFarm 2050, Design Indaba (2011). http://www.designindaba.com/protofarm2050

Re:Farm The City (2011). http://www.refarmthecity.org/

Seago, Alex and Anthony Dunne. 'New Methodologies in Art and Design Research: The Object as Discourse', Design Issues 15 (2, 1999):11–17.

Sonnino, Roberta & Terry Marsden. 'Beyond the divide: rethinking relationships between alternative and conventional food networks in Europe', Journal of Economic Geography 6 (2006): 181–199.

Sterling, Bruce. Interview. 'SciFi Writer Bruce Sterling Explains the Exciting New Concept of Design Fiction' By Torie Bosch. Slate (online magazine). Posted Friday, March 2, 2012. Retrieved March 19, 2012. Available at http://www.slate.com/blogs/future_tense/2012/03/02/bruce_sterling_on_de-sign_fictions_.html

Twilly, Nicola. 'How to Clone Mineral Water., Edible Geography.' Posted January 7, 2012. Retrieved March 19, 2012. Available at http://www.ediblegeography.com/how-to-clone-mineral-water/

Suggested Additional Readings

Allison Carruth. 2013. "Culturing Food: Bioart and In Vitro Meat." *Parallax* 19(1): 88–100.

Heather Looy, Florence V. Dunkel, and John R. Wood. 2014. "How Then Shall We Eat?: Insect-Eating Attitudes and Sustainable Foodways." *Agriculture and Human Values* 31: 131–41.

Susan McHugh. 2010. "Real Artificial: Tissue-cultured Meat, Genetically Modified Farm Animals, and Fictions." *Configurations* 18(1–2): 181–97.

Heather Paxson. 2011. "The 'Art' and 'Science' of Handcrafting Cheese in the United States." *Endeavor* 35(2–3): 116–24.

Sophia Roosth. 2013. "Of Foams and Formalisms: Scientific Expertise and Craft Practice in Molecular Gastronomy." *American Anthropologist* 115(1): 4–16.

Alexandra Sexton. 2016. "Alternative Proteins and the (Non)Stuff of 'Meat.'" *Gastronomica* 16(3): 66–78.

Hervé This. 2006. "Food for Tomorrow? How the Scientific Discipline of Molecular Gastronomy Could Change the Way We Eat." *EMBO Reports* 7(11): 1062–6.

Index

access to food 6, 7, 16, 96, 99, 105, 106, 113, 155, 162, 164, 255, 262
advertisements 173, 211
  baby food industry 278–80, 283
  tea 46, 49
advice about food 88, 121, 181, 231, 238, 239, 250, 272, 273, 277
advice manuals 115
aesthetics 329
affect 60, 102, 241, 299, 319, 321
agency 4, 68, 113, 177, 178, 183, 189, 217, 250, 251, 264, 283, 318
  abduction of agency 135
  agency of fat 245–6
agrarian imaginary 51
agriculture 99, 106, 124, 134, 136, 138, 141, 147, 154, 195–6, 232, 276, 276, 295–8, 313, 318, 319–20, 328
  agriculture and design 326, 327, 329–30
  agricultural transition 224
  alternative agriculture 61, 189, 194, 294
agro-resistance 189
alimentary dignity 96, 97, 98, 99, 100, 102, 104–6
alternative foods 164, 226
alternative food movements 2, 29, 194
antipolitics machine 120
appetite 174, 216, 238, 239, 246
  appetite regulation 240–50
apps 209, 210, 213
aroma 171, 173–7, 183, 206, 306, 316, 321
artisanal foods 29, 38, 49, 50, 60, 328, 329, 331, 332
authenticity 4, 49, 192, 194, 206, 328
authority 28, 68, 114, 116, 118, 122, 123, 131, 142, 143, 145, 154, 206, 231, 273, 274, 311
  unitary authority 138–9

babies 272, 274–6, 278, 279, 280–3
baby food 271, 272, 274–8, 281–3
bacon 39, 40
bacteria 5, 10, 28, 178, 182, 290, 297
banquets 133, 139, 176

Beck, Ulrich 153–5, 161
beer 189–99, 218, 298
bidding 6, 27–9, 30–1, 32–41
biomedicine 8, 87, 90, 91, 130, 206, 224, 229, 239
BMI 226, 237, 238, 260
body
  theories of 4, 5, 7–10, 75, 76, 77, 97, 132, 141, 170, 171–2, 175, 178, 182, 183, 206, 210, 211, 212, 214, 218, 224, 226, 238, 239, 244, 245, 259, 316, 323, 333
body image 212–15, 217, 225, 230–2, 237, 259
body politic 145, 175, 184
botulism 129, 130, 132, 133, 136, 139–41, 145, 146
Bourdieu, Pierre 97, 118, 212
bureaucracy 133, 146, 193

canning 130, 133, 136, 139, 140, 142, 145
capitalism 22, 23, 28, 29, 39, 98, 170, 175, 179, 198, 259, 266, 272, 330
  salvage capitalism 32
censorship 66, 67, 74, 116
Centers for Disease Control (CDC) 129, 258
charity 30, 41, 130
chilblains 75, 76
children 135, 140, 156, 248, 256, 257, 258, 261, 273, 283
  feeding of 23, 85, 86, 96, 103–5, 117, 119, 120, 121–4, 174, 179, 181, 256, 277, 280
  health concerns 275, 276, 277, 279
circulatory sociality 293, 295, 299
citizens 4, 7, 8, 41, 67, 71, 120, 132, 134–5, 142, 173, 174, 178, 181, 183, 257, 259, 264, 266, 308, 309–10
citizenship 148, 164, 174, 209, 212, 214
citizen-consumer (also consumer-citizen) 4, 145, 172
civic life 114, 173, 175
civil society 98, 131
civility 97, 98, 105, 106, 273
climate change 298, 327

Codex Alimentarius 142–4, 147
coffee 30, 32, 38, 42, 46, 49, 51, 99
colonialism 46, 47, 48, 49, 50, 51, 52, 56, 57, 59, 60, 61, 99, 133, 147, 190, 296. *See also* postcolonialism
commensality 7, 115, 117, 156, 189
commodity 16, 22, 29, 32, 34, 38, 41, 51, 304
  unfinished commodity 38
communication styles 69–71, 72–4, 76–8
community building 2, 7, 35, 96, 106, 193, 195, 231, 232
cosmopolitanism 190, 194, 198, 303, 304, 306
cost
  theories of 34, 138, 264, 281
Cubanidad 99, 105
cuisine 96–100, 103, 104, 106, 157, 158, 326

dairying 314, 316, 317–20, 322
danger 118, 120, 137, 140, 141, 146, 157, 170, 181, 194, 239, 258, 260, 266
death 72–6, 129, 266, 297, 318
dégustation 237, 243
deprivation foods 176–7
design 325, 326, 327, 331
  speculative design 325, 326, 327, 330, 333–4
development 51, 59, 120, 133, 142, 145, 271, 272, 275, 277, 280, 282, 283, 294, 296
diabetes 225, 229, 246, 258, 259, 328, 329, 332
diet 115, 117, 124, 158, 181, 224, 231, 238, 264, 281, 316, 319–20, 322
dietary habits 49, 100, 103, 145, 155, 156, 162, 171, 182, 197, 212, 218, 230, 232, 242, 247, 257, 264
dieting 49, 122, 206, 210, 211, 212, 213–17, 237, 239–40, 263
diet industry 209, 218, 243, 261, 262
digestion 171, 177, 178, 180, 181–3, 316
digital technology 4–5, 210, 214, 217. *See also* apps
dignity 95, 98, 105, 106, 197, 264. *See also* alimentary dignity
discipline 132, 210, 211, 214, 215, 216, 217, 218, 294, 298, 299
discourse analysis 211
discourses about food 19, 47, 48, 49, 50, 51, 68, 70, 72, 90, 115, 157, 158, 171, 178, 190, 209, 262–3, 265, 271, 272, 273, 274, 281, 329
  famine discourse 65, 66, 70, 74
disease
  as cultural construct 136, 141, 145
disposal 6, 10, 16, 84, 332
disruptive behavior 121

distinction 48, 49, 50, 51, 55, 58, 59, 89
distribution 16, 28, 29, 30, 31, 34, 35, 37–39, 41, 42, 99, 104, 136, 154, 257, 267
division of labor 56, 124, 135
DIY 21, 22
Douglas, Mary 7, 97, 103, 106, 140

economy
  conceptions of 21, 22, 30, 37, 51, 99, 137, 139, 144, 170, 197, 224, 232, 250, 310
ecosan initiatives 298
education programs 49, 76, 154, 225, 238, 240, 241, 245, 248, 256, 271, 276, 281, 282, 294
Elias, Norbert 97, 106
emotional responses to food 67, 68, 71, 73, 78, 106, 117, 121, 122, 123, 125, 156, 210, 215, 218, 242, 244, 248
environmental issues 48, 50, 83, 153, 154, 158, 160, 163, 164, 190, 194, 240, 245, 248, 255–67, 294, 295, 298, 299, 311, 326
environmental sustainability 51, 295
epidemiological change 224
epistemic community 274
exchange 29, 118, 123, 130, 148, 229, 230
excrement 161, 197, 293, 296, 297, 298, 299, 305
expired food 36, 89–90

family
  role of 15, 33, 36, 39, 77, 78, 136, 155, 156, 163, 273, 299
family meal 7, 85–9, 97, 105, 115–25, 226, 228. *See also* meals
famine 225, 237, 245–7, 271, 274
  North Korea 65–7, 69, 71, 72, 74–8
  Soviet Union 133, 136
farmwork 19–23, 50, 51, 60, 68, 69, 75, 76, 118, 196, 294, 315
fatness
  attitudes toward 211, 212, 215, 217, 218, 225, 230, 255, 257, 259, 260, 262, 263, 265, 266, 267
Fat Studies 212, 217
feeding practices 85–6, 104, 122, 227, 248, 272, 274, 277, 278, 297, 316–19, 320, 322
female bodies 212, 217, 273
female workers 52, 53, 54, 57, 59, 295
femininity 210, 215, 216, 218
feminist approaches 211, 212, 217, 255, 256, 259, 260, 262, 264, 266, 267, 273
fertilizer 156, 157, 161, 196, 197, 293, 297, 298, 299, 303, 309
fetishization 22, 30, 51, 57, 60, 61, 329

food banks 30
food manufacturing 8, 16, 60, 320
food poisoning 8, 72, 170
food processing 58, 59, 133, 134, 135, 138, 139, 140, 144, 147, 242, 282
food relief 75, 180–1, 182
food security 98, 106, 155, 281
food shortage 69, 70, 72, 76, 97, 99, 100, 102, 134, 145, 176, 225
food sovereignty 96, 98, 106, 197, 198
food waste 31, 32, 37, 39, 41, 42, 83, 84, 85, 87, 89, 90, 91. *See also* waste
food work 19, 20, 32, 36, 39, 206
foraging 176, 195, 304, 328–32
forest ecologies 310
forests 28, 175, 303, 307, 308–11
fortification of food 271, 272
Foucault, Michel 23, 132, 141, 211, 217
free speech 66, 72, 74
freshness
  as a value 158, 160, 161, 163, 262, 313
fungi 10, 303–5

gardening 19, 271, 272, 281, 326
gardens 47, 48, 52, 56, 57–61, 156, 175, 195, 196
gender 116, 118, 121, 123, 124, 209–218, 228, 273, 283. *See also* feminity, masculinity
Geographical Indication 46, 47, 52, 53, 54
goodness 36, 50, 116, 117, 281
governance 53, 131, 142, 147, 148, 178, 264, 265, 273, 299
governmentality 130, 141, 142, 145, 206
Gramsci, Antonio 124
Great Leap Forward Famine 67, 68
grocery auction 27–9, 30, 31–42
guerrilla gardening 189–90, 191, 192, 197

habitus 317
Haraway, Donna 318, 319
hay 313–16, 321
health 8, 21, 30, 40, 49, 58, 69, 86, 87, 89, 90, 91, 106, 115, 123, 130, 135, 140, 144, 154, 156, 157, 158, 161, 162, 164, 171, 174, 175, 177, 181, 182, 183, 195, 196, 206, 209, 212–13, 215–17, 223, 224, 226–33, 238, 240, 255, 256–8, 259, 260, 262, 264, 266, 276, 283, 319, 321
health education 237
health practitioners 223, 224, 225–6, 227–33, 237, 244
healthism 4, 214, 262, 263
heritage 47, 49, 58, 59, 60, 99, 121, 172, 175

hidden hunger 271, 272, 274, 275, 276, 281
humor 35, 40, 227
hunting 303, 308, 327, 328, 330, 332
hygiene 123, 142, 154, 157, 159, 162, 164, 181
hygiene manuals 174, 181

immaterial labor 49
inclusion 147, 148, 242, 308
  arts of inclusion 303, 304, 306
indigestion 171, 180, 181, 182
ingestion 97, 171, 172, 173, 177, 178, 183
industrially produced food 33, 37, 47, 50, 51, 133, 134, 135, 136, 138, 140, 144, 158, 175, 190, 191, 192, 198
industrial food production 50, 55, 56, 134, 154, 157, 190, 195, 197, 242, 318, 329, 331
industrial food system 28, 29, 30, 32, 34, 37–42, 99, 100
inequality 74, 120, 189, 211, 232, 265
insecurity 71, 155
intellectual property 45, 46, 53, 54, 57, 61
intersubjectivity 314, 318, 322
invention of tradition 50
Israeli occupation 189, 190, 192–9

kamān 48, 56–61
knowledge systems 9, 54, 57, 59, 61, 130, 135–6, 140, 156, 212, 214, 223, 224, 272, 280–1, 308, 311, 313, 315, 316
  control of 135, 274, 310

labor
  conceptions of 16, 19, 20, 21, 22, 23, 29, 30, 42, 46, 47, 48, 49, 50, 51, 57, 58, 61, 122, 123, 124, 206, 228, 259, 296. *See also* migrant labor, work
Lakoff, George 122, 331
Latour, Bruno 135, 143
leftovers 85, 123, 296
listening
  as social strategy 77
local food 29, 51, 189, 190, 194, 198, 231
love/hate opposition 78, 83, 85, 88
luxury
  as quality of distinction 47, 48, 49, 50, 99

manure. *See* excrement
March of Suffering 66, 70
marketing 46–8, 49, 50, 51, 56, 57, 60, 61, 192, 218, 241, 245, 247, 272, 278–81, 328
masculinity 210, 212, 213, 215–18. *See also* gender

materiality 3, 10, 56, 60, 87–9, 136, 239, 290
matsutake 306–11
meals 36, 85, 86, 88, 96–8, 100, 102–6, 115, 117, 137. *See also* family meal
memory 67, 68, 74, 77, 146, 316
metabolic disorders 223–5, 227–8, 231–3, 320
metabolism 178, 183, 184, 237, 239–40, 246, 251, 260
metaphor 66, 75–6, 78, 118, 122, 331
microbes 5
microbial contamination 154, 157
microbiome 4
microbiopolitics 5, 8, 178, 183
micronutrients 271, 272, 274–8, 280–3
micronutrient deficiency 271, 272, 275, 281, 282–3
migrant labor 49, 50
Mintz, Sidney 157, 171
modernization 155, 158, 159, 163, 164, 196, 225, 276
molecular gastronomy 3
moral economy 37, 197
morality 3, 4, 6, 9, 16, 97, 98, 116, 120, 122, 125, 174–5, 177–8, 181, 183, 206, 241, 255–7, 259, 262–4, 267
moral personhood 4
motherhood 212, 272, 273, 278, 280, 283
mothers 179, 262, 272–3, 275–8, 280–1, 283
mycology 304

national body 76
national identity 47, 48, 50, 77, 99, 133, 173
national myths 51
nationalism 51, 75, 78, 137, 172, 175, 179, 181, 192, 193
nature
    as idealized place 57, 60, 61, 124, 134, 192, 294–6, 309, 310, 311
nurturing
    as value 117, 122, 319
nutrition 212, 224, 239–42, 261, 271–2, 274–83, 316–22
nutritionism 4, 183
nutritionists 237, 247, 281, 314, 316–22

obesity 115, 224, 225, 232, 237, 238, 239, 240, 241, 245, 246, 248–50, 255–67
obesity epidemic 9, 178, 245, 258
obesogenic environment 241, 255, 261

ontological gambit 39–40, 41
organics 48, 51, 58, 61, 158, 159, 178, 190, 197, 294, 295
organic farms 19, 161
organic movements 51

pain
    as food-related experience 71, 72, 75, 77, 78, 117, 179, 180, 259, 313
palatability 47, 61, 68, 76, 238, 242, 245, 246, 247, 262, 266, 313, 315–17, 319, 321, 322
palate 5, 9, 59, 169, 170, 171, 172, 177–8, 182–4, 206, 315
parents
    role of in food-related decisions 21, 115, 117, 118, 120, 121–2, 156, 163, 174, 181, 261
paternalism 135, 322
pathologization 178, 248, 260, 273
perception
    as legal distinction 48
picky eating 117, 121, 123
place-making 50, 51, 53, 55, 65, 143, 161, 163, 176, 197, 198
plantations 45–50, 52, 54, 56–61
    as gardens 58, 61, 99, 140, 225, 303
plantation labor 47, 48, 228
plantation science 311
pleasure
    as aspirational quality 19, 20, 21, 56
political economy
    conceptions of 30, 137, 250
politics
    as discursive structures 22, 23, 29, 121, 178, 196, 274, 296, 322, 333
pork 4, 29, 35, 49, 50, 96, 99, 100, 103, 157–63, 230, 231, 320. *See also* bacon
postcolonialism 58, 61 99, 190, 192, 296
postsocialism 97, 130
potato 69, 98
poverty 145, 146, 263, 265, 266, 267, 282, 328
    poverty of time 121
power
    conceptions of 28, 113–14, 115, 116, 118, 121, 124, 132, 189, 211
power relations 114, 124, 211, 318
precarity 20–3
privilege 20, 23, 74
production 29, 30, 41, 46, 47, 48, 50, 51, 53, 55, 175, 189, 206
projection 322, 325, 329

proper eating 89
protection 48, 50, 53

racialized food differences 260, 261. *See also*
    whiteness
rationing 99, 154
"real" food 95, 96, 97, 100, 104, 105,
    115, 178
recipes 85, 87, 102, 115, 142, 172, 174, 181, 216,
    297, 327, 329
refuge 55, 56, 61
refugees 28, 137, 193, 322
religion
    role of 49, 97, 115, 117, 119, 173, 294,
        295, 314
regulation
    as system of order 132, 133, 140, 141, 145,
        147, 164, 206, 238, 239, 243, 245, 246, 247,
        249–51, 256, 299
    self-regulation 142
resistance 61, 114, 189, 190, 193, 194, 195,
    197–8, 211, 314
responsibilization 83, 90, 120, 154, 164, 178, 183,
    209, 214, 215, 224, 226, 232, 233, 239, 247,
    256, 257, 264, 265, 266, 273, 280, 282, 319
risk 89–90, 141, 153, 161, 229, 233
risk society 153, 154, 155

salvage capitalism 32
scarcity 97, 99, 100, 102, 103, 106, 175
science
    as system of knowledge 49, 50, 51, 67, 76, 116,
        120, 124, 131, 142, 143, 178, 206, 238, 239,
        242, 244, 248, 249, 271, 273, 277, 304, 306,
        308, 310, 311, 331
scientization 272, 273, 274, 280, 283
Scott, James C. 131, 189
sensorium 176, 183, 184, 314, 316
sensory experiences 48, 61, 154, 170, 171, 172,
    174–84, 206, 238–44, 246, 248–50, 295, 310,
    313–18, 322–3
shopping 33, 34, 88, 123, 153, 155–63, 175,
    216, 262
silence 66–7, 72, 229
Situationists 330
Slow Food 2, 29, 177, 190, 196–8
speculative design 325–7, 330, 332–4
speech
    as cultural expression 65–8, 71, 74, 78. *See
        also* free speech
starvation 58, 65, 70, 72–8. *See also* famine

subjects
    as conceptions of the person 22, 23, 132, 148,
        211, 217, 257, 264, 283, 314, 322
subjectivity 10, 76, 171, 214, 299
subsidies 21, 100, 101, 191, 198, 250, 257,
    259, 264
suffering 65–6, 67, 68, 72, 75–7, 132, 318
surplus 6–7, 10, 30, 37, 83, 84, 100
surplus value 32, 41
survival 21, 28, 30, 39, 41–2, 67, 68, 71, 74, 76,
    77, 98, 136, 138, 245, 247, 289
survivors 65–72, 74, 75, 77–8, 177,
    225, 237
sustainability 29, 41, 124, 263, 267, 295, 296,
    326, 327

taste
    as quality of distinction 48, 49–51, 55, 58, 61,
        89, 97, 98, 130, 133, 135, 139, 145, 158, 162,
        173, 174, 178, 211, 223, 241, 290
    as physiological response 170, 171, 177, 183,
        239, 243
    as transcorporeal knowledge 313–19,
        322–3
taxonomy 304–5
Taybeh beer 189–94, 198
technology. *See* apps and digital technology
terroir 4–53, 60, 197
Third World 146, 265, 271, 272, 274–6,
    281–2
TMR (Total Mixed Ration) 320, 322
tourism 58–61, 161
tradition
    as ideal quality 48–9, 50–1, 99, 100, 103, 105,
        116, 118, 123, 172, 173, 194, 198
traditional knowledge 50, 54, 57, 59, 61
transcorporeality 314, 316–18, 322–3
translation 224, 320
    translation machine 28
trauma 67, 68, 71, 72, 77

unfinished commodity 38
University Extension 313, 316

value 3, 5, 6, 15–16, 23, 28–32, 34, 35, 37–42,
    48–50, 61, 74, 98, 209, 212, 218
violence 68, 76, 232
voluntarism 5, 6, 20–1, 23, 60, 158, 194

waste 28, 32, 39, 40, 41, 83–4, 87, 89, 293,
    294–9. *See also* excrement and food waste

wealth 224, 230
well-being 223, 224, 226, 229, 230, 232, 260,
    263, 308–9, 311
whiteness 21, 23, 124, 190, 212, 214, 231, 257,
    260, 263, 273

work
    conceptions of 6, 19, 20, 21, 22, 23, 50, 59,
        85, 316. *See also* food work, labor
Worldwide Opportunities on Organic Farms/
    Willing Workers on Organic Farms (WWOOF)
    19, 20, 21, 23